Deep Politics and the Death of JFK

Books by Peter Dale Scott

Crime and Cover-Up: The CIA, the Mafia, and the Dallas-Watergate Connection (1977; reissued 1993)

The War Conspiracy: The Secret Road to the Second Indochina War (1972)

(With Paul L. Hoch and Russell Stetler, eds.) *The Assassinations: Dallas and Beyond—A Guide to Cover-Ups and Investigations* (1976)

(With Jonathan Marshall) *Cocaine Politics: Drugs, Armies, and the CIA in Central America* (1991)

(With Jonathan Marshall and Jane Hunter) *The Iran-Contra Connection: Secret Teams and Covert Operations in the Reagan Era* (1987)

(With Franz Schurmann and Reginald Zelnik) *The Politics of Escalation in Vietnam* (1966)

Coming to Jakarta: A Poem About Terror (1989)

Listening to the Candle: A Poem on Impulse (1992)

Deep Politics
and the Death of JFK

Peter Dale Scott

UNIVERSITY OF CALIFORNIA PRESS
Berkeley · *Los Angeles* · *London*

University of California Press
Berkeley and Los Angeles, California

University of California Press, Ltd.
London, England

© 1993 by
The Regents of the University of California

Library of Congress Cataloging-in-Publication Data

Scott, Peter Dale.
  Deep politics and the death of JFK / Peter Dale Scott.
    p.   cm.
  Includes bibliographical references and index.
  ISBN 0-520-08410-1 (alk. paper)
  1. Kennedy, John F. (John Fitzgerald), 1917–1963—
Assassination.   I. Title.
E842.9.S35   1993
364.1′524′0973—dc20   93-3209
                                                           CIP

Printed in the United States of America

9 8 7 6 5 4 3 2 1

Contents

Acknowledgments   vii

Abbreviations   ix

PART ONE: DEEP POLITICS, VIETNAM,
AND THE ASSASSINATION

1. The Kennedy Assassination, Deep Politics,
   and Denial   3
2. Kennedy, Johnson, and Vietnam:
   A Tale of Two NSAMs   24
3. The Dialectical Cover-Up   38
4. The Key to the Cover-Up:
   The FBI, COINTELPROS, and the Case   58

PART TWO: LEE HARVEY OSWALD

5. Oswald, Intelligence, and the Mob
   in New Orleans   77
6. Oswald, Intelligence, the Mob,
   and the Banana Companies   93
7. Mexico, Somoza, and the Martino-
   Rosselli Story   107

PART THREE: JACK RUBY

8. Ruby and Narcotics:
   The Heart of What Was Suppressed   127
9. Ruby's Background:
   Narcotics, the Teamsters,
   and the Racing Wire Service   144
10. The Nationally Protected Drug Traffic
    and Ruby's Relation to It   164
11. Blakey and the Politics of Fighting Crime   182
12. Ruby, Narcotics, and the Establishment   197

PART FOUR: THE PLOT AND THE COVER-UP

13. The Coalitions against the Kennedys   211
14. Intrigue, Murder, Cover-Up:
    The Continuity of Manipulation   226
15. Oswald as an Informant for the Government   242
16. Oswald as a Double Agent for Hoover   254
17. Army Intelligence and the Dallas Police   267
18. The Assassination and the Great Southwest
    Corporation   283
19. Who Killed JFK? The Deep Political System   295

Notes   315

Bibliography   383

Index   393

Acknowledgments

The origins of this book go back over two decades, to two book manuscripts (first *The Dallas Conspiracy* and then *Beyond Conspiracy*) that have somehow become cited without ever being published. I cannot now begin to remember, let alone recount, all those who have helped me over those years, from research to typing to the compilation of laborious indexes. I must, however, pay a special tribute to Sylvia Meagher, an early pioneer who did not live to see the fruits of her work, and to Mary Ferrell, whose researches in Dallas have been an inspiration to so many investigators. I owe thanks also to my former collaborators Russell Stetler and Josiah Thompson, to Richard Popkin, who first persuaded me to join ranks with other researchers, and to the late Bernard Fensterwald and Jim Lesar of the Assassination Archive in Washington, who did so much to make documentation available, particularly through their efforts to secure passage of the Freedom of Information Act and successor legislation.

The present manuscript, written in less than a year, could not have been completed without the help of many who may not agree with all of it. My first thanks must go to Paul L. Hoch, whose scrupulous analysis and control of so many complex facts helped me (as many others) more than once from venturing down false paths. I wish to pay tribute to Paul's labors over almost three decades to focus on truth, in a field so easily taken over by myths. I owe a similar long-term debt to my best friend Daniel Ellsberg, who was mostly absent while this book was written, but who before that had helped sharpen my mind to the nuances of bureaucratic intrigue. Jonathan Marshall has been similarly helpful with his keen eye for cant, bad research, and bad logic. In the writing of the book I have also been helped by John Newman, Alan A. Block, Eugene Scheiman, Michael Lerner, Dick Russell, Wesley McCune of Group Research, Inc., Frank Mather, Sue Robinson, William Anderson, Mary Ferrell yet again, and by my patient editors Naomi Schneider, Tony Hicks, and Ellen Stein. I owe another enormous debt to my inveterate indexer, Mary Marshall.

My biggest debt is to the person who has suffered most through this project along with myself, Ronna Kabatznick, my beloved partner and hopefully (by the time of this publication) my bride.

Abbreviations

In this book, WH and WR refer to the Hearings and Report of the Warren Commission (1964), AH and AR to the Hearings and Report of the House Select Committee on Assassinations (1979), WCE to Warren Commission Exhibits (published), and WCD to Warren Commission Documents (unpublished, in the National Archives).

PART ONE

Deep Politics, Vietnam, and the Assassination

The Kennedy Assassination, Deep Politics, and Denial

In America we are now approaching a consensual state of mind about the Kennedy assassination that is perhaps as bizarre as the assassination itself. Increasingly, it is admitted that the facts of the President's murder are not fully known, let alone understood. Some of the major findings of the first official investigation, the Warren Commission in 1964, have now been authoritatively demolished by the second, the House Select Committee on Assassinations in 1979.

The new findings prove that there was something seriously wrong, not just with the initial investigation (i.e., a cover-up) but with the legal and political systems that needed a cover-up to conceal their criminal shortcomings. For example, we now know that one of the Warren Report's discredited propositions, that Lee Harvey Oswald's killer, Jack Ruby, "was not involved with Chicago's criminal element" (WR 785), was the result not of inadequate intelligence but of a deliberate deception of the Warren Commission by the FBI, designed to keep organized crime out of the picture.

There are allegations of deliberate deception on even more central matters, such as the handling of the President's autopsy and the physical evidence. Most of these allegations are hotly disputed. The physical and medical evidence present ordinary citizens with a profound dilemma of credibility. Either the evidence is true, in which case the President and Governor John Connally were hit by only two bullets causing a total of

3

eight wounds; or, if this result defies our credulity, we must accept that there has been massive falsification of the evidence.[1]

But with respect to the Warren Report's portrait of Jack Ruby as a loner there is now no such dilemma: this portrait was false, and the FBI had gone out of its way to conceal Ruby's organized-crime connections. If considered objectively, the acceptance that the Warren Commission findings were falsified, even in this one area, should lead to questions about the political succession of the United States that was ratified by the Commission's findings. Outside the United States one customarily does find such questioning, if not indeed a complacent cynicism that without either knowledge or curiosity simply assumes guilt on the part of the U.S. political establishment itself. And yet within the United States there is not only disinterest but psychological resistance, from the right and left as well as the mainstream, to examining the question further. As a result there is still little or no institutional will to address and deal with the highest-level American political crime of this century.

Instead the search for the truth has been left, by default, to a small band of self-selected critics, usually derided as "buffs" or "assassinologists." These, often disagreeing among themselves, have certainly failed to produce a generally persuasive alternative account of how the President was killed. Indeed their often strident disagreements may have only strengthened the general impression that the President's murder was a mystery which will never be solved.

I believe this failure has been an unnecessary one, caused by the tunnel vision of most critics and their opponents. They have been too fixated on the least answerable question: Who really killed the President? And they have paid far too little attention to the contextual question, both more important and paradoxically more easy to answer: What were the structural defects in governance and society that allowed this huge crime to be so badly investigated (or, in other terms, to go unpunished)? In simpler words, how could American institutions harbor and protect such evil?

Let us for a moment consider two revealing areas in which false claims put forward in the Warren Report have been definitively and finally refuted by the Report of the House Committee. Significantly, these do not bear on the hotly contested question of the President's murder; instead they concern Jack Ruby, the murderer of the President's alleged assassin Lee Harvey Oswald. The first false claim by the Warren Commission was that Ruby acted alone and spontaneously in killing Oswald. The House Committee showed quite convincingly that Ruby's entry to the Dallas police basement had been assisted by members of the Dallas police department. Ruby probably entered the basement through an unlocked and unguarded stairwell; yet this disturbing probability was obscured by a false alternative story corroborated by at least four police officers. One of these officers failed a polygraph test on these questions in 1964, yet this failure was kept a secret until the House Committee revealed it in 1978.

What is now known about Ruby's entry into the basement suggests collusion and corruption among the Dallas police. The second false claim of the Warren Commission, that the evidence "does not establish a significant link between Ruby and organized crime" (WR 801), indicates corruption of our political institutions at the highest national level. The FBI had transmitted to the Commission the assurance of one of Ruby's friends that Ruby was "not outfit connected" (22 WH 372); only those knowledgeable about crime who bothered to consult the footnoted citations could learn that this friend was Dave Yaras, one of the syndicate's top killers at the time, and that a similar assurance given to the FBI had come from a head of organized crime in Chicago—two sources who should not have been considered persuasive. The FBI did not tell the Warren Commission that these interviews exonerating organized crime came from organized crime itself.

Thanks to the revelations of the House Committee, which produced a staff report of over one thousand pages on Ruby's organized-crime connections, we can now see that in 1964, as on many other occasions, the FBI, in blandly transmitting such worthless assurances, was covering up the existence of organized crime in America. But it is hard for most Americans to accept that there was such collusion and corruption at the top of the U.S. government, paralleling that in the Dallas police. Such an acceptance would compel most Americans, particularly those with status in the present regime, to alter their conscious relations to the society which protects them.

The collective response to the Kennedy assassination, in short, has been marked by psychological denial. This denial is even shared by those of the assassination critics or buffs who have spent years looking for external killers of the President: whether Communists, Cubans,

Corsicans, the CIA, or even "organized crime" itself, if demonized and projected outward as some kind of external enemy rather than an integral element of our domestic deep-political economy.

This need to deny ugly facts about our civilization is a universal one. Through writing poetry I have come to accept its presence in myself. My own early researches into the Kennedy assassination, as into the related topic of the Vietnam War, focused on external conspiratorial forces, impacting on a victimized body politic. What none of us (myself included) wish to accept is that the unsolved assassination is a symptom of something wrong today, not just in 1963, in the heart of the society in which we live.

And now we come to the heart of the paradox. Today virtually everyone concedes that there *is* something profoundly wrong with American society. Psychological denial cannot repress this fundamental perception. Try, however, suggesting that the Kennedy assassination was a symptom of something structurally wrong in American society, and you will see this suggestion rejected, energetically, by intellectuals from the right, center, and left of the American political spectrum. Rejected, indeed, with an almost desperate energy. What is going on here?

In this book I will argue that, just as repression of these ugly facts is psychological, so the exploration of them can be psychotherapeutic, for both the writer and the audience, and in the end for society itself.

POLITICS, PARAPOLITICS, AND DEEP POLITICS

Let me for a moment digress on the superficiality of my own early researches into the Kennedy assassination. I used to summarize them collectively as the investigation of *parapolitics,* which I defined (with the CIA in mind) as "a system or practice of politics in which accountability is consciously diminished."[2] This term referred chiefly, but not exclusively, to the world of intelligence agencies and similar organizations, where secrecy and covert operations were adopted as a matter of deliberate policy.

I still see value in this definition and mode of analysis. But parapolitics as thus defined is itself too narrowly conscious and intentional to describe the deeper irrational movements which culminated collectively in the murder of the President; it describes at best only an intervening layer of the irrationality under our political culture's rational surface.

Thus I now refer to parapolitics as only one manifestation of *deep politics,* all those political practices and arrangements, deliberate or not, which are usually repressed rather than acknowledged.

The chapters in this book explore many processes of politics at levels usually not acknowledged or reported and indeed repressed and denied. Normally, these deep political processes are not brought to the public eye: for example, the way in which major drug traffickers are recurringly protected by the U.S. Justice Department, or the way in which some of the top traffickers have been recurringly named in connection with the systematic sexual corruption of members of Congress. Such arrangements are in fact widely known, but rarely written about. One way or another, scholars and journalists learn to back off.

The resulting social system is relatively stable, and the fact that certain procedures are repressed from public consciousness becomes itself suppressed. Occasionally, however, such "connections" between overworld and underworld impact radically upon the public realm, and we have unexplained crises such as the Kennedy assassination, Watergate, and Contragate.

One thesis of this book is that, because of the underlying continuities of deep politics, such crises are interrelated. To study any one of them is to acquire knowledge about some of the principal players, and their procedures, in the others. In this way we become aware of a violent milieu underlying American politics, including the ex-CIA Cuban exiles and their American handlers (such as the Watergate burglar Frank Sturgis, who earlier, as we shall see, had figured in the Warren Commission files on the Kennedy assassination).

In the United States, just as in other countries, parapolitics, including the activities of government and private intelligence agencies, recurringly has recourse to persons from such a milieu. Thus parapolitics has always been close to, dependent on, and interactive with deep politics. An example of deep politics is the way Tammany Hall, in alliance with ethnic gangsters, refined patronage and corruption into a working system for dividing the spoils in an ethnically divided New York City. This arrangement grew by itself, was never consciously designed, and hence was not truly parapolitical.

A seminal example of parapolitics was the use of the Tammany connection by the U.S. government in 1945, for the first postwar occupational government of Italy and Sicily. A number of former New York politicians were installed in AMGOT, the Allied Military Government, while Lucky Luciano and other mafiosi were released and deported to Italy or Sicily. Vito Genovese, a mafia family leader, was installed as an interpreter at AMGOT headquarters; through organized black-marketing in U.S. army trucks (as described in *Catch 22*), he became the connection or go-between.[3]

This particular scandal has been chronicled in histories of organized crime, rather than histories of U.S. foreign relations. In fact it is probably more paradigmatic of the latter than of the former. Such arrangements were repeated in Vietnam, where subordinates of Santos Trafficante, a Tampa mafioso with CIA connections, arrived not long after the first U.S. combat troops.[4] They were repeated again in Contragate.

The phenomenon was not just one of corruption, but of governance. The U.S. government, like Tammany in the nineteenth century, wished its own gangs to control others, especially on the left—which is to say it preferred organized crime to either disorganized crime or radicalism. That the AMGOT-Genovese arrangement pleased the overworld as well as the underworld is best documented by the fact that Charles Poletti, the army colonel responsible for Genovese's appointment, and once described by Luciano as "one of our good friends," went on to become an Overseer of Harvard University.[5]

This parapolitical connection was a continuing, not an ad hoc arrangement. It survived, with progressive modifications, to become part of the deep political underpinnings of first Watergate and then Contragate, both of which, at a deeper level, involved drug-trafficking Cubans in Miami.[6] The common denominator, linking U.S. organized criminals in Italy, Vietnam, and Central America, was the highly centralized international drug traffic. Luciano, Trafficante, and the ex-CIA Miami Cubans assisting the Nicaraguan Contras were all successive parts of an ongoing and influential trafficking arrangement; and even a CIA agent has acknowledged that this arrangement was influential in part because of its services to friendly intelligence networks, including the CIA. (The agent, Thomas Tripodi, wrote in secret CIA and DEA reports on drugs that "the American authorities were instrumental in the revival of the Sicilian Mafia," and that the largest non-Sicilian importers of heroin into the United States were "the Corsicans, who had also been buttressed by the CIA as an anti-Communist force.")[7]

I first became aware of all this in the course of my years of anti-war research into the origins of the U.S. commitment to fight a war in Vietnam. As a former Canadian diplomat I had been exposed very peripherally to the secret Canadian cable traffic of the 1950s on Indochina (where Canada was a member of the three-nation International Control Commission). By 1963 I could no longer remember what I had read a few years before, but I had been rendered more sensitive than most to the arguments of rational moderates (such as Walter Lippmann and Hans Morgenthau) that it would be the sheerest folly for the United States to repeat the disastrous experience of the French in Indochina.

At the outset, my anti-war speeches and writings were naive appeals to rationality. Later, as it became increasingly obvious that folly would for some time prevail, I wished to establish why. My first researches, heavily influenced by my friend and sometime coauthor Franz Schurmann, focused on bureaucratic intrigue and in-fighting, as reflected in Chapter 2 of this book. My later essays, beginning with the final chapters of *The War Conspiracy* (1972), went behind bureaucratic rigidities and conflicts to the competing economic interests underlying them. Above all they looked at the tension between those interested in stabilizing the U.S. domestic economy and balance of payments, and those (particularly some U.S. oil companies) interested in providing a secure shield for U.S. investment in Southeast Asia—and particularly the development of offshore oil in Indonesian and other waters of the South China Sea. This in turn led to increasing focus on the symbiosis between governments (and in particular their intelligence agencies) and criminal associations, particularly drug traffickers, in the stabilization of right-wing terror in Vietnam, Italy, Bolivia, Afghanistan, Nicaragua, and other parts of the world. This focus was increasingly documented by revelations in the 1970s and 1980s about the "strategy of tension," whereby government intelligence agencies, working in international conjunction, strengthened the case for their survival by actually fomenting violence, recurringly in alliance with drug-trafficking elements.[8]

Dishonesty, manipulation, and even self-deception are widespread in our nominal political democracy. So little of what really goes on is acknowledged that the notion of deep politics as earlier defined, "political practices and arrangements that are usually repressed rather than acknowledged," needs to be defined more fully. I will henceforth use *deep political analysis* to refer to the progress in research I have just described, looking beneath public formulations of policy issues to the bureaucratic, economic, and ultimately covert and criminal activities which underlie them.

STRUCTURALIST REJECTION OF "CONSPIRACY THEORIES"

My experience has been that the degree of psychological resistance to and denial of each of these levels increases geometrically. Bureaucratic struggles, even when not officially acknowledged, could (I learned personally) be discussed in mainstream journals like the *New York Review of Books*. My articles which focused on underlying economic motives for U.S. intervention were denied such outlets, but could still be published in journals like the *Nation,* or what I have since come to think of as the establishment left. But even the *Nation* is fiercely hostile to the notion that criminal interventions, such as the assassination of President Kennedy, can themselves be part of the system or process by which we are governed.[9] Analyzing U.S. foreign policy in the midst of the Vietnam War, Gabriel Kolko spoke for this establishment left when he wrote that "a ruling class makes its policies operate" through a pervasive "business-defined consensus," and that "to understand this essential fact is also to reject conspiracy theories."[10]

Underlying this resistance is I believe the legacy of the Enlightenment that has left us in this century with the unattractive choices of academic social science and scientific socialism. The rationalistic structuralism of both resists "conspiracy theories," which, in the words of Alexander Cockburn, undermine "any sensible analysis of institutions, economic trends and pressures, continuities in corporate and class interest and all the other elements constituting the open secrets and agendas of American capitalism."[11]

The same resistance has been expressed more moderately by G. William Domhoff, a sociologist whose analyses of the American ruling class heavily influenced my own economic essays. Domhoff concedes that

> if "conspiracy" means that these men are aware of their interests, know each other personally, meet together privately and off the record, and try to ham-

mer out a consensus on how to anticipate and react to events and issues, then there is some conspiring that goes on in CFR, not to mention the Committee for Economic Development, the Business Council, the National Security Council and the Central Intelligence Agency.[12]

But Domhoff shares Cockburn's resistance to the idea that an assassination conspiracy could have had a lasting impact on our political arrangements: "We all have a tremendous tendency to want to get caught up in believing that there's some secret evil cause for all of the obvious ills of the world." Conspiracy theories "encourage a belief that if we get rid of a few bad people, everything would be well in the world."[13]

I should make it clear that I propose deep political analysis of the Kennedy assassination not as a substitute or alternative to the structural analysis desired by Cockburn and Domhoff but as an extension of it. I have always believed, and argued, that a true understanding of the Kennedy assassination will lead, not to "a few bad people," but to the institutional and parapolitical arrangements which constitute the way we are systematically governed. The conspiracies I see as operative, in other words, are part of our political structure, not exceptions to it.

This was the natural course and conclusion of my Vietnam researches, as I collected them into essay-chapters for my 1972 book *The War Conspiracy*. That book, like my subsequent researches, began with bureaucratic demystifications, and proceeded, via economic analysis, to a closer look at the power role in Southeast Asia exercised by organized crime and the international drug traffic. I explained my title, *The War Conspiracy*, to

> mean the sustained resort to collusion and conspiracy, unauthorized provocations, and fraud by US personnel, particularly intelligence personnel, in order to sustain or increase our military commitment in Asia. . . . War conspiracy itself is as much a symptom as a cause of the war mentality it furthers, for where the management and censorship of the news are commonplace, the manipulation and outright invention of it are invited. The war conspiracy is to be seen as a general syndrome, not . . . [a] private cabal.[14]

In other words, my own analysis at this stage was primarily parapolitical, rather than the deep political analysis which would have frankly accepted the extent to which the drug traffic was more than simply a conscious device of imperialistic control.

PSYCHOLOGICAL RESISTANCE
TO DEALING WITH THE KENNEDY ASSASSINATION

Today I have come to recognize that the structural arrangements which incorporate organized crime and the drug traffic into imperial systems are not all parapolitical stratagems designed by those in power. My emphasis in this book, in other words, is more on deep politics, as well as on the parapolitical exploitation of them. Speaking more generally, irrational forces, which have always been there, must be included as part of our social structure. But to say this, of course, is to redefine the notion of structure, as less rational, and hence less amenable to a rational takeover, than Marxists once believed.

So powerful indeed is the resistance to acknowledging a successful assassination conspiracy that we should admit that such resistance is not just ideological, it is also affective. The notion that unreason as well as reason rules us from above is psychologically painful. This intolerability has given rise to the consoling world-views of religions, literature, and more recently enlightenment structuralism. One has perhaps to have dealt seriously with the Kennedy assassination to be aware just how intense is the resistance to discussing it, on both the personal and the institutional level.

Consider, for example, the impressive, indeed ground-breaking, biography of J. Edgar Hoover by Athan Theoharis and John Stuart Cox.[15] Although the book devotes much attention to Hoover's illegal COINTELPRO programs against the Fair Play for Cuba Committee and other left-wing groups, the book does not mention the outcome of what may have been Hoover's only fully successful COINTELPRO: how the FPCC, shattered by the disclosure of Oswald's unsolicited activities for it, decided to close itself down. Indeed the book says not one word about Oswald, Ruby, and the Kennedy assassination, although Hoover played a crucial role in protecting the assassins (see Chapter 3); and murder, even of a President, should surely be considered a form of oppression.[16]

This central omission in Theoharis's excellent study is the more glaring because Theoharis accurately describes Hoover's bias in favor of Johnson over Kennedy before and after the assassination, including "Hoover's and Johnson's shared interests in purging the Justice Department of Kennedy loyalists [which] continued after the November 1964 presidential election." The assassination itself, however, is treated as "fate in the guise of an assassin," almost as an act of God.[17]

One can appreciate his dilemma: with enough controversial revelations about Hoover's other illegal activities, Theoharis did not wish needlessly to challenge reader resistance and thus marginalize his standing as a social critic. By the same token, Hoover's treatment of Ethel Rosenberg, an egregious instance of inquisition, is not discussed at all.

The result is a distortion of the Hoover legacy, and a continued repression of its worst features. One must turn to the more recent Hoover biography by Curt Gentry to learn that Ethel Rosenberg was very likely indicted and convicted on faked evidence, as part of an FBI stratagem to get her husband, and that the Dostoievskian perpetrators of this judicial murder were FBI officials Hoover, Alan Belmont, and William Branigan, precisely the team (as we shall see in Chapter 4) that Hoover contrived to put in charge of the Kennedy assassination investigation.[18]

This resistance to raising the awkward topic of the assassination is so great that it spills over into technically unrelated areas. A flagrant example is that treated in my next chapter: the significant change in U.S. Vietnam policy after the assassination of President Kennedy. This change in policy ought to be treated as a factual question, and separated in our minds from the assassination, about which, by itself, it tells us nothing. (That is, the policy change is a fact, even if Kennedy had been killed by a lone nut, or for that matter by a falling meteorite.)

But the change has not been so treated. On the contrary, a significant hiatus in Vietnam documentation has emerged for the months of November and December 1963, precisely the period in which America made the initial shift from an advisory to a combat role. This hiatus first occurred in the Pentagon documents and studies compiled for the Defense Department under Secretary Robert McNamara in the late 1960s, and then released to the *New York Times* (as the Pentagon Papers) in 1971. This understandable hiatus can be explained as a normal bureaucratic phenomenon: those analyzing policy inside the Johnson Administration were unlikely to admit (even to themselves) that the policy they had been implementing was in part the consequence of a presidential murder.

But the resistance, denial, and cover-up of this fact have not died away with time. On the contrary, they have increased, climaxing as I write with the frenzied media reaction to the use of two high-level National Security Action Memoranda on Vietnam (NSAMs 263 and 273 of 1963) in Oliver Stone's movie *JFK*. It will be interesting to watch the critical response to the new scholarly history, *JFK and Vietnam* by John Newman, which documents this policy change with meticulous scholarship.

The success and thoroughness of Newman's demonstration point to an anomalous feature of preceding Vietnam histories. In 1971–72 the Pentagon Papers were published, along with my comparison (based on them) between Kennedy's last Vietnam policy statement and Johnson's first one, NSAMs 263 and 273. Thus it was now in the public record that in October 1963 Kennedy had authorized the implementation of a plan to withdraw 1,000 troops from Vietnam in 1963, and that in November Johnson had quietly replaced this by secret planning for U.S. escalation.

Nothing about any of this will be found in the 750 pages of Stanley Karnow's *Vietnam: A History* (1983), which skip from the Diem coup (November 1, 1963) to the situation in late December. William J. Rust's *Kennedy in Vietnam* (1985), despite its subject, is silent about NSAM 263 and the troop-withdrawal plan, although it does underline the importance of the commitment to win made by Johnson's NSAM 273.[19]

George Kahin's *Intervention: How America Became Involved in Vietnam* (1986) is perhaps the most significant example of this hiatus, not just because it is so carefully and exhaustively compiled, but because he himself is aware of the bureaucratic bias in the Pentagon Papers, and draws attention to it in his own, divergent narration. His historical account notes (correctly) that plans for phased withdrawal of U.S. troops were approved generally in March 1963 by the Joint Chiefs of Staff, who directed in May that "a plan for the withdrawal of about 1,000 U.S. troops before the end of the year should be developed."[20] Yet there is nothing about the implementation of the plan in October, or what happened to the plan after that. His explanation to me for the omission is that "I probably was influenced by what others had written on the subject."[21]

This explanation appears to contain an inversion that is both curious and instructive. Much more plausibly, it was what people had *not* written that influenced Professor Kahin. Earlier histories had marginalized the issue of the implementation and annulment of the withdrawal plan by not discussing it, by avoiding it, and thus leaving it to be speculated upon in the sub-literature circulating about the Kennedy assassination. The marginality of this sub-literature is usually apparent from its out-of-the-mainstream publishers. The subject, in short, had become controversial, and indecorous.

THE NEED FOR A PARADIGM SHIFT

Unfortunately it is hard for me to address this subject disinterestedly, since I am often the source cited in the assassination sub-literature.[22] But what I see is the phenomenon of a paradigm shift as discussed by Thomas Kuhn in *The Structure of Scientific Revolutions*. Paradigms, Kuhn wrote, "determine large areas of experience at the same time." Evidence challenging that paradigm tends to be suppressed, the more so as the extant paradigm becomes codified in textbooks. Eventually the accumulation of enough anomalous evidence produces a competing paradigm, but one shared by a new population in poor communication with the old one: "the proponents of competing paradigms practice their trades in different worlds." Kuhn notes the resistance that arises to the new paradigm, "particularly from those whose productive careers have committed them to an older tradition." And he quotes from Max Planck that "a new scientific truth does not triumph by convincing its opponents and making them see the light, but rather because its opponents eventually die, and a new generation grows up that is familiar with it."[23]

If such resistance and discontinuous progress can prevail in the realm of science, how much more so in the realm of history, where the psychological and social investment in continuity and rational evolution (and hence in resistance to counterevidence) is so much greater. Most readers may resist the notion that interpretations of the Kennedy assassination, and of circumambient events such as the change in Vietnam policy, are central and profound enough to be called paradigmatic. But as a foreigner who lived through it, I could not but observe the depth and centrality of everyone's response to the assassination of the President. How one saw that assassination affected, and was affected by, how one interpreted the rest of the world.

It is certainly true, as the establishment press reiterates from time to time, that many people are psychologically disposed to conspiratorial explanations for events like political murder. Many leftists repeat this

cliché, adding that conspiratorial explanations allow people to externalize evil and separate it from the political system under which they
live. Such psychological explanations can be put forward in an open-
minded and truth-seeking spirit, but only if their proponents concede
that the opposite is also true. That is, many people, particularly those
whose productive careers have prospered under the status quo, are
equally disposed on psychological grounds to reject conspiratorial explanations for events that affect the legitimacy of the society they live
in. For some years, whenever I have been treated to a short sermon
about the paranoid style in American politics, I have asked the preacher
if he (it is never a she) did not recognize the psychological grounds for
his anti-conspiratorial position as well. Few do.

And yet the evidence is there: not just with respect to the central
event of the assassination itself, but with much smaller, ancillary matters, such as the repression and denial of the Vietnam policy change
which occurred in the same time period. What is at stake here is a competition between paradigms of how politics works. One is the establishment paradigm, codified in textbooks and taught in universities as "political science," whether pluralist or Marxist: this sees politics as a
system of overtly identified interactive forces, and offers an inclusive
chart of political behavior in which, for example, there is little or no
room for assassinations.

ALTERNATIVES TO THE ESTABLISHMENT
MODEL OF GOVERNMENT

At present there is more than one alternative to this establishment
model. What I propose as a competing paradigm, that of deep politics,
is certainly not the most commonly encountered alternative. Many
more people, convinced that overt politics is not the true arena of
power, postulate a kind of Satanic reflection of it. Thus they talk reactively of some unified "shadow government," "invisible government,"
or "secret team."

Unified "shadow" models are, in my experience, usually based less
on research than on reactions to the resistance and denial which have
been observed with regard to sensitive topics, such as the political assassinations in this country, or the CIA, or elite institutions such as the
Council on Foreign Relations, or the drug traffic. The moment one be-

gins to gather extensive data on any one aspect of deep politics, such as organized crime, it is only too easy to pass from one extreme reception of it, the systematic underacknowledgment of its power, to its opposite, and to conclude that one has found the key to all political mysteries. Actually, shadow-government theories, by their very totalizing, do not seriously challenge the most sensitive feature of the conventional power paradigm. This is the belief that overt politics and deep politics have little to do with each other, a belief in which establishment media, hyperstructuralist Marxists, and even shadow-government conspiratorialists, all paradoxically concur.

The deep-politics paradigm, in contrast, attempts to go beyond all such restricted, unified explanations. It is essentially an extension of conventional political investigative methods to consideration of a much larger field of evidence, including, but not restricted to, the unacknowledged processes and events which conventional decorum excludes from our current "political science" textbooks. By thus examining overt events in this larger field of deep political arrangements, it breaks down the distinction between overt and covert power, and thereby hopefully avoids the frequently asked question: Which forces are in control, the public or shadow powers?

It also responds to those who object that no conspiracy to kill the President could have remained a secret for so long in a society as open as America's. We shall see in this book that beneath the open surface of our society lie connections and relationships of long standing, virtually immune to disclosure, and capable of great crimes, including serial murder. To the stock objection that it would be virtually impossible to assemble a murder conspiracy without leakage, the response is that an existing conspiratorial network or system of networks, already in place and capable of murder, would have much less difficulty in maintaining the discipline of secrecy.

I shall focus on the intelligence-sanctioned international narcotics network as a candidate for such a conspiracy, because of the involvement, directly or indirectly, of so many relevant players. The drug traffic, when we look at it more closely, will be seen to consist of overlapping networks, relating official to private power through collusion and corruption.

We shall see that a key reason to suspect drug involvement in the assassination is the sustained effort of administration and congressional officials, in 1964 and again in 1978, to conceal the extent of Jack Ruby's involvement with both drug traffickers and law enforcement. I have not assumed, and certainly cannot prove, that this network arranged the assassination. I suspect, however, that the need to keep this particular secret helped explain the cover-up, particularly with respect to Ruby, even if the other principals were only indirectly related to it.

This book analyzes diverse forms of deep politics and parapolitics, acknowledging the historical relevance of splits within bureaucracies, within economic systems, and within the clumsily named phenomenon of organized crime. In other words, the model for deep politics put forward in these pages, although aiming at a more integrative view of politics than the conventional model, is also roughly pluralistic both above, in the public arena, and also below. Above all, the fact that an area of political activity (such as CIA covert operations) is unacknowledged, or even actively suppressed, should not lead us, reactively, to exaggerate its importance. That these pages focus on areas of facts usually unacknowledged or denied does not mean that I believe them to be the determinant areas or facts of our political life; only that fuller understanding of our politics, toward the goal of public control of political life, requires a fuller understanding of these areas as of others.

The common method in these chapters is to look at areas where there is such resistance and denial. The findings I reach in them are still too scattered and incomplete to be labeled a competing paradigm. What I put forward here is not a new system, but only a method. And if I apply it to the Kennedy assassination, the goal is not so much to solve that beleaguered case as to better understand the society that engendered it.

A DEEP POLITICAL READING
OF THE KENNEDY ASSASSINATION

The Warren Commission investigation of the murder of John F. Kennedy, however unsatisfactory it may have been, at least released an unprecedented flood of FBI and other official documentation surrounding both Lee Harvey Oswald and Jack Ruby. Most researchers who have pored over this evidence have done so for the narrow purpose of "solving" the case, in the sense of establishing "Who did it?" This goal has proven difficult to achieve, especially as the hottest clues have been recurringly neutralized by still more new and contradictory evidence.

The same documentation proves much more fruitful if we study it not to pinpoint assassins but to understand more about the deep politics of this country, the ongoing, unacknowledged processes linking so-called legitimate political and economic activities to their criminal underpinnings. Both Ruby and Oswald, when studied in this broader political context, emerge as operators within the world where political and criminal activities interface. By studying them, we learn more about the assassination and its political context. We also learn more about the deep involvement of criminals in the deep political processes of our country.

We learn more, finally, about how and why the whole question of "organized crime," and above all the so-called Cosa Nostra, has been systematically misrepresented by law enforcement investigators and prosecutors. For this active misrepresentation has deformed the two official investigations into the Kennedy assassination itself, not in marginal ways, but so as to conceal central truths about the assassination, truths that were embarrassing to those conducting the investigation. In the end one comes to recognize that the history of organized crime and the history of the investigation and prosecution of organized crime are closely intertwined processes affecting one another. Processes, one must add, which mutually affect the true, but concealed, seats of political power in this country.

It is now recognized that the Warren Commission investigation was a deformed one. A recent history of the CIA notes that, "as historians would comment," the Warren Commission's most active member, Allen Dulles, "blanked out whenever the discussion touched Castro," because of his unwillingness to let the Commission's investigation get into a most pertinent project, the CIA-Mafia plots against Castro.[24] Robert Blakey, general counsel for the second official investigation, the House Select Committee on Assassinations, documents in his book how the Warren Commission investigation was deflected from the CIA-Mafia plots.[25]

But Allen Dulles was far from the only Warren Commission member with a special turf to protect. A true examination of Lee Harvey Oswald and his family would have led to the influence of New Orleans mob figure Carlos Marcello on Louisiana Democratic party politics; but somehow, with the presence on the Commission of Louisiana Congressman Hale Boggs (himself deeply indebted to Marcello for help on his political campaigns), this never happened.[26] One of the Commission's senior counsels, Albert Jenner, was a Chicago attorney with a history of representing figures, such as Allen Dorfman, from Ruby's milieu. In the 1970s he would even represent one of the men (Irwin Weiner) who had been phoned by Jack Ruby.[27] Jenner in 1963 was counsel for General Dynamics, which, as we shall see, was at the time deeply embroiled in a series of Texas-based scandals being exposed by the Kennedys, and should perhaps have been under investigation itself.

Few informed observers would now doubt that the purpose of the Warren Commission was not to find out who killed the President; as we shall see in Chapter 3, the purpose was damage control. Even the second official investigation, that of the House Select Committee on Assassinations, had to conclude that the performance of the Warren Commission, which "acted in good faith," "was in fact flawed":

> Virtually all former Warren Commission members and staff contacted by the [House] committee said they regarded the CIA-Mafia plots against Fidel Castro to be the most important information withheld from the Commission. They all agreed that an awareness of the plots would have led to significant new areas of investigation and would have altered the general approach of the investigation. (AR 258)

Among the deficiencies the Committee identified in the Warren Commission's performance were "Oswald's activities and associations during the periods he lived in New Orleans," and "the background, activities, and associations of Jack Ruby, particularly with regard to organized crime" (AR 260). The Committee was quite right to identify these areas; and, to its credit, shared much previously suppressed information with the public.

Despite this, after a decade of reflection, I have come to the troubled conclusion that, at bottom, the House Committee investigation, like the Warren Commission's, was also seriously flawed. And for the same reason: despite some excellent individual performances, the search for the truth was still limited by the need for damage control.

Later I shall have kinder and more exculpatory things to say about the House Committee investigation. But I should say at the outset that the errors and distortions to be found in its report mostly do not originate with the Committee, but are transmitted as part of an evidentiary record which had been distorted or falsified much earlier, some of it by the FBI.[28] The methodological problems of working with falsified evidence are immense, as I shall discuss in Chapter 4, and the House Committee's work should therefore be appreciated for the many ways in which it definitely has advanced our understanding.

This book has been distorted by the same problem. I have avoided major topics to which I earlier attached great importance, such as Oswald's visit to the Soviet Union, because of the unresolved issues pertaining to such relevant evidence as the Defense Department's reports of Oswald's service record.[29] Unlike some other authors, I have also been wary of new witnesses who have come forward. In 1977 I did a film for television with the Canadian Broadcasting Corporation; and, long before this project became common knowledge, we almost instantly had one such new witness, a French-speaking Québecois who claimed to have known Oswald. His story quickly collapsed during our interrogation; I learned from it, however, that the problem of falsification is an ongoing one.

To sum up: official investigations of the Kennedy assassination have failed, not because the case is inherently insoluble, but because both the case and the investigations have been governed by deeper political processes, which have not yet been discerned.

These forces are still with us, and they are not benign. Much has been made of the number of witnesses who were murdered or wounded at the time of the Kennedy assassination.[30] To the twenty-one or more who are supposed to have died violent deaths during the Warren Commission investigation, Anthony Summers adds a supplementary list of sixteen, who died at the time of the Garrison investigation of 1967, Church Committee investigation of 1975–76, and House Committee investigation of 1977–78.[31] Some of the names in the secondary list are far more prominent than any in the first. We shall see that at least two of the murders, of mobsters Sam Giancana and John Rosselli, have been said by credible informants to have been occasioned by their testimony to the Church Committee, pending or just delivered, about the Kennedy assassination.

THE KENNEDY CASE AGAIN? WHY BOTHER?

Let me conclude with a brief articulation of my personal political beliefs as to why deep political analysis of events such as the Kennedy assassination is useful. This book is written in an age of declining belief in Enlightenment, when grandiose designs for political change, such as socialism or communism, have in most cases been thrust aside.

The shadow of the unsolved Kennedy case has only increased the skepticism of many as to reason's ability to address major social events. Even among former assassination researchers, one finds the cynical assumption that the more important a political mystery, the less likely we are to learn the truth behind it. The response of Bob Katz, who spent nearly ten years in the 1970s working on the Kennedy assassination, spoke for many of the Chilled Generation when he wrote that "the truth in this case lies buried forever. The Unsolved Murder of the Century has entered the realm of myth."[32]

What has failed here, in my view, is not human rationality itself, but that imperfect ideological crystalization of it which we call the Enlightenment. Both Marx and Weber, following Hegel, hypostatized rationality and neglected competing factors in history. Others, acting in the opposite direction, have hypostatized the irrational, or (in the case of the later Freud) the return of the repressed.

The defect here has not been that of rationality, but only of the historic ideologies put forward in reason's name. In my poetry I take issue with the Enlightenment contempt for poetry and religion; I propose that, in the spirit of Dante or the *Tao Te Ching*, we should move instead toward a deeper Enmindment that respects the truths of darkness, as well as those of light.

Deep political analysis is one specific attempt at enmindment in the political area. It grounds the processes for political change in a larger context less amenable to control, not to reject the inspiring vision of change, but to render it more possible. In the case of the Vietnam War, I now concede that it was naive, or what I call the cognitive fallacy, to believe that that intervention could have been prevented simply by publishing facts such as those in this book. However, I still believe that better understanding of history can better prepare us for change, and thus contribute to a better future.

This book is an act of faith, not just in history but in America. Jungian psychologists write of the buried shadow in the psyche, the repository for repressed unpleasantness. In a sense this book is about the collective shadow, or shadows, of America. Good citizens will rightly feel, as they read, that this is not the whole story of America, that I am leaving out the good side. This is true. No one can write the complete book of America, and this one is too long already.

But psychologists explore shadows, not because they prefer darkness, but because they believe that healing can come from an enlargement of insight. Obviously the only justification for this book is a similar optimism. If America were no more than its shadows depicted here, logic and common sense would rule out the writing and publication of this book.

Just as there is more to life than logic, there is more to America than its shadows. I believe that America, for all its shortcomings and present difficulties, is still an unusually open society, where it is still possible to strive for even greater openness and justice. This book is an appeal to America's residue of humanity, an appeal based more on faith than on logic.

Consider for a moment the contrary situation prevailing in eastern Europe. No one there could write and publish about the monstrosities of Stalinism, until Stalin was dead. Years later, after the collapse of the Soviet empire, survivors reproached themselves for not having criticized their regimes more severely and candidly. They had been silent because they thought to protect the ideals of socialism, and later recognized that by their silence they had contributed passively to the corruption of those ideals.

One should not expect too much from merely exposing and understanding the corruption of our society. The original investigation of Watergate, as we shall see in Chapter 14, did not get to the heart of the matter and had only limited results. And yet, at a time when America was disengaging from Vietnam, one fallout from the Watergate inquiries was the partial scaling back of an oppressive domestic security apparatus which had become anachronistic. Now, with the closing down of the Cold War, one can hope that a further scaling back might result from even partial disclosures of bureaucratic responsibility for what happened in 1963.

TWO

Kennedy, Johnson, and Vietnam

A Tale of Two NSAMs

Whatever is done against Vietnam will be felt in America
too. . . . I can predict to you all that the story in Vietnam
is only at its beginning.

Madame Ngo Dinh Nhu, November 2, 1963

NSAM 263 AND NSAM 273

While there were undoubtedly fictions in Oliver Stone's movie *JFK*,
many critics at the time of its release in 1991 concentrated on denying
two of Stone's incontrovertible facts. The first was that in late 1963
Kennedy had authorized an initial withdrawal of 1,000 U.S. troops
from Vietnam, as the first step of a pull-out to be substantially completed by the end of 1965. The second was that, in a high-level meeting
right after Kennedy's murder, Johnson redirected U.S. Vietnam policy
from this graduated disengagement to graduated escalation.[1]

These divergent decisions were encoded in two divergent National
Security Action Memoranda, NSAMs 263 and 273. NSAM 263 of October 11, 1963, was Kennedy's last NSAM policy directive on Vietnam.
NSAM 273 of November 26, 1963, dated four days after the assassination, was Johnson's first. The two NSAMs (once pronounced "nas-
sums," now usually "ensams") were flashed in the Stone movie, but
only for about six seconds. These six seconds engendered an intense
counterattack in the establishment press. The subject is indeed sensitive, even explosive.

The language of both documents was convoluted and misleading,
but for different reasons. NSAM 273 was partly designed to reassure an
anguished nation that murder and/or conspiracy had not changed national policy, whether or not it had. To this day, many leading critics of

Stone's handling of the two NSAMs have this same establishment urge, not to find truth, but to soothe the anxieties of the nation, and possibly themselves. Thus it is that six seconds of NSAMs in *JFK* engendered a cover-up, as did the earlier six seconds of gunfire in Dallas.

But Kennedy's NSAM 263 was also misleading, reflecting the intense conflicts raging within the Administration at the time. This brings up another important fact that is not contested: Vietnam in late 1963 divided the Kennedy bureaucracy like no other issue. (NSAM 273 even acknowledged these policy differences, by ordering that all senior officers end their criticisms of one another.) One faction (the "military" one, although it included civilians) gave priority to "winning" the war. The other, "political," faction had also hoped to "win," but had subordinated this chimeric goal to more realistic considerations of both international and domestic politics. Conspiratorial bureaucratic plotting in Washington between these two factions was exacerbated by the killing of Diem and his brother in Saigon on November 2. Both factions had been divided internally over the coup, but key personnel in the "military" faction, notably Vice-President Johnson, had opposed it bitterly.

The two NSAMs, seeking to balance these vivid tensions, are indeed so convoluted that perhaps only bureaucrats can make sense of their language.[2] But after the death of Kennedy the bureaucratic interpretation of NSAM 273 became extremely simple. General Maxwell Taylor, Chairman of the Joint Chiefs of Staff, told the Pentagon on January 22, 1964, that NSAM 273 "makes clear the resolve of the President to ensure victory. . . . To do this, we must prepare for whatever level of activity may be required."[3]

And indeed the root issue dividing the two NSAMs had always been a simple one. Kennedy's NSAM 263 reflected the "political" priority of avoiding an unlimited commitment to the war, by the signal (important politically but not militarily) of withdrawing 1,000 troops. Johnson's NSAM 273, while deceptively reiterating language from a still earlier and lower-level document about withdrawal, chose instead the "military" option of escalation, and also reversed Kennedy's most recent Vietnam policy NSAM.

Time after time Stone's critics, from Leslie Gelb in the *Times* to Alexander Cockburn in the *Nation,* have replaced this verifiable issue of fact by an unverifiable one: whether or not JFK would have pulled the

United States out of Vietnam. One can agree with Gelb that what Kennedy would or would not have done, had he lived, is a "mighty unknown."[4] But Stone talks about something much more specific, and undeniable: Kennedy's "political" decision to withdraw 1,000 U.S. troops by the end of 1963.

Kennedy's policies at the moment of his death are a matter of record: a fiercely suppressed record, to be sure, but a record I was able to reconstruct deductively in 1971 from the Pentagon Papers. My tentative reconstruction of the two NSAMs and their significance has now been massively documented in a new book, *JFK and Vietnam,* by the professional historian John Newman. Newman and I essentially agree on the following propositions.

1. Despite vigorous bureaucratic opposition, Kennedy used NSAM 263 to give his authorized disengagement plans, "to withdraw 1000 U.S. military personnel [from Vietnam] by the end of 1963," their first implementation. This was in accordance with his more long-range program to train Vietnamese, making it "possible to withdraw the bulk of U.S. personnel . . . by the end of 1965."

The sources for this quoted "political" language are not anti-war senators Mike Mansfield and Wayne Morse, as Cockburn has implied. The language is taken from the top-secret Military Recommendations to the President by Defense Secretary McNamara and General Maxwell Taylor on October 2, 1963. The "presently prepared plans" to withdraw 1,000 troops, which they now recommended announcing, had in fact been approved at a SecDef Conference the preceding May.

2. In NSAM 263 of October 11, Kennedy secretly approved the recommendation by Defense Secretary McNamara and General Taylor "to announce in the very near future" withdrawing 1,000 troops, "as an initial step in a long-term program to replace U.S. personnel" (*Pentagon Papers* [Beacon], II, 752, 769–70). He directed then "that no formal announcement be made of the implementation" of these plans, but in November the secrecy was lifted, with the hint that the details would come from a top-level Honolulu conference on November 20, 1963. This happened, and the *New York Times* wrote on November 21, one day before the assassination in Dallas, of the "plan to bring home about 1,000 . . . by January 1."

3. Two days after the assassination, Johnson and his top advisers (all Kennedy holdovers) approved a new policy statement, finalized as

NSAM 273 of November 26. With respect to the 1,000 troops, the text was highly ambiguous and deliberately misleading: "The objectives of the United States with respect to the withdrawal of U.S. military personnel remain as stated in the White House statement of October 2, 1963." In that statement McNamara and Taylor had "reported their judgment" that the United States could basically complete its military task "by the end of 1965," and "should" be able to withdraw 1,000 men by the end of 1963 (*Pentagon Papers* [Beacon], II, 188). This conditional and personal "judgment" was obviously not binding, unlike the unconditional presidential "implementation" of secret plans, three days later, in NSAM 263 (*Pentagon Papers* [Beacon], II, 769–70).

Of course the *objectives* of NSAM 273 with respect to withdrawal remained the same: no one wanted the U.S. troops to fight there forever. But the *implementation* of this withdrawal under NSAM 263, a decision so controversial that to this day there are those who cannot talk candidly about it, had been replaced by the earlier objectives and nothing more. Furthermore, NSAM 273 directed that military and economic assistance programs should not appear to be lower than they had been under the Diem government (a directive distinguishable technically, but not in substance, from the issue of U.S. troop levels).

The best proof of the difference is that, despite frequent lies to the contrary, the planned withdrawal of units advising combat troops was never implemented. Although differing figures have been given for U.S. troop strength at the year's end, none of these figures represents a decrease of 1,000 from the October high level of 16,500. It appears that instead only a few hundred individuals, not units, were withdrawn, and these from non-combat elements.[5]

4. The key policy innovation of NSAM 273 was for the United States to begin carrying the war north. For the first time in any presidential directive, NSAM 273 authorized prompt planning for "different" (i.e., escalating) levels of military activity against North Vietnam, up to and including bombing. These operations, which led to U.S. destroyer patrols and the August 1964 Tonkin Gulf incidents, had in fact been discussed for some time inside the Pentagon, but had never before been presented for presidential authorization. Allegedly, McNamara himself never saw the plans until November 20.

5. In its final form, NSAM 273 was crafted to deceive, by launching a public, but false, illusion of continuity with Kennedy's policies. Spe-

cifically, the language reaffirming Kennedy's "objectives" with respect
to withdrawal was published on November 25, 1963, in the *New York
Times* and the *Washington Post,* but with no hints about carrying the
war north. This deception in 1963 can presumably be blamed on the
Administration, not on the press. But the *Times* and the *Post* had no
such excuse for continuing the deception in 1991–92.

6. Ultimately, the issue of what these nuanced NSAMs "meant" is
made clear, not just by the texts alone, but by how the texts were interpreted at the time by the restricted audiences to whom they were addressed. Here there is abundant corroboration for General Taylor's
"military" interpretation of NSAM 273 as authorization for something that Kennedy had turned down in 1961 and again in October
1963: an unlimited commitment to win in Vietnam. (As Taylor wrote in
January 1964, NSAM "273 makes clear the resolve of the [new] President to ensure victory.") On November 26, the day of NSAM 273, the
Joint Chiefs used its language to launch accelerated planning for escalation against North Vietnam. Since then, members of the "political"
faction have confirmed their understanding that the era of Kennedy's
limited engagement, as exemplified by NSAM 263, had ended with his
assassination.

THE ILLUSION OF POLICY CONTINUITY
IN THE PENTAGON PAPERS

In the late 1960s the illusion of continuity was reinforced by some of
the secret Pentagon Studies of the war (known to the public as the Pentagon Papers), which were prepared secretly for Defense Secretary
McNamara. The principal author of this "continuity" cover-up in the
secret Pentagon Papers was Leslie Gelb, then in the Pentagon but later
a columnist for the *New York Times.*

The year 1963 was a difficult one for the McNamara-authorized histories to treat coherently. From the May SecDef Conference on, there
had been planning for withdrawal, and simultaneously for escalation.
The Pentagon Studies avoided reconciling these two divergent tracks by
assigning them to separate Studies, attributing the former track to "optimism," the latter to a sense of deepening gloom.

Gelb had the task of writing "Summaries" for these conflicting accounts of the Kennedy-Johnson transition. Thus in one Summary (*Pen-*

tagon Papers [Beacon], III, 2) Gelb wrote of the "aura of optimism" which led NSAM 273 of November 26 "to endorse policies pursued by President Kennedy" (on withdrawal). In another (*Pentagon Papers* [Beacon], II, 207) he described "the real gravity of the economic situation" and the "deterioration of the military situation" which already "dominated the discussions at the Honolulu Conference on November 20" (about escalation).

Few will agree with the first of these two conflicting mood descriptions. Gelb himself admitted elsewhere that the "rosy picture" being painted "as late as July 1963" had been replaced by a "more balanced evaluation" by the time of "the McNamara-Taylor trip report late in September and October, 1963" (*Pentagon Papers* [Beacon], II, 164).

This admission by Gelb in 1968–69 (which vastly underestimates the actual degree of official pessimism) is perhaps the best rebuttal to his absurd claim, in the *Times* of January 6, 1992, that NSAM 263 (of October 11, 1963) "was grounded in one of the few periods of genuine optimism about the war. So Kennedy had some basis for believing the war might be won soon and that U.S. forces could be withdrawn." By October 1963 optimism survived only in the false rhetoric of those seeking by deception to maintain budgetary and congressional support for the war; it seems clear (from the NSC minutes in question) that Kennedy was not fooled by it.[6]

But Gelb's inaccuracies in 1968–69 went far beyond debatable issues about mood. In another Summary (*Pentagon Papers* [Beacon], II, 163), Gelb wrote that "the U.S. did effect a 1,000 man withdrawal in December of 1963," a claim underlying the press distortions of 1991 (in response to Stone's movie) and sometimes repeated in them. But the Study Gelb purported to summarize said quite the opposite: the withdrawals were an "accounting exercise" that "did not even represent a decline of 1000" (*Pentagon Papers* [Beacon], II, 191). Its Chronology confirmed that "no actual reduction of US strength was achieved. The December figure was *not* 1,000 less than the peak October level" (II, 171; italics in original).

In rebuttal to Stone's movie, Gelb's distortions in the *Pentagon Papers* were revived and repeated everywhere in the press. Although both NSAMs were declassified in the 1970s, the obfuscation of the record in the *Post*, the *Times*, and even the *Nation*, continued. In June 1991, George Lardner wrote in the *Post* that NSAM 273 "ordered the withdrawal [of 1,000 troops] to be carried out."[7] (It didn't.) Michael Specter wrote in the *Times* that NSAM 273 "continued Kennedy's policies, and historians have shown that it was drafted the day before Kennedy journeyed to Dallas."[8] But on November 21, the day in question, Kennedy was in Texas, and he never saw the draft prepared for his signature. He may of course have heard it over the telephone. But the draft spoke only of additional resources for activities against North Vietnam by the *GVN* (the Saigon government). NSAM 273 deleted this restriction and sanctioned plans for U.S. operations which began shortly thereafter. This deletion of the GVN restriction is by itself proof of the change in policy which occurred between November 21 (under JFK) and on November 24 (under LBJ).

LBJ'S INTRIGUES WITH THE MILITARY
FOR U.S. INVOLVEMENT, 1961–63

That this policy change followed so closely on the assassination does nothing to prove the contention that differences over Vietnam became a motive for killing Kennedy. But Newman's 1992 book, *JFK and Vietnam,* which documents the November 24 policy shift more clearly than I could ever have done in 1971, also proves that Johnson had been, since 1961, the ally of the Joint Chiefs (and in particular Air Force General Curtis LeMay) in their unrelenting efforts, against Kennedy's repeated refusals, to introduce U.S. combat troops into Asia.[9]

In May 1961, according to Newman, LBJ had briefly been a "linchpin" in an attempted end-run around Kennedy's reluctance. On May 10 the Joint Chiefs sent a recommendation to Defense Secretary McNamara that Ngo Dinh Diem of Vietnam be "encouraged to request" U.S. combat troops. A copy of this memo (which McNamara failed to endorse) was sent in an urgent OPIMMEDIATE cable to Saigon for Johnson to see, just before his scheduled meeting with Diem. In circumstances which Newman finds "too coincidental not to have been planned," Johnson acted on the unapproved recommendation, raised the issue of U.S. combat troops, and obtained from Diem the response that he "did want an increase in U.S. training personnel." Moments later, Diem had accepted the compromise proposed by Johnson's companion, General McGarr, that U.S. combat troops be introduced "for direct training purposes." Johnson's own military aide, Colonel

Howard Burris, who was also present, recalls that McGarr's talk of "training" was really just a "guise."[10]

As Newman points out, McGarr's compromise "parallels precisely" a formula inserted into policy documents two weeks earlier in Washington by General Lansdale, saying that 16,000 U.S. combat troops were required in Vietnam as trainers. That General McGarr proposed the same number, 16,000, is for Newman a certain sign of back-channel coordination. He sees Lansdale's hand in the scenario; but he also finds it hard to rule out the idea "that Johnson was rehearsed for the combat troops discussion." Johnson's coach was possibly his military aide, Colonel Burris, who admitted to Newman that he "was specifically instructed, by persons he calls 'the boys in the woodwork,' " with respect to the combat troops issue.[11]

Kennedy of course turned down the spring 1961 proposals to dispatch 16,000 combat troops, and also turned down General Taylor's recommendation for 8,000 the following November. But the formula of U.S. "combat-trainer units" endured, was gradually implemented, and had led to the first U.S. casualty in Vietnam before Christmas 1961.[12] On December 19, 1961, a Burris memo to Johnson noted that Lemnitzer had pointedly failed to tell the President about the shift to a combat role. By March 1962 the Vice-President was being regularly informed of what was being withheld from the President.[13]

A back channel had been established whereby "the boys in the woodwork" were feeding Burris and Johnson a steady stream of accurate Vietnam intelligence reports which were denied to the President. With what Newman calls deception and subterfuge, the U.S. military MACV Intelligence Chief in Saigon (like Burris an Air Force colonel) prepared one series of false and optimistic intelligence reports, which were delivered to McNamara and the President and helped ensure their ongoing support for the war. Meanwhile, U.S. Army Intelligence in Honolulu kept producing a second series of reports, more accurate and gloomy. These were denied to the President and McNamara, but supplied by a secret intelligence back channel to Vice-President Johnson. Newman calls this duplicitous intelligence relationship with the Vice-President "one of the great mysteries of the Vietnam War during the Kennedy years."[14]

What is most unsettling about this selective deception of the President and McNamara is that General Maxwell Taylor, whom Kennedy had appointed Chairman of the Joint Chiefs of Staff, was part of it. Colonel John Paul Vann came from Vietnam to Washington in April 1963, with a report highly critical of MACV's optimistic assessments of the war, which were supported by Taylor. When Taylor learned from Marine General Krulak (another "optimist") about the contents of Vann's dissident report, he immediately canceled Vann's scheduled briefing before the Joint Chiefs of Staff.[15]

These divisive intrigues came to a head at the Honolulu conference of November 20, 1963, two days before the assassination. At this meeting the truth about the deterioration of the ineffective war effort "was presented in detail to those assembled, along with a plan to widen the war, while the 1,000-man withdrawal [first publicly announced at the same meeting] was turned into a meaningless paper drill."[16]

The tone of the meeting, in other words, was in keeping with the policies of the man who would not become President until the shootings in Dallas two days later. On the most important issue of all, the introduction of U.S. combat troops, the published documentary record is inadequate to determine if this was agreed to at Honolulu. It was, however, achieved by the change of presidents:

> Kennedy had told [Kenneth] O'Donnell in the spring of 1963 that he could not pull out of Vietnam until he was reelected, "So we had better make damned sure I *am* reelected." . . . [A]t a White House reception on Christmas eve, a month after he succeeded to the presidency, Lyndon Johnson told the Joint Chiefs: "Just get me elected, and then you can have your war."[17]

Thus there are two interlocking mysteries about the events of November 1963: the assassination, and the pre-assassination preparations for a reversal of Vietnam policy endorsed almost immediately by the incoming president. Newman is careful to make clear that the assassination is a topic beyond the scope of his book. He thus does not examine, as we shall, the disturbing role of army intelligence in both mysteries (see Chapter 17).

THE NEED FOR DISCLOSURE

The interface between the two mysteries lies in the genesis for the policy reversal encoded in NSAM 273. Clearly in 1991–92, as earlier, the documentary record and significance of the two NSAMs were still being systematically, and indeed predictably, distorted. I would suggest that distortions and cover-ups, when systematically repeated, testify to the perceived importance of the material they conceal.

If I am wrong, if there is nothing but continuity between the two NSAMs, then national discomfort about the events of 1963 will be all the better served by what I have repeatedly called for: complete disclosure of the remaining documents pertaining to NSAM 263, NSAM 273, and the intervening Honolulu conference. For it is truly ironic that, after thousands of words of rebuttal against Stone's movie, so many of these crucial Vietnam policy documents remain classified. Stone's critics have all argued that there is no significance to this documentary record; if so, there is no reason today to keep it secret.

I predict, however, that there will be intense resistance to declassifying these central documents, and that we shall more easily obtain the files of the House Select Committee on Assassinations. As I see it, the Vietnam documents may well prove to be explosive either way. We may learn that the escalations discussed at Honolulu were for operations against North Vietnam by the Saigon government alone. In this case we would have proof that NSAM 273, which lifted this restraint, represented a turning point in the Vietnam War (and that a Pentagon Study was wrong when it claimed that in NSAM 273 "no new programs were proposed or endorsed" (*Pentagon Papers* [Beacon], II, 458]).

Alternatively, we may learn that the "advisory" restriction on the U.S. role had already been effectively eroded in the plans discussed at Honolulu but never seen by the President. This would show that a group within the military command, dissatisfied with Kennedy's limited support, had already begun secretly to plan for the option preferred by the Vice-President.

A third possibility, of course, is that some of the key documents will prove to be "missing." This is already the case with respect to the minutes of the secret discussion which authorized this covert-operations planning the previous May. It is also the case with the Army Intelligence file on Lee Harvey Oswald, which was never given to the Warren Commission and was later destroyed (AR 221–25). The Vietnam documentary record, in short, could serve either to strip away the mystery from this tale of two NSAMs, or alternatively to point to deeper political mysteries. By either outcome, both truth and the nation would be served.

BUREAUCRATIC POLITICS AND DEEP POLITICS

We must expect, however, that the parapolitical infighting inside the Pentagon bureaucracies will prove to have been grounded in deeper political conflicts dividing the nation as a whole. In Chapter 13 we shall see that such conflict had escalated in late 1963, with strident voices for a more aggressive Vietnam policy coming from the American Security Council.

The ASC was not just the leading group lobbying for the use of air power in Vietnam. It called also for the displacement of Fidel Castro from Cuba, and for a more militant posture toward the Soviet Union. In its ranks were veteran anti-Communist activists, like William Pawley, General Charles Willoughby, and Robert Morris from the old China Lobby (and names we shall deal with below). But the key to ASC's clout was its financial support from the leading defense contractors of the nation, such as General Electric, Lockheed, Motorola, Honeywell, and General Dynamics.[18]

Such industries also subsidized other far-right voices for escalation, like the so-called Christian Crusade of Billy James Hargis. The Kennedys had tried to curb this lobbying apparatus of the Cold War, as when they secured the dismissal of General Edwin Walker from the U.S. Army, for indoctrinating his troops with propaganda supplied to him by Hargis.[19]

In this inconspicuous and indirect way, the government-based defense industries, a structural part of the postwar American economy, were contributing to the exotic and marginal world inhabited by Lee Harvey Oswald, who for one or another reason (see Chapter 16), "spied upon and photographed the home of General Edwin Walker" in 1963.[20]

EPILOGUE

After this book was first written, and while I was out of the United States, Noam Chomsky published an analysis of Kennedy's NSAM 263 and Johnson's NSAM 273, to rebut the claim of John Newman (and myself) that the assassination of John F. Kennedy was followed almost immediately by a more escalatory U.S. policy in Vietnam.[21] I regret that I can now reply to it only briefly.

Chomsky relies heavily on what he calls "the internal planning record" (9), not noting that a good deal of this record (the Pentagon Papers) is in fact an edited version of the primary documents, in the Pentagon Studies prepared for McNamara inside the Pentagon in the later 1960s. Much of Chomsky's case, for continuity between the two NSAMs and administrations, is in fact the case made by Leslie Gelb and some of the other editors of the Pentagon Studies. Two decades ago I first argued, as now, that much of Gelb's case for continuity was based on selective editing and sometimes blatant distortion. Two decades ago, when others declined to publish my article, noting its political incorrectness in discriminating between presidential policies, it was Chomsky (who even then must not have agreed with it) who arranged for it to appear.[22]

It is painful for me, as a long-time admirer of Chomsky's striving for truth and honesty in politics, to deal with our present disagreements. In my view, they derive partly from Chomsky's too-uncritical acceptance of the Gelb case for continuity, supported by Chomsky's own rationalist analysis of texts outside their bureaucratic setting, often without regard for how they were interpreted at the time.

1. Following Gelb, Chomsky alleges that Kennedy's withdrawal planning was in response to an "optimistic mid-1962 assessment" (10), repeating what Gelb had to say about "the euphoria and optimism of July 1962" (*Pentagon Papers* [Beacon], II, 160). But in fact the planning was first ordered by McNamara in May 1962.[23] This was one month after ambassador Kenneth Galbraith, disenchanted after a presidentially ordered visit to Vietnam, had proposed a "political solution" based in part on a proposal to the Soviets entertaining "phased American withdrawal."[24] One cannot prove that Galbraith's recommendation was responsible for McNamara's order; but neither can one rely naively on Gelb's suspect chronology and explanation.

2. Chomsky argues that the position advocating "withdrawal *without victory* . . . received scant support until well after the Tet offensive of January 1968" (11). But it was at least contemplated in a question raised by Robert Kennedy in September 1963, whether victory could be achieved "with any government. If it could not, now was the time to get out of Vietnam entirely, rather than waiting."[25] Chomsky might well retort that this is far less than a principled advocacy of withdrawal; but in my view it is a startling and authoritative divergence from the bureaucratic consensus.

3. Chomsky argues that withdrawal plans were carried forward into late 1963 "under the same optimistic assumptions" (12). Here again

Chomsky echoes Gelb, though (as we have seen) even Gelb concedes
that the "rosy picture . . . as late as July 1963" was discredited by the
"more balanced evaluation" of the McNamara-Taylor Report in
September.[26] At this point, admittedly, the documentary record becomes more cryptic and incomplete. But we can safely say that NSAM
263's reference to "the implementation of plans to withdraw" (the first
such reference) was *not* made under the same optimistic assumptions
(cf. Newman, 367). Chomsky's reading of NSAM 263 ("Presumably,
the intent was to implement the withdrawal plans if military conditions
allow," 13) begs the question: his case for this assumes the continuity of
mind-set that he is trying to prove.

4. Chomsky writes that "two weeks before Kennedy's assassination,
there is not a phrase in the voluminous internal record that even hints
at withdrawal without victory" (14). Indeed not! But the documentary
record is conspicuously defective for this crucial period. As I wrote
twenty years ago, "in all three editions of the Pentagon Papers there are
no complete documents between the five [coup] cables of October 30
and McNamara's memorandum of December 21; the 600 pages of documents from the Kennedy Administration end on October 30."[27] Since
then this striking lacuna has been partly corrected. But as a result we
know more clearly than before that some documents are still missing,
and others almost certainly have been destroyed. The record we have is
an edited one; Chomsky should admit that this weakens the force of his
argument about a missing "phrase."

5. Reading Johnson's NSAM 273 as if it were as contextless as a
Dead Sea Scroll, Chomsky dismisses the claims for its novelty and importance as having "no known basis in fact" (15). He ignores the early
accounts of it as a "major decision," a "pledge" that determined "all
that would follow," from journalists as diverse as Tom Wicker, Marvin
Kalb, and I. F. Stone (in Scott, *Pentagon Papers* [Beacon], V, 218, 235).
More significantly, he ignores General Taylor's memo to the President
of January 22, 1964, using NSAM 273's determination "to ensure victory" as authority to prepare to *escalate* operations against North Vietnam, including the "aerial bombing of key North Vietnam targets, using U.S. resources under Vietnamese cover."[28] What NSAM 273 meant
to Washington insiders in 1963–64 was clear.

6. Chomsky, looking only at the Pentagon Studies, concludes that
NSAM 273 and the plans flowing from it proposed no U.S. involvement

"beyond what was already underway under JFK" (15). I have argued that the Studies claiming this were clumsily falsified, as Taylor's reference to U.S. aerial bombing should corroborate.[29] I have not seen the plans, but the De Soto patrols by U.S. destroyers, which led swiftly to the Tonkin Gulf incidents and retaliatory bombing, were probably part of them.[30]

In support of Chomsky's position, it must be pointed out that OPLAN 34-63 plans for U.S.-backed covert operations against North Vietnam had been prepared after May 1963 by CINCPAC in Honolulu, approved on September 9, 1963, by JCS Chief Maxwell Taylor, and approved again on November 20 at Honolulu, two days before the assassination, by McNamara.[31] At present there is no evidence that Kennedy knew about, let alone authorized, these plans; and for what it is worth I have been assured by Kennedy-Johnson insiders that he did not know about them, and that such military plans would not ordinarily have been seen in the White House. The record indicates that OPLAN 34-63 received its first presidential authorization with NSAM 273, and that detailed plans first reached the White House (under Johnson) in December 1963. The OPLAN 34-63 story remains unclear, and so in particular does McNamara's relationship to it. It is on this crucial issue that many documents are missing and probably destroyed.

7. Chomsky seems to assume that counter evidentiary statements, that Kennedy told intimates such as Kenneth O'Donnell and Senator Mansfield he intended to get out of Vietnam, can be attributed to "Camelot memoirists" who shared the official U.S. disillusionment with the Vietnam War after the Tet offensive of 1968. I can assure him that Senator Wayne Morse told me of such Kennedy talk, albeit imprecisely, in 1966. As Newman reports, in the spring of 1964 Daniel Ellsberg heard from his Pentagon boss John McNaughton of a Kennedy-McNamara agreement to get out of Vietnam after the 1964 election.[32] Specifically, Ellsberg "recalls that John McNaughton, who was close to McNamara, told him that McNamara said he had an understanding with Kennedy that they would close out Vietnam by 1965, *whether it was in good shape or bad*."[33] Yet Chomsky writes that, in his case for "the withdrawal-without-victory thesis" (20), "Newman relies almost exclusively on the virtually meaningless O'Donnell-Mansfield post-Tet reconstructions" (21–22).

THREE

The Dialectical Cover-Up

COVERING UP A COVER-UP

On November 25, 1963, before the Warren Commission had even been established, its eventual conclusion, and more importantly the source for it, were revealed in an AP wire story: "FBI Director J. Edgar Hoover said today all available information indicates that Lee Harvey Oswald acted alone in the assassination of President John F. Kennedy."[1] When an FBI assistant director objected the next day "that a matter of this magnitude cannot be fully investigated in a week's time," Hoover's response was one of impatience: "It seems to me we have the basic facts now." On November 29, summarizing his conversation that day with the new President, Hoover stated in a memo:

> I advised the President that we hoped to have the investigation wrapped up today, but probably won't have it before the first of the week, due to an additional lead being pursued in Mexico. (AR 244)

Leads from Mexico were, in fact, the hidden key to what I have called the two-phase dialectical cover-up, in which (phase one) a false but plausible story of an international Communist conspiracy (supported by superficially credible evidence from intelligence sources too sensitive to be publicly disclosed) was eventually (phase two) replaced by a second false story of Oswald as a lone assassin. Many who found the second false story much more implausible than the first nevertheless came forward to support it, as preferable (even if manifestly untrue) for reasons of state: the avoidance of an unnecessary and unjust war.

The best (but, as we shall see, not the only) example of a plausible phase-one story from sensitive sources in Mexico is the following SECRET pre-assassination cable to CIA Director McCone on October 9, 1963, from Winston MacKinlay Scott, the CIA station chief in Mexico City:

> 1. Acc [deleted] 1 Oct. 63, American male who spoke broken Russian said his name [was] Lee Oswald, stated he [was] at Sov[iet] Emb[assy] on 28 Sept when [he] spoke with Consul whom he believed [to] be Valeriy Vladimirovich Kostikov. Subj[ect] asked Sov[iet] Guard Ivan Obyedkov [deleted] if there [was] anything new re telegram to Washington. Obyedkov upon checking said nothing received yet, but request had been sent.
>
> 2. Have photos male appears be American [long deletion] 1 Oct. Apparent age 35, athletic build, circa 6 feet, receding hairline, balding top, wore khakis and sport shirt, source [deleted]
>
> 3. No local dissem[ination].[2]

Today few believe that the man in this cable was the 23-year-old from Dallas known to the world as Lee Harvey Oswald. Yet, whether he was or was not, we almost certainly have evidence of a high-level intrigue. Kostikov had recently been identified by the CIA and FBI as a member of the KGB's Thirteenth Department, responsible for sabotage and murder.[3] Other CIA sources (as we shall see) were alleging that the KGB's Thirteenth Department had a training school for assassins in Minsk (where Oswald had lived from 1959–61 as an apparent Marine defector).

Just before the assassination, the FBI had intercepted a letter to the Soviet Embassy, dated November 9, 1963, and signed Lee H. Oswald. It referred to "my meetings with comrade Kostin in the Embassy of the Soviet Union," and added the mysterious innuendo, "had I been able to reach the Soviet Embassy in Havana as planned, the embassy there would have had time to complete our business" (WR 309–11; WCE 15, 16 WH 33). Although the letter might appear ambiguous to some, in the paranoid anti-Communist world-view espoused by James Jesus Angleton, the CIA's counterintelligence chief, the letter "suggested that Oswald had been involved in some undercover dealings with Soviet officials in Mexico, Cuba, and Washington."[4]

The alleged Oswald-Kostikov contact remains mysterious, if not sinister. Even as released by CIA Director Robert Gates in 1992, the Mexico City cable remains censored at certain points. The Warren Report, in its superficial treatment of Oswald's letter, reported the CIA's identification of "Kostin" as Kostikov, but was understandably silent about the KGB's Department Thirteen (WR 309–11). The House Committee, as we shall see, also tiptoed around the implications of the Kostikov story (AR 225, 249–50).

Right after the assassination, James Angleton's Counterintelligence staff inside the CIA (sometimes referred to as a second or "alternative CIA") suggested in a memo that the Oswald-Kostikov "connection might not be totally innocent."[5] Of course not! And yet a message from the CIA to the FBI on October 10, the day after the cable, combined misinformation about "Lee Henry Oswald" with astonishing silence about Kostikov, presumably the more important subject of inquiry. If the man we know as Oswald had "business" with Kostikov, that business should have been investigated. If he did not, and above all if an older and heavier man impersonated Oswald, we have evidence of a different conspiracy (serving the phase-one needs for a cover-up): to simulate an international Communist conspiracy where none existed.

Either way, the treatment of the story by the Warren Commission and the House Committee constitutes a cover-up, as some of their members and staff must have been aware. What they were covering up, however, was not necessarily a conspiracy of either variety, "Communist" or phase-one, so much as an earlier cover-up of the Kostikov story by both the CIA and FBI, before the Warren Commission had begun its business.

THE EARLIER CIA-FBI COVER-UP
OF THE KOSTIKOV STORY

The CIA never gave the Warren Commission all the data it had accumulated in response to the Mexico City cable about "Lee Oswald" and Kostikov. What we do have suggests that the response of CIA headquarters at Langley was a cautious one. Their outgoing cable of notification the next day to State, the FBI, and the Navy was careful to speak (like the incoming cable) of a "man who identified himself as Lee Oswald," who had *said* (to a Soviet embassy guard) that he had spoken with Kostikov three days earlier.[6] This account clearly leaves room for the possibility that an impostor, not Oswald, was planting a false trail to the KGB. But a member of the CIA's Mexico City station turned this allegation into purported fact when he reported on October 16 that "this officer [i.e., himself] *determined* that Oswald . . . had talked with . . . Kostikov."[7] In other words, the officer reported the alleged Oswald's claim as fact; and if the alleged Oswald's claim was false, so was the officer's.

If as I believe the memo was part of a phase-one conspiracy to induce a cover-up, then the author of the memo was probably part of it. The name of the author is deleted from the censored versions released in 1976 and 1992, but seems to have appeared on the file copy. Almost certainly the author was either CIA Station Chief Win Scott, or CIA Officer David Phillips, both of whom are now dead. This is just one case where the release of all the files on the Kennedy case would give us important new information.

Most critics now think the alleged Oswald was an impostor. The CIA, right after the assassination, sent to Dallas photos it claimed were of this man; clearly they are shots of someone heavyset, balding, and middle-aged (WR 364, 20 WH 691, 11 AH 490–93). House Select Committee researcher Edwin Lopez studied all the CIA surveillance photos during Oswald's alleged visits to the Cuban Embassy in this period, and concluded, as he later said on televison, that the visitor was not Oswald but an impostor.

This conclusion is reinforced by an FBI report about a CIA recording of the alleged Lee Oswald's voice; the report said that the Dallas FBI heard the recording and rejected it as not being of Oswald. The recording itself, an important possible clue to a conspiracy, apparently disappeared some time after the assassination, and a solitary documentary reference to it did not reach any audience outside intelligence circles until 1975.

Retired CIA officer David Phillips then claimed that the recordings of "Oswald" in Mexico were destroyed prior to the assassination. But this claim is challenged by an FBI memo to the Secret Service of November 23, 1963, which was not released until a dozen years later:

> The Central Intelligence Agency advised that on October 1, 1963, an extremely sensitive source had reported that an individual identified himself as Lee Oswald, who contacted the Soviet Embassy in Mexico City inquiring as

to any messages. Special Agents of this Bureau, who have conversed with Oswald in Dallas, Tex., have observed photographs of the individual referred to above and have listened to a recording of his voice. These Special Agents are of the opinion that the above-referred-to individual was not Lee Harvey Oswald. (AR 249–50)[8]

One thus gets the impression that the CIA, possibly quite innocently, had both photographs and a voice recording of a conspirator, not Oswald, who was consciously inducing the future cover-up of the assassination of the President by laying a false ("phase one") trail to the doorstep of the KGB's assassination bureau in Mexico City. Such a conspirator would of course be no "maniac" or "societal outcast," as the "lone assassin" Oswald has been depicted, but a sophisticated planner who was counting on the CIA's surveillance of the Soviet embassy in Mexico City to detect his reported contact with Kostikov. In 1963 such a person would almost certainly have had to be associated with the global intelligence milieu, or at least privy to special knowledge about the CIA's procedures.

Richard Helms, then the CIA's Deputy Director for Plans, took steps to dispel this impression, so far as the photograph was concerned. In a belated explanation to the Warren Commission, which was itself withheld from the public until 1967, Helms assured the Commission that the photograph was taken on October 4, 1963—two days after Oswald was supposed to have left Mexico City. (He misleadingly neglected to mention that the other photographs of the heavyset man *had* been taken at the time of Oswald's visit and the alleged Oswald–Soviet Embassy conversation.) He gave the alternative impression that Oswald and the unidentified middle-aged man had only been confused ex post facto in some innocent CIA mix-up. Such an explanation could work for the photograph, since photos do not identify themselves. If the FBI report is correct, however, the recording could not have been sent by mistake; it recorded the voice of someone, apparently not Oswald, who "identified himself as Lee Oswald."

The House Committee's discussion of the Mexican Oswald seems determined to accept the misleading explanations offered by Helms and the FBI:

The overwhelming weight of the evidence indicated to the Committee that the initial conclusion of Agency employees that the individual was Oswald was the result of a careless mistake. It was not, the committee believed, because the individual was posing as Oswald. *In fact, the committee established* [i.e., from Helms] *that the photograph was not even obtained at a time when Oswald was reported to have visited the Soviet embassy in Mexico City* [italics added; the Committee did not add that other photographs of the heavyset man had been obtained at the time of Oswald's visit].

In response to a committee inquiry, the FBI reported that no tape recording of Oswald's voice was in fact ever received. . . . On November 25, the Dallas office again apprised the Director that "[t]here seems to be some confusion in that no tapes were taken to Dallas. . . ." Finally, on the basis of an extensive file review and detailed testimony by present and former CIA officials and employees, the committee determined that CIA headquarters never received a recording of Oswald's voice. The committee concluded, therefore, that the information in the November 23, 1963, letterhead memorandum was mistaken and did not provide a basis for concluding that there had been an Oswald imposter. (AR 249–50)

The Committee did not consider, let alone refute, the commonsense possibility, that the recording of Oswald's voice, instead of being "taken" to FBI agents in Dallas, was simply played to them by long-distance radio or telephone. Nor did it mention the testimony it received from Cuban Consul General Eusebio Azcue, that the Oswald he encountered in the Cuban consulate "in no way resembled" the Oswald he saw later in Dallas newsreel footage; the Oswald who made a scene at his consulate was "maybe thirty-five years old," and with an unyouthful, "deeply-lined face."[9]

Supporting Azcue's allegation that the "Oswald" in his office was not the Dallas Oswald is the fact that the CIA had arranged to photograph surreptitiously all visitors to the Soviet Embassy and Cuban Consulate on a routine basis. As the Committee noted, "Oswald paid at least five visits to the Soviet Embassy or the Cuban consulate," yet the CIA could not come up with even one photo that resembled the Dallas Oswald, at the same time that they had to explain the six or more photographs they possessed of the heavyset man (AR 125).[10]

The Committee's explanation ("photographs of Oswald might have been taken and subsequently lost or destroyed") might allay suspicions in the case of someone in whom the CIA had no interest. But "Lee Oswald" was supposed to have met with Kostikov, a KGB agent from Department Thirteen, dealing with sabotage and assassination!

A Committee staff report by Edwin Lopez, still not released, confirms how sensitive the matter was. According to someone who has seen it, the staff report established that, on the death of Win Scott, the by-then retired Mexico City station chief who had sent out the Kostikov cable, CIA Counterintelligence Chief Angleton flew immediately to Mexico City, retrieved a photograph of "Oswald" from the family safe, and destroyed it.[11] This staff report, said to run to three hundred pages, is an example of important file information on the assassination that deserves to be released.[12]

Angleton may have undertaken this mission on behalf of the agency. Another possibility is that he undertook it on behalf of a cabal within the government who had conspired to create the "Oswald"-Kostikov story. Later we shall look at other indications of a cabal linking CIA Officer David Phillips, Win Scott, James Angleton (who handled for the CIA the supposed Kostikov link to the Kennedy assassination), and Angleton's FBI friend and colleague William Sullivan, who during World War II had directed Win Scott's intelligence work in Mexico and Latin America for the FBI.

COVER-UPS BY HOOVER
AND THE JUSTICE DEPARTMENT

If it concealed the recording, however, the CIA was not acting like a "rogue elephant," since it had help from the other agencies that shared its information, in particular the FBI. Following an official rebuke by a Senate subcommittee for ignoring "significant leads," the FBI declassified its files on Oswald and the Kennedy assassination and, after security deletions, made them public. These files show the FBI's role in covering up to have been much more deliberate than was suggested by the report of senators Richard Schweiker and Gary Hart, which spoke merely of "deficiencies," and of efforts "focused too narrowly to allow for a full investigation."[13] The FBI did not simply fail to interview certain important witnesses to a possible conspiracy; we shall see that at least once FBI headquarters sent a telegram vetoing the interview of one such witness (John Wilson Hudson). And it campaigned vigorously through the media to win support for its hasty finding that Oswald was the lone assassin.

The same files show J. Edgar Hoover ordering the release of information to "very friendly" journalists like Jeremiah O'Leary, later of the *Washington Times*, who in December 1978 was the first journalist to propose the hypothesis of two lone nuts in Dealey Plaza firing within the same half-second. These files also show "corrective" interviews with the employers and backers of journalists who had published stories deemed unfriendly: from these memos we learn how sensitive was the subject of Oswald's pre-assassination contacts with the FBI—a subject unclear to this day. For example, when Drew Pearson reported that the FBI had interviewed Oswald six days before the assassination, yet failed to warn the Secret Service about him, the FBI tried to silence the columnist. FBI Assistant Director Cartha DeLoach interviewed one of the chief stockholders of Pearson's distribution syndicate, "furnished him sufficient ammunition to refute all of Pearson's facts," and arranged for the apparently sympathetic stockholder to report back in person on his rebuke of Pearson. The idea of a contact between Oswald and the FBI on November 16 faded until 1975, when the FBI first revealed that some two weeks before the assassination, Oswald did visit the Dallas FBI office, to leave a threatening note.[14]

The FBI even resorted to "dirty tricks" to suppress dissent over its conclusions. In February 1964, when Mark Lane was planning to present the case for a grassy-knoll assassin before a public meeting at Town Hall in New York, the FBI tried unsuccessfully to prevent the meeting from taking place. At one stage, using what its files call "counterintelligence action," the FBI succeeded in having Town Hall (a private auditorium) cancel the meeting; when Lane's contract was later upheld in court the FBI took comfort from the fact that Lane had been required to put up a costly $25,000 performance bond.

In 1966 the FBI prepared memos linking Lane and other prominent assassination critics to allegedly subversive activities; these were supplied on request to Marvin Watson, President Johnson's political trouble-shooter. (This request from the White House seems particularly cynical in the light of subsequent revelations that Johnson himself shared the belief that the assassination in Dallas had been part of a conspiracy.)[15]

In the FBI's own files Hoover does not appear as the inducer of cover-up through false allegations of international conspiracy, but rather as the one so induced, attempting by the lone-assassin hypothesis to put such allegations to rest. White House files, as reported by the Schweiker-Hart committee, confirm this impression. On November 24, 1963, in a phone conversation with White House aide Walter Jenkins,

Hoover stated, "The thing I am concerned about, and so is [Deputy Attorney General] Katzenbach, is having something issued so we can convince the public that Oswald is the real assassin" (3 AH 469, 472; cf. AR 244).

The next day Katzenbach himself wrote to another presidential assistant, Bill Moyers, suggesting that an FBI report on Oswald and the assassination be released as soon as possible, to convince the public that "Oswald was the assassin," and that "he did not have confederates who are still at large." Noting that "the Dallas police have put out [phase-one] statements on the Communist conspiracy theory," Katzenbach argued that "we should have some basis for rebutting thought that this was a conspiracy or (as the Iron Curtain press is saying) a right-wing conspiracy to blame it on the Communists" (3 AH 567).[16]

In these early hours of the new Administration, Katzenbach, as much as Hoover, was a driving force for the phase-two lone-assassin story. FBI files show him pressing on November 24 for the FBI to go public with a statement "that Oswald killed the President," and the FBI responding "that the FBI would not put out the statement and we are opposed to any statement being put out along this line" (3 AH 667).

Another memo from FBI Assistant Director Courtney Evans shows Katzenbach sharing in the FBI's desire to reinforce the lone-assassin hypothesis:

> One of the dangers [!] which Katzenbach sees is the possibility that the state hearing to be held in Texas may develop some pertinent information not now known. In an effort to minimize this, he is having Assistant Attorney General Miller confer with the state officials in Texas in an effort to have them restrict their hearing to the proposition of showing merely that Oswald killed the President.

As late as December 9, after the FBI had prepared a lone-assassin report, Katzenbach urged the newly appointed Warren Commission to announce officially that the FBI had identified Oswald as the assassin, and that there was no evidence to show a conspiracy (3 AH 675). Informed in a memo that Commission member Ford was opposed to such a press release, Hoover scrawled in the margin, "This is my view point too" (3 AH 594).

It is unclear whether or not Hoover and the FBI, by such notes, were simply protecting themselves for the record. Already by December 3 someone had leaked the contents of the FBI report to the press:

On December 3, 1963, the UPI wire carried a story . . . under the following lead: "An exhaustive FBI report now nearly ready for the White House will indicate that Lee Harvey Oswald was the lone and unaided assassin of President Kennedy, Government sources said today." When he was informed of these news articles, Director Hoover wrote, "I thought no one knew this outside the FBI." According to [Assistant FBI Director] William Sullivan, Hoover himself ordered the report "leaked" to the press, in an attempt to "blunt the drive for an independent investigation of the assassination."[17]

There can be little doubt that this leak was itself a stratagem, designed to constrain the Warren Commission before its first meeting on December 4. The leaker may have been Hoover. Or Sullivan, who when interviewed was Hoover's enemy, may have lied to protect someone else.

FBI MANIPULATION OF THE WARREN COMMISSION

For its part, the FBI undoubtedly tried to ensure that the Warren Commission would reach the same conclusion. Hoover even intervened at the *Washington Post* to block a proposed editorial calling for the establishment of such a presidential commission; he claimed that, given the FBI's "intensive investigation," a further review would "muddy waters."

Later, when Commission member Allen Dulles warned his old CIA colleague James Angleton that the Warren Commission was considering hiring its own investigative staff, Angleton passed the warning along to the FBI. FBI Deputy Associate Director Alan H. Belmont noted that the Commission "should be discouraged from having an investigative staff" and as a first step moved to limit the number of copies of the first secret FBI report made available to the Commission.

Thus it was by no accident, but Justice Department policy, that the Warren Commission found itself dependent for facts on the FBI, which had already (as Commission counsel J. Lee Rankin complained in January 1964) "decided that it is Oswald who committed the assassination" and that "no one else was involved."

This dependence made it virtually impossible for the Commission to check out independently published allegations—backed by a hearsay report that the name and phone number of FBI Agent James Hosty were in Oswald's address book—that Oswald was an FBI informant. The FBI, when it learned of the Commission's interest in Oswald's pre-assassination FBI contacts, did belatedly confirm this report. Earlier, however, the FBI had provided a typewritten transcription of Oswald's address book in which the Hosty entry was omitted: the relevant page of this transcript was actually retyped, and its contents then failed to fill the page by just the number of lines of the missing Hosty entry. The House Committee confirmed that the Hosty entry had been deleted in the retyping of the memo. It called this incident "regrettable," but "trivial" (AR 186–90), even though what was at stake was an apparently false statement by FBI officials under oath.

FBI documents released in 1979 show other instances in which key information was either altered before it reached the Warren Commission, or else withheld altogether. For example, judging from Warren Commission records, the FBI covered up Jack Ruby's connections to organized crime. The Commission did not receive an important interview with Luis Kutner, a Chicago lawyer who had just told the press (correctly) about Ruby's connections to Chicago mobsters Lennie Patrick and Dave Yaras. All the FBI transmitted was a meaningless follow-up interview in which Kutner merely said he had no additional information (WCD 104.23).

Apparently the FBI also failed to transmit a teletype revealing that Yaras, a national hit man for the Chicago syndicate who had grown up with Ruby, and who had been telephoned by one of Ruby's Teamster contacts on the eve of the assassination, was about to attend a "hoodlum meeting" of top East and West Coast syndicate representatives, including some from the "family" of the former Havana crime lord Santos Trafficante.[18]

It is therefore significant that the FBI also suppressed a report that a British freelance newsman, John Wilson-Hudson, claimed to have been in a Havana prison in 1959 with "an American gangster named Santos" (presumably Trafficante), when "Santos" was visited by someone called Ruby whom the newsman believed was Jack Ruby. Wilson-Hudson had offered to look at photographs of Jack Ruby to see if he was indeed that visitor, but FBI headquarters, in an urgent cable to London, vetoed the suggestion: "Prior information available at Bureau that Ruby in Havana, Cuba, in 1959. Bureau desires no further investigation re Wilson." In this way the Warren Commission never heard about the alleged Ruby-"Santos" contact. Nor did it see allegations in the FBI files that linked Ruby at that time to Trafficante's Miami asso-

ciate Dave Yaras "through shylocking and girls." (The House Committee report, while also ignoring the Yaras allegation, found the Ruby-
Trafficante meeting "a distinct possibility" [AR 152–53].)

Such blatant interference by FBI headquarters in the investigative
process is recorded in the files only rarely. But this only confirms that
the bureau's professed lack of interest in a lead to "Santos" probably
derived not from ignorance but from knowledge—perhaps knowledge
of the CIA's use of Trafficante and Chicago crime boss Sam Giancana
in plots to assassinate Fidel Castro, since CIA embarrassment about
this relationship had already led the Justice Department to drop criminal charges in another case involving Giancana. That would be a
relatively nonconspiratorial explanation for the bureau's intervention—an example of "induced cover-up" through appeals to "national
security."[19]

THE FBI'S COVER-UP OF A PRIOR WARNING

Such an explanation is less plausible for the FBI's interference with
leads that appeared to be guiding its agents to the actual assassins of the
President—a case, seemingly, of obstruction of justice, or worse. How
else should one assess the response of FBI headquarters to a report from
Miami that Joseph Adams Milteer, a white racist with Klan connections, had in early November 1963 correctly warned that a plot to kill
the President "from an office building with a high-powered rifle" was
already "in the working"? These words are taken from a tape-
recording of a discussion between Milteer and his friend, Miami police
informant Bill Somersett. Miami police provided copies of this tape to
both the Secret Service and the FBI on November 10, 1963, two weeks
before the assassination, and this led to the cancellation of a planned
motorcade for the President in Miami on November 18.[20]

Although an extremist, Milteer was no loner. Southern racists were
well organized in 1963, in response to federal orders for desegregation;
and Milteer was an organizer for two racist parties, the National States
Rights party and the Constitution party. In addition he had attended an
April 1963 meeting in New Orleans of the Congress of Freedom, Inc.,
which had been monitored by an informant for the Miami police. A Miami detective's report of the Congress included the statement that
"there was indicated the overthrow of the present government of the

United States," including "the setting up of a criminal activity to assassinate particular persons." The report added that "membership within the Congress of Freedom, Inc., contain high ranking members of the armed forces that secretly belong to the organization."[21]

In other words, the deep politics of racist intrigue had become intermingled, in the Congress as elsewhere, with the resentment within the armed forces against their civilian commander. Perhaps the most important example in 1963 was that of General Edwin Walker, whom Oswald was accused of stalking and shooting at. Forced to retire in 1962 for disseminating right-wing propaganda in the armed forces, Walker was subsequently arrested at the "Ole Miss" anti-desegregation riots. Nor was the FBI itself exempt from racist intrigue: Milteer, on tape, reported detailed plans for the murder of Martin Luther King, Jr., whom Hoover's FBI, by the end of 1963, had also targeted for (in their words) "neutralizing . . . as an effective Negro leader."[22]

Four days after the assassination Somersett reported that Milteer had been "jubilant" about it: "Everything ran true to form. I guess you thought I was kidding you when I said he would be killed from a window with a high-powered rifle." Milteer also was adamant that he had not been "guessing" in his original prediction. In both of the relevant FBI reports from Miami, Somersett was described as "a source who had furnished reliable information in the past."

What was the response of FBI headquarters to the second report? An order was sent to Miami to "amend the reliability statement to show that some of the information furnished by [Somersett] is such that it could not be verified or corroborated." The headquarters file copy noted that "investigation by Atlanta has indicated there is no truth in the statements by [Somersett] and that Milteer was in Quitman, Georgia, during perti[n]ent period."

This notation referred to an interview by the Atlanta FBI with Milteer himself, who quite understandably denied ever having threatened Kennedy, or even having "heard anyone make such threats." This simple denial was forwarded to the Warren Commission in December 1963 (WCD 20.24); but the reports from Somersett (duly rewritten to make them less credible) were not forwarded until August 7, 1964, when the Commission had almost completed its work (WCD 1347.119–24). Nothing was ever said to the Commission about the tape in the FBI's possession that proved conclusively that Somersett had reported his conversation truthfully, and that Milteer, in his denial, was lying. Nor did the Commission hear about this tape from the Secret Service.

THE WATERGATE ANALOGY:
REACHING THE CONSPIRACY THROUGH THE COVER-UP

In their cover-up of the Milteer tape, the FBI and the Secret Service concealed the fact that they had both had prior warning of "plans . . . to kill President John F. Kennedy." But Milteer had predicted, correctly, not merely the modus operandi of the assassination but also the cover-up:

SOMERSETT: Boy, if that Kennedy gets shot, we have got to know where we are at. Because you know that will be a real shake, if they do that.

MILTEER: They wouldn't leave any stone unturned there no way. They will pick up somebody within hours afterwards, if anything like that would happen, just to throw the public off.

(Cf. 3 AH 450)

Since 1963 both Milteer, the extremist, and Somersett, the informant, have died. Their deaths might seem to corroborate the *Washington Post*'s opinion in 1978 that it was by then too late to pursue the "cold trails" of the John F. Kennedy assassination. But the important leads here pertain not so much to the crime as to the cover-up, not so much to events in Miami or in Dallas as to those inside the FBI and other government agencies. For example, following the analogy of Watergate, one candidate it might be useful to interrogate is Robert P. Gemberling, a retired special agent under whose supervision the page with the missing Hosty entry was retyped, and through whose hands the important Somersett interviews reached the Warren Commission nine months late. It is not likely that Gemberling, an apparently modest and mild-mannered man, has important knowledge bearing directly on the assassination; but, like the Kroghs and Deans of Watergate, he could perhaps lead interviewers to those involved at a higher level in conspiratorial cover-up.

The existence of a cover-up does not prove that the U.S. government itself was somehow involved in the crime. It does however suggest that the crime was plotted in such a way that to unravel it would threaten major governmental interests, thus inducing a cover-up. The stakes might have been world peace, if a foreign power was, or falsely appeared to be, implicated; or a sensitive government operation, with which Oswald may well have been connected, whether or not he was involved in the actual killing.

Neither of these examples is hypothetical. Within hours of the assassination, officials in Dallas and elsewhere were suggesting, on the flimsiest of evidence, that Oswald was part of a Communist conspiracy, acting on orders out of Havana or Moscow. Worse yet, highly dubious reports, already in U.S. intelligence files, provided some backing for these false conspiracy stories—which soon began to circulate about Jack Ruby as well. Thus, in the context of rumors that were as dangerous as they were misleading, reasonable men may well have settled on a "lone assassin" hypothesis for pragmatic reasons, as less misleading and less dangerous than the alternative theories already circulating. One need not, therefore, assume malevolent motives on the part of all those who engaged in the cover-up.

The motives of Hoover and the FBI cannot be so rationalized. On the Milteer matter alone, they clearly intervened to prevent the examination of legitimate leads. As we shall see in the next chapter, they helped invent misleading biographies of both Ruby and Oswald as "loners," in such a way as to ignore, and thus protect, the almost certain involvement of organized crime.

Nor, unfortunately, can Hoover and the FBI be isolated as the "bad apples" solely responsible for this corruption of justice. By most accounts, the "phase two" story that Oswald acted alone could not be reconciled with initial reports, from the Dallas doctors who treated Kennedy and from others, that the President had received wounds in the front of his body. Attention is thus focused on the extraordinary military autopsy of the President at Bethesda Naval Hospital near Washington, and the evidence (too complex to explore here) that the President's body had been surgically altered, while in the control of federal authorities, somewhere between Parkland Hospital in Dallas and Bethesda.[23] While a strong case can be made that military authorities played a key role in this medical cover-up, this aspect of the cover-up can hardly be attributed to the FBI.

HYPOTHESIS: P.R. FOR A DIALECTICAL COVER-UP

What I have said so far is based chiefly on the internal documentary records of the FBI and other agencies. These make it clear that Hoover and the FBI covered up evidence in order to promote their prejudged finding of a lone assassin, and also engaged, by selective and strategic leaks, in what can only be called a public relations campaign to make sure that the Warren Commission would reach the same conclusion. Since I first published a version of the preceding sections over a decade ago, the evidence has grown even stronger that Hoover, more than any other individual, was a major architect within the government of the lone-assassin cover-up.[24]

In this book we shall come to look at evidence that Hoover and the FBI may have played a larger and more serious role. We have seen that in effect there were two false myths or cover-ups. Both of these, phase one and phase two, were conspiratorial artifacts, in the sense that false evidence was systematically planted, with privileged knowledge of the government's intelligence files, in a well-organized p.r. campaign to support each of them. Hoover's p.r. role in producing and disseminating the second myth is clear. But what about the first?

Evidence will be developed in the following chapters that the two p.r. campaigns, to promote the "international Communist conspiracy" and to replace that with the "lone nut" myth, were in fact two phases of the same p.r. campaign. Just as the Navy will ask for two carriers in order to generate pressure to be granted one, so Hoover and the FBI fed the rumor mills with sophisticated hints of conspiracy, in order to pressure the FBI's usual liberal foes into accepting the "lone nut" compromise.

The documentary evidence for the FBI's role in the second phase of this dialectical p.r. cover-up is unambiguous. That Hoover and the FBI played a key role in the first phase as well is also suggested by the documentary record, but in a much more tenuous, indirect, and debatable way. In Chapter 14 we shall come to look closely at what appear to be informed FBI leaks of a "Red conspiracy" to their press contacts, notably Guy Richards of the Hearst *New York Journal-American*. (One of these leaks was shortly after Hoover and his aide DeLoach heard from their informant on the Warren Commission, Allen Dulles via James

Angleton, that a majority of the Commission wished to have their own investigators to go beyond the FBI's already leaked finding of a "lone assassin.")[25]

Hoover's scribbled comments on at least one of these "Red conspiracy" stories ("Be certain to go over this thoroughly") generated internal FBI memos focusing on Richards's allegations. What might look like a low-key response from the FBI director becomes more sinister in the whole pattern of Richards's informed stories. It is even more alarming in the light of a British journalist's accusation (see Chapter 14) that Hoover, before the assassination, was leaking to Richards what may have been his most scandalous and damaging information about President Kennedy.[26]

Equally sinister, in this perspective, is the role of Dulles and Angleton (who managed a "second CIA" within the CIA, to match Hoover's "second FBI" within the FBI) in preventing the Warren Commission from acquiring its own investigative staff.[27] One can of course imagine that this was to support Hoover in reaching the "phase two" conclusion of a lone assassin. But Dulles was both one of the President's enemies (having been fired by him) and one of Angleton's closest friends; and Angleton and his deputy Ray Rocca were allegedly the two top proponents within the CIA of the phase-one Communist conspiracy version, as well as proponents of the importance of the supporting Kostikov story. We shall have occasion to look later at pre- and post-assassination collaboration between CIA officials and the Senate Internal Security Subcommittee, to publicize within the United States alleged KGB assassination activities, which Guy Richards also wrote ominously about and linked to Oswald.[28]

The dialectical cover-up, in other words, was carried out by some of President Kennedy's bitterest pre-assassination opponents. It is important, however, to understand that the FBI and CIA, in both phases of the p.r. cover-up, were not acting alone or solely with the support of their press and congressional contacts. On the contrary, as we shall see, some of the alarming clues to an "international Communist conspiracy" were planted with the assistance of Army Intelligence in Dallas.[29]

In fact what has delayed for years my coming to believe in a single, dialectical, p.r. cover-up campaign, has been precisely the abundant appearances of pressure *on* Hoover, by recurring (and sometimes well-informed) stories that Oswald was an FBI agent or informant, or that the FBI had (or should have had) Oswald under surveillance.[30] It is inconceivable that Hoover was responsible for these stories. If they were concerted (and, without being certain of it, I suspect they were), they were probably concerted by someone outside the FBI. In the course of this book, we shall be looking at the role of p.r. agents in creating the "legend" of Oswald as a left-wing assassin, and later in coordinating and coaching the very malleable testimony of Marina Oswald, to support first "phase one" and then "phase two" of the dialectical cover-up.

We shall also look at the loud and irresponsible campaign of the American Security Council, the largest p.r. lobby for the military-industrial complex, to support the intelligence-fed claim that a KGB assassin "had been trained at an assassin's school in the USSR for assignment later on the North American continent."[31]

THE P.R. COVER-UP:
POLYCENTRIC OR COORDINATED?

P.r., the influencing of public opinion, is known inside the CIA and government as "psychological warfare." One veteran of both p.r. and psywar was C. D. Jackson, the publisher of *Life*, who had *Life* buy the rights to the Zapruder film and to Marina's story, and who allegedly stopped *Life*'s presses to alter the selection of frames of the President's fatal head-snap.[32] In an arrangement covered up by Warren Commission testimony, Jackson and *Life* arranged, at the urging of Dulles, to have Marina's story ghost-written for *Life* by Isaac Don Levine, a veteran CIA publicist. In 1953, when Jackson was Eisenhower's special assistant for psychological warfare, the Jackson-Dulles-Levine team had collaborated on the U.S.-CIA psychological warfare response to the death of Stalin.[33]

Carl Bernstein called Jackson "Henry Luce's personal emissary to the CIA," and claimed that in the 1950s Jackson had arranged for CIA employees to travel with Time-Life credentials as cover.[34] If Bernstein is right, then Jackson may have coordinated Luce's subsidy through *Life* of Cuban exile raids on Castro's Cuba which were explicitly designed to challenge Kennedy's steps towards detente with the Soviet Union.[35] In that case, it would have been Jackson who arranged for Richard Billings, then one of his in-laws, to represent *Life* on board a joint *Life*- and mob-backed raid, the Bayo-Pawley mission, whose later involvement in "phase one" conspiracy allegations may have impelled both the CIA and *Life* itself into the ranks of "phase two" supporters.[36]

Since Jackson's death in 1964, Time-Life has continued to influence American perceptions of the case, from its publication of Gerald Ford's "inside account" of the Warren Commission (October 2, 1964) to Time-Warner's backing of the fictionalized film *JFK* in 1991. So has Richard Billings, as coauthor of the Blakey-Billings Report of the Select Committee on Assassinations, which will be critiqued at length in this book.

Some have seen in C. D. Jackson a power center adequate to explain the original p.r. manipulation of the dialectical cover-up. In our discussion of the Bayo-Pawley affair, the pressures leading to dialectical cover-up will appear more dispersed, involving a key figure in the CIA-mob connection (John Martino), in Congress (the Senate Internal Security Subcommittee) and in the Administration (J. Edgar Hoover), as well as at Time-Life itself (Jackson). The evidence suggests that Martino, although a relatively low-level CIA-mob figure, was manipulating Jackson and Billings, not plotting with them.

Thus, if behind Bayo-Pawley there was a coordinated phase one– phase two p.r. effort, that coordination must probably be sought at a higher level than that of Jackson, Hoover, et al. This book cannot prove that there was such a higher p.r. effort; nor can it disprove it. What leads me to conclude that we cannot rule it out is disquieting evidence (see Chapter 14) linking a rarely mentioned mob associate of Martino's, Joe Nesline, to p.r. men in Washington, to Hoover's sexual blackmail files, and to ongoing manipulation of government in Washington (manipulation both of Congress and the Administration) at the very highest level.

That one of these p.r. men could have coordinated the whole scenario is at least possible. The 1960s, with their intense lobbying in favor of an expanded Vietnam War, were also the first decade in which p.r. agents combined the manipulation of public opinion with intelligence agentry and traditional lobbying (including the use of sexual favors and possibly blackmail).[37]

The evidence presented in this book can be interpreted in more than one way. At times we shall be pointing to a plurality of forces behind both phase one and phase two of the cover-up: a competition of cover-ups, just as some have spoken of competing conspiracies to kill the President.[38] At times we shall look at clues suggesting that, beneath the polycentric and diverse cover-up activity for phase one and phase two, there was skilled p.r. coordination.

Coordination, furthermore, with the acts leading to the assassination itself.

FOUR

The Key to the Cover-Up

The FBI, COINTELPROS, and the Case

A DEEP POLITICS METHODOLOGY: DEFINING WHAT HAS BEEN SUPPRESSED

As noted in Chapter 1, I have come to evaluate the mixed performance of the House Select Committee on Assassinations in much the same way as that of the Warren Commission: as a combination of selected revelations of truth with other selected areas, where the overriding collective purpose was not so much the truth as damage control.

This does not mean that we should disregard the procedures and findings of the House Committee. On the contrary, they should be closely examined, for in this case damage control (as well as truth) is evidence: a clue to what relevant truths are being concealed. But one must be methodical in this selective use of official material. Just as we believe the defendant who pleads guilty more readily than the one who pleads innocent, so we will pay more attention to the official record when it raises questions about its own reliability.

In studying the Warren Commission performance, I came two decades ago to focus precisely on what was not being transmitted. For example, the Warren Report described the person who met Oswald at dockside on his return from Russia as "a representative of the Travelers' Aid Society" (WR 713); not mentioned was the surely relevant fact that the man, Spas T. Raikin, was also a revanchist Bulgarian émigré and sometime Secretary-General of the American Friends of the Anti-Bolshevik Bloc of Nations.[1]

This detail is intriguing, since Raikin's group was supported by U.S. intelligence and was part of a shadowy anti-Communist network (known later as the World Anti-Communist League) which was linked to Oswald's career in many ways. We shall see that one of its associates, Maurice B. Gatlin, frequented the anti-Communist address, 544 Camp Street, stamped on Oswald's pro-Communist literature in New Orleans.

At the same time, the non-transmission of this particular detail is not very informative. We cannot tell if the omission is accidental or deliberate, nor, if there has been suppression, who was responsible for it. It most definitely does not implicate Raikin in the Kennedy assassination (as opposed to the truth about Oswald's visit to the Soviet Union, quite possibly an unrelated matter). It does not even indicate that the Warren Commission knew of Raikin's double role; almost certainly most of the Commission's members and staff did not.

What it does corroborate, no more and no less, is that the Warren Report's official biography of Oswald is an inadequate one. Time after time, Oswald was not the "loner" that he appeared to be: there were hidden forces at work, long before the assassination, to conceal his true activity. This example of omitted evidence is a relatively ill-defined and possibly innocent example; it might indicate no more than an intelligence interest (a legitimate one, from the U.S. government's point of view) in Oswald's trip to the Soviet Union.

In another case, however, the omission of evidence appears to have been deliberate. As I first wrote two decades ago, the Justice Department in 1964, when Robert Kennedy was still nominally the Attorney General, compiled an index for the Warren Commission staff of all those Ruby acquaintances who had been interviewed by the FBI before February 4, 1964 (WCD 355 of 2/4/64). By 1973, when I saw it, both the index and the FBI interviews (many of them also indexed by the FBI) could be reviewed at the National Archives. I soon became aware that those interviews which most interested me—men with either organized-crime or corrupt political backgrounds—were more likely than not to be missing from the Justice Department index.[2]

It developed that the Justice Department index, when correlated with the FBI interviews received by the Warren Commission, was defective by almost one hundred names.[3] Nor were these omissions random: for a name to be missing meant almost certainly, from the examples I could identify, a link to organized crime or politics, or both together. Two decades ago I cited the examples of

> Benny Barrish (a former co-worker with Ruby for Moe Annenberg), who went on to become a Democratic bagman in San Francisco (22 WH 349; cf. below, p. 158).
>
> Maurice "Frenchy" Medlevine (22 WH 329), a veteran with Ruby of the old Dave Miller gang, who in 1970 was arrested with a Marcello associate as part of a national stolen-securities ring.[4]
>
> Erwin Horwitz (22 WH 311), a Democratic politician in Chicago's 24th Ward, where (as we shall see) Ruby was launched into politics and crime together; Horwitz was a friend of hoodlum Lenny Patrick's protégé Alderman Ben Lewis, murdered in February 1963.[5]
>
> Irwin Weiner (WCD 84.12, 229), "thought to be the underworld's major financial figure in the Midwest,"[6] whom Ruby telephoned on October 26, 1963 (25 WH 246).

These missing names were recurringly so sensitive that I formed the testable hypothesis that the index itself, or more specifically the residue of names missing from it, provided a negative template or clue for further investigation. In simpler language, for a name to be missing from the Justice Department list was itself a lead, fallible to be sure, that the name might turn out to be that of a significant figure in the political underworld. What was being protected, it appeared, involved politicians as well as mobsters. This hypothesis did indeed help me to focus fruitfully on new individuals whose names were suggestively omitted, notably Dallas Assistant District Attorney William Alexander, of whom more hereafter.

By 1973, when I saw the index, it was not clear when it had been sanitized, whether at the moment of its compilation in the Justice Department, while in the possession of the Warren Commission, or conceivably (but perhaps least likely) even later, during or after its transmittal to the National Archives. What remained unmistakable, and as I say disturbing, was prima facie evidence of a political cover-up protecting organized-crime figures and their allies in politics—a cover-up apparently conducted by those who should in theory have been committed to the exposure of organized crime.

The sanitized index was in short a phenomenon of our deep politics, a symptom that our justice establishment was by no means at arm's length from the criminals it was supposed to prosecute. It was a clue, finally, to the problem of expecting an honest investigation of the Kennedy assassination from an arm of the U.S. government. In this case the false Warren Commission picture of Ruby as a "loner" was clearly an artifact, where one of the hidden forces responsible for generating this false impression lay inside the justice establishment.

THE SOURCE OF THE "TWO LONERS" MYTH: HOOVER AND THE FBI

The House Committee, to its credit, isolated the origins of the false Warren Commission "Ruby-as-loner" myth, which paralleled the Hoover pre-investigation conclusion that "Oswald acted alone." Both derived from the warped arrangements for the investigation of Ruby and Oswald by the FBI.

> Within the General Investigative Division [of the FBI], the probe of Jack Ruby was delegated to the Civil Rights Division on the theory that Ruby violated Oswald's civil rights by killing him. While the committee, in its investigation, found that Ruby's links to various organized crime figures were contained in reports received by the FBI in the weeks following his shooting of Oswald, the Bureau was seriously delinquent in investigating the Ruby-underworld connections. The committee established that the Bureau's own organized crime and Mafia specialists were not consulted or asked to participate to any significant degree. The assistant director who was in charge of the organized crime division, the Special Investigative Division [Courtney Evans], told the committee, "They sure didn't come to me. . . . We had no part in that that I can recall." The committee also determined that the Bureau's lack of interest in organized crime extended to its investigation of Oswald. (AR 243)

Courtney Evans was the FBI's liaison with both John and Robert Kennedy, and his Special Investigative Division was a monument to Hoover's belated conversion, under the Kennedys, to belief in the existence of organized crime. The warped investigation of Ruby shows Hoover's regression to his pre-Kennedy protection of organized crime, rather than investigation of it. "With Kennedy's death, Evans had be-

come persona non grata in the Bureau, and organized crime had immediately ceased to be a priority. The director wasn't even speaking to
Evans."[7]

But if Hoover was the author of this "Ruby-as-loner" myth, the
man he chose to implement the parallel "Oswald-as-loner" myth was
William Sullivan, the man who, in the Committee's words, "coordinated the FBI's [foreign] conspiracy investigation" (AR 242n). As the
Committee observed, Sullivan

> had been one of several FBI officials and agents [including James Hosty] who
> were disciplined by Director Hoover for what the Inspection Division deter-
> mined to have been defective performance in the investigation of Oswald
> prior to the assassination. The disciplinary action was kept a Bureau secret.
> Not even the Warren Commission was informed of it. Within [Sullivan's]
> Domestic Intelligence Division, the investigation of Oswald and a possible
> conspiracy was assigned to a team of agents from the Bureau's Soviet section
> because Oswald had been an avowed Marxist who had defected to the So-
> viet Union. While numerous experts on Cuban affairs and exile activities
> were assigned to the Domestic Intelligence Division, the committee found
> that they were seldom consulted on the assassination or asked to participate
> in the investigation, despite the reported connections between both Oswald
> and Ruby and individuals active in Cuban revolutionary activities. (AR
> 243–44; cf. 3 AH 478–79)

We do not yet know what events or secrets motivated Hoover to select
Sullivan and the Soviet section; we do, however, know that Hoover re-
ferred to prior "actions which have resulted in forever destroying the
Bureau as the top investigative organization."[8]

One thus learns the powerful bureaucratic consequences of the Mexico City CIA station's Kostikov cable, and the follow-up "Kostin" letter
which Oswald supposedly mailed to the Soviet Embassy in Washington. Oswald, even by Angletonian "phase one" accounts, had had no
other contacts with the Soviets since his return to the United States in
June 1962, unless one counts his wife's notification to the Soviet Embassy of their Fort Worth address, one week after their return.[9]

With these two belated and very dubious documents, the Kostikov
cable and the Soviet letter, Sullivan's Intelligence Division had an embarrassing Oswald problem, since it had not yet responded to them.
(Allegedly, the report on Oswald's activities in Mexico City was "sit-
ting on a pile of documents on [an FBI] Headquarters Supervisor's
desk" in Washington on November 22, the day that news of the "Ko-

stin" letter reached Oswald's FBI handler James Hosty in Dallas.)[10] But the FBI also, belatedly, had a pretext for handling Oswald within the Bureau's Soviet section. If Epstein's account of how the FBI handled Oswald is accurate (and Sullivan himself was a major source for his book), then there is probably still a major secret hidden in the Soviet section files. Did this secret make Oswald look like a "phase one" Soviet assassin, which blackmailed the Bureau into treating him as a "phase two" loner? Or, an even more embarrassing possibility, had the FBI failed to treat the Oswald file according to its own house rules because of Oswald's special relationship to the FBI or to some other intelligence agency?

There is authoritative evidence of such special treatment. FBI Inspector James H. Gale, assigned by Hoover to review the Bureau's handling of Oswald, reported his feeling that, at least after reports of the Oswald meeting with Kostikov, "the field should have been instructed to intensify investigation . . . and Oswald placed on Security Index."[11] Prior to that time, Oswald should have had a "stop" on his file in the State Department, which would have prevented his successful application for a passport in June 1963. As Gale noted, the FBI had already advised the Warren Commission by letter "that the facts did not warrant placing a stop on the passport"; but in Gale's view this was a justifiable duplicity:

> Inspector [i.e., Gale] feels it was proper at that time to take this "public" position. However, it is felt that with Oswald's background we should have had a stop on his passport, particularly since we did not know definitely whether or not he had any intelligence assignments at that time.[12]

Quite clearly, the only "intelligence assignments" for Oswald which Gale could have envisaged to rationalize this position, would have been assignments from a U.S. agency. Had Oswald been a spy for any other country, the need for a stop would have been even greater.

MOBILIZING THE FBI-CIA ANTI-SUBVERSIVE TEAM AGAINST RUBY AND OSWALD

On the basis of Inspector Gale's internal critiques, Hoover secretly disciplined seventeen FBI agents for their "failures" and "deficiencies" in the pre-assassination handling of Oswald—most notably for not putting him on the Security Index.[13] The Committee Report rightly noted the inappropriateness of assigning the investigation of Oswald, and of a possible foreign conspiracy, to the very FBI Assistant Director (Sullivan) who was the senior agent to be disciplined (AR 243).

This double move by Hoover, of assigning the case to those he simultaneously rebuked, went far beyond Sullivan. In his headquarters alone, the Domestic Intelligence Division personnel handling the Oswald case *after* the assassination were Inspectors Joseph Sizoo and Donald E. Moore, Espionage Section Chief William Branigan, and Supervisors Elbert Turner, W.M. Gheesling, and Lambert L. Anderson, along with Leonard M. Linton of the Espionage Section (3 AH 478–79). All of these men had handled the Oswald case *before* the assassination; and at least three of them (Sullivan, Branigan, and Gheesling, as well as probably Sizoo, Moore, and Linton) were then disciplined by Hoover for their pre-assassination treatment of Oswald (3 AH 517, 519, 521–22; cf. AR 245).

As we shall see, the same phenomenon was true in the field: men like James Hosty in Dallas, disciplined for failure to put Oswald on the Security Index (3 AH 519), were assigned crucial roles in investigating the most promising conspiracy leads (such as the so-called Odio story; see Chapter 7).

With the Kostikov cable and Kostin correspondence (and little else) to justify him, Hoover had now placed the investigation of Oswald in the hands of his top anti-subversive specialists: Alan Belmont, William Sullivan, and William Branigan of the Espionage Section (3 AH 478–49). What all these Hoover subordinates had in common (along with Sizoo, D. E. Moore, and others) was responsibility for COINTELPROs, the FBI's "dirty tricks" and illegal activities against people (such as Martin Luther King) who were considered "subversive." Belmont had secured Justice Department approval for the FBI's use of illegal wiretaps. As the head of Division Five, the Domestic Intelligence Division, Sullivan was in charge of the department's COINTELPROs against (for example) Martin Luther King, the Socialist Workers' party, and the Fair Play for Cuba Committee. Branigan, the head of the Espionage Section (later renamed the Soviet Section) was responsible for the Bureau's illegal mail-opening program.[14] Other Seat of Government (SOG) FBI agents handling the Oswald case along with COINTELPRO matters included C. D. Brennan, W. R. Wannall, Fred J. Baumgardner, and G. C. Moore.[15]

It is difficult to assess the real meaning of Gale's censures. Despite Gale's rebukes to Sullivan and Branigan, they, and others handling the Oswald case before and after the assassination, continued to thrive in the Bureau. So did the COINTELPROs. A memo envisaging a "continued aggressive approach" to COINTELPRO goals was sent out by Hoover on July 15, 1964, as the Warren Commission was winding up its business. Hoover's memo was addressed to all field offices, and also to Belmont, Sullivan, D. E. Moore, Branigan, F. J. Baumgardner, Smith, and Ryan at FBI headquarters.[16] The first five of these men all handled the Oswald case; the first four did so before the assassination and except for Belmont were apparently reprimanded by Gale. Clearly, however, the FBI continued on its earlier illegal course. At the same time, it appears that agents on the Oswald case who were not reprimanded (C. D. Brennan, W. R. Wannall, G. C. Moore) may have been promoted more rapidly than some of those who were.[17]

As we shall see, the FBI, in its hounding of alleged subversives, relied on assistance from friends of Hoover like Lewis Rosenstiel, who could be helpful because of their contacts in organized crime. Thus it will come as no surprise that Alan Belmont, one of the top anti-subversives of the 1950s, was also the author of a 1953 memo stating that "Maffia [sic] is an alleged organization. . . . The organization's existence in the U.S. is doubtful."[18] After the mob Apalachin meeting of 1957, Belmont accepted the responsibility for the FBI's complete ignorance of such participants as Vito Genovese of New York, Santos Trafficante of Tampa and Havana, and Joseph Civello of Dallas.[19]

With the election of Kennedy, Belmont authorized the creation of a new Special Investigative (i.e., Organized Crime) Division, run by Bobby Kennedy's friend Courtney Evans. But it was also Belmont, as the superior to both Sullivan and Evans, who must take responsibility for the exclusion in 1963 of Evans and his men from the assassination investigation (AR 243; cf. 3 AH 484–85). Belmont in effect channeled the case to the anti-subversives of Division Five, for whom the leaders of organized crime were not targets, but potential allies.

Back in the 1950s, moreover, Hoover, Alan Belmont, and William Branigan had already been guilty, bloody co-conspirators in what must be called the judicial murder in 1953 of the alleged spy Ethel Rosenberg. (This case was so weak, and based so heavily on FBI-induced testimony, that apparently "no one in the hierarchy of the FBI, including its director, favored a *death* penalty for Ethel.") Belmont and Branigan were the two senior FBI agents at Sing Sing when the Rosenbergs were electrocuted, still hoping, in vain, that impending death for his wife would induce Julius Rosenberg to confess.[20]

In 1950 Belmont had suggested to Hoover that charges be placed against Ethel, "if possible," as a "means to bring pressure on [her husband Julius] Rosenberg to make him talk." Hoover wrote on the memo, "Yes by all means," adding that if necessary "I will see the A.G," Attorney General J. Howard McGrath. A compliant witness, who had earlier testified that Ethel was not involved, was "reinterviewed" and, after a total of four hundred hours of FBI interviews, supplied the needed incrimination.[21]

Today it is common to concede that the Rosenbergs were convicted on flimsy evidence; and to retort that the true case against them was contained in decrypted intercepts of Soviet cable traffic, which the U.S. government was unwilling to use, since the revelation would alert the Soviets.[22] Having read this so many times, one is disconcerted to learn that the intercepts spoke of "a husband-and-wife team . . . identified in the traffic only by cryptonyms," with the wife's brother (supposed to be Ethel's brother David Greenglass) a part of the plot.[23] One would prefer to live in a country where stronger evidence was required for execution.

Interestingly, these decrypted intercepts had been supplied to the FBI by members of the CIA's Counterintelligence "Staff C," the two chief members of which were William Harvey and James Angleton. Harvey, in 1963, no longer supervised the anti-Castro activities of William "Rip" Robertson and John Rosselli; Richard Helms had "parked William Harvey as Station Chief in Rome to keep him as far away as possible from a smouldering Robert Kennedy."[24] (Bobby "found Harvey and his meaningless melodrama detestable." Harvey, according to a CIA colleague, "hated Kennedy's guts . . . with a purple passion.")[25]

Angleton and his Counterintelligence Staff, however, were picked in the CIA to handle the Kennedy assassination opposite Belmont and Branigan. Within the CIA, a quite parallel investigative warp occurred, analogous to that in the FBI. There too the investigation of a possible foreign conspiracy, originally lodged with Latin American experts in the Western Hemisphere Division (WH), had after two weeks been snatched away by CIA Counterintelligence Chief James Angleton, William Sullivan's colleague and counterpart in the CIA (4 AH 10; 11 AH 476–77). Angleton's pretext for doing so was a cable from Win Scott, linking Kostikov to WH's agent Rolando Cubela.[26]

In the CIA, as in the FBI, there are signs that some hidden agenda dictated the pre-assassination handling of the Oswald file. Years later Angleton recalled that he and his office had been given the assignment of liaison with the Warren Commission because they "knew the mechanisms of the KGB [and] of the Cuban DGI." He spontaneously "raised the specter of the KGB's [and Kostikov's] Department 13," whose specialties were defined in a 1964 CIA report from his staff to the Warren Commission as "abduction and murder."[27] Both Angleton and his deputy Ray Rocca are known to have argued, along with Mexico City Ambassador Thomas Mann, that the KGB might have been responsible for Kennedy's murder. Given this CIA anxiety in 1963 about Department 13's capacity for murder, why then did the CIA suppress all reference to the sinister Kostikov when notifying the FBI, on October 10, 1963, of the "Oswald" contact with the Soviet Embassy in Mexico City?

In Chapter 7 we shall examine the bad performance of the Mexico City CIA station concerning another "phase one" allegation, that of the Nicaraguan Secret Service agent "D." One has to wonder about the CIA station's handling of the "phase one" Kostikov story as well. Was the cable about "Cubella" a plant, to give Angleton leverage over his colleagues, and gain control of the case? In any event, the JFK assassination investigation was soon dominated by two Hoover allies: by Angleton (a "phase one" believer) on the CIA side, and on the FBI side by his very close associate Sullivan, a "phase two" believer, but also Win Scott's former chief from the days of the wartime FBI SIS service, and an Angleton crony above all.

A third interested party to this coterie appears to have been Allen Dulles. Now no longer in the CIA but on the Warren Commission, he remained very close to Angleton and his counterintelligence set, including Donald E. Moore in the FBI.[28]

JACK RUBY'S DEEP POLITICS
AND ITS SUPPRESSION BY THE HOUSE COMMITTEE

In 1977 I brought Ruby's organized crime connections, along with his 1963 phone calls to mob associates, and much else, to the attention of the House Select Committee on Assassinations, at a meeting of assassination researchers with Committee Chief Counsel Blakey, arranged at his request. I urged that the Committee focus on Ruby's suppressed links to the worlds of crime and politics, not at all sure that a Congressional Committee, with a former Justice Department official as its Chief Counsel, could honestly deal with politics.

My skepticism was justified. Where the Warren Commission had suppressed Ruby's crime links, the House Committee now focused on them to the exclusion of all else, while his political connections continued to be ignored. The effort was a second instance of official denial, of resistance to the proposition that President Kennedy was murdered by forces operating within and through our social system, rather than by external forces.

Thus both the Warren Commission and the House Select Committee have falsified evidence in order to label Oswald and Ruby as such external forces: as "loners" in the Warren Commission version, or, in the House Committee version, as people having "connections" or "contacts" or "associations" with the world of "organized crime" or "the national crime syndicate" (AR 156, 162, 170–71).

While the House Committee version is certainly more truthful than the Warren Commission's, it is still demonstrably committed to an externalized, indeed demonized explanation: what it hypothesized as a possible "syndicate-authorized" hit "by organized crime" (AR 162). It can be shown that both versions involved systematic falsification of known facts about Ruby and Oswald that raised the possibility that official forces are part of, rather than extraneous to, the complex of forces leading to the assassination.

In the case of Ruby, Blakey and the House Committee distorted the true relationship of Ruby to organized crime, in order to conform to and reinforce a false picture of organized crime itself as dominated by an ethnic "Cosa Nostra." This false picture had by 1978 already been discredited by historians; yet it remained the prevailing ideology of the FBI and Justice Department; and it continued as before to be sold to the American public via successive congressional committee hearings.

Central to these hearings had been the coached testimony of Joseph Valachi in 1963 about an Italian "Cosa Nostra," testimony before a Senate committee of which Blakey himself would become chief counsel. Blakey was not a disinterested transmitter of Valachi's disinformation; as we shall see, Valachi's falsified testimony about a controlling "national commission," created after the alleged "purge" of the old mafia "Moustache Petes," created the necessary legal justification for federal anti-crime legislation of which Blakey himself was the author.

In saying this, I am not trying to characterize the entire performance of Blakey, the House Committee, and its staff, some of whom (especially among the junior staff) made major contributions to what we now know about the case. It must be kept in mind that the House Committee, almost as much as the Warren Commission, was under external pressures to produce a report quickly, and to resolve public doubts about the matter, with limited power and under conditions of external political restraint. The Committee, like the Warren Commission, was unable to force either the FBI or the CIA to cooperate fully.[29] Justice Department officials were similarly, and sometimes publicly, hostile.[30] Finally, we should not forget that the Committee's finding of a probable conspiracy to shoot the President, with "a high probability that two gunmen fired at him" (AR 1), aroused feverish and derisive dismissals from those guardians of sane non-conspiratorial thinking, the *Washington Post* and the *New York Times*.[31]

Conceding all this, one still has to recognize that, in certain specific areas, cover-up in the Warren Report was perpetuated by the House Committee Report. Nowhere is this more evident than in the area of Ruby's connections to law enforcement, politicians, judges, and corporate figures. Here the evidence of suppression is even clearer than in the case of the Warren Commission, for the Committee produced a staff report of 1,044 pages, "Possible Associations Between Jack Ruby and Organized Crime" (9 AH 125–1169), including two chronologies (9 AH 1080–1118). There is much useful information in this staff report. And yet key events in Ruby's criminal background are either ignored altogether or else falsified. With so much data as background, one can see even more clearly than before that the omissions are Ruby's links to law enforcement, the judicial system, and politics.

THE SYMBIOSIS OF ORGANIZED CRIME AND POLITICS

This staff report, like the earlier Justice Department index, can be used to supply us with a negative template: what is perversely omitted is, as before, a clue to the missing truth. I hope in later chapters to demonstrate that, for whatever reason, the Committee studiously avoided the following important propositions:

> From as early as 1946–47, Ruby was involved in major narcotics dealings; and yet he was protected from arrest, most probably because he was also a U.S. government informant.
>
> Ruby was, as reported, involved in payoffs to the Dallas police, for whom he was unquestionably a narcotics informant.
>
> Ruby was on good, but probably illicit, terms with judges and other high members of the Dallas political establishment.
>
> According to his lawyer, Ruby was an informant for the Kefauver Committee; and in exchange for this service the Kefauver Committee agreed to ignore contemporary organized crime and police corruption in Dallas, specifically with respect to the 1946 takeover by organized crime of the national racing wire service.
>
> The wire-service operation was a key organizing force for criminal activity in that era, including narcotics. Profits from the resulting system of protected crime (in which Ruby was somehow implicated) were invested in legitimate businesses (such as international hotels and defense industries like General Dynamics) which formed part of the expansive postwar U.S. military-industrial establishment.

To sum up, the Warren Commission, like the Justice Department index prepared for it, suppressed Ruby's links to organized crime and the political establishment. The House Committee rectified the first half of this suppression, but not the second. An example of this continuity in suppression is the name of Dallas Assistant District Attorney William Alexander (of whom more later). Just as the Justice Department index of 1964 suppressed the fact that he was a Ruby associate interviewed by the FBI, so the House Committee Chronology of 1978 omitted the fact that he was visited by Ruby on November 21, 1963, one day before the assassination.

Defenders of the Committee will object that the Committee was studying organized crime connections, not political ones. This is true, and goes to the heart of the problem. The House Committee had chosen to focus on an externally projected Justice Department ethnic model of organized crime as "La Cosa Nostra" or "the National Crime

Syndicate" (AR 160). It chose to ignore the following evidence from Ruby's own career in Dallas:

1.   Organized crime, at least in Dallas, was an intrinsic part of the way that Dallas was governed.

2.   Political corruption, at least in Dallas, was an intrinsic part of the way in which local crime was organized.

3.   In this symbiosis of crime and politics, the deep politics of Dallas, Ruby was in some way an important figure.

Ample evidence for these three rather obvious and elementary propositions was given to the House Committee. As we shall see, it neither confirmed nor refuted this evidence; instead the Committee either ignored or falsified it. Analysis of the Committee's performance leads to three further propositions on a higher and more disturbing level:

4.   Ruby was part of this symbiosis of crime and enforcement on a federal level, not just a local one.

5.   This symbiosis, especially as organized by Federal Bureau of Narcotics officers at the highest level, used and/or protected international narcotics traffickers (in what we shall call "Operation X") as agents against communism, not just informants.

6.   The resulting flood of drugs into this country since World War II was one of the major "unspeakable" secrets leading to the ongoing cover-up of the Kennedy assassination.

The reasons for these new allegations will be expounded in the following chapters.

A study of the Committee's distortions and omissions also leads us to a consideration of the true status of organized crime in this country, and the related subject of how organized crime has been distorted and demonized, by federal agencies and responsive congressional committees, as the "Mafia" or "La Cosa Nostra." By 1978, when Blakey became Chief Counsel to the House Committee, prosecutorial accounts of "La Cosa Nostra," and the falsified "history" given the world by Valachi (and his FBI handlers) in 1963, had already been exposed by scholars as falsehoods to support an "alien-conspiracy" theory or "alien conspiracy myth" of "La Cosa Nostra."[32] We shall have to draw attention to the lawyerly way in which Blakey, clearly aware that some of the historical claims he makes had already been refuted, presented "alien conspiracy" fictions in such a way as to make them appear, falsely, to be consensually accepted facts.[33]

The problem here is certainly not Blakey per se. At stake rather is the ideological world-view of the Justice Department, and indeed of American law enforcement. Not surprisingly, they have rewritten the history and sociology of organized crime so as to justify studying, and prosecuting, what is alien to them, not the larger sociological system of which they themselves are a part.

It would be disturbing enough to think that facts about the JFK assassination have been ignored, and in some cases falsified, to fit into this ideological world-view. To some, the facts might suggest an even more alarming hypothesis, that Justice Department officials cling to this "alien conspiracy" myth in part because, if they were to revise it as scholars have done, they might have to look more seriously at the role of the Justice Department, and more particularly of Hoover and the FBI, in the cover-up of President Kennedy's assassination. And this in turn might prove to be only one chapter in an even more extended cover-up, a cover-up of organized crime's role in the domestic and international security arrangements of U.S. society.

A NEW ASSASSINATION HYPOTHESIS: NOT AN EXTERNAL CONSPIRACY, BUT A SYSTEMIC ADJUSTMENT

Over twenty years ago my inquiry into the origins of the U.S. commitment to the Vietnam War led me to investigate the Kennedy assassination which preceded that commitment by only hours. My researches into both topics, and particularly into the career of Jack Ruby, led me to look more closely at the international drug traffic. One of the most disturbing findings in that research has been the extent to which agencies of the U.S. government, including the Justice Department, have been involved in actively protecting international drug traffickers, and indeed the traffic itself.[34] I have published on this topic in four books, beginning with *The War Conspiracy* (1972). With each new phase of research, I have had to conclude that the degree of official complicity in this protection and cover-up is even greater than I had previously realized.

Although I had not anticipated this, the writing of this book has re-turned me yet again to the ongoing cover-up of U.S. official involve-ment, for security reasons, with international drug traffickers. My latest and most alarming account of this involvement and cover-up will be found in Chapter 10. It is alarming for two different reasons: because the involvement presented is even more sustained and systemic than I had previously realized, and because the cover-up of this involvement directly affects, to a far greater extent than I had previously realized, what we know about the assassination.

On reviewing what I have written on this topic, I am compelled to pose the question, which is still only a question, of whether this in-volvement and cover-up did not lead to the events of the assassination, and to their inevitable cover-up as well.

The inquiry into Jack Ruby's background will lead us ultimately to men of enormous private wealth and power who both sustained and profited from the symbiosis of crime and government. We shall see that just one of these men, the late Clint Murchison, Sr., was in a position to manipulate and control J. Edgar Hoover in 1964, at a time when Hoover and the FBI were simultaneously perverting the investigation of John F. Kennedy's murder, and also (to use historian Arthur M. Schle-singer's term) in "revolt" against their nominal superior, Attorney Gen-eral Robert Kennedy.[35]

A good part of the Murchison fortune derived from loans from the mob-dominated Teamsters' Pension Fund, at a time when corrupt Teamster locals played a prominent part in bringing heroin (and later cocaine) into the United States. We shall see also how this corporate-Teamster milieu of Clint Murchison and his friends had powerful mo-tives to hate Kennedy and promote his successor Lyndon Johnson, and how some of them intervened conspiratorially in the manipulative cover-up described in Chapter 3.

This probing of history and politics to the depth of those who could control Hoover, and even the new President, leads us beyond politics to deep politics. The methods of official history, though not to be faulted as far as they go, facilitate denial. We all know that public power in America is supplemented by private power, and that in moments of cri-sis like 1963 it can be subordinated to it. To some this subordination is perhaps the major defect of a political system which (despite its one re-sidual merit, its superiority to the known alternatives) is visibly under extreme duress. Yet the subject, being sparsely documented, is only sparingly and marginally written about.

It will be written about in the ensuing chapters, using documents to define what has not been documented. At the end I shall propose that most hypotheses of the Kennedy assassination hitherto, whether the designated culprits have been Communists or Minutemen, the CIA or the Mafia, have suffered from a common defect. This is to look for an external conspiracy violating a systemic political order from without.

We shall offer an enlarged and deeper perspective of power as a symbiosis of public government, organized crime, and private wealth with deep connections to both government and crime. From this perspective, the forces behind the assassination no longer appear as extraneous, but as deeply systemic; and the violation to the enlarged power system can be seen as coming from the Kennedys, with their policies of detente abroad and an attack on a CIA-sanctioned Hoffa-crime connection at home. From this perspective, the assassination was not a corrupt attack from outside on an honest system. The assassination was a desperate, extraordinary defense, or adjustment, of a system that was itself corrupt.

To establish this enlarged perspective, let us look more closely at the two official investigations of Oswald and Ruby, to evaluate just what the distortions and suppressions of their true roles have been.

PART TWO

Lee Harvey Oswald

FIVE

Oswald, Intelligence, and the Mob in New Orleans

Jack Ruby grew up in the political underworld of Chicago, where he and his brother, through their gang activities, became part of the notorious political machine of Jake Arvey in Chicago's 24th Ward.[1] Lee Harvey Oswald's family in New Orleans was likewise part of the political underworld of that city, where the uncle with whom he lived, Charles "Dutz" Murret, was a former boxer turned fight manager and professional bookmaker, and his mother had worked for a corrupt assistant district attorney.[2] Oswald's links to local deep politics are illustrated by his mother's appeal to mob politician Clem Sehrt (whom she knew as an old family friend) about Lee's desire to enter the Marines. Sehrt was identified by Robert Blakey of the House Assassinations Committee as "a lawyer and financial adviser to a business associate of Marcello," omitting the information (supplied to him) that Sehrt was also chairman of the Democratic "Old Regulars" in New Orleans.[3]

This omission is typical of Blakey's tendency to externalize and indeed demonize the mob as a force alien to, rather than part of, the deep structure of U.S. politics. Yet in New Orleans, as in Chicago, criminal power and local politics had been deeply intertwined for decades. Sehrt and the "Old Regulars" elected one of the mob's more dependable congressmen, Jimmy Morrison, who once introduced a private bill in a vain effort to prevent the deportation of convicted narcotics trafficker Silvestro "Sam" Carolla, and who was identified by Jack Anderson as one of the "boon companions" of Syndicate lobbyist Murray Olf.[4]

Oswald's overseas duties with the U.S. Marines in 1957–58 plunged him into an intelligence milieu which seemed remote from the world into which he was born.[5] His Marine Air Control Squadron was assigned to the naval air station at Atsugi, Japan, one of the major bases for the CIA's U-2 reconnaissance overflights of the Soviet Union. For some months in the Philippines he was also part of Operation STRONGBACK, a Seventh Fleet military task force apparently backing up a 1958 CIA attempt to overthrow Indonesian President Sukarno. His apparent defection to the Soviet Union in 1959, part of a wave of similarly suspicious defections by men with intelligence backgrounds, has been frequently interpreted as part of a program by U.S. intelligence (possibly the Office of Naval Intelligence) to penetrate the Soviet Union with false defectors.[6]

We shall see that on his return to Dallas in 1962, Oswald continued to live in a milieu with intelligence overtones, particularly when he was employed at Jaggars-Chiles-Stovall, a graphic arts company doing classified work for the U.S. Army.[7] For most critics, Oswald's intelligence connection in Dallas is personified by the mysterious Baron George de Mohrenschildt. A suspected spy during World War II, de Mohrenschildt acted very much as a classic intelligence "baby-sitter" for the Oswalds (or at a minimum for Marina), driving them to parties and other appointments, and possibly arranging for the job at Jaggars-Chiles-Stovall. De Mohrenschildt and his wife claimed that, before cultivating the Oswalds, they received assurances that Oswald was "okay" from an overt CIA employee in Dallas, George's friend J. Walton Moore. (Moore has consistently denied giving this assurance, or that he even knew of Oswald.)[8]

The House Committee added to what was known about the de Mohrenschildts' intelligence connections. It revealed that, when leaving Dallas in May 1963 for Haiti, the de Mohrenschildts traveled to Washington and took part in a Pentagon-CIA meeting with de Mohrenschildt's business ally, a Haitian banker named Clemard Joseph Charles. A former CIA contract agent has since suggested that one of de Mohrenschildt's purposes in moving to Haiti was to oversee a CIA-approved plot to overthrow Haitian dictator François "Papa Doc" Duvalier.[9]

This seems quite possible. Clemard Charles did advocate the overthrow of Duvalier in the Washington meeting (12 AH 57); and in 1967, the year in which the de Mohrenschildts were smuggled secretly out of Haiti, Charles was reportedly jailed for his role in an anti-Duvalier plot. Charles was jailed again for having financed an abortive military revolt of April 1970, in which a major role was played by the French intelligence agent André Labay, later arrested as a major drug trafficker. At the time of the meeting in May 1963, a U.S. task force of eight ships with 2,000 Marines was menacing Duvalier by their presence just outside of Haitian waters.

From the outset Clemard Charles may have had mob contacts and assistance for his intrigues in Haiti. His influence there increased in 1964, when he helped Duvalier break a U.S. arms embargo and acquire two T-28 fighter planes, possibly with help from U.S. organized crime.[10] After his exile to the United States in the late 1970s, Charles's business deals involved a number of intelligence and organized crime figures. In 1979 Charles discussed yet another possible ouster of Duvalier with veteran guerrilla warfare expert Mitchell WerBell III, a veteran of Cuban exile missions against Castro, and a representative of the Nugan Hand Bank, a bank involved in both intelligence operations and the financing of drug deals.[11] During the savings-and-loan scandals of the 1980s, Charles laundered money for Mario Renda, a leading mob money-broker for failed savings-and-loan banks, a number of them controlled by alleged Carlos Marcello associate Herman Beebe.[12] Charles also became an officer or director of Florida corporations with Albert Krieger, the attorney for convicted drug figures Larry Freeman and Jack DeVoe, and with Frank Sturgis, of whom more shortly.[13]

De Mohrenschildt was also in contact with the dubious milieu of Herman Beebe and his associates, from as early as 1960. In that year the de Mohrenschildts embarked on a mysterious walking trip from Mexico to the Panama Canal, stopping first at the ranch of "some very close friends who own a big ranch" at Piedras Nigras on the Mexican side of the U.S.-Mexican border. These friends were Tito Harper and his wife Conchita (9 WH 213). Tito's brother Richmond Harper in Eagle Pass, Texas, across the river, was a banking associate of Herman Beebe. Richmond Harper was indicted in 1972 for his alleged part in a complex arms-for-drugs smuggling plot, along with Barry Seal, later a notorious drug pilot, and Murray Kessler, an associate of New York's Gambino crime family.[14] According to Barry Seal, Richmond Harper had "very deep ties right into the [Nixon] White House;" this claim was corroborated when Nixon's top drug enforcer, Myles Ambrose, was revealed to have visited the Harper ranches straddling the border, and subsequently resigned.[15]

In other words, George de Mohrenschildt, so often described in assassination books by his intelligence connections, may have had links to the world of crime as well. But such intriguing connections should not make us forget that first and foremost de Mohrenschildt was an oil exploration geologist, and that his travels overseas were above all to countries like Haiti where oil was being sought. His repeated visits to Haiti, in 1956, 1961, 1962, and March 1963, led to a proposal for a holding company with Charles for various investments, including a casino (19 WH 551).[16] De Mohrenschildt's self-described role in the deal was to obtain the support of oil companies, along with U.S. aid sources in Washington (19 WH 550, 555).

So de Mohrenschildt was not just a "spook," as he has often been described;[17] and his operation in Haiti should not be projected abstractly as an intelligence plot, or even an intelligence-mafia plot, so much as another export overseas of the U.S. way of doing business. This tripartite example of an intelligence-mob-corporate gray alliance, one of many in this period, is an example of the kind of milieu in which a plot against the President could have developed. It was characteristic of many such alliances in Texas, the state which figured so largely in the illicit financing of the Watergate burglars and later in the S & L scandals of the 1980s. More importantly for our purposes, it is a paradigm for how we should understand the milieu, in New Orleans, of Lee Harvey Oswald.[18]

OSWALD AND THE NEW ORLEANS
ANTI-CASTRO CUBANS

Since the revelations of the Garrison investigation and of the House Committee, there has been a belated recognition that at least some of Oswald's political performance in New Orleans was consciously deceptive. There is really no other explanation why Oswald, posing as a pro-Castro sympathizer distributing Fair Play for Cuba Committee literature, should have stamped that literature with the address "544 Camp Street," the headquarters for local *anti*-Castro activities coordinated by a militant anti-Communist, Guy Banister. This relationship was not accidental or feigned: at least three witnesses, including a former Banister employee not interviewed by the House Committee, placed Oswald in Banister's presence at the 544 Camp Street address.[19] Meanwhile, Oswald was in contact with at least five *anti*-Castro Cuban members of the CIA-backed Cuban Revolutionary Council, which was connected to Banister and had until late 1962 been housed in the same building.[20]

A House Committee staff report, reviewing only two of these contacts (Carlos Bringuier and Frank Bartes), and ignoring the three others, concluded that "the New Orleans chapter of the CRC had no relationship with Oswald other than the brief encounter with Bartes" (10 AH 62). But to reach this conclusion it had to falsify the record, and declare that Bringuier was "not a CRC member" (10 AH 62).[21]

OSWALD'S ARREST AS PUBLIC RELATIONS

Bringuier, however, was not only a former member of the CRC but (as he himself had reported in a Who's Who of Cuban exiles) its Secretary for Publicity and Propaganda.[22] And in 1963 Bringuier was now conducting propaganda activities for the anti-Castro group DRE (Directorio Revolucionario Estudiantil), a group which "continued to accept U.S. funding," and yet "was, of all the anti-Castro groups, one of the most bitter toward President Kennedy" (10 AH 81–82). The funds supplied to the DRE were for propaganda activities, and its self-avowed chief propaganda goal was to "do battle with" the Fair Play for Cuba Committee, in the United States and abroad.[23]

For most of August 1963 Carlos Bringuier's propaganda activities involved Oswald, with whom he had at least four encounters. The second of these was an alleged street scuffle with Bringuier and two of his DRE friends, in which (according to Bringuier) Oswald's most aggressive act was to say, "O.K., Carlos, you want to hit me, hit me" (10 WH 38); yet at the subsequent court hearing, it was Oswald alone who was fined.

Bringuier and his allies arranged for WDSU-TV cameras to be present after the court hearing, when Oswald and a number of CRC Cubans engaged in a shouting match. Bringuier and his friends also arranged later for the celebrated Bringuier-Oswald WDSU radio "debate," in which Oswald revealed himself to be both a Marxist and a liar. Oswald and the FPCC fared very badly in this debate, thanks largely to a third participant, Ed Butler, who was a professional practitioner of anti-Communist psychological warfare. Armed with Washington newspapers he had obtained from an undisclosed "third party in Washington," Butler was able to expose the self-appointed FPCC spokesman as a defector to the Soviet Union who had turned in his passport in Moscow and "applied for Soviet citizenship" (21 WH 639).

We shall have more to say about Ed Butler, a key figure wholly ignored by Blakey and the House Committee. But it is worth noting that another gray eminence behind the Oswald story in Dallas, a CIA-linked anti-Communist propagandist called William Gaudet, later agreed with an interviewer's suggestion that Oswald's street scuffle was "a sort of a PR operation," and volunteered that "That was put in, I think, mostly by [Ed] Junior Butler," Gaudet's personal friend.[24] Gaudet's testimony is particularly significant, because this lifelong anti-Communist, with government experience, confirmed to many interviewers (including myself), his belief that the President had been killed by an anti-Communist conspiracy.

There is at least one other indication that Oswald's street scuffle was in fact being managed by invisible forces. This was the fact that his bail was paid by Emile Bruneau, a state boxing commissioner who was another of the prominent political friends of Oswald's mob-linked uncle Dutz Murret.[25] The House Committee, eager to link Oswald and Ruby together to the world of organized crime, made a point of noting that Bruneau was both "connected to Dutz Murret" and also "an associate of two of Marcello's syndicate deputies. (One of the two, Nofio Pecora . . . also received a telephone call from Ruby on October 30, 1963, according to the committee's computer analysis of Ruby's phone records)" (AR 170).[26]

But Bruneau also presented the Committee with a dilemma, given the resolutely anti-Castro politics of organized crime in 1963. Thus the more Oswald's political activity was attributed to control by Bruneau or any other organized crime figure, the less credible Oswald's pro-Castro affectations would appear. Blakey's lawyerly solution to this dilemma was to portray Oswald as a genuine pro-Castro sympathizer who was being *tracked*, not controlled, by organized crime, with Dutz Murret "a likely conduit of information about Oswald" (including "his assault on General Walker") to persons in the mob "who had the motive and the capability to plot the assassination."[27]

One can only sustain this ingenious theory by keeping Bruneau at a safe distance from Oswald's pro-Castro performance. Thus Blakey wrote that Bruneau paid the bail at the request of Oswald's family, having been telephoned by Oswald's aunt and cousin (Uncle Dutz being out of town), after "Oswald telephoned the Murrets and arrogantly demanded that they use their influence to get him out of jail."[28] But Oswald's aunt, Lillian Murret, who spent that day in a hospital, made it clear that the initiatives to get Oswald out of jail were taken at Bruneau's end and then communicated to the family, not the other way round:

> [My daughter] Joyce said she didn't know what to do, so we talked about it awhile, and then we decided to call this man that we knew, and we called him, *and he told us what had happened,* that Lee had had a fight with some Cubans, and everything, and *we were still wondering what to do about Lee being in jail and everything* when, a little while after that, he called back and said that everything was all right, *that Lee was out.*[29]

The House Committee's depositions of Bruneau and Mrs. Murret have not yet been released. It will be interesting to learn if Bruneau was asked how he found out about Oswald's "fight" and arrest; and if the Murrets were asked how they came to telephone someone who was already apprised of Oswald's activity. The true answers to these questions would, I suspect, establish that Oswald was not a loner, but playing a pro-Castro role for a hidden political agenda, about which Bruneau, certainly not a leftist, was knowledgeable.

In Chapter 16 we shall look behind Oswald's public p.r. performances to his secret interviews with enforcement officials on August 10, just prior to being bailed out by Bruneau.

OSWALD'S FURTHER P.R. PERFORMANCES
FOR TV AND RADIO

Oswald continued in the next two weeks to appear on both TV and radio, appearances which would be used after November 22 to condemn him as a leftist and a liar. One of Oswald's other TV performances, his celebrated leafleting for the FPCC outside the New Orleans Inter-

national Trade Mart, was clearly staged for TV rather than to garner
FPCC supporters. For two dollars Oswald hired a youth (Charles Hall
Steele, Jr.) at an employment agency to distribute FPCC literature with
him. Steele later testified: "I said, 'About how long will it take?' and he
said 'About 15 or 20 minutes at the most' " (10 WH 64). The Warren
Commission ascertained from Steele that in fact he leafleted for only
"12 or 15 minutes" (10 WH 66); an FBI report said, "only a few moments" (FBI File NO 97-47-67). The TV cameras from WDSU and
WWL which covered this swift event, the leafleting by Oswald, Steele,
and a third "sort of Cuban looking" person, were therefore probably
alerted before the leafleting began.[30] Those with either media or protest
experience will find it hard to believe that two TV stations would have
responded so promptly to a call from Oswald alone, if he were truly an
unemployed loner who had just been fired from a coffee factory.[31]

Common sense declares that of Oswald's conflicting political pos-
tures, pro-Castro and anti-Castro, at least one, if not both, must have
been a dissembling performance. Almost as clearly, common sense
would suggest that the public performance (handing out left-wing
FPCC literature) was the dissembling one, and that the unrecognized
relationship (to a 544 Camp Street address that was right-wing, and
to at least five Cubans linked to this address) was the key to Oswald's
real role.

The FBI agents in New Orleans seem to have understood that Oswald's self-appointed FPCC leafleting was for anti-Castro purposes. On
August 10, 1963 (the day Bruneau arranged for his bail), Oswald gave
FBI Agent John Quigley one of his pro-Castro pamphlets, stamped
"FPCC 544 Camp Street." A few days later a second copy was mailed
in by an informant to the FBI Field Office, where someone filed it in the
Field Office file (NO 97-105-1095) on anti-Castro activities.[32] Next to
the Camp Street address was the notation "ck out," presumably meaning "check out." After the assassination an FBI agent assured the Secret
Service "that they had checked this angle out thoroughly but with negative results" (22 WH 831). Yet there is no trace of any such check in
the released New Orleans FBI files on either Oswald or the FPCC, despite orders from Hoover at this time to be on the alert for FPCC
activities.

After the assassination, FBI agents carefully covered up the anti-
Castro nature of the Camp Street address and the FBI's involvement

with it.[33] A key figure here was New Orleans FBI Agent Warren deBrueys, the agent charged with monitoring the FPCC, anti-Castro Cubans,
and other political groups. DeBrueys should have known the significance of 544 Camp Street, since Banister's reports to the FBI on anti-
Castro Cubans allegedly came to him, and since one of the CRC Cubans, Orest Pena, was used by him as a source of information (AR 193).

Soon after November 22, deBrueys was sent by FBI headquarters
from New Orleans to Dallas, to coordinate the collection of information on Oswald and the transmission of it to the Warren Commission.
DeBrueys compiled a vast file for the Commission on Oswald in New
Orleans. In this file (Commission Document 75) the significance of the
544 Camp Street address is systematically expunged.[34] DeBrueys's role
in preparing this file, WCD 75, was thus a significant one.[35]

The cover-up was perpetuated both by the Warren Commission in
1964 (WR 408) and the House Committee in 1979, even though the
latter attached considerable importance to the 544 Camp Street address
from a *mafia* perspective.[36] Assuming for public purposes that Oswald's "Marxism" was genuine, they discounted both the alleged links
of Oswald to the New Orleans FBI (AR 191–94) and his repeated associations with right-wing Cubans in New Orleans:

> The committee found his actions and values to have been those of a self-
> proclaimed Marxist who would be bound to favor the Castro regime in
> Cuba, or at least not advocate its overthrow. For this reason, it did not seem
> likely to the committee that Oswald would have allied himself with an anti-
> Castro group or individual activist for the sole purpose of furthering the
> anti-Castro cause. The committee recognized the possibility that Oswald
> might have established contacts with such groups or persons to implicate the
> anti-Castro movement in the assassination. Such an implication might have
> protected the Castro regime and other left-wing suspects, while resulting in
> an intensive investigation and possible neutralization of the opponents of
> Castro.[37]

To imagine that Hoover's FBI would have thus launched a witch-hunt
of the right is of course ludicrous. Oswald's links to the right have been
downplayed from that day to this, by the House Committee as by the
Warren Commission. Instead the FBI, predictably, went after the Fair
Play for Cuba Committee, with which Oswald had no relationships except those initiated by himself. It was and could only have been the
FPCC which suffered because of Oswald's political performances; indeed it closed down forever in December 1963, precisely because of

Oswald. To be more precise, it was the DRE that, as soon as Oswald's name was broadcast on November 22, released to the press and the FBI the tape in which Oswald identified himself as an FPCC organizer (10 AH 85–86), thus ensuring the FPCC's demise.

The House Committee resolutely refused to consider the possibility that Oswald's FPCC performance was intended to bring this about, even though it was an explicit DRE propaganda objective to destroy the FPCC. In addition, an earlier congressional investigation had established that the CIA and FBI were collaborating in CIA plans for "countering the activities" of the Fair Play for Cuba Committee (with "some thought to planting deceptive information which might embarrass the Committee").[38] In response to the CIA's request, the FBI had already, before the assassination, broken into the FPCC headquarters in New York and photographed a number of documents. After the assassination, an urgently expedited review of these photos revealed Oswald's letter to FPCC National Director Ted Lee about his alleged FPCC activities in New Orleans.[39]

In Chapter 14, we shall see how Hoover and his allies in Congress and the press used timely leaks from this correspondence to increase the pressure for his p.r. compromise on Oswald as a lone assassin.

544 CAMP STREET:
INTELLIGENCE, MAFIA, OR SOME OTHER FORCE?

One simple explanation for decades of official cover-up about the Kennedy assassination is precisely that Oswald's "legend" as an arrogant Marxist had been the outgrowth of a CIA- and FBI-sanctioned propaganda campaign against the FPCC. For those exploring such a disturbing hypothesis, it thus becomes imperative to establish who was directing Oswald: intelligence, the mob, or some third force.

Most assassination researchers agree that Guy Banister was probably involved in Oswald's political performance. The great dissenter is Edward Jay Epstein, whose well-informed but perverse biography of Oswald is silent about 544 Camp Street, Banister, and Banister's investigator David Ferrie. His silence is the more eloquent, because his biography is one of the few to see that Oswald on August 9 and 10, 1963, when he was bailed out by Emile Bruneau, was creating a "legend," and adding "one more bit of documentation for the dossier he was preparing on his pro-Castro activities."[40]

As we shall see in Chapter 16, Epstein even tells us the response of his good friend James Angleton's Counterintelligence staff of the CIA to the documentation supplied by Oswald on August 10.[41] Both in what he reveals and equally in what he suppresses, Epstein tells us quite a lot about the Angletonian world-view, which the CIA fortunately came in time to reject. That Epstein could focus on Oswald's interviews of August 10, and also be silent about the 544 Camp Street address that Oswald gave on that day to the FBI, strengthens rather than weakens the proposition that Banister's Camp Street address is an important key to Oswald's performance.

Generally there is agreement about the importance of the 544 Camp Street address, and also of Oswald's initiative in planting this address in FBI files. Disagreement arises, however, as to who was paying for Banister's anti-Communist activities: governmental intelligence, the New Orleans mafia, or some third force allied with both together. Those stressing *intelligence* (Garrison, William Turner, Anthony Summers) have pointed to Banister's years of service in the FBI and the Office of Naval Intelligence, his association with the CIA-sponsored Cuban Revolutionary Council, and his work for the Louisiana State Committee on Un-American Activities.[42] Those stressing the *mafia*, following the lead of G. Robert Blakey and the House Committee on Assassinations, have argued that Banister was "closely associated with G. Wray Gill, an attorney for Mafia leader Carlos Marcello, and David W. Ferrie, who performed investigative services for both Banister and Gill."[43]

A third and more likely possibility is that Oswald and Banister were working for what was in effect a third force: an intelligence-mafia gray alliance, rooted in the deep political economy of New Orleans. Since I first proposed this intelligence-mafia hypothesis two decades ago, new revelations about Oswald and 544 Camp Street have strengthened the evidence linking both the man and the address to all three aspects of this intelligence-mafia-corporate milieu.

Guy Banister, to begin with, was undoubtedly working with the FBI. A declassified CIA document has confirmed that Sergio Arcacha Smith, the chief delegate of the Cuban Revolutionary Council at 544 Camp Street, "maintained extensive relations with the New Orleans FBI. . . . Two of his regular FBI contacts were a [name deleted] and the deceased Guy Banister."[44] The fact that Banister served as a contact or cut-out for the FBI does not diminish his independence. In fact, his split-second resignation from the FBI in 1957 had become a legend within the Bureau, as an example of someone fed up with Hoover's dictatorial treatment of his agents.[45]

At the same time, moreover, Banister was also working with Marcello. Banister's former secretary has confirmed that in 1963 Banister, as well as Ferrie, were working with Carlos Marcello's lawyer Wray Gill to block the deportation of Marcello to Guatemala.[46] The New Orleans FBI failed to reveal these incriminating links between Banister and Marcello, but this is hardly surprising. According to Curt Gentry, the New Orleans FBI investigation of the President's murder was coordinated by Special Agent Regis Kennedy, who later told the House Committee "that he did not believe Carlos Marcello was a significant organized crime figure," and that Marcello earned his living "as a tomato salesman and real estate investor."[47]

In addition Banister is said by one of his former associates to have "participated in every important anti-Communist South and Central American revolution which came along."[48] This included the anti-Castro activities of Sergio Arcacha Smith, whose Friends of Democratic Cuba fund-raising group Banister helped to incorporate.[49] The House Select Committee later revealed that, according to an FBI report of April 1961, Arcacha Smith had been offered financial support by Carlos Marcello, possibly through David Ferrie, in return for concessions in Cuba after Castro's overthrow.[50]

Marcello may not have been Banister's only mob contact. Banister worked also with the Anti-Communist Legion (or League) of the Caribbean, a group funded by Trujillo of the Dominican Republic, Anastasio Somoza of Nicaragua, and former Cuban secret police chief Orlando Piedra (a frequent visitor to 544 Camp Street).[51] As the alleged Louisiana organizer of the right-wing paramilitary Minutemen, moreover, Banister may have had prior knowledge of an arms cache seized by the FBI on July 31, 1963. The arms were seized on the Lake Pontchartrain property of William McLaney, brother of Havana casino operator Mike McLaney. Among those arrested were Sam Benton, Mike McLaney's go-between with the mob-financed Cuban exiles, and Richard Lauchli, co-founder of the Minutemen.[52] The cache was for a nearby Somoza-backed Cuban exile training camp, which according to Warren Hinckle and Bill Turner had been "set up a year earlier by

Gerry Hemming and Frank Sturgis at the request of the New Orleans branch of the Cuban Revolutionary Council."[53]

In short, Banister had unmistakable links both to the mob-linked arms cache, and to the FBI which seized it in July 1963. The degree of contacts in both directions suggests that the original question—which side was he working for?—was a naive one: Banister had no problem working for both.

The record suggests that, even if the FBI would carry out raids at the Kennedys' request, Hoover's heart was not into making trouble for Lauchli and his Minutemen. Despite their involvement in illegal bomb-making and sabotage plots, Hoover did not see them as dangerous. In 1965 he told a California Senate Committee that "little real evidence" existed "that the Minutemen are anything more than essentially a paper organization with just enough followers over the country so that they can occasionally attract a headline."[54]

Hoover's remarks are consistent with his career of treating mob-financed anti-Communist operations as supportive of, rather than inimical to, his notion of proper law enforcement. In this he was not alone. Mob-backed intelligence operations, such as the New Orleans branch of the Cuban Revolutionary Council, served the purposes of all U.S. interests which hoped to reverse Castro's expropriation of their Cuban assets.[55]

Thus the Lake Pontchartrain arms cache and training camp, a promising lead for establishing an Oswald-Ruby link, was not pursued by the FBI and the Warren Commission. They failed to note that Sam Benton was connected to a nationwide betting network involving a number of Ruby associates such as Dave Yaras, and possibly Ruby himself.[56]

The House Committee did not pursue the possibility of a Benton-Ruby link. Instead it presented an alternative account of the organized-crime backing for Gerry Patrick Hemming and Rich Lauchli, which it claimed to have found in unreleased FBI and CIA files. This was that Hemming and Lauchli had been contacted and supported by Paulino Sierra Martinez, head of a Chicago-based and mob-financed Junta del Gobierno de Cuba en Exilio, or JGCE (10 AH 95–101; cf. AR 134, 236–37; 3 AH 377–78). After extensive investigation, I believe the mob allegations against Sierra to be false but significant, part of a high-level pre-assassination disinformation campaign to implicate Sierra falsely in the assassination. The purpose of this campaign was presumably to embarrass Sierra's true backers, who probably (as he believed) included Robert Kennedy.[57]

THE NEW ORLEANS CRC, VARONA, AND SOMOZA

The New Orleans Cuban Revolutionary Council was close to Banister, and indeed had migrated with him in early 1962 from the Balter Building to the Newman Building at 544 Camp Street (10 AH 110). Moreover, it had mob as well as CIA origins.

The House Committee revealed that the New Orleans CRC had been set up, and regularly visited through November 1963, by the former Cuban Premier Manuel Antonio de Varona, perhaps the prime exemplar of the CIA-mafia connection. On the one hand "Tony" Varona had been the CIA's first choice to head the political front (the Frente Revolucionario Democratico) it had set up in connection with the 1961 Bay of Pigs invasion, and in 1963 he was the head of the Frente's successor organization, the Cuban Revolutionary Council of Miami (the CRC's only other chapter).

At the same time, Varona was a go-between at the mafia end of the CIA-mafia plot to assassinate Castro, having been brought into the plot by Santos Trafficante and a Cuban ("Macho" Gener) who was "Trafficante's top man in his and the Mafia's relationship with Cubans." A CIA Inspector General's Report of 1967, investigating this plot, commented that Varona may have been brought in because of his links to what the FBI called the efforts "being made by U.S. racketeers to finance anti-Castro activities in hopes of securing gambling, prostitution and dope monopolies in the event Castro was overthrown."[58] The House Committee later confirmed that Varona had met with Meyer Lansky to secure financing for the Frente, and benefited from the "promotional efforts" of the Washington, D.C., public relations firm of Edward K. Moss & Associates, supposedly a conduit for funds supplied by the Lansky gambling executives Dino and Eddie Cellini.[59]

In the anti-Castro plotting, Varona represented the interests and fortune of former Cuban President Carlos Prío Socarras, whose investments were intermingled with Lansky's.[60] As such, Varona became more prominent in the 1962 CIA-mafia plots to assassinate Castro, when William Harvey, who was now in charge of the CIA's Cuban

Task Force W for Operation Mongoose, proceeded without explicit orders to resume the mafia connection.[61] Harvey's unauthorized green light to mafia operations in 1962 was swiftly followed by the mob-financed training camp on Lake Pontchartrain.

According to a well-informed and apparently leaked story, the chief trainers at the camp were "Fiorini" (Frank Sturgis) and "Patrick" (Gerry Patrick Hemming), both with connections to Prío that went back to the Batista era. The story then added, "It's an educated guess that Patrick's big backer might be Prio, who reportedly left Cuba with a huge fortune."[62] The leaker of the story to journalist William Stuckey was presumably Carlos Bringuier, press secretary of the New Orleans Cuban Revolutionary Council; one year later, Bringuier called Stuckey again, about Lee Harvey Oswald; and Stuckey thereupon arranged for the notorious "debate" between Bringuier and Oswald (WR 729).

In mid-1963, Varona again became head of the Miami Cuban Revolutionary Council, which by then had apparently lost all CIA financial support. Varona resumed his visits to New Orleans; in particular he contacted at least two Cuban exiles (Chief Delegate Frank Bartes and Agustin Guitart) who personally witnessed the televised "pro-Castro" behavior of Oswald at his court appearance for "disturbing the peace" with Carlos Bringuier. Varona also flew with Prío, Paulino Sierra, and Laureano Batista Falla to Nicaragua, where they met the Somoza brothers.[63] This trip was apparently linked to a brief resumption of activities at the underworld-financed DRE training camp on Lake Pontchartrain, backed by Batista Falla, Prío, and Somoza.[64]

Very few critics have been struck by the recurrence of Somoza contacts and agents in the pre- and post-assassination stories of Lee Harvey Oswald. We shall consider the example of "D," a Somoza secret agent in Mexico who briefly claimed that he had seen someone recruit Lee Harvey Oswald to kill President Kennedy.[65] Significantly, none of the major books that present the Kennedy assassination as a simple mob hit (Blakey and Billings, John Davis, and Scheim) deal with this indication that the mob, even if it shot the President, was not "acting alone."

In fact, as we shall soon see, the Somozas did have ongoing deep connections to both U.S. intelligence and U.S. organized crime. But they had a much more obvious and continuous connection to New Orleans in particular, via the two giant U.S. fruit companies, then called United

Fruit and Standard Fruit & Steamship, which shipped their bananas from Nicaragua to the United States. These connections were particularly active in late 1963: both Anastasio Somoza and the banana companies backed an October 1963 military coup in Honduras which John F. Kennedy, to the day he died, declined to recognize.[66]

The banana companies, moreover, had connections not only to the Somozas, but to the anti-Communist propaganda mills of New Orleans, which in August 1963 made a media celebrity out of Lee Harvey Oswald.

SIX

Oswald, Intelligence, the Mob, and the Banana Companies

We have seen how Oswald's family was part of the mob-dominated local political milieu in New Orleans, exposing Oswald, like Ruby, to the twinned worlds of law enforcement and organized crime. But few critics have related Oswald's activities in New Orleans to firms, like the big banana companies, whose business depended on maintaining "friendly" (i.e., client) governments in Central America.

Yet in August 1963 men working with both of the two biggest banana companies, United Fruit and Standard Fruit & Steamship, interacted with Oswald at the moments of his most suspicious activities in New Orleans.

The banana companies' preference for military client governments had by 1963 created tension with the Kennedys' preference in the same area for governments that were democratically elected. In late 1963 the banana companies, together with Nicaraguan strong man Anastasio Somoza, plotted together against the rhetoric of social reform and political democratization which the Kennedy Alliance for Progress proposed for Latin America. In the spirit of this rhetoric, liberal president Ramón Villeda Morales of Honduras had promoted a moderate social revolution, and had become known as a "responsible leader who cooperated closely with John Kennedy and the Alliance for Progress."[1] The response of the banana firms and of Somoza was to support a military coup against Villeda on October 2, 1963, which began (like so many coups) with an attack on the presidential palace by U.S.-trained army pilots.[2]

In the weeks left to him, Kennedy refused to recognize the new government of General Oswaldo López Arellano. Recognition was granted in December 1963 by President Johnson's new undersecretary of state for Latin American affairs. The new undersecretary, whose appointment was understood to mean a more business-oriented policy in Latin America, was Thomas Mann, a personal enemy of Robert Kennedy, who is said to have figured in Central American coup planning. In June 1963 Mann, then U.S. ambassador in Mexico City, had announced his impending retirement from the foreign service; instead he was promoted, on December 14, 1963.[3]

What should be considered, as we shall see, is the possible involvement of the banana companies, their mob contacts, Somoza agents, and even Ambassador Mann, in attempts to portray Oswald as a conspiratorial Communist killer.[4]

OSWALD, INCA, AND THE BANANA COMPANIES

Employees of the banana companies, to begin with, were involved with Oswald himself. It was for example a Standard Fruit employee, Manuel Gil, who arranged for and managed the Bill Stuckey program that aired the televised Oswald-Bringuier "debate" (the footage used on November 22 to tell the world that Oswald was a dishonest, Marxist, Castro sympathizer).[5] It is true that Gil (a veteran of the New Orleans CRC) probably did so as an associate of Ed Butler's INCA, the Information Council of the Americas, a New Orleans right-wing propaganda operation that almost certainly did work for the CIA.[6] But so many Standard Fruit employees were associated with INCA that one may perhaps conclude that Standard Fruit, at least as much as the CIA, was sponsoring INCA's propaganda activities in Latin America. As I wrote in a monograph submitted to Robert Blakey and the House Committee on Assassinations,

> Standard Fruit's employees at INCA included its General Counsel Eberhard Deutsch (Jim Garrison's former law partner and political mentor); Cuban refugee activist and CRC-veteran Manuel Gil . . . and William I. Monaghan, who later resigned and joined Oswald at the William B. Reily [coffee] Company. And a "Charter Member" of INCA was Standard Fruit's

Director Seymour Weiss, a veteran anticommunist and political heavy from the Huey Long era. Weiss was said to have run New Orleans for the National Crime Syndicate along with the more famous mafioso Carlos Marcello.[7]

Many U.S. multinationals supported INCA, through foundations such as the Cordell Hull Foundation. INCA's anti-Communist activities in Latin America, in practice, meant opposing all political parties advocating nationalization of U.S. corporations. Thus INCA clearly served the economic interests of U.S. firms doing business there.

These included not only Standard Fruit but the William B. Reily Company, the coffee company that ostensibly employed Lee Harvey Oswald while he was in New Orleans. I say "ostensibly," because at least some of Oswald's alleged paychecks from the Reily company are apparently not genuine as transmitted to the Warren Commission; the FBI was aware they had a problem in this area; and they went out of their way to conceal the problem.[8] The distinct possibility that these checks are artifacts, not real, draws our attention to the coincidence that the chief source of information to both the Secret Service and the FBI about Oswald at the Reily Coffee company was INCA charter member William I. Monaghan, an ex-FBI agent, who left Standard Fruit to join the Reily Company about the same time Oswald did, and also left the Reily Company at about the same time as Oswald.[9] The Reily family's engagement in Caribbean anti-Communist politics is exemplified by the fact that one Reily brother (Eustis Reily) was a backer of INCA, and another (William B. Reily) was a backer of the Crusade to Free Cuba Committee, which raised cash for the New Orleans CRC.[10]

Extensive cover-up has hitherto obscured the evidence linking the Oswald story in New Orleans to the other major banana company, United Fruit. This activity was the trip he, or someone else using his passport, took to Mexico City, where an employee of the Somozas' Nicaraguan Secret Service would later claim, falsely, that Oswald had been recruited by agents of Fidel Castro to assassinate President Kennedy.[11] Perhaps the best documentary evidence for that trip was the Mexican tourist card for Oswald, obtained from the New Orleans Consulate of Mexico on September 17, 1963. We must, however, scrutinize this supposed evidence carefully, inasmuch as at least one other document "proving" the trip is now admitted to have been forged. This was the

Mexican bus manifest with Oswald's name on it (24 WH 673, 682; 25 WH 736); it was later admitted that the manifest had been altered deceptively (probably by a member of the Office of the Mexican President) by adding the name "Oswld" (24 WH 619–22; 25 WH 599, 646, 736). (Relying on testimony from another employee of the Mexican government, the Warren Commission later located Oswald on a different bus: WR 736; 22 WH 233; 24 WH 602–9; 25 WH 650, 739–42).

At the same time it transmitted the falsified bus manifest, the Mexican Interior Ministry (Gobernación) also provided U.S. authorities with a list of the names of those tourists whose tourist cards immediately preceded or followed the permit, FM8 24085, issued to Oswald (24 WH 679, 685). From this list exactly one name and number was omitted, the name for FM8 24084, immediately preceding the Oswald permit.[12]

In fact, however, the FBI possessed the name, William Gaudet, and had confirmed from Gaudet on November 27 that he had picked up his travel permit the same day as Oswald. Gaudet also told the FBI that "he has in the past been an employee of CIA."[13] After this FBI interview was declassified, many researchers, including me, interviewed and wrote about Gaudet. To all his story was consistent: he had worked for the CIA; he had seen Oswald on occasion, even in the presence of Guy Banister; but he had never spoken to Oswald. Above all he had not seen Oswald in the Mexican Consulate on September 17; and he did not travel with Oswald to Mexico.

I now believe that all of these answers, and especially the last two, are possibly true. The man who called himself Lee Oswald in Mexico City, we now suspect, was not the man using that name in New Orleans. I wish that I had had the wits to ask Gaudet (who is now deceased) a different question: "Did you, or someone with you, arrange to bring the Oswald birth certificate to the consulate and pick up a tourist card issued in the Oswald name?" For that could have been the full extent of Gaudet's participation in the plot.[14]

It is relevant here that Gaudet was an expert in public relations, like so many others linked to Oswald in those two months when Oswald briefly became a television figure in New Orleans.[15] For years he edited a journal, *Latin-American Report*, which justified his extensive travels in Latin America and which was sponsored by men like Dr. Alton Ochsner, a consultant to the U.S. Air Force "on the medical side of subversive matters." Ochsner ran his own foundation dealing with Cuban exiles. He was also the president of INCA, and close to Standard Fruit (which had funded his clinic).[16]

Every published account of the Gaudet-Oswald story, including my own, has repeated Gaudet's description of himself as working for the CIA.[17] They have failed to note the revelation of a former United Fruit public relations man, Thomas McCann, that United Fruit, in its public relations campaign, "supported for many years a publication named *Latin American Report,* published by William Gaudet."[18] It would be wrong to deduce from this that Gaudet was a simple employee of United Fruit; we should conclude rather that his operation, much like INCA, represented not just the fruit companies but all businesses which had cause, like Gaudet himself, to be dissatisfied with Kennedy's rhetoric and policies for Latin America.

STANDARD FRUIT, SEYMOUR WEISS, AND ORGANIZED CRIME

We must now consider why in 1963 Standard Fruit & Steamship, the second largest banana company in America, would contain on its board Seymour Weiss, a man three times indicted and once jailed on criminal fraud charges, and accused of illicit business deals in New Orleans with New York mobster Frank Costello and J. Edgar Hoover's friend Lewis Rosenstiel (see Chapter 13).[19] The superficial answer is that Seymour Weiss, like his political mentor Mike Moss before him, managed the New Orleans Roosevelt Hotel, in which the Vaccaros, the founding family of Standard Fruit, had a major interest. More importantly, Weiss had been the political bagman for Huey Long, and Mike Moss and the Vaccaros among Long's original big donors.[20]

Behind the deep politics of the Kennedy assassination lie those of the Long assassination, when Seymour Weiss was at the focal point of organized-crime deals, corporate payoffs, and the hidden manipulation of government. Standard Fruit, or what we might better call the Vaccaro-Moss-Hecht interests (for during the early Long era, the Mosses and Hechts managed the Vaccaro interests, including Standard Fruit), were the surviving powers behind the rise and fall of Huey Long.[21] Long's murder in 1935, some say, was arranged to prevent men like Weiss, then a "prime target" of the IRS, from going to jail.[22] Certainly Weiss was prominent in helping to establish the official version of the killing, which was that Long had been killed by a deranged physician (Dr. Carl Weiss, no relation), who was himself immediately shot.[23] Summary accounts of the Kingfish's career often do not add that there was abundant pre-assassination evidence of well-organized plots to kill him. One plotting group, the paramilitary Square Deal Association, united a number of Long's most influential enemies, including Standard Oil employees, New Orleans Mayor T. Semmes Walmsley, and former Louisiana Governor John M. Parker.[24] Shortly before the assassination, Mayor Walmsley had brought back from Central America Guy Maloney or Molony, a mercenary, who, we shall see, had organized several revolutions there for the banana companies.[25]

The Long-Weiss-Costello business deals which brought Costello's slot machines from New York to Louisiana contributed to a permanent alteration in the patterns of organized crime. On the local level, the slot machines conferred eventual wealth and influence upon Carlos Marcello, who at the time he was picked in 1934 was a twenty-two-year-old immigrant just out of jail for having robbed a grocery.

As a right-hand man to Huey Long, Weiss "arranged payoffs to Long at the hotel from three members of the national crime syndicate, Frank Costello, Jake Lansky, and "Dandy Phil" Kastel."[26] The purpose of these payoffs was to consolidate a Louisiana slot-machine empire under Long's protection. According to Messick, Jake's brother Meyer Lansky worked out the details face to face with Huey Long in Weiss's hotel.[27] Marcello's first lucrative business was the slot-machine franchise for the west side of New Orleans; later, Marcello was cut into another Lansky-Costello operation, the posh Beverly Club casino.[28]

On the national and international level, Costello brought his financial adviser, Meyer Lansky, to New Orleans, where Lansky developed a national clearinghouse for underworld money-laundering. Lansky made financial history by opening accounts in Switzerland for Huey Long and the other principals, making a channel for the postwar flow of mob money to overseas havens from the Bahamas to Vanuatu.[29]

As Roosevelt became increasingly concerned with Huey Long's demagogic ambitions for the Presidency, he ordered the IRS to investigate Long and his associates for tax fraud. Unable to trace Long's rumored profits from the slot machines, the Treasury's hottest lead was something called the Win or Lose corporation, in which Huey Long was only a hidden owner, while the leading officers were oilman Jimmy Noe and Seymour Weiss.[30] After Long's assassination, the IRS interest in its "prime target," Seymour Weiss, diminished, although five years later Weiss went to jail on unrelated charges.[31]

In 1946–47, when Frank Costello, Meyer Lansky, and Sam Carolla met several times in New Orleans to establish the Beverly Club, Carlos Marcello was picked to represent the New Orleans interests, while Frank Coppola, a Luciano-Costello lieutenant, was sent south to represent New York.[32] The resulting Coppola-Marcello connection would come to dominate postwar drug trafficking. As we shall see in Chapter 10, Coppola and Sam Carolla were soon deported to Sicily, where they became part of what we shall call "Operation X," a postwar intelligence-mafia collaboration, which both helped massacre Sicilian leftists and simultaneously laid the foundations for the postwar trans-Atlantic drug traffic.[33]

A final consequence of the Rosenstiel-Costello-Weiss business deals was that the influence which both Rosenstiel and Costello enjoyed with Hoover was thenceforth shared by Weiss as well. In 1939, amid rumors that Louisiana Governor Richard Leche and Weiss would be indicted, Leche entertained Hoover and Attorney General Frank Murphy at his governor's mansion. One week later Hoover's assistant Louis B. Nichols gave Leche and Weiss a personally guided tour of FBI headquarters in Washington.[34] Hoover's partiality for Weiss's brand of anti-communism helps explain the clear bias in his handling of the Kennedy assassination.

THE BANANA COMPANIES, THE MOB, AND THE WATERFRONT

But behind the story of the Vaccaros, Weiss, and the mob in the Huey Long era is a still older story: not only Standard Fruit, but also United Fruit, were deeply involved with organized crime, for reasons going back to the nineteenth century.

The first need of the fruit companies was to control the waterfronts where their produce was loaded and unloaded. Because their imports were perishable, fruit shippers were vulnerable to labor demands, which could easily degenerate into corrupt extortion. In the early days of ruthless competition, the successful companies were those with the best connections to organized gangs. One firm, owned by the half-brothers of New Orleans Sicilian waterfront crime boss Joe Macheca, later was merged into United Fruit.[35] Another, that of the Sicilian Vaccaro brothers, became Standard Fruit & Steamship.[36]

We have already seen how Seymour Weiss of Standard Fruit became involved with Frank Costello. Later, Blaise d'Antoni, a Vaccaro grandson who was president of Standard Fruit from 1949–53, would become involved in the mob-linked sports of boxing and racing; and would allegedly boast of the watch which Frank Costello had given him.[37] Boxing financier James Norris once told a Senate committee that Paul "Frankie" Carbo of the Lucchese mafia family had drawn a line across a map of the United States, offering him boxing in the top half, with Blaise d'Antoni getting the bottom half.[38] In 1940, the year that Seymour Weiss went to jail for fraud, the entire New Orleans dock board was indicted for embezzlement and extortion, along with former Louisiana governor Earl Long, Huey's brother and successor. Among those indicted was Lucca Vaccaro, a Standard Fruit founder and vice-president.[39]

Standard Fruit in particular has been cited in connection with the recent domination by the mafia of corrupt longshoremen's union locals in the United States.[40] As we shall see, the desire of the U.S. government in World War II to exploit this mafia domination of the waterfront led to the OSS-mafia Operation Underworld, where U.S. intelligence worked with Frank Costello and Meyer Lansky.[41] But the symbiosis on the waterfront between firm and gang should not be blamed on any one company.

Consider the New Orleans Matranga-Provenzano gang wars of 1888–90, which gave rise to the first hue and cry in the United States against the "Mafia." The mafia charge was raised by the Provenzanos, against their waterfront opponents, the Matrangas, after the murder of New Orleans Police Chief David Hennessey, an ally of the Provenzanos. That murder remains an unsolved one, in which one of the strongest clues was that Hennessey allegedly died with the suggestive words, "The Dagoes!" on his lips.

Nevertheless, the original "mafia-did-it" allegations of the Provenzanos about the Hennessey murder are still repeated, uncritically, in some "mafia-did-it" books on the Kennedy assassination. John Davis even labels as "justice" the lynch scene that followed Hennessey's death, the largest lynching in American history, in which eleven Sicilians died, including not only Joe Macheca but five who had not even been on trial.[42]

Based on the Provenzanos' mafia allegations, *Harper's* soon raised a specter that is still with us, "of a perfectly organized secret society in America, with ramifications in New Orleans, New York, St. Louis, and San Francisco, and possibly Chicago."[43] According to Professor Humbert Nelli, however, the Matranga-Provenzano dispute, even if it involved some "low-level members (*picciotti*)" from the Sicilian mafia, was essentially a struggle between competing stevedore firms, with the fruit companies making their decision, on business grounds, to go with the so-called "mafia" Matrangas:

> From 1878 to 1886, in the words of Joseph P. Macheca (a leading Italian fruit importer in New Orleans) the Provenzanos "had the exclusive business of discharging fruit vessels." This monopoly ended in 1886 when a new stevedore firm, that of Matranga and Locascio, appeared on the docks. For the next two years that firm offered stiff competition to the established Provenzanos, and in June 1888 (as described in a *Times-Democrat* article of October 21, 1890) "the fruit merchants concluded to change their stevedores and employed the Matranga brothers because of certain disagreements with the Provenzanos." ... The shippers then organized an association, discharged the Provenzanos, and gave all their business to the Matranga-Locascio firm. The new employers retained most of the laborers who had worked under the Provenzanos. Vincent Caruso, for example, one of the men later accused of Henness[e]y's murder and himself a lynch victim in 1891, had worked for twelve years for the Provenzanos before joining Matranga. ... From the evidence available, the shippers apparently based their decision on business factors. The Irish and black workers who controlled the docks were in the process of unionizing during this period, and the Matrangas may have been brought in to head a company-type union (it was this union that many New Orleanians meant when they alluded to the *mafia*).[44]

Those who describe Matranga as continuing to be, until 1922, the "boss of the local Mafia" or "head of organized crime" inevitably fail to mention that he continued to work "as a stevedore for the Standard Fruit Company, later the United Fruit Company, until his retirement after fifty years of service in 1918."[45] When Matranga finally died in 1943, his funeral "was large and attended by executives of United Fruit, Lykes, Standard Fruit, and other large steamship companies which had benefited from his good will."[46]

In the same way, something is lost when authors, following Robert Blakey, describe Oswald's uncle "Dutz" Murret's career as a professional gambler, handbook operator, and manager of prizefighters.[47] All of this is true and relevant, but no more so than the fact that for most of his life he worked on the docks (8 WH 93, 99; 9 AH 96). And briefly, at the beginning of his career, so did Lee Harvey Oswald himself (WR 680; 9 AH 101–02).[48]

THE BANANA COMPANIES, THE MOB, AND CENTRAL AMERICA

Another reason for the fruit companies to maintain a mob connection was their reliance on corruption and even violence to maintain their influence over the client governments of the banana republics. The bribing of Central American politicians was a practice dating back to United Fruit's founder Henry Meiggs, and revelations about payoffs from both United Fruit and Standard Fruit to Honduran President López Arellano (in the so-called Bananagate scandal) led to the latter's overthrow in 1975.[49] In the course of these and other revelations, both United Fruit and Standard Fruit changed names and ownership; but the era of gray alliances was not over. Given the exigencies of waterfront and banana republic politics, it is not surprising to find the banana companies caught up in the intrigues of Contragate and Noriega; and today United Fruit/United Brands, now known as Chiquita Brands International, is owned by Carl Lindner, a business ally of Michael Milken and Charles Keating, two of the major figures convicted in the Wall Street and savings-and-loan mess.[50]

The twentieth-century banana republics of Central America can be seen as creations of the fruit companies and the New Orleans milieu. In particular, New Orleans organized crime played a historic role in the 1911 Honduran revolution that ended the ascendancy of European bankers and bondholders over Honduras, "and left it free to be conquered by the fruit companies."[51] For that change in government had been financed by Samuel Zemurray of the Cuyamel banana company (itself partly financed by, and later incorporated into, United Fruit); the revolt was actually plotted by the future Honduran President and two corrupt American "soldiers of fortune" (both non-Sicilian) in a New Orleans brothel.[52] Although the U.S. government made a show of neutrality in the ensuing revolt, the tilt of the U.S. Navy toward the rebels facilitated the incumbent's overthrow.[53] U.S. Marines played a similar role in the comparable Nicaraguan revolt of 1909–10, also backed by U.S. commercial interests.[54]

This symbiosis of the fruit companies, their local client rulers, the U.S. military, and organized crime, became more institutionalized with the passage of years. In the 1930s, the collapse of the banana economy saw its role in the Honduran political economy being extensively supplemented by that of narcotics. Both the government and opposition factions financed themselves by drug smuggling to New Orleans. One of the two Americans in the 1911 Honduran revolt, former New Orleans police chief Guy Molony, was by the 1930s suspected by U.S. authorities of involvement in a well-organized heroin traffic involving the Honduran government-owned airline, TACA, and the Honduran Vice-President and Minister of Gobernación, General Abraham Williams. The government at this time was securely controlled by United Fruit's preferred strong man, President Tiburcio Carías Andino.[55]

Meanwhile, the opposition Liberal party, no longer energetically supported by Zemurray after his company merged into United Fruit, was caught up in heroin dealings with the New Orleans *mafioso* Nofio Pecora, the friend of the Oswald family who may have been telephoned by Jack Ruby on the eve of the Kennedy assassination.[56] The newly organized U.S. Federal Bureau of Narcotics cracked down on the Liberal opposition's New Orleans heroin connection, but let the government's connection continue unhindered.[57]

> In fact, the State Department ordered all surveillance of the TACA group curtailed for a time. . . . The security of tenure in office provided an atmosphere of stability out of which Carías could pursue his primary political goal: domestic peace through suppression of revolutionary discord. This emphasis placed Carías in line with the evolving security emphasis of the Good Neighbor Policy.[58]

(One of the more intriguing papers found in Guy Banister's office after his suspicious death in 1964 was "a memorandum to attorney Guy Johnson, an Office of Naval Intelligence reserve officer, reporting, 'We apparently have cut across a CIA operation in the Taca affair,' Taca being a Central American airline company.")[59]

We see that the merger of Zemurray's Cuyamel Company (backing Liberal Honduras politicians) into United Fruit (backing Conservatives) was followed by the collapse of the Honduran two- or three-party system into the strong-man *continuismo* of Carías, who lasted from

1932 to 1963. There was a parallel move away from electoral instability in the other banana republics, with the emergence in Guatemala of Jorge Ubico (1931–1944), and in Nicaragua of the Somoza dynasty (1933–1979).[60]

No single factor can explain the emergence of strong men in the 1930s. We see a similar stabilization at this time of the Mexican presidency under Lázaro Cárdenas. Clearly the consolidation of the banana companies was not a factor in the stabilization of Mexico; at the same time, government-sanctioned heroin trafficking may have been a factor. So too may have been the strategies of the U.S. State Department and FBI in the era of Roosevelt's Good Neighbor Policy, which clearly favored local strong men to replace U.S. Marines being withdrawn. This apparently evolved into an American tolerance of, and even symbiosis with, governmental drug connections in Latin America. The example of Mexico is worth pursuing, since as we shall see the Mexican gray alliance involved people who would become involved in the story of the JFK assassination.

The governmental drug connections tended to be centered in ministries of Gobernación, which used funds outside the official budget (whether from the banana companies, or later from narcotics) to pay off competing factions in the army and civilian establishment, and keep them from rebelling. In the 1930s the Honduran narcotics trafficking was divided between that of the incumbent minister of Gobernación, Abraham Williams, and that of his Liberal predecessor, José Maria Guillen Velez. Similarly in Mexico the PRI minister of Gobernación, Carlos Riva Palacio, announced his resignation in 1931, because of "alleged complicity in a smuggling operation which was introducing illegal drugs into Mexico and then transporting them to the United States." His replacement was Lázaro Cárdenas, who held the post until 1934, when he became President.[61]

For the next forty years, the PRI candidate for the Mexican presidency would be the incumbent minister of Gobernación. The pattern was only broken in 1976, when the minister of Gobernación, and official "Precandidate for President," was discovered to have been flying around Mexico in the Lear jet of Alberto Sicilia Falcón, then Mexico's leading drug trafficker.[62] A decade later it would emerge that the Federal Security Directorate (DFS), an agency created out of the Gobernación Secretariat in the 1940s, was PRI's chief link to the highly institutionalized Mexican drug traffic; through it Sicilia and other highest-level traffickers acquired official cards identifying them as agents of the Gobernación.[63] According to Elaine Shannon, "most DEA agents who worked in Mexico and on the border considered the DFS the private army of the drug traffickers. They called the DFS badge 'a license to traffic.' "[64] At the same time, DFS was the chief point of contact for both CIA and FBI officials with the Mexican government. When the DFS Chief, Miguel Nazar Haro, was secretly indicted by a U.S. grand jury in San Diego, for his participation in North America's largest stolen-car ring, the CIA blocked the indictment because of Nazar Haro's "indispensability as a source of intelligence in Mexico and Central America."[65]

One is struck by the recurring importance of this U.S.-protected Mexican gray alliance as a source of disinformation, both before and after November 1963, about Oswald and the JFK murder. Nazar Haro was a long-time personal friend of the CIA's Mexican station chief, Win Scott, to the extent of giving him a Cadillac for his own use; and Win Scott's station in turn played a key role in the transmission of false stories about Oswald in Mexico.[66] The Gobernación of Mexico also transmitted a number of altered or suspicious documents on Oswald, such as the forged bus manifest (24 WH 673) and the list of tourist cards which suppressed the name of William Gaudet (24 WH 679, cf. 24 WH 609, 25 WH 616). As we shall see in the next chapter, Noe Palomares, the Gobernación official transmitting these documents (24 WH 682, 680), was also connected indirectly to witnesses implicating Oswald in a "phase one" Communist conspiracy (3 AH 301). And Bernardo de Torres, a Cuban-exile drug trafficker with intimate links to Nazar Haro, became in 1966–67 a source of dubious reports about Miami for the hapless Garrison investigation.[67]

The Mexican government, of course, was no banana republic and had no particular reason to be close to the American banana companies. The Mexico City CIA station, however, was another matter. As we shall see confirmed in the next chapter, the CIA station was a base for regional operations in Central America; and it had a long history of co-operation with both the banana companies and Somoza. Indeed, one could argue that the CIA in this region enjoyed the same kind of special arrangement with Somoza's Nicaragua as it did in the Far East with Chiang Kai-shek's Taiwan, and in the Middle East and Africa with Israel. This special arrangement further explained the collaboration of these three scattered countries with one another, both abroad and in Washington.

It is well known that in the 1950s and 1960s the Israel Lobby and the Taiwan Lobby were both powerful in Washington and sometimes collaborated on common projects. For example, the publicist Marvin Liebman, a Zionist, helped set up a steering committee in 1958 for what eventually became the Taiwan-dominated, and drug-tainted, World Anti-Communist League (WACL).[68] There was also a Nicaragua Lobby, or perhaps more accurately, a Somoza Lobby, which also overlapped with the Israel, China, and Cuba lobbies. We shall look later at the example of Irving Davidson, a registered lobbyist for both Nicaragua and Israel Aircraft Industries, who by no accident was also close to J. Edgar Hoover. Davidson promoted Somoza through his connections with the Teamsters.

In the next chapter we shall see how closely Standard Fruit had worked in Latin America with the mob, specifically John Rosselli, as well as with the Somozas and the Mexico City CIA station.

SEVEN

Mexico, Somoza, and the Martino-Rosselli Story

In this chapter we shall be looking at the genesis of a key "Castro-did-it" Oswald story told by two men at the very juncture of the intelligence-mob connection, and at the role played by their story in legitimating the "phase two" version that Oswald acted alone. But before doing so we must look at the role played in Central America by the two men, John Rosselli and John Martino, and their relation to Somoza, the Mexico City CIA station, and Standard Fruit.

The Mexico City CIA station was perhaps unlike any other. In 1963 it had been headed for seven years by an FBI veteran, Winston Mac-Kinlay Scott, who was one of a regional cabal of ex-FBI agents going back to World War II. At that time the FBI had built a Special Intelligence Service spy network in Latin America, and particularly Mexico, which paralleled that of OSS elsewhere, and also competed with it. When in 1947 Hoover was ordered to merge his FBI/SIS assets in the newly created CIA, he "did not do so gladly. Under his direct orders . . . the FBI/SIS agents burned their files and dismissed their informants, rather than turn them over to their new rival."[1]

At this time a number of Hoover's men moved over to CIA, including Raymond Leddy, Winston MacKinlay Scott, and William King Harvey, all of whom would later work on Central America and/or Cuba.

> According to William Corson, Hoover did not bemoan these losses: in some cases he secretly arranged them. Even those who were not "witting" spies

for the FBI director usually maintained their fraternal old-boy-network ties with the Bureau and, if the need arose, could be called upon for assistance.[2]

But there were deeper reasons for the special CIA problems in the Caribbean than Hoover's quirky personality and empire-building. Around most of the world the CIA collaborated with global U.S. multinationals, such as the major oil companies and ITT. These companies' interests were long-term, complex, and diversified. In 1963 their traditional anti-communism was undergoing sophisticated mutations, as they moved toward an understanding with the Soviet Union on dividing up the markets of eastern and western Europe.

The interests of the fruit companies in countries like Honduras and Guatemala were quite different: narrowly regional, exploitative, often more opposed to local capital development than hoping to profit from it, and thus quite happy with rule by gang and military coup. Franz Schurmann wrote an entire book, *The Logic of World Power*, about the contrast between these two types of imperialism, global and regional, and the resulting tensions between New York corporate-financial boardrooms and direct Texas investors in Central America (such as the Murchisons, investment partners with Somoza).[3]

STANDARD FRUIT, GUATEMALA, AND JOHN ROSSELLI

Both types of imperialism were represented in the CIA cadres of 1954, when the U.S. government, spurred on by psy-war advisers like C. D. Jackson, collaborated with Somoza and United Fruit to bring about the military overthrow of the elected government in Guatemala.[4] The much-told story of that overthrow is a story of conflicts between the CIA's central overseers and their "cowboy" operators like "Rip" Robertson, who soon took orders from Somoza rather than Washington. Robertson was fired by the CIA, after authorizing one of his pilots (at the urging of the first Anastasio Somoza) to drop a bomb down the smokestack of a British cargo carrier (the CIA later had to pay $1.4 million to the insurers, Lloyd's of London).[5]

Among the lasting baneful results of the 1954 death-blow to Guatemalan democracy has been the ongoing presence in Guatemala of American organized crime, operating specifically in the areas of gambling and narcotics. By 1958 Carlos Marcello was thought, rightly or wrongly, to be a major criminal presence in Guatemala. In the same year a regional conference of an anti-communist confederation, organized by E. Howard Hunt and the CIA in connection with the 1954 coup, was chaired by a right-winger, Antonio Valladares, who doubled as Marcello's lawyer.[6] Attending the same conference, which eventually became part of the World Anti-Communist League, was Maurice B. Gatlin, one of Banister's associates at the 544 Camp Street address.[7]

Gambling in Guatemala City was in the hands of Ted Lewin, a Lansky representative already active in the Philippines, in collaboration with the CIA and with such up-and-coming politicians as future president Ferdinand Marcos.[8] More interesting to students of the JFK assassination were the occasional visits to Guatemala of two major figures in accounts of CIA-Mafia assassination plots, John Rosselli and John Martino.

Charles Rappleye has written that he learned of Rosselli's presence from

> two sources who said they worked with Rosselli on frequent occasions in Guatemala. . . . The first source . . . [an] underworld operator . . . said he joined Rosselli in Guatemala City and Mexico City on half a dozen separate trips beginning in 1956. Mexico City served at the time as a nerve center for plots in Guatemala, which borders on Mexico . . . and as the base for all CIA operations in Central America. . . . The second source was a longtime government field worker assigned to Guatemala with the International Cooperation Administration (ICA). . . . The ICA source was extremely reluctant to talk, but confirmed that he had become acquainted with the underworld source in Guatemala, and Rosselli had been "a major force" beneath the surface of events in Guatemala City and in other states in Central America. "John had access to everyone and everything that was going on there," the government source asserted. That included the fruit companies, the Guatemalan Army, and the American delegation. . . . According to both sources, Rosselli's primary concern in Guatemala was to protect and advance the interests of Standard Fruit and Steamship Company.[9]

This account of Rosselli's operations in Guatemala implies that he was being run out of the CIA station in Mexico City, which from 1956 through 1969 was headed, as we have seen, by Win Scott.

Standard did not own plantations in Guatemala, as did its larger competitor United Fruit. Instead it purchased bananas from independent growers, through a specially incorporated subsidiary, Standard Fruit Company of Guatemala; and exported them through United Fruit's port facility at Puerto Barrios.[10] After the United Fruit–CIA success in toppling the elected Arbenz government in 1954, United Fruit apparently used its power over the affiliated International Railway of Central America, and over the new Castillo Armas government, to make it difficult for Standard to operate in Guatemala.

Apparently, Rosselli made contact with an anti-Castillo army faction, tempting them with "the potential financial rewards of casino gambling," which Castillo opposed. Rosselli visited Guatemala in 1957; Castillo was promptly murdered by a palace guard; Ted Lewin's casino flourished under the successor governments; and Rosselli's army contact, Lieutenant Colonel Enrique Trinidad Oliva, "was elevated to chief of the secret police."[11] In the next few years Rosselli also supplied rebel bands led by dissident army leaders with munitions and cash "in exchange for occasional raids on United Fruit facilities when talks over rail access [by Standard Fruit] and freight rates stalled." By this means Rosselli could supply intelligence on rebel activities to Oliva and the secret police, and no doubt to the CIA as well.[12]

In 1962, following a bad hurricane, Standard Fruit decided to withdraw from Guatemala altogether.[13] But the importance of drug-trafficking in Guatemalan politics continued, as did organized crime's simultaneous connection to both the military secret police and the insurgents.[14] By 1975 Guatemalan insurgents were being not only armed but trained in Mexico by employees of the Cuban exile narcotics trafficker Alberto Sicilia Falcón, who, like Rosselli, was "treated like royalty" by the men running the Guatemalan Government.[15] U.S. DEA agents speculated that the CIA itself had recruited Sicilia, a U.S. Army veteran who had trained at Fort Jackson in 1963.[16]

Sicilia himself told Mexican police that "the U.S. government had turned a blind eye to his heroin shipments, while his organization supplied CIA weapons to terrorist groups in Central America, thereby forcing the host governments to accept U.S. conditions for security assistance."[17] Sicilia's close associate and chief intelligence officer, José Egozi, had been trained by the CIA and taken part in the Bay of Pigs invasion. Egozi in turn was close to a Cuban exile who acted as chief liaison to wealthy Latin American gamblers at Caesar's Palace, one of the casinos in Las Vegas which had been financed by the Central States Pension Fund, thanks to the influence of Jack Ruby's Chicago friends the Dorfmans, working with John Rosselli.[18]

The man running Guatemala from 1970 to 1974, Carlos Araña Osorio, had earlier succeeded Rosselli's old contact Colonel Oliva as the

chief of counter-insurgency operations in Guatemala. In this capacity
he had earned the nickname, "The Butcher of Zacapa"; for it was under his tutelage that Guatemala inaugurated the death squad activities
that had led to forty thousand "disappeared" people in Guatemala by
the 1980s.[19]

After he was elected President of Guatemala in 1970, his CIA contact was an old Rosselli and Trafficante crime associate called John
Martino, who also became Araña's business partner. Araña knew Martino as an American mafioso, which he was; but Martino also was
working with the CIA. At this time he became the CIA's case officer for
a Guatemalan veteran of the 1954 plot against Arbenz: Mario Sandoval
Alarcón.[20] In this period Sandoval was a leader of the private death
squads which supplemented the army's reign of terror in Guatemala; by
the 1980s he was known as the Godfather of all the death squads of
Central America, as well as an early patron of the Contras.[21]

THE MARTINO-ROSSELLI RETALIATION STORY

Just as Sandoval is an unseen force behind the Contras in the 1980s, so
his former handler John Martino is an unseen force behind the so-
called Rosselli story, that Castro used Oswald to kill Kennedy, that was
essential to inducing the dialectical cover-up. In 1963, moreover, Martino and Rosselli were living together in Miami, using their similar mob
and CIA connections to assemble assassination teams, allegedly against
Castro.[22]

Martino had begun with the Atlantic City mob, and then installed
security systems in the Havana casinos for Santos Trafficante. His career thus closely resembles Rosselli's: from Sicilian mafia to Havana casinos to the Nixon-authorized CIA-Mafia plots at the time of the Bay of
Pigs. Martino would appear by most accounts to be a relatively low
member of the mob or mafia. At the Deauville Casino in Havana, however, he had worked with Joe Nesline, who as we shall see was close not
only to Meyer Lansky but to the very center of organized criminal corruption in Washington, D.C.

In 1963, after the Bay of Pigs debacle and Martino's release from a
Havana prison, Rosselli and Martino set up shop together in Key Biscayne, to mobilize a new Cuban-exile resistance to Fidel Castro. From
what is known of their work in this period, they seem to have had only
limited support from the CIA; their main encouragement came rather

from old Nixon contacts like William Pawley and Nathaniel Weyl (who in 1963 ghost-wrote a book for Martino, "I Was Castro's Prisoner.") They also worked with men from the old CIA-mob alliance authorized under Nixon's (and Pawley's) urging: Carlos Prío Socarras, Tony Varona, Gerry Patrick Hemming, and Frank Sturgis.[23] All four of these men, it should be noted, had been associated with the Lake Pontchartrain training camp, the relevance of which will become evident when we see the role of Martino and his Bayo-Pawley mission (like the training camp) in the Kennedy assassination story.

Pawley's prewar and postwar career had been one of generating increased regional U.S. commitments, often in alliance with organized crime, in areas of the Third World, like China and Cuba, where he held personal investments.[24] For years there has been speculation that Pawley and J. Edgar Hoover (perhaps in conjunction with Robert Maheu and his partner Robert King, a former FBI man and Nixon aide) worked with Richard Nixon to generate the authorization for the 1960 CIA-Mafia plots.[25] By his own account, Pawley may have played a key role in reviving them in 1963.[26]

The chief trainer for these operations was William "Rip" Robertson, the CIA contract agent for the Bay of Pigs invasion whose primary allegiance since the 1950s had been with the Somoza family.[27] According to Pawley, Robertson was put in touch with Martino as a result of Pawley's request for assistance to the CIA's military deputy director, General Marshall "Pat" Carter, this being more or less the full extent of CIA support for Pawley's initiative at that time.[28]

It is possible that after June 1963, CIA support for Martino's operations may have increased. That month saw the authorization of "autonomous operations," a "track two" of irregular ops to supplement the regular CIA- and army-controlled "Operation Second Naval Guerrilla" of Manuel Artime (10 AH 77, 140, 142). Under this concept, financial assistance would be offered to anti-Castro Cuban guerrilla operations mounted outside the United States, with U.S. participation limited to an "experienced liaison officer."[29]

Truly or falsely, both Rosselli and Martino claimed to have special knowledge about Lee Harvey Oswald and the John F. Kennedy assassination; and their suggestive claims significantly affected, perhaps crucially, how the U.S. government handled the case. For both men told the FBI that the assassination of John F. Kennedy had been Castro's retaliation for Kennedy's CIA-Mafia plots against himself, even to the point of Castro's having "turned" an assassination team and sent it back to Dallas.[30]

We now know that Lyndon Johnson himself, despite his public lip-service to the Warren Report's verdict of a lone assassin, believed in fact that the killing was the work of a "conspiracy," a "retaliation" for "a CIA-backed assassination team . . . picked up in Havana."[31] Johnson allegedly used the rumors of Cuban involvement to persuade a reluctant Earl Warren to head the Warren Commission: "If the public become aroused against Castro and Khrushchev, there might be war."[32] And Warren in turn referred privately to Cuba as "one of the principal suspects."[33] Yet another person concerned about the possibility of a Castro retaliation or retribution was Robert Kennedy.[34]

The intense reaction, or overreaction, of U.S. investigators suggests that there may have been at least this much possible truth to the Rosselli-Martino story: that there were grounds for suspecting that the hit team against Kennedy (with or without Castro's intervention) was one which Rosselli and Martino had themselves recruited, with or without CIA sanction.[35]

THE MARTINO STORY
AND THE BAYO-MARTINO-PAWLEY MISSION

What must have particularly threatened establishment insiders, including C. D. Jackson at *Life,* was the fact that Martino himself had shepherded one such hit team into Cuba in June of 1963, the same month in which Rosselli is known to have met with CIA Officer William Harvey. The Martino mission was especially sensitive to the establishment, because it had been backed simultaneously by the CIA, organized crime, *Life* magazine (which planned to write it up as a photo feature), and a New York financier described as close to the Kennedy White House.[36] The Cuban hit team was taken close to the Cuban shoreline on Pawley's boat, loaded with men then unknown who would later play a role in the Warren Commission and later investigations of the Kennedy murder.

One was Trafficante associate John Martino, whose story of the murder as an act of retaliation attracted the interest of a Warren Commission staffer, until he was told the FBI had determined that Martino's story did not stand up.[37] Another was Loran Eugene Hall, by his own account a former worker in a Havana casino owned by Santos Trafficante. Hall later told writer Dick Russell that Trafficante and Chicago organized-crime boss Sam Giancana (one of Bobby Kennedy's leading enemies) helped plan the Bayo-Martino-Pawley raid.[38] Hall came to Dallas shortly before the assassination and was later used by the FBI to refute (falsely) a provocative story linking Oswald in Dallas to Cuban exiles.[39]

In 1963 Hall was attending West Coast meetings of the paramilitary Christian Defense League, whose leader, Lieutenant Colonel William Gale, was a Minutemen ally and the California chairman for James Milteer's racist Constitution party (see Chapter 3).[40] Hall, Hemming, and Martino all are said to have had racist associations in this period, raising questions about the role in the Bayo-Pawley raid of Senator Eastland, at the time the most powerful racist in the Senate and perhaps indeed in the country. In Chapter 16 we shall ask whether Oswald's secret agenda was not also to feed the segregationist propaganda mills of Eastland's Senate Internal Security Subcommittee.

A third and important member of the Bayo-Martino-Pawley team was the hit-team leader Eddie Bayo (alias Perez), a veteran of the anti-Kennedy Cuban exile group Alpha 66. Bayo's brother-in-law Luis Castillo later floated the Martino-Rosselli retaliation theory in the Philippines. When Rosselli went public with the story of the Kennedy assassination as a retaliation for the CIA-Mafia plots, a secret CIA Inspector-General investigation of his claim noted its similarity to Castillo's.[41]

According to published accounts and photographs, a fourth member was a Rolando Martinez, presumably the Cuban exile and contract CIA employee who would later be caught and convicted in the 1972 Watergate affair.[42] One has to ask of his presence on this Bayo-Martino-Pawley mission the same question one has to ask of his participation in the Watergate burglary attempt: Was he present precisely to force the CIA into colluding in a subsequent cover-up?

A fifth person on the boat was William "Rip" Robertson, the veteran of the CIA's Guatemala and Bay of Pigs operations. Robertson is described in all early accounts of the Bayo-Martino-Pawley mission as a CIA agent or officer.[43] In fact, as we have already noted, Robertson had fallen out of favor with the CIA leadership in 1954, after arranging to sink a British freighter at the urging of the first Anastasio Somoza.[44] In the aftermath Robertson was fired by the CIA; he thereupon transferred his allegiance to the Somozas and became a business partner with them in a gold mine.[45]

Robertson, a mystery man, may well hold the key to the Pawley-Martino mission. He cannot be defined as simply a Somoza agent. Somehow in 1961 he met Robert Kennedy, then still gung-ho for covert operations against Castro; he then returned to tell his Cuban exile protégés that "Kennedy was all right."[46] By 1963, moreover, as we shall see, he had developed a "close friendship" with his drinking partner John Rosselli, who by then was John Martino's roommate in Key Biscayne.[47] There is veritably a black hole in the evidence concerning this 1963 trio of Robertson (who may have used the CIA as a cover), Martino (who claimed privileged knowledge about Oswald), and Rosselli (said by intelligence sources to have met Ruby in October 1963).[48]

A sixth person on the boat was Richard N. Billings, along to write up a story for *Life* magazine, where he was an editor; an important early investigator of the Kennedy assassination and a man of high personal integrity, he would later be selected by Robert Blakey as the editorial director of the House Select Committee's Report.[49]

Billings was there under an arrangement that was common for "unauthorized operations" in this period: a story with pictures for *Life* would help pay for the operation. On an earlier Alpha 66 (Comandos L) raid which blew up a Soviet freighter, the designated "journalist" was a freelancer for *Life* named Andrew St. George, said to be connected to U.S. army intelligence.[50]

MARTINO'S PURPOSE: PROPAGANDA, MURDER, OR PRE-ASSASSINATION BLACKMAIL?

Like the earlier Alpha 66 raid, the avowed purpose of the Bayo-Martino-Pawley mission was overtly political, to embarrass the Kennedy-Khrushchev understanding over Cuba. Bayo had shown Pawley and *Life* a letter, purportedly smuggled out of Cuba, claiming that two Soviet colonels stationed there wished to defect with knowledge of where the Russians had hidden offensive missiles in violation of the Cuban-missile-crisis settlement. The agreed plan was to bring the defectors to the United States, but not turn them over to the government. Instead, a press conference would be held, to present the Russians "as living proof that Soviet missiles were still in Cuba."[51]

No matter how it is viewed, the Bayo-Pawley raid is a symptom of the profound opposition developing in 1963 against the Kennedys' Cuban policies. Its anti-Kennedy purpose had gained Bayo and Martino the support of Pawley, *Life,* the Senate Internal Security Subcommittee of Senator Eastland, and (to a limited extent) personnel of the CIA. The House Assassinations Committee learned that Julien Sourwine, counsel to the Senate subcommittee, "was involved in financing the operation which has come to be known as the Bayo-Pawley raid," and that it "saw evidence that the CIA knew of Sourwine's involvement" (11 AH 65).

But a deeper purpose of the mission, according to Loran Hall and another source, was quite different: to assassinate Castro and collect an organized-crime bounty for killing him (allegedly offered, according to Hall, by Sam Giancana, at a meeting with Hall, Martino, Bayo, and two Cubans).[52] Bayo and his commandos left Pawley's boat for the Cuban mainland, and never returned; Hall later was told by Bayo's brother-in-law, Luis Castillo, that Bayo and two of his team were captured and imprisoned in Havana.

Whatever the facts, one can see the potential embarrassment for Pawley, Time-Life, and the CIA in the "retaliation" theory for the Kennedy assassination floated by Castillo, Martino, and Rosselli. As long as it was even possible that Bayo's team, ostensibly recruited to kill Castro, had in fact killed Kennedy, the Martino-Rosselli story provided a powerful motive to advance the alternative hypothesis, that Oswald had acted alone.

There is little reason to think that the retaliation story is a true one: the sources for it, all mob or mob-connected, were not in a good position to report authoritatively on Castro's covert operations. Nevertheless, the so-called Rosselli story, when progressively leaked by Jack Anderson in 1967 and 1971, produced powerful bureaucratic reactions. In 1967 it engendered the CIA Inspector-General's Report on the CIA-Mafia Plots and their relationship to the Kennedy assassination. In 1971 it produced a spate of memos in the Nixon White House that led to the ill-starred involvement with the future Watergate burglar, E. Howard Hunt.[53]

The 1967 CIA Report even included a section titled, "Should we try to silence those who are talking or who might later?" (10 AH 194). We shall see that in 1975–76, just before Sam Giancana was to testify to the Church Committee about the CIA-Mafia plots, Giancana was murdered, allegedly by a "CIA guy" and mob killer (whom someone else called "the same people responsible for killing the Kennedys").[54] In 1976, after Rosselli testified, he too was murdered. About the same time, Martino died: according to his widow, "the Company [i.e., CIA] or the government" picked up the body to establish the cause of death, which was determined to have been a heart attack.[55]

The coordinated stories of Martino, Rosselli, and Castillo could theoretically have been hatched after the Bayo-Martino-Pawley mission, and even after the Kennedy assassination, to make the most of a botched anti-Castro attempt. Alternatively, the trip could have been planned precisely to blackmail the CIA and *Life* into an assassination cover-up. On November 22, *Life*, hearing of the assassination, dispatched Billings to coordinate the hyperactive *Life* team in Dallas that swiftly bought up the Zapruder film and the rights to Marina's story. A principal in both preemptive purchases (the Zapruder film was never publicly screened, as long as *Life* had exclusive ownership of it) was Billings's relative-in-law C. D. Jackson, a veteran of CIA propaganda activities with Allen Dulles.[56]

It is not clear, in other words, if the Bayo-Martino-Pawley mission was designed to blackmail the CIA and *Life* magazine, or was exploited for that purpose by Martino and others at some later date. But Martino's behavior in September 1963 suggests prior knowledge of the assassination conspiracy.

In September 1963, having set up the first half of the "retaliation" scenario, John Martino traveled to Dallas. There he made contact, indirectly or possibly directly, with the world of Lee Harvey Oswald.

MARTINO, OSWALD, AND THE SILVIA ODIO STORY

Subsequent investigation of the Martino-Rosselli story has added to the seriousness of the two men's claims. Both men, for example, are said to have met Jack Ruby. Martino told a friend he worked with Ruby in Havana in 1959, when both men were acting as couriers or bagmen to smuggle casino cash profits to the U.S. mainland. (The House Committee "reached the judgment that Ruby most likely was serving as a courier for gambling interests" in his successive trips out of Cuba at this time; AR 152).[57] Scott Malone, an investigator with good contacts inside the U.S. government, claims that there exists an FBI report of two meetings between Ruby and Rosselli in Miami, in early October 1963.[58] If such meetings occurred, it is possible that Martino (who was living with Rosselli in Key Biscayne) may have seen Ruby again. Conceivably, it may even have been Martino who set the meetings up, since one month earlier he had visited Dallas. (A former co-worker of Martino's at the Hotel Deauville casino, R. D. Matthews, now resided in Dallas and knew Ruby; 9 AH 525, 530–31.)

The purpose of Martino's trip to Dallas was to make contact there with anti-Castro Cubans, Cubans whom Oswald is said also to have contacted. While imprisoned in Cuba, Martino had made friends with a Cuban trucker, Amador Odio, who had been jailed in 1961 for his role in concealing a terrorist, Reinaldo Gonzalez, who hoped to assassinate Fidel Castro.[59] In September 1963 Martino addressed an anti-Castro meeting and made reference to Amador Odio, and to his daughter, whom he knew to be living in Dallas.[60]

The daughter was Silvia Odio, whose story of meeting Oswald in Dallas is one of the most provocative and revealing stories about Oswald, and also one of the stories most obscured and covered up by the FBI and the Warren Commission. Because of the obvious pressures on Silvia Odio, I shall repeat the story as it was originally communicated to the FBI, not by Odio herself, but by her social worker, Lucille Connell.

According to Connell, Odio told her six days after the assassination

> that she knew Lee Harvey Oswald, and that he had made some talks to small groups of Cuban refugees in Dallas in the past. Odio stated she considered Oswald brilliant and clever, and that he had captivated the groups to whom he spoke. . . . A call had been made in recent months by a Cuban associate of hers to an unknown source in New Orleans, Louisiana, requesting information on Lee Harvey Oswald. . . . Oswald was considered by that source in New Orleans to be a "double agent." The source stated Oswald was probably trying to infiltrate the Dallas Cuban group, and that he should not be trusted. (26 WH 738)

Mrs. Connell referred also to an arms dealer, "Mr. Martin," and to a U.S. Army Colonel "Caster" (i.e., Castorr) who (as another witness corroborated) had been trying to exploit the political emotions of the Cuban refugees in Dallas (26 WH 738; cf. 26 WH 837).

To help the reader, let me interpolate that (as we shall see) there is other evidence to suggest that Oswald was indeed trying to infiltrate

Cuban groups in Dallas. Moreover, this early version of the Odio story, of Oswald as a suspected "double agent," correlates very well with what was believed at this time by her friend Carlos Bringuier and his cabal of CRC Cuban exiles in New Orleans (including Miss Odio's uncle, Agustin Guitart, who had attended the Oswald-Bringuier court trial; 11 WH 378). Others, including John Martino and his friend Frank Sturgis, were quoted as saying that Oswald had "tried to infiltrate Cuban anti-Castro organizations" in Miami.[61]

Connell's version of the Odio story, in which Oswald had attended anti-Castro meetings, is also corroborated by a DRE sympathizer, Edwin Steig. Steig reported seeing Oswald at a DRE meeting in October (WCD 205.646) which may also have been attended by General Walker (WCD 246.22). There were, as we shall see, still other reports linking Oswald to the Alpha 66 group in Dallas, which he may well have been trying to penetrate—for the U.S. government.

But the "double agent" version of the Odio story soon disappeared and was replaced with a simpler story of a visit by Oswald to Odio's home. The FBI and Warren Report in turn made this story disappear, by using rebuttal testimony from a convenient witness who recanted his testimony just as the Warren Report was being sent to press (WR 322–24; cf. 10 AH 19–21).

The witness was Loran Hall, associate of both John Martino, in charge of the Bayo-Martino-Pawley mission, and Frank Sturgis, who had helped plan it. The FBI's handling of Hall, and of the whole Odio story, suggests they had something to hide. To begin with, the agents they sent to interview Silvia Odio, and who asked no questions about the "double agent" story, were James P. Hosty, Jr., and his partner, Bardwell D. Odum. Hosty also interviewed Juan B. Martin, the man Odio had been interested in buying arms from (11 WH 375; 26 WH 349); yet his write-up of this interview is utterly trivial and makes no reference to gunrunning at all (WCD 205.645).

James Hosty was hardly the right agent to send for an impartial investigation. As the FBI agent assigned to handle both arms trafficking and the Oswalds before the assassination, Hosty quickly became a party to some of the FBI's most serious cover-up activities. On November 24, 1963, long before he finally interviewed Silvia Odio in December, Hosty had already destroyed a threatening note which Oswald had left for him at the Dallas FBI office. He had done so on orders from his boss, Gordon Shanklin, which almost certainly came from Washington.[62]

William Sullivan, who investigated the Hosty-Oswald matter for Hoover, later told Curt Gentry that he had no doubts that Hoover ordered the destruction of the note. He also recalled that some other documents were missing, the nature of which he could not recall. One possibility, which we shall explore in Chapter 16, is that Oswald was indeed an FBI informant, as Bringuier had rightly guessed, and that in Dallas James Hosty, the FBI liaison on gunrunning cases, was using Oswald to investigate gunrunning by Odio's and other Cuban groups.

If so, Oswald (and Hosty) would have been investigating the gunrunning of Odio's Cuban group and "Juan Martin," who may or may not have been John Martino. Alternatively, John Martino, already intent on assassinating the President, may have traveled to Dallas to implicate the government's agent, Oswald, as a "patsy" for his retaliation theory.

Fanciful as this hypothesis may seem, consider that by the time of Martino's visit to Dallas, those with whom he worked would be well aware of Oswald's apparent efforts to infiltrate the training camp at Lake Pontchartrain. The trainers there, Hemming and Sturgis, had been involved from the beginning in the planning for the Pawley-Martino mission. In addition DRE activists had, with Hemming, helped move the dynamite to the nearby house of the McLaneys, raided by the FBI in July 1963; the DRE was subsidized by Pawley and his friend Clare Boothe Luce (10 AH 83, 85), and the DRE head office in Miami had received a report from DRE delegate Carlos Bringuier on his meetings with Oswald, along with one of Oswald's FPCC leaflets and a tape recording of the Oswald-Bringuier radio debate (10 AH 85).[63]

But it might appear that Hemming and Sturgis had given information about Oswald not just to Martino but also to the man who (according to a deposition given in 1967), had given the "green light" for the training camp in 1963, General Luis Somoza, brother of the then Nicaraguan dictator Anastasio II.[64]

SOMOZA, THE MEXICO CITY CIA STATION, AND THE "D" STORY

The role of Martino and Rosselli in spreading the "phase one" story of Oswald as a Castro-sent assassin does not enable us to reduce it to a "mafia-did-it" conspiracy. As already noted, corroborating "evidence" of Oswald as a Castro assassin was supplied in Mexico City after the assassination by an agent of the Somozas, who patronized "Rip" Robertson, the alleged CIA trainer for the Bayo-Martino-Pawley mission. This so-called "D" story is a significant one, because of the support lent to it by someone, almost certainly David Phillips, inside the Mexico City CIA station.

What interests us most in the "D" story is the power struggle between Phillips, who supported it, and the FBI officials who sought to discredit it.[65] Gilberto Alvarado, or "D," as he was called in the Warren Report, was an agent in Mexico City of the Nicaraguan Secret Service. On November 25, presenting himself as a pro-Castro Cuban, he told a CIA officer (David Phillips) that on September 18, 1963, he had seen a "Negro with red hair" in the Cuban Consulate speak to Oswald about assassination and pass him $6,500 "to kill the President" (26 WH 857; WR 307).

"D"'s story did not hold up for long, especially after he was told that Oswald did not arrive in Mexico City until September 27. After the U.S. government had expressed its concern about the implications of the story, "D" was reinterviewed by Mexican Internal Security Police at the request of the FBI (i.e., the Embassy's legal attaché Clark Anderson), and he retracted his story on November 30:

> "D" said that his motive in fabricating the story was to help get himself admitted into the United States so that he could there participate in action against Fidel Castro. He said that he hated Castro and hoped that the story that he made up would be believed and would cause the United States to "take action" against him.[66]

Reinterviewed again with a CIA officer present, "D" now claimed that the Mexican police had pressured him into a false retraction. He then repeated his story about Oswald, and took a polygraph test, apparently administered by the FBI, which indicated that he was lying. In the words of the "phase two" FBI report, "D" then "stated that he had heard of the polygraph and respected its accuracy. He added that if the polygraph indicated he was lying, then that must be so" (WCD 78.5).

"D," in short, comes across as a confused agent responding to opposing indications from CIA and FBI as to whether to stick to his "phase one" story, or disown it. In his account of the "D" story,

David Phillips says he was one of two CIA station officials interviewing "D," when apparently he was the only one.[67] Much more misleading, but also instructive, is Phillips's effort to present himself as the discreditor of "D"'s phase-one story, when in fact he had originally been its proponent:

> After President Kennedy was assassinated there was a walk-in to the American embassy in Mexico City. He was a young Nicaraguan, who said that he had been inside the Cuban embassy when Oswald visited there, and that he saw a red-haired black pay Oswald $6,500 in American money. . . . John and I were assigned to interrogate him. It soon was apparent that he was lying, and not very well. A lie-detector test . . . soon confirmed that he was a fabricator. . . . (I have a theory, almost a conviction, that in fact this man was dispatched to Mexico City by the Somoza brothers [Anastasio II and Luis] . . . in what they considered a covert action to influence the American government to move against Cuba. If so, it was a nice try, but a transparent operation.)[68]

Unfortunately for Phillips's own "nice try," we have the CIA cables which he must have drafted and which must in the ordinary course have been approved by his station chief, Win Scott. They present "D"'s claims, not as "transparent," but as credible and important. "D" is called a "well-known Nicaraguan Communist underground member" (rather than a member of the Somozas' anti-communist secret service). He is described as a "quiet, very serious person, who speaks with conviction." In a second CIA cable the next day, "D," who said he had once received U.S. training for the Nicaraguan army at Fort Gulick, Panama, was described as "completely cooperative."[69]

"D's" story, which the FBI so quickly discredited, apparently received some initial high-level support from the CIA and its friends. Gerald Ford, the FBI's informant on the Warren Commission, told Cartha DeLoach of the FBI that CIA Director John McCone had told him "that CIA had uncovered some 'startling information' " that "a source of CIA's in Mexico had seen money exchange hands between Oswald and an unknown Cuban Negro." In DeLoach's words, "Ford stated this excited him greatly inasmuch as it definitely tended to show there was an international connection involved in the assassination of the President."[70] DeLoach swiftly redirected the pliant congressman's thinking, assuring Ford that "D" "was obviously either unstable or a psychopathic liar" (3 AH 595; cf. 3 AH 596).

Much later, "D"'s story received belated confirmation from an apparently independent second source, the well-known and eccentric Mexican writer Elena Garro de Paz. In 1965 she reportedly told contacts in the American embassy that she had met Lee Harvey Oswald in early September 1963, at a party also attended by "a Latin American Negro man with red hair" (3 AH 297; cf. 3 AH 300). Garro's anticommunist story, soon modified, was part of a larger phase-one assassination scenario that also incriminated two members of the Cuban Consulate in Mexico City, Eusebio Azcue and Silvia Durán (3 AH 300, 297); Garro's left-wing cousins Ruben and Horacio Durán (Silvia's husband, 3 AH 299, 301); and possibly leading members of the liberal faction in Mexico's ruling party, the PRI (3 AH 297–98, cf. 304). Apparently she told her story in 1964 to "two Embassy officers (presumably from the [FBI] Legal Attaché's office)" who "did not give much credence to it" (3 AH 299; cf. 286).

What is striking here is not the overlap or concatenation of Garro's story with "D"'s account. "D"'s story of a "Negro with reddish hair" had been published in September 1964 in the Warren Report (WR 307), shortly before she went to the U.S. Embassy (3 AH 301). Of much greater interest is Garro's statement that in the week following the assassination, she had been hidden in a Mexico City hotel by Manuel Calvillo, "an undercover agent of the Secretariat of Gobernacion." Calvillo was also a "close personal friend" of former Gobernación Chief Gustavo Díaz Ordáz (reportedly in Win Scott's "pocket"), and of Gobernación's Secretary Noe Palomares.[71] It was Palomares, readers may recall, who transmitted falsified documents about Oswald's Mexican visit from the Gobernación to the U.S. authorities (see Chapter 6).

The House Committee's thorough investigation of the Garro de Paz story disclosed in passing that the Gobernación Security Police, the DFS, had arrested Silvia Durán right after the assassination (3 AH 82–102, 292), and had pressured her in vain to admit that she was the "link" in an international Communist conspiracy to kill Kennedy (3 AH 91, cf. 86, 102). Like Garro de Paz a year later, the DFS clearly suspected not only Silvia Durán, but her husband Horacio Durán and his brother Ruben (Garro's cousins).[72] Details of this DFS effort to back a phase-one conspiracy story suggest that, only one day after the assassination, they had been fed a mixture of facts and rumors that would be repeated later by Garro. One of these rumors (that Oswald was Silvia

Durán's lover) was apparently supported by a fact (that Durán's name and phone number were in Oswald's notebook) that DFS most likely learned from American law-enforcement or intelligence sources.[73]

Both Phillips's distortions inside the Mexico City CIA station and the Gobernación pressures on Silvia Durán suggest a concatenated effort to hoodwink the U.S. government into an unwarranted response against Castro's Cuba. At the time of his cables, the Castro-did-it theory was still supported by the CIA officials closest to Hoover: Counterintelligence Chief James Angleton, and his deputy Ray Rocca, who was assigned the responsibility of representing the CIA to the Warren Commission.[74] It was also supported by Thomas Mann, the U.S. ambassador in Mexico City, the man who, when promoted by Lyndon Johnson in December 1963, arranged for U.S. recognition of the Somoza–United Fruit coup in Honduras.[75]

If there was prearranged conspiracy to present a phase-one falsehood ("Castro did it") in order to justify the phase-two falsehood ("Oswald acted alone"), these men—"D," Phillips, Win Scott, Angleton, Sullivan, Hoover—seem the logical candidates for its coordination. This sinister hypothesis will become more plausible when we see that Phillips would later team up with Gordon McLendon, whom Jack Ruby described as one of his six closest friends in Dallas (20 WH 39), and who is said to have embarked on a sudden and secret trip to Mexico City in the fall of 1963.

But to see this, we must turn from the narrow, covert world of Lee Harvey Oswald, to the much more complex world of Jack Ruby.

PART THREE

Jack Ruby

EIGHT

Ruby and Narcotics

The Heart of What Was Suppressed

JACK RUBY, THE MAFIA, AND DRUGS: THE TWO OFFICIAL SUPPRESSIONS

Jack Ruby has to be studied in a very different way from Lee Harvey Oswald. Oswald's life was narrow, constricted, endlessly conspiratorial, marginal, his known social contacts (even with his mother and brothers) almost incredibly scanty. Jack Ruby, on the other hand, "knew everybody," or at least a broad cross-section of Dallas, from its politicians, millionaires, cops, and judges, to its dope traffickers, thieves, and prostitutes. He communicated with key figures in the deep power structure of other cities as well. Thus we study Oswald intensively, to learn more about intelligence intrigues and the forces involved in them. Ruby must be studied extensively, to see the many ways in which the overworld and underworld intersect.

In no respect have the findings of the Warren Commission been more universally discredited than in their specious effort to claim that "the evidence does not establish a significant link" between Jack Ruby, Oswald's assassin, "and organized crime."[1] This splendid absurdity was no accidental oversight: the Warren Report section on Ruby was allegedly rewritten so as to downplay Ruby's more obvious organized crime connections. The Commission even used a close criminal associate of Sam Giancana who knew Ruby (Lenny Patrick) to support the manifestly false claim that Ruby "was not involved with Chicago's criminal element" (WR 785; 22 WH 318; AR 150).[2]

At least one of the Warren Commission exhibits was censored, to delete an eyewitness account of (to quote David Scheim) "Ruby's frequent
visits with Dallas Mafia boss Joseph Civello."[3] Among the deleted sen-
tences was the conclusion of the eyewitness, Bobby Gene Moore, an
employee at Civello's Importing Company, that because his employers
would not allow him to open certain cartons of cheeses from Italy,
"they might be importing narcotics." Moore added that two policemen
were obviously aware of Civello's bookmaking operations at the store-
front, "if they were not actually involved," and that a local municipal
judge was a regular recipient of Civello's hams and other foodstuffs.

What Moore depicted, in short, was a small but accurate glimpse of
how gambling and narcotics corrupted local law enforcement in Dallas,
with Ruby "a frequent visitor and associate." Many other witnesses,
similarly ignored, corroborated this picture. And what Moore narrated
about the judge was corroborated by official testimony. Some years earlier a Dallas police officer, Lieutenant George Butler, told a Senate committee that Chicago mobsters, some of whom Ruby knew, controlled
"certain judges . . . which practically handcuffed the law-enforcement
field in their fight against narcotics."[4]

The House Select Committee in 1979, while still minimizing Ruby's
involvement in the deep political corruption of Dallas, abandoned the
Warren Commission's attempt to deny his involvement with organized
crime. Summarizing a 1,044-page staff report (9 AH 125–1169), it
found that Ruby "had a significant number of associations and direct
and indirect contacts with underworld figures" (AR 149), and in his
1959 visits to Cuba "most likely was serving as a courier for gambling
interests" (AR 152). In their subsequent book, the Committee chief
counsel, Robert Blakey, and editor of the Committee Report, Richard
Billings, were even blunter. They concluded that "the murder of Oswald by Jack Ruby had all the earmarks of an organized-crime hit, an
action to silence the assassin, so he could not reveal the conspiracy."[5]

But Blakey and the House Committee, even if more candid than the
Warren Commission, had launched a new caricature of Ruby to replace
the earlier one, both caricatures downplaying Ruby's relevance to local
politics, to law enforcement, and even to narcotics.

The Blakey correction of the record is epitomized by his partial, but
very selective, resurrection of the Moore interview suppressed by the
Warren Commission. Moore was important to Blakey, who wished to

demonstrate that Ruby was connected, not just to organized crime (which is obvious), but to what he called "a particular national syndicate known as the Mafia," or "in New York City, 'La Cosa Nostra.' "[6]

Having thus decided, very arbitrarily, to focus on the Italian mafia, Blakey inevitably focused on "Joseph Civello, who took over the Mafia family in Dallas in 1956."[7] If Civello was important to Blakey, then Moore was a useful witness: "Moore, who had worked both in a store owned by Civello and as a piano player for Ruby, said, 'Ruby was a frequent visitor [at Civello's store] and [an] associate of Civello.' "[8]

Blakey chose to believe Moore, but only for a trivial fact, corroborated by Civello himself and not in dispute, that Ruby and Civello knew each other.[9] Note that Blakey transmits nothing about narcotics, nothing about the involvement of local and state policemen, nothing about the hams for a local judge. The omission of the hams is the more striking, given that Blakey reported on the very same page that Civello's deputy Joe Campisi, who also knew Ruby, sent 260 pounds of Italian sausage every year to the Marcellos and other friends in New Orleans (cf. 9 AH 396). It was clear that Blakey was interested only in the food linking mafiosi to mafiosi, not mafiosi to the local power structure. And of course Blakey said nothing, above all, about the censorship of Moore's remarks by the Warren Commission.

What is most striking here is not that Blakey, a political appointee to a politically delicate position as chief counsel, would omit the politically embarrassing references to policemen and a judge. The surprise is that he would omit Moore's allegations about narcotics. Blakey's rhetorical purpose here was to link Ruby to the Italian mafia, many of whose leaders (notably Santos Trafficante and Carlos Marcello, Blakey's chosen suspects) have been linked to narcotics trafficking. Civello himself had been convicted for narcotics trafficking in the 1930s; and the Federal Bureau of Narcotics (FBN), having seen him with New York trafficker John Ormento at New York's Idlewild airport in 1957, suspected Civello of being a major trafficker.[10]

THE JOE CIVELLO PROBLEM:
THE DALLAS MAFIOSO AS NARCOTICS INFORMANT

The House Committee's voluminous documentation about organized crime has much to say about the narcotics involvement of "Mafiosi" generally (9 AH 27), of Trafficante (5 AH 382), of Marcello (9 AH 62–63), and of Ormento (9 AH 9), but is curiously silent about Civello. For example, Ormento and Civello both attended a 1957 meeting, known as the Apalachin meeting, which House Committee consultant witness Ralph Salerno described as "a national underworld meeting" (5 AH 382), to discuss "future involvement in narcotics" (9 AH 9). The Committee Report mentioned Ormento's attendance and his later conviction for heroin trafficking (5 AH 382, 9 AH 9) but said nothing in this context about the attendance and drug conviction of Civello, the Ruby associate.

The strange treatment of Civello originated, however, not with Salerno, a former New York City Police detective, but with his FBI sources. His own staff report for the Committee established that the Dallas FBI in 1962 found "no evidence of illegal activity by Joseph Francis Civello," a finding which may have helped provoke J. Edgar Hoover's complaint to his regional offices in 1963 that "some cities have blind spots about La Cosa Nostra" (9 AH 59–60). Indeed, the Dallas FBI's blind spot about Civello was even more flagrant than Salerno indicated. A report to a different Senate committee from Customs and the Federal Bureau of Narcotics reveals that Civello had been sentenced in 1960 to five years for conspiracy to obstruct justice.[11]

The report by Salerno confirms that the FBI knew that its own offices were suspiciously complacent about organized crime figures they were supposed to have under surveillance:

> The memorandum [by Hoover] reads in part: "Some cities have blind spots about La Cosa Nostra. It is well to note that we have experienced situations in which certain offices took the position that La Cosa Nostra did not exist in their respective territories, only to learn at a later date that this organization, with its typical family structure, is in fact in existence in the area and has been for many years. . . . That the results of efforts against Carlos Marcello and Santos Trafficante were less than those experienced against other targets was confirmed to the committee by a former official of the FBI. . . . Dallas was another area in which the FBI was far less active against La Cosa Nostra. Although Joseph Francis Civello, a 'counselor to the Italian community at large' according to the FBI, attended the Apalachin meeting in 1957, the Crime Condition Report filed by the Dallas field office for the period ending February 26, 1962, stated, 'There is no evidence of illegal activity by Joseph Francis Civello.' This same report concluded that 'Texas is not a place where the Mafia has the kind of control it has elsewhere.' " (9 AH 60)

One can suspect that the good FBI reputation of Marcello in New Orleans, and of Civello in Dallas, derived from their status as unofficial or official informants. I myself heard Dallas police sergeant Patrick Dean, who was in charge of security in the Dallas police basement when Oswald was murdered (and who later failed a lie detector test about Ruby's access to it) tell me without embarrassment of his longtime relationship with Civello. He justified being on good terms with Civello by the information Civello supplied him, in "many, many dope cases I made."[12] In other words, he knew Civello because he used Civello as a narcotics informant.

Blakey's book, to be fair, breaks the Committee silence about Civello's earlier drug record, and in such a way as to corroborate Civello's symbiosis with law enforcement:

> After serving six years of a fifteen-year narcotics conviction in 1937, Civello was paroled. He then applied for a pardon, and one of his character witnesses was J. E. (Bill) Decker, the Dallas County sheriff in 1963 [of whose payoff involvement more below], into whose custody Oswald was being transferred when he was murdered.[13]

But Blakey's omission of the Ruby-narcotics story was systematic, indeed total. He ignored, above all, a story from a reliable FBN informant, transmitted back in 1956 by the Los Angeles FBI to the Dallas FBI, suggesting that Ruby was, as many other witnesses had suggested, a payoff or liaison connection between narcotics activities and the Dallas Police Department. The informant, Eileen Curry, reported that "her husband [James Breen] had made connection with [a] large narcotics setup operating between Mexico, Texas, and the East. . . . In some fashion James got the okay to operate through Jack Ruby of Dallas."[14]

This report, made long before Ruby became notorious, was important enough for the FBI to take seriously in 1956. It was of course entirely predictable that the Warren Report would ignore it in 1964. But why did Blakey, who unlike the Warren Commission was *searching* for Ruby's crime links, ignore it in 1978? It had been brought specifically to his attention, along with corroborating reports that Ruby had the same status with respect to gambling activities: that Ruby "was supposed to have influence with the police" (23 WH 363), that "in order to operate in Dallas it was necessary to have the clearance of Jack Ruby" who "had the 'fix' with the county authorities" (23 WH 372), that "Ruby is the payoff man for the Dallas Department and whenever liquor and gambling raids were to be made on the Dallas underworld Ruby would always be contacted first" (WCD 4.529).[15]

The Warren Commission, of course, declined to interview these witnesses, and instead wrote that "it found no evidence of any suspicious relationships between Ruby and any police officer" (WR 224). Why would Blakey and the House Committee, professedly open to Ruby's criminal background, suppress, much more thoroughly than the Warren Commission, all reference to these witnesses? It might of course have developed that they were not credible; but apparently Blakey and the Committee could not know that: they never bothered to check them out![16]

Was this because of a predetermined political decision to downplay Ruby's importance? Indeed, in the subsequent mainstream books on the Kennedy assassination, Ruby, having first been depicted as a loner, now became "a classic two-bit pawn in the hierarchy of organized crime."[17] The assassination of the President, as well as of Oswald, became similarly marginalized as an external onslaught on our political establishment, and shrunken to an outcast mafia's revenge against the President for his "domestic crusade against organized crime."[18] Or, as the jacket subtitle of Blakey's book epitomized his findings: "Organized Crime Assassinated J.F.K." Period.

But Blakey, as a Justice Department veteran (like his Justice Department colleague Howard Willens on the Warren Commission staff), may have ignored the narcotics and payoff stories to protect the Justice Department itself. For it seems highly probable that Ruby was a narcotics informant not just at the local level but at the federal level as well.

What was to be concealed here was not just the Justice Department's relationship to Ruby, but its true relationship to organized crime. Since about 1961 the FBI and Justice Department had been projecting a falsified picture of organized crime as a predominantly ethnic "La Cosa Nostra," or LCN, organized not around corrupt local politics and law enforcement, but by an alleged "national commission of LCN bosses."[19] For some years academic criminologists have been debunking this FBI "alien conspiracy myth"; it is time to suggest that the FBI has floated it to disguise its own sustained dependence on protected informants in organized crime, such as (as we shall see) Ruby himself in 1959.

ZEROING IN ON THE PROBLEM:
RUBY AND THE DALLAS POLICE

The "two-bit pawn" portrait of Ruby, assuredly, was almost as defective as the "loner" portrait, in its downplaying of Ruby's links to both local and federal law enforcement. These links were clear enough to define Ruby not as a "member" of organized crime, but as a "connection" or go-between between law enforcement and the underworld. As I informed the House Committee in 1978, Ruby

> enjoyed excellent relations with the Special Services Bureau (including the Vice and Narcotics Squads) of the Dallas Police, many of whom worked after hours for pay in his nightclub the Carousel. For years Ruby had been a police informant for members of the Narcotics Squad. At the time of his travel to Cuba in 1959 he was also a PCI (Potential Criminal Informant) for the FBI, who interviewed him eight times over a period of seven months.[20]

Blakey and the House Committee repeated much of what I and others told them about Ruby and organized crime, but only after straining out most of the links between Ruby and government. The Committee reported that

> Ruby had a friendly and somewhat unusual relationship with the Dallas Police Department . . . but the committee found little evidence of any significant influence by Ruby within the force that permitted him to engage in illicit activities. (AR 156)

The Report then conceded that Dallas policemen may have assisted Ruby's entry into the Dallas police basement to kill Oswald, surely an "illicit activity." Quite rightly, both the Report and Blakey's subsequent book made much of the fact that the policeman most probably involved, Sergeant Patrick Dean, failed a polygraph examination "on questions related to Ruby's access," and was "on good terms" both with Ruby and with Dallas mafia boss Joe Civello.[21] As already noted I spoke at length to Dean about these matters, and I was personally satisfied that

1. Dean's contacts with Civello could be explained by his use of Civello as a source of information for narcotics arrests.

2.   Whether or not Civello played a role in Dean's suspicious behavior on November 24, the fundamental responsibility for the security breakdown which led to Oswald's murder had to rest with Dean's superiors in the Dallas Police Department.

The circumstances of this breakdown suggest a high-level police-Ruby collusion which Blakey downplayed. Those who have seen the murder of Oswald on camera will recall the crowd of Dallas detectives surrounding him. But, over-reacting to an anonymous phone threat to the FBI the night before (that "about 100 men were going to take the prisoner Oswald" and kill him; 21 WH 587, 660), the Department had decided to give priority to protecting Oswald rather than the building; as a result, nearly all the detectives were with Oswald in front of the cameras.

Although TV viewers could not be aware of this, in the darkness behind the cameras there were almost no remaining patrolmen and reserve officers. Nearly all of them had been reassigned at the last minute (again in response to the phone threat) to control traffic along Oswald's approach route; this left only a couple of guards in the dark area (9 AH 145). Thus, there was nobody guarding the stairwell down which Ruby, as the Committee confirmed, probably made his entry (AR 157; 9 AH 143–44); the policemen assigned to this area (Patrolman Alvis R. Brock and Reserve Officer Gano E. Worley) had been reassigned to cover traffic (24 WH 65, 189; cf. 19 WH 179, 431–33; 9 AH 145).

Dean (as he conceded in 1964) played a big role in these crucial reassignments (12 WH 425; 19 WH 434), along with two other sergeants, James A. Putnam (24 WH 156) and Don F. Steele (24 WH 167), whose very presence in the basement (12 WH 354) was cited by critic Sylvia Meagher as a "mystery" to be explained.[22] But Dean acted under orders from his superior, Captain Cecil Talbert, as both Steele (12 WH 354–55) and Talbert himself corroborated (24 WH 172; cf. 21 WH 664).

It is also the case, as Blakey pointed out in the Report and in his book, that Dean and three other officers corroborated an alternative story of Ruby's access by a garage ramp, offered belatedly by Ruby himself, that was probably not true.[23]

Further testimony by Dean was used by state prosecutors Henry Wade and William F. Alexander to convict Ruby. What Dean said he

heard Ruby say about his premeditation occurred during Ruby's inter-
rogation after Oswald's murder; it was inadmissible evidence under
Texas law. Thus it led to a reversal of Ruby's conviction on appeal.
Some have seen in this a collusion to secure Ruby's acquittal.[24]

In short, there are ample grounds for believing, along with virtually
every foreign critic of the Kennedy assassination story, that Ruby's killing of Oswald and subsequent account of the killing show ample evidence of collusion between Ruby and the Dallas police. One can agree
with the Committee staff report on Ruby that "Dean is a key figure" (9
AH 139). But it is equally clear that in none of his suspected intrigues
could Dean have acted alone. Still less could his moves have been or-
chestrated from outside the police hierarchy by Joe Civello. If Dean col-
luded, so did higher circles of Dallas law enforcement.

You would certainly not know this from Blakey's account of Dean's
behavior. In his Report, you will find that "the committee believed that
it was less likely that Ruby entered the police basement without assistance" (AR 157), followed by a reference to the fact that Dean had
" 'failed' " a polygraph test administered for the Warren Commission
in 1964 (9 AH 158). Nothing, either here or in a more extended staff
report on the reassignment of Brock and Worley (9 AH 144–45), questions the entire Police Department's strategy of surrounding Oswald,
rather than the building.

THE HEART OF THE RUBY PROBLEM:
JACK RUBY AS A NARCOTICS INFORMANT

When I spoke to Sergeant Dean about all this in 1979, he added some
new and intriguing details. One was the curious fact that he had first
met Civello at a place frequented by "senators, judges, councilmen,"
suggesting that Civello had his own place in the deep political structure
of Texas politics. This is corroborated by the acquaintanceship of Civello and Joe Campisi, through gambling, with Clint Murchison, Jr.[25]

Dean also claimed that "I was aware of the stairway; Jack Revill
says that he wasn't and he was Captain down there but I was aware of
it" and had it covered. No other account of Oswald's transfer and
shooting has said that Revill played a role in the security arrangements.
Revill is some critics' candidate for Most Conspiratorial Policeman on
the weekend of November 22–24, 1963. Sylvia Meagher assigns him

no less than fourteen intriguing pages in her book *Accessories After the Fact,* or more than any other police officer except Police Chief Jesse Curry.

I myself had suggested that the Committee interview Revill, to learn more about the "Army Intelligence man" whom "Lieutenant Revill knew" and drove back to his office right after the President's murder (5 WH 57). I speculated that the Army Intelligence agent might have been James Powell, an Army Intelligence agent present on the sixth floor of the Texas School Book Depository (WCD 329.57–58) when Revill organized the search there which produced the famous Mannlicher-Carcano (4 AH 604). Whoever the man was, Revill omitted his name when testifying under oath to the Warren Commission as to the occupants of his car (5 WH 34).

The Committee did publicly interrogate Jack Revill, a former "lieutenant commanding the narcotics unit" (4 AH 569) at length (5 AH 568–608)—not, however to explain his own behavior, but to give the Committee a clean bill of health on Ruby's relationship to the Dallas police. This included the statement Committee staffers Donald Purdy and Howard Shapiro would use in their staff report on Ruby, that "Ruby was not used as an informant by the intelligence unit" (4 AH 571; cf. 9 AH 128, 1119–20).

This staff report gave less attention to Revill's next sentence: "Whether or not Jack Ruby was used as a source of information, and there is a difference, this I don't know" (4 AH 571). Yet Revill himself told the Committee that

1. Prior to 1958 he "was a lieutenant commanding the narcotics unit." (4 AH 569)

2. He "had known Jack Ruby since 1953." (4 AH 570)

3. His relationship to Ruby was "no relationship whatsoever other than a professional relationship of a police officer to an individual such as Jack Ruby." (4 AH 570)

What could this mean, if not that, when in the narcotics unit (as opposed to the intelligence unit) he had used Ruby, either as an informant, or (a distinction we shall hereafter ignore) as "a source of information"?[26]

As already noted, the Committee found "little evidence of any significant influence by Ruby within the force" (AR 156). As citation for its finding, it referred to a staff report on Ruby, which traced the "belief . . . that Ruby was an informant for the police" to Ruby's habit of making unsolicited phone calls to Dallas police officers (9 AH 128–29). This claim had to ignore the contrary statement of Dallas Narcotics and Vice Squad Detective Richard L. Clark (to the FBI, a statement supplied later to the Committee) that he "contacted Ruby on investigative matters [not the other way round] on an average of once a month."[27]

That Ruby was indeed an ongoing informant is corroborated by the FBI's decision in 1959 to develop him as a PCI (Potential Criminal Informant) with reimbursement for "expenses . . . on a COD basis" (5 AH 213). The FBI evidently regarded Ruby as well "connected," as a man whose potential range of information was wide-reaching. Agents quizzed him about bank robberies and burglaries in Dallas, Houston, Baltimore, Chicago, Kansas, and California, as well as on interstate trafficking in stolen property from Kansas, Kentucky, and Illinois. Despite the negative results from these contacts (at the time of his 1959 trips to Cuba), his PCI rating in his first three monthly reports was "Good," and for the remaining two, "Average" (5 AH 206–20). Richardson Preyer, chairman of the Subcommittee on the Assassination of John F. Kennedy, found Ruby's PCI file interesting enough to be entered in the Hearings record (5 AH 205). Yet the only reference to Ruby's PCI status for the FBI in Blakey's House Committee Report is a negative one, in a footnote about Ruby's movements in 1959 (AR 151).[28]

Of course, much of the evidence had been hidden away before the Committee was ever asked to look for it. Right after the assassination, a former Dallas FBI agent told the FBI in San Diego that he had known Ruby in Dallas back in 1948 and believed him to have been influential even then in the Dallas Police Department.[29] This is exactly the sort of information from credible sources that one will not find in the Warren Commission Exhibits, which published such miscellaneous rumors as the allegation (via Jack Revill from Dallas Police Lieutenant George Butler, about whom we shall have more to say) that Oswald was "the illegitimate son of Jack Ruby" (25 WH 166).

The "little evidence" also meant ignoring the 1956 story in FBI files linking Ruby to a "large narcotics setup operating between Mexico,

Texas, and the East," in which one "got the okay to operate through Jack Ruby of Dallas" (23 WH 369). This story is corroborated by the revelation that Ruby was an informant for the Dallas police; high-level informants frequently are the men with the "fix," sanctioning some deals and turning in others.

RUBY'S FALSE FBN ALIBI
IN THE PAUL JONES DRUG CASE OF 1947

The 1956 FBI report linking Ruby to narcotics smuggling through Mexico did not mention that Ruby had been interrogated in a major 1947 FBN drug case, involving forty-eight pounds of opium which had been smuggled from Mexico into Texas by Paul Roland Jones, an important Ruby associate about whom we shall say much more. The Warren Commission exonerated Ruby in that case, but on evidence which strengthens, rather than weakens, the impression that he was involved, and protected from arrest, as an informant:

> On October 24, 1947, [Jones] was arrested for violating Federal narcotics statutes . . . and 5 days after Jones' arrest, Jack and [his brother] Hyman Rubenstein were interrogated in Chicago by agents of the Bureau of Narcotics. . . . Intensive investigation to determine whether Jack Ruby was criminally or otherwise connected with Jones' narcotics violation leads the Commission to conclude Ruby probably was not involved. A search of the files of the Bureau of Narcotics disclosed no record that either Hyman or Jack had been prosecuted by Federal authorities in 1947. . . . One of Jones' confederates reported after the shooting of Oswald that although Jones "propositioned" the two brothers concerning narcotics, they refused to participate. (WR 792–93)

One eyewitness in the FBN files on the 1947 arrest indeed claimed that Ruby was "propositioned" in Chicago by Jones but "refused to [have] any part of it" (23 WH 206). This account of the meeting, corroborated by Jones, has the problem, however, of demolishing Ruby's own alibi. Ruby himself told the FBN that he had met Jones "on numerous occasions" in Dallas, but never in Chicago; and he claimed that he was in Dallas on August 2 and 3, 1947, the days in question (23 WH 203; cf. 24 WH 516). Jones and the first witness spoke of meeting Ruby in Chicago, and Jones supplied Ruby's Chicago address (22 WH 300, 478).[30] The FBN had Jones and his friend under surveillance on August

2, 1947, and confirmed that the two men made several phone calls to a Chicago number listed to Hyman and Jack (9 AH 522).

These conflicting accounts of Ruby's whereabouts on August 2, 1947, reached the Warren Commission from different agencies. Ruby's Dallas alibi was supplied to the Warren Commission by the Federal Bureau of Narcotics, in the FBN file on the case (WCE 1708; WCD 101 f.), which as published is apparently incomplete. The report putting Ruby at the Chicago narcotics meeting was from a post-assassination account of the FBN file supplied by the Secret Service:

> The meeting between Jones, Hyman and Jack Ruby was arranged by [Ruby's sister] Eva Grant. . . . They met in Jack Ruby's room at the Congress Hotel, Room 6-142. Co-defendant Melton stated that Hyman and Jack Ruby when propositioned concerning narcotics refused to [have] any part of it. (WCD 87, SS.194; 23 WH 206)

Note how the Warren Report, by choosing to believe this version, and quoting selectively from it, had the effect of demolishing the alibi transmitted by the FBN itself.

Blakey and the House Committee on Assassinations staff had been alerted to these problems with the Ruby alibi, and to the need to secure the complete FBN file on the case. Instead their staff report's twenty-two pages on the Jones-Ruby relationship (9 AH 149–58, 513–24) show extensive citations from the copious FBI files on Jones, but no FBN sources except those already published with the Warren Report (9 AH 1129, 1150–54). They did make the conflicts over Ruby's alibi disappear, but only at the cost of falsifying the record. Their elaborate "Jack Ruby Chronologies," twenty-two pages long, have this and no more to say about the relevant years 1946–47:

> October 1946—Ruby builds log cabin across the street from Mr. and Mrs. Yates (Log Cabin nightclub)? Visits it mostly on weekends and entertains mostly men. [W]CD 4, p. 410.

> August 1947—Jack Ruby occupies a room in a Chicago hotel where Paul Rowland Jones, John Melton, Maurice C. Melton, and Taylor Crossland are meeting. Ruby denies meeting these men. Vol. 22, p. 307.[31]

Once again, predictably, there is nothing about narcotics; instead, awkward paraphrase obscures the fact that Ruby and the four men are said to be in the same *room,* not just the same hotel. And no reference is made to Ruby's claim that "he was visiting in Dallas on August 2 and 3, 1947, which are the dates that Paul Jones, Taylor Crossland and Maurice Melton were in Chicago" (23 WH 203). Elsewhere, in a long House Committee staff report on Paul Roland Jones, this claim is misquoted, concealing the conflict in testimony: "Ruby stated that 'he was visiting in Dallas, Texas, on *October* 2 and 3, 1947' " (9 AH 522, emphasis added; citing 23 WH 203).

House Committee Staff Counsel Donald Purdy, it would seem, was aware of the problem. He depicted Ruby as a man with significant organized-crime "associations" (AR 149), without disputing the Warren Commission finding that "Ruby was not involved with Paul Roland Jones . . . in the narcotics case" (9 AH 523). The Warren Report at least mentioned the narcotics case; it is, however, ignored in the Committee's seven-page discounting of "Ruby's Alleged Involvement" in "Organized Crime's Move to Dallas, 1947" (9 AH 152–58), a move in which Paul Jones is presented as a central figure (9 AH 149–52).

These seven pages even mention that Ruby told "Federal narcotics agents" that he "had never spoken to [Jones] in Chicago" (9 AH 153), without any indication of why Ruby was talking to the FBN. Blakey's account of Ruby's organized-crime career omits, once again, the incriminating fact that Jones and Ruby had been placed in the same room (as opposed to the same hotel):

> Jones himself acknowledged to the FBI in 1964 that he had represented "syndicate" interests in jukeboxes and slot machines in Dallas in the 1940s. . . . He also admitted he had met Ruby at the Congress Hotel in Chicago. (We learned from the U.S. Bureau of Narcotics that Ruby had, for a period in 1946–1947, kept a regular room, number 6-142, at the Congress Hotel).[32]

What is being concealed here is the national, even international, scope of this organized-crime connection. Paul Jones was by his own account in 1946 only a small part of an international "syndicate" which "operates from coast to coast, and in Canada and Spain."[33] As a representative of Chicago mob figures Marcus Lipsky and Paul Mann, Jones had made "political arrangements with the Mexican officials" and established a casino in Mexico City.[34] He was also in communication with those running the Copacabana, then perhaps the largest casino in Havana.[35]

This syndicate was large enough to attract the special attention of the Kefauver Committee, in its Third Interim Report five years later: "The syndicate, according to Jones, controlled such cities as St. Louis, Kansas City, New Orleans, and Little Rock. In addition the syndicate had connections in every large city, and if Jones ran into trouble anywhere, money and help would be forthcoming."[36] They also reported elsewhere on a 1944 case involving Nick de John (a member of Jones's syndicate, 9 AH 153), the Antinori family (predecessors in Tampa and Havana of Santos Trafficante), and other mafiosi from Kansas City and St. Louis, in a "New York–California–Mexico smuggling ring."[37]

As has been pointed out by scholars, the Kefauver Committee used what it learned about these two surfacings of the Jones syndicate, the wartime Kansas City case, and the 1947 murder in San Francisco of Nick de John, as central evidence in its case for "a Nation-wide syndicate known as the Mafia."[38] We shall return to the politics of this claim, derided by academic critics as a "myth," and also to the politics of its author, George White of the FBN, who served as a government liaison with organized crime and as a deceptive consultant to the Kefauver Committee on the Kansas City and San Francisco cases. We shall see that White's first postwar investigation was of a famous Chicago shooting in 1946, attributed to Jones's syndicate, in which Ruby may have been an informant. This murder, of racing wire service king James Ragen, will be discussed in Chapters 9 and 10.

THE PROTECTED MEXICAN DRUG CONNECTION AND RUBY IN 1963

It is certain that Ruby was investigated for his role in Jones's international drug-trafficking syndicate, involving corruption of government officials in Mexico City. At this time the top American syndicate representative in Mexico City was Harold "Happy" Meltzer, identified in Senate Narcotics Hearings as an associate of Meyer Lansky (who had the "in" with Cuban authorities) and John Ormento (the trafficker seen with Joe Civello of Dallas), as well as of Louis Tom Dragna and Mickey Cohen in Los Angeles.[39]

Right after World War II this was probably the biggest drug-smuggling channel into the United States, organized by Lansky and Meltzer. According to government sources,

The Federal Bureau of Investigation reported Lansky and [Nig] Rosen [of Philadelphia, alias Harry Stromberg] likely financed the expansion of Mexico's heroin industry. The Mexican heroin connection running to New York and Philadelphia started around 1939 and became increasingly important as older routes were disrupted by World War II. Former major suppliers such as Japan were knocked out of the world market when war engulfed the Pacific. In the latter stages of the war Lansky and Rosen decided to increase their interests in Mexican drugs. They reportedly bankrolled a smuggler [Meltzer] who moved to Mexico City to manage the operation. The syndicate's reach included Mexico City, Miami, New York, Philadelphia, Havana, and Los Angeles.[40]

We must at this point say a few words about this Mexican drug connection, which underlies many aspects of the Kennedy assassination story, including Oswald's Mexico trip and sources for some of the false stories which derailed the Garrison investigation of 1967. Above all, this particular Mexican connection was huge, and it was well connected, on both sides of the Mexican-U.S. border. In 1947 the FBN estimated illicit opium imports from Mexico equaled the combined amount from India, Turkey, and Iran, in large part because of high-level corruption in the Mexican government. As we have seen, there were already disturbing signs that this corruption reached to the highest levels of Mexican narcotics enforcement and internal security.[41]

Indeed there were areas of Mexico where internal security and drug trafficking were closely symbiotic, even interfused. When in the late 1940s Mexico created its own CIA, the DFS (Dirección Federal de Seguridad), the DFS soon came not only to draw upon, but to protect, the major drug-trafficking organizations. (The DFS founder, Captain Rafael Chavarri, later went to work for Mexico's leading international trafficker, Jorge Moreno Chauvet, who in turn received drugs from the Lansky-Luciano connection in Europe.) And soon after its creation the CIA itself became enmeshed in the drug intrigues and protection of the DFS, its sister agency, as well of the interrelated flow of drugs from Luciano to Ormento and Moreno Chauvet.[42]

These intelligence-drug intrigues may have been barely developed in 1947, when the FBN apparently began to protect Ruby. A more likely, though clearly hypothetical, reason for this protection is that Ruby was an informant in the case. It is not uncommon for large-scale traffickers to stay in business by turning in for prosecution those smaller clients to whom they have no particular loyalty. Jones may well have been set up in this case by the mob itself, operating with the FBN. There is no doubt that the FBN saw the Jones case as a syndicate case: their file is cross-referenced to "Mafia," the term used in charts about the Jones syndicate presented by FBN agent White to the Kefauver Committee.[43]

There were two leads linking the 1947 Meltzer Mexican connection to the assassination of the President. The first is that Jim Braden, alias Eugene Hale Brading, a convict friend of Meltzer and suspected major courier for Meyer Lansky, was picked up by a Dallas sheriff's deputy near the Texas School Book Depository right after the shooting and then released without fingerprinting.[44] What is particularly intriguing about Braden's background, as explored by former CBS producer Peter Noyes, are his connections to a number of Minutemen and their associates, such as Loran Eugene Hall, Dennis Mower, Albert Tarrants III, Philip Earl Scheib, and Keith Gilbert, suspected in a number of assassination plots, including plots against John Kennedy, Robert Kennedy, and Martin Luther King.[45] In 1963 an associate of this right-wing set employed a Teamster hoodlum, Barney Baker, who as we shall see was telephoned by Jack Ruby before the assassination.[46]

The second reason is that another associate of the Harold Meltzer–Mickey Cohen crowd in Los Angeles, Alexander Gruber, visited Ruby in early November 1963, and then had a number of long-distance phone conversations with him before and after the assassination.[47]

The House Committee took both of these leads seriously, especially the second. It deposed Gruber, and pointed out disturbing inconsistencies in his various accounts of why, in 1963, he suddenly resumed contact with a former close friend, Ruby, whom he had not seen for ten years.[48] But it asked no questions about Meltzer, to whom Noyes had drawn attention, nor about Gruber's friend Eli Lubin, a Meltzer associate who had been arrested with Meltzer and Cohen back in 1949.

Gruber's unexplained visit to Ruby in November 1963 paralleled the movements of Paul Roland Jones, who after a similar ten-year gap had visited with Ruby in Dallas about a week or ten days before the assassination, possibly on the same day. Of course this was significant. For some reason, which the Committee failed to explore, Ruby's 1940s contacts with Jones and the Mexican connection, long moribund, had been restored in the last days before the assassination.[49]

NINE

Ruby's Background

Narcotics, the Teamsters,
and the Racing Wire Service

THE MEXICAN CONNECTION, MEYER LANSKY, AND FEDERAL LAW ENFORCEMENT

Why would Ruby's informant status in narcotics, and his links to drug traffickers like Paul Roland Jones, have engendered so much cover-up since 1947? One possible answer is that Ruby may not have been acting alone, and that what is being protected is not a one-time arrangement, or even an arrangement through Ruby's lifetime, but a more institutionalized arrangement between the mob and the government, initiated in the era of Hoover and Lansky but outlasting them and perhaps enduring down to the present.

Lansky is the central figure in both the FBN's and the FBI's special, and still not fully understood, relationship to organized crime. Except for a brief period when Robert Kennedy was pursuing the issue of the "skim" from Las Vegas casinos (most of which went to Lansky), Lansky was one of the three top organized crime figures never tapped or bugged by the FBI. (The other two, both also relevant to the Ruby story, were Carlos Marcello and Santos Trafficante.)[1]

Meyer Lansky, the key figure in the Meltzer syndicate, had in 1937 established a special relationship with both FBN Chief Harry Anslinger and FBI Chief J. Edgar Hoover, by arranging to turn over to them Louis Lepke Buchalter, who was then probably America's major drug trafficker, and designated by Hoover as "the most dangerous man in

America."[2] Shortly afterwards, as America geared up to enter World War II, it was Lansky who worked with Naval Intelligence and OSS officers to help create Operation Underworld, "an Intelligence/Organized Crime project" which organized the mob's waterfront locals in the New York port area.[3]

At that time Lansky's main narcotics operation was the Mexican one. It is known that the FBI and FBN had other informants in the Lansky-Meltzer syndicate, and these arranged for the government's indictment of Meltzer himself when he failed to make payments on "the original mob money invested in his Mexican scheme."[4] We shall soon see that George White, the top OSS officer on Operation Underworld, left the Army in 1946 and began immediately to monitor the Jones end of the drug connection, as head of the Chicago FBN office.

Lansky appears to have been protected at the top of the FBI. According to Hank Messick, writing from IRS sources, that protector was Hoover himself. After Robert Kennedy engaged Hoover in the war on organized crime, the FBI, in pursuit of "La Cosa Nostra," instituted wiretaps on Italians; but Hoover (according to Messick) ordered that there be no electronic surveillance in Las Vegas at the Flamingo and Thunderbird, two casinos, built by Hoover's friend Del Webb, where the skim went to Lansky.[5]

Why did Lansky enjoy such protection at the FBI? As this book went to press, a new biography of Hoover by Anthony Summers presented evidence for an old rumor: that Hoover protected Lansky because Lansky possessed photographs of Hoover in sexually compromising behavior.[6] This allegation is particularly relevant to the argument of Chapter 14: that Meyer Lansky and his colleagues in organized crime (Joe Nesline and Charles Tourine) systematically used sexual blackmail to compromise a number of people in Washington who were politically influential.

At the same time, it may be trivializing the suspicious symbiosis between the FBI and organized crime to reduce it to the personal vulnerability of Hoover. As we have seen, others beside Hoover in the Justice establishment have had recourse to distorted pictures of organized crime which minimized Lansky's influence; and this habit clearly persisted after Hoover was dead. Thus, institutional as well as personal explanations must be sought for Lansky's immunity from prosecution, which only ended after Lansky apparently retired from his organized-crime activities (at an important mob meeting of February 1970 in Acapulco) and moved to Israel.[7] There are those who argue that the FBI's primary institutional goal was never the prosecution of crime, but the surveillance and repression of political dissent.[8] In this very different battle, as we shall see in Chapter 16, mob figures like Meyer Lansky and John Martino were not enemies of the FBI, but allies.

For whatever reason, protection for Lansky, and for the postwar international drug traffic he helped consolidate, was not confined to the FBI. The Federal Bureau of Narcotics, in particular, diverted attention away from the key traffickers, some of whom were used by the U.S. government for covert operations. George White and Charles Siragusa, the FBN's top liaison officers with these protected traffickers, were also seconded to the Kefauver Committee to create a misleading portrait of a "mafia," the prototype for Hoover's "La Cosa Nostra," in which Lansky was irrelevant.[9]

Hoover had a particular Lansky problem. Some of his strongest political backers and most intimate associates, notably Lewis Rosenstiel of Schenley Industries and the American Jewish League Against Communism, were intimate with Meyer Lansky and his organized-crime milieu (see Chapter 13).[10] Rumors persist that these compromising relationships evolved in part out of the secret of Hoover's homosexual liaisons, of which Lansky obtained proof in the 1930s. For the next three decades this left Lansky and the Bureau chief in a symbiotic relationship, each protecting the other.[11]

The Italian mafia leaders themselves, increasingly resentful of the concentrated FBI attention they got after 1961, began to talk more and more, in conversations they rightly suspected were monitored, about Meyer Lansky. In 1962 one Italian said, "Meyer owns more in Vegas than anybody—than all of ours put together. He's got a piece of every joint in Vegas." Another mafioso complained in May 1961 that it was difficult to touch the Jews "helping our country," and added: "That Lansky is a stool pigeon for the FBI—they're working on sugar."[12]

BLAKEY'S STAKE IN THE VALACHI VERSION OF HISTORY

Before beginning the following section, I should warn readers that I am about to do something uncomfortable both for myself and for them, and that is to challenge the popular view (which happens to be Robert Blakey's) of the mafia as a nationally controlled, isolatable threat.

This is uncomfortable for me because of my limited knowledge, and consequent agnosticism, as to how to talk about the "mafia." As indicated in my notes to some passages above, I find it necessary at times to subscribe to both of two opposing views of the mafia, each partly true: "Mafia" is both a reality, perhaps unfortunately named, and also a myth fostered by law enforcement.

The way to understand the "mafia" phenomenon is to absorb the best of both the "mafia-as-myth" critiques and the reasoned responses to them in rebuttals such as that of Stephen Fox.[13] The truth is not so much in between as embracing both. "Mafia," in the United States, is an attempt to define the dark areas of society where ordinary definitions do not work. It is an effort to name the unnameable: we both need such names and must distrust them. This is the point of my critique of the FBI and Blakey which follows: that they have attempted to present a hard-edged definition of "La Cosa Nostra," and to build a legal apparatus upon this definition, when in fact such hard-edged definitions are, in this sphere of the dimly known, inappropriate and misleading.

Let me here present unobtrusively what I myself believe about the reality and the myth of the "mafia": (1) there really is a "mafia" in Sicily, and a roughly analogous organization of *borgate*, or "families," in New York and some other cities; (2) the FBN and later the FBI have presented the "mafia" or "La Cosa Nostra" as a national organization controlled (as opposed to adjudicated) by a national "Commission"; this claim, although it underpins federal anti-mafia legislation such as Blakey's, is largely a myth; (3) while men like Joseph Civello in Dallas and Carlos Marcello in New Orleans undoubtedly dealt with mafiosi in other cities and can thus perhaps be called mafiosi themselves, talk such as Blakey's of "the Mafia family in Dallas" is unsubstantiated and should probably be treated as part of the myth.

The disagreement over the nature of organized crime in this country focused for many years on the status of Meyer Lansky. Was he the true organizer of a multi-ethnic crime confederation, as argued, apparently on the basis of Treasury IRS sources, by Hank Messick?[14] Or was he a mere associate of the more powerful Luciano, incorporating Jewish mobsters into a larger, Italian "La Cosa Nostra," or "LCN" (the official Hoover-FBI view after 1962, based largely on the revelations of its informant Joseph Valachi; 9 AH 15). We shall see that there were many problems with the Valachi version of history, which in 1978 became the Blakey version.

In this radically polarized controversy between Italian and multi-ethnic organized-crime theories, the House Committee came down heavily on the side of the FBI, Valachi, and the LCN, thus marginal-izing Lansky. Their staff report, by Ralph Salerno, describes Lansky first as a member of "a tightly disciplined organization" during Prohi-bition, in which, despite the presence of "people of other ethnic back-grounds . . . the core unit was still Italian" (9 AH 5). The next reference is in a discussion of "skim" money from Las Vegas casinos, taken from the FBI's "La Cosa Nostra file"; Lansky is described here only as "a Florida mob figure" (9 AH 25). The staff report concludes that "there was a national, conspiratorial, criminal organization within the United States which members referred to as La Cosa Nostra" (9 AH 28). And Blakey's book, despite its more numerous references to Lansky, presents the same biased account of La Cosa Nostra, while specifically attack-ing, as "mistaken," Messick's case for "a national syndicate of which the Mafia was only a part."[15]

Blakey and Salerno were logical candidates to perpetuate in 1978 the LCN story presented in 1963 by Valachi, after months of FBI coaching, to the Senate's McClellan Committee. Ralph Salerno had been the first witness after Valachi to testify to that committee, to interpret the LCN story, about which he later wrote a book. Blakey had subsequently served as the committee's chief counsel.

More significantly, Valachi's memoirs, *The Valachi Papers,* had been published as a Justice Department–authorized exception to Bureau of Prisons policy prohibiting such memoirs; Attorney General Katzen-bach's letter authorizing publication noted "that law enforcement can be benefited by publication of the book," and Blakey was the author of the subsequent legislation.[16] Blakey served in 1967 on the President's Commission on Law Enforcement, whose *Task Force Report* became the first "official government statement that 'Mafia' (or 'Cosa Nostra') and 'organized crime' were one and the same."[17] Blakey's own submis-sion to that commission was a legal analysis that (in the words of a critic) allowed the thinking man "to accept modifications to the tradi-tional limits on evidence in order to attack the organized crime conspiracy."[18]

Also in 1967, Blakey had given legal advice for a "hard-hitting series of articles on the Mafia" in *Life* magazine. This was his first encounter with Dick Billings, then associate editor of *Life* in charge of the articles, who in 1978 rejoined Blakey as co-author of the House Committee Report and Blakey's book.[19] Blakey's analysis for the President's Commission on Law Enforcement led Congress in turn to pass the Organized Crime Control Acts of 1968 and 1970. Enacted at the height of the Vietnam anti-war protest movement, these new laws disregarded Blakey's civil-liberties safeguards and effectively authorized wiretaps in the investigation of any conspiracy to commit a felony.[20]

THE VALACHI "REVELATIONS" AND WHAT IS WRONG WITH THEM

By 1978, however, the two chief "revelations" in Valachi's testimony, the two which "benefited" federal law enforcement, had been seriously challenged by three academics, Humbert S. Nelli, Dwight C. Smith, Jr., and Alan A. Block:

1. Valachi had testified about a "Castellammarese War" and "Purge" or "Sicilian Vespers" of 1930–31, national in scope, which left an interstate, "Americanized" organization in which (to quote Smith) "non-Italian groups were of secondary importance." According to the separately published *Valachi Papers*, on the day that warring mafia leader Salvatore Maranzano was killed, in September 1931, "some forty Cosa Nostra leaders allied with him were slain across the country." Newspaper searches by Nelli and Block reduced this figure from forty to a maximum of four or five: three in New York, one in Pittsburgh, and possibly one in Denver.[21]

2. A *Commissione*-dominated national "organization structure" for LCN, which (to quote Smith again) "was reassurance for the existing belief that organized crime is an entity apart from the criminal activities of its members. It was the reassurance for which successive investigations had searched for more than a decade. . . . It was a case of a story being true because it sounded like what ought to be heard. Valachi was not really as specific concerning organized crime structure as the subcommittee thought he was."[22]

In his challenge to the Valachi testimony, and what he called the "alien-conspiracy theory" of the Mafia, Smith explicitly questioned the "tightly reasoned analysis by G. Robert Blakey" for the 1967 President's Crime Commission.[23] In 1978, quite aware of this challenge to the credibility of Valachi, Blakey and Salerno chose to reaffirm him before the Assassinations Committee and to ignore the contrary evidence, or, worse, misrepresent it. They even revived the myth of the "Purge" or "Sicilian Vespers," though by accounts so casuistical they virtually concede that it was (as even Salerno called it) a "myth" (9 AH 6). The following account of it by Blakey could indeed have only been written by a lawyer:

> The Maranzano murder was not an isolated event. According to many sources, Luciano had been planning a purge of old-line Mafia leaders across the country, although Humbert S. Nelli, author of *The Business of Crime*, suggested the murders were largely restricted to New York. There was no record of just how many men died, but Thomas E. Dewey, who later was to prosecute Luciano, represented the general view when he estimated it at "some 40."[24]

Blakey's words omit, of course, the fact that Nelli, who unlike Dewey had researched the matter, had (like Block) found "only three victims" in New York, and one other, almost certainly unrelated, in Denver.[25]

Blakey chose to bolster the Valachi account of a Castellammarese war and resulting "national syndicate," with what he presented as an independent "eyewitness account." This was from another mafioso, Nicola Gentile, who had "returned to Sicily" and there written "a long, rambling memoir entitled *Vita di Campmafia*" [sic; i.e., *Capomafia*].[26] But this appearance of corroboration was misleading, and indeed suspicious. As we shall see, Gentile himself was a part of U.S.-supervised covert operations in Sicily.[27] According to Smith, Gentile's memoir had been first used in a *Saturday Evening Post* article in 1960 ("revealed here for the first time by Narcotics Commissioner Harry J. Anslinger") to corroborate the very dubious FBN claim that the Apalachin meeting of 1957 had been a Mafia "Supreme Council" (as opposed to an ad hoc meeting) to discuss narcotics.[28] And as Block had noted, Gentile's memoir is suspect; for it repeats, without corroborating detail, the often-repeated but baseless FBN story of a "Sicilian vespers" followed by an Americanized national "commission."[29] Even more suspiciously, Gentile's "confession" had been circulated within the FBI before its publication, translated for the benefit of J. Edgar Hoover ("FBI insiders say that Gentile's story finally convinced Hoover that there was a Mafia"), and shown, as a skeptic might have predicted, to Joe Valachi.[30]

In effect, Blakey was defending his Organized Crime Control legislation, which was developed in response to Valachi's testimony about an organizing national LCN Commission. If the "Purge" was discredited, then Valachi was discredited; and if Valachi's testimony about a "national syndicate" and "commission" (9 AH 18) was discredited, where was the basis for the legislation of which Blakey was the author?

Blakey and Salerno, almost certainly, were not consciously lying. It is easier to imagine the two of them as Captain Ahabs who had spent their lifetimes in pursuit of a "Black Hand," rather than a white whale. The institutional environment which had shaped their clichés is one which (I know from personal experience) discourages fresh thinking and independent assessment of known facts. One can, however, say that their account of "La Cosa Nostra" is a projection externalizing the organized-crime demon. And their supporting accounts of the "Purge," of the "Commission," and of organized crime in general are bureaucratically distorted to the point of falsehood. We shall see that this distortion involved systematic distortion of the facts, not just about Ruby, but about other aspects of the Kennedy assassination.

JACK RUBY, LIEUTENANT BUTLER, AND CONGRESSIONAL INVESTIGATIONS OF DALLAS

What both the Warren Commission and the House Committee downplayed, in sum, is the evidence supporting the picture of Ruby as influential in the worlds both of organized crime and of law enforcement. There is political power inherent in such status as a "connection." This would be consistent with Ruby's reported appearance before the staff of the Kefauver Senate Rackets Committee in 1950. According to Luis Kutner, the well-known lawyer who accompanied him and subsequently spoke about it, Ruby offered high-level information about mob activities in Chicago, on the condition that the Kefauver Committee stay away from Dallas.[31]

The performance of the Kefauver Committee would seem to corroborate Kutner's claim, for the Committee did give Dallas a clean bill of health. It did so by hearing the testimony of a Dallas policeman, George

Butler, that the same Paul Roland Jones had tried, but failed, to bribe a new Dallas County sheriff, Steve Guthrie, on behalf of Chicago syndicate elements who wished to move down into Dallas. Butler's self-censored testimony was so bland that Senator Kefauver congratulated Butler for his city's honesty: "I think you deserve to be complimented on catching this thing before it got started down in Dallas."[32]

Eight years later the same Lieutenant Butler was more candid. He told the McClellan Committee on Labor Racketeering that the Jones group had failed to infiltrate unions in the Dallas area (the Committee's explicit charge). For the first time, however, he revealed that the Chicago group "took over coin machine and amusement companies in Texas, Louisiana and Arkansas," making $18 million a year in Dallas alone. These admissions rather undercut the grounds for Senator Kefauver's compliments.[33]

In 1964, the same yea-saying Lieutenant Butler told the FBI (in an interview accepted, perhaps too easily, by the Warren Commission and the House Committee) that Jack Ruby "was not involved in the bribery attempt" by Jones.[34] There can be no doubt, however, that Jones and Ruby came from the same powerful Chicago milieu. Jones was offering a deal based on the impending takeover of the nationwide racing wire service by the Chicago mob, after the shooting of the former wire service's manager (James M. Ragen) by Lennie Patrick and Dave Yaras, two longtime acquaintances of Ruby.[35]

The man believed to have ordered Patrick and Yaras to shoot Ragen, Jake Guzik, was reported in FBI files to have been in Dallas in December 1946, where Dave Yaras's brother Sam was already engaged in the slot-machine business (9 AH 518; cf. 9 AH 155). FBI files also reported that Jones had presented himself as an organizational man for the Guzik syndicate (9 AH 516), and the surviving transcriptions of the Jones-Guthrie bribe discussions corroborate this (9 AH 517).[36] As Butler summarized it, it was the "Dallas group" (meaning Guzik and Jones) that muscled into the wire service by killing Ragen.[37]

The House Committee itself concluded that "Ruby had probably talked by telephone to Patrick during the summer of 1963" (AR 151); while Patrick, who denied this (9 AH 973), conceded that Ruby "might have talked to my partner," Dave Yaras (9 AH 968, cf. 972). Telephone records confirm that in November 1963 Ruby twice phoned Barney Baker, a former Teamster hoodlum and Lansky employee (9 AH 274), who in turn telephoned Dave Yaras on November 21, the eve of the Kennedy assassination.[38] We shall have more to say about Patrick and Yaras, because of the overlap of their interests, and Jack Ruby's, in Cuba.

Jones also told Guthrie and Butler about the Chicago mob's intention to use the Teamsters in Dallas to "bring industry to its knees, and even the Government."[39] Meanwhile the Teamsters' mob connection in Chicago was Paul Dorfman, whose union career had begun by taking over the presidency of a junk-handlers' local where Jack Ruby was secretary.[40] Dorfman became president after his predecessor, Leon Cooke, was murdered in Ruby's presence; Ruby himself was arrested on the same day and "was held at the Police station in the investigation." This little-known detail is found in a Chicago police homicide report which reached the Texas attorney general's investigation of the Kennedy assassination but not the Warren Commission's. Jones himself told the FBI in 1964 that "he knew that the syndicate had an interest in this union and presumed this was Ruby's connection."[41] Robert Kennedy later pinpointed this murder and Dorfman takeover as central to the mob control of the Teamsters' Central States Pension Fund under Hoffa.[42]

THE HOUSE COMMITTEE
AND THE CONTINUING DISTORTION

Both the Warren Commission and the House Committee appear to have gone out of their way to conceal the wire-service and Teamster aspects of the Jones-Ruby relationship.[43] As noted below, a House Committee history of organized crime omits the 1946 wire-service war, despite Ruby's known involvement with the wire service; and a staff interview of Lenny Patrick (9 AH 942–77, cf. AR 150–51) asked no questions about Patrick's key role in the 1946 takeover of the wire service.

Blakey's book linked Jimmy Hoffa's "rapid ascent to leadership" in the Teamsters to "his associations with a number of organized crime figures, including . . . Paul Dorfman of Chicago," and recalled the McClellan Committee's description of Dorfman as an "associate of Chicago mobsters and a head of a local of the Waste Material Handlers Union" in Chicago. This account was quite accurate, though it failed to

note that Ruby was secretary of the local.[44] Ninety pages later, in accurately describing the Dorfman-Ruby connection, Blakey mentioned
nothing about the Teamsters.[45]

The result was to leave no trace of a Ruby-Hoffa connection, other
than the rather minor detail that, after Oswald was murdered, Ruby's
brother approached one of Hoffa's attorneys to represent Ruby.[46] The
Committee wished to represent Ruby's suspicious phone calls in 1963
as leads to "the national syndicate known as La Cosa Nostra or the
Mafia" (9 AH iii); even though, of eight such calls, only one was to an
Italian American, while three were to close Hoffa associates (Barney
Baker, Dusty Miller, and Irwin Weiner).[47]

There were a number of allegations linking Ruby to Hoffa and the
Teamsters; the Committee, despite its interest in organized crime, did
not publicly pursue them. Perhaps the most significant of these allegations left uninvestigated was

> a Justice Department internal memorandum of November 26, 1963, "indi-
> cating a connection between Rubenstein [i.e., Ruby] and Frank Chavez and
> Tony Provenzano." Both these Teamster hoodlums had been indicted by
> Robert Kennedy: it was Chavez who threatened to kill Robert Kennedy in
> March 1967, and Provenzano has figured since 1975 as a prime suspect in
> the disappearance of Jimmy Hoffa.[48]

I supplied this information (which was also known to, but not pursued
by, the Warren Commission) to Blakey in 1978; it was also contained in
a book by Dan Moldea, *The Hoffa Wars*, which Blakey used for his
own treatment of Provenzano and Hoffa's death.[49]

It is necessary to explain Blakey's lack of interest in a Justice Department memo linking Ruby to Provenzano, whom Blakey himself identified as "a *caporegime* in the Genovese family of La Cosa Nostra."[50]
What is most striking here is that the November 1963 memo came from
a unit of the Justice Department whose members, at the time, included
both Howard Willens, who later served on the Warren Commission
staff, and Blakey himself.

The explanation for this Committee disinterest probably lies in
Ruby's past involvements in the deep-political history of the nation. For
example, it quite possibly has to do with Ruby's proximity to the Ragen
shooting of 1946, after Ragen had agreed to talk to the FBI in return for
protection. Having handled the mob relationships of the wire service
for his former boss Moe Annenberg (who in 1940 went to prison for

tax evasion), Ragen knew not only the Capone outfit in Chicago but gamblers and mob bosses all over the country, "including Annenberg's close friend Meyer Lansky."[51]

We learn from the diaries of the late journalist Drew Pearson that it was Pearson who had persuaded Ragen, one month before his death,

> to meet with the FBI. I sold the idea to Tom Clark, then Attorney General, and the FBI interviewed Ragen at great length. They brought back a multitude of tips, leads, and evidence. Tom Clark told me afterward that it led to very high places. J. Edgar Hoover intimated the same thing. He said the people Ragen pointed to had now reformed. I learned later that it pointed to the Hilton Hotel chain, Henry Crown, the big Jewish financier in Chicago [involved in Cook Country real estate deals with Jake Arvey, the local Democratic political boss], and Walter Annenberg [son of the prewar wire-service owner Moe Annenberg].[52]

The liberal Pearson's information is partly corroborated by the right-wing crime writers Jack Lait and Lee Mortimer, who reported that Henry Crown bankrolled Jake Arvey in real estate, just as he put up $3 million for Conrad Hilton to purchase the Waldorf Astoria. "The Syndicate," they noted elsewhere, "owns a controlling interest in three of the most important hotel chains in the country."[53]

Pearson's disclosure about the Hilton Hotels is corroborated by the longtime business relationship between Barron Hilton, head of Hilton Hotels, and Sidney Korshak, a lawyer frequently identified as the representative in Los Angeles of the Chicago mob.[54] Korshak had also done business for Henry Crown; and the Hilton-Korshak retainer was in fact recommended by Patrick Hoy, a vice-president of Henry Crown's company, General Dynamics, and "a close friend of both Hilton and Korshak."[55] In 1963 Crown was the major stockholder (with 20 percent of the shares) of General Dynamics, the defense contractor whose controversial TFX created a major political scandal just before the Kennedy assassination.

THE NATIONAL IMPORTANCE
OF THE 1946 WIRE-SERVICE WAR

That both the Warren Commission and the House Committee would suppress the role of Paul Roland Jones and Jack Ruby in the 1946–47 wire-service war is consistent with their overall avoidance of the deep

politics of organized crime. For gambling authority Rufus King has depicted the wire service as the very key to law enforcement corruption
and political influence:

> To attribute half the gang killings and mob violence of the forties and fifties
> to battles over control of this gambling empire would be a very conservative
> speculation. Whoever controlled the wire service "drops" in a town became
> master of gambling activities there. And more often than not he con-
> trolled—the word is responsibly chosen, controlled—the community's local
> law enforcement agencies. . . . once you have got the patrolman—his lieu-
> tenant and his captain and the Chief—taking bribes from your organization
> for "protection" of a harmless little gambling enterprise, *you have got them
> for all purposes.*[56]

Subsequent to the Chicago mob's wire-service move of 1946, Marcello
took over the wire service in New Orleans, where one of the wire-
service clients (as we have seen) was Lee Harvey Oswald's uncle "Dutz"
Murret.[57]

The wire service had been built into a nationally organized network
by Moe Annenberg and his lieutenant James Ragen in the 1920s, when
the two men also "hired gangs of sluggers and ex-boxers" to defend the
Hearst newspaper empire in its vicious circulation wars with competing newspapers.[58] First Annenberg and then his successor Ragen used
the corporate resources of Hearst to establish themselves nationally;
sluggers and ex-boxers, notably Jack Ruby himself in the 1930s,
worked for both networks.[59] This national organization was approved
by the first recorded gathering of organized crime heads across the
country, at Atlantic City in 1929. Following this meeting, John Rosselli,
who had moved to Los Angeles from Chicago in 1924, "was appointed
Annenberg's primary business representative in Los Angeles." As such
he soon became a dominant figure in Los Angeles organized crime, and
above all corruption; the need for payoffs to the police made Rosselli
"the Mafia's bridge to the mayor's brother."[60]

The social costs of this corruption are being borne by the American
people down to the present. Above all the Los Angeles police, being
paid off to ignore gang activity, concentrated their efforts instead on
strike-breaking, espionage against leftist groups, and the suppression of
political dissent:

> Earle Kynette, head of the department's notorious "Intelligence Divi-
> sion," . . . operated out of his own building a block from city hall and

served as a personal emissary and enforcer for [the mayor's brother] Joe Shaw. Critics of the city administration were spied upon and threatened. If they persisted, their homes or offices were bombed, with at least five documented attacks beginning in 1935, including one on a Methodist minister. In addition to his political duties, Kynette managed vice enforcement in the city, harassing racketeers not connected with Shaw [or Rosselli], and monitoring payments from those who were.

Kynette helped Rosselli and the local Jack Dragna mafia family end local gang wars by driving an "older, more civilized gambling syndicate, the one headed by Guy McAfee and Farmer Page," out of Los Angeles.[61]

The killers of Ragen in 1946 were backed in Los Angeles by Ben "Bugsy" Siegel. Siegel hoped to control a new competing wire service, Trans-American, that had been founded to put pressure on Ragen. Although the details are disputed, it seems clear that Siegel's reluctance to fold Trans-American back into the national wire service was discussed at two 1947 national crime syndicate meetings, in Havana and New York, that discussed Siegel's murder.[62] The murder of Siegel led briefly to a new gang war between Siegel's lieutenant Mickey Cohen and Rosselli, with the LAPD organized-crime division under newly appointed Police Chief William Parker assisting Rosselli by tracking Cohen.[63] The notorious right-wing slant of the Los Angeles police continued; in 1965 John Rousselot of the John Birch Society claimed that his organization had two thousand members among Los Angeles County law officers.[64]

In the 1950s Rosselli also served as a conduit to political fixers like Bill Graham in Reno and California's "Governor of the Legislature," Artie Samish, who, "within beckoning distance of the legislature . . . handed out bribes and favors for his shady clients and his gangster friends." In 1933, starting as a lobbyist, Samish

co-authored the bill that legalized horse racing in the state. Thereafter he represented the Santa Anita track [a Rosselli operation, where Jack Ruby also worked in the 1930s]. . . . [Representing California brewers and distillers] brought Samish the fat Schenley account and the friendship of its president, Lewis Rosenstiel [see Chapter 13]. . . . Grounded in Schenley and the brewers, Samish's power through the liquor business reached into wholesalers, retail outlets, advertising, nightclubs, bars, delivery trucks: a half-million workers behind "the damndest political machine you ever saw," Samish said fondly. . . . In Los Angeles, Samish was often seen with his home boy Mickey Cohen; they talked on the phone once a week. . . . Frank Costello of New York was asked if he considered himself a "fairly good friend" of Samish. "Yes, I would say so," Costello replied.[65]

THE WIRE-SERVICE WAR IN CHICAGO

In Chicago, Moe Annenberg's brother Max (from whom he became permanently estranged) organized rival gangs for the competing *Chicago Tribune*. In the 1946–47 Chicago wire-service war newspapers lined up on opposing sides. Hearst's *Chicago Herald-American*, Ragen's former employer, championed the two policemen, Drury and Connelly, who had dared to arrest Patrick, Yaras, and William Block for the Ragen shooting; and it hired Drury as a reporter when he was fired for making the arrests.[66] The *Tribune*, meanwhile, gave prominent coverage to Assistant State Attorney Richard Austin's attack on Drury's "deliberate, dastardly plot to indict three innocent men" and faulted Drury for having as a cop leaked wiretap reports to the *Herald-American* on a gambling joint (Putty's Place, at 3613–15 West Roosevelt Road) frequented by Dave Yaras.[67]

It is not too much to say that Hearst's employment of goons nationally helped disseminate Chicago gangsters into the deep politics of corrupt cities across the nation. This was corroborated in 1975, when a San Francisco bail bondsman called Benny Barrish was named in connection with the controversial lease of a city-owned golf course to a recently arrived East Coast mafia figure. In the Warren Commission Exhibits, Barrish is identified as someone who hung out with Ruby at the Lawndale Poolroom (a gathering-place on West Roosevelt Road for many of Ruby's friends).[68] In the 1930s Barrish had gone out West with Ruby to hustle papers for the *San Francisco Call-Bulletin*, a Hearst newspaper which Annenberg had placed under his questionable protection a decade earlier.[69]

Even before Ragen's death, his killers Patrick, Yaras, and Block supplied muscle for Democratic political boss Jake Arvey's machine in Chicago's Jewish 24th Ward. A Republican-dominated Senate committee in 1947, investigating the parole in that year of John Rosselli and other mob leaders in the Browne-Bioff extortion conspiracy, drew attention to the fact that Patrick, Yaras, and Block all hung out at Putty's Place on West Roosevelt Road (where Patrick was involved in gambling operations). After Jake Arvey admitted this was his 24th Ward Democratic Headquarters, the committee heard from Lieutenant Connelly, one of the policemen who arrested the killers, that the place was "a hangout for thieves and gangsters."[70] They also learned that Maury Hughes, a Dallas attorney who traveled to Washington to obtain the parole, was offered employment in Dallas by Chicago mob figure Pat Manno, as part of the group Jones claimed to represent.[71]

These revelations did nothing to weaken Arvey's hold over the Democratic party in Chicago. On the contrary, it was the Arvey machine that successfully nominated Adlai Stevenson to be the Democratic presidential candidate in 1952 and 1956. Nor did Arvey distance himself from Patrick: a 1961 federal crime report revealed that Patrick was the gambling boss of the 24th Ward, and could not be stopped "since he was backed politically by Jake Arvey," in whose ward he grew up. Arvey "would often call upon him for strong arm tactics in connection with stuffing ballot boxes."[72]

Such tactics had of course been part of Democratic politics in Chicago for decades. On the model of other gang leaders such as Dion O'Banion and Big Jim Colosimo, who delivered the Irish and Italian ethnic vote, so gambling boss Dave "Yiddles" Miller and his gang in the 1920s and 1930s mobilized the votes of the Jews.[73] A famous study by John Landesco in 1929 noted that, despite their multiple convictions, Chicago police records were negative for Dave Miller and his brothers (including Harry Miller, who, "while a member of the police force, was involved in the narcotics traffic").[74] The Kefauver Committee heard Dave Miller's restaurant (frequented by Ruby) mentioned in connection with the recruitment of young toughs for the Hearsts in their newspaper wars, and for the related sales of racing scratch sheets for Moe Annenberg and James Ragen.[75]

The Warren Commission staff learned quickly that "Ruby's group was known as the Dave Miller gang" (26 WH 469; cf. 22 WH 322, 22 WH 425). They also knew that Ruby was reportedly (22 WH 327), and his brother Hymie admittedly (15 WH 11), in the Arvey 24th Ward political machine (cf. 21 WH 314). But the Warren Report went out of its way to disguise the deep politics of the Dave Miller gang. It described Ruby and his poolhall companions as "not organized adherents of any political creed," but young men "who gathered on the spur of the moment" to oppose activities of the anti-Semitic German-American Bund (WR 789).

The fact is that in Chicago, as in some other cities, organized criminal activity and organized political activity were difficult to distinguish. Ballot-box stuffing by Arvey's machine, with the help of Sam Giancana and other mob figures, had of course helped elect Kennedy in Illinois, and thus the nation, in 1960. Small wonder that the Warren Commission and House Committee averted their eyes from the politically sensitive Ruby-Patrick-Arvey connection.

Yet this may have been the key to the assassination. Virtually the only interest shared by Oswald and Ruby in 1963 was Cuba, and Ruby later made it clear to his attorney that his initial interest in Cuba was in connection with Jake Arvey's business concerns there.[76] Even the Warren Commission knew that this had brought Ruby into contact with a Robert Ray McKeown, a former gunrunner for ex-Cuban President Carlos Prío Socarras, who had been arrested with Prío on smuggling charges in 1958.[77] We have already seen that Carlos Prío Socarras, the backer with Varona of the Cuban Revolutionary Council at 544 Camp Street, had taken part in the early planning of the Martino-Pawley mission.[78]

RUBY, THE WIRE SERVICE, AND CORRUPTION IN DALLAS

As in Los Angeles, certain consequences seemed to follow the Chicago mob's move into Dallas in 1946: warring local gangs (those of Herb Noble and Benny Binion) ceased their street-fighting and murders (Noble ended up killed, and Binion was forced out of town), and special political power became concentrated in the Dallas police force and its Special Service Bureau, which handled intelligence, vice, and narcotics. As we shall see when discussing Oswald, the SSB showed its politics by targeting such threats to public safety as the local affiliate of the American Civil Liberties Union. According to an organizer for the Ku Klux Klan in 1961, "half of the police force in Dallas were members of the KKK." This organizer, a former head of the Dallas Policeman's Union and speaker for anti-Communist causes, was someone we have already encountered, Lieutenant George E. Butler.[79]

The House Committee, like the Warren Commission, reached the very dubious conclusion that "Ruby apparently did not participate in the organized crime move to Dallas in 1947" (AR 151). It did so partly on the say-so of Butler, who told the Committee that Jones (who became his informant in 1946) told Butler that Ruby was "no part of us" (9 AH 157). They also cited a memo on the move from the Chicago Crime Commission, with a list of names which mentioned neither Jack Ruby nor his Dallas club, the Silver Spur (9 AH 155). However, Sheriff Guthrie himself recalled that, "Whenever I wanted to find anyone from the syndicate, I went to Ruby's Silver Spur."[80] If so, Luis Kutner would appear to be corroborated in his claim that "Ruby was a syndicate lieutenant who had been sent to Dallas to serve as a liaison for Chicago mobsters."[81]

Even more predictably, in its review of the actual notes and transcripts of the 1946 discussions between Jones, Guthrie, and Butler, the Committee underreported the revelations therein about the extent of political corruption in Dallas and Washington. Jones promised Guthrie that when he stood for re-election, Jones could guarantee supporting letters from President Truman and his postmaster-general Bob Hannegan. Whether he could have delivered on this promise is unknown; but one year later, in August 1947, Hannegan was the payoff recipient in the controversial parole of John Rosselli and other Chicago mobsters.[82]

The same transcripts reveal corruption in Dallas which is relevant to the Kennedy assassination. At one point in the transcript, Sheriff Guthrie stated that "we all know that Bill Decker [the county under-sheriff, whom Jones described as an "old-time bootlegger here"] is a payoff man with Bennie Binion"; and George Butler agreed (9 AH 517). (This would be consistent with Decker's having served as a character witness for Dallas mafioso Joseph Civello in 1937, when Civello applied for a pardon from a narcotics conviction.)[83] In 1963 Bill Decker was Dallas County sheriff; and one of his men, Deputy Sheriff Eugene Boone, helped discover the controversial 6.5-mm Mannlicher-Carcano, which he first identified as a 7.65 Mauser.[84]

Jones also noted that the Chicago mob already had the new Dallas District Attorney, Will Wilson, "in the bag"; this revelation may or may not help explain why in 1954 Wilson's successor, Henry Wade, dismissed arrest charges against Ruby for reasons which are apparently not true.[85] Wade also played a large and controversial role after the arrest of Oswald; at a press conference on November 22, he identified Oswald as a member of the "Free Cuba Committee," and the correcting voice in the crowd ("Fair Play for Cuba") was Jack Ruby's.[86]

Jones also identified the Dallas law firm (of T. K. Irwin) through which the payoffs were distributed. As I pointed out to the House Committee, one member of this family firm, Ivan Irwin, was in 1963–64 sharing a law office with two other lawyers, Pete White and William McKenzie, who appeared to supply the otherwise missing link between the worlds of the Oswalds and of Ruby. For Pete White was one of Ruby's attorneys (it was Pete White who had arranged with Henry Wade for the charges against Ruby to be dismissed); and his officemate William McKenzie (see Chapter 18) became the attorney for Marina Oswald. Instead of being interested in this Ruby-Oswald link (which would explain why the phone number for Marina's lawyer was in the notebook of a Ruby employee), the Warren Commission systematically avoided it.[87] The House Committee did not interview Ivan Irwin or his two officemates; instead a Committee staff report noted that "the committee was unable to locate T. K. Irwin," a notorious lawyer who at the time (1978) had been dead for several years (9 AH 1152).

In short, the Kefauver Committee conspicuously failed, as Ruby's lawyer Luis Kutner alleged, to expose the extent of the Chicago mob's takeover of Dallas gambling in 1946–47, when Ruby himself moved from Chicago to Dallas. Lieutenant George Butler, a longtime friend of Ruby's, contributed to this performance, and again to the Warren Commission's concealment of Ruby's status with the mob in Dallas. Butler was also in the Dallas police basement when Ruby shot Oswald, and one journalist was struck that this normally phlegmatic man was so "extremely nervous" just before the shooting that his lips were trembling.[88]

The House Committee rightly noted, and criticized, the Warren Commission's "overall failure to investigate [Ruby's] possible organized crime connections," especially with respect to the wire service and Teamster connections represented by Patrick, Yaras, and Paul Dorfman (9 AH 1040, cf. 943). But the inability to address this politically sensitive area persisted. Although Blakey and Billings in their book repeated the well-known story that Patrick and Yaras were prime suspects in the shotgunning "of James M. Ragen, the owner of Continental Press Service," a twenty-two-page staff interview of Patrick does not once ask about this, even though Patrick was questioned about an earlier and much more minor murder of which he was suspected, that of Ben ("Zuckie the Bookie") Zuckerman.[89] This omission is inexcusable: the Committee had been alerted to the fact that many of Ruby's phone calls in late 1963 had reportedly been to the Teamster and wire-service mob elements, including Patrick and Yaras. The Committee itself concluded that "Ruby had probably talked by telephone to Patrick" (AR 150–51), despite Patrick's testimony under oath that "I am positive that he [Ruby] never called me" (9 AH 973).[90]

The House Committee did show that Ruby's phone calls with crime-linked individuals increased in the weeks before the assassination, especially to men with influence in the Teamsters. But it failed to recount, let alone expand upon, the discovery by a Warren Commission staffer that one of Ruby's suspicious phone contacts, the convicted Teamster organizer Barney Baker, had phoned Dave Yaras the night before the assassination.[91]

TEN

The Nationally
Protected Drug Traffic
and Ruby's Relation to It

As we have seen, both the postwar mob takeover of the Teamsters and the 1946 wire-service war are important events in any objective history of organized crime in America.[1] Ruby's associates in Chicago were deeply implicated in both events, thanks to the murders of Leon Cooke (which launched Paul Dorfman's union career) and James Ragen (which reorganized the nationwide wire service more securely under mob control). We have already seen that gambling authority Rufus King attributed half the gang killings and mob violence of the forties and fifties to battles over control of the wire service.

There was also an important narcotics angle to the Ragen shooting. The *Chicago Tribune* revealed, five days after the shooting, that Colonel George White, head of the Chicago federal narcotics office, "said he wanted to study Ragen's statement because most of the hoodlums mentioned in it also are mentioned in his secret studies dealing with the narcotics racket."[2]

White's information is richly corroborated by other sources. Jake Guzik, the mob boss of Yaras and Patrick, and Police Captain William Drury's top suspect in the Ragen shooting, was said to be in charge of prostitution and narcotics for the Chicago syndicate.[3] Later, Patrick was similarly suspected of involvement in narcotics and prostitution; as late as 1966 a government report stated that "Patrick was believed to be the largest dealer of narcotics on [Chicago's] west side" (9 AH 948).

And Dave Yaras and Barney Baker in the 1950s helped organize Teamster Local 320 in Miami, "which served as a front for many of the mob's gambling and narcotics activities." (Santos Trafficante, one of the nation's top traffickers, "occupied a small office in the union hall.")[4]

The intrusion into the case of George White, the veritable "Mr. Deep Politics" of the U.S. intelligence-mob connection, was much more intriguing than most people would have known at the time. As one of the Federal Bureau of Narcotics' top users of mob informants, he had been during World War II a senior officer in the counterespionage, or X-2, component of OSS (perhaps its most secret unit), and he would later play a similar role in the lethal MK-ULTRA operations of the CIA.[5] While in OSS he had taken part in Operation Underworld, the World War II deal between U.S. intelligence and Meyer Lansky, whereby Lucky Luciano was released from prison to pave the way for the U.S. invasion of Sicily.[6] Indeed, it was White who gave the Kefauver Committee, for which he was a consultant, the first sanitized account of Operation Underworld, suggesting, falsely, that "OSS remained aloof."[7]

What we shall examine in this chapter will support the thesis of the noted criminologist Alan A. Block that continuously, from Operation Underworld in 1943 down through the CIA-Mafia plots against Fidel Castro, "the FBN under the leadership of [Harry] Anslinger, [Garland] Williams, [George] White, [Charles] Siragusa, etc., was one of the lead organizations involved in foreign counterintelligence activities in pursuit of anti-communist objectives."[8] Unfortunately we have no name to describe this continuous postwar exploitation of international drug traffickers for covert operations purposes. For convenience, I shall call this ongoing use of the narcotics traffic and traffickers "Operation X," after a similar French use of Indochinese narcotics traffic and traffickers in the 1950s.[9]

The CIA and other agencies appear to have collaborated closely with the FBN in this operational use of drug traffickers. As we shall see, the CIA helped establish important institutional support for the traffic in postwar Sicily, on the Marseille waterfront, and throughout Southeast Asia. U.S. intelligence operative Paul Helliwell was particularly prominent in establishing this connection, first by arranging for the CIA to take over and protect a drug-trafficking airline, and then by helping to establish the Castle Bank in the Bahamas, one of a series of banks through which both CIA funds and drug profits were laundered.[10] One way to study the continuity of the global narcotics networks is to follow the connections between Helliwell's Castle Bank and successor drug-laundering banks, such as the Nugan Hand Bank of Australia, the World Finance Corporation (WFC), and the Bank of Credit and Commerce International (BCCI).[11]

The inevitable result of this use of drug traffickers was a nationally protected drug traffic, in which many key traffickers, because of their government connection, were not prosecuted. We shall see that one of the highest-level architects of this traffic was Meyer Lansky, owner of the Tropicana casino in Havana, which was managed by Ruby's friend Lewis McWillie (9 AH 802). By the time Lansky retired and was then indicted in 1970–71, his place had been taken by Santos Trafficante.

But, although they are convenient, terms like *Operation X* or *CIA-Mafia connection* are also, from a deep-politics perspective, superficial and thus misleading. It was not only intelligence operatives who had a motive to protect drug traffickers. There were also those entrepreneurs, particularly in the southern sunbelt from Florida through to Southern California, who profited from the flow of laundered drug money and other crime-controlled funds into real estate and other investments.[12]

OPERATION UNDERWORLD, "OPERATION X," AND THE CIA-MAFIA PLOTS AGAINST CASTRO

Thus, the intelligence-mob collaboration established with Operation Underworld did not end after World War II. On the contrary, postwar narcotics operations overseas were subordinated to anti-Communist activities; and they were used as a cover for ongoing use of mob assets, above all drug traffickers, around the world. In developing these postwar mob contacts, White and his FBN associates, notably his former supervisor Garland Williams, and his protégé Charles Siragusa, even while formally back in the FBN hierarchy, "functioned as a counterintelligence unit, attached to the CIA and, at times, the Army." Such is the conclusion of criminologist Alan Block from the George White diaries:

> In 1948, for instance, while the CIA was conducting one of its first operations, the subversion of Italian politics, White showed up in Rome for a meeting with his former OSS boss William Donovan. More importantly,

however, the diaries disclose that White, and his FBN protege, Charles Siragusa, were part of the "inner circle" of CIA officials who planned and carried out various lethal secret operations.[13]

In the 1950s and 1960s it would appear that the FBN systematically subordinated the prosecution of drug cases to a second, hidden agenda, the use of traffickers as agents against communism. We can see this in the selective arrests made by George White in a 1959 heroin case involving the anti-Communist (and pro-Kuomintang) Hip Sing tong or gang (this was at a time when anti-Communist, drug-trafficking KMT guerrillas were being supported by the CIA in Burma). The arrests were delayed until after the ringleader, Chung Wing Fong, a former Hip Sing president and official of the San Francisco Anti-Communist League (a KMT front) had been ordered by the U.S. consulate in Hong Kong to travel to Taiwan. In this way Fong became no more than an unindicted conspirator, and the KMT disappeared from view; White then told the U.S. press that the heroin had come from *Communist* China ("most of it from a vast poppy field near Chungking").[14]

White's projection of an ally's trafficking onto the Communist enemy was typical of the FBN as long as it was headed by Harry Anslinger. In this way FBN officials protected top-level international drug traffickers who were also anti-Communists, not just in the KMT, but all around the world. For example, Alan Block reports that FBN Commissioner Anslinger and OSS agents, doubtless in coordination with the CIA, set up a private intelligence organization in the Middle East. Forty years later Dennis Dayle, a veteran of Middle Eastern drug enforcement and former chief of the DEA international intelligence unit, said for the record that "in my 30-year history in the Drug Enforcement Administration and related agencies, the major targets of my investigations almost invariably turned out to be working for the CIA."[15]

If what Block has written is correct, then what Blakey and the House Committee published about Ruby and Jones (and also, as we shall see, about the CIA-Mafia plots against Castro) can perhaps be characterized as a watered-down and restricted version, for public consumption, of a more sinister ongoing story, the use of organized crime, and in particular of international narcotics traffickers, for overseas covert operations, including assassinations. As noted earlier, I have chosen for convenience to call this governmental use of drug traffickers Operation X. In talking of Operation X, however, we should understand that this continuation of Operation Underworld by White, Siragusa, and other FBN officers in the postwar period was not restricted to any single operation or any single agency.

Despite the many revelations about the CIA since the mid-1970s, the story of Operation X has continued to be treated as an unspeakable one. Virtually none of the recent histories of CIA mention White's and Siragusa's use of underworld drug traffickers (like Rosselli and Trafficante), except in the single instance, revealed by Rosselli himself while facing prosecution, of the plots against Castro.[16] The reason, we shall suggest, is that these ongoing operations, those of White in particular, have contributed to the flood of narcotics this country and others have experienced since World War II. As recently as the 1980s, this country's problems with a flood of heroin from Afghanistan, and a flood of cocaine coming via Honduras, could be attributed in part to CIA operations in those countries.[17]

Following the lead of Blakey and the House Committee in 1978, many mainstream historians have now acknowledged that the CIA was at fault in failing to disclose the CIA-Mafia plots against Castro to the Warren Commission. I ask the reader to contemplate a much more disturbing possibility. Were these plots, confirmed by the Church Committee in 1975, only one phase of a much more sustained collaboration between intelligence and drug traffickers since World War II? And, insofar as this connection is still operative, does it still drive government officials to cover up the truth about the Kennedy assassination, as well as other events in our history? For there have indeed been recurring instances in which intelligence-linked drug traffickers and their allies (such as Miguel Nazar Haro, discussed in Chapter 6) have been protected from prosecution, and otherwise assisted by the U.S. government, sometimes explicitly as a result of their parapolitical connection to it.[18]

Very soon after VJ-Day, if not indeed continuously, the FBN counterintelligence set maintained or resumed contacts with underworld representatives in anti-Communist operations around the world. An early documented instance, in late 1949, is a particularly relevant one. Garland Williams, who went into deep-cover work in the Far East, was pretty clearly the "Col. Williams from the Army" who arranged for a mob associate, Satiris "Sonny" Fassoulis, to become an officer of Commerce International China, a company which "had definite ties with

Army intelligence."[19] Fassoulis thus became a principal agent in the "private" procurement of military supplies and advisers for Chiang Kai-shek in Taiwan, a project originally proposed to the U.S. government by William Pawley. Funds for CIC's "volunteers" came "through 'Texas oil people,' presumably including H. L. Hunt"; and many of the advisers came from General Charles Willoughby's intelligence G-2 in Japan, itself working with elements from Japan's yakuza underworld.[20]

Fassoulis and his associates continued through the decades to be named in major mob financial scandals. In the 1970s a witness before a Senate committee investigating stolen securities linked Fassoulis to the Texas-Adams stock swindle, a case for which Paul Roland Jones was under indictment in 1963, at the time of the assassination.[21] (Some of those named by the witness would in the 1980s be accused of nationwide looting in the savings-and-loans scandal.)[22] We shall return to the possibility, for which there is other corroboration, that White addressed himself to the intrigues of the Ragen killing, not just or even primarily to make drug cases, but to "turn" some of those involved into intelligence assets.

One of these assets may have been Ruby himself, who has been linked to Rosselli and others in the postwar intelligence-mob connection. At the time of Ragen's shooting on June 24, 1946, George White was still in the U.S. Army. His diaries show that White left the army three days later, on June 27, and, in his new appointment as FBN Chief in Chicago, immediately immersed himself in the Ragen case.[23] One suspects that White somehow already knew that this shooting would play a key role in the postwar reorganization of organized crime—as was confirmed when Lansky (White's collaborator in Operation Underworld) and the New York and Chicago mobs decided they had to kill Bugsy Siegel, for his attempt to take over the national wire service.[24]

George White's diaries contain the following entry, possibly important but as yet undeciphered, concerning the situation in Chicago:

Tues July 23 1946 Met Ruby—Interview Kehler def. Chicago Miller say met Kehler. Pete o.k.'d R's for $25/ week. Intv Dr [?] M. Boyer. Says Pete o.k.'d R for Kehler and Woodin

It is not clear that this Ruby is our Jack Ruby, who did not officially change his name from Rubenstein (giving as a reason that he was "well known" as Jack L. Ruby) until December 30, 1947 (WR 793–94). We have seen, however, that there are strong independent reasons for thinking that

1.   Ruby told authorities about the Ragen killing;

2.   Ruby was somehow involved with Paul Roland Jones, the focus of the first FBN case to involve the Guzik crowd; and

3.   Ruby, by the time of this case, was an FBN informant.

More significantly, the House Committee, like the Warren Commission, omitted the information leading to precisely these three conclusions. Indeed the omission is so consistent and well defined as to again constitute what I have called a negative template, and to justify invoking the conclusion that, here again, the omission is a symptom of something important.

VALACHI AND BLAKEY RECONSIDERED: PROTECTING OPERATION X'S LINKS TO THE ASSASSINATION

The House Committee, to be sure, did not completely ignore the intelligence-mob connection. On the contrary, it looked intensely at the CIA-Mafia plots against Castro from 1960 to 1963; it had no choice but to do so, given the earlier suggestions by the Church Committee that these plots might have had something to do with the Kennedy assassination itself. These earlier suggestions derived from the disturbing claim by John Rosselli, the CIA's principal mafia contact, that a CIA hit team dispatched to Cuba had been "turned" and used to kill the President.[25]

Blakey himself pinpointed Rosselli and Giancana, two central figures in the 1960–63 plots, as prime suspects in the killing of the President. No one was particularly threatened by this: Giancana and Rosselli had already been murdered in 1975–76, the first just before, and the second just after, scheduled testimony to the Church Committee. Blakey wondered if "Roselli was killed for what he knew about the [Kennedy] assassination"; and he repeated the opinion of Giancana's daughter that her father had been killed "by the same people responsible for killing the Kennedys."[26]

There were many excellent reasons for believing this, but Blakey, intent on seeing a mob plot and not a CIA-mob one, had to ignore a much better source than Giancana's daughter. This was the information supplied by Charles Crimaldi, a former contract killer and longtime FBN informant, reporting for many years to George White's FBN (and CIA) protégé, Charles Siragusa:

> Claiming that the mobsters involved with the CIA were responsible for Giancana's murder, Crimaldi told his biographer, John Kidner, an official of the Bureau of Narcotics, "Momo [Giancana] knew too much, and was ready to talk to the Senate investigating committee about the Chicago underworld's part in the CIA assassination plot against Fidel Castro. . . ." "I told him [Crimaldi] that that would take some proving," Kidner wrote. "He didn't bother to prove it, but replied: 'I don't need proof. I say he was hit by the CIA guy. He didn't pull the trigger himself. He used one of our guys [in the underworld]. An import.' " The Giancana gunman turned government informer later claimed that Jimmy Hoffa had also participated in the plots. And at that time Hoffa's chief contact with Trafficante . . . had set up locals in Miami with the help of reputed Giancana executioner David Yaras. According to Crimaldi, Hoffa had been the "original liaison" between the CIA and the underworld.[27]

Crimaldi also told Kidner that John Rosselli's death was the work of the same top mob people who ordered the deaths of Giancana and Hoffa.[28]

If Crimaldi is right, a CIA-mob assassination connection survived into the 1970s, when it carried out a series of high-profile killings in the United States to cover up truths about the CIA-Mafia plots of the 1950s and early 1960s. Giancana was hit by a "CIA guy," who "used one of our guys"; if Blakey's quote from Giancana's daughter is correct, this would mean that, as others have suspected, a mobster and "the CIA guy" were "responsible for killing the Kennedys." And Giancana's killers would appear to have been involved in the anti-Castro plots as well.[29]

Moldea's book supplements Crimaldi's information with that of unnamed government agents and secret internal reports to which they had access. According to these, one of the key murders, that of Hoffa, was authorized by Russell Bufalino, who had given the contract to New Jersey mobster Tony Provenzano.[30] We shall see in a moment that Bufalino was a key member of the Hoffa–Operation X–Cuba connection, while Provenzano (we have already seen) was the mob Teamster official linked by the Justice Department to Jack Ruby. Other investigators with government connections have seen still other murders in this

1970s series, such as that of Leo Moceri in 1976, after he had supplied information about the Hoffa killing. Two that concern us most are the murder of Dave Yaras's son Ron in 1974, possibly by the gunman in Rosselli's murder, and also Dave Yaras's death in the same year.

What is most striking here is the certification of Crimaldi's reliability by Charles Siragusa, George White's protégé and former deputy director of the Bureau of Narcotics. Siragusa, "who used Crimaldi's information about the underworld's narcotics traffic in numerous successful prosecutions by the bureau, called the former syndicate figure 'absolutely reliable.' "[31] And Siragusa himself hinted at the importance of "Davie Yaras" in Giancana's anti-Castro plots with the CIA against Castro:

> During his stay down there [Davie Yaras] was second only to the Lansky-Trafficante people in the number of Cuban contacts he had. He ran a number of gambling operations on the island and was also the Chicago mob's [i.e., Giancana's] liaison to the Cuban exile community after the fall of Batista.[32]

The Committee's own closely reasoned analysis of the CIA-Mafia plots noted testimony that "Roselli contacted Giancana to provide Cuban contacts," one of whom was Cuban exile leader Tony Varona (10 AH 167); and it concluded that Giancana "served solely" in this contact role. If so, and if Siragusa is right, Yaras (as well as his officemate Trafficante, the connection named by the Committee) would appear to have been involved in the first CIA-Rosselli-Varona plot to kill Castro.

If Crimaldi as a Giancana gunman was a well-located source, his FBN handler, Siragusa, was even more so. We have already seen that Siragusa and White together, according to criminologist Alan Block, "were part of the 'inner circle' of CIA officials who planned and carried out various lethal secret operations."[33] Siragusa himself has confirmed that "a friend who was a CIA agent" asked him, because of his "contacts with the underworld . . . to put together a team to conduct a series of hits" against "foreign leaders," meaning Fidel Castro. Siragusa told Moldea and Jack Anderson that he replied softly, "This is peacetime. If we were in war, maybe I could do it. But not like this; I just couldn't do it."[34]

Siragusa's CIA friend may have been Dr. Sidney Gottlieb, expert in lethal toxins for the CIA's "Executive Action" assassination program, as well as overseer of the MK/ULTRA LSD experiments which first George White, and then Siragusa, supervised in New York. Alan Block heard from a former high official in the FBN and DEA that Siragusa, far from turning Gottlieb down, was put in charge of ZR/RIFLE plots to kill Castro.[35] White's diaries also suggest that Siragusa's response was not negative: they show that Gottlieb and Siragusa together flew out to visit White in San Francisco, right after Gottlieb's failed attempt to assassinate Congolese Premier Patrice Lumumba.[36]

The CIA officer principally in charge of ZR/RIFLE was William Harvey, working in collaboration with Jim Angleton.[37] Harvey, the CIA officer who came to hate Robert Kennedy "with a purple passion," first recruited Rosselli under the ZR/RIFLE program.

THE INTELLIGENCE-MOB CONNECTION
BEFORE CASTRO

On two points at least, Crimaldi's account of the CIA-mob plots against Castro is indeed more reliable than Blakey's: the CIA contacts with the mob began much earlier than 1960, and included not only Rosselli but Hoffa and others. Hoffa is indeed likely to have been, as Crimaldi claimed, the "original liaison" for the CIA-mob contacts. Back in 1940, with help from some Justice Department indictments, Hoffa had been the key figure in an AFL-Teamster drive in Minneapolis to defeat "reds" in a rival union which had defected to the new and more militant CIO. The drive, which was also supported by local police and allegedly the FBI, had overtones of "national security," since at the time Communists supported the Hitler-Stalin pact of 1939. It was Hoffa's success in this purge which launched him toward national leadership.[38] It also launched him into closer ties with mob elements in Chicago and elsewhere, notably Paul Dorfman, who brought Ruby's Waste Handlers' Union into the Teamsters, and, through Dorfman, John Rosselli's mentor Paul "the Waiter" deLucia, alias Ricca.[39]

Dan Moldea, who interviewed Siragusa, suggests that "it was Hoffa who persuaded [Russell] Bufalino, [Salvatore] Granello, [John] La-Rocca, [Gabriel] Mannarino, and [James] Plumeri to cooperate with the agency" (CIA).[40] These men were all Mafia, all Teamster-related. All of them had casino investments in Havana. And like Trafficante and Marcello, virtually all of them, except possibly LaRocca, had been linked to narcotics trafficking, usually through corrupt Teamster locals.[41] Gabriel Mannarino and John LaRocca, at least, enjoyed CIA protection; they were acquitted in a 1971 Teamsters kickback trial, after "one of the star witnesses [Mario Brod, for the defense] turned out to be the local head of the CIA."[42]

This CIA-narcotics-Teamsters alliance was first established back in 1946, when the U.S. government paroled a number of Mafia figures and deported them back to Sicily. The two key deportees for this connection were Lucky Luciano and Jimmy Hoffa's first mob contact, Frank Coppola of Detroit, the godfather of Hoffa's foster son Chuck O'Brien. In Italy Coppola, along with more than sixty other deported American mafiosi, became political muscle to help elect politicians of the CIA-favored Christian Democratic party.[43] Coppola was said to have been behind a 1947 May Day massacre in Sicily, allegedly financed by former OSS chief William Donovan, in which eight people were killed and thirty-three wounded; 498 people, mostly left-wingers, were killed in 1948 alone.[44]

One result of this anti-Communist campaign was to restore, down to the present, a Mafia rule of terror in Sicily that had been largely eliminated by Mussolini. Another result was to restore, down to the present, the unimpeded flow of drugs into the United States, which had been largely eliminated by World War II.

Even CIA sources have now attested to the intelligence aspect of this post-OSS, pre-CIA covert operation, when Angleton was chief of the SSU intelligence station in Rome. Former CIA officer Miles Copeland, defending the CIA-Mafia connection, wrote that "had it not been for the Mafia the Communists would by now be in control of Italy."[45] Thomas Tripodi, an agent who went from FBN to CIA counterintelligence, confirmed that "American authorities were instrumental in the revival of the Sicilian Mafia."[46]

From 1946 on, heroin from Coppola in Italy was shipped back to Detroit, and from there to New York and elsewhere, via a number of genealogically interrelated mafia families; these families included those of Russell Bufalino, James Plumeri, and John Ormento.[47] The genealogical relationships are mind-boggling, but important, because they establish the continuity between the Coppola operation of 1946–47 and the Plumeri-Bufalino anti-Castro plots of 1960. They also supply a postwar sketch of how the postwar national Mafia became consolidated laterally, through kinship exploitation via the Teamsters of an intelligence-sanctioned drug traffic, rather than downward from a hypothetical ethnic "national commission."[48]

In the resulting drug traffic, a key organizing role was played by trucking companies (like that of Ormento), and Teamster locals like those controlled by the Dioguardi brothers and Plumeri. Hoffa himself protected the "key receivers" in Detroit, John Priziola and Raffaele Quasarano, by assigning them to Teamster Local 985, a mob local dealing with jukeboxes, run by Russell Bufalino's cousin William.[49] Plumeri had helped Dave Yaras establish Teamster Local 320 in Miami, which supplied an office to Santos Trafficante; and allegedly created the Hoffa-Trafficante connection for the CIA-Mafia plots. Non-Italians from the Dioguardi-Plumeri Teamster locals (such as Bernard Blaustein, Abe Gordon, and Milton Holt) were frequently the connections, not only with the international narcotics smugglers, but also with other Mafia leaders, such as James Licavoli in Cleveland.[50]

FBN LIES ABOUT OPERATION X: "WE PUT AN END TO THE TRAFFIC"

All of this was watched knowledgeably in the FBN, first by White and later by his protégé Siragusa. Siragusa later told author Dan Moldea that Luciano, the hero of White's Operation Underworld, "ran the whole show." He also gave Moldea (p. 64) the false story that, thanks to busts made by himself, "the Luciano network had crumbled, and by 1954 it was replaced by French Corsican drug traffickers Giuseppe and Vincent Cotroni" (in Montreal).

A Canadian book based on RCMP files totally discredits this optimistic account of the FBN's efficiency. To begin with, the Cotronis were not "Corsican," as one often reads in FBN-inspired accounts, but Calabrians, that is to say, ethnically close to Luciano and his associates.[51] More importantly, the Cotronis began to receive heroin in 1954, when New York mafioso Carmine Galente (number two in the Joe Bonanno family) came to Montreal, having met in the same year with Luciano in Italy.

As the FBN well knew, the Cotronis were getting their heroin thanks to the Luciano connection. The FBN itself warned the RCMP in October 1954 that, "a few weeks earlier Frank Petrula, one of Galente's

Montreal partners, had paid a visit to Luciano in Italy and had apparently returned with a stock of heroin." By 1959, the Cotronis, each month, supplied about fifty kilos of pure heroin to John Ormento, Carmine Galente, and Vito Genovese of the New York crime families.[52]

In 1957, as Luciano prepared to retire, Quasarano's father-in-law, Vito Vitale, attended a senior Mafia international summit in Palermo with Frank Coppola, Santo Sorge, and others, about which we shall have more to say (see Chapter 12). That the original Luciano connection had incorporated the Corsican connection was demonstrated again in 1965, when a seizure of ninety pounds of heroin destined for the Trafficante organization led to the arrest and conviction of several high-ranking Corsicans (including Paul Mondoloni, a former Saigon chief of police), and also Frank Dioguardi, brother of Hoffa's mafia Teamster ally John Dioguardi.[53]

What Siragusa undoubtedly did do in April 1952 was arrange for the busts of Detroit receivers Priziola and Quasarano, and eventually of their supplier Salvatore Vitale, who made the mistake of returning to the United States.[54] But this bust only happened after Priziola and Quasarano had already become marginalized to the main Operation X drug connection. Back in 1950 Luciano's diverted supplies of legally produced Italian heroin had begun to dry up; a timely visit to Europe by Meyer Lansky apparently arranged for Corsican leaders around Marseille to provide Luciano another source—from Marseille and ultimately Indochina.[55]

The new flow of heroin from Marseille in 1950–51 coincided with renewed CIA support for anti-Communist operations in that city, because of Marseille's importance in the French government's supply route for its deepening war in Indochina. Anti-Communists in the AFL, working with CIA agent Paul Sakwa, had already established close relations with Luciano's new suppliers, the Corsican Guérini gang.[56] The heroin was being processed from Indochinese opium, supplied after 1950 from the French army's Operation X via Corsicans in Saigon.[57] Responsible French sources claim that even the chemist in the Guérini's heroin lab, Jo Cesari, had his own CIA connection.[58]

In short, Siragusa lied blatantly to Moldea when he claimed that "we put an end to the traffic in the early 1950s."[59] The Canadian account of the trafficking is a continuous one, from 1946, when Luciano and Coppola were strategically deported to Italy, down to 1976, when the book was written; indeed the traffic has continued to involve Montreal and the Detroit Teamsters down to the present day.[60] With or without the assistance of the Cotronis, French Corsicans continued for over twenty years to supply Luciano's Mafia connections in New York, and when necessary to meet with them directly.[61]

One also learns from Canadian sources that an early source of Luciano's drugs was "medical supplies destined for the U.S. military when the cases arrived in Sicily at the end of the war." This was in an era when the army employed both Vito Genovese, Luciano's eventual successor in drug trafficking, and Nicola Gentile, a trafficker and longtime informant for both the FBN and the FBI.[62]

One can guess that Siragusa was lying to Moldea for the same reason that George White lied to the Kefauver Committee, when he suggested that OSS had declined an offer of collaboration from Luciano. Both were trying to protect Operation Underworld, the wartime collaboration of OSS with Luciano, and what we have called Operation X, its postwar extension. Here the government's heavy use of what Blakey called Gentile's "rambling memoir," to present an "externalized" rather than a "symbiotic" Mafia, is both ironic and instructive. Gentile was part of Operation X; one should not be surprised that his "memoir" should serve to make Operation X invisible.

OPERATION X, THE ARMY, ROSSELLI, AND RUBY

Operation X, as we have seen it, should not be conceived of restrictedly as a CIA-Mafia connection. Indeed, Coppola and Gentile collaborated with the U.S. Army in Sicily, and as we have just seen, received drugs from it, even before the CIA was created in 1947. At least one of the U.S. mafia figures deported in 1946–47, former New Orleans mafia boss Silvestro "Sam" Carolla, was returned to Sicily on a U.S. military transport.[63]

George White's closest CIA contact, James Angleton, was still working for the U.S. Army at this time, reporting to future Army G-2 and DIA chief William Quinn.[64] And when White turned up in Italy to meet with his former OSS boss William Donovan, Donovan was not working for CIA, but for the elusive World Commerce Corporation, a private intelligence service representing wealthy Americans like Nelson Rockefeller. Donovan is said to have personally involved himself with the supply of arms for the 1947 May Day massacre in Sicily.[65] CIC (China), a subsidiary of Donovan's World Commerce Corporation, was the firm that employed mob figure Sonny Fassoulis, at the urging of army colonel (and FBN agent) Garland Williams, to procure arms for Taiwan in the period of private procurement before the Korean War.[66] From 1946 on, Major-General Charles Willoughby, General MacArthur's G-2 chief in Japan, used Japan's dope-dealing yakuza gangs to break up left-wing strikes and demonstrations, just as the CIA backed the Corsican Guérinis in Marseille.[67]

Like Operation Underworld before it, Operation X, with FBN agents at its center, operated both within and outside the CIA, and particularly with the military. This arrangement continued. In the late 1950s, U.S. Army Colonel Jack Y. Cannon or Canon, a veteran of the Willoughby-yakuza operations in Japan, penetrated Castro's guerrilla operation against Batista in Cuba.[68]

Associated with Cannon in Cuba was a U.S. Marine reservist, Gerry Patrick Hemming, whose services in 1962–63 for a mob-financed training camp of Cuban exiles in Louisiana would bring him into the fugitive world of Lee Harvey Oswald. With Hemming was another Marine reservist, future Watergate burglar Frank Sturgis, who has claimed that his "first intelligence work" was with the U.S. Army Security Agency. Yet another of these self-appointed soldiers of fortune was William A. Morgan, named by the McClellan Committee as being paid by one of the fixers (Dominic Bartone) in Jimmy Hoffa's mysterious (and possibly intelligence-related) Caribbean plane deals.[69]

Castro appears to have accepted the service of Cannon, Hemming, and also Sturgis, because of their ability to procure surplus or allegedly stolen U.S. military supplies for his troops. Hoffa and mob casino operator Norman Rothman both were part of this arms flow, for which in exchange Castro initially selected Sturgis, a Rothman associate, to be his liaison in 1959 with the Havana casinos.[70]

In 1962, when Rosselli was assigned by the CIA's William Harvey to assassinate Castro, Army Captain Bradley Ayers (himself assigned to work with CIA), thought and later wrote of him as " 'Colonel' Rosselli," even though Rosselli, despite his lack of CIA credentials, "had virtual carte-blanche into the highest levels" of the CIA's JM-WAVE station in Miami.[71]

We have seen, when talking of Oswald and the fruit companies, that Rosselli's government work had begun much earlier than the Bay of

Pigs, probably about the time he met CIA operative Robert Maheu in the middle 1950s.[72] Maheu's CIA-linked detective agency, Robert A. Maheu Associates, was set up in the offices of lawyer Edward Bennett Williams, and had already been involved in a murder contract, along with New Jersey mobster "Bayonne" Joe Zicarelli, against a critic of Dominican Republic dictator Rafael Leonidas Trujillo.[73]

At this time Rosselli also went to Havana, where his contacts seem to have been made through his prewar work for Moe Annenberg's wire service. Blakey chose to link Rosselli to Trafficante, by citing his "management role" in the Havana Sans Souci casino.[74] More pertinent was probably the fact that the Sans Souci was operated, at this time, by Dave Yaras and Lenny Patrick, the suspected killers of James Ragen (9 AH 948). Also at this time, Rosselli's most constant companion was "Major" Charles "Babe" Baron, a suspected murderer who was also a brigadier-general in the Illinois National Guard.[75] Baron was a protégé of Chicago Democratic machine leader Jake Arvey, as were Yaras and Patrick; and an even closer friend of Patrick Hoy, the Henry Crown employee at General Dynamics who arranged for Sidney Korshak to work for Hilton Hotels.[76] Hoy was also the general manager of the Sherman Hotel in Chicago, a hangout frequented by Ruby and Jones in 1947 (22 WH 366; 24 WH 518).

There have been a number of stories linking Ruby, and his casino operator friend Lewis McWillie, to arms trafficking to Cuba, one of which involved an eyewitness account of a meeting in Dallas between Ruby and a U.S. army colonel in uniform.[77] After Ruby had been convicted of Oswald's murder, he reportedly told a friend in his jail cell, "They're going to find out about Cuba. They're going to find out about the guns, find out about New Orleans, find out about everything."[78]

What is certain is that, when Ruby visited him in 1959, McWillie was by his own account manager of Meyer Lansky's Tropicana casino in Havana (5 AH 20; 9 AH 802). Norman Rothman, the architect of the syndicate arms smuggling with which Ruby was said to have been involved, was said to be a co-owner of the Tropicana, although this claim was ignored by the House Committee.[79]

One might think that, since his predecessor Dino Cellini came to know both Lansky brothers well as the Tropicana's manager, McWillie, too, must have known them both well. McWillie however admitted only to knowing both Cellini and Jake Lansky ("very fine man"), claiming that he "never laid eyes on" Meyer Lansky in his life (5 AH

109–10). Nevertheless, McWillie, at the time of the assassination, was working at the Thunderbird in Las Vegas, where the Lansky brothers also had an interest (23 WH 163, 172). In other words, McWillie was working for the Lanskys when Ruby made seven phone calls to him in 1963.

But the key link between Ruby and Operation X may even have been Rosselli himself, at whose Santa Anita racetrack Ruby had worked in the 1930s.[80] Scott Malone, an investigator with good government sources, has said that in early October 1963 there were two meetings in Miami between Ruby and Rosselli.[81] According to Malone, Rosselli told a close friend that "Ruby was hooked up with Trafficante in the rackets in Havana."[82]

The House Committee heard stories of a Ruby-Trafficante meeting in Havana, and judged them to be circumstantial evidence making such a meeting "a distinct possibility" (AR 153). But what had been reported by their major source for Ruby's movements in Havana, Ruby's casino-operator friend Lewis McWillie, involved very much more than a possible meeting with Trafficante. McWillie had gone out to Trescornia, a luxury prison where Castro had detained a small group of mob figures involved in Operation X; and McWillie conceded reluctantly that "Jack Ruby could have been out there one time with me" (5 AH 167).

McWillie had gone to Trescornia "to see a fellow named Guiseppe. He had been a dealer around the Capri [where McWillie was manager] and he was a fanatic gambler, gambled his money away" (5 AH 163). Besides seeing Trafficante, McWillie recalled seeing "Jake Lansky, Dino Cellini, and Guiseppe" (5 AH 165), whom he identified, after prodding, as "Guiseppe de George" (5 AH 163).

In its tortuous search for links between the Kennedy assassination and the CIA-Mafia plots (10 AH 147–95), the Committee made no reference to this visit, at which Ruby, it conceded, may have been present. Yet Dino Cellini was involved in the anti-Castro plotting (10 AH 171), as was Jake Lansky's brother Meyer (10 AH 171), the man who had put together both the World War II Mexican connection with Happy Meltzer, and the postwar Luciano-Corsican connection which we have called Operation X.

This "Guiseppe," the "primary reason" (5 AH 109) for McWillie's visit, was Giuseppe de Giorgio, alias Pierre Canavese (5 AH 325), named in the Senate narcotics hearings as one of the two chief couriers for the Italian-Corsican-Cotroni connection, traveling between Italy, France, the United States, Canada, and Cuba.[83] Ruby may even have had business to negotiate with de Giorgio, because of the couriers' connection to a case at that time concerning stolen Canadian securities. This was a case against one of the Cotronis, one of the CIA's mob contacts, Sam Mannarino, and Norman Rothman, represented by Ruby's longtime associate and former lawyer, Luis Kutner.[84]

But the Committee was interested only in a meeting between Ruby and Trafficante, not these other figures who might have indicated a higher-level link between Ruby and Operation X. A symptom of this disinterest is the index of over one hundred names which the Committee prepared from a preliminary deposition of McWillie. In this list, the name of de Giorgio, the "primary reason" for the Trescornia visit, is omitted (5 AH 13–14). By itself, this could well be a coincidence. The alert reader will recall from Chapter 3, however, that the best-documented instance of an FBI cover-up was the order from FBI headquarters in 1963 vetoing a proposal to reinterview John Wilson-Hudson, at that time the only known witness to Ruby's Trescornia visit.

In general, as we have seen, the House Committee in 1978, like the FBI in 1963, systematically averted its eyes from Ruby's connections to the protected narcotics traffic. It is time to hypothesize that what made this topic unmentionable was an illicit connection between that traffic, the U.S. government, and the assassination.

ELEVEN

Blakey and the Politics of Fighting Crime

A PREFATORY NOTE: BIAS AND CONTRIVED BIAS

This chapter will take a closer look at the House Committee's biased determination to reduce Ruby's crime contacts to the FBI-Justice crime model of an Italian "Cosa Nostra." To make the accusation of bias is of course to invite retribution; no one, perhaps not even God, can be free from all bias. It is only natural that Senator Kefauver's crime hearings should focus on the Mafia and men like Marcello, while going lightly on the Teamsters, so strong in his own state of Tennessee. Later, Senator McClellan would focus on the Teamsters at the expense of Marcello, who was strong in *his* own state of Arkansas. Nor does one have to be a senator to exhibit such natural bias. I myself was guilty of it in my earlier parapolitical researches into links between the CIA and the conspiratorial right; it was some time before I began to discern similar deep political underpinnings to the careers of liberal Democrats as well.

Our human capacity for denial in such matters is universal. The late Sidney Lens, a man of the highest probity and ideals, managed to write an entire history of the U.S. labor movement without once mentioning the role of organized crime. But we must distinguish between the unconscious bias which is the product of innocent self-deception, the semi-conscious bias which is the product of self-adaptation to bureaucratic groupthink, and the conscious bias, or what might be called contrived bias, the purpose of which is to deceive others. Readers of the following section will have to decide for themselves the extent to which the performance of the House Committee exhibits an unconscious or a conscious bias.

THE COMMITTEE'S TAKE ON RUBY:
STUDY "LA COSA NOSTRA"

In the House Committee's flawed account of organized crime, one is struck by their aversion to the interrelated stories of drug trafficking, the Teamsters, and the wire-service wars. The most glaring instance is the "History of Organized Crime in the United States," commissioned by the Committee from Ralph Salerno, part of a "consultant's report" which was admittedly censored by the Committee, because (among other factors) it "contained allegations of gross personal immorality involving a variety of public figures" (9 AH 3). In its published form, there is not a word about the wire-service wars; and the reason for this is the law-enforcement habit, grounded in the Valachi testimony (see 9 AH 15–18), of raising the topic of "organized crime" (9 AH 3) and then switching to "La Cosa Nostra" (9 AH 16) and its national "commission" (9 AH 18).

The Committee justified this by a stunning exhibition of bureaucratic doublethink:

> A major reason for suspecting conspiracy was Oswald's murder by Jack Ruby. Organized crime—specifically the national syndicate known as La Cosa Nostra or the mafia—was a logical choice for study. A number of leads to organized crime existed, mostly through Ruby:
>
> —Ruby had moved from Chicago to Dallas in 1946, at a time when the Mafia was said to be moving into that city. It has been alleged that Ruby was a front man. . . .
> —Ruby had made several unexplained phone calls to underworld figures in the months preceding the assassination.
>
> (9 AH iii; cf. AR 160)

Only from officials can logic like this be encountered. Oswald was killed by Ruby, a Jew; therefore, we should study La Cosa Nostra. Fifteen Chicago mobsters (according to the same memo, 9 AH 155) move into Dallas; only three of these are Italian; nine were Jewish (including Dave Yaras's brother Sam Yaras, who also knew Ruby); therefore we should study La Cosa Nostra.[1] Ruby called (according to the staff report, 9 AH 192–96) seven or eight "suspicious" (i.e., mob-linked) individuals; only one of these was Italian; therefore we should study the Italian mafia.[2]

Blakey's book gives a more sophisticated and less racial account of what he calls the "national syndicate" of organized crime. At times his version of what happened seems to diverge significantly from Salerno's, as when he quotes the account (from a first-hand but controversial witness, Edward Grady Partin) of a 1962 conversation "in which Hoffa had talked about assassinating Robert Kennedy."[3] But it still relies heavily on Valachi, and in the end his model for the "national structure" of organized crime, like that of the House Committee Report, is still the so-called *commissione* of La Cosa Nostra.[4]

An example of the reductionism in this externalized projection is his account of Ruby's suspicious phone calls in 1963, which he analyzes in terms of organized crime, rather than the Teamsters. Blakey's list of such calls was a short one already familiar to researchers and drawn to the Committee's attention: twelve calls involving five individuals— Lewis McWillie (7 calls), Irwin Weiner (1), Nofio Pecora (1), Barney Baker (2), Murray "Dusty" Miller (1).[5]

These calls, along with some others, had been originally identified in 1964 by Burt Griffin, an alert staffer with the Warren Commission. The Committee's one significant piece of new information, an important but politically neutral one, was to pinpoint a "significant upsurge" in the total number of Ruby's long-distance phone calls in the weeks before the assassination, and to graph a similar upsurge in the "suspicious" phone calls as well (4 AH 561).

Blakey's book calls the recipients of these calls "individuals who have been identified as being in some way associated with organized crime" (4 AH 562). But three of these five men (Weiner, Baker, and Miller) were conspicuously identified, not with La Cosa Nostra, but with the Teamsters. (Baker had actually begun his Teamster career by helping a progressive Teamster official, Harold Gibbons, fight the Italian mafia in St. Louis.)[6] Furthermore, as I argued years ago in *Crime and Cover-Up*, these men were not just Hoffa associates, but associates with strong political connections inside both political parties. Once when Baker was arrested he was found to be carrying on his person the unlisted telephone number of New York governor Averell Harriman.[7]

As is recorded in a book by Walter Sheridan, the head of Robert Kennedy's so-called "Get Hoffa" squad in the U.S. Justice Department,

Baker and Weiner had been targeted, along with Hoffa, in Robert Kennedy's vigorous campaign to purge criminals from the Teamsters (and, not coincidentally, from the Democratic party).

Blakey knew of such matters from his own years of service under Kennedy in the Justice Department. His book opens with a poignant, and obviously sincere, recollection of spending the morning of November 22, 1963, with Robert Kennedy, as a young prosecutor "about to be assigned to a field unit [in Chicago, Weiner's city] in the government's stepped-up drive on organized crime." Blakey would have worked on the contemplated prosecution of Sam Giancana, whose son-in-law (Anthony Tisci) was on the payroll of a congressman (Roland Libonati) lobbying in Hoffa's defense. But, as Blakey notes wryly, "The meeting was not reconvened, and I never made it to Chicago."[8]

Blakey's projection of organized crime as a nationally organized enemy clearly derives from that of his mentor Bobby Kennedy, the author of *The Enemy Within,* and the man who ordered the FBI to go into organized crime "like they went into the Communist Party."[9]

Despite his good memories of Robert Kennedy, Blakey obviously does not share his former boss's penchant for seeing the world in the light of Jimmy Hoffa. In his brief account of Kennedy's "Get Hoffa" campaign, he relies principally on Sheridan's book; yet he omits the very relevant fact that Baker, Weiner, and Miller, whom Ruby phoned shortly before the assassination, are all prominent in Sheridan's account of the war between Hoffa and Bobby Kennedy, the latter two in his narration of late 1963.[10] In Blakey's account, Miller is never introduced by his title, the head of the Southern Conference of Teamsters; instead, he is introduced only twice, first as one of "several syndicate figures" (a possible libel?), and then as "a Hoffa associate with links to organized-crime figures."[11]

THE POLITICS OF TARGETING:
LA COSA NOSTRA VERSUS THE TEAMSTERS

As noted earlier, the most logical common denominator for investigating Ruby's phone calls would have been corrupt unionism, above all in the Teamsters. But the Committee's much-touted computer analysis had effaced, rather than clarified, Ruby's interest in the Teamsters. It ignored, for example, Ruby's telephone call to Oscar Mauzy, leader of the

Dallas liberal Democrats, and the law partner of Nat Wells, a former court-appointed monitor of the Teamsters (WCD 1254).[12]

Such a phone call was hardly relevant to the pursuit of La Cosa Nostra. But it would, I am sure, have interested Walter Sheridan, who had gone to Dallas in 1962, "at Wells' invitation, to talk to him and [Murray] Miller about the grand jury investigation we had in progress there at the time." Sheridan's next contact with Miller was on November 7, 1963, when Miller visited Sheridan in his Washington office.[13] This was the day of Ruby's first phone call with Barney Baker, and the day before Ruby's two successive phone calls with Miller and Baker.

In Salerno's fifty-eight-page "History of Organized Crime," there are only three trivial references to the Teamsters. The first concerns a contribution "for a camp for the underprivileged, sponsored by [Congressman Roland] Libonati" transmitted by "Murray Humphreys, a Chicago mob figure," from a Teamsters vice-president, "for favors in Congress" (9 AH 22). The second concerns information from a wiretap to the effect that Milwaukee mafia leader Frank Balistrieri might go to jail "so as not to jeopardize his position with the International Brotherhood of Teamsters" (9 AH 31). The third summarizes a conversation in October 1963 between Sam Giancana and three of his Chicago mafia associates, one of whom "spoke of the possibility of the Teamsters Union going back into the AFL—it would hurt Kennedy if they were to take Hoffa back" (9 AH 42).

This "history" was in effect a rewriting of history, to delete the Bobby Kennedy agenda for fighting crime. Take for example the Apalachin meeting of November 1957, which had given rise to the McClellan hearings (with Bobby Kennedy as counsel) into the subject of labor racketeering. The McClellan Committee's analysis of Apalachin, as summarized by Sheridan, noted that, of fifty-eight men known to have attended, "twenty-two had been involved in either labor unions [including the Teamsters] or labor-management activities."[14] In the House Committee history, "labor union matters" is the last item of a four-item agenda, and the Teamsters are not mentioned: "Many of those attending were involved in legitimate businesses. . . . Their profits were being threatened by a nonunion enclave of manufacturing shops that had sprung up in the anthracite coal mining region of northeast Pennsylvania, when mining declined" (9 AH 9). Nor is there any mention of the Teamsters when the Apalachin meeting is discussed in Blakey's book.[15]

By such rewritings, the Committee's staff "history" suppressed the intertwined stories of Patrick, Yaras and the wire service, Dorfman and the Teamsters. We learn from it that the FBI was aware of organized criminal "Control and Domination of Police Agencies" (9 AH 10). But as for corruption, or even symbiosis, on a higher level, its concerns seem to be limited to Italians in or from Chicago (9 AH 14, 22–25). Meanwhile the "history" served up such standard official fare for congressional committees (wholly irrelevant to the Ruby story) as the admitted myth of the mafia "Sicilian Vespers massacre" of 1931.[16]

What Robert Kennedy had meant by the "syndicate" was very different from what Salerno meant by La Cosa Nostra. In saying this I must repeat what I said earlier, that anyone speaking about organized crime from a Justice Department or congressional perspective does so under conditions of great political constraint. The Sheridan account of Bobby Kennedy's war on organized crime, so dramatically different from Blakey's, is by no means flawless: it omits such obviously relevant names as those of Meyer Lansky, Barney Baker's former employer; and Dave Yaras, who had used Barney Baker to set up Teamster Local 320 in Miami.

However limited, Sheridan's account of organized crime is a reasonable facsimile of Bobby Kennedy's. It focuses on the Teamsters, to which it subordinates the question of the Mafia. By overriding this focus with Valachi's testimony about La Cosa Nostra, it could be said that Blakey and Salerno in effect replaced the Kennedy agenda for fighting crime with that of Bobby's dangerous rival, J. Edgar Hoover.[17]

PROTECTING A WITNESS: EDWARD PARTIN, THE TRIAL OF HOFFA, AND THE ASSASSINATION

But one can imagine that Blakey and the Committee chose the discredited Valachi scenario for organized crime, not to betray Bobby Kennedy's memory, but to protect it. Kennedy's first conviction of Hoffa, for jury tampering in Chattanooga, had been secured on the hotly disputed basis of the testimony of a Louisiana Teamster official, Edward Grady Partin. Sheridan felt that Dusty Miller's visit to him on November 7, 1963, was "to feel us out about Partin," at that stage still a secret witness.

The Chattanooga trial began in January 1964, when John Kennedy was gone but his brother was still a lame-duck attorney general. In the same month the Warren Commission began to crank up its own investigation; and in numerous small ways, too petty to examine here, some of the individuals involved in the trial began to be named in connection with either Ruby or Oswald, in reports reaching the Commission.

To judge by their sources, some of these stories appear to have been planted by Hoffa's supporters, in an effort to disrupt the Justice Department's case against their client, or even to blackmail the government's witnesses.[18] One of these stories, however, appears to be possibly true, extremely sensitive, and (according to Sheridan) an eventual factor in what he called the "intrigue" of the Garrison investigation of the Kennedy case.[19]

It is the claim that Partin, quoted in Blakey's book for his allegation that "Hoffa had talked about assassinating Robert Kennedy," was himself somehow involved with those implicated in the Kennedy assassination. This claim about Partin has taken various forms. One version is that Partin knew Ruby (and perhaps even Oswald), from their common activity in smuggling arms to Cuba. The story has been told in various ways: in one version (attributed to Hoffa's lobbyist I. Irving Davidson) there may have even been a photograph of "Partin in the presence of Jack Ruby."[20] Another version is that Partin's Cuban activities had involved David Ferrie, an alleged associate of Oswald, whom Jim Garrison later named, on very questionable evidence, as a key conspirator in the Kennedy assassination. All that need concern us here is that Jack Martin, the associate of Guy Banister who denounced David Ferrie to Garrison's investigators (10 AH 105), became (according to Sheridan) part of the well-organized campaign to pressure Partin on behalf of Hoffa.[21]

Whether or not there is any truth to these allegations about Partin, they seem to have affected both the conduct of Hoffa's Chattanooga trial and the subsequent history of inquiries, including both Garrison's (anti-Partin) and Blakey's (presumably pro-Partin), into the Kennedy assassination. One can perhaps believe Partin's own assurance to investigators that he never knew Ruby (who clearly is part of the JFK murder story). As to whether or not he knew Ferrie (not so clearly involved), the record is more murky.

As for smuggling arms to Cuba, Partin has since admitted it: "I was right up there on several occasions when they were loading the guns. . . . Hoffa was directing the whole thing."[22] His account of the smuggling named three Teamster organizers, Hoffa, William Presser, and I. Irving Davidson, "a dapper Washington public relations man who did business with government officials in Israel and Latin America."[23] (It was Davidson who may have been involved in Haiti with George de Mohrenschildt and Clemard Charles [see Chapter 5], and who in 1967 let the FBI know that he had heard of a photo showing Partin in the presence of Jack Ruby.)

The story that Ferrie was once Partin's pilot, however, seems for whatever reason to have been taken very seriously by Partin and his government protectors, notably Walter Sheridan, in 1967. This was after Jim Garrison launched his investigation of Ferrie and the Kennedy assassination, which, in the view of Sheridan and Moldea, "became an ideal means of intimidating Partin."[24]

Both Partin and Sheridan moved to Louisiana in 1967, in reaction to the rumors leaking out of the Garrison office that Partin would be named. A June 1967 radio broadcast, claiming that Garrison had linked Ruby and Oswald to Partin, left Partin scared:

> "Soon after that, [Hoffa's attorney] Frank Ragano called me," Partin says, "and he said he could get Garrison off my back. In return he wanted a signed affidavit saying that I lied in Hoffa's trial. Naturally I didn't sign. But later it came out that Ragano was in touch with both Trafficante and Marcello during that period of time."[25]

If it is true that the Garrison investigation was being used to pressure Partin, and that Partin knew Ferrie, this would offer a hidden motive behind those who denounced Ferrie, on no clear evidence, as being behind the assassination.[26]

The Garrison pressure on Partin is a central panel in Sheridan's story of the contest between Hoffa and Robert Kennedy. Particularly interesting, therefore, is Sheridan's inability to mention Partin's gunrunning to Cuba for Hoffa. On February 27, 1964, Hoffa's defense attorneys asked a character witness for Partin, Victor Bussie, "Are you aware that Partin was under investigation for smuggling arms to Cuba?"[27] The judge would not allow the question; and, when he was insistent, the defense responded by moving for a mistrial. In his book Sheridan described the dramatic scene, but omitted the question, as did those "responsible" newspapers the Washington Post and the New York Times.

The question reached a national audience, however, thanks to Congressman Libonati, the congressman who employed Giancana's son-in-law. Libonati placed the *Chicago Tribune* story of the trial, which did repeat the forbidden question, in the *Congressional Record*.[28] Soon after, Fred Cook would write in the *Nation* that Partin had been training and gunrunning for Castro; this story too would be placed in the *Congressional Record* by Libonati.[29]

"MAFIA" VERSUS "SYNDICATE":
ROBERT KENNEDY AND OPERATION X

What the protracted struggle between Robert Kennedy and Jimmy Hoffa shows, as I have written before, is that organized crime is deeply embedded in American society, and that its opponents must therefore adopt an aggressive political strategy for fighting it. All too often, the FBN, FBI, and IRS have made convictions of marginal organized criminals, by tolerating criminals at a higher level whom they have used as informants. The strategy of Bobby Kennedy was much more confrontational. Kennedy also used informants, but lower-level ones, to go after figures like Jimmy Hoffa whose removal would significantly alter the structure of organized crime in America, and above all American politics.

To say this is not to make a hero of Bobby Kennedy. On the contrary, a cynical view of the Kennedys' attack on organized crime is to see it as a struggle for dominance of the Democratic party, a campaign to weaken big mob-based city machines such as Chicago's (which had backed Adlai Stevenson) and New Orleans's (which had backed Lyndon Johnson).

An extreme reduction of Kennedy gang-busting to political vendetta was made during a 1970 interview between Carlos Marcello and respected crime writer Michael Dorman. An unnamed racketeer, who was present at the interview because he had helped set it up, argued:

> You know, the Federal government has been harassing Carlos [Marcello] for the last ten years, and it's all because of politics. . . . In 1960, when Bobby Kennedy was managing his brother's presidential campaign, he sent a guy down here to see Carlos. This was before the Democratic National Convention. He wanted Carlos to use his influence to swing the Louisiana delegation for Kennedy at the convention. Carlos said that he was sorry, but that he'd already promised his support at the convention to Lyndon Johnson. The Louisiana delegation went for Johnson. Even though Jack Kennedy got the nomination and picked Johnson for Vice President, Bobby was pissed off

at Carlos and promised he'd get even. When he became attorney general, the first thing he did was start a campaign to put Jimmy Hoffa in the pen. The second thing he did was go after Carlos's ass. . . . All the Feds have been harassing Carlos ever since. . . . Once these things get started in Washington, it's hard to stop them no matter who's President.[30]

A different account of the Marcello-Kennedy split in 1960 is that Marcello, a supporter of Jimmy Hoffa, was throwing big money at both the Democrats and the Republicans to defeat Hoffa's biggest political enemies, the Kennedy brothers. Edward Partin has since claimed to have been present at a September 1960 meeting between Carlos Marcello, Irving Davidson, and Hoffa, at which a suitcase containing $500,000 was passed from Marcello to Hoffa for the election of Richard Nixon.[31] There is no doubt that in 1966–67 Marcello, his lawyer G. Wray Gill, Senator Russell Long from Louisiana, and Irving Davidson were part of a concerted effort to acquit Hoffa by pressuring Partin to change his testimony in the Chattanooga jury-tampering trial. Central to this effort was an alleged $1 million in mob money to secure Hoffa's release. The money was said to be administered by Paul Dorfman's stepson and close associate, Allen Dorfman, one of the defendants with Hoffa in the 1963 jury-tampering case. Partin was informed of Dorfman's million by D'Alton Smith, a Marcello associate who was the brother-in-law of Ruby's phone contact Nofio Pecora.[32] (Senator Long and G. Wray Gill were also important in laying the foundations for the Jim Garrison investigation which became part of this dispute.)

Certainly Marcello, Davidson, and Jimmy Hoffa supported elements in the Democratic party to which the Kennedys were opposed. But the same conflict can also be seen from a Kennedy viewpoint. One reason why the Kennedy strategy to "get" Hoffa became devious, and focused on a case in Tennessee instead of larger cases in Michigan, was that Hoffa's longtime attorney George S. Fitzgerald had been for some years a Democratic national committeeman from Michigan, and had helped place politically sympathetic judges on the federal bench in that state.[33]

Reformers and civil libertarians will continue to disagree about the rights and wrongs of the Kennedy-Hoffa struggle; certainly each side cut moral corners, convinced that it was facing a ruthless opponent. Three favorable things can be said, however, about the model of organized crime as a "syndicate" which Robert Kennedy projected, when compared to the competing bureaucratic models of organized crime as a "Mafia" (from the FBN via the Kefauver Committee) or "La Cosa Nostra" (from the FBI via the Valachi hearings):

1.   Whatever its shortcomings, the "syndicate" model was less ideologically distorted than either the "Mafia" or "LCN" model.

2.   The Kennedy campaign against the "syndicate" resulted in the highest-level convictions since those of Annenberg and Luciano (also for political reasons) in the 1930s.

3.   Whether or not he knew it, Robert Kennedy, by targeting Jimmy Hoffa, Meyer Lansky, and related figures such as Paul and Allen Dorfman, Barney Baker, Sam Giancana, Johnny Dioguardi, James Plumeri, and Irwin Weiner, had targeted the milieu of "Operation X," where intelligence connections facilitated the flow of drugs into this country.

A small but relevant corollary to the last point is that, without knowing it, Robert Kennedy had targeted men (like Paul Dorfman, Barney Baker, and Irwin Weiner) from the milieu of a man he was not yet aware of, namely Jack Ruby.

It is relevant that Kennedy did not use the word "Mafia" when presenting, in his 1960 book *The Enemy Within,* his model of organized crime as an endemic, multi-ethnic, partially institutionalized syndicate ("The gangsters of today work in a highly organized fashion and are far more powerful now than at any time in the history of the country. They control political figures and threaten whole communities. They have stretched their tentacles of corruption and fear into industries both large and small").[34]

Compared to this model, both the FBN "Mafia" model and the FBI "LCN" can be seen as bureaucratically self-serving, designed to exempt from scrutiny their chief informants and collaborators in the underworld. It is particularly striking that the Kefauver Committee, for all the "Mafia" and narcotics talk fed to it by its special consultant George White, targeted only one of the Operation X mafiosi about which White and Siragusa were by 1950 knowledgeable.[35] Instead the "Mafia" attacked by the Kefauver Committee were losers like Paul Jones, Nick de John, and the La Ducas of Kansas City, possibly because the Kansas City mob had tried, and failed, to take over the crumbling Pendergast political machine of that city which had promoted Harry Truman.[36] Though there were many diverse political forces at work to distort the Kefauver Committee Report, one can still say that the "mafia" presented therein, far from being a revelation of Operation X, was virtually a cover for it.

Much the same must be said of the La Cosa Nostra model, virtually composed for Valachi by the FBI, which took over in the Justice Department following President Kennedy's murder and his brother's resignation. Hank Messick has carefully reconstructed how the FBN supplied Valachi to the FBI as an informant, and how the FBI, disappointed with the limited area of Valachi's personal experience, supplied him with a copy of the manuscript prepared for the FBN by Operation X veteran Nicola Gentile "to supplement his education."[37] The new (and probably invented) name "La Cosa Nostra" enabled Hoover (who had always scoffed at the Anslinger/FBN talk of a "Mafia") to join the Justice Department's stepped-up war on organized crime under Bobby Kennedy. But it was the FBN's "Mafia" that was described by Valachi and the FBI, with big names like Lansky and Yaras either omitted altogether or subordinated to the minor category of "non-member associates."[38]

With the death of John Kennedy, the "LCN" model came gradually to displace the old RFK syndicate-Teamster model of organized crime. How much this change of thinking eviscerated serious law enforcement has been disputed. Blakey speaks for many when he says that "the organized-crime program faltered after the President's death."[39] Although the Justice Department followed through on key Kennedy cases, such as those against Hoffa, Plumeri, and Weiner, charts of the Justice Department organized-crime program show a falling-off after 1964 in almost all the key areas: in the number of convictions, attorneys employed, days in court, days in the field, and (after 1963) days in grand jury (9 AH 21).

When Blakey and the House Committee used the "LCN" model, the result was an oblique and trivial investigation of the Barney Baker–Irwin Weiner–Dave Yaras–Jack Ruby milieu. Virtually omitted was any reference to what we have called Operation X, the ongoing, drug-fueled, intelligence-mob connection.

THE INTELLIGENCE-MOB CONNECTION
AND THE DEATH OF KENNEDY

To sum up, it would appear that Bobby Kennedy, consciously or not, had targeted a number of figures, such as Sam Giancana, James Plumeri, and perhaps even Jimmy Hoffa, who were simultaneously in-

telligence assets. Well-placed informants and/or their government handlers have furthermore implicated members of this intelligence-mob
connection in the coalition of forces that retaliated by killing the President. The House Committee Report, steadfastly refusing to look at
Ruby's very pronounced connection to this intelligence-mob milieu,
provided instead a distorted governmental account of "La Cosa Nostra," from which the intelligence connections had been systematically
expunged. But if Blakey was responsible in repeating the opinion that
those who killed Kennedy killed Giancana as well, it becomes even
more important to know who was the "CIA guy," who (according to
FBN and DEA informant Charles Crimaldi) used someone from the underworld to kill Giancana.

After so many years, some of the mob members of this milieu are
now notorious—notably John Rosselli, Santos Trafficante, Carlos Marcello, and Sam Giancana. Others—Barney Baker, Dave Yaras, Irwin
Weiner—have been known for years to researchers. About the "CIA
guy" implicated by Crimaldi, we know much less.

Moldea, the author who reported Crimaldi's remarks, also wrote
that "a trusted underworld informant who was close to [Giancana] told
a House committee investigating the CIA that Sam Giancana was ex-
ecuted by underworld associates who had also been involved in the
[anti-Castro] assassination plots."[40] This informant would appear to
be Crimaldi; the House committee is certainly the Pike Committee, the
only committee ever prevented (probably by CIA intervention) from
presenting its completed report to Congress.[41] If this informant is
Crimaldi, then his allegations may also define the "CIA guy" as someone involved in the CIA-Mafia plots against Castro.

If we focus narrowly on those plots as officially narrated, e.g., by the
Church Committee, then the CIA men involved would include Bill
Harvey, Desmond FitzGerald, Sheffield Edwards, Jim O'Connell, Miami Station Chief Ted Shackley, or possibly the contract officer Robert
Maheu. But of this partial list, only a few are known to have had the
intimate, ongoing relationship to mob figures which would make such
conspiring conceivable.

There were, however, others in the CIA, such as Jim Angleton,
George White, and Mario Brod, whose relationships to the mob lasted
over decades, and were inherently conspiratorial even when on official
operations. Angleton had been SSU chief in Italy under Army Lieuten-

ant Colonel William Quinn when the U.S. mafia deportees were turned against the Communists in Sicily, and he continued to use such "Operation X" connections, at least for intelligence, in years thereafter. Of particular relevance here are Angleton's ongoing contacts with George White, one of the principal FBN architects of Operation X.[42]

In particular, Angleton developed a "close and mutually beneficial association" with Jay Lovestone of the AFL's Free Trade Union Committee, set up in 1944 by Lovestone's sponsor, Dave Dubinsky of the International Ladies Garment Workers' Union.[43] Lovestone and Irving Brown of the AFL (later AFL-CIO) Free Trade Union Committee had passed funds from the ILGWU and later the CIA to French strong-arm gangs on the Marseille waterfront, which in turn worked with the Corsican heroin labs and traffickers integrated by Meyer Lansky into the Luciano-Coppola-Gentile drug-trafficking network.[44]

The AFL, and Dubinsky in particular, had of course been dealing with anti-Communist mob figures in New York for many years, before reaching out to their opposite numbers in Marseille.[45] Angleton appears to have been have been interested in mob intelligence from both sides of the Atlantic. As we shall soon see, he also used Mario Brod for his American mafia contacts, which led to Brod's appearance as a character witness for veterans of the Hoffa-centered anti-Castro plots.

In 1976, after his retirement, Angleton told an investigator that he knew which mob figures, from the New York and Chicago mafia families, had killed Sam Giancana. He also blamed the Church Committee for causing the death of Giancana and Rosselli, by demanding testimony concerning topics on which the mafia code of silence (*omertá*) could not be broken.

Most interestingly, he intimated that Harvey had been concerned about what Giancana might tell the Church Committee. Angleton spoke as if he, not Harvey, was the man on the inside, and knew what would happen: "I warned Bill that Giancana would not appear."[46]

Jim Angleton figures prominently in other phases of the Kennedy assassination background as well, particularly through his programs of mail interception, which had picked up Lee Harvey Oswald from the time of his visit to the Soviet Union.[47] It was Angleton's counter-intelligence staff who drew attention to Oswald's alleged contacts in Mexico City with Valery Kostikov, a Soviet KGB station chief and suspected assassination specialist.[48]

Finally, there is the recurring presence of Angleton in the background of the Warren Commission investigation. For a while, Angleton himself was responsible for all CIA dealings with the Warren Commission, and he enjoyed an unusually close, extra-institutional relationship with former CIA Director Allen Dulles, the most active member of the Warren Commission.[49] Angleton apparently manipulated two ongoing CIA operations (one with Russian KGB defectors Golitsyn and Nosenko, a second with potential Cuban assassin "AMLASH," or Rolando Cubela Secades) in such a way as to virtually guarantee a cover-up of the Kennedy assassination.[50] And, as we have seen, when the Mexican CIA station chief died in 1971, years after his retirement, Angleton flew to Mexico City, rifled the family safe, and removed key documents on the CIA's handling of Oswald.[51]

But before we conclude that we have reached the center of the assassination mystery, we must recall that military intelligence, as well as the CIA, had made operational use of the mob. And before returning to the role of military personnel in Dealey Plaza, we must see how Ruby's connections, like Oswald's, cannot be simply reduced to the dimensions of organized crime and intelligence, but were on the contrary located in the deep economic and political structure of his adopted city, Dallas.

TWELVE

Ruby, Narcotics, and the Establishment

When we compare the world of Ruby to that of Oswald, we are struck by the common milieu shared by these two men who may never have met each other: namely, the realm where intelligence and mob intersect. In the case of Oswald, his known connections helped define more clearly a solution to the enigma of what Oswald was up to in New Orleans. Because he was a marginalized individual with relatively few business or personal contacts, it is relatively easy to identify those who might have manipulated his behavior and directed the hidden agenda for his brief and striking burst of media appearances in that city.

In exploring Oswald's intelligence-mob milieu, moreover, we saw that it involved not only intelligence veterans (notably former FBI agent Guy Banister at the notorious 544 Camp Street address) and mob associates (his uncle and father-figure "Dutz" Murret, like Ruby a former boxer and gambler), but men from corporations, notably the two great banana companies Standard Fruit and United Fruit, whose dominance of Central America depended on both intelligence and mob figures, especially those with links to the narcotics traffic. The key men in this last category may have been John Rosselli and his 1963 roommate, John Martino, two men whom Ruby is alleged to have known as well.

The full solution to the Ruby enigma, I am satisfied, would involve his contacts not just in the worlds of intelligence and organized crime but from the business establishment as well. Some critics have even attempted to reconstruct a possible conspiracy by retracing Ruby's contacts with business figures, notably his apparent visit on November 21 to the offices of Lamar Hunt, the son of the right-wing Texas oilman, H. L. Hunt, an extreme and vocal foe of President Kennedy.[1]

Unfortunately, Ruby, in contrast to Oswald, did not appear to lead the life of a "loner"; and his contacts with the overworld, far from being meager and easily enumerated, are so manifold as to defy enumeration. If, however, we restrict our focus to the negative template of such contacts, to those overworld contacts which the official investigations suppressed or obscured, then we get a much clearer picture: that Ruby was in contact, up to the very hours before the assassination, with establishment figures who in turn interfaced with the intelligence-mob connection.

Let us begin with a few examples where the facts have been clearly distorted or suppressed.

RUBY, ZOPPI, AND LAS VEGAS

The House Committee Chronology of Ruby's movements on Friday, November 22, 1963, reports, deadpan, Ruby's own story to the FBI that, just before the assassination, Ruby went to the office of *Dallas Morning News* columnist Tony Zoppi, "but Zoppi was not there" (9 AH 1101). It even repeats Ruby's testimony under oath to the Warren Commission: "So I went down there Friday morning to Tony Zoppi's office, and they said he went to New Orleans for a couple of days" (9 AH 1102; 5 WH 183).[2] It did not mention the allegation by Lewis McWillie, Ruby's main contact in the Havana casinos and a friend of Zoppi's, that Ruby "was in Tony Zoppi's office right *after* [the assassination] happened and he was crying and carrying on, what I read in the paper and you did, too, I'm sure" (5 AH 38, emphasis added). As McWillie's memory is possibly confused, this omission could be quite innocent.

The problem is rather that Zoppi, by his own account, was there in his office (and not in New Orleans) when Ruby called. Zoppi reported at some length to House Committee investigators what Ruby's last words to him were that morning ("Zoppi believed him [Ruby] to be too calm that morning to have been involved in a conspiracy" [5 AH 170]).[3]

Did the House Committee notice this discrepancy? Zoppi was for them a suspect, along with Lewis McWillie. More specifically, Zoppi had in 1978 corroborated a new explanation by McWillie for Ruby's visit to him in Cuba in 1959. The Committee had so completely demolished the new story that Zoppi, at least, retracted it, admitting "that he must not have been involved in Ruby's trip to Cuba after all."[4]

Zoppi's 1978 story, even if false, reveals that, as entertainment editor for his newspaper, he knew personally not just McWillie, but a number of figures (such as Jack Entratter and Al Freeman) representing the mob's casinos in both Havana and Las Vegas.[5] Zoppi's chief contacts in Las Vegas were at the Sands, where the official greeter was Charles "Babe" Baron, the associate of Meyer Lansky and Jake Arvey who was also a general in the Illinois National Guard (5 AH 171; 9 AH 167–68).

By 1978, when the Committee interviewed him, Zoppi himself worked in Las Vegas at the Chicago mob's Riviera casino, as did Charles Baron and Ruby's early friend Dave "Dingy" Halper. It was in this interview that Zoppi revealed that Baron was a close friend of General Curtis LeMay, another well-known enemy of President Kennedy; and the Committee investigators confirmed that "Baron was visiting LeMay the following week" (5 AH 170).[6]

Inasmuch as Ruby spent two or three hours at the *Dallas Morning News* on November 22, much of it in Zoppi's office, the Committee surely failed in its own search for organized-crime links when it failed to explore the possibility that Ruby used Zoppi's office that day for liaison with Las Vegas, the city that Blakey and the Committee believed that Ruby had secretly visited the previous weekend.[7]

(The Rosselli biography records an allegation that Ruby met with Rosselli in Las Vegas that weekend; but discounts it, "as the FBI reported Rosselli in Phoenix from November 16 to 19."[8] It seems more likely that Ruby would have seen his former Cuban contact McWillie, who in late 1963 was working at Lansky's Thunderbird casino. McWillie was interviewed in Las Vegas on November 20, two days before the assassination, presumably about CIA-Mafia figure Sam Giancana's hidden ownership of the Cal-Neva Lodge on Lake Tahoe, where McWillie had worked a few months earlier).[9]

In other words, Ruby in late 1963 apparently reactivated his McWillie casino connection, which in 1959 had taken him to Cuba to see McWillie, and possibly such top "Operation X" narcotics traffickers as Santos Trafficante and Giuseppe di Giorgio. This impression is confirmed by the list of organized-crime–related phone calls made by

Ruby in the second half of 1963; of the thirteen suspicious phone calls, eight, or more than half, were placed by Ruby to McWillie or his Las Vegas work address, the Thunderbird casino (4 AH 563–64).

It is time to examine just how closely the McWillie-narcotics milieu of Havana embodied all of the influential crime connections in Ruby's Chicago background.

RUBY, CUBA, AND NARCOTICS

As early as 1946, the Jones-Chicago-Dallas connection involved Cuba; and by 1953 there was a Chicago Crime Commission report that Ruby's old acquaintances Dave Yaras and Lenny Patrick were operating the Sans Souci gambling establishment in Havana.[10] By the late 1950s the Sans Souci casino was operated by Norman "Roughhouse" Rothman, the key figure in smuggling money to the forces of Fidel Castro from the U.S. mob, and from Cuban ex-president Carlos Prío Socarras.[11] Whether or not we believe the witnesses who linked Ruby himself to Rothman's smuggling network, it is clear that Ruby was extremely close to Lewis McWillie, Rothman's employee at the Havana Sans Souci and Tropicana casinos; and Ruby visited McWillie at Rothman's Tropicana casino, most likely on mob business, in 1959.[12]

Rothman, like Jake Arvey, was allied in Cuba with the mob connection behind former Cuban president Carlos Prío Socarras. Rothman's own political clout was revealed in 1962, when he beat an indictment for his gun-running activities. The House Committee chose to disbelieve Rothman's statement to an FBI agent in 1961 that he "expected to avoid imprisonment for a 1960 gun running conviction," because the deal had been sanctioned by high-level members of the Kennedy Administration (10 AH 183). The fact remains that Rothman *did* avoid imprisonment, along with his fellow defendants Sam Mannarino of Pittsburgh and Giuseppe Cotroni of Montreal, despite their having been caught red-handed for illegally pledging $8.5 million worth of securities stolen from a Canadian bank, in what the FBI then called "the biggest burglary in the world."[13]

We have already identified Sam Mannarino as part of the CIA-Hoffa connection and Cotroni as part of the FBN-protected "Operation X." Sam Mannarino (whose brother Gabriel attended the 1957 Mafia Apalachin convention) and Cotroni (head of the Montreal mafia) were

Rothman's casino partners at the Sans Souci and Tropicana respectively. Cotroni was in addition one of the most important smugglers of Marseille heroin into the United States, both through his home city of Montreal and (like Paul Roland Jones) through Mexico.[14]

In 1978 Rothman told a CBC television interviewer that he had avoided conviction because of the CIA's interest in his gunrunning activities. This is corroborated by the CIA's intervention in an unrelated trial in 1971, when Sam Mannarino and two other mafia leaders went on trial for charges arising out of a Teamsters' Pension Fund kickback scheme. FBI men in the New York courtroom were astonished to discover that the star witness for the defense was Angleton's mafia case officer Mario Brod, following whose testimony the defendants were acquitted.[15]

A clue to the political and intelligence importance of the Rothman-Mannarino gunrunning case is the fact that Rothman's successful defense attorney was the same Luis Kutner who had intervened with Ruby in 1950 before the Kefauver Committee. Whatever his role, Kutner also was part of the wire-service war and cover-up story: in 1950 he was also representing James Ragen's avenger on the Chicago police force, Captain William Drury, who was about to testify as a witness before the Kefauver Committee when he was murdered, along with another witness, in September 1950.[16]

Kutner, by his own account, had known Ruby since 1936, when he had used Ruby to "run errands" in his unsuccessful 1936 congressional campaign. Later Kutner had inserted himself into what can only be described as international intelligence operations, ranging from Latin American coups to the defense of ousted Congolese leader Moise Tshombe. His involvement with Ruby confirms that Ruby should not just be thought of as a man with local influence with the Dallas police, but as a player in international deep politics.

RUBY, THE SICILIAN MAFIA, AND THE OIL COMPANIES

This impression is corroborated by his contact in Dallas with an attorney who, via his corporate-mafia connections, clearly played a role in the mafia's penetration of the Third World. Though this exposure may have been merely casual and anecdotal, the anecdote is worth recounting, since it demonstrates that Ruby could be exposed to a high-level corporate mob connection, as well as a political and law-enforcement mob connection.

Many books critical of the Warren Commission draw attention to Jack Ruby's fruitless appeal in Dallas to the Chief Justice of the United States Supreme Court: "Unless you get me to Washington, you can't get a fair shake out of me. . . . get me to Washington. . . . Gentlemen, my life is in danger here."[17] However, almost none of these books note that Ruby in his dialogue with Warren dropped a name of a Dallas attorney with whom he had once had dinner, apparently in an effort to collect a debt contracted in one of the mafia-dominated casinos in Havana. The fact that Ruby was called into this discussion is itself a tribute to his status as a "connection" or "fixer," rather than (in Henry Hurt's words) "a classic two-bit pawn."

The lawyer's name was badly mangled in the official transcript (as "Mark Lane," "Dave Lane," or "McClain"). But Earl Warren recognized and responded to Ruby's apparent digression, with the intriguing information (not generally available) that "Alfred was killed in a taxi in New York" (5 WH 206).

The lawyer was Alfred E. McLane, member of the prestigious Dallas petroleum-law firm Turner, Atwood, doing business for such oil and gas interests as the Murchisons' Delhi-Taylor and Wofford Cain's Southern Union Gas Company.[18] The petroleum affairs of Clint Murchison, Sr., and Wofford Cain made them deeply political: Murchison and Cain underwrote the bills for President Eisenhower's farm at Gettysburg, and J. Edgar Hoover's annual racing holidays in California at the Murchison resort motel, the Del Charro.[19] Hoover's Del Charro holidays were a matter of particular sensitivity, since (as we shall see) "some of the nation's most notorious gamblers and racketeers" would register there when Hoover came out to gamble at the (Murchison-owned) Del Mar racetrack.[20]

In 1959–60 Alfred McLane served as general counsel of an oil-exploration company, Rimrock Tidelands. Rimrock's subsidiary, Rimrock International, found its way into a Senate investigation of the international narcotics traffic, since (in the view of U.S. Customs investigators), its managing director was probably using the company as a cover for liaison, at the highest level, between the Sicilian and American mafia. The following memo was supplied to the Committee by Customs.

SANTO SORGE. Managing director of the Rimrock International Oil Co., 680 Fifth Avenue in New York. Member of the Foreign Economic Research Association. Modus operandi: one of the most important Mafia leaders. Travels extensively between Italy and the United States in furtherance of ostensibly legitimate international ventures which probably cover for liaison duties between highest ranking Mafiosi in the United States and Italy. Has considerable political influence in Italy.[21]

Santo Sorge, without question, was one of the highest-level Sicilian mafiosi; and his counsel was sought in high-level decisions affecting the American mafia as well. For example, he participated in the meetings from October 10 to 14 in the Hotel des Palmes, Palermo, which apparently cleared the way for the murder, eleven days later in New York, of Albert Anastasia, mafia boss of the mob-dominated International Longshoremen's Association.[22]

The question then arises why Rimrock would pick such a figure to head up an oil-exploration company. A possible answer is suggested by a report in the oil journal *World Petroleum* about oil-exploration farmouts in Tunisia, an Arab country that for decades was kept friendly to American interests, and those of the major oil companies, by corruption. A map of the oil-exploration leases shows that much of the land was allocated to Rimrock, with smaller concessions for the parent company, Canadian Husky.[23] Rimrock International was, however, a desktop company, not an operating one. Its role was to secure the lease from the Tunisian government and then lease it out, in what the oil industry calls a farmout agreement, to larger development companies, and ultimately to the oil majors themselves.

It is normal, not unusual, for the entry of major U.S. firms into Third World countries to be facilitated and sustained, indeed made possible, by corruption. More often than not, from China and Southeast Asia to Lebanon and South America, the key corrupters have been simultaneously CIA-connected and major figures in the international narcotics traffic.

This is not the place to fully assess the relationship of Santo Sorge, and the other key members of the Luciano international narcotics network, to the CIA. Even CIA and DEA internal memos concede the role of U.S. intelligence in establishing Luciano and his mafia narcotics-trafficking network in Sicily after World War II.[24] French authorities such as *Le Monde* have charged that this CIA gray alliance survived into the 1970s. American sources have suggested that this particular

CIA-mafia alliance broke down about the time of Sorge's travels between Sicily and New York, after some mafia members defied a collective mafia decision to cease importing heroin into the United States. (Anastasia's death is said to have been ordered precisely because he was one of the dissidents defying the decree.)[25]

What can we say of Rimrock Tidelands, the oil company that chose to set up a subsidiary headed by an international mafia leader? Rimrock Tidelands itself was a subsidiary of a middle-rank oil company, Canadian Husky Oil Company, that had both CIA-mafia and high-level political connections. On its board was a director of an insurance company, American National of Galveston, Texas, which had a history of investments in casinos, and interlocked with a bank controlled by the CIA-mob lawyer-banker Paul Helliwell (see Chapter 10). And in 1964 Canadian Husky's board was joined by J. W. Bullion, a personal attorney for Lyndon Johnson, whom the new President had tried hard to reach in the first hours after the assassination of John F. Kennedy.

Up through the 1960s, many U.S. industrial corporations, hotel chains, and banks operating overseas developed various forms of business relations with organized crime, for the latter's expertise in corrupting and managing local governments. In Havana, for example, Meyer Lansky consolidated his local operating base by leasing the local racetrack from National City Bank of New York, allied financially with what was then Havana's largest hotel-casino (the Hotel Nacional, where Lansky operated the casino), as well as Cuban plantations and the local power company.[26]

Perhaps the classic historical example of this was the alliance which we saw forged between the two major U.S. banana companies, United Fruit and Standard Fruit and Steamship, and representatives of the New Orleans mafia, for the sake of overthrowing and then dominating the so-called banana republics of Central America. Let us now examine the high-level connection in Dallas which, amongst all others, had most to lose from the Kennedy attack on Jimmy Hoffa and his political and CIA allies.

RUBY, MURCHISON, HOOVER, AND THE "DEL CHARRO SET"

The story of Ruby and Alfred McLane illustrates how Ruby's intimacy with the world of gambling gave him an entrée to the overworld of

Dallas oilmen and lawyers, men with considerable political influence. Beyond question, Ruby knew a number of such individuals. A businessman told the FBI, for example, that Ruby had once introduced him to Dallas businessman E. E. Fogelson and his wife, Greer Garson (23 WH 346). Like McLane's employers Clint Murchison, Sr., and Wofford Cain, Fogelson was a member of the "Del Charro set." This was a group of Texas millionaires who frequented Clint Murchison's resort, the Hotel Del Charro, near Murchison's racetrack, the Del Mar, in La Jolla, California. Clint Murchison and some of his associates would pay for the annual racing holidays of their good friend J. Edgar Hoover.[27]

Fogelson was not the only member of the Del Charro set whom Ruby knew personally. Authoritative corroboration of Ruby's gambling, police, and Del Charro connections was supplied by a friend of Ruby's from the heart of the Hoffa-underworld milieu investigated by Bobby Kennedy when counsel at the McClellan Rackets Committee.

The witness's name was Harry Hall (alias Haler, Haller, or Helfgott), and he knew much about gambling and organized crime. In 1961 he had been convicted with Lucchese gunman Frankie Carbo and Frank "Blinky" Palermo for defrauding Truman Gibson of the International Boxing Club, as part of a corrupt boxing milieu which Kennedy and the McClellan Committee had linked to both Hoffa and Paul Dorfman.[28]

After the murder of Oswald, Hall, by then an inmate in the Los Angeles federal prison on Terminal Island, contacted the Secret Service, who reported that Hall's previous "information in many cases had proven reliable" (WCE 1753; 23 WH 362). Hall knew Ruby well enough to talk of one of Ruby's friends in San Francisco (Solly Schulman, cf. 22 WH 426); and his story was deemed so important by the Los Angeles Secret Service that the agent-in-charge there dictated the report himself, then went to Dallas with Hall's information the next day. Yet there is no sign that either the FBI (which sat in on the Hall interview) or the Warren Commission followed up on the matter.

Hall's story was that he and Ruby would travel together to cities such as Chicago, Tulsa, and Shreveport, where Ruby had "good connections" with gamblers. Ruby helped Hall set up large bets with Texas oilmen on sporting events. On one occasion Ruby and Hall won a large amount of money by betting Dallas oil billionaire H. L. Hunt on the Cotton Bowl and Rose Bowl games. Ruby took forty percent of Hall's gambling profits, because he "was supposed to have influence with the police, so that [Hall] would have no worry about any gambling arrest" (23 WH 363).

Hall also linked himself and Ruby to the Del Charro set. He said that he and Ruby knew a "Texas millionaire named Bill Byers [i.e., Byars], who came from Tyre [i.e., Tyler], Texas, and who was friendly with two other Texas millionaires named [Clint] Murchison and Andraddy [C. Dick Andrade]." Ruby had wanted Hall to help rob Byars of his bankroll; and Hall heard later that Byars "was robbed while at the Del Charro Hotel, La Jolla, California. This hotel is owned by Mr. Murchison" (23 WH 363).

Much of what Hall claimed checked out. Billy Byars was indeed close to Clint Murchison, Sr.; and had joined with Murchison, Wofford Cain, and George E. Allen in underwriting the costs of President Eisenhower's farm at Gettysburg.[29] Like Murchison, Cain, and E. E. Fogelson, he was also part of the Del Charro set that would join J. Edgar Hoover once a year for a gambling holiday at the Del Mar racetrack in La Jolla.[30] According to Anthony Summers, Hoover was close to Byars, and the two men "used adjacent bungalows at [the Del Charro] each summer. The phone log for the Director's office shows that, aside from phone calls to Robert Kennedy and the head of the Secret Service, Edgar called only one man on the afternoon the President was shot—Billy Byars." Summers also confirmed from Hall and other close witnesses that Byars had indeed known Ruby.[31] The House Committee learned from Ruby's Havana gambling friend Lewis McWillie that Billy Byars, along with other oilmen like H. L. Hunt and Sid Richardson, gambled at Benny Binion's legendary Top of the Hill Terrace when it was managed by McWillie between 1940 and 1958.[32] McWillie was not asked about Byars's and Richardson's gambling partner Clint Murchison, Sr.

We learn however from Lieutenant George Butler's notes of the 1947 Paul Jones attempt to bribe Sheriff Guthrie that the top oilmengamblers who (it was hoped) would bring big money to the gambling tables were Clint Murchison, his friend Toddie Lee Wynne, and Ray Ryan.[33] These are presumably Clint Murchison, Sr., who was Hoover's host at the Del Charro, and Toddie Lee Wynne, Sr., father of Toddie Lee Wynne, Jr., chairman of the board of the Great Southwest Corporation, which (as we shall see in Chapter 18) supplied a manager to handle the affairs and testimony of Marina Oswald.

Whether the Murchison mentioned on the Jones recording was the father or the son, it is clear that the FBI did not want Hoover's friend to be embarrassed. The FBI transcript of the same recorded interview completely garbled the two names, giving them as "Cling Masserson" and "Jimmy New Yorker."[34] The FBI's habit of garbling politically sensitive names was a recurring one. Ruby, for example, had on the day before the assassination gone to the office of H. L. Hunt's son Lamar Hunt (WR 368); the FBI however filed a report on "Mr. LARMAR HUNT . . . whose name appeared as 'LAMAR HUNT' in a book which was the property of JACK RUBY" (25 WH 381).[35]

It must be understood that Clint Murchison, Sr., was in a position to insist upon favors from J. Edgar Hoover. The free racetrack holidays for Hoover at the $100-a-day Del Charro (a princely sum in the 1950s) constituted an impropriety in themselves. They were also the scene for further intrigues: it was at the Del Charro, for example, that Clint Murchison arranged for Hoover to lend his name to, and thus earn a small fortune from, an anti-Communist tirade, *Masters of Deceit*, which Murchison then placed with his own publishing company, Henry Holt.[36]

Others besides Hoover opened themselves to compromise and even blackmail by accepting Murchison's hospitality during the Del Mar racing season. The chief political objective of Murchison and Richardson was to safeguard the oil depletion allowance and expand the offshore state boundaries of Texas, both of which goals they achieved by liberal gifts to both parties, and by labeling as "red" those who opposed them in Congress.[37]

But particularly compromising to Hoover were the Murchisons' undoubted links to organized-crime figures, including friends of Ruby. On the national level, almost 20 percent of the production of the Murchison Oil Lease Company was allegedly owned by Gerardo Catena of the drug-trafficking Vito Genovese family.[38] In Texas, Murchison banking activities intermingled with those of Herman K. Beebe, which in turn intermingled with those of Carlos Marcello and of George de Mohrenschildt's banking friend Richmond Harper.[39] In the city of Dallas, Ruby's friend Joe Campisi, a figure "linked with gambling and bookmaking" (9 AH 335), was close to Clint Murchison, Jr., when he was an owner of the Dallas Cowboys.[40] The Committee learned that Joe Campisi ran gambling tours from Dallas "to the Flamingo Hotel in Las Vegas, a substantial part of which was owned by three prominent underworld figures: Meyer Lansky, Anthony Accardo, and Gerardo Catena."[41] According to Joe Campisi's brother Sam, Ruby ate dinner at the Campisis' restaurant, the Egyptian Lounge, the night before the assassination. This interested Blakey and Billings, who transmitted a 1967 FBI informant's report that Joe Campisi was going to replace Joseph Civello as the Mafia leader in Dallas.[42]

In its heyday, the Murchisons used the Del Charro to consolidate their political influence. One of Clint Murchison, Sr.'s top congressional allies in red-baiting, Senator Joe McCarthy, was a guest at the Del Charro. Other "special guests" in the 1950s included Vice-President Richard Nixon, Senator John Connally, Senator George Smathers, Murchison lobbyist Robert Thompson, Lewis S. Rosenstiel of Schenley Liquors, the California mob-linked lobbyist Arthur Samish, and (according to Hank Messick) "a wide assortment of top gangsters from Las Vegas."[43]

All of these anti-Communist politicians, but J. Edgar Hoover above all, exposed themselves to political blackmail by visiting the Del Charro in the company of mobsters. Hoover even had a special detail of FBI agents to ensure that mobsters would not come up to him in public at the racetrack. But his love of horse racing and gambling meant that his holidays recurringly exposed him to the milieu of organized crime, whether at the Del Charro or (his other annual freeloading holiday) the Gulfstream Hotel owned by the family of McCarthy staffer G. David Schine.[44]

In the next chapter, I shall argue that this fatal compromise of Hoover was exploited by the killers, whoever they were, of John F. Kennedy. But to understand Ruby's role in this, it is important to see that he was neither a "loner" nor a simple "mob" figure, but someone whose links to sex and gambling gave him easy access to the upper realms of the special Texan political economy, one which progressed from the scandals of Ben Jack Cage, Fred Korth, and Bobby Baker in the Kennedy era, to the much more widespread savings-and-loan scandals of the 1980s.

PART FOUR

The Plot
and the Cover-Up

THIRTEEN

The Coalitions
against the Kennedys

The Hotel Del Charro did not open its doors until June 1953; but the potent alliance of mob, intelligence, and "high rollers" like Clint Murchison and Lewis Rosenstiel had been around for some time before. Rosenstiel was perhaps the prime go-between between Meyer Lansky's world and Hoover's; his Schenley Products Corporation had helped bootleggers like Johnny Torrio make the transition from Prohibition to repeal. It was Rosenstiel who had made the arrangements between Lansky and the FBI for the surrender of Murder Inc.'s Louis "Lepke" Buchalter; and his wife later told a State crime committee how she and her husband had been given unlimited credit by Meyer and Jake Lansky to gamble while at the Hotel Nacional in Havana.[1] Later, Rosenstiel, and his fellow ex-bootlegger Joseph Kennedy, helped launch the J. Edgar Hoover Foundation, to which a number of organized-crime figures contributed.[2]

Hoover and Rosenstiel had helped to invent McCarthy's anti-Communist shtick, before even Murchison got into the act. They did so by playing upon the internecine feuds splintering the postwar U.S. intelligence and political communities. McCarthy's famous list of Communists in government was originally prepared inside the FBI, then leaked to a member of military intelligence with instructions to transmit it to members of the American Jewish League Against Communism, a group founded by the China Lobby leader Alfred Kohlberg and largely funded by Rosenstiel. The league in turn gave the report to Senator McCarthy, who in February 1950 used it to charge that there were two hundred and five "security risks" in the State Department.[3]

Messick says that the military intelligence officer was "in the Pentagon";[4] it seems more likely, however, that he was a member of the rump military-intelligence group, "The Pond," headed by Colonel John V. ("Frenchy") Grombach. In 1947 Hoover and Grombach had both opposed the integration of their overseas intelligence activities into the newly created CIA; and Grombach in particular had hidden some of his intelligence assets in a new corporation, Universal Service Corporation, which had been created in the same year (1947) as a wholly owned subsidiary of Rosenstiel's Schenley Distilleries.[5] It would appear that Hoover and Grombach, abetted by Rosenstiel and the China Lobby, used McCarthy to attack alleged subversives like William Bundy in the CIA.[6]

Hoover and Rosenstiel were not the only source of McCarthy's poison. Others who used McCarthy to settle old scores included the Chinese Nationalists of the China Lobby, their spokesman Alfred Kohlberg, and General MacArthur's Prussian-born intelligence chief in Japan, General Charles Willoughby.[7] Willoughby in 1963 was still active in his opposition to CIA internationalism, through a network of private intelligence operatives which were supported by the family of H. L. Hunt.

THE HUNTS, WILLOUGHBY, AND THEIR PRIVATE INTELLIGENCE NETWORKS

The intra-bureaucratic feud of the 1950s between the CIA and Hoover was much more than a matter of personalities: it was a conflict between alternative visions (globalist/internationalist versus nationalist/expansionist) of how the United States should expand into the rest of the world. Where the major oil companies and their allies in the CIA thought of creating and dominating a global economy, their nationalist opposition in the United States preferred unilateralist expansion into specific areas, above all Latin America and the Far East. The latter group allied dissident generals, resentful of civilian control, with exploiters of minerals and independent oilmen opposed to the oil majors, like William Pawley and H. L. Hunt.[8]

In 1951, when General MacArthur was dramatically relieved of his Korean command by President Truman, H. L. Hunt and Clint Murchison, Sr., brought him out to speak in Texas, and eventually Hunt set up a national MacArthur-for-President headquarters in Chicago.[9] Sometime afterwards, MacArthur's now jobless intelligence chief General Willoughby (the same man who had forged alliances with Japanese war criminals, the yakuza, and Jack Cannon) was set up in a right-wing intelligence network called the "International Comité for the Defense of Christian Culture" by H. L. Hunt's sons Nelson Bunker Hunt and Lamar Hunt.[10]

In the 1960s this group's self-named "Foreign Intelligence Digest" network incorporated some of Kennedy's most outspoken ideological opponents in the United States: men like Frank Capell (the first to break the explosive story of the Kennedy–Marilyn Monroe affair) and Billy James Hargis, the "Christian Crusade" ally of General Edwin Walker's army indoctrination program in West Germany. German neo-Nazis and Abwehr veterans rounded out this group, along with a Cuban exile, José Ignacio Rasco, whose group (the MDC, or Christian Democratic Movement) funded the Cuban exile guerrilla training camp on Lake Pontchartrain in Louisiana (discussed in Chapter 7 on Lee Harvey Oswald).

One avowedly racist member of this network was Austin J. App, chairman of the Federation of American Citizens of German Descent. According to a British book, the West German intelligence network, the BND, may have funded App's federation, to the tune of $280,000 in 1964.[11] If so, the Hunt-Willoughby connection can be called transnational, in that it melded assets, and probably funds, from overseas to supplement the Hunt family's assets. The Hunts' own marginal status in U.S. society should not therefore mislead us into subordinating Willoughby's network still further. In a postnational era, transnational influences flood into our country by vehicles whose apparent marginality is misleading. For example, Nixon's friendship with a Key Biscayne banker, Bebe Rebozo, looks less peripheral when we read rumors that foreign funds may have flowed in and through his Bank of Key Biscayne.[12]

In late 1963 the most conspicuous transnational feature of the Hunt-Willoughby network was their close identification with Madame Nhu, the widow of the recently assassinated Ngo Dinh Nhu in Vietnam. The ongoing Willoughby interest in the Far East was represented by the presence of Father Raymond de Jaegher of the Free Pacific Association, the patron in America of Ngo Dinh Diem and his brother Ngo Dinh Nhu. This Hunt-Willoughby-Walker intelligence network seems to have taken care of Madame Ngo Dinh Nhu when she came to Dallas in the fall of 1963 and was presented with a bouquet of flowers at an October 1963 "U.S. Day" rally in Dallas, organized by General Walker (23 WH 516).

The Hunts and the Murchisons present the images of different versions of right-wing politics, with the Hunts allied to opponents of Washington, particularly when they were supporting southern resisters to integration, and the Murchisons playing their connections to Washington, Johnson, and Hoover, for all they were worth. Nelson Bunker Hunt was behind the hostile ad that confronted Kennedy in the November 22 edition of the *Dallas Morning News* (23 WH 690), an ad which, at a sponsor's insistence (5 WH 507–09) attacked the CIA for "arranging coups [i.e., against Diem] and having staunch Anti-Communist allies of the U.S. bloodily exterminated" (18 WH 835).

After the assassination, Frank Capell was active in disseminating conspiratorial "phase one" stories linking Oswald to Russia and Ruby to Castro's Cuba (20 WH 75, 26 WH 608), some of them apparently from intelligence sources such as Carlos Bringuier's colleagues in the DRE (26 WH 610). Capell was not acting alone: "phase one" stories linking Oswald and Ruby to Communists were circulated by Willoughby's associates Philip J. Corso, a veteran of army intelligence who had retired by 1963 to work for the segregationist Senator Strom Thurmond, and Cuban exile Salvador Diaz Verson, a former chief of Cuban military intelligence.[13]

Corso, the army intelligence veteran, was like Willoughby a foe of the CIA from the right, having tangled with the Agency in his years under C. D. Jackson as a member of Eisenhower's Operations Control Board.[14] In 1963–64 Corso and Willoughby were part of a secret right-wing group, the "Shickshinny Knights of Malta" (so called after their headquarters in Shickshinny, Pennsylvania, to distinguish them from the more famous Roman Catholic Sovereign Military Order of Malta based in Rome). The group provided a home to dissident retired military officers dissatisfied with the CIA's internationalism, many of them, like Willoughby and General Bonner Fellers, veterans of the old Hunt-MacArthur-Pawley coalition in the early 1950s. By 1963 the group's leading asset in their anti-CIA propaganda was a Polish intelligence defector, Michal Goleniewski, who had claimed to audiences inside and outside the CIA that the Agency was penetrated by the KGB at a high level.[15]

Corso built on this anti-CIA paranoia by telling his friend and fellow Senate staffer Julien Sourwine, who made sure it was relayed to the FBI, that Oswald was tied to a Communist ring inside the CIA, and was doubling as an informant for the FBI.[16] Shickshinny Knight Herman Kimsey, who claimed to have been Goleniewski's handler inside the CIA, also spun an elaborate story about how his CIA duties had put him in touch with Kennedy's assassin—the mystery man in Mexico.[17] Finally, the chief press contact of the Shickshinny Knights, Guy Richards of the *New York Journal-American,* published the claim (soon taken up by Frank Capell, by the John Birch Society, and by Willoughby's American Security Council) that Oswald, like another alleged KGB assassin (Bogdan Stashynsky), had been trained at a KGB assassination school in Minsk.[18] A toned-down version of the story was subsequently published by Julien Sourwine's Senate Internal Security Subcommittee, with help supplied via Senator Thomas Dodd from within the CIA.[19]

Frank Capell was also a source for an anti-CIA "phase one" assassination article in the John Birch Society publication *American Opinion,* by yet another Hargis associate, Revilo Oliver. Oliver was not just a Bircher, but a featured speaker and award-winner at the Congress of Freedom meeting in New Orleans attended by Joseph Milteer, where plans to assassinate politicians were allegedly discussed.[20]

As summarized by Warren Commission counsel Jenner, Oliver's article claimed that the JFK assassination

> was part of a Communist plot engineered with the help of the Central Intelligence Agency, that Lee Harvey Oswald was a Communist agent trained . . . in a school for international criminals near Minsk, Russia, under order from Secretary of Defense Robert S. McNamara. (15 WH 710)

Oliver argued that the assassination grew out of a conspiracy between Khrushchev and Kennedy to enact a "fake 'revolt' " against Castro, and replace Castro with a crypto-Communist " 'agrarian reformer.' " Roughly the same story was circulated at this time by John Martino and by the Minutemen.[21]

Questioned by the Warren Commission about the sources for his article, Oliver identified his "research assistant," Frank Capell, "a private

expert on Communism and Communistic information, who, I understand, has the cooperation of many former intelligence officers of the
Army and former members of the FBI" (15 WH 718, 714; cf. 742–43).
It seems clear that the Foreign Intelligence Digest network (FID),
through Corso, Capell, and possibly Kimsey, enjoyed connections inside the official intelligence world. Though their claims were distorted
to the point of absurdity, there may have been a germ of truth to their
claims, enough to have embarrassed and possibly even blackmailed
the FBI.

Meanwhile Capell had other, even more dubious associations. In
1965 he was indicted for the criminal libel of California's liberal Republican senator Thomas Kuchel, along with J. D. Clemmons, a Los
Angeles policeman who had been the first police officer to go to Marilyn
Monroe's home the night of her death, and John Fergus, a public-
relations man for the right-wing Schick-Eversharp Corporation.[22]

The Hunt-Capell-Minutemen constellation was not short-lived. In
1967, when some Minutemen helped form a new Patriotic party, John
Martino and his ghost-writer Nathaniel Weyl became speakers for it; a
financial backer for it and related paramilitary activities is said to have
been H. L. Hunt's son Nelson Bunker Hunt.[23]

But, as William Turner showed some years ago in his book *Power on
the Right*, the ramifications of this milieu went far beyond the Hunt
family and their FID network. Willoughby in particular was also part
of the leading defense-industrial lobby, the American Security Council,
along with politically active army reserve officers like Lieutenant Colonel Lev Dobriansky, who first brought the issue of Bogdan Stashynsky
and the alleged murder training school to the attention of Sourwine
and the Senate Internal Security Subcommittee.[24] In the early 1960s the
American Security Council was the leading public group campaigning
to use U.S. military force to oust Castro from Cuba, and to escalate the
war in Vietnam. Senator Dodd was on the ASC payroll when he generated the Senate subcommittee report on Stashynsky's supposed murder training school.[25]

In the same manner, Schick-Eversharp sponsored not only John Fergus but a number of other p.r. activities, notably the ASC's campaigns
in the 1960s for wars against Cuba and Vietnam. Billy James Hargis's
Christian Crusade enjoyed financial support not just from the Hunts
but from a number of national defense contractors, while some of his
right-wing propaganda was quoted in an official Air Force manual.[26]

In short, the conspiratorial right was not just the invention of exotic Texas millionaires but was rooted in the deep politics and defense lobbying of the nation. The Hunts and their immediate associates, like retired general Edwin Walker (forcibly retired in 1961 after using Hargis propaganda in a compulsory army training program), were, from a sociological viewpoint, small adjuncts to this large private intelligence complex.

From the point of view of the assassination, however, this Dallas milieu was more important, as we shall see in Chapter 18.

THE MURCHISONS
AND THEIR WASHINGTON LOBBYISTS

Unlike the Hunts, Clint Murchison, Sr., is not known to have hired a full-fledged intelligence organization circulating "phase one" stories of a Communist conspiracy. Murchison preferred to rely on personal connections and patronage, such as the compromising services he continued to offer to both J. Edgar Hoover and Senator McCarthy. But one close intelligence contact the family developed was with a former naval intelligence officer, Gordon McLendon, who owned a network of radio stations, and who also became a co-owner, with Clint Murchison, Jr., of the Dallas Cowboys.

McLendon continued in the 1960s to have excellent intelligence connections. These kept him, for example, abreast of the developing Bobby Baker scandal in Washington in 1963, about which he was able to tell me things still not generally known in 1977 (when I interviewed him for the Canadian Broadcasting Corporation). McLendon also represented a kind of a link between the usually separated worlds of Jack Ruby, who listed him as one of his six "closest friends" in Dallas (20 WH 39), and Lee Harvey Oswald.

McLendon knew CIA Officer David Phillips, who in September 1963 strangely mishandled the Lee Harvey Oswald visit to Mexico City for the CIA station there. When Phillips retired in the 1970s, he went into business with McLendon, and the two men also cofounded the Association of Former Intelligence Officers (later called the Association of Retired Intelligence Officers).[27]

But Murchison's most powerful intelligence connection was probably through the man he engaged in the 1950s to be his Washington lobbyist, I. Irving Davidson. The amazing spread of Davidson's contacts— to Carlos Marcello, J. Edgar Hoover, the CIA, Israel, the Somozas, and

Haiti—has been forcefully summarized by Marcello's biographer John H. Davis:

> He was a registered lobbyist for the Teamsters and . . . a friend of Jimmy Hoffa. He was the registered lobbyist for the Somozas of Nicaragua, the Duvaliers of Haiti, the Trujillos of the Dominican Republic, and the wealthy Murchisons of Dallas, owners of the Dallas Cowboys. . . . He shared his close friendship with the Murchisons with another good friend, J. Edgar Hoover, who, it has been said, relied on Davidson for inside information no one else was able to provide. . . . Irv Davidson's activities ranged the entire globe. He once sold seventy Israeli-made staghound tanks to Nicaragua. He lobbied on behalf of the CIA on Capitol Hill. He represented Fidel Castro's interests in the United States. As the registered lobbyist for Coca-Cola, he personally escorted Coca-Cola soft drink teams on missions all over the world. He did a good deal of business with the sultan of Oman and was instrumental in getting Carlos Marcello involved in business with Oman and other Persian Gulf countries.[28]

After Bobby Kennedy started to put pressure on Jimmy Hoffa at the McClellan hearings, Davidson, who already knew both Carlos Marcello and Clint Murchison, became Hoffa's protector and go-between with both the Nixon forces in the Republican party and the Johnson forces in the Democrats.[29] This put Davidson in a position to obtain huge Teamsters' Pension Fund loans, first for the Murchisons, and eventually for himself (in a deal which led to his conviction for bankruptcy fraud).[30] Up to the time of his legal difficulties, Davidson used his international connections to be of service to the CIA and National Security Council.[31]

A third source of political power for Clint Murchison was through his political protégé Lyndon Johnson, along with Johnson's Senate secretary and bagman Bobby Baker. The same Murchison trouble-shooter who had brought McCarthy to Murchison, Robert Thompson, later arranged for Murchison to deal directly with Baker.[32]

While working for Johnson, Baker became the epitome of Washington wheeler-dealer sleaze. Repeatedly, he fronted for syndicate gamblers Cliff Jones and Ed Levinson, in investments which earned super-profits for himself and another military-industrial lobbyist, his friend Fred Black, Jr. In exchange he intervened to help Jones and Levinson obtain casino contracts with the Intercontinental international hotel system (before Castro, Jones and Levinson, both associates of Meyer Lansky, had the casino in the Havana Hilton).[33]

Like Ruby, Baker also used women to consolidate his political influence. Baker once billed an airline seeking government charter business for a plane trip carrying Washington lobbyists and party girls to a
fund-raiser for Senator Howard Cannon in Las Vegas. A small club
with which he was associated, the Quorum, became a place of assignation between politicians and call girls, some of them with intelligence
connections.

THE NOVEMBER DENOUEMENT
BETWEEN THE KENNEDYS AND THEIR OPPONENTS

In short, the Murchison-Hoffa-Baker triangle of influence, cemented
chiefly by Carlos Marcello's longtime lobbyist Irving Davidson, presented by 1963 an awesome power base in Washington for Clint
Murchison and Lyndon Johnson. From another point of view, it also
represented a sinkhole of criminal influence; and by 1963, for whatever
reason, that point of view had come to be shared by Bobby Kennedy.

From the moment he took office, Bobby Kennedy had, as expected,
targeted both Jimmy Hoffa and Carlos Marcello. In early March of
1961 he took steps to have Marcello deported to Guatemala (the country Marcello had falsely listed as his birthplace); and this was accomplished on April 4, 1961, by a swift and forcible trip to the airport that
some have called a virtual kidnap.[34]

But Marcello's was only one of the forty names on the initial list
worked up by the beefed-up Organized Crime Section in the new
Kennedy Justice Department. Under a new policy of targeting sus-
pected crime bosses, the list also included the CIA's contacts Sam Gi-
ancana and Santo Trafficante, the Teamster-linked mobsters Frankie
Carbo and Tony "Ducks" Corallo, and longtime Lansky allies Mickey
Cohen of Los Angeles and "Trigger Mike Coppola" of Miami. Mean-
while a new "labor and racketeering unit" within the Organized Crime
Section (the "Get Hoffa" squad, headed by Walter Sheridan) targeted
Hoffa and his Teamster allies.[35]

These incursions into the CIA-Teamster-mob world accelerated in
1963, with new (and ultimately successful) indictments of Hoffa, Philadelphia mafia boss Angelo Bruno, and James Plumeri of the Hoffa-
CIA plots.[36] From 1962 on, Davidson spent more and more time in the
courtrooms where Hoffa was being tried.[37]

The Kennedy Justice Department and the IRS were also looking at the "skim" from Las Vegas casinos through Lansky financial institutions like the Bank of World Commerce in the Bahamas. Bobby Baker's investment partners Ed Levinson (an old Lansky ally) and Ben Siegelbaum (a Hoffa ally) became key figures at both ends of the investigation; and the Kennedys can hardly have been unaware of what this might mean for Baker and his political patron Lyndon Johnson.[38]

In late 1963 these hidden threats to Johnson's political future began to break into the nation's press. Baker's lobbying operations surfaced in September 1963, with (for example) a number of New York Times stories linking Baker to both Davidson and Murchison.[39] Stories about Ed Levinson and the Las Vegas skim by Ed Reid and Ovid Demaris were published in the New York Times in the week preceding the assassination.[40]

Concurrently, there were a number of interrelated congressional committee investigations, of Bobby Baker (with his mob connections), of Murchison lobbyists Robert Thompson and Thomas Webb, and of Irving Davidson. It was the perception of the Johnson and Hoffa camps that the Kennedys had inspired them all.[41]

According to President Kennedy's secretary, Evelyn Lincoln, Bobby Kennedy was also investigating Bobby Baker for tax evasion and fraud. This had reached the point where the President himself discussed the Baker investigation with his secretary, and allegedly told her that his running mate in 1964 would not be Lyndon Johnson. The date of this discussion was November 19, 1963, the day before the President left for Texas.[42]

A Senate Rules Committee investigation into the Bobby Baker scandal was indeed moving rapidly to implicate Lyndon Johnson, and on a matter concerning a concurrent scandal and investigation. This was the award of a $7-billion contract for a fighter plane, the TFX, to a General Dynamics plant in Fort Worth. Navy Secretary Fred Korth, a former bank president and a Johnson man, had been forced to resign in October 1963, after reporters discovered that his bank, the Continental National Bank of Fort Worth, was the principal money source for the General Dynamics plant.[43]

On November 22, 1963, the day of the assassination, a closed session of the Senate Rules Committee heard sworn testimony from a Baker business associate, Don Reynolds. Reynolds was telling the com-

mittee of a big lobbyists' sex party in New York, and also of a suitcase he had seen, full of money which Baker described as a $100,000
payoff to Johnson for his role in securing the Fort Worth TFX contract. His testimony was broken off by the news that the President had
been shot.[44]

Bobby Baker has since denied the payoff story. There is, however, no
doubt that Lyndon Johnson felt threatened by the TFX case and more
specifically by Don Reynolds's testimony. On his return from Dallas the
same day, the new President made time to telephone Abe Fortas, who
had represented Bobby Baker at the closed hearing, to learn what Reynolds had said.[45] Thanks to what one senator called "string-pulling by
Johnson and Abe Fortas," only a highly bowdlerized version of the
Reynolds testimony reached the public and the press, who declined to
pursue the matter.[46]

Johnson was even more effective in closing off the parallel Senate investigation of the TFX contract, by Robert Kennedy's former Senate
boss Senator McClellan. The McClellan subcommittee had closed its
TFX meeting on November 20, 1963, with the chairman's undertaking
"to resume hearings next week"; *Business Week* predicted that Fred
Korth would be the next witness.[47] But the hearings promised for "next
week" were not resumed until 1969, after Johnson had left office; and
Korth never had to testify.

Finally, according to Victor Navasky, the Bobby Baker case was expanded to bring the Murchisons themselves under FBI investigation; yet
Hoover, as if to show his defiance of the attorney general he hated, continued to "allow Clint Murchison to pay his California health-resort
bills."[48] Nor, as far as is known, did either Hoover or the CIA lessen
their involvement with Irving Davidson, who became actively involved
in the defense of Hoffa at the same time he came under investigation for
his role in arranging for thousands of dollars in "finders fees" to Bobby
Baker from a Murchison meat-packing firm in Haiti.[49]

WHO HAD THE MEANS? NOT THE MOB, HOFFA, OR CIA, BUT THE GET-KENNEDY COUNTERCOALITIONS

By November 1963, when this scandal reached the *New York Times*,
Davidson was indeed, as John H. Davis has described him, "the representative of all that Jack and Bobby fought against—Trujillo, Hoffa's

Teamsters, the Somozas' Nicaragua, the Texas rich, the CIA, Castro, Nixon, the mob"; he was also "a representative in good standing of the interests that profited most conspicuously from the destruction of the Kennedy brothers."[50] The Kennedys had put together a formidable coalition to purge the Democratic party of mob alliances; and Davidson, as much as any other individual, had mobilized a countercoalition to resist this.

By 1963 this political contest had escalated to a level which many observers have described metaphorically as a war, a war being fought on many fronts. Some have talked of the attorney general's war on organized crime, or against Jimmy Hoffa. Others have pointed to the Kennedys' disaffection with the CIA hawks and with lobbyists for a sustained or expanded defense effort. But in 1963, as conflict within the Administration intensified over Vietnam, Cuba, and the future of the Cold War, the various fronts merged into a polarized contest between the supporters of the President and of the Vice-President.

In this contest, Davis's countercoalition of Davidson friends and clients is a good working list, not only of the Kennedys' enemies, but of those in a position to have organized the Kennedy assassination plot. For example, as we have seen, one of the Somozas' agents, "D," contributed to the phase-one legend of "Lee Harvey Oswald."

But it is misleading to enumerate, among the constituents of this coalition, only these exotic elements. By late 1963 the most powerful members of this countercoalition were the Kennedys' leading opponent in the Democratic party (Lyndon Johnson) and in their Administration (Davidson's personal friend J. Edgar Hoover). Their status in Washington, threatened by the Kennedys, was clearly consolidated in the days after the assassination. To give just one example, as soon as Johnson became President, Hoover and the FBI stopped sending the Justice Department reports on the Bobby Baker case.[51]

It is at this high level that we find those who benefited from the assassination. In the end, the assassination did not stop those most commonly accused of it, such as Carlos Marcello, from eventually going to jail. Marcello, Hoffa, Bobby Baker, Rosselli, Giancana, even Davidson, all sooner or later were indicted and convicted. But Johnson, Hoover, and their backers like the Murchisons, although they never faced indictments, did face in late 1963 an imminent loss of the political power which they had enjoyed for years. From this they were saved by the assassination.

That they so benefited does not of course prove their involvement in the assassination plot; and the purpose of this chapter, indeed of this book, is not to identify the assassins. We are talking instead of a powerful milieu with the motive, by one means or another, to get rid of the Kennedys. In the next chapter we shall show that many of those in this milieu were actively intriguing, in a get-Kennedy coalition, to neutralize the Kennedys' threat to their power. Although we should not confuse this intriguing with the assassination plot, it will be striking to observe how many of those involved in pre-assassination intrigues were the same individuals who surfaced, along with Hoover, at the center of the post-assassination cover-up.

This cover-up was of course essential to consolidate the political legitimacy of Lyndon Johnson. Hoover's crucial role in establishing Oswald as the lone assassin (see Chapter 4) must have helped guarantee his being allowed to stay on as FBI director, past the statutory date for his retirement at the age of seventy in 1964.

But an entire Cold War status quo in Washington was preserved along with Lyndon Johnson. Surviving with him were Johnson-allied power-movers in the Democratic party like Edward Bennett Williams, Thomas Corcoran, Corcoran's junior law partner James Rowe, Ed Weisl, Eugene Wyman, and Morris Shenker, Vietnam and Cold War hawks like Dean Acheson and Clark Clifford (the architects of containment), a dependent tribe of military-industrial lobbyists like Fred Black, and the two Murchison employees Robert Thompson and Thomas Webb (a former assistant to J. Edgar Hoover).[52] It was this power base for the Vietnam War whose power was preserved by the assassination; and key elements of it survived to play a similar, equally hidden, role in Watergate.[53]

It is time, finally, to apply the House Committee's own test for identifying suspects: Who had the motive, the means, and the opportunity to kill the President? The Committee came up with three candidates: Marcello, Trafficante, and Hoffa, although they added arguments making Hoffa's involvement "improbable" (AR 169–79). Marcello has in fact emerged as the media's favorite candidate, producing such obvious questions as how he could have had the "means" to place Oswald and the parade route in conjunction, or to produce a story about the "hiring" of Oswald to kill Kennedy in the Mexico City Cuban Consulate, or the staging of even more conspiratorial contacts between Oswald and alleged KGB assassination expert Valeriy Kostikov.

For the complicated Oswald-Kostikov charade, which we looked at in Chapter 3, help from the Mexico City CIA station was necessary. The CIA certainly had the means to kill as well, with or without mob gunmen. Some have asked if it had a motive. The case that the CIA had no motive, as presented for example by John H. Davis, rests on denials that the CIA was going to pull out of Vietnam or make peace with Castro. In his 620-page book, Davis does not deal with the contrary evidence presented in Chapter 2. Nor does he mention the talks in fall 1963, authorized by the President and his brother, between Kennedy's Ambassador William Attwood and the Cuban ambassador at the UN, concerning an opening toward Cuba and a possible normalization of relations.[54]

While discounting the case made by Davis, I would not suggest that the CIA had a motive to kill Kennedy. It is a simplistic anthropomorphism to treat the CIA as if it had a single-minded point of view, when in fact the CIA is, like "Washington" or "the Democratic party," a cockpit for conflicting viewpoints.[55]

In fact, as I tried to show in Chapters 3 and 7, individuals in or close to the CIA may have been involved in pre-assassination plotting to set up Oswald as a KGB-directed assassin; and we shall soon try to show that this intrigue became merged with pre-assassination sexual blackmail of the Kennedys. The use of a wide brush to whitewash the CIA, in these circumstances, is ridiculous.

But (lest anyone imagine it) not even the CIA could have "acted alone." Officials of other agencies acted conspiratorially on or before November 22: the FBI (whose relationship to Oswald remains unknown); the Secret Service; Alcohol, Tobacco and Firearms (ATF—see Chapter 17); and army intelligence, to name only those agencies in our narrative.

Of all the components to this nexus of anti-Kennedy intrigues, the most crucial and powerful input, both before and after the assassination, was that of J. Edgar Hoover. Although Hoover could and did command the resources of the entire FBI to preserve his personal career against the Kennedys, the key to his power lay in the "O & C" (Official and Confidential) files which he kept in his own office, and which he used from time to time to leak material to friendly journalists against his enemies, including the Kennedys.

As we shall soon see, the fate of these files, on the occasion of Hoover's suspicious but hardly premature death in 1972, is unknown.[56] I believe that we know enough today to say that, if these Hoover O & C files still existed, the information in them would resolve some of the extant mysteries about the assassinations of the two Kennedy brothers. I do not mean by this that they would contain the names of the true gunmen involved. I mean that they would illuminate the pre-assassination intrigues setting off Hoover against the Kennedys (such as the sexual blackmail we are about to consider), which twice eventuated in murder as their denouement.

In short, a key to the successful murder of the President, and the ensuing cover-up, is the deep political countercoalition of intrigue we have been describing, involving Hoover with lobbyists, CIA officers, and mobbed Hoffa contacts of the type Ruby got in touch with. There is no comparable suspect. Compared to the diverse assets of this conspiratorial countercoalition, the means available to Marcello, Hoffa, the whole of "La Cosa Nostra," or even the CIA, were puny.

This does not mean that the killers themselves are necessarily to be found in this specific coalition. As activists threatening the status quo in many ways, the Kennedys had generated more enemies than can be listed in a single chapter. We have not, for example, even mentioned the resentment of Cuban exiles who felt betrayed by the Kennedys at the Bay of Pigs (or what Revilo Oliver called "Operation Judas" [15 WH 735]).

Nor have I mentioned the concern of defense contractors that (as I have argued elsewhere) the President's public hints about withdrawal in Vietnam were only part of preparations for a broader U.S.-Soviet strategic parity, "perhaps even at a lower level." This tentative language from Defense Secretary McNamara, in the very week leading up to the assassination, was given a much simpler reading by *Business Week:* "The word came loud and clear this week. . . . A major cut in defense spending is in the works."[57]

But in 1963, as the tensions increased between the Kennedys and their enemies, the various anti-Kennedy coalitions found themselves more and more in a common camp, with Hoover their strongest ally.

FOURTEEN

Intrigue, Murder, Cover-Up

The Continuity of Manipulation

In the last chapter, we looked at the emergent signs in late 1963 of a showdown between the Kennedys and their opponents, particularly those in the Democratic party. In this chapter we shall see how a number of power-movers in Washington, notably J. Edgar Hoover, the mob, Bobby Baker, and John Rosselli, intrigued to restrain the Kennedys by the crudest forms of sexual blackmail. In the ensuing chapters we shall see how a number of apparently unrelated people, who were engaged in these intrigues, later surfaced in the post-assassination cover-up.

The overall picture, in other words, is of a prevailing continuity at the level of deep politics. A momentary threat to the Cold War status quo, presented by the Kennedys in 1963, was successfully overcome. Some of the same players in maintaining this continuity survived to blackmail the Nixon Administration in 1972, at a time of renewed presidential interest in detente with the Soviet Union, and possible disengagement from Vietnam.

In 1963, the conspiratorial get-Kennedy countercoalitions not only had the means to execute the crucial cover-up after the assassination, they did help to execute it. In Chapter 18 we shall look at the role in the cover-up of the Great Southwest Corporation, and its chief counsel Bedford Wynne, who prior to the assassination was close to Johnson's former Senate aide Bobby Baker, while Baker blackmailed the Kennedys.

Bedford Wynne had both frequented the "Bobby Baker set" in Washington and invested in wheeler deals with Baker, Thomas Webb, and men who would later play a recurring role, along with Clint Murchison and Gordon McLendon, in the desperate and protracted fight to keep Jimmy Hoffa from going to jail.[1]

By one of history's ironies, *Life*, in its pre-dated issue of November 22, 1963, identified Bedford Wynne as a nonresident member of Bobby Baker's assignation club, the Quorum. For fourteen years after that day Bedford Wynne would virtually disappear. But in 1977 his name would again surface—in a Senate hearing into a Teamster-related insurance scandal. The witnesses were Wynne's two business partners I. Irving Davidson and Clint Murchison's lobbyist Tom Webb, along with Allen Dorfman, who appeared with his counsel Albert E. Jenner, formerly of the Warren Commission.[2]

HOOVER, HOFFA, AND SEXUAL BLACKMAIL

It is not known that Johnson himself plotted against Kennedy, or needed to; his backers included men far more experienced in intrigue. But the mob, Hoffa, and Hoover all took common steps to defend themselves against the Kennedys: the mob by supplying the brothers with women, and Hoffa and Hoover by documenting these liaisons for potential blackmail. According to Anthony Summers, Hoffa wiretappers Fred Otash and Bernard Spindel obtained recordings of both brothers making love to Marilyn Monroe; and Hoover was aware of this. In addition Hoover's own agents "discovered Kennedy liaisons with no fewer than thirty-two women during his brief presidency."[3]

The CIA may have been involved in this countercoalitional defense as well. John Rosselli, the CIA-mob go-between, was "almost certainly" the man who at Sam Giancana's request brought Judy Campbell (Exner) to her first tryst with John Kennedy (at a Frank Sinatra "Rat Pack" revel in February 1960, after Sinatra's show at the Las Vegas Sands).[4] February 1960 was also the month in which Bobby Kennedy published *The Enemy Within*, which named the little-known Giancana and Trafficante as mobsters; soon afterwards, the CIA gave both men protection, by involving them in the Bay of Pigs assassination plots.[5] Thereafter, FBI records established more than seventy phone calls between Campbell and the President, as a result of FBI surveillance of Rosselli, which Bobby had ordered.[6]

John H. Davis has written that the FBI files on the President's sexual escapades, and also Bobby's, were a key factor in making Bobby, after November 1963 "a virtual hostage to his enemies, including, above all, J. Edgar Hoover":

> Hoover . . . knew of John F. Kennedy's innumerable affairs with women of dubious reputation . . . the two most imprudent of which were with Sam Giancana's girlfriend Judith Campbell and the actress Marilyn Monroe. Recently he had received persuasive reports from Scotland Yard that the President had been involved with one of the call girls from the [Christine Keeler] ring that had brought down Great Britain's minister of defense, John Profumo. And he had evidence in his files also of the attorney general's brief fling with Miss Monroe and of the tapes Jimmy Hoffa's wireman, Bernard Spindell, had secretly recorded of their encounters.[7]

Anthony Summers's new book on Hoover, published just before this one went to press, gives a more intricate three-way picture of the sexual-blackmail triangle involving the Kennedys, Hoover, and Lansky. According to Summers, Lansky had by the 1930s acquired compromising evidence of Hoover's homosexual activities. In the 1950s, Meyer Lansky, and other mob figures such as Sam Giancana, supplied women to John F. Kennedy, some of whom were logged into Hoover's growing files of dirt on the young senator. In the 1960s this deep-political equilibrium was threatened by Robert Kennedy's war on organized crime, which alienated Hoover. Feeling increasingly threatened, especially after the Kennedys began to collect their own files on Hoover, both Hoover and the mob began to escalate their collection of Kennedy sexual dirt. At first Hoover gained White House influence by protecting the Kennedys against mob blackmail, but in 1963 Hoover, desperate, began to leak some of his own dirt on Kennedy to the public.[8]

Hoover's sexual dirt on the Kennedys began to surface in late June 1963, after the President's "peace speech" at American University with its appeal, "Let us reexamine our attitude toward the Cold War." On June 20, the United States and the Soviet Union signed an agreement establishing a "hot line" between the Kremlin and the White House.[9] A week later, there was a flurry of veiled hints linking the President to the Profumo story, such as the Drew Pearson–Jack Anderson column for June 29: "Britishers who read American criticisms of Profumo throw back the question 'What high American official was involved with Marilyn Monroe?' "[10]

On the same day, in a front-page story, the Hearst paper in New York, the *Journal-American,* linked the Christine Keeler–Stephen Ward sex ring itself to a "high U.S. aide," "one of the biggest names in American politics."[11] Back in 1960, after his election but before his inauguration, the President had slept with two members of the ring, including Mariella Novotny (a former stripper in London's Club Pigalle).

In June 1963, following Profumo's resignation in England, Novotny began dropping hints of American involvement. What draws our attention to this source of pressure on Kennedy is the recent revelation that the British security agency MI5 had been using the Stephen Ward sex ring for some time to compromise the Soviet agent, Yevgeniy Ivanov, with whom Christine Keeler had slept.[12] In the intrigues that follow, it is important to remember that MI5, as Britain's counterintelligence agency, maintained direct relations with both Hoover in the FBI and James Angleton in the CIA.

The Cold War politics of this MI5 Keeler-Ward sex-ring operation are indicated by the fact that the Keeler story first began to surface in October 1962, in the midst of the Cuban missile crisis. At the time, Ivanov and Ward were talking to the private secretary of Sir Harold Caccia, permanent undersecretary of the British Foreign Office, in a plan to resolve the crisis through a summit conference in England.[13] The surfacing rumors about his involvement with Keeler were enough to neutralize Ivanov, and to ensure his abrupt recall to Moscow.

We have seen that Cold War politics could also explain the timing of the *Journal-American* revelations in June 1963, after Kennedy's "peace speech." Anthony Summers has written that the paper's editor, Guy Richards, "was a rightwinger with excellent intelligence contacts"; and that Richards published the story after bringing to America an anti-Communist friend of Keeler's called Michael Eddowes.[14]

Although Summers does not mention it, both Richards and Eddowes would later play major roles in the post-assassination story. Both men helped advance the sophisticated KGB-killed-Kennedy stories which were used to justify the equally false story of Oswald as the lone assassin. We shall see that in that effort, also, Richards had help from his intelligence contacts.

In June 1963 Richards arranged for Eddowes to talk to FBI assistant director John Malone, the bureau chief in New York, before publishing the Novotny story. According to Summers, the Novotny story

> was manna from heaven for Hoover, for it apparently touched not only John, but also Robert. . . . It was probably Hoover who saw to it that the *Journal-American* got its stories on Novotny. It was a Hearst Corporation newspaper, and throughout the fifties Hoover had seen to it that Hearst papers fanned the flames of the Red Menace. Some of the Hearst star writers— like Walter Winchell—were personal friends of Hoover. There were even former FBI men on the paper's staff. In 1963, this cozy relationship was still flourishing. Red-baiting continued, as did fierce editorial opposition to the policies of the Kennedy administration.[15]

Bobby Kennedy used the full Kennedy treatment to silence the *Journal-American*, threatening the paper with a government anti-trust suit if it did not cease to pursue the matter. The paper desisted.

HOOVER, BOBBY BAKER,
AND THE ELLEN ROMETSCH STORY

On July 3, however, one day after Robert Kennedy had asked Hoover for what he knew about the whole Christine Keeler story, Robert learned of new allegations linking "highly placed government officials" with an East German woman called Ellen Rometsch.[16]

Apparently, it was true that the President had compromised himself in the same manner as Profumo, by sharing a sex partner, Ellen Rometsch, with a member of the Soviet embassy. Rometsch was one of the women at Baker's Quorum Club and N Street "love nest"; and Bobby Baker has since written that it was he who led John Kennedy into the compromising relationship, which Bobby Kennedy took care of by having Rometsch deported. Hoover may have played a role in leaking this story as well, perhaps even in making it happen.[17]

A contemporary story by Clark Mollenhoff reported that Rometsch had associated "with congressional leaders and some prominent New Frontiersmen"; and that, after the FBI investigated Rometsch in the summer of 1963, "she and her husband were sent back to Germany August 21, 1963, at the request of the State Department." Mollenhoff also noted that Ellen Rometsch had been born in East Germany and still had relatives there: "The possibility that her activity might be connected with espionage was of some concern to security investigators because of the high rank of her male companions." The story was put into the *Congressional Record* by Congressman H. R. Gross, perhaps Hoover's chief spokesman in the House.[18]

Not surprisingly, Baker's memoir depicts himself only as a "playboy," not, as the press had portrayed him, the pimp of Capitol Hill. Nevertheless, his account of the Rometsch affair is instructive: it strengthens the impression of an ongoing, sophisticated blackmail operation, and tells us that the affair was surfaced by Irving Davidson's ally and office-mate, Jack Anderson:

> The fat was in the fire, of course, when the ever-bellicose senator John J. Williams [chairman of the Rules Committee investigating Baker], an avid reader of Jack Anderson's column, learned there that I was an official of the Quorum Club and that Ellen Romesch—who'd once had an affair with a Soviet embassy attaché—had been seen in that club. Suddenly, Ellen Romesch was the greatest threat to national security since Alger Hiss. Attorney General Robert Kennedy had her rush-deported to Germany—sending as her escort, oddly enough, a trusted aide with whom the lady fell in love, causing her to write a series of embarrassingly intimate letters to him, which now are in my possession—in order to save the Republic. What the newspapers did not say, possibly because I've never admitted it before—but which Robert Kennedy definitely knew—was that Ellen Romesch had been one of the women Jack Kennedy had asked me to introduce him to. I accommodated his request.[19]

Note here how professionally Rometsch performed for Baker's purposes: Bobby Kennedy's "trusted aide" may never even have seen the intimate letters which could later be used for potential blackmail. Nor is it likely to have been a coincidence that Baker compromised the President with a woman who (as Hoover was more likely than Baker to have known) was sexually involved with a Soviet attaché. Exactly what had happened to Profumo in Britain had just repeated itself in America with a member of a similar call-girl ring: a sexual liaison had exposed a prominent politician—in this case, the President—to blackmail as a potential national security risk.[20]

According to Michael Beschloss, it took Hoover (who had already bailed out the Kennedys when Marilyn Monroe died) to rescue the Kennedys once again from this even bigger scandal:

> The Attorney General asked J. Edgar Hoover to help persuade the Senate leaders, Dirksen and Mansfield, to avert a Senate investigation that, he

warned, would taint Republicans as well as Democrats. . . . As a result of
Hoover's meeting with the two Senators at Mansfield's home, Rometsch's
relationship with the President remained a national secret. FBI agents
stormed the office of a congressional photographer, confiscating prints and
negatives of the German woman. The President and his brother acquired one
more unwanted debt to Hoover.

And he speculates on the extent to which the highest policy considerations can be affected by the operations of deep politics:

> Had the Attorney General and Hoover failed to get the Rometsch matter
> "under control," were the President forced to resign in 1963 or 1964 in a
> sex-and-security scandal, the politics of the United States could have been
> poisoned for a generation. The American right and others might have ex-
> plained Kennedy's failure to exploit the American nuclear advantage at the
> Bay of Pigs, in Laos and Berlin, and during the Missile Crisis as the result of
> the President's compromise by Soviet bloc intelligence.[21]

BOBBY BAKER, SEX POLITICS, AND JACK RUBY

As soon as the Rometsch story broke, Bobby Kennedy "asked his
trusted friend LaVern Duffy, an investigator who had worked closely
with him . . . on the Labor Rackets Committee, to fly immediately to
West Germany, calm the woman down, and keep her quiet." Soon afterwards Hoover told the President that Rometsch "wanted to return to
the United States to marry a Senate investigator."[22] In other words,
LaVern Duffy, Bobby's "trusted friend," is almost certainly the "trusted
aide" whose liaison with Rometsch had become compromising intelligence shared by Bobby Baker and J. Edgar Hoover.

At the time Kennedy dispatched Duffy to deal with Rometsch, Duffy
had just finished assisting the McClellan Government Operations Committee in investigating a Teamster-dominated union's relationship to
mob-organized prostitution, and an alleged "nation-wide white slavery
ring under the syndicate."

The union in question was the American Guild of Variety Artists,
the subject of so many of Ruby's pre-assassination phone calls.[23] The
corrupt, mob-dominated union supplied the legal fiction that the
women were "independent," rather than the exploited workers in a
string of brothels. But in fact, in Blakey's words, "girls were passed
from club to club in New York, Miami, Houston, Dallas, Phoenix, Las
Vegas, Denver, and Seattle."[24]

Not surprisingly, the testimony pointed to Ruby's milieu in a number of ways. For example, the licensee of a strip club in Miami Beach was also an officer of Teamsters Local 320, which had been organized by Ruby's old associate Dave Yaras, where Santos Trafficante had an office.[25]

Much of the testimony was directed to the clubs' practice of ordering women against their will to "mix" or "mingle" with the audience; at least one of Ruby's strippers had complained to AGVA that "Ruby ordered her to 'date' some of the customers" (9 AH 423). Blakey does not mention this, nor does he mention the recurring testimony that Ruby made outside assignations for his women and took half of their earnings. He does, however, report that Ruby's former partner in the Vegas Club, Joe Bonds (alias Joe LoCurto) was convicted in 1954 of white slavery.[26]

Prostitution, as much as gambling, invites the corruption of local politicians and law enforcement. Joe Bonds himself told the FBI that Ruby "made women available" to Dallas police officers (22 WH 335). No one has yet documented the rumors one hears in Dallas that Ruby's relationship to the wealthy oilmen and "high rollers" of the Del Charro derived from his practice of supplying girls for them, their parties, and their private clubs.

What remains unexplained is the story of Ruby's relationship in 1963 to Candy Barr, a nationally known stripper and protégée of Mickey Cohen in Los Angeles. In 1957, Barr had been arrested and convicted on trumped-up marijuana charges, by the same players (prosecutor Bill Alexander and Judge Joe B. Brown) who in 1964 would convict Ruby on evidence that led to a reversal; Barr's defense attorneys, Joe Tonahill and Mel Belli, also represented Ruby.[27]

In 1963 Ruby was regularly in telephone contact with Candy Barr, who was then out on parole but not permitted to visit Dallas. The rumor persists that the phone calls related to the stripper's attempt to blackmail someone of prominence. The rumor is reinforced by the knowledge that sexual blackmail was a practice for which Mickey Cohen was famous.[28]

For some reason the Barr case also drew the attention of Gordon McLendon, who was one of those who told me in 1977 that she had been framed on the marijuana charge (by members of the Dallas Police Narcotics Squad). McLendon's brother-in-law Lester May became her first attorney. McLendon told me this when I asked him for information about his friend Bedford Wynne. While not giving me the answers I was hoping for, he volunteered the detail, which seemed trivial at the time, that Wynne's intimate friend George Owen, later the first husband of Maureen Dean, had been the man present at Candy Barr's arrest who may have helped set it up.[29]

He also volunteered to me the detail, which at the time seemed unrelated, that when Bobby Baker emerged in 1972 from his time in prison for tax evasion and fraud, he went to stay with McLendon at his Cielo Ranch north of Dallas. I thought later that McLendon here was possibly standing in for Bedford Wynne and Clint Murchison, Jr., two of McLendon's friends who had been mentioned in the Bobby Baker hearings and were now unwilling to be publicly associated with Baker.

Since recent revelations about Watergate, I now wonder if the real link was not George Owen. Owen was extremely close to Bedford Wynne, and would party with him in Mexico, or even in his law office, where William McKenzie (of whom more in Chapter 18) was a partner.

George Owen also introduced to Bedford Wynne (the friend of Bobby Baker and member of his Quorum Club) the woman Owen would later marry: Maureen Biner, who played a much-underestimated role in Watergate as the girlfriend, and then the wife, of John Dean.

SEX, THE MOB, AND INTELLIGENCE IN WASHINGTON

One of the most underreported political topics is the extent to which prostitution in Washington has been the key to ongoing corruption and scandal in that city. Like other researchers, I have listened to a retired Washington detective, one who played a small but important role in Watergate; he is convinced that the systematic sexual seduction of Congress and the Administration is an ongoing, highly organized, and protected operation. This claim has long formed part of the anti-establishment rhetoric of puritanical right-wing extremists, but there is also empirical evidence to support it.

Subsequent revelations about Watergate in 1972, and the so-called Koreagate scandal of 1978, corroborates his hypothesis that mob-supplied call girls, with their phones bugged by intelligence agents, have driven the major scandals of Washington since at least the beginning of the Cold War. Scholarly memories, possibly because of denial, tend to be short when it comes to sexual politics. Few now remember, for example, that the first congressional investigation of military lobbying by Howard Hughes, in 1947, drew attention to the women that Hughes's press agent, John Meyer, had "procured" for military men, including President Roosevelt's son Elliott.[30]

Though Baker denies that he drew on such resources, he does tell us that his friend Fred Black, Jr., a major defense lobbyist, "kept a hotel suite at the Sheraton-Carlton in Washington where he and his friends—and I was among them—repaired to conduct business . . . or entertain ladies. Though we did not then know it, that suite was bugged by the FBI."[31]

Black was a close friend and admirer of John Rosselli over many years; Rosselli stayed at Black's apartment in the Watergate before testifying to the Church Committee in 1975; and Black phoned Rosselli from Los Angeles with an urgent message, "Get out of Miami," on July 27, 1976, the night before Rosselli (who ignored the warning) was murdered.[32] It is known that Rosselli supplied at least one woman, Judith Campbell, to President Kennedy. Could he, through his Las Vegas connections, have supplied women to Fred Black as well? An affirmative answer would help explain why two files on "Black, Fred B. Jr." were maintained by J. Edgar Hoover in the "Personal and Confidential" files which he kept in his FBI suite, the files "containing damning information that gave the Director a lasting hold over many men of power—including the Kennedy brothers."[33]

Hoover's "Personal and Confidential" files disappeared at the time of his death in May 1972. According to a staff member of the House Intelligence Committee who was interviewed by Jim Hougan, they may have later been burned in a mysterious fire at a hunting lodge which served "as the weekend retreat of more than two dozen top FBI agents and CIA officers (including John Mohr and James Angleton)."[34] Of the remaining "Official and Confidential" (O & C) files from his office, many, even though censored, clearly contain information on the sexual activities of members of Congress and other prominent persons, including the Kennedys.[35]

Baker also confirms that there was a party in a suite maintained by a defense-industry executive (and attended by Rometsch) in which naked women cavorted in a bathtub filled with champagne.[36] The Baker-

Rometsch story overlaps with later scandals in Washington involving politicians, call girls, and assignations recorded by intelligence experts for intelligence purposes. The most important of these is Heidi Rikan's call-girl operation, a few doors from the Democratic National Committee headquarters in Watergate, which two separate and well-researched books have now seen as the key to the 1972 Watergate break-in and scandal.

According to both books, the phone line inside the DNC which was supposed to be tapped by Howard Hunt's Watergate burglars (including Frank Sturgis) was a special line (not going through the central switchboard), which DNC staffers and friends used to phone the Heidi Rikan call-girl operation.[37] Jim Hougan adds that the phone line was already being tapped by a stringer for Jack Anderson, Lou Russell.[38]

Lou Russell was a former FBI agent who had helped Nixon with the Hiss case when he was both HUAC's committee counsel and also Hoover's informant on the Committee.[39] An employee in 1963 of Watergate burglar James McCord, Russell was close to Heidi Rikan's call girls whose line was the target of the Watergate burglars. Russell also had an unexplained financial relationship to McCord's attorney, Bernard Fensterwald (a longtime backer of the Garrison and other investigations of the John F. Kennedy assassination) and may have been working for Fensterwald as well.

In Jim Hougan's summary,

> Russell had been involved in the June break-in; he had almost certainly planted false evidence at the DNC in September; and throughout the fall and winter he had been instrumental in McCord's defense, helping him to secure bail and to switch attorneys. That switch had not been of mere tactical value; it represented a strategic change. Alch saw the case as a criminal one, whereas Fensterwald saw it in political terms. According to Alch, Fensterwald's entry into the case was marked by the assertion "We're going after the President." Which, as it happened, is precisely what McCord did.[40]

The climax of this campaign was McCord's book of 1974, which made his Angletonian suspicions of Nixon and Kissinger all too plain.[41]

Russell had knowledge, not only of the Rikan call-girl ring and of successful taps on the phone line, but also of McCord's plans to break into the DNC. Russell was apparently present at the scene of the June 16 break-in, and may have been source of a detailed warning to the Democrats about it the previous April (via Joe Shimon, Jack Anderson's source when breaking the Martino-Rosselli story).[42]

Whatever Russell's role, to which Hougan devotes fifty inconclusive pages, he was sought as a witness by the Republican minority staff on the Ervin Committee. On May 18, 1973, one week after declining a committee subpoena for his records, Russell suffered his first massive heart attack. On July 2, 1973, soon after he was approached again about his knowledge, he had a second, and died. The Republican investigator who approached him, John Leon, was "convinced that Watergate was a setup, that prostitution was at the heart of the affair, and that the . . . burglary had been sabotaged from within." He too died of a heart attack: one month later, on July 13, 1973, the day he was scheduled to hold a Watergate press conference.[43]

It would appear that Jack Anderson, the friend of Watergate burglar Frank Sturgis, and the recipient of sexual intelligence from Bobby Baker's Quorum Club in 1963, may have been getting inside dope from Heidi Rikan's operation in 1972. But there is another link between the two operations, more complicated, which is more revealing, and which will take us back, for the last time, to Jack Ruby's sex clubs in Dallas.

It is also clear from Hougan's account that Heidi Rikan's sex ring was only one instance of an ongoing operation. When Washington police raided the apartment, they seized a trick book including the names of "at least one U.S. senator, an astronaut, a Saudi prince, a clutch of U.S. and KCIA (South Korean) intelligence agents and a host of prominent Democrats."[44] Among the names were two, Ed Wilson and "Tungsten" [Tong Sun] Park, who would later be named as forces behind the similar George Town Club, which in the later 1970s the KCIA listed among its "assets" for the manipulation of Congress, the White House, U.S. intelligence agencies, and the press.[45]

It is generally recognized that at the George Town Club, Park was working for the KCIA, and Ed Wilson for the U.S. CIA, possibly spying on Park. The KCIA, meanwhile, was both corrupting and observing some of the club's members, one of whom, Congressman Richard Hanna, went to jail for his role in Koreagate. Behind the club was the influence of Tong Sun Park's friend Anna Chennault, at the time perhaps the leading overt lobbyist (on behalf of Taiwan) to keep the United States involved in Vietnam.[46]

Despite a Congressional investigation of Koreagate and the sexual favors it dispersed, "South Korea's intelligence operations grew stronger, not weaker in the aftermath of the scandal."[47] Two spinoffs from the KCIA-controlled Unification Church, the political group CAUSA and the *Washington Times,* would play important, but under-chronicled, roles in the Iran-Contra affair.[48]

Robert Gray, a founder with Park of the George Town Club as well as one of Washington's leading lobbyists, was investigated in 1982 by a House Ethics Committee concerning allegations of "using drugs and sexual activity to lobby Congressmen." Two members of the Committee's staff, both veterans of the Blakey-Billings House Committee on Assassinations, were assigned to interview a Washington police detective, Carl Shoffler, who agreed that the committee should take a close look at Robert Keith Gray. Shoffler told one of the pair, investigator Jack Moriarity, of a male-prostitution service on Capitol Hill, which he believed to be linked to Gray, to the charges of sex and drugs involving the pages in the House of Representatives, and to organized-crime figure Joe Nesline.[49]

The outcome of this inquiry would seem to confirm the impossibility of reform. First, Shoffler learned that his supposedly confidential information had become known to Neil Livingston, an employee of Gray who (like Gray himself) had intelligence connections. Then Shoffler learned that Moriarity's private-detective firm was working not just for the House Ethics Committee but for Gray as well. Finally, Shoffler was given an offer of employment with a private investigations agency working for one of Gray's companies, which Shoffler took to be a bribe. The offer was made, in Moriarity's presence, by Moriarity's business partner.[50]

In the end no charges were brought in connection with the male-prostitution ring. No action was taken against Moriarity or his business partner, who eventually went back to work for the House Ethics Committee. Shoffler retired from the Washington Police Force, believing that his investigation into Gray had hurt his career. Unscathed, Gray went on to handle p.r. for such lucrative accounts as BCCI, the drug-laundering bank which would also be accused of corrupt influence and sexual favors.[51]

After investigators on the House sex and drugs case were told to stop their work, one of them voiced to author Susan Trento the hypothesis, which I myself heard in Washington, of systematic sexual corruption by intelligence and organized crime forces:

> If a lobbyist wants to use hookers to influence legislation, there's a pool of talent he draws from. There are certain madams in town that they make connections with. By simple logic if you're in the business of influencing people with male prostitutes or kids, there has to be that supply chain. So by looking into these rings, we were trying to identify that aspect of it. If you're an intelligence service, foreign intelligence service or a friendly intelligence service or a corrupt lobbyist or an organized crime entity, and you want to influence political figures in Washington, D.C., the bottom line is you're all dipping into the same pool. . . . [If] we start to identify some of the clients, it's possible we would find the suppliers for intelligence, organized crime, and lobbyists.[52]

With this ongoing hypothesis in mind, one is struck by the recurrence in it of two names. The first is that of organized-crime figure Joe Nesline, in the background not just of the male prostitution ring referred by Carl Shoffler to the House Ethics Committee but also of the call-girl ring whose operation is said by two books to have precipitated the 1972 Watergate break-in. The second is that of Bedford Wynne, whose former girlfriend, Mo Biner, is alleged to have been the reason for the Watergate break-in, because of her presence in the address book of the call girls' madam. As already noted, Bedford Wynne was also a member of Bobby Baker's Quorum Club; and his family's company, the Great Southwest Corporation, figured in the assassination cover-up (see Chapter 18).

WATERGATE, THE WASHINGTON SEX SCENE, AND MCWILLIE

From *Silent Coup*, by Len Colodny and Robert Gettlin, we learn that the call girls' madam, Heidi Rikan alias "Cathy Dieter," a girlfriend of Joe Nesline, the top organized-crime representative in the Washington area (associated at this time with Meyer Lansky, Charles Tourine, and Dino Cellini, in sex-club operations in Amsterdam and Hamburg).[53] These men were at the very summit of international gambling, call-girl operations and narcotics, the key to mob influence in politics:

> There is no doubt that Lansky, Nesline, Tourine, etc., made up a very powerful criminal cabal with associations seemingly everywhere. Their notoriety

was such that in the early 1960s [i.e., when Robert Kennedy was Attorney General] law-enforcement agencies closely monitored their activities. For example, in 1962 narcotic officers following them noted that Nesline's wife and Tourine left the U.S. and travelled to Paris. Later that year, Nesline and Lansky were spotted in England and that summer Nesline and Tourine were spotted in Bermuda.[54]

These were also men close to the Havana casinos which Ruby had visited and where his friend McWillie worked. In pre-Castro Cuba, Nesline had been employed at the Havana Tropicana, where Lansky's man Dino Cellini was manager and where McWillie had also worked, before shifting jobs to work for Tourine at the Capri.[55] When Ruby and McWillie went out to Cuba's Trescornia Prison in 1959, both Tourine (5 AH 331) and Cellini (5 AH 109) were there. In June 1963, Tourine and Nesline were arrested together outside Washington, along with Frank "Lefty" Rosenthal of the Chicago mob.[56]

At the time of Watergate, Rikan's current protector was a Washington attorney, Phillip Bailley, whose self-professed model for his political activities was Bobby Baker.[57] But Bailley, like Baker before him, came to the attention of local law authorities, and was indicted on sex charges in June 1972. The resulting news publicity ("Capitol Hill Call-Girl Ring Uncovered") produced an immediate response from John Dean in the Nixon White House: within an hour, he had a chauffeured limousine bring the prosecutor on the case to his office, where he photocopied Bailley's address book.[58]

Dean's motive for doing so, according to *Silent Coup*, was personal: a roommate of his girlfriend, Maureen Biner (later his wife), was Heidi Rikan, whose name appeared in Bailley's address book.[59] But the swiftness and efficiency with which the Bailley case disappeared from the court dockets cannot be attributed to John Dean alone. *Silent Coup* does not consider the possibility that Dean and "Mo" Biner had been compromised, by a hostile force, in order to gain leverage over Dean, possibly to get his compliance in the matter of Hoffa's pardon in 1971.[60]

Here it becomes relevant that the man who introduced Mo Biner to Heidi Rikan was George Owen, "then a scout for the Dallas Cowboys who would become Maureen's first husband."[61] More precisely, George Owen, like Mo Biner, was a close personal friend of Bedford

Wynne, the nonresident member of Bobby Baker's Quorum Club when Baker compromised Jack Kennedy.

The name Bedford Wynne will mean more to the reader after we have considered the strange collaboration of army intelligence, the Secret Service, and the Wynne family firm, the Great Southwest Corporation, in the Dallas cover-up of the Kennedy assassination.[62]

FIFTEEN

Oswald as an Informant for the Government

The question of whether Oswald had any relationship with the F.B.I. or the C.I.A. is not frivolous. The agencies, of course, are silent. Although the Warren Commission had full power to conduct its own independent investigation, it permitted the F.B.I. and the C.I.A. to investigate themselves—and so cast a permanent shadow on the answers.

Walter Cronkite, June 28, 1967

The sensational development, [Warren Commission Counsel] Rankin explained, was the claim of Attorney General Waggoner Carr of Texas that Lee Harvey Oswald had been a paid FBI informant. The [commission] was stunned. "If that was true and it ever came out and could be established," Rankin said, "then you would have people think that there was a conspiracy to accomplish this assassination that nothing the Commission did or anybody could dissipate."

BOGGS: You are so right.
DULLES: Oh, terrible.
BOGGS: The implications of this are fantastic, don't you think so?
WARREN: Terrific.
RANKIN: Now it is something that will be very difficult to prove out. . . . I am confident that the FBI will never admit it, and I presume their records will never show it.

Transcript of Warren Commission
executive session, January 22, 1964,
quoted by Curt Gentry in J. Edgar Hoover

We saw in the last chapter that for some years the control of Washington was consolidated in the sexual and other blackmail deposited in Hoover's personal files. Hoover deflected the interest of the Commission away from Ruby's involvement with organized criminal prostitution and transfered the case from the Criminal Investigative Division (where it belonged) to his trusted allies Belmont and Branigan in Counterintelligence. Given Hoover's central role in the cover-up of the assassination, it is time to consider what virtually forced, or if you prefer blackmailed, Hoover into his "phase two" cover-up, which included the effacement of Ruby's obvious links to organized crime.

What forced Hoover's hand was the combination of rumor and evidence linking Oswald to the FBI as some kind of informant. The rumor (even if false) was persuasive. On January 24, 1964, the Warren Commission heard from Dallas district attorney Henry Wade and Texas attorney general Waggoner Carr that Oswald had been an FBI informant since September 1962, that he had a federal government voucher for $200 at the time of his arrest, and that FBI Agent James Hosty's name and phone number were in his address book (5 WH 242).

This last piece of hearsay proved to be true (16 WH 64), but the Commission had trouble learning this. As we have seen, the FBI initially supplied it with a list of the names in Oswald's notebook, from which Hosty's had been omitted.[1]

As to the story that Oswald was an FBI informant, I doubt that Oswald was directly on the FBI payroll.[2] A more likely possibility is that he worked for a private security agency which in turn reported to the FBI, the way that ex-FBI and ex–Office of Naval Intelligence agent Guy Banister, according to a CIA document, reported to the FBI in New Orleans.[3]

It is time to look more closely at Oswald's extraordinary career, in which he appeared to develop revolutionary sympathies while in the Marines, established communications with the Communist party, and nevertheless was able to gain an employment at a firm (Jaggars-Stiles-Stovall in Dallas) which did classified work for the U.S. Army requiring a security clearance.

REVOLUTIONARY MARINES
AND U.S. INDUSTRIAL SECURITY

Revolutionary U.S. Marines are unusual but not unique. The case of Gerry Patrick Hemming, who went from Marine service to Castro's army (and later the Lake Pontchartrain training camp), suggests that some of them are churned out by the military intelligence services, to infiltrate the forces of America's potential enemies. But I know of only one other Marine who, like Oswald, became a revolutionary sympathizer in a sensitive workplace.

His name was Robert C. Ronstadt, and we know what made him tick. In 1946, on leaving the Marines, Ronstadt went to work for a Los Angeles firm, Allied Records, that was concerned about possible Communist employees. At the same time, Ronstadt began to sell subscriptions to the Communist *Daily People's World;* and after some months he became a Communist party member in the spring of 1947.

Ronstadt, who had originally passed his FBI entrance exam in 1942, later explained to a friendly House Un-American Activities Committee that his job had been to smoke out potential Red sympathizers. His actual employer was the private investigative firm of Joseph P. McCarthy and Joseph Dunn, industrial security consultants to Allied Records. At Allied Records Ronstadt was not an FBI informant; but his job was to report on possible Communist infiltration of the plant to McCarthy and Dunn, who in turn reported to the FBI. After Ronstadt succeeded in joining the Communist party, he ceased to work for McCarthy and Dunn, and for the first time was paid directly by the FBI as an informant.[4]

Ronstadt's activities at Allied Records were duplicated throughout America during the Cold War. All defense contractors were eventually required by law to conduct industrial-security investigations, under legislation for which both the FBI and the American Legion had helped to lobby. This legislation created work both for veterans and for the Legion itself. During World War II the Legion had built up a network of confidential information contacts, on the model of the so-called vigilantes of the American Protective League during World War I.[5] The key man in this effort, an FBI agent named Lee Pennington, Jr., left the Bureau for the Legion in 1953, where he began to develop a massive "library" of information on alleged subversives. Future Watergate burglar James McCord, in search for subversives in the CIA, made his first contacts in the 1950s with Pennington, his library, and Lou Russell of HUAC.[6]

Pennington thus became a CIA consultant, a status which continued when he transferred his by-now-massive files on Americans from the

American Legion to the newly formed American Security Council. However, the principal users of his library were large corporations, including defense contractors such as the large oil companies, who consulted the file-card index when screening employees as part of their industrial-security program.

WAS OSWALD
AN INDUSTRIAL-SECURITY INFORMANT?

Oswald's business career is suggestively like Ronstadt's. In late 1962 this allegedly Marxist Marine veteran was able to get employment at the photographic firm Jaggars-Chiles-Stovall in Dallas, a firm doing classified work for the Army Security Agency (ASA). While there he exhibited "Communistic tendencies" (WR 246); yet "Oswald had complete access to the worktables on which the secret lists of place-names for the Army Map Service were kept. In theory, these were supposed to be 'restricted areas' in which only employees with a security clearance from the FBI were allowed to be present."[7]

According to the Warren Commission, Oswald's new job was found for him by the Texas Employment Commission (WR 719). However, according to investigative journalist Anthony Summers, George de Mohrenschildt's wife and daughter both said that de Mohrenschildt, who as we saw had CIA connections in both Dallas and Washington, arranged for the job.[8]

At work his most frequent companion was apparently Dennis Ofstein, a young veteran about Oswald's age, who had learned Russian while he served in the Army Security Agency.[9] Shortly after beginning work, in the same month of October, Oswald and his wife established social contact with Max Clark, the chief of industrial security for the General Dynamics plant in Fort Worth which secured the controversial TFX contract in the fall of 1963.

Thereafter, Oswald's proximity to potential subversives, worthy of investigation, seems to have been continuous. April 21, 1963, two weeks after he left Jaggars-Chiles-Stovall, is the date on which his FBI file shows his first alleged contact with another FBI target, the Fair Play for Cuba Committee. Even during his next job, at the Reily Coffee Company in New Orleans, both he and his co-workers talked of moving soon to the newly opened NASA Space Center in nearby Michoud (10 WH 226; 26 WH 772; cf. WCD 75.45–46, 336, 348).[10]

Even at the Texas School Book Depository, Oswald's workplace on November 22, there was a potential security target, the TSBD's credit manager, Joe R. Molina. Molina had a rough time of it during the early "phase one" investigation by the Dallas police of Oswald as an international terrorist. A veteran like Oswald, he had joined the American G.I. Forum, which "the Dallas police considered possibly subversive" (WR 237). Thus Molina had become the subject of FBI reports as well as of a Dallas Police Department security file (WR 237; 24 WH 259; FBI 105-82555-4427A).[11]

All this suggests that, like Ronstadt, Oswald's true employer may not have been the firms, but a private investigative agency doing industrial-security work. This would explain the FBI's zeal to cover up the pay-check anomalies, and the reluctance of the government, to this day, to release Oswald's income-tax records.

A DIGRESSION:
DAVID FERRIE AS A SELF-INCRIMINATING PATSY

Even without the suggestive analogy of Robert C. Ronstadt, there are numerous signs that Oswald's employment recurrently coincided with opportunities for surveillance of FBI subversive targets. But Oswald's activities appear to have focused on the targets of other investigative agencies as well, the federal Social Security system, and above all the Alcohol, Tobacco, and Firearms unit (ATF) of the U.S. Treasury. This multiple targeting by Oswald increases the likelihood that he was an employee not of the FBI but of a private agency with contracts to more than one federal government agency.

Consider for a moment the well-documented employment of David Ferrie, a former army reservist (10 AH 107) and a known employee of two private detectives, Guy Banister and Jack Martin, as well as an investigator for G. Wray Gill, attorney for Carlos Marcello (AR 143).[12] The House Committee rightly linked Ferrie to Marcello through his work for Gill. More questionably, it also linked Ferrie to Oswald, re-lying on disputed testimony which I shall not here try to resolve.

For what it is worth, I personally believe that Ferrie was most prob-ably in the same position as Oswald: an employee of a private investi-gator, who at some point was hired, probably unwittingly, to create a record or "legend" falsely linking himself to the assassination. Viewers of the movie *JFK* know of Ferrie's frenzied trip to Galveston right after the assassination (10 AH 113), and his improbable explanation for it (duck shooting, ice skating).[13]

Garrison made much of this trip, and these implausible explanations, in his 1967 case against Ferrie and Clay Shaw. To do so he had to omit the additional explanation for the trip which Ferrie gave one of Garrison's investigators on December 15, 1966: "I took a weekend vacation and I had some business for Gill to take care of."[14] This explanation seems quite plausible. While in Houston, Ferrie apparently made a collect call to the Town and Country Motel of Carlos Marcello, Gill's client (10 AH 113). If it is true, then Ferrie may have been hired to act as a decoy, or patsy. This is just what I shall argue Oswald was hired to do, when he told the FBI about his links with "Hidell."

More suspicious than Ferrie, in my view, is the man who drew attention at the time to Ferrie's trip, his other employer, Jack Martin (associated with Banister at 544 Camp Street, where the two men established an alibi on November 22). Then and later, Garrison and Martin made much of Ferrie's alleged membership in a phony church.[15] However, in an earlier lawsuit protesting his dismissal as an airline pilot, Ferrie had testified that he "became involved with these religious orders only to assist Martin in a Department of Health, Education, and Welfare organization investigation into the sale of phony certificates of ordination and consecration" (10 AH 130, cf. 110). The Select Committee, after investigating Ferrie extensively, agreed that "Martin . . . and Ferrie had performed some investigative work on a case involving an illegitimate religious order in Louisville, Ky." (AR 143; citing 10 AH 110; cf. WCD 75.293).

But this finding radically discredits Martin's multiple allegations against Ferrie, which Blakey took so seriously in his book.[16] If Martin and Ferrie conducted this investigation, it would seem highly disingenuous of Martin later to attack Ferrie for the very membership he hired Ferrie to purchase; and to tell Garrison's investigators that Ferrie, quite independently, had "conned" a bishop into "ordaining" him.[17]

I personally prefer to believe Ferrie's account, that, working for a private investigator on federal government contract, he was investigating the sale of fraudulent religious certificates. It accords so neatly with what I have long believed of Lee Harvey Oswald: that Oswald, working for a private investigator on federal government contract, was investigating the use of interstate mails for illegal arms sales.

OSWALD, KLEIN'S SPORTING GOODS, SEAPORT TRADERS, AND THE ATF

As we shall see in Chapter 17, the FBI and the Warren Commission had problems linking Oswald to the alleged murder weapon, or indeed any gun. Many witnesses claimed to have seen Oswald shooting, but often their stories, incompatible with the FBI version and indeed dubious, had to be discredited. In the end the key witness was Marina, who, under pressure from her government interviewers, told them what they wanted to hear.[18]

No credible witness ever saw Oswald shoot, although some *discredited* witnesses have claimed that they did. The evidence, so weak on Oswald's use of weapons, is very much stronger on his interest in ordering them by interstate mails. If anything, the evidence is excessive. After Oswald's arrest, Dallas police discovered among his effects at least five mail-order coupons for firearms (mostly from Klein's Sporting Goods and Seaport Traders, the stores from which he allegedly ordered his murder weapons), plus additional complete ads for guns. One of these, a Klein's mail-order coupon for the notorious Mannlicher-Carcano, was matched by researcher Paul Hoch to a magazine retrieved in New Orleans, a copy of the June 1963 *American Rifleman,* one of whose torn pages exactly complemented the ripped-out coupon. To complete the chain of evidence, FBI lab technicians found Oswald's thumb-print on the page from which the coupon had been removed.[19]

The magazine in question was one of several seized by the FBI and Secret Service on November 23, 1963, the day after the assassination. They had been found in a search of the waiting room in the Crescent City Garage, next to the William B. Reily Company where Oswald worked from May to July 1963. The operator of the garage, Adrian Alba, later testified that Oswald frequented the garage, talked to him about guns; and that "Oswald's special interest seemed to be in how one goes about ordering guns by mail."[20] In Alba's own words, Oswald asked "how many guns had I ever ordered, and how long did it take to get them, and where had I ordered guns from" (10 WH 220–22).

Whatever Oswald's motive in asking such questions, it was not to learn how to do it. According to the FBI and Warren Commission, Oswald (or more strictly "A. Hidell") had already ordered his Mannlicher-Carcano in Dallas back in March, from the *February* issue of the *American Rifleman* (WR 119). If Oswald really planned to use the *June* coupon, it would have been to order a *second* example of the gun he was never seen to use.

To order guns by interstate mail is of course an irrational way for a potential assassin to purchase his murder weapons: it lays a paper trail linking the weapon to the purchaser, or at least his post-office box. Conversely, if one is investigating firms known to sell weapons illegally through the mails, a paper trail is precisely what is needed.

In Texas anyone in 1963 could go to a gun shop and purchase a weapon untraceably over the counter. Only in interstate purchases did the law require identification, and Oswald was interested only in making interstate purchases. In the words of the Warren Commission,

> Using the name of A. J. Hidell, Oswald had ordered a Smith & Wesson .38 revolver from [Seaport Traders in] Los Angeles on a form which he dated January 27 [1963]. On March 12, he ordered a rifle from Klein's Sporting Goods in Chicago under the name of A. Hidell. (WR 723)

The Warren Report did not mention that in 1963 Seaport Traders and Klein's Sporting Goods were being *investigated,* by the ATF unit of the U.S. Treasury's Internal Revenue Service, as well as by Senator Dodd's Juvenile Delinquency Subcommittee of the Senate Judiciary Committee. Treasury and the Committee sought to demonstrate the need for more restrictive federal legislation to control the burgeoning mail-order traffic in firearms.[21]

As Senator Dodd announced, the existing situation had been studied, by actually tracing firearms through the mail, from firms under investigation. "A. J. Hidell's" purchase of a pistol from Seaport Traders on January 27, 1963, without even minimum proof of identification, was only two days before the Dodd subcommittee hearings on the matter opened on January 29. Sometime later, a corresponding purchase in Texas from Seaport Traders was duly noted in the committee's sample statistics.[22]

What made the FBI and Secret Service converge so swiftly, only one day after the assassination, on the magazines in Adrian Alba's garage?

Here it may be relevant that the garage housed and serviced cars in a U.S. government motor pool, used by such agencies as the FBI and Secret Service.[23] It was, in short, a locale already known to the U.S. government, and conceivably used by the ATF to order gun magazines for testing interstate weapons purchases.

Years afterwards, Alba added to his testimony before the Warren Commission, claiming that one day in 1963 an FBI agent took a car from his garage, and later "Alba observed the FBI agent in the car handing a white envelope to Oswald in front of the Reily Coffee Co." (AR 193). The House Committee discredited this story, I suspect correctly (AR 194). But by impeaching Alba's credibility, the Committee only raised further questions about the flood of FBI "evidence" determining, or overdetermining, Oswald's link to the Mannlicher-Carcano.

In my view it is uncertain whether the "Hidell" who ordered the rifle was in fact our Lee Harvey Oswald. (We shall see in the next chapter that Oswald did use the name "Hidell," and incriminated him, but as if "Hidell" were someone else). The superfluity of gun ads could even have been planted among Oswald's possessions (as some have argued his "Hidell" draft card was). For our present argument, it is irrelevant: both Oswald and "Hidell" (whether one man or two or more) were apparently part of a sustained investigation into illegal and improper gun sales.

This investigation would explain Oswald's (or "Hidell's") desire for the wretchedly inaccurate and indeed dangerous Mannlicher-Carcano, a gun which sold wholesale for as little as two dollars. The federal government and Dodd subcommittee, as it happened, were concerned about "so-called 'junk' guns that foreign governments [in this case the Italian government] have found obsolete."[24] The investigation would also explain the names and addresses of American Nazi party officials found in Oswald's address book. The American Nazi party, in 1963, was being investigated by the U.S. government and the Dodd subcommittee, for its mail-order purchase of firearms.[25]

OSWALD AND ARMED CUBAN EXILES

Above all, the ATF investigation would explain why Oswald, an alleged Marxist, also had reported contacts with at least three groups of violently anti-Marxist and anti-Castro Cubans. These three groups were the DRE in New Orleans, Silvia Odio's JURE group in Dallas, and Alpha 66. These three groups had more in common than their anti-Marxism. They were all suspected of involvement in illegal arms purchases and movements. The FBI, whether directly, or through cut-outs like Guy Banister, was keeping files on all three.

The best-known case is Oswald's initial meeting of August 5, 1963, with the DRE's Carlos Bringuier, only five days after the FBI had raided the dynamite cache next to the DRE's secret training camp. Bringuier, with good reason, took Oswald's offer to him "to train Cubans in guerrilla warfare" as proof that he was not a "loner," but someone with knowledge of the DRE's secret links to both the arms cache and the training camp.

Bringuier's argument was indeed an almost unanswerable one. As he pointed out to the Warren Commission, the presence of the training camp "was not generally known. . . . I believe that that was the only time here in New Orleans that there was something like that" (10 WH 43–44). Bringuier went on to suggest that Castro might have given Oswald this privileged information. Back in August, however, Bringuier had had the opposite reaction: "I thought he might be an agent from the FBI or the CIA, trying to find out what we might be up to."[26] Bringuier's logic here is of major importance. Oswald had to be working for one side or the other; he could not have been acting alone.

Not till years later did the rest of us learn how accurate was Oswald's knowledge. Only in 1976 did the Church Committee reveal, from U.S. government sources, that "underworld figures" were (as the FBI had known) involved in the training camp along with the arms cache.[27] Yet Oswald talked as if he were investigating this involvement back in 1963. According to one bystander at the first meeting, Oswald asked Bringuier "was he connected with the Cosa Nostra" (10 WH 77). According to another witness, Oswald brought up the subject by saying that he had "recently visited something called the Casa Nostra"—in Florida, the source of the dynamite and trainees (10 WH 84–85; WCD 75.533).

What is most suggestive in these two reports is Oswald's use in August of a term, "Cosa Nostra," that did not gain general currency until later, after Joseph Valachi's celebrated testimony of September 25, 1963. Inside the FBI, "La Causa Nostra," later reinterpreted as "La

Cosa Nostra," had been an in-house term for the Mafia, since Valachi's first FBI debriefing in September 1961 (9 AH 19–20). If Oswald was not being directed by the FBI, how did he come to use a term current within the FBI and (because Valachi had made it up) current nowhere else?

If Oswald had read the *New York Times* of that very morning, August 5, or an early copy of the August 10 *Saturday Evening Post,* he could have had access to the first public use of the term which would soon become so famous. But no one has ever presented Oswald to us as a voracious newspaper reader. In any case, one still needs to explain Oswald's apparent linkage of Bringuier to the "underworld figures" at the camp.

The investigation of illegal arms would explain not only the Oswald-Bringuier meeting of August 5, but also the alleged Oswald-Odio meeting in Dallas one month later. Silvia Odio herself told the Warren Commission that Oswald had come to her at a time when she was engaged in discussions with a Mr. Martin about buying arms.

> We had been trying to establish a contact with Mr. Johnny Martin, who is from Uruguay. He is from there, and he had heard that I was involved with this movement [JURE]. And he said that he had a lot of contacts in Latin America to buy arms, particularly in Brazil, and that if he were in contact with one of our chief leaders of the underground, he would be able to sell him second-hand arms that we could use in our revolution. . . . I jumped at the possibility.[28]

At the time Odio learned from a source in New Orleans that Oswald "was considered to be a 'double agent' . . . was probably trying to infiltrate the Dallas Cuban refugee group, and . . . should not be trusted" (26 WH 738).[29] The term "double agent" is resonant with the conflicting evidence we shall examine in the next chapter. Silvia Odio may very well have heard this story from her uncle, Dr. Agustin Guitart of the New Orleans CRC, who attended Oswald's trial (11 WH 378; 26 WH 405); and in turn Guitart would probably have been transmitting the concern of Carlos Bringuier that Oswald had come from the FBI.

But Bringuier had described Oswald to the world as an agent, not a double agent. As a double agent, Oswald would be playing both sides, acting covertly to fulfill some of the goals of the Cuban exiles (such as denouncing peace activists and integrationists in New Orleans) at the same time he was reporting against them.

Complex and improbable as this notion may seem, we shall see in the next chapter that there is good evidence for it. Oswald indeed was helping secretly to defame Bringuier's enemies, and thus acting as a conspiratorial part of the illicit gun-trafficking coalition on which (we have postulated) he was supposed to be reporting.

This double role may well have resulted in his being chosen for the fatal role of "patsy" on November 22. Although one can imagine many scenarios which would lead Oswald to play a double role, one is much simpler than the rest. It is that ultimately Oswald's movements were being directed by the circle of J. Edgar Hoover, a man who worked simultaneously for the Kennedys (against targets such as the Lake Pontchartrain arms cache) and against them (against integrationists like Martin Luther King).

SIXTEEN

Oswald as a Double Agent for Hoover

OSWALD, ALPHA 66, MILITARY INTELLIGENCE, AND THE ATF

In the last chapter we saw how many of Oswald's unexplained approaches to anti-Castro Cubans could have been (as Carlos Bringuier suspected) as an informant for the U.S. government, perhaps to investigate illicit arms trafficking. It is now time to consider the most suggestive and least understood example of all, Oswald's alleged dealings in Dallas with the bitterly anti-Kennedy Cuban-exile faction, Alpha 66, a group that we know to have been under investigation by the Treasury's Alcohol, Tobacco, and Firearms unit (ATF).

Dallas deputy sheriff Buddy Walthers, in a report never officially pursued, told his superiors that Oswald had attended meetings of Cubans ("possibly connected with the 'Freedom for Cuba Party' of which Oswald was a member") at "3128 Harlendale" (19 WH 534).[1] The FBI never pursued Walthers's lead. It did, however, report independently that there were Cubans at "3126 Hollandale," Dallas (WCD 1085U.4); these Cubans were members of the local chapter of SNFE–Alpha 66, a militant anti-Castro group associated (just as at Lake Pontchartrain) with the DRE, the Minutemen, and attempted arms deals. Researchers in Dallas have confirmed that Alpha 66 Cubans were in fact living on Harlandale Street.

Like the DRE, and in concert with it, Alpha 66 was violently anti-Kennedy in 1963. With the active support of Henry Luce and Time-

Life, which is said to have spent a quarter of a million dollars, Alpha 66 made a point of attacking Russian targets in Cuba, in an attempt to shatter the growing convergence of U.S. and Soviet policies in the Caribbean after the nuclear scare of the 1962 Cuban missile crisis.[2] When the President appealed separately to Luce and to the exiles to cease their attacks, both rebuffed him. Alpha 66 leader Tony Veciana "publicly snubbed the President and said that Alpha 66 would continue. If anything, the activities of Alpha 66 were stepped up."[3]

Through 1963 there were reports that the nuisance raids of Alpha 66, despite Kennedy's disapproval, were being tolerated (against orders) by middle-level ranks of the U.S. Navy.[4] Indeed it seems likely that at the same time Alpha 66 was being used operationally by the U.S. Army. In 1976 the Schweiker-Hart Senate subcommittee revealed that in 1963 the army was using operationally one of the four Cuban exile groups about which the Warren Commission was curious, that the FBI knew this, and that the FBI failed to transmit this information to the Warren Commission.[5] Reports persist that the group was Alpha 66, specifically in Dallas.[6] The House Committee confirmed that army intelligence had "had an operational interest in Antonio Veciana," the leader of Alpha 66; and that Veciana had been registered with the Army Information Source Registry from November 1962 until July 1966 (10 AH 51). In this same period Alpha 66's leaders had been negotiating for the use of aircraft with which to conduct raids, with those involved in the Lake Pontchartrain training camp (Schweiker-Hart Report, 65)—that is to say, with Frank Sturgis *alias* Fiorini and Gerry Patrick Hemming, the former of whom was one of six men publicly given "strong warnings" by the Kennedy Administration, in the same month of September, to cease their anti-Castro activities.[7]

Was Oswald sent to investigate Alpha 66's gunrunning activities? We happen to know that the Dallas chapter of Alpha 66 was under investigation by the ATF. The Warren Commission heard this from Treasury Agent Frank Ellsworth, the ATF's top expert on the illegal arms traffic in Dallas, whose FBI contact was James Hosty, the agent handling the Oswald case. Ellsworth told the Commission staff:

An organization known as the Minutemen is the right-wing group most likely to have been associated with any effort to assassinate the president. . . . The Minutemen are closely tied to General [Edwin] Walker and H. L. Hunt. Mr. Ellsworth described in some detail his undercover efforts in procuring the arrest of a local gunshop owner [Thomas Masen] who is an ardent member of the Minutemen. As a result of these undercover activities Agent Ellsworth learned that Manuel O[rcarberro] Rodriguez, apparently a Cuban survivor of the Bay of Pigs episode, was attempting to purchase arms in Dallas for Alpha 66. Mr. Rodriguez is also a member of the DRE. Agent Ellsworth indicated that virtually all information gathered by the FBI with respect to [such] activities was the responsibility of Agent Hosty.[8]

The FBI heard elsewhere that the Dallas Alpha 66 chapter's president, Manuel Rodriguez Orcarberro (who was also a Dallas DRE leader), was "violently anti-Kennedy" (WCD 853a, SS 3670; WCD 1085 U.1).[9]

Ellsworth's throwaway remark about Hosty's responsibility for investigating Cuban arms purchases resurrects the question of whether Hosty himself (despite his denials) was using Oswald as an informant. This would explain many anomalies: why, for example, the FBI and the Warren Commission apparently never checked out Oswald's reported links to the Alpha 66 address, with contacts presented by Ellsworth as suspicious. Above all, it would explain why Hosty, having already destroyed evidence about Oswald, was assigned to conduct the belated interview with Silvia Odio in which he avoided reference to the arms deals. If Oswald, directly or indirectly, had been reporting to the FBI about these groups and their arms deals, one would expect just this erasure of obviously important leads.

But if Ellsworth's testimony about Hosty makes Hosty look more suspect, Hosty returned the compliment. Fourteen years later Hosty told the Select Committee that at the time of the assassination "Frank Ellsworth . . . had indicated that he had been in the grassy knoll area and for some reason had identified himself as a Secret Service agent" (AR 184). The Committee pursued this lead because a Dallas policeman, Joseph M. Smith, had told the Warren Commission he encountered a man on the grassy knoll who (although no regular Secret Service were present) "stated that he was a Secret Service agent and offered supporting credentials" (AR 184).

Ellsworth, deposed by the Committee, denied Hosty's allegation (AR 184). We know, however, that he *was* in the immediate area. Interestingly, he and seven other ATF agents were among the first law-enforcement personnel of any description to reach the sixth floor of the Texas School Book Depository where the controversial Mannlicher-Carcano was found.[10] Here it becomes relevant that the interstate sales of foreign governments' "junk" guns (like the Mannlicher-Carcano) were being investigated by the U.S. government—presumably by the ATF.[11]

If Ellsworth was in the vicinity, it remains to be asked how Hosty knew about it. One explanation would be that Ellsworth was the un-identified ATF agent who met with Hosty (Ellsworth's usual contact) and "an Army Intelligence agent" for most of the morning of November 22, until forty-five minutes before the assassination (4 WH 461).

As we shall suggest in the next chapter, this agent may well have been James W. Powell, who, like Ellsworth, was inside the Texas School Book Depository at the moment the Mannlicher-Carcano was recovered (WCD 354, SS 1009; cf. WCD 329.58). In any case, one has to be interested in a three-way meeting between the FBI agent on the Oswald case, army intelligence, and the ATF, which ended forty-five minutes before the shots were fired.[12] One can see the possibility of a conspiracy where Oswald's covert employers, just like Ferrie's, turned their manipulations of Oswald's behavior for investigative purposes into a much more sinister scenario.

OSWALD AND MILITARY INTELLIGENCE

The preceding chapter considered the possibility that Oswald associated with anti-Kennedy Cubans in order to investigate them on behalf of a federal agency. But we saw it alleged that Oswald was a double agent collaborating with some of these groups, either (as I suspect) because he or his handlers shared their goals, or possibly because he or his handlers had been "turned" by those they were supposed to investigate. Such a possibility was particularly likely with targets, like Alpha 66, about which the government itself was conflicted, of two minds.

Here it is relevant that Alpha 66, although anti-Kennedy, was being used operationally by military intelligence. There are signs, albeit complex and inconclusive, that Oswald's strange and self-incriminating behavior in New Orleans and Dallas was staged to be documented in the secret files of military intelligence. A key moment appears to have been on the day after Oswald's arrest in New Orleans on August 9, 1963, when he gave self-incriminating and conflicting stories to both the New Orleans police and the New Orleans FBI.

On August 10, before being bailed through the intervention of Emile Bruneau, Oswald had been busy, creating a false documentary record of his activities (or what in intelligence circles is called a "legend").[13]

No doubt he thought his lies of that day would injure others, but in November they would end with his own murder. He established this false paper trail by talking (and apparently lying), first to Lieutenant Francis Martello of the New Orleans Police Intelligence Division (22 WH 822), and then (before being bailed out) to John Lester Quigley of the New Orleans FBI office (who allegedly had come to the New Orleans jail on a Saturday morning at Oswald's request [4 WH 432; 17 WH 758]). Both men, after interviewing Oswald, initiated contacts with military intelligence: Martello's information was relayed to the 112th Army Military Intelligence Group, while Quigley got in touch with the Office of Naval Intelligence in Algiers, Louisiana.[14] It is worth recalling that, as was shown in the McCarthy period, one of Hoover's techniques for spreading non-attributable data was to arrange for it to be parked in the files of military intelligence (see Chapter 13).

What exactly was relayed about Oswald to military intelligence remains unknown. It would appear, however, that to both Martello and Quigley Oswald showed two Fair Play for Cuba Committee cards. The first was signed by V. T. Lee, national director of the FPCC; the second was signed "A. J. Hidell," whom Oswald described as his local FPCC overseer (WR 728; 10 WH 53–57). In response to Martello's information, the 112th MIG "opened a file under the names Lee Harvey Oswald and A. J. Hidell" (AR 222).[15] Oswald also piqued Quigley's curiosity about a "Hidell" who was directing Oswald's Fair Play for Cuba activities in New Orleans.[16]

On November 22, the 112th MIG file was instrumental, perhaps crucial, in clinching the superficial case against Oswald as an assassin. For both the rifle said to have killed the President and the pistol said to have killed Officer Tippit had been ordered by "A. J. Hidell." Almost immediately after the assassination, the name "was fed into various circuits that transmitted it to government agencies that might yield pertinent information." By 3:15 P.M., Colonel Robert E. Jones of the 112th MIG at Fort Sam Houston contacted the FBI in Dallas, and linked Hidell to Oswald.[17]

Why was the name "Hidell" sent out to other agencies? According to the Dallas police, an obviously forged Selective Service card for "A. J. Hidell," with Oswald's photograph on it, had been found in Oswald's wallet when he was arrested (WR 181; 7 WH 187–88; WCE 795). Sylvia Meagher, by examining the record carefully, has shown that there is no contemporary reference to this card before an FBI report dated Saturday, November 23 (of an interview the day before), and that the claim it was found in Oswald's wallet is almost certainly false.[18]

Common sense supports her question as to why Oswald would go to the trouble of inventing an alias to buy the guns, and then carry evidence linking himself to this alias on the day the guns were used, and (so far as is known) on no other occasion. (It was not, for example, in the list of the contents of Oswald's wallet itemized by Lieutenant Martello on August 10, and indeed was incompatible with Oswald's story on that day [10 WH 52–54].) What other purpose could the forged card serve, other than identify Oswald as "Hidell," the supposed assassin? (Real Selective Service cards did not carry photographs, as was well known in the days when all men had to carry them. The Hidell card might have functioned as ID in Outer Mongolia, but not the United States.)

The result of Oswald's behavior on August 10, considered in context, was to call attention to "Hidell," and through him to the FPCC—something he would hardly have done had he imagined that Hidell would eventually be identified with himself. What he had done, and may or may not have intended to do, was leave a bureaucratic record linking the FPCC to "Hidell," and through "Hidell" to the gun that would kill the President. No wonder so many left-wingers, sympathetic to the FPCC, were willing to live with the second falsified cover-up, Hoover's false story that Oswald (alias "Hidell") had acted alone.

And not just the left, but moderates within the U.S. government (including Chief Justice Warren) as well. Henry Hurt has concluded of the Oswald-Hidell story:

> There is but one sure point buried in this shifting conclusion. If the Hidell evidence on that black Friday afternoon had led the United States to the conclusion that an agent of Fidel Castro had killed President Kennedy—and if there had been rash military retaliation against Cuba—certain elements of the military-intelligence establishment, long frustrated by the official toleration of Castro, would have been neatly satisfied.[19]

But there is another sure point to be made. Oswald on August 10 fed information to the New Orleans police and FBI which went straight to military intelligence, from which (if we can believe the record) it was returned to the Dallas FBI on November 22. In the same intervening period, FBI headquarters ordered additional investigation of Oswald "in view of the activities which had led to his arrest" (WR 437). Yet the crucial linking of Oswald to the "Hidell" who ordered the weapons reached the attention of the FBI on November 22, thanks to Colonel Jones of the 112th MIG. Allegedly, the FBI treated the Oswald file lethargically, despite the information learned by the FBI in September linking Oswald to a suspected KGB assassination expert (Kostikov), in Mexico. Thus the Oswald case only arrived in Dallas on November 21, as was learned after the assassination the following day by Oswald's FBI case officer James Hosty, who had just spent the morning with an army intelligence agent (4 WH 461–62). For some reason, it was also the 112th Army Intelligence Group at Fort Sam Houston that first notified the FBI Oswald was carrying a fraudulent "Hidell" Selective Service card. How the military knew this has never been explained.[20]

Was it in fact military intelligence that directed Oswald to link himself to Hidell? One possible indication of an Oswald-military link in 1963 was his Marine Corps Reserve ID Card, not mentioned in the Warren Report but found on his person, which had been issued in September 1959. This ID was a DD Form 1173, which according to a Marine spokesperson could have been issued to him for one of two reasons: because of an injury on active duty entitling him to medical privileges, or because he was a civilian employee overseas needing a military ID.[21]

OSWALD'S STEPS TO INCRIMINATE OTHERS BESIDES "HIDELL"

Understandably, because of "Hidell's" link to the notorious Mannlicher-Carcano, students of the assassination have focused on this aspect of his seminal interviews on August 10. But if we look at what is known of these interviews, it is clear that Oswald, in collaboration with his questioners, was making statements to embarrass a number of people targeted controversially by law enforcement.

Let us turn, for a moment, to the other FPCC card in Oswald's wallet, the one signed by V. T. Lee. Lee, the national director of the FPCC, was in 1963 a major target of both the FBI and Hoover's primary Senate ally Julien Sourwine, counsel to Senator Eastland's Senate Internal Security Subcommittee.[22] Lee had been grilled by Sourwine in a subcommittee hearing on February 14, 1963; on May 28, Oswald began a correspondence with Lee that was especially active in August.

The FBI had a double interest in Lee, as director of the FPCC which it and CIA had targeted, and as an alleged member of the Progressive Labor Movement. Both FPCC and PL were targets of FBI COINTELPROs and break-ins in 1963. Under the direction of Special Agent in Charge John Malone, the New York FBI had broken into Lee's FPCC headquarters in April and in October 1963, and into the office of the *Progressive Labor* magazine in May.[23] Consequently they had photographed Oswald's correspondence with Lee before the assassination.

On December 7, 1963, after Hoover had been overruled in his proposal to close off the murder investigation with a brief FBI report, the press published six of the Oswald-Lee letters, apparently from copies given by Lee himself to the FBI, after the assassination. The "responsible" face of the FBI was reflected in the *New York Times* the next day: "Asked about the exchange of letters between Mr. Lee and Oswald, the FBI said it had no comment."[24]

In the more lurid Hearst *New York Journal-American*, however, a much more conspiratorial story was planted. Its author, Guy Richards (who was close to John Malone, as we saw in Chapter 14), postulated that the assassination might have been a Lee-directed FPCC conspiracy. Almost certainly the FBI was behind the planted story, which was entered into the FBI's assassination file with the telling admonition from J. Edgar Hoover himself, "Be certain to go over this thoroughly."[25]

According to Richards,

> Lee was the friend and adviser who guided Oswald on many moves down South. . . . Lee's name and the extent of his role as a mentor for Oswald have been kept secret by the FBI and Dallas authorities. . . . It was reported in Dallas that pictures shown to Mrs. Oswald on Nov. 23 [the Mexico mystery man] . . . were of one or more figures from the militant pro-Castro [PL] faction of the Communist Party. . . . The FBI is maintaining enormous interest in the elusive and violently pro-Castro Mr. Lee—Oswald's friend and sponsor—and the group of key figures in the FPFCC who are oriented to the Red Chinese anti-coexistence Progressive Labor Movement.[26]

As we have seen, this was not the only relevant story leaked to Guy Richards, both after and more importantly before the assassination.

What is relevant about the targeting of V. T. Lee here is his persecution by Senate Committee counsel Julien Sourwine, whose hostile grilling of Lee was quoted prominently in Guy Richards's story. As I wrote in 1976, Sourwine was at the power center of the right-wing "Cuba Lobby" in Congress, working with Cuban exiles, wealthy businessmen like William Pawley, and venal congressmen supported by Caribbean dictators Trujillo (d. 1961) and Somoza.[27] Since then it has been revealed that Pawley (a friend of Allen Dulles, and supporter of Bringuier's DRE) and Senator Eastland (Sourwine's committee chairman) together planned a 1963 raid against Castro, which (we suggested in Chapter 7) helped trigger the massive cover-up of the JFK assassination.[28]

OSWALD AND THE ANTI-INTEGRATIONIST AGENDA

By means unlikely to have been accidental, Oswald facilitated the work of Hoover, Eastland, and Sourwine in their coordinated pursuit of a quite different target, the integration movement. At least two of the men Oswald implicated in his FPCC activities, the black Communist leader Ben Davis, and the civil libertarian Corliss Lamont, were the targets of both Hoover and the Senate Internal Security Subcommittee because of their friendship with Martin Luther King.[29] On August 10 Oswald gave FBI Agent Quigley a pamphlet by Corliss Lamont. This provoked a lengthy "Appendix" to the FBI Oswald file, linking the FPCC to the Communist party in 1963, on the basis of informer Louis Budenz's very dubious testimony to the Senate Internal Security Subcommittee (on "September 28, 1963," i.e., 1953) that Corliss Lamont had been a CP member in the late 1940s (17 WH 766–67). Oswald also made Ben Davis an honorary member of his FPCC Chapter.[30]

According to Martello, Oswald told him that he knew a Dr. Leonard Reissman at Tulane, and that his FPCC meetings were held on Pine Street, near Reissman's home (26 WH 763). In reporting this to the Secret Service after the assassination, Martello found it significant that Oswald's leaflets had been found near the 1100 block of Pine Street, close to the Reissman residence. He added that Reissman frequently entertained a Dr. James Dombrowski, and noted that both men were "said to be active in the integration movement." He added further that Reissman and Dombrowski's lawyer were both affiliated with a

Quaker-associated liberal group, the New Orleans Council for Peaceful Alternatives, or NOCPA (26 WH 763; cf. 10 WH 54–55). Martello reportedly told the Secret Service he had learned that one of the FPCC pamphlets "had blown out of Dr. Reissman's car."[31]

Martello was not making all of this up. Oswald (as we shall see in a moment) also told his aunt that he had been to the Reissman home, and he told someone else that his FPCC organization "was affiliated with Tulane University" (10 WH 68).[32] Martello's account of Oswald's remarks suggests that Oswald and Bringuier were allies, not opponents, in their propaganda activities; for Bringuier, back in the spring of 1963, had already targeted the Quaker-linked New Orleans Council for Peaceful Alternatives as pro-Communist and pro-Castro.[33]

New Orleans in the summer of 1963 was inflamed over the school-integration issue, and Oswald's apparently innocent remarks would add fuel to the flames. Some of Oswald's information soon reached a private detective, J. D. Vinson, working for the Louisiana Joint Legislative Committee on Un-American Activities, which responded to the Kennedy assassination with a provocative press release linking Oswald and the FPCC to Dombrowski's organization, the Southern Conference Educational Fund.

Before reporting any more of this right-wing paranoia, I should make clear that, having interviewed Mrs. Reissman about her late husband's activities, I am satisfied that Oswald had no contact whatever with the Reissmans. At the time of Oswald's "FPCC" activities, Reissman, a distinguished scholar, was on leave from Tulane University to a research center at Stanford University in California. According to Mrs. Reissman, her husband, although a liberal, had no dealings with James Dombrowski; it was she herself who had infuriated local racists, by arranging for an integrated birthday party of seven-year-olds at her daughter's school.

Despite the improbability of Oswald knowing Reissman, it is likely that he told Martello he did. Oswald's aunt (the same one who phoned Emile Bruneau) also told the Secret Service that Oswald had "mentioned that he knew, or was acquainted with, Dr. Reissman" (26 WH 766). She went on to link Oswald and Reissman to another integrationist, the Quaker Ruth Paine:

It was her impression that Oswald came into contact with Dr. Reissman through the Russian woman [sic; this was Marina's friend, the American

Quaker Ruth Paine]. Mrs. Murrett said that one of the two told her that Dr. Reissman had a daughter who was studying in Russia (26 WH 766).

Mrs. Murret, finally, urged this specter of a seditious left-wing cabal on the Warren Commission:

> He also said that Mrs. Paine knew a Tulane professor. . . . I remember him [Oswald] saying that he [Reissman] had a daughter that was attending the university in Moscow, and they either went to his home or they came to Lee's house (8 WH 147; cf. 8 WH 170).

At the time that Oswald was linking his FPCC chapter to the beleaguered integrationists in New Orleans, similar link-ups were being made by the Louisiana State Joint Legislative Committee on Un-American Activities, and their Washington allies, the Senate Internal Security Subcommittee under Senator Eastland of Mississippi, and his committee counsel Julien Sourwine. Dombrowski and the Southern Conference Educational Fund (SCEF) were among their chief targets. But through SCEF, which the Senate Internal Security Subcommittee had called Communist, they were hoping to pin the red label on its most famous associate, Martin Luther King.[34]

On October 4, 1963, State Representative James H. Pfister, head of the Louisiana Un-American Activities Committee, announced that as a result of an eleven-month investigation by his committee (for which Banister was an investigator), Louisiana state and New Orleans city police had raided the offices and homes of SCEF's leaders, and arrested three of them for conspiracy under the 1962 Communist Control Act. The three were SCEF's executive director, James Dombrowski, its treasurer, Benjamin Smith, and Smith's law partner Bruce Waltzer, a SCEF member. The *New York Times* report of the arrests added that "charges will be presented formally to Jim Garrison, Orleans Parish District Attorney, tomorrow."[35] Later developments make it clear that Smith and Waltzer had been singled out for arrest because they were simultaneously registered as foreign lobbyists representing the Castro government of Cuba in legal matters.

Despite the urging of Representative Pfister, the three men were ultimately booked, but not formally charged. A Louisiana state judge, J. Bernard Cocke, ruled that there was insufficient legal evidence to create a probable cause for the arrests. Thus the men were released, but not their records. Eastland and Sourwine had already subpoenaed their documents, which then vanished from Louisiana.[36]

Shortly after the assassination, the FBI was told that Pfister's State Un-American Activities Committee was now investigating the links between Oswald, SCEF, and the Fair Play for Cuba Committee. Apparently one of the keys to this sinister link-up were the FPCC pamphlets found in the 1100 block of Pine Street. The Committee's detective, Joseph Vinson, told another professional anti-Communist, Myers G. Lowman of Circuit Riders, Inc., in Ohio, about the Pine Street circulars, and Lowman in turn told the FBI.[37] Meanwhile, the Eastland-Sourwine subcommittee stepped up its attacks on Smith and Waltzer, since they were "registered as agents of the Castro government."[38]

Eastland and Sourwine could in theory have been sincere in suspecting the hidden direction of foreign Communist governments behind the integrationist movement. The same cannot, however, be said of Lee Harvey Oswald's linking of his own provocative activities to people like the Reissmans who knew nothing about them. This false-flag propaganda was conspiratorial, even if directed by men of some authority.

Can we say who was directing Oswald's anti-integrationist propaganda? A reasonable guess, once again, would be the segregationist Guy Banister. From his office in the 544 Camp Street building, Banister published the racist *Louisiana Intelligence Digest,* "which depicted integration as part of the Communist conspiracy."[39] His collecting of anti-Communist intelligence focused on the campuses of universities like Tulane. A former Louisiana State University student who did investigative work for Guy Banister on that campus told me that anti-integrationist activists picketing the Fifth District Federal Court in 1963 would regularly store their picket signs in Banister's office, and that he himself had seen Oswald there at the time.[40]

Banister's ideological proclivities were corroborated after his death by the fact that "several books from Banister's collection went to Banister's associate, Kent Courtney."[41] Kent Courtney, the organizer of the Conservative Society of America, had been the States' Rights candidate for governor of Louisiana in 1960. Like Myers G. Lowman, he was also a featured member of Billy James Hargis' Christian Crusade.[42] In addition, Courtney was a member of the California-based American Committee to Free Cuba, a group that gave money in late 1963 to the

Minuteman Loran Eugene Hall.[43] The night of the assassination, the radio tape of Oswald's "debate" with Ed Butler was released to the press by the DRE. Soon afterwards the tape was sold as a commercial recording by Key Records, owned by an associate of the American Committee to Free Cuba's organizer.

But the mentality which linked integration to communism was not restricted to the South alone. J. Edgar Hoover, when ordering a "Disruption Program" against the Socialist Workers' party in 1961 (or what later became known as a COINTELPRO), began his authorizing memo with the same link-up as Pfister's Un-American Committee: "The Socialist Workers' Party (SWP) has, over the past several years, been . . . strongly directing and/or supporting such causes as Castro's Cuba and integration problems arising in the South."[44] Meanwhile, Hoover had been searching for years in vain for proof linking the Communist party to Martin Luther King. On May 11, 1963, two days after Oswald began to work in New Orleans for the Reily Coffee Company, Hoover ordered (without any evidence) "that King be 'tabbed Communist' in 'Section A of the Reserve Index,' his current secret list of those slated to be arrested and held during a 'national emergency.' "[45]

Oswald, of course, linked himself simultaneously to the SWP and to the ideologically antithetical Communist party (CPUSA), as well as to the Fair Play for Cuba Committee. His task, wittingly or not, may have been to discredit all three groups through his own activities, and with them also the cause of integration. This would not just have satisfied Guy Banister's agenda, or State Representative Pfister's, or the Eastland-Sourwine Senate Internal Security Subcommittee's. It would also have served the deep political agenda of the master manipulator, J. Edgar Hoover.

SEVENTEEN

Army Intelligence
and the Dallas Police

In this chapter we shall draw heavily on official documents in reconstructing suppressed facts about the John F. Kennedy assassination.[1] It is of course unlikely that any document will identify the true conspirators and their specific crimes; and certain that many documents were suppressed or even falsified as part of the ensuing cover-up. But by unraveling and exposing the cover-up we come a little closer to what really happened. The analogy of Watergate is helpful here: the Ervin Committee, though it never fully established the reasons for the original Watergate break-in, was able from documentary evidence to expose many of the principals in the ensuing conspiracy to cover up. By focusing on some initially technical details, we can pick up a trail that leads to the conspiratorial involvement of army intelligence, not just in the cover-up, but in the circumstances surrounding the assassination itself.

THE DARK AND SCOPELESS RIFLE

The first clues we shall look at are minute, and apparently insignificant until placed in context. They concern certain tiny distortions of Marina Oswald's initial testimony linking her husband to the alleged murder weapon. Apparently inconsequential in themselves, they were in fact used to reinforce the allegation, later rejected by the Warren Commission, that the President was killed by a dark rifle which Oswald had used earlier in the Soviet Union, at which time it lacked a scope and had

267

a longer stock. In other words, the false and eventually discarded story of a dark and scopeless rifle was used to reinforce what we have called the "phase one" illusion of an international Communist conspiracy, which the Warren Report later replaced with the "phase two" myth of Oswald as a lone assassin.

Even in the final phase-two incrimination of Oswald, the Warren Commission had to rely heavily on quite different testimony from Marina linking her husband to the rifle. We shall see that Marina "repeatedly lied" (to quote an internal Commission memo) on such vital matters; that she did so after illicit coaching from her mentors; and that even the Warren Report recognized that some of her gun allegations were "of no probative value" (WR 189). Our attention to details in such a morass will not lead to the truth about the rifle; it will, however, help us to identify one of the important groups contributing to the phase-one illusion of an international Communist conspiracy: an Army Intelligence Reserve unit in Dallas.

Marina's alleged story in Russian of a "dark and scopeless rifle" was presented to English listeners by two émigré Russian interpreters in Dallas, Peter Gregory and Ilya Mamantov, who had known each other for many years. Both men had worked together to set up a CIA-subsidized anti-Communist "church" in Dallas, and Gregory had known Oswald before the assassination. We know that distortions of Marina's testimony occurred, because for some reason a transcript was prepared of a long Secret Service interview of Marina Oswald on November 24, 1963. At a few points, the transcriber noted small deviations between what Marina actually said and what the interpreter, the Oswalds' friend Peter Gregory, translated.

Two of these small deviations, by a strange coincidence, added the same details about Oswald's rifle as were put down in Marina's police affidavit on November 22, two days earlier, after translation by Gregory's friend Ilya Mamantov: "This (i.e., the alleged murder weapon) was like the rifle my husband had. It was a *dark* gun. But *I don't remember the sight* on it" (Senkel affidavit, 24 WH 219, emphasis added). Ruth Paine, who was present at the first interview, also recalled specifically that Marina "said her husband had a *dark* gun, dark in color. . . . She *couldn't definitely recall the sight*" (3 WH 82, emphasis added).

Keeping in mind the consensus as to the italicized details on November 22, it is disturbing to learn that on November 24 these details did not originate with Marina, but with her interpreter. On both points Marina's testimony was significantly different, enough so to attract the attention of the transcriber:

> (Q) This gun, was it a rifle or a pistol or just what type of gun? Can she answer that?
>
> (A) It was a gun.
>
> Mr. Gregory asked: Can you describe it?
>
> NOTE: Subject said: I cannot describe it because a rifle to me like all rifles.
>
> Gregory translation: She said she cannot describe it. It was sort of a *dark* rifle just like any other common rifle. . . .
>
> (Q) Can you describe this rifle that you saw?
>
> (A) Mr. Gregory in Russian: Same size as they are showing to you?
>
> Subject: I think so, but,
>
> Gregory translation: She says that a rifle approximately the same length as you are showing her; however, *the stock was longer.*
>
> Subject in Russian: It was a hump (or elevation) but I never saw through the telescope, but it was the same kind of hump (or elevation).
>
> Gregory translation: She says there was an elevation on the rifle but *there was no scope*—no telescope.
>
> (Q) Would you recognize a rifle scope if you saw one?
>
> (A) Yes. She says that now she knows the difference between a rifle with a scope and one without a scope. She says until she saw the rifle with a scope on TV the other day she did not know that rifles with scopes existed.[2]

Even if we knew no more than what has been said, this transcript would constitute prima facie evidence of a cover-up conspiracy. Gregory had not been present at the first interview, and (in theory at least) he knew nothing about the rifle and its color. How then, if not by conspiracy, did Gregory supply the seemingly innocuous word "dark," which Marina had not used, and to which so much attention had been paid on November 22? In fact the word was not so innocuous. On November 22 it was reported that the Dallas authorities would arrest Oswald "as part of an international conspiracy" (5 WH 218), and Marina's first FBI interview was "interpreted" and reported in such a way as to strengthen the impression that the murderer had brought his weapon with him from the Soviet Union:

> MARINA OSWALD advised that LEE HARVEY OSWALD owned a rifle *which he used in Russia* about two years ago. She observed what she presumed to be the same rifle in a blanket in the garage at 2515 West Fifth, Irving [where Marina stayed with her friend Ruth Paine]. On November 22, 1963, she observed the same blanket in the garage but the rifle was missing. MARINA OS-

WALD stated that on November 22, 1963, she had been shown a rifle in the Dallas police Department, reportedly found at the Texas School Book Depository, and was unable to positively identify it as the one she had observed in the above mentioned garage. She stated that it was a *dark* color like the one she had seen, but she *did not recall the sight.* (WCE 1778, 23 WH 383–84, emphasis added)

Here the story of the dark and scopeless rifle acquires political importance: Marina appeared (according to her interpreter) to be identifying the rifle as one which Oswald had used in the Soviet Union. This was presumably part of the evidence with which Assistant District Attorney Bill Alexander promptly "prepared to charge Oswald with murdering the President 'as part of an international Communist conspiracy.' "[3]

Ilya Mamantov, Gregory's friend who was the interpreter at the first interview, himself later went on television to argue that the assassination was an international Communist "underground conspiracy" (WCD 385.269–72). The case was plausible. As Mamantov himself explained to the Warren Commission, no ordinary person "had a gun in the Soviet Union" (9 WH 114); nor would he be allowed one. Mamantov added no less than seven times under oath that Marina had used the word "dark" to describe Oswald's rifle on November 22. Her actual words to Gregory only two days later ("I cannot describe it because a rifle to me like all rifles") suggests how much had been gained as well as lost in translation.

Gregory's interpolation of the word "dark" can hardly have been coincidental. There was thus no excuse for Secret Service agent Leon Gopadze (who in turn became Marina's interpreter) to report that Gregory's translation "was faultless without deviation and at no time was there any indication that Mr. Gregory was translating otherwise" (23 WH 405). The same Gopadze decided it would be "beneficial" to use Gregory in his own first interview with Marina, when she first said she had taken the picture of Oswald and the rifle, including the disputed scope (23 WH 406, 408). Later the Warren Commission decided to use Gopadze and Gregory together as Marina's interpreters on September 6, 1964 (5 WH 588; cf. 11 WH 275).

It may seem idle to make too much of Gregory's apparently invented story of a dark and scopeless rifle, since the story was soon abandoned. Four days later, Marina changed her story, telling the same Leon Gopadze and Peter Gregory that she had taken the famous photograph of Oswald with pistol and scope-fitted rifle ("she does not remember noticing the scope but . . . it was Lee's rifle," 23 WH 408). Later, she told the Commission under oath that Lee sold his Russian gun in Russia (1 WH 14) and that "I recognized the telescope . . . in New Orleans" (1 WH 15) on his later gun, which she no longer called dark. The Commission relied on Marina's testimony that the Mannlicher-Carcano "was the 'fateful rifle of Lee Oswald' " (WR 128, citing 1 WH 119, 14); even though it knew very well that, as its counsel Norman Redlich wrote in a memo of February 28, 1964, "Marina has repeatedly lied to the Secret Service, the FBI, and this Commission on matters which are of vital concern." It chose to ignore the abundant indications that Marina, faced with not-so-subtle threats of deportation back to the Soviet Union (1 WH 410; cf. 23 WH 405), frequently changed her story to meet the latest demands of her interviewers.

The Warren Commission wisely abandoned some of Marina's wilder gun stories as "of no probative value" (WR 189), since they were discredited by FBI investigators.[4] Yet the Commission relied on Marina's testimony anyway, presumably because there was virtually no indisputable evidence linking Oswald to murder, the rifle, or indeed to any gun. For example, when it concluded that the rifle in the controversial photograph "is the same" as the Mannlicher-Carcano (WR 125) it had to pass over the FBI's initial report that the photo showed too little detail to permit this identification (WCD 7.335). Before concluding that the Warren Commission were the chief culprits of the cover-up conspiracy, however, one has to consider the many constraints, of time, budget, and both public and bureaucratic politics, on the scope of their enquiry. Rightly or wrongly, they saw part of their task as being "to lay the dust"; and the "one lone nut" hypothesis which they offered to the nation, even if not true, may have been less untrue and less harmful than Mamantov's alternative phase-one hypothesis of an international Communist conspiracy.

For the Mamantov-Gregory story of a dark and scopeless rifle, even if soon discarded, had strong corroborating evidence at the time (which the Commission was thus forced also to reject): testimony suggesting that someone called Oswald had had a scope mounted on a rifle just before the assassination.

Dial D. Ryder, an employee of the Irving Sport Shop, has stated that he found on his workbench on November 23 [i.e., one day after the Mamantov interview] an undated work tag with the name 'Oswald' on it, indicating that sometime during the first 2 weeks of November three holes had been bored in a rifle and a telescopic sight mounted on it and boresighted. . . . The Commission concluded that it is doubtful whether the tag produced by Ryder was authentic. (WR 646)

This was just the story needed to explain how Oswald's scopeless Soviet rifle could have been converted into the assassination weapon.

The Commission and FBI exhaustively demolished the case that Oswald visited Ryder's gun shop (WR 315–18; 22 WH 529–58), even though this meant discarding the informed corroborative testimony of two other Irving witnesses as well. It did not, however, consider the alternative hypothesis that the inauthentic work tag reported by Ryder and the "anonymous telephone calls" (WR 316; 24 WH 328) which brought it to the attention of Dallas police and the FBI, constituted prima facie evidence of conspiracy.

This impression of coordinated disinformation will be strengthened in the next chapter; we shall see there that another of the details added by Gregory (that in the original gun "the stock was longer," WCD 344.23) was also corroborated by supporting testimony (rightly rejected by the Warren Commission) that Oswald had practiced firing at a local rifle range with a "foreign" gun, on which "it appeared that the front end of the wood stock had been cut off" (26 WH 371; cf. 372, 370).

There were men on the Dallas police force who should have been questioned about this apparently coordinated disinformation. For example, the Warren Report failed to note that F. P. Turner, the Dallas policeman who received and investigated the Ryder story (24 WH 328), was the partner of B. L. Senkel who, with Mamantov as interpreter, prepared Marina's November 22 affidavit about a dark and scopeless rifle (24 WH 219, 325).

AN APPARENT DIGRESSION:
ARMY INTELLIGENCE AND DEALEY PLAZA

Senkel and Turner are among the couple of dozen policemen who on November 22 and 24 managed to be at all the crucial scenes of action, often in the company of the Secret Service. Senkel and Turner had searched the Texas School Book Depository (TSBD) after the shooting,

Senkel arriving on the sixth floor shortly before the controversial Carcano was found (24 WH 324; cf. 19 WH 502). Both men, after separating briefly between City Hall and the sheriff's office, converged on Oswald's room at North Berkeley, where they discovered the leather holster that linked him to the pistol (7 WH 223; 24 WH 325, 344, 350). Turner later testified that he obtained the warrant for that search on November 22, although police records would indicate that it was dated November 23 (24 WH 344; cf. 7 WH 222). With Turner and Senkel at the search was Assistant District Attorney Bill Alexander (24 WH 327), the man who (as we saw) then "prepared to charge Oswald . . . 'as part of an international Communist conspiracy.' "[5]

Before the assassination, Senkel and Turner were in the pilot car of the Kennedy motorcade, along with Deputy Chief George Lumpkin (who chose Mamantov to be Marina's interpreter, 9 WH 106) and two alleged members of the Secret Service (20 WH 497, 24 WH 329). In fact (21 WH 578) these "Secret Service" personnel were Lieutenant Colonel George Whitmeyer, a local army-reserve commander, and Jack Puterbaugh, the local advance man for the Democratic National Committee who was present when the parade route in front of the TSBD was set (17 WH 611–19).

The pilot car's behavior on November 22 is certainly peculiar. Driving "about 3 minutes ahead of the motorcade," the pilot car made one recorded stop along the parade route—exactly in front of the TSBD. ("Deputy Chief G. L. Lumpkin . . . stopped momentarily at the corner of Houston and Elm Street" and spoke to the policeman "working traffic at that corner," 21 WH 579). None of the three policemen assigned to that corner reported this conversation in their affidavits (22 WH 598, 600, 604); one of them (J. M. Smith) did, however, report his part about ten minutes earlier in the police request of 12:19 P.M. for an ambulance for "a white male who had an epileptic seizure" (22 WH 600; cf. 23 WH 839).

Eight pages of police-radio Channel One transcript at the precise period of the assassination (23 WH 839–42) relate to this epileptic "emergency" and the resulting need to open a route directly and exactly to Parkland Hospital ("cut all traffic for the ambulance going to Parkland" 23 WH 841)—not for the President, who was shot only midway through this "emergency," but for the man with the "epileptic seizure." The Commission later learned, but did not report, that the man, who walked away from the ambulance at Parkland, had not had an epileptic seizure at all (WCD 1245.6–10).

Considering that Deputy Chief Lumpkin in the pilot car was (I have been reliably informed) a member of the Army Intelligence Reserve, and considering that the pilot car also contained the local army-reserve commander as an unscheduled occupant (4 WH 170), it is intriguing to learn that one of those near the "epileptic seizure" in Dealey Plaza was an army-intelligence agent, James W. Powell (WCD 206.19–20). Special Agent Powell was soon afterwards "trapped inside the Texas School Book Depository after the Depository doors had been sealed."[6] The man who had ordered the TSBD sealed was Lumpkin (21 WH 580), who had driven there with Lieutenant Colonel Whitmeyer, Senkel, Turner, and Dallas Secret Service Chief Sorrels (24 WH 324). Yet Lumpkin later reported that, apart from a Channel 8 photographer whom Powell saw in the TSBD, and two Alcohol, Tobacco, and Firearms agents, "all other persons, including the press, was [sic] kept outside the building" (21 WH 581). This statement is contradicted by a police report that in the TSBD were FBI Agent Pinkston and a Secret Service agent (probably Sorrels, 21 WH 512; cf. 23 WH 926).

As many as three army-intelligence agents may have figured in the events surrounding the Kennedy assassination; alternatively, one or both of the two "other" agents may have been Powell. There was the army-intelligence agent who with a member of the ATF (Frank Ellsworth?) spent the morning of November 22 with James Hosty (4 WH 461), the FBI agent whose name was in Oswald's notebook (16 WH 64), and who reportedly described Oswald to Dallas Police Lieutenant Revill as "a member of the Communist Party . . . capable of committing the assassination" (17 WH 495; cf. 17 WH 780–84). And there was the "Army intelligence man" whom "Lieutenant Revill knew" and drove back to his office from the TSBD (5 WH 57), shortly before Revill encountered Hosty (5 WH 34). This agent may well have been Powell, since Revill had organized the search of the TSBD which discovered the famous rifle on the sixth floor, where Powell (along with Lumpkin) was present (WCD 329.57–58). Whoever he was, Revill omitted his name when testifying as to the occupants of his car (5 WH 34).[7]

For ten years it might have seemed unwarranted to see anything conspiratorial in this convergence of army-intelligence personnel on Dealey

Plaza. But on May 16, 1973, the day before the first of the Senate Watergate hearings which would help drive President Nixon from office, army intelligence declassified an extraordinary army telegram about Oswald dispatched late in the evening of November 22, 1963. The cable, from the Fourth Army Command in Texas to the U.S. Strike Command at McDill Air Force Base in Florida, linked Oswald to Cuba via Cuba's alleged Communist "propaganda vehicle," the Fair Play for Cuba Committee. It also transmitted two statements about Oswald, both false, which had come via army intelligence from the Dallas police: "Assistant Chief Don Stringfellow, Intelligence Section, Dallas Police Department, notified 112th Intelligence Group, this Headquarters, that information obtained from Oswald revealed he had defected to Cuba in 1959 and is a card-carrying member of Communist Party." Stringfellow was a member of the police intelligence unit headed by Jack Revill (19 WH 120), while the Fourth Army's 112th Intelligence Group (with offices in Dallas and New Orleans) was the unit of James Powell (WCD 329.58).

USSTRICOM, the U.S. Strike Command, is an extraordinary two-service command (army and air force) set up in 1961 in response to the "Lebanon crisis" of 1958. Designed to provide a swift strike force on short notice, its location in Florida made it singularly appropriate for a surprise attack on Cuba. Since mid-1963 its commander had been General William D. Rosson, a CIA-related general who in 1954 had formed part of General Lansdale's team in Vietnam. Fletcher Prouty, in his book *The Secret Team*, lists him as one of the six who "made rapid promotions to the grade of brigadier general and higher as a result of the CIA, Special Forces, and Vietnam."[8]

Once again, one can see the abundance of reasons behind the consensus, apparently generated by Hoover, for establishing that Oswald was just a nut who acted alone.[9]

ARMY INTELLIGENCE, THE OSWALDS, LEIU, AND THE KENNEDY PARADE ROUTE

All of these facts add some interest to the unusual fashion in which Mamantov was recruited for the first interview about the "dark and scopeless rifle." I have already mentioned that he was phoned by Deputy Chief Lumpkin, but the initial contact with Mamantov had been made two minutes earlier by Jack Alston Crichton, a right-wing Republican, oil operator, member of Army Intelligence Reserve (9 WH 106), and head of "a local Army Intelligence Unit" (WCD 386, SS 1058). Crichton knew Mamantov personally as a fellow petroleum geologist. He also knew him because Mamantov was a precinct chairman of the Republican party, for which Crichton became the 1964 candidate for governor of Texas.

It is not known how many Dallas policemen were also (as is apparently a widespread practice) members of the U.S. Army Reserve. One such reservist was Detective Adamcik (7 WH 203), a member of the party which retrieved the rifle-blanket from the Paine garage and later reported what he overheard at Mamantov's interview of Marina about the rifle ("She said that it looked like her husband's rifle. She said that it was dark"; 24 WH 291). Another member of Army Intelligence Reserve was Captain W. P. Gannaway, Revill's supervisor as head of the Dallas Police Special Service Bureau (WCD 1426.26; 19 WH 120); Gannaway's secretary was reported by an out-of-town police chief to be "closely connected" to Jack Ruby (WCD 86.151). This story was plausible, given the close connections between Jack Ruby and the SSB, including men who participated in the search of the TSBD and the arrest of Oswald. Since the protection of visiting dignitaries was one of the SSB's responsibilities (5 WH 48), Gannaway was involved in the meetings arranged by Secret Service advance man Winston Lawson for the Kennedy visit (5 WH 39; 7 WH 580).

According to a news story in FBI files, in 1963 both Captain Gannaway and his subordinate Lieutenant Revill were assigned a special responsibility for "espionage and subversive activities" in Dallas. This was in conjunction with

> Federal Bureau of Investigation agents, military intelligence teams from the army, navy, and air force, and other federal agencies with investigators operating from headquarters here. . . . The job of [Revill's] intelligence section in Capt. Gannaway's bureau . . . requires the closest cooperation with these other governmental agencies gathering intelligence on subversive groups suspected of espionage. . . . With membership in a national police intelligence organization known as LEIU (Law Enforcement Intelligence Units) the local officers are able to get information almost immediately on suspected subversives when they move into Dallas. This information is exchanged by police units as these persons move from city to city. . . . Employes in [industrial] plants are carefully screened by security conscious personnel officers, and in

key jobs are given strict government security clearances. Industry is taking great strides to upgrade security practices. One such group in this area is the American Society for Industrial Security.[10]

The possibility that Oswald was an informant for this centralized security team would explain his visit to the Dallas American Civil Liberties Union, a liberal group being investigated by Revill's intelligence section, in the company of an extreme right-winger (Michael Paine).[11]

One can see how easily a false legend for Oswald could have been generated in the shared files of this coordinated security campaign, involving the Dallas SSB, FBI, military intelligence, and the American Society for Industrial Security. Such a centralized file system could be the source for the recurring (and unexplained) inversion of Oswald's name, as Harvey Lee Oswald, in the files of the Dallas police (e.g., 19 WH 438, 24 WH 259), FBI (e.g., 23 WH 207, 23 WH 373), Secret Service (16 WH 721, 748), army intelligence, and naval intelligence.[12]

The most intriguing "Harvey Lee Oswald" document is Jack Revill's list of employees at the Texas School Book Depository, compiled right after the assassination, before Oswald had been apprehended for the Tippit murder. For some unexplained reason, Oswald's inverted name ("Harvey Lee Oswald") was at the very head of that list, accompanied by an address, "605 Elsbeth," that slightly misrepresented the address (602 Elsbeth) where he had resided a year earlier (24 WH 259).[13] The Elsbeth address does suggest that Oswald's data had been parked for some time before the assassination in an intelligence file, not hitherto identified. One possibility would be the files of LEIU, the Law Enforcement Intelligence Unit, the intercity police-intelligence organization of which Revill was the lead local representative. LEIU's files, unlike ordinary police files, cannot be given to any civilian authorities and are treated as exempt from the Freedom of Information Act. As we shall see, it was also a frequent practice for the LEIU member intelligence units to collaborate with army intelligence.[14]

Another army reserve officer in Dealey Plaza may have been Winston Lawson, the White House Secret Service agent responsible for the choice of the Kennedy motorcade route (4 WH 318). Lawson's first three reports of what happened on and before November 22 raise considerable questions about his performance. For example he reported that motorcycles were used on "the right and left flanks of the President's car" (17 WH 605; cf. 17 WH 624, 18 WH 741), although photographs show that they accompanied at the rear (21 WH 768–70). Numerous later reports from the Dallas police agreed that at Lawson's own instructions the proposed side escorts were redeployed to the rear of the car (7 WH 581, 3 WH 244, 18 WH 809, 21 WH 571). This change, ostensibly for the sake of security, would appear to leave the President more open to a possible crossfire.

Lawson also noted that "the motorcycles cleared a path to the Parkland Hospital" (17 WH 629), and later that his own car (the lead car, between Lumpkin's and the President's) "assisted the motorcycles in escorting the President's vehicle to Parkland Hospital" (17 WH 632; cf. 21 WH 580). These claims are inconsistent with the radio orders on police channels to clear a route to Parkland (and block off the side streets), which had been issued, not for the President's car, but for the ambulance summoned by the pseudo-emergency of the so-called "epileptic seizure" (23 WH 841; cf. 17 WH 368, 395).

Lawson's sworn testimony to the Warren Commission said nothing about the motorcycle escort; and it painted a picture even harder to reconcile with the orders for a route to be cleared: "We had to do some stopping of cars and holding our hands out the windows and blowing the sirens and the horns to get through" (4 WH 354). No one on the Commission asked about the orders on the police radio transcript, by which other cars had already been blocked from the route.

ARMY INTELLIGENCE AND THE SECRET SERVICE

Events since the Kennedy assassination have alerted us to the possibility of illicit collaboration between members of army intelligence and the Secret Service. In 1970 the *Washington Star* reported that "plainclothes military intelligence agents played a questionable—and still secret— surveillance role at the 1968 national conventions" in Chicago, where the Secret Service admitted borrowing agents from the Illinois-based 113th Intelligence Group.[15] These borrowed "security" forces conducted extensive domestic intelligence operations, and (according to George O'Toole) there were stories of provocations as well.

> In Chicago, the [CPD] Red Squad [a member unit of the LEIU] was in daily contact with the army's 113th Military Intelligence Group during the late 1960s and early 1970s, passing along intelligence reports and receiving a variety of technical assistance. The 113th also provided money, tear-gas

bombs, MACE, and electronic surveillance equipment to the Legion of Justice thugs whom the Chicago Red Squad turned loose on local anti-war groups. On at least two occasions, the fruit of the Legion's burglaries turned up in army hands. In one case documents stolen from the defense attorneys in the famous Chicago Seven trial growing out of the disturbances at the 1968 Democratic Convention were turned over to the army by the Legion of Justice hoodlums.[16]

There were similar rumors about the 1972 party conventions and the 111th Intelligence Group in Miami, where one provocateur (Pablo Fernandez) was said to be a former CIA agent working with Watergate burglar E. Howard Hunt.[17] What we know from these later disturbances suggests that it is common practice for the Secret Service, whose local offices are scantily staffed, to augment their staff for special events with auxiliary personnel from military intelligence and other sources.

Quite by accident, we know that the Dallas Secret Service recruited thirty men from the Fort Worth Chamber of Commerce Sports Committee (of whom the informant, at least, was a former Army Air Force intelligence officer) to "assist the Secret Service at the breakfast for president Kennedy" on November 22 (18 WH 691). In Dallas, where Adlai Stevenson had been attacked only one month earlier, one would expect the Secret Service, which gave "special attention" to this event (2 WH 108), to have recruited even more such auxiliaries. Yet the reports and testimony of Lawson and other Secret Service agents are silent on this score. Meanwhile, the FBI reported that its offer of assistance had been declined (17 WH 821). The Warren Commission, faced with reports and rumors of unexplained additional "Secret Service" on the grassy knoll (6 WH 196), with Lumpkin (4 WH 162), behind the TSBD (6 WH 312), in front of the TSBD (19 WH 524; 20 WH 443), and even at the Tippit killing (3 WH 332; cf. 12 WH 202, 24 WH 204, 12 WH 45), asked no questions and learned nothing (cf. AR 222).

We recognized earlier the political constraints which made it difficult for the Warren Commission, which had questionable constitutional authority and no independent investigative staff, to pursue the documentary indications of a possible conspiracy linking army intelligence and the local Dallas police (who engaged Mamantov as interpreter) to the Secret Service (who engaged Gregory [2 WH 344; WCD 5.291]). Thus, one might exculpate the Warren Commission for not having asked more questions of high-level witnesses, such as Washington Secret Service Inspector Thomas J. Kelley. It was Kelley who ratified the strange and possibly illegal arrangements under which the Secret Service, after being telephoned by Gregory himself, sequestered Marina from other investigative agencies for thirty-six hours and brought in Gregory as her interpreter (2 WH 344; WCD 5.292; WCD 87, SS 533.1–2; cf. 20 WH 445).[18]

THE WARREN COMMISSION
AND ARMY SURVEILLANCE

Considering the Warren Commission's difficulties in the face of so many unanswered questions about the role of the Secret Service, the failure to pursue these questions is less surprising than the Warren Commission's controversial recommendations that the Secret Service's domestic surveillance responsibilities be increased (WR 25–26). Somewhat illogically, the Warren Report concluded both "that Oswald acted alone" (WR 22), like most American assassins (WR 463), and also that the Secret Service, FBI, CIA, should coordinate more closely the surveillance of "organized groups" (WR 463). In particular, it recommended that the Secret Service acquire a computerized data bank compatible with that already developed by the CIA (cf. WR 464–65; 5 WH 125; 472–75; 577–79).

Thanks to Senator Ervin's investigation into federal data banks, in the wake of the army-intelligence espionage scandals of 1970, we know that these recommendations were eventually implemented, under the direction of the same Thomas J. Kelley, who by now was assistant director for protective intelligence of the Secret Service. The Warren Commission's recommendation was by 1970 "widely cited in the government as the authority for citizen surveillance" by any agency, including the controversial army-intelligence program.[19]

Federal domestic surveillance increased after November 22, 1963, even before this recommendation; and it increased again after the Watts and Detroit riots. For army intelligence, "the big build-up in information gathering, however, did not come until after the shooting of the Rev. Martin Luther King, Jr. in April 1968."[20] Army-intelligence agents were assigned to spy at the 1968 political conventions because the Secret Service "had been handed the job of protecting presidential candidates after the June 5, 1968, assassination of Senator Robert F.

Kennedy—and didn't have enough men of its own."[21] The termination of these army-intelligence programs after disclosure in 1970 led directly to the Huston Plan and succeeding series of White House intelligence operations, which climaxed with the so-called plumbers' unit of Watergate burglar E. Howard Hunt. Once again, Thomas J. Kelley was the Secret Service participant in at least one of these clandestine White House units.[22]

This rapid glance at the post-assassination increase in domestic surveillance operations does not tell us anything about who committed those assassinations. It does, however, refute the absurd but frequently encountered hypothesis that assassinations have had no impact on the U.S. structure of government. Not only did assassinations (or attempts at assassination) have a very direct bearing on the outcome of the next three presidential elections (in 1964, 1968, and 1972), they also helped inaugurate a new era of domestic intelligence operations which, as one Nixon official conceded, "would have been unthinkable, and frankly, unattainable from Congress in a different climate."[23]

EPILOGUE

"Thus the failure of the Warren Commission to establish the true facts about the John F. Kennedy assassination, and the subsequent failure of Congress to rectify that deficiency, have a direct bearing on America's current political crisis and erosion of Congressional power." I so concluded a survey of domestic intelligence operations published in early 1976.[24]

Later that year, in response to congressional revelations by the Church and Pike Committees in the wake of Watergate, Attorney General Edward Levi issued new guidelines to prevent the indiscriminate monitoring of political dissenters. Although this executive order was apparently honored through the Carter years, it also engendered a backlash: the Reagan-Bush promises in the 1980 presidential campaign to "unleash" the intelligence agencies. The new Reagan Administration moved promptly to overrule the Levi guidelines, and progressively augment the collection of "dirt," not only on dissenters, but also on members of Congress.[25]

Thus the abuses of the Watergate plumbers were soon reduplicated and enhanced in the Iran-Contra affair, with government-financed covert domestic operations, in conjunction with one of the nation's largest p.r. firms, directed against individuals, the Democratic opponents of the Contras in Congress, and the press.[26] Again, as in the Nixon years, Congress went through the motions of investigating these abuses, and the Iran-Contra committees' staff drafted a chapter for their report. As summarized later by Robert Parry and Peter Kornbluh, the subject matter of the draft chapter was of major constitutional importance: "The Administration was indeed running a set of domestic political operations comparable to what the CIA conducts against hostile forces abroad. Only this time they were turned against the three key institutions of American democracy: Congress, the press, and an informed electorate."[27] As a mark of the new fear in Congress and the press, however, the draft chapter was covered up, with the connivance of those who had been successfully intimidated: above all Congress and the press.

There are, of course, those who say that these abuses—and not the unsolved mystery of how the assassination of a President could be carried out and covered up three decades ago—are what citizens should investigate and protest today. This chapter has attempted to suggest how the two concerns are in fact one and the same.

EIGHTEEN

The Assassination and the Great Southwest Corporation

In the last chapter, we examined Peter Gregory's distorted "translation" of Marina Oswald's testimony, to supply the baseless story, already reported by Gregory's friend Mamantov, of Oswald's "dark and scopeless" rifle.[1] Because this story was ultimately not used, and the "corroboration" for it painstakingly discredited, it might appear that Gregory's role in the Dallas cover-up, even if improper, was a small one not worth examining in such detail.

As part of a conspiracy to promote a preplanned second cover-up, however, such stories are more sinister, and indicative of conspiracy. In this chapter we shall see that those who spoke of an "international Communist conspiracy," and those who arranged for a "lone assassin" cover-up, were in deep contact with each other.

Gregory, moreover, played a second and more lasting role in the post-assassination history of Marina Oswald. It is Gregory who assumed responsibility for delivering Marina into the hands of employees and lawyers of the Great Southwest Corporation, a real-estate venture controlled in Dallas by the wealthy family of Bedford Wynne.[2] One Great Southwest employee, James Herbert Martin, who managed the firm's Inn of the Six Flags motel, soon became Marina's manager. After he was fired, William A. McKenzie, a lawyer from the Wynne family law firm (which represented Great Southwest) became Marina Oswald's lawyer. Both men, along with still other employees of Great Southwest, were responsible for highly questionable "links" between

Oswald and the Mannlicher-Carcano rifle, some of which were again discarded by the Warren Commission.

It was Martin who negotiated the sale of the backyard photograph of Oswald with the rifle (1 WH 496). McKenzie, according to the testimony of two witnesses under oath, coached his client as to what she should tell the FBI about her husband and his rifle (2 WH 321, 336–37). Shortly after Gregory altered Marina's rifle testimony to add the gratuitous details that when she first saw it, "there was no scope" and "the stock was longer" (WCD 344.23), two Great Southwest employees told the FBI of seeing Oswald at a rifle range before the assassination; one of them specified that Oswald had "a foreign gun and it appeared the front end of the wood stock had been cut off" (26 WH 371; cf. 372, 370). The Warren Report, quite properly, found "no substantial basis" for believing this identification of Oswald (WR 318); quite improperly, it converted at least three similar apparently independent and corrobative reports of a shortened "stock" (WCE 2915, 2916, 2935; 26 WH 370, 371, 383; cf. 10 WH 374, 381) into less suspicious accounts of a shortened "barrel" (WR 320).

Once again we are faced with a prima facie case of a conspiracy to deceive; especially since one of these witnesses, M. H. Price, testified under oath that "Oswald" had told him in early November, 1963, that he had just had a Japanese scope "mounted" and "boresighted" locally (10 WH 370, 372). Readers will recall the local work ticket "with the name 'Oswald' on it" to have a scope "mounted . . . and boresighted" in early November, which the Commission rightly doubted was "authentic" (WR 315, 646; 20 WH 27). Other evidence showed that Oswald (or at least "Hidell") had bought the rifle with the scope already mounted on it in March; yet this scope was indeed, just as Price testified, Japanese (22 WH 528).

Since 1963 the Great Southwest Corporation has drawn the attention of investigative journalists for a quite different reason: allegations of bankruptcy fraud with organized-crime overtones. It is certain that highly questionable transfers of assets to Great Southwest contributed to the spectacular bankruptcies of the Webb & Knapp real estate empire in 1965 and the Penn Central in 1970—the world's two greatest bankruptcies up to that time. After the Penn Central bankruptcy, two Great Southwest directors were indicted on criminal charges.

NEW AND OLD WEALTH IN THE GREAT
SOUTHWEST CORPORATION, WEBB & KNAPP,
AND PENN CENTRAL

We noted earlier the pattern of Teamsters' Pension Fund investments with the Murchisons, their lobbyist Irving Davidson, and the mob in Las Vegas.[3] One tends to hear less of the Teamsters' Central States Pension Fund favors to the old establishment, although these were probably just as large. In the Kennedy years, FDR's son John Roosevelt at Bache and Co. in New York handled about 25 percent of the fund's $160 million investments.[4]

There is a deep pattern in this country where mob-controlled funds, licit and illicit, are brought in to revitalize declining "old wealth" firms. In 1963, the largest Teamsters' fund loan to that time, $25 million at 6.5 percent, went to the aging and almost bankrupt New York realty firm Webb & Knapp, which declared bankruptcy two years later.[5] That $25 million loan (or gift) kept the cash-hungry Webb & Knapp alive for two more years, at a time when (as *Esquire* pointed out in May 1963) much of its capital was tied up in a joint yankee-cowboy Dallas–Fort Worth real-estate venture on which it was earning no return.[6]

This investment was the Great Southwest Corporation, a realty development where control, in late 1963, "was tightly centered in the Rockefeller and Wynne families."[7] We owe this revelation to a congressional investigation of the 1970 Penn Central Railroad bankruptcy, in which it appeared that, as in the case of the Teamsters' Pension Fund loss in Webb & Knapp, a dying publicly held corporation had been looted for the benefit of this major Wynne-Rockefeller investment.[8] Worse, the surviving Penn Central Corporation's ongoing manipulation of the U.S. tax laws' "net loss relief provision" is said to have "charted the course" for increasing exploitation of this relic tax provision by more and more bankrupted U.S. corporations, many of them in Texas.[9]

The Wynnes had been longtime close associates of the even more influential Murchisons. Toddie Lee Wynne, Sr., the founder of the Wynne family fortunes, had begun in the 1930s as attorney for Clint Murchison, Sr.[10] Bedford Wynne, the senior partner in the family law firm of Wynne, Jaffe, and Tinsley, was a Washington troubleshooter for the powerful Murchison oil and construction interests in Texas; we have already seen that in 1963 his questionable lobbying activities were beginning to attract the attention of the federal government.

In August 1963 Bedford Wynne was the subject of a highly critical army audit of his "salary" from a firm with federal-government contracts (Sweetwater Development), which had been set up by the Murchisons' Tecon Corporation through the law firm of Wynne, Jaffe, and Tinsley.[11] To Wynne this must have seemed like gross political ingratitude. As recently as January 1963, Bedford Wynne had raised a half-million dollars for the depleted treasury of President Kennedy's Democratic party, after which Clint Murchison's son John was granted a mutually satisfactory interview with President Kennedy about preserving the oil depletion allowance.[12]

But it was unlikely that Wynne could escape being noticed in the mounting publicity about the scandalous activities of Lyndon Johnson's Senate protégé, Bobby Baker. As noted earlier, it was in the *Life* issue of November 22, 1963 (p. 92A), that Bedford Wynne was first named as a member of the "Bobby Baker set" at Washington's Q Club. Subsequent Treasury and congressional investigation of Bedford Wynne and Clint Murchison established that their Sweetwater company had made payments (which looked very much like political kickbacks) to the legal firms of Bobby Baker and of Democratic Congressman Emmanuel Celler.[13] Dallas Republican leader Robert H. Stewart III, a director of Great Southwest, had also arranged for questionable loans to Bobby Baker, via the same two Murchison employees (Robert Thompson and Thomas Webb) who figured in the Baker payoffs from Bedford Wynne.[14]

THE GREAT SOUTHWEST CORPORATION AND THE WARREN COMMISSION

For whatever reason, the Great Southwest Corporation was not investigated, but protected, by the Warren Commission investigation. An FBI report linking its former employee James Herbert Martin to a semi-underworld character with an FBI record (WCD 1039) remained withheld until 1972. There was no scrutiny of the interlocking relationships between Peter Gregory, the Oswald family, the Secret Service, the Wynnes, and the Great Southwest Corporation. No one examined Gregory's baseless addition to Marina Oswald's rifle story, and its corroboration by a Great Southwest employee. No one challenged the circumstances under which a phone call from Gregory led (as we shall see) to reservations for Marina at Great Southwest's motel—reservations arranged for by Gregory's contact in the Secret Service. No one asked questions as to how the same Secret Service agent came to select Gregory as an "interpreter" on Saturday, November 23 (WCD 5.291; 2 WH 344).

This was not an objective choice. The Secret Service agents who chose Gregory had already learned from him that he knew Lee Harvey Oswald (23 WH 421). Indeed, the Gregory family were so close to Lee and Marina as to have helped support them (2 WH 340). This fact may have been recognized as embarrassing, for somebody took Lee's certificate of proficiency in Russian, which had included Gregory's letterhead and signature, and retyped it, deleting the reference to Gregory (WCE 384; 16 WH 976; cf. 2 WH 340, 24 WH 342). Gregory himself gave an elaborate story under oath, corroborated in its details by Oswald's mother Marguerite Oswald, to suggest that his selection by a Secret Service agent to translate on Saturday (which came to naught when Marina proved to be unavailable) had nothing whatsoever to do with Gregory's request on Sunday to the same Secret Service agent to protect Marina and Marguerite Oswald, following which Gregory *did* translate for the Secret Service (2 WH 344; cf. 1 WH 155).

Gregory's story (WCD 5.290), which was later corroborated by Marguerite Oswald under oath (1 WH 156), went as follows: ten days before the assassination, Marguerite Oswald, who had not seen her son and daughter-in-law for fourteen months, began a course of Russian instruction in response to a newspaper advertisement. The instructor, by what Marguerite called "a very unusual coincidence" (1 WH 155), was Peter Gregory, who knew her sons Lee and Robert (1 WH 400); yet neither Marguerite nor Peter Gregory was aware of this "very unusual coincidence" until November 24, two days after the assassination. At 6:30 A.M. Sunday Marguerite Oswald suddenly decided she needed "help" and a place to stay (1 WH 156); she therefore telephoned, not her son Robert, but her new Russian instructor, whose classes she had attended exactly twice with several other women (1 WH 156; 2 WH 344). Mr. Gregory thereupon telephoned Secret Service agent Mike Howard at his home at 7:00 A.M., and Mr. Howard said, "We will find a hiding place for her" (2 WH 344). It was thus completely by accident that Marguerite and Marina spent most of Sunday in the company of Secret Service agent Howard, who was looking for them on Saturday night (16 WH 902), and of Peter Gregory, who had already been chosen by the Secret Service on Saturday to be Marina's interpreter (2 WH 344).

The effect of this "very unusual coincidence" story is to give Marguerite Oswald and Peter Gregory, rather than the Secret Service, the responsibility for Mike Howard's having hidden the Oswalds on November 24 from all authorities, including the FBI, at an Arlington motel called the Inn of the Six Flags, which at this time was one of the chief assets of the Great Southwest Corporation. Marguerite's and Gregory's testimony, in other words, explained away the embarrassing anomaly that Howard had arranged for a reservation for the Oswalds (at government expense) by 11:00 A.M. on Sunday, *before* Lee Oswald was shot; even though the Secret Service had no standing authority for such action and was only authorized by Lyndon Johnson to do so on compassionate grounds *after* Lee Oswald had died on Sunday afternoon (WCD 87, SS 533.1–2; cf. 1 WH 471–72).

Robert Oswald later wrote that in the next few days the Inn of the Six Flags "seemed to be serving now as a kind of regional headquarters" for the Secret Service.[15] If so, the Secret Service was dealing with its regular landlord; for the Dallas Secret Service office was housed in the building of the Reliance Life and Accident Insurance Company, of which the brothers Bedford and Angus Wynne were directors. Furthermore, the landlords had a special relationship of sorts with Marina Oswald as well, inasmuch as Morris Jaffe of the Wynne, Jaffe, and Tinsley law firm was attorney for Marina's mysterious friend and protector, Baron George de Mohrenschildt (9 WH 201), whom Marina's own attorney from the same law firm, William McKenzie, also knew (1 WH 395).

Howard's choice of the Inn of the Six Flags was, as we have seen, a momentous decision, since the motel's manager, James Herbert Martin, soon became Marina's agent and lodged her in his home (16 WH 770; 1 WH 473–75). Martin, who sold *Life* the dubious photograph of Oswald posing with a rifle (2 WH 23), later had Marina's life story taped and "interpreted by Ilya Mamantov" (2 WH 22), the friend of Peter Gregory. Later still, Martin arranged for Marina's story to be ghost-written by Isaac Don Levine, a veteran China Lobbyist who had previously collaborated on anti-Soviet projects with the CIA and the CIA-subsidized Tolstoy Foundation. Like Mamantov, Levine reportedly "was trying to tie in Oswald . . . with the Communist Party" (1 WH 487) and with "a Russian connection, conspiracy concept."[16]

THE LAW OFFICE THAT REPRESENTED
BOTH THE OSWALDS AND JACK RUBY

Despite appearances, Howard's choice of the motel (introducing Martin) was probably not accidental but deliberate. For in February, when Marina fired Martin and engaged a new lawyer, William A. McKenzie, she had not really changed protectors. Martin had been an employee of the Great Southwest Corporation. McKenzie, a close college friend of Bedford Wynne, had only just resigned from Bedford Wynne's family law firm of Wynne, Jaffe, and Tinsley in order, so his colleagues said at the time, to become the lawyer for Marina.

On February 17, 1964, the day that McKenzie and his new law-officemate Pete White signed a contract with Robert Oswald (16 WH 762), McKenzie informed the FBI of a new story that would help bridge the problematic gap between Oswald and his alleged rifle (1 WH 336). According to one version of this latest story from Marina, Oswald had "intended to shoot Nixon" in Dallas; and she "had locked Lee Harvey Oswald in the bathroom the entire day . . . to prevent him from doing so" (22 WH 596; cf. 1 WH 482, 2 WH 321). Faced with the fact that the Oswald bathroom, like all others, locked from the inside, Marina then told the FBI (in the company of McKenzie's law partner Henry Baer, another veteran of Wynne, Jaffe, and Tinsley) that in April 1963 "she forcibly held the bathroom door shut by holding on to the knob and bracing her feet against the wall" (23 WH 511; 22 WH 786). Finally she would tell the Warren Commission (in McKenzie's presence) that she and her much stronger husband "struggled for several minutes" *inside* the bathroom (WR 188; 5 WH 389–90). Faced with other, irreducible difficulties in this Nixon story, the Warren Commission discreetly concluded it was of "no probative value" (WR 189).

What is interesting about the story is not its content, but the corroborating testimony (later withdrawn) that Nixon had indeed been invited to Dallas in April 1963. This testimony came from Maurice Carlson, then the Dallas County Republican party chairman as well as a "close friend of Richard Nixon" (23 WH 414; cf. 22 WH 631), and also "independently" from William McKenzie (1 WH 339) and even from Richard Nixon himself (who "vaguely thought there was some invitation extended during the early part of 1963, probably in April" (23 WH 831).

Despite this authoritative corroboration, this invitation story was swiftly retracted, under suggestive circumstances. Maurice Carlson was the president of the Reliance Life and Accident Company, the Dallas landlords of the Secret Service, and the secretary of this company (of which Bedford Wynne and his brother Angus were directors) was McKenzie's partner Henry Baer. On February 25, 1964, just one day after Secretary Baer heard Marina tell of "bracing her feet against the wall," President Carlson prudently retracted his story of the Nixon invitation ("Since refreshing his memory, he remembered it was Senator Barry Goldwater . . . and not Nixon" [23 WH 416]).

This retraction is not particularly embarrassing to Nixon, who only "vaguely" remembered being invited. It does draw attention to Nixon's "quick business trip" to Dallas on November 20–22 for Pepsi-Cola (23 WH 941)—presumably about Pepsi's impending land deal with the Wynne family's Great Southwest Corporation, which would normally have been handled by the latter's law firm Wynne, Jaffe, and Tinsley. Nixon also planned to talk to "several Dallas Republican leaders" (23 WH 942); that description fits Crichton (the 1964 gubernatorial candidate), Mamantov, and Carlson.

Carlson's timely retraction of the invitation story on February 25 leaves McKenzie, the veteran of Wynne, Jaffe, and Tinsley, with the task of explaining his unequivocal corroboration of it to the Warren Commission on February 21 ("I recall when Mr. Nixon was coming to Dallas at the invitation of Mr. Carlson" [1 WH 339]). The Warren Commission never pursued this anomaly. It also failed to pursue unsolicited sworn testimony that McKenzie had "coached" Marina in the problem area of the Carcano rifle ("He advised her 'They will ask you if there were two guns, you tell them there was one gun that was used,' he told her" (2 WH 321; cf. 336–37). We learn elsewhere that Marina, on the very same day, told the FBI in McKenzie's office precisely that ("Oswald had only one rifle" [22 WH 785]).

If the Warren Commission had looked more closely at McKenzie, it would have found what it was ostensibly looking for, links between the world of Oswald and the world of Ruby. The Report rightly concluded that the Commission "was unable to find any credible evidence to support the rumors linking Oswald and Ruby directly or through others" (WR 661). The rumors it chose to investigate were indeed false, but certain other facts would have been more profitable to investigate. One of these facts was the appearance of the new office telephone number (RI 1–1295) of William McKenzie, Marina Oswald's lawyer in the notebook of Jack Ruby's assistant Larry Crafard (19 WH 73; 14 WH 34). The Commission was interested in Crafard, who fled Dallas right after the assassination. It apparently suspected that Crafard, who was thought by some to resemble Oswald, might have impersonated Oswald at a Dallas rifle range with the shortened-stock rifle.[17] Thus it asked witnesses at the rifle range if they could recognize pictures of Crafard as the man in question: one witness, M. H. Price, did answer yes (10 WH 375).

Just as Marguerite Oswald assumed responsibility for securing the Great Southwest reservation, so Robert Oswald assumed responsibility for choosing McKenzie as his and Marina's lawyer. His letter appointing McKenzie was witnessed by McKenzie's law partners Henry Baer, of Reliance Life, and Pete White, the name entered in Crafard's notebook (16 WH 763; 1 WH 282). The Commission asked Crafard about Pete White (14 WH 34) but did not ask Robert Oswald. They should have. Pete White, who together with McKenzie had once served as an assistant district attorney, told the FBI that he had got Ruby's charge of pistol-carrying dismissed back in 1954 and that he "ran into" Ruby on November 20, 1963, two days before the assassination (WCD 273.120). The FBI duly incorporated this encounter with White in its chronology of Jack Ruby's movements before the assassination (WCD 360.130). In the Warren Commission's published chronology (which included such trivia as Ruby's thirty-minute treatment for baldness on the same day), his encounter with White was omitted (25 WH 321). Worse, when Ruby's roommate George Senator was asked about more than fifty names in the Crafard notebook, that of Pete White was for some reason skipped (14 WH 295).

THE FIRM, THE HUNTS,
AND THE CONSPIRATORIAL RIGHT

Questions about Pete White might have opened up several possible connections to the underworld past of Jack Ruby, and also to the

Minutemen–Cuban exile–General Walker milieu supported by H. L. Hunt and his two sons. In 1962 one of White's two partners was Ivan Irwin, formerly of the family law firm identified to the FBI (by Paul R. Jones, the convicted dope trafficker and associate of Ruby) as the conduit for payoffs by organized crime to local law enforcement officials (22 WH 298). Irwin's son, Ivan Irwin, Jr., was a lawyer for the Hunt oil interests, and more particularly for Nelson Bunker Hunt (23 WH 690), to whose office Ruby drove on November 21, 1963, one day after seeing White.[18]

Irwin represented Nelson Bunker Hunt in the matter of the black-bordered anti-Kennedy advertisement which appeared in the *Dallas Morning News* on the morning of November 22. This ad, paid for in part by Hunt and other John Birch Society sponsors (22 WH 690), had, at a sponsor's insistence (5 WH 507–09), attacked the CIA, in an obvious reference to the coup against Ngo Dinh Diem, for "arranging coups and having staunch anti-Communist allies of the U.S. bloodily exterminated" (18 WH 835). The ad had been arranged for by a young right-winger, Larrie Schmidt, who with help from General Walker had organized the anti-Stevenson demonstrations which became one of Dallas police chief Curry's pretexts for recruiting outside security personnel on November 22 (22 WH 623, 625, 630). Robert Hatfield, the only member of Schmidt's group arrested at the Stevenson incident, engaged Pete White as *his* attorney (20 WH 420–21). These anti-Stevenson demonstrations may have been a reason to have army intelligence and ATF personnel backing up the Secret Service in the Dealey Plaza area at the time of the assassination.

Larrie Schmidt's semi-conspiratorial CUSA ("Conservatism, U.S.A.") cabal, which had captured the local chapter of the right-wing Young Americans for Freedom (18 WH 874), included Warren Carroll, whom Schmidt described to a friend as a scriptwriter for H. L. Hunt "and a former CIA man (don't worry)" (18 WH 875). Among Schmidt's other contacts were Dr. Robert Morris of the American Security Council (18 WH 886), who in 1962–63 lobbied actively on behalf of General Walker and Otto Otepka (the former State Department officer and Hoover ally who had handled Oswald's file) and against Kennedy's policies toward Cuba, the Soviet Union, and Vietnam. Another associate of Schmidt was Morris's protégé, Professor Anthony Kubek of the ASC, author in 1963 of *How the Far East Was Lost* (a belated but timely McCarthyite attack on the State Department), who was present with General Walker at a Cuban exile DRE meeting in Dallas, which Oswald also may have attended (WCD 246.22; WCD 205.646). Larrie Schmidt's brother Bob became General Walker's chauffeur, possibly to spy on him.[19]

Larrie Schmidt's proximity to the milieu of General Walker may have made him aware, before the assassination, of Lee Harvey Oswald. Reviewing the conflicted evidence linking Oswald to Walker, Henry Hurt concludes that "there is convincing circumstantial evidence that Oswald spied upon and photographed the home of General Walker."[20] This is quite compatible with our suggestion in Chapter 15 that Oswald investigated men suspected by the U.S. government of gun trafficking. Walker and his entourage were so suspected after Walker's participation in the Ole Miss riots of 1962. Arrested in Dallas at that time, "with several guns and a large quantity of ammunition," was Ashland Frederic Burchwell, who "admitted working for General Walker" (23 WH 516). Richard Lauchli, the Minuteman arrested near the Lake Pontchartrain training camp (see Chapter 5), is also said to have transported arms to the Ole Miss confrontation.

According to information provided to Dick Russell, Larrie Schmidt's true mentor was neither General Walker nor H. L. Hunt, but General Charles Willoughby, who met with Schmidt on more than one occasion.[21] There is no trace of this connection in the Schmidt documents published by the Warren Commission. We learn there that Schmidt's CUSA member in charge of public relations, Art Franzwald, was at the "Bedford Wynne PR Agency" (18 WH 839). This indicates that CUSA had not only conspicuous links to extreme right-wingers like Morris and the Hunts but also more secretive links to the "center" world of the Wynnes and their Murchison and Rockefeller allies (as embodied in the Great Southwest Corporation).

This was not the only rapprochement between the right wing and the center, between the world of Oswald and the world of Ruby, between the Pete White–Ruby–Irwin–Hunt netherworld and the Bedford Wynne–Rockefeller overworld. A potentially more significant example was the movement in late 1963 of Marina Oswald's attorney, William A. McKenzie, from the office of his old friend Bedford Wynne to that of his old friend Pete White.

EPILOGUE

The prominence of Great Southwest employees in the JFK assassination case did not cease with my first circulation of these observations some twenty years ago. Since then Beverly Oliver, the "Babushka Lady," has come forward with a story of seeing "Lee Oswald of the CIA" in Jack Ruby's nightclub, two weeks before the Kennedy assassination.[22] Most responsible accounts of the assassination (such as those of Anthony Summers and Henry Hurt) have declined to use her story, but that does not mean that it has lacked influence. On the contrary, the problem of how to handle the "Babushka Lady," and some of her wilder claims, bedeviled the first months of the House Select Committee on Assassinations. It can be said that this problem helped precipitate the crisis of confidence which almost wrecked the Committee, led to the departure of its first chief counsel, Richard Sprague, and his replacement (with a constrained time frame and budget) by Robert Blakey. Her story also contaminates the Time-Warner film *JFK*, rendering less credible the film's message about Vietnam.

Beverly Oliver's history of employment is part of her exotic story. In all accounts of it I have seen, it focuses on her work at the Colony Club, a strip joint next door to Jack Ruby's.[23] But in 1961, when she was dating a member of the Wynne family, she also worked, like James Martin, at the Great Southwest Corporation's Inn of the Six Flags, where Marina was taken.

NINETEEN

Who Killed JFK?
The Deep Political System

Practically all the Cabinet members of President Kennedy's
Administration, along with Director J. Edgar Hoover of the
FBI and James Rowley of the Secret Service, . . . testified
that to their knowledge there was no conspiracy. To say now
that these people, as well as the Commission, suppressed,
neglected to unearth, or overlooked evidence of conspiracy
would be an indictment of the entire government of the
United States.

Chief Justice Earl Warren

To believe them [the Rosenbergs] falsely condemned, one
would have to believe the judges monsters, insensate beasts.

Leslie Fiedler, Encounter, *1953*

At the first meeting of the newly constituted Warren Commission,
Allen Dulles handed out copies of a book to help define the ideological
parameters he proposed for the Commission's forthcoming work.
American assassinations were different from European ones, he told the
Commission. European assassinations were the work of conspiracies,
whereas American assassins acted alone. Someone was alert enough to
remind Dulles of the Lincoln assassination, when Lincoln and two
members of his cabinet were shot simultaneously in different parts of
Washington. But Dulles was not stopped for a second: years of dissembling in the name of "intelligence" were not to fail him in this challenge. He simply retorted that the killers in the Lincoln case were so
completely under the control of one man (John Wilkes Booth), that the
three killings were virtually the work of one man.[1]

Dulles's logic here (or, as I prefer to call it, his paralogy) was not id-
iosyncratic, it was institutional. As we have seen, J. Edgar Hoover had
already, by November 25, committed his own reputation and the Bu-

reau to the conclusion that Oswald had done it, and acted alone. Chief Justice Warren knew this, yet said at the same meeting, "We can start with the premise that we can rely upon the reports of the various agencies that have been engaged in the investigation."[2] John J. McCloy spoke for the extra-governmental establishment when he added that it was of paramount importance to "show the world that America is not a banana republic, where a government can be changed by conspiracy."[3]

Members of the Commission knew they could count on help in this demonstration. The *New York Times* had already assured its readers that American assassinations were the work of "loners," before the Warren Commission had even begun its predictable course toward its predictable finding: that Oswald, and for that matter, "Charles J. Guiteau, Leon F. Czolgosz, John Schrank, and Guiseppe Zangara" (note that Booth has now been conveniently omitted) "were all men who acted alone" (WR 463).[4]

This was not just psychologically motivated denial. What was at stake here was a definition of the supreme power in the land. The universally taught doctrine is that the United States functions under a rule of law, and that that rule, however imperfect, is the highest power there is. If Oswald was the assassin, acted alone, and was apprehended, then the hypothesis (or fiction) of a rule of law had been reaffirmed.

But what system of power do we live under, if Oswald was not the assassin, and if the constitutionally designated powers of the land, beginning with President Johnson and the Warren Commission he appointed, guaranteed that the true powers behind the assassination would not be apprehended? The mickey-mouse paralogies of Allen Dulles, the Warren Commission, and later the House Committee have helped to keep our thinking simple-minded on this point. Our very vocabulary is impoverished, even to describe the event of November 22, 1963, let alone the system of power which absorbed the event and covered it up.

WHAT HAPPENED?
NOT AN EXTERNAL PLOT, NOT A COUP D'ETAT

If a loner did not kill the President, the alternatives are usually construed as being either an external *plot* or *conspiracy* (the thesis of nearly all critical accounts, inspiring the titles of many of them, including Blakey's), or alternatively a *coup d'état* (the thesis of A. J. Weberman's *Coup d'Etat in America* and also of Oliver Stone's movie). From a layman's perspective, the difference is whether the President was killed by a group in office, or a group out of office.

When we reflect on this distinction, however, it begins to blur, particularly when we seek to clarify it with help from a dictionary. According to the American Random House dictionary, a "coup d'état" is "a sudden stroke of state policy involving deliberate violation of constitutional forms by a group of persons in authority." The Oxford English Dictionary slants the same definition away from unconstitutionality and toward *change:* "a sudden and decisive stroke of state policy: *spec.* a change in the government carried out violently or illegally by the ruling power."

A "coup d'état," in other words, is an extreme and exotic (as the use of a foreign language would suggest) form of conspiracy in the legal sense: "an agreement between two or more persons to commit a crime or accomplish a legal purpose through illegal action." I myself believe that some individuals in scattered parts of the federal government either contributed to the conspiracy, or at a minimum were knowledgeable of it and contributed wittingly to a cover-up of the crime.

I have no idea whether these individuals did, or did not, include Vice-President Lyndon Baines Johnson. At this time important allegations remain unresolved concerning the relations between Johnson (and his vice-presidential office staff) and Hoover, the Vietnam War lobby and its industrial backers, and organized crime. With respect to Hoover, Anthony Summers has charged that Hoover secured Lyndon Johnson the vice-presidential nomination in 1960, by giving Johnson enough dirt on Kennedy's sexual activities and background to blackmail Kennedy into making this choice.[5] With respect to Vietnam, John Newman has established that Vice-President Johnson had a secret back channel to army intelligence about Vietnam that was being denied to the President (see Chapter 2). And there are allegations, not yet proven, that at least one organized-crime figure was receiving, via the Vice-President's office, copies of federal investigative reports on his activities.

Lyndon Johnson's role, if any, remains uncertain. There are, however, two good reasons for saying that what happened on November 22, 1963, was not a coup d'état. The first is that, despite certain dra-

matic scenes in the movie *JFK,* the channels of authority do not appear
to account for the assassination plot, even though other, authorized intrigues may have been subverted to serve the purposes of the plot. Too
much of what we have observed about the case appears to have been
plotted outside the government, indeed in such a way as to force the
hand of the government, to use sanctioned operations perversely toward an unsanctioned result.

The second reason is that a coup does indeed usually suggest a
change in government personnel and policy. The presidency did change
hands, but in the areas we have studied this change served more
to perpetuate a status quo (graduated escalation in Vietnam, the
intelligence-mafia symbiosis, the fostering of the military-industrial
complex), and to stave off a threatened change of it by the incumbent
President.

The evident combination of what we may loosely call "inside" and
"outside" elements in the assassination has given rise to the fall-back
version of the coup explanation: that what happened should be attributed to a second, invisible, secret, or shadow government. Here again,
there do seem to have been powerful, but extra-constitutional, forces at
work on November 22, such as networks of former intelligence agents
in the pay of wealthy entrepreneurs like William Pawley or private
Texan oilmen, men who were both extremely wealthy and exposed to
organized-crime figures like John Martino and Jack Ruby.

I would accept that secret networks or teams have indeed worked
vigorously since World War II, inside official agencies, outside them,
and transcending their borders. They appear to have operated in the
Kennedy assassination and other, related character assassinations, such
as the Hiss case. However, the very plurality and ubiquitousness of such
networks makes it inappropriate to talk of them as something more
highly organized and unified, a shadow *government.* America's deep
politics, like its politics, is partly centralized but also profoundly plu-
ralized, indeed conflicted. I have argued consistently in this book that
we should look within, not outside, the political status quo, if we hope
to understand the assassination. The shadow-government model might
be called the extreme instance of the externalized conspiracy theories
which I believe are contradicted by the complexities of the known facts.

In my view it is clearly an oversimplification to say that the President
was killed by the power structure, the establishment, or even the polit-

ical system. The scene in the movie, where General Y speaks into his Pentagon phone, and says, "Bill, we're going," is not my idea of how Kennedy was murdered.[6]

To the notion that the political system killed Kennedy, I propose a more capacious alternative formulation: the President was murdered by a coalition of forces inside and outside government, of the type described in this book. In short, Kennedy was killed by the deep political system.

To understand the assassination, analysis, in the sense of isolating constituent agents, will not be enough; it must be complemented by synthesis, the relating of apparently separate elements in a coherent whole. To take just one example, far too much has been written about the roles in the case of Texas oilmen, organized crime, the Dallas police, and army intelligence, without looking at the ways these superficially separate elements in fact functioned together. The key to a credible model for what happened, through the murders and also the cover-up, is not to think of it as an externalized conspiratorial disruption of our deep political system (analogous to the invasion of an otherwise healthy body by an external germ or virus to be isolated). It is to think of it as a synergetic performance by internal ingredients of that deep political system itself.

There are those who object that no conspiracy, of the scale contemplated in this book, could have remained a secret for so long in a society as open as America's. Admittedly, the open surface of our society is no mere facade. However, as I suggested at the beginning of this book, beneath the open surface lie connections and relationships of long standing, immune to disclosure, and capable of great crimes including serial murder.

The postwar international alliance between intelligence and drug traffickers is perhaps the best-documented instance of such a connection, one where denial persists despite limited revelations about the 1960–63 plots to murder Fidel Castro. It is not the only such connection, and indeed merges with others, notably unassailable networks responsible for gambling and prostitution in the United States.

There are two other special reasons for suspecting the intelligence-sanctioned drug networks in particular. One is their role in connecting so many disparately centered different networks, from FBN and FBI to foreign casinos to local corruption in Dallas and elsewhere. The other is their key role in transnational connections to the deep politics of Mexico and Nicaragua, two countries clearly involved in the assassination story.

TRANSNATIONAL CONNECTIONS AND THE KENNEDY ASSASSINATION

By the distinction between political and deep political systems, I intend to move toward a more pluralistic and, I hope, empirical view of the case. A first step is to suggest that one ingredient in the complex, multi-centered intrigues that climaxed in the Kennedy assassination was the participation of diverse unaccountable transnational connections, each transcending the limits of American political society, and each with distinctive motives for the murder of the President.

I apologize for the clumsy neologism, "transnational connections." If I were to use more normal speech, I would talk instead of the many international aspects of the Kennedy assassination, such as the intelligence assets ("D") and lobbying elements (like Irving Davidson) working for Anastasio Somoza, or the coalition of forces working to involve the United States in Vietnam, or those with a vested interest in laundering the proceeds and profits of the international drug traffic.

Such more conventional language can, however, be misleading, and in a dangerous way. If one talks of "foreign" or "international" involvement, one is likely to think only that other *governments* could have been involved, either those of other countries (some authors have tried to implicate Cuba, China, or the Soviet Union) or else (the theory of Revilo Oliver and the John Birch Society) the United Nations.

"D"'s lies about Oswald's alleged recruitment to kill Kennedy, which were clearly conspiratorial, prove that there was a transnational aspect to the Kennedy assassination. Unfortunately, they do not clearly prove what that transnational aspect was. It may have involved "D"'s ostensible employers, the Somoza family and their Nicaraguan Secret Service: there is certainly corroborating evidence to implicate the Somozas in the 1963 intrigues of the Cuban exiles, the Murchisons, William Pawley, "Rip" Robertson, Hoffa lobbyist Irving Davidson, and the coup of October 1963 in Honduras. But then again, it may not: "D" may just as easily have been "turned," to accept employment from another intelligence agency, such as the Mexico City CIA station, or the

DFS of the Mexican Government, both of which were involved in the manipulation and disclosure of "D"'s story.

One way or another, the "D" intrigue is relevant here, not to establish who killed Kennedy, but to demonstrate the transnational dimension of the case, and also to suggest how tenuous this transnational connection is, as well as how difficult for a merely national investigation to pin it down. Above all, we must not fetishize the Somoza connection, or Ruby's apparent links to international drug trafficking, simply because the Warren Commission suppressed them. The Somozas, or international drug traffickers, could no more have accounted for the whole of the Dallas conspiracy than could Lee Harvey Oswald or Carlos Marcello.

As we have said repeatedly, the Kennedy assassination was the product of ongoing relationships and processes within the deep American political process. To now recognize a transnational dimension to the case is not to refute our earlier model, but to refine it: to recognize that the American political system is of necessity an open one, and thus increasingly susceptible to the growing influence of money and intelligence penetration from abroad. The systemic adjustment of which we have spoken is thus one not confined to the perimeters of U.S. sovereignty.

Transnational connections are common modes of interaction between intelligence agencies, often in intrigues of which heads of government may be, at best, only dimly aware. Sometimes they may give rise to more overt, structured arrangements or forums, such as the World Anti-Communist League, a forum, financed over the years by countries like Nationalist China and Saudi Arabia, with recurring links to the international drug traffic.[7]

These transnational connections can be thought of as rather clumsy efforts to fill what I see as the great governmental vacuum which has existed, especially since World War II, when sovereignty has not expanded to deal with the multinational society, economy, and even polity in which we live. Transnational connections have thrived in this vacuum, some to fill human needs, and many, many others to exploit them.

Turning now to more relevant, but still very marginal examples of structured transnational connections, I would point to private intelligence coalitions, such as the Foreign Intelligence Digest network compounded for the Texas Hunt family by General Willoughby, with both very broad ideological goals and more hidden practical intentions, such as the entry of the Hunt Oil Company (for which General Willoughby became an agent) into Mozambique.[8]

Despite the Hunt family wealth, this network remained marginal, virtually impotent to achieve its stated goals. Like all other transnational connections transcending national boundaries, however, it enjoyed one relevant advantage: it was relatively unaccountable. For this very reason, it entered into play with other, better established networks, such as the Gehlen Organization, which despite its technical nationalization into the West German intelligence agency, the BND, remained largely an unaccountable multinational transnational connection itself.

I would propose that such unaccountable transnational connections have played an important and increasing role in the politics of all countries since World War II, including the politics of the United States. I would offer as a general proposition that unaccountable transnational connections (usually with intelligence overtones) have contributed to most of the major postwar scandals, such as Koreagate in the United States, the Suez crisis in Great Britain, or the various Indochina *affaires* that afflicted and ultimately brought down the Fourth French Republic. (There are also intriguing transnational connections to the murders of Martin Luther King and Robert Kennedy.)[9]

Those who study such scandals develop a deepening sense that they compose a common parapolitical subject matter; and that to learn more about any one of them is usually to learn more about the others as well. One example, which may or may not bear upon the Kennedy assassination, is the concerted effort of de Gaulle after the assassination attempts on him in the 1960s to disperse the conspiratorial elements plotting against him, by finding them jobs elsewhere—such as training and leading the unmanageable Cuban exiles which the Kennedys were dropping from the CIA payroll and paying to relocate to Central America.

I think it helps to recognize that when the intelligence networks of three different countries (France, the United States, and Nicaragua) become thus involved in keeping intelligence assets alive and fed, a transnational connection has been created that wholly transcends the primitive oversight capabilities of any one nation.

DALLAS, WATERGATE, CONTRAGATE
AS INTERNAL ADJUSTMENTS OF AN OPEN SYSTEM

There have been four incapacitating political crises in Washington since World War II: McCarthyism, Dallas, Watergate, and Contragate. Students have been struck by the deep continuities between them: continuities of personnel, transnationality, and outcome.[10] What we are about to say here is far too superficial to "solve" any of these mysterious intrigues. The point is rather that, by their decadic regularity, they deserve to be regarded as periodic readjustments of the open political system in which we live.

At the center of all four crises have been perceived threats to the prosecution of the Cold War. Those suspected of advocating disengagement from China and South Korea (above all, John Stewart Service and Owen Lattimore) were persecuted and ultimately driven from power, ostensibly by McCarthy, but ultimately by Hoover.[11] Kennedy's death followed by only two days the first announcement of his detailed plans for phased disengagement from Vietnam. The Watergate break-in of 1972 (in which, I have always been convinced, Nixon was not so much a guilty perpetrator as a guilty victim) followed Nixon's secret negotiations with Hanoi for disengagement from Vietnam, significantly advanced by his May 1972 visit to Moscow, where he signed the first Strategic Arms Limitation Agreement.

Even the Iran-Contra scandal presents an analogy for further investigation: the flood of Iran-Contra revelations which embarrassed and weakened Reagan in December 1986 followed his return from the Reykjavik conference with Gorbachev one month earlier, where major arms cuts had first been discussed between the two leaders. And as new revelations about the Bank of Credit and Commerce International (BCCI) teach us more and more about the deep structure of Iran-Contra (a scandal which might better be called Iran-Contra-Afghanistan-BCCI), we see more and more clearly how drug trafficking and money-laundering were a central factor in that scandal, as earlier in the China Lobby, and in the Cuban aspect of Watergate.[12]

I am not suggesting that the four crises were part of some single conspiracy, only that we should recognize that in all cases the outcome was roughly the same: a prolongation of a system committed to the Cold War. Concerning Watergate, for example, a leading student of U.S.-Soviet relations has written that "Over the long run Watergate was undoubtedly a serious blow to American-Soviet détente. While its effects on Soviet interest in détente were peripheral and ephemeral, its indirect and direct effects on American politics were very far-reaching."[13]

Those skeptical of such a sweeping approach to American crises may particularly doubt the example of Iran-Contra, since in this limiting case the Cold War was almost over, and the check to détente caused by the crisis was short-lived. But there is no question that the investigation of the crisis by Congress was extremely muted, for the explicit reason that those in charge of the congressional investigation did not wish to weaken President Reagan to the point where the détente process would be destroyed.[14]

Given what we now know about the McCarthyism (or, as we might better call it, the Hooverism) of the early Cold War, how can we be astonished that Hoover and co-conspirators from that era (such as Alan Belmont, William Branigan, and James Angleton) would collaborate in presenting a false account of the Kennedy assassination?[15] But as long as we continue to talk of "McCarthyism," and thus marginalize it, we conceal from ourselves how rooted that phenomenon was in the deepest politics of our establishment. In this way we shall continue to resist seeing the continuity between the two scandals.

Hoover of course proved to be mortal in 1972, just before Watergate. But the in-house coalition of conservatives who opposed the Nixon-Kissinger moves toward détente in 1972 was similar to the one which opposed the Kennedy-Harriman détente initiatives in 1963. It still included James Angleton in the CIA, who in the 1960s had suspected Harriman of being a Soviet spy, and who in the 1970s "reportedly 'objectively' believed Kissinger to be a Soviet spy."[16] Nixon, like Kennedy, was having trouble with his Joint Chiefs of Staff, one of whom, Admiral Zumwalt, resigned over his differences with Kissinger.[17] Those who believe that Nixon's betrayer "Deep Throat" was a real official, and not a composite, advance well-argued reasons that he must have been a senior FBI official, probably Mark Felt, John Mohr, or L. Patrick Gray.[18]

In all four crises, one sees the recurrence of CIA and other intelligence officials and assets, repeatedly those with more militant anti-Communist stances than the Presidents they have worked under. Another common denominator for such individuals has been an exposure to narcotics trafficking, from the China Lobby of the 1950s to the Contra support networks of the 1980s.

In the case of Dallas, Watergate, and Contragate, a common denominator at a lower level has been former CIA Cubans working with Rosselli and Martino at the JM/WAVE CIA station in Miami. I suspect this continuity is more of a symptom of deeper relationships than a major causal factor in itself, but the symptoms are overt and hardly marginal. I wrote in 1971 how Frank Sturgis alias Fiorini had worked with Cubans and others in Miami to disseminate false stories about Lee Harvey Oswald in 1963; and I did so before Sturgis became famous as a Watergate burglar in 1972. I can now add that one of the DRE Cubans suspected in the July 1963 shipment of dynamite to the Lake Pontchartrain training site (José Basulto Leon) became in 1986 a leading Cuban-exile spokesman for the other ex-CIA Cubans, some of them allegedly from Alpha 66, named in the Contra support effort.[19]

FROM DALLAS TO WATERGATE:
SOME COMMON DENOMINATORS

Though I have spoken of four postwar crises as having certain features in common, two of them, Dallas and Watergate, have more in common than the rest. In each case an incumbent President was removed from office, after a build-up of suspicion and resentment inside his administration because of his announced plans and/or negotiations for disengagement from Vietnam.

Each event has been described as a "coup d'état." Watergate has been called a coup d'état by Roger Morris, former Nixon NSC staffer and biographer of General Alexander Haig, who has been accused of being a principal plotter in the Pentagon espionage on Nixon's Vietnam negotiations, as well as in the eventual plans to force the President's resignation.[20]

It has not, of course, been proven that Haig played a conspiratorial role in the toppling of Richard Nixon, in a plot where ex-CIA Cubans and their handlers like Frank Sturgis would also appear to be involved. If it ever is confirmed, historians will wish to look more closely at the role played by Haig in the summer of 1963, when his job under Army Secretary Cyrus Vance was to assimilate some of these same Cubans

into the U.S. Army.[21] Haig's successor in this post was Alexander Butterfield, whose unforced disclosure to the Senate Watergate Committee
of the White House taping system became a major factor leading to
Nixon's resignation.[22] Nixon's White House Chief of Staff H. R. Haldeman later suspected that Butterfield may have been the leading example of "CIA 'plants' in the White House," for reasons to which critics
like Jim Hougan have given some credence.[23]

It has even been alleged by a Marine officer who worked in 1963
with Haig that Haig's and Vance's close colleague Joe Califano
"worked hand in hand" checking out Cuban exiles "for the hit teams"
against Fidel Castro.[24] If the Califano-Haig team did this in 1963, when
they took up their jobs, then the chances are high that this operation
also involved John Rosselli and John Martino, the two central figures in
the 1963 hit-teams planning. In this case, one would have to investigate
much more closely the informed allegation that E. Howard Hunt and
James McCord, who are supposed to have met for the first time in connection with Watergate, actually had collaborated on Cuban-exile operations under Kennedy in 1963.[25]

A final point of similarity, one that many readers will have difficulty
accepting, is the suspicious deaths of witnesses in both cases. Of the
more than a dozen suspicious deaths in the case of Watergate, we have
already mentioned the deaths in rapid succession of Lou Russell,
among the first to have believed that the Watergate break-in had to do
with Heidi Rikan's call-girl ring, and John Leon, who intended to develop the Watergate call-girl hypothesis.[26]

Perhaps the most significant death was that of Dorothy Hunt in the
crash of a United Air Lines jetliner in December 1972. The crash was
investigated for possible sabotage by both the FBI and a congressional
committee, but sabotage was never proven.[27] Nevertheless, some people assumed that Dorothy Hunt was murdered (along with the dozens
of others in the plane). One of these was Howard Hunt, who dropped
all further demands on the White House and agreed to plead guilty.[28]

HOOVERISM, POST-HOOVERISM, AND FBI MURDERS

Common sense, fortified by our psychological resistance, tells us that
the government could have had nothing to do with such deaths. However, government documents, released since the 1970s, show that the

FBI, having illegally persecuted its opponents for years through the Cold War, resorted increasingly in the 1960s to arranging, in collaboration with local police, for the deaths of those whom it did not like.

In saying this, I am not referring to the suspect governmental presence at the murder of Malcolm X in 1965 (one of the men closest to Malcolm X when he died, his bodyguard Eugene Roberts, was revealed later to have been an undercover cop for the New York Police Department's Bureau of Special Services, which worked closely with FBI anti–"black extremist" COINTELPRO personnel).[29] Nor am I referring to the FBI's mishandling of the Martin Luther King case in 1968, although we should not forget that there were exultant cheers ("They got Zorro! They finally got the SOB!") when the Atlanta FBI field office first received the news that King had been shot.[30]

I will deal only briefly with the murky and suppressed role of the FBI, CIA, and army intelligence (behind that of the Los Angeles Police Department) in the investigation of the Robert Kennedy assassination (which came soon after William Sullivan heard Hoover's longtime FBI associate Clyde Tolson say, in 1968, "I hope someone shoots and kills the son of a bitch").[31] Like King, Robert Kennedy was murdered after he had called publicly for disengagement in Vietnam. Sirhan, like Oswald, acknowledged pro-Communist sympathies in a diary-like notebook (which Sirhan did not remember writing). A more arresting analogy is that Sirhan's allegedly radical sympathies, like Oswald's, were recorded in federal intelligence files, including those of army intelligence, possibly before the assassination.[32] Manuel Pena, the Los Angeles police lieutenant who was one of the pivotal officers in the LAPD investigation of the RFK case, had a federal intelligence background (according to his own brother, he had worked with the CIA). He had also worked, along with the Dodd subcommittee, in the investigation of interstate firearms sales, at the time of Oswald's (or "Hidell's") purchase of a revolver from a Los Angeles gun shop).[33] After John F. Kennedy was killed, it was Pena who traced the telescopic sight on the Mannlicher-Carcano to another California gun shop (22 WH 528).

When I talk about FBI murders, I mean murders in which the instigating role of the FBI is now well understood, and the responsibility widely dispersed through the FBI. For this reason we can talk of a violent and even murderous system, even if the seeds of it can be traced

back to the ruthlessness, well understood by his key agents, of J. Edgar
Hoover.

Certainly the level of FBI persecution, as well as the contempt for
law and judicial process, reached new heights after the adoption of the
secret National Security Council document NSC-68 in 1950, in which
it was accepted that the United States, to survive, must adopt the ruthless tactics it attributed to the Soviet Union.[34] But Hoover's personal
vendettas extended the sanctioned war against communism to targets
of his own eccentric choosing, such as integration leaders like Martin
Luther King. Not even presidential disapproval was able to stop this
perversion of the deep political process.[35]

We now know that, by the late 1960s, colluding in the murder of
nonwhite Bureau opponents had become endemic in the FBI, and a
cause for self-gratulation when successful. Perhaps the best documented case is that of the shooting of Chicago Black Panther leaders
Fred Hampton and Mark Clark in December 1969, in a predawn
apartment-building shoot-out with the Chicago police involving
eighty-three or more shots, only one of which was from a Black Panther
weapon. Fred Hampton died in his bed.

> He probably died in his sleep, for there was evidence he had been drugged
> prior to the raid. It was rare for the FBI to hide its light under a bushel, but
> in most of the COINTELPRO actions it was forced to do so. This didn't
> keep the Chicago SAC from claiming credit when he airteled Hoover on De-
> cember 11, "The raid was based on information supplied by [William
> O'Neal, an FBI] informant." . . . This being the case, "it is felt that this in-
> formation is of considerable value in consideration of a special payment for
> informant." Hoover agreed and on December 17 responded, "Authority is
> granted to make captioned informant a special payment of $300 over and
> above presently authorized levels of payment for uniquely valuable
> services."[36]

In blunter language, a payoff for a successful killing.

For reasons too complex to explore here (see WCD 47.4–9; 26 WH
342), Kennedy-assassination researchers were already aware (from
studying the allegations in 1964 of a black Secret Service agent, Abraham Bolden) of Chicago Police Sergeant Daniel Groth, leader of the
special police attack unit which killed Hampton. Research into the raid
indicated that Groth, apparently a Chicago policeman,

> *never* had a normal police assignment, but was deployed all along in a coun-
> terintelligence capacity, having earlier focused his attentions upon such en-

tities as the Fair Play for Cuba Committee. Groth's record also reveals several lengthy "training leaves" to Washington, D.C., where it is believed he underwent specialized counterintelligence training under the auspices of both the FBI and CIA.[37]

In other words, he was trained under William C. Sullivan and James Angleton, the FBI and CIA counterintelligence chiefs, and the driving forces behind the FBI's COINTELPROs.

A more common FBI COINTELPRO practice in this era was to deliberately create (in FBI language) "dissention" and "retaliatory action" and "reprisals" within and between black activist groups, with a focus on the Black Panther party. In response to Hoover's demands for "hard-hitting counter-intelligence measures aimed at crippling the BPP," false-flag letters and hate literature were disseminated, successfully provoking the murders of other leaders in shoot-outs between blacks for which the Bureau, in its internal memos, took credit.[38] As legal scholar Frank Donner has written about just one of such incidents, and there were many, "The Bureau, it is clear, was criminally complicit in the violence" that ensued.[39]

Since the release of FBI documents concerning COINTELPROs, which ended in 1971, it has become customary to blame these programs on Hoover. No one was more responsible for this focus than William Sullivan, fired by Hoover the same year, a few months before Hoover's death. But the tactics of COINTELPROs survived, against Puerto Rican nationalists from 1976 through 1985 (with political assassinations remarkably similar to those of Hampton and Clark), and also, just as murderously, against the American Indian Movement (AIM) from 1972 through 1976.[40] Both of these repressive campaigns have, quite rightly, led to the indictment of U.S. political repression before international tribunals. Yet many of the surviving victims, such as Leonard Peltier, remain in jail, while most white Americans, even those aware that something is wrong, repress the details and find persuasive psychological reasons not to "get involved."

As a symptom of the continuity between Hoover's COINTELPROs and post-Hoover murders, though not as an explanation of them, consider that Richard G. Held, a Chicago bureau chief who coordinated the FBI cover-up of the Hampton murder (for which judicial sanctions were later imposed) also commanded a murderous 1974 attack against Oglala Sioux Indians at Wounded Knee.[41] His son, Richard Wallace

Held, Los Angeles bureau chief at the time of the COINTELPRO murders, was then sent to Puerto Rico for the repressive campaign there.[42]

The point of this FBI kinship digression is not to blame the Helds for a generalized FBI problem; it is to counter the rhetoric of a "new FBI" in the post-Hoover era. When Richard G. Held retired in 1981, under the directorship of the supposedly benign William Webster (who went on to be director of Central Intelligence under Reagan and Bush) he was assistant FBI director for Internal Security, the post held earlier by William Sullivan. And President Reagan, the same year, began a series of FBI guideline relaxations to authorize FBI surveillance of Americans for their political activities, thus undoing the temporary reforms of the post-Watergate era.[43]

The problem of FBI murders, clearly, did not end with Hoover. Nor did the problem of FBI perjury. Despite a massive FBI cover-up in the Hampton and Clark murder cases, a federal judge finally ruled in 1983 that there had been an active government conspiracy to deny Hampton and Clark their civil rights, and awarded $1.85 million to their families and the other survivors.[44] Does one imagine that the FBI would lie less vigorously about their malfeasance in the Kennedy case?

IDENTIFYING THE SYSTEM:
A SYSTEM OF ACCOMMODATIONS, NOT A RULE OF LAW

In describing what has gone murderously wrong here, I spoke earlier of Hooverism, to avoid marginalizing the problem by associating it with the ephemeral and ultimately pathetic figure of Joe McCarthy. It is easy from our vantage point to see that the Soviet Constitution was a facade, behind which functioned the repressive system we call Stalinism and/or post-Stalinism. Turning to our own society, it is easy now to acknowledge the excesses of what became known as McCarthyism, especially after McCarthy made the tactical error of directing his attacks against the CIA and the U.S. Army.

But should historians still talk of "McCarthyism" today? If what we mean by it is the ruthless destruction of opponents and dissidents, without regard to legal or judicial restraint, then surely McCarthy was no more than a temporary foot soldier in a much more extended, far-reaching, and vicious system. Even Hooverism is too superficial and externalized a label for a system which both antedates, and has outlived, the man who survived every attempt of Presidents, Congress, and the law to displace him.[45]

What is most striking about this sanctioned law-breaking is its continuity. Hoover dropped McCarthy after the latter's foolish challenge to the U.S. Army.[46] By 1956, however, Eisenhower had been persuaded (apparently by the example of the Rosenbergs) to authorize COINTELPROs. No one knows how many individuals, from ordinary workers to university professors, were driven from their jobs by false allegations in the ensuing years. The lack of challenge to such tactics led in the Vietnam era into such widespread governmental violence that, in the case of the targeted top Black Panther leaders, there was little choice but to get out, get jailed, or get killed.

What shall we call such a society? If we are to identify and then change the forces deforming it, we must begin by calling them something. But the process of naming is double-edged. On the one hand it empowers, by bringing an unspoken problem more clearly into our realm of discourse. At the same time naming distorts those problems which are internal to ourselves and our society, by projecting them outward onto some externalized force.

Earlier, I suggested the label of Hooverism for the system of governmental violence, because it increased during Hoover's incumbency and eventually abated somewhat after his death. But it was more institutional than personal; and unlike Hoover it is not dead. From their experience down through the 1980s, few activists on the left, especially among ethnic activists, doubt that, if opposition were to escalate, so would the so-called counterintelligence tactics of the FBI and other agencies.

A parapolitical analysis of this system would focus on the responsibility of these institutional agencies. But the problem is one of deep politics, not just parapolitics, and involves more than just institutions. What is really operating here is a widely disseminated willingness, not to be blamed on any single individual or agency, private or public, to resort to fraud, violence, and even murder.

Organized crime in this sense could also be called tolerated crime: it is the milieu which private and government interests have turned to when there was fraud, violence, or murder to be done. This symbiosis has gone on so long that no President or Congress can now easily change it. It is engrained in our way of life, and perhaps increasingly threatens it. The recent savings-and-loan crisis, involving many of the names named in this book, is an example of how costly to the nation this toleration of lawlessness can be.[47] For this reason, a better name for our system would be a system of accommodations, one which is characterized by alliances or symbiosis with lawless forces, such as the drug traffic, which the system is nominally committed to eradicating.

In an age of recurring suspicious political crises, how should we view the government which recurringly is adjusted by them? If, in moments of crisis like 1963, a profound intra-administration division is resolved by an assassination, and the organs of government prevent the truth about that assassination from emerging, how should we characterize that system?

Not, surely, as a democratic Republic. Not, surely, as a rule of law. What we have seen is an open system embracing both power-holders in office and power-movers behind them. The assassination was an example, and not such an isolated one, where there was an adjustment at the level of power-holding, to meet the overriding political priorities of the power-movers and -shakers.

The dictionary has a word for "one dependent upon the patronage of another." The word is "client." It would, I think, be helpful to ask ourselves how far our office-holders, including our Presidents, have been reduced to the status of clients, dispensable when that more enduring patronage is withdrawn. To what extent has our visible political establishment become one regulated by forces operating outside the constitutional process, rather than through it?

These are not rhetorical questions, nor are there simple answers. In the system we have described, power is dispersed rather than concentrated. The constitution is not yet an empty shell; even office-holders possess some power; and Nixon, after conspiring forces had been launched against him, did not leave office without a struggle.

It is an agenda we are left with, not an answer. The enigma of the Kennedy assassination presents us with a challenge of constitutional seriousness. In the name of honest government, we must strive to bring to light, not so much the gunmen of Dealey Plaza, but the hidden powers which on that day were successful in their struggle for political dominance.

EPILOGUE

A century before the Roman Republic perished, two brothers, the Gracchi, emerged as popular leaders who were determined to check the corruption by wealth of the city's institutions. They were both killed. The murderers, who were never punished, came from the senatorial class which had felt threatened by the brothers' reforms.

The institutions of the city were preserved. Rome, however, was ceasing to be just a political city; it was becoming an empire for which civic institutions were ill-adapted. Its armies cut wider and wider swaths around the Mediterranean; their conquests impressed more and more men and resources into the armies, which became the real source of power. Eventually the generals (*imperatores*) became accustomed to occupying Rome as well as foreign cities.

Even after the *imperator* Augustus took up permanent residence in Rome, the Senate continued to meet. Tribunes and consuls were elected. Historians wrote about decadence, and moralists vowed to revive the old family virtues. A class accustomed to participate in civic institutions continued to do just that and no more, for generations. People found it preferable to ignore the fact that real power had migrated out of these institutions, into an imperial regime, the armies and the courts of the army commanders. The self-respect of the senatorial classes depended on this denial.

I do not wish to make too much of this clichéd analogy, only to draw attention to the social function of denial in masking political change. We still talk of an America of constitutional government. But in crisis after crisis the real power centers turn out to be institutions like the CIA, or the National Security Council, which the Constitution never contemplated and arguably cannot survive.

If we do not wish to close our eyes to political reality, if we are not frightened of investigating the truth, it is quite clear what should be done as the first next step. All the existing documents about the assassination which are being withheld should be released. If by national security we mean the security of the Constitution (rather than the security of extraconstitutional contrivances like the CIA), then there should be no documents concerning the assassination, and related events of 1963, withheld in the name of national security.

This seems obvious. Nevertheless, as one who is optimistic about the grand course of events, but not at all optimistic about the health of U.S. deep politics, I predict confidently that it will not happen without a struggle. Those who continue to insist that Oswald acted alone will continue to add that the full truth is too important (to national security, of course) to be fully revealed.

Win or lose, the struggle will be worth the effort. Already the urge to know the truth about the case has helped to generate new legislation, most notably successive versions of the Freedom of Information Act, that have helped make ours a more open society, even before solving the murder. It has also reinforced the awareness, in myself and in others, that in a commitment to the search for truth, one may begin in loneliness but is ultimately never alone. Slowly we have watched the emergence of a new community, still small but undeniably growing, that will not be satisfied with the old false answers. How far this new community can reform the deep politics of the old society remains unclear. But in the long perspectives of historical time, we see that the communities dedicated to truth, and justice, and decency, tend to outlast those of their vilifiers.

Notes

CHAPTER ONE

1. The fullest treatment of this area remains David Lifton, *Best Evidence* (New York: Macmillan, 1980). Overviews of the problems with the medical and physical evidence can be found in Sylvia Meagher, *Accessories After the Fact* (New York: Random House, 1975), 134–78; and Henry Hurt, *Reasonable Doubt* (New York: Holt, Rinehart and Winston, 1985), 35–86.

2. Peter Dale Scott, *The War Conspiracy* (New York: Bobbs Merrill, 1972), 171.

3. Alan A. Block, *East Side–West Side: Organizing Crime in New York, 1930–1950* (New Brunswick, N.J.: Transaction Books, 1983), 109.

4. Scott, *War Conspiracy,* 212, 218; Alfred W. McCoy, *The Politics of Heroin* (New York: Lawrence Hill Books, 1991), 252–54. Nicholas Deak, former OSS agent and CIA money-launderer, played a financial role in both the AMGOT and the Vietnam arrangements (Scott, ibid., 217–18n).

5. See below, Chapter 10.

6. For details, see Jonathan Marshall, Peter Dale Scott, and Jane Hunter, *The Iran-Contra Connection* (Boston: South End Press, 1987), 23–49.

7. Peter Dale Scott and Jonathan Marshall, *Cocaine Politics* (Berkeley and Los Angeles: University of California Press, 1991), 85.

8. Marshall, Scott, and Hunter, *The Iran-Contra Connection,* 68–70; Peter Dale Scott, "Transnationalised Repression," *Lobster* (Hull, England, 1986), 1–30; Frédéric Laurent, *L'Orchestre noir* (Paris: Stock, 1978); Magnus Linklater et al., *The Nazi Legacy* (New York: Holt, Rinehart, and Winston, 1984), 266–84; Jeffrey Bale, "Right-Wing Terrorists and the Extra-Parliamentary Left in Post–World War II Europe: Collusion or Manipulation?" *Berkeley Journal of Sociology* 32 (1987): 193–236.

9. See *Nation*, January 6/13, 1992, 6–7; March 9, 1992, 318–20; reprinted in Oliver Stone and Zachary Sklar, *JFK: The Book of the Film* (New York: Applause Books, 1992), 379–83, 466–83.

10. Gabriel Kolko, *The Roots of American Foreign Policy* (Boston: Beacon, 1969), xii–xiii.

11. *Nation*, January 6/13, 1992, 6.

12. G. William Domhoff, "Who Made American Foreign Policy, 1945–1963?" in David Horowitz (ed.), *Corporations and the Cold War* (New York: Monthly Review Press, 1969), 34. Quoted in Jonathan Vankin, *Conspiracies, Cover-Ups, and Crimes: Political Manipulation and Mind Control in America* (New York: Paragon House, 1991), 209. Cf. G. William Domhoff, *The Higher Circles* (New York: Random House, 1970), 298–308.

13. Vankin, *Conspiracies*, 125–26, quoting interview of Domhoff by Tai Moses, "The Cult of Conspiracy," Santa Cruz *Sun*, January 26, 1989.

14. Scott, *War Conspiracy*, xvi.

15. Athan G. Theoharis and John Stuart Cox, *The Boss: J. Edgar Hoover and the Great American Inquisition* (Philadelphia: Temple University Press, 1988).

16. Neither is there one word about the assassination in Hank Messick's seminal *John Edgar Hoover* (New York: David Mackay, 1972); but Messick, unlike Theoharis, has the excuse that Hoover's role was at that time not yet properly documented.

17. Theoharis and Cox, *The Boss*, 344–51.

18. Curt Gentry, *J. Edgar Hoover: The Man and the Secrets* (New York: Penguin, 1991), 419–28. Gentry does not mention the equally conspiratorial role in the Rosenberg case of the CIA's Counterintelligence, or "C," staff, led by William Harvey and James Angleton. As we shall see, Harvey and Angleton both figure prominently in our extended narration of the Kennedy assassination as well.

19. Stanley Karnow, *Vietnam: A History* (New York: Viking, 1983); William J. Rust, *Kennedy in Vietnam* (New York: Scribner's, 1985). Roger Hilsman, in 1963 the Assistant Secretary of State for Intelligence and Research, confirmed in 1992 that Kennedy "had begun to implement a plan to withdraw from Vietnam," and that Rust, in his book, "systematically ignored" this fact. He added that "Rust interviewed me twice for that book and for a magazine article that preceded it. I told him the truth about Kennedy's plans. Rust did not mention what I told him, and on several other points he distorted what I said. When I wrote a letter to his magazine repeating what I had actually said to Rust, the editor refused to publish it" (*Tikkun*, July/August 1992, 2–3).

20. George M. Kahin, *Intervention: How America Became Involved in Vietnam* (New York: Alfred A. Knopf, 1986), 143.

21. Telephone conversation, 2/3/92.

22. E.g., Jim Marrs, *Crossfire: The Plot That Killed Kennedy* (New York: Carroll and Graf, 1989), pp. 308, 603; Harrison Livingstone, *High Treason 2* (New York: Carroll and Graf, 1992), 480–91.

23. Thomas S. Kuhn, *The Structure of Scientific Revolutions* (Chicago: University of Chicago Press, 1970), 129, 150–51.

24. Burton Hersh, *The Old Boys: The American Elite and the Origins of the CIA* (New York: Scribner's, 1992), 450.

25. G. Robert Blakey and Richard N. Billings, *The Plot to Kill the President* (New York: NYT Books, 1981), 78–80; Arthur M. Schlesinger, Jr., *Robert Kennedy and His Times* (New York: Ballantine Books, 1978), 663; Curt Gentry, *Hoover,* 556. The Committee also reprinted a CIA memo discussing how Dulles was "persuading" his Warren Commission colleagues to eliminate references from the Report which the CIA found sensitive (4 AH 15). This referred to the matter of the Russian defector Yuri Nosenko, and was thus not sinister in itself; but it confirms how the background of CIA secrets constrained the work of the Warren Commission (see below, Chapters 4 and 11).

26. John H. Davis, *Mafia Kingfish* (New York: New American Library, 1989), 302–3. Davis adds that Chief Justice Warren's election campaign to become Governor of California had been managed by "his good friend Murray Chotiner . . . attorney for several notorious Mafia leaders and . . . particularly close to mob front man D'Alton Smith . . . brother-in-law of Marcello's top associate, Nofio Pecora" (302).

27. Blakey and Billings, *The Plot,* 84–86 (request); Dan E. Moldea, *The Hoffa Wars* (New York: Paddington Press, 1978), 358 (Jenner-Weiner).

28. A small but instructive example of how evidence was massaged by the FBI is Warren Commission Document 5.129, referring to the paper of a paper bag in which Oswald is supposed to have brought the murder weapon to his place of work at the school book depository (WR 130–37). As received by the Warren Commission, this FBI memo reported that the FBI lab found paper from the Book Depository "to have the same observable characteristics as the brown paper bag." But WCD 5.129 had been retyped. In another version, found years later in the Archives, the same memo stated that the FBI lab found this paper "not to be identical with the paper gun case." The two versions are reproduced in Hurt, *Reasonable Doubt,* 138; cf. Meagher, *Accessories After the Fact,* 45–64. We shall examine a more important example of FBI retyping in Chapter 3.

29. See my article in Peter Dale Scott, Paul L. Hoch, and Russell Stetler, *The Assassinations* (New York: Random House, 1976), 365, citing 19 WH 658, 23 WH 796.

30. Discussion at 4 AH 453–68.

31. Anthony Summers, *Conspiracy* (New York: McGraw-Hill, 1981), 496–503. Most relevant to this book are the organized-crime murders of Sam Giancana (1975) and John Rosselli (1976), and the unsatisfactorily explained shotgun deaths of William Pawley (1977) and William Sullivan (1978). Sullivan's shooting death, allegedly in a hunting accident, came "a few days before his scheduled appearance" before the House Select Committee (Gentry, *Hoover,* 546n).

32. *Chicago Tribune,* December 20, 1991. Reprinted in Stone and Sklar, *JFK,* 281. Establishment liberals like Anthony Lewis have long sounded the

same note: "We want to open some file and find the conspiracy. But we never shall" (*New York Times*, January 9, 1992; reprinted in Stone and Sklar, ibid., 389). The response of a still younger writer puts despair even further behind him: "It was on that autumn day in Dallas that postmodernism came home to roost.... We'll never know who killed John Kennedy. But we know enough.... To survive, we need to walk away from the quagmire of Dallas" (Andrew O'Hehir, "JFK: Tragedy Into Farce," *San Francisco Weekly*, December 18, 1991; reprinted in Stone and Sklar, ibid., 270–73).

CHAPTER TWO

1. The argument in this chapter is based on an article published in *Prologue: Newsletter of the Committee for Open Archives* 1.2 (July 1992): 1, 9–10. That article was a radically condensed version of my essay, "Vietnamization and the Drama of the Pentagon Papers," in the Gravel edition of *The Pentagon Papers* (Boston: Beacon, 1972), V, 211–46; reproduced in Scott, Hoch, and Stetler, *The Assassinations*, 406–42. The chapter includes material published as a letter to the *Nation*, March 9, 1992, and reprinted in Stone and Sklar, *JFK*, 473–76. A much fuller treatment of the material discussed in this chapter will be found in John M. Newman, *JFK and Vietnam* (New York: Warner Books, 1992).

2. For the texts of NSAM 263 and NSAM 273, see U.S. Dept. of State, *Foreign Relations of the United States, 1961–1963: Vietnam*, IV, 395–96, 635–37. NSAM 263 was originally released as part of the Pentagon Papers (Department of Defense edition), Book 12, 578. NSAM 273, despite its importance, was not reproduced as a whole in the Pentagon Papers, but it was partially quoted so many times that I was able to reconstruct a substantially correct version of the text as an Appendix to my article in *Pentagon Papers* (Beacon), V, 240–42.

3. Memorandum of January 22, 1964; *Pentagon Papers* (New York: Bantam, 1971), 274–75; discussion in Scott, *Pentagon Papers* (Beacon), V, 214–18; *The Assassinations*, 412–18.

4. Leslie Gelb, *New York Times*, January 6, 1992, A15; Alexander Cockburn, *Nation*, January 6/13, 1992, 6–7.

5. Newman, *JFK and Vietnam*, 432–34.

6. U.S. Dept. of State, *Foreign Relations of the United States, 1961–1963: Vietnam*, IV, 350–52. See discussion in Newman, *JFK and Vietnam*, especially 404–11. At an NSC meeting on October 2, the President originally objected to the projected timetable of withdrawing 1,000 men "by the end of this year," fearing that, if this could not be done, "we would be accused of being over optimistic." Later, "the draft announcement was changed to make both of the time predictions . . . [1,000 in 1963 and all out by 1965] a part of the McNamara-Taylor report rather than a prediction of the President." As Newman comments: "In other words, the President had been adamant that McNamara and Taylor recommend a withdrawal from Vietnam and was now publicly accepting it, while making clear that the optimistic timetable was theirs alone."

7. *Washington Post*, June 2, 1991, D3.

8. *New York Times,* December 23, 1991.

9. Newman, *JFK and Vietnam,* 18, 83, 96–97 (Johnson), 162 (Joint Chiefs, LeMay).

10. Ibid., 57–58, 69–73.

11. Ibid., 73.

12. In October 1961 Diem formally requested "US combat unit or units to be introduced into SVN [South Vietnam] as 'combat-trainer units' " (U.S. Embassy Cable of 13 Oct. 1961; Pentagon Papers (Beacon), II, 81–82, 651–52). When turning down Taylor's proposal for an 8,000-man task force, the President approved the introduction of small helicopter and other units, some of which had already been put in place prior to authorization; these began air combat operations with the covering device of putting South Vietnamese "trainees" in the back of the planes (Newman, *JFK and Vietnam,* 147, 160–61).

13. Newman, *JFK and Vietnam,* 161.

14. Ibid., 223–34.

15. Ibid., 318.

16. Ibid., 435.

17. Ibid., 449, citing Kenneth O'Donnell, *Johnny, We Hardly Knew Ye* (Boston: Little Brown, 1970), 16 (O'Donnell); Karnow, *Vietnam,* 326 (Johnson).

18. William W. Turner, *Power on the Right* (Berkeley: Ramparts Press, 1971), 199–207.

19. Ibid., 26–27, 130–34.

20. Hurt, *Reasonable Doubt,* 223.

21. Noam Chomsky, "Vain Hopes, False Dreams," *Z Magazine* (October 1992): 9–23.

22. Noam Chomsky and Howard Zinn, eds., *The Pentagon Papers,* V, *Critical Essays,* Senator Gravel edition (Boston: Beacon, 1972), 211–47.

23. Newman, *JFK and Vietnam,* 254.

24. *Pentagon Papers* (Beacon), II, 670–71; Scott, *Pentagon Papers* (Beacon), V, 219; Newman, *JFK and Vietnam,* 236–37.

25. Hilsman, 501; Scott, *Pentagon Papers* (Beacon), V, 221.

26. *Pentagon Papers* (Beacon), II, 164.

27. Ibid., V, 217.

28. *Pentagon Papers* (Bantam), 274–77; *Pentagon Papers* (Beacon), III, 151; V, 217–18.

29. *Pentagon Papers* (Beacon), V, 228–29.

30. Newman, *JFK and Vietnam,* 434, 446.

31. Ibid., 375–77, 434–35.

32. Ibid., 321.

33. Deborah Shapley, *Promise and Power: The Life and Times of Robert McNamara* (Boston: Little Brown, 1993), 262.

CHAPTER THREE

1. Gentry, *Hoover,* 548. This chapter contains material from an article by me, "The Kennedy Assassination Cover-Up," in *Inquiry* 2.11 (May 14, 1979): 18–22.

2. CIA Incoming 36017 of 9 Oct. 1963; 8 May 1992 CIA release # 5-1A (cf. 4 AH 212). This cable was originally released in April 1976, with the additional deletions of those words (e.g., "Obyedkov upon checking said"), which indicated that the source of the information was a recorded conversation (see below).

3. Edward Jay Epstein, *Legend: The Secret World of Lee Harvey Oswald* (New York: Reader's Digest Press/McGraw-Hill, 1978), 16.

4. Ibid. The language is Epstein's, and it is unclear whether Epstein means that the letter "suggested" this objectively, or merely to "the CIA." He does not begin to mention Angleton's name until ten pages later. The entire book, however, like other publications by Epstein, presents without criticism or respite the world-view of Angleton and his favorite Soviet defector, Anatoli Golitsin. Since Epstein's case for Oswald as a KGB agent reflects Angleton's, it is significant that his first paragraph about Oswald, and indeed his whole case, refers to the Oswald-Kostikov cable (p. 7). Much privileged information was leaked to Epstein to support the Angletonian world-view. According to Angleton's biographer Tom Mangold, this included details about an FBI double agent ("TOP HAT") inside the Soviet U.N. Mission, whose *bona fides* was doubted by the Angletonians (the leak led to TOP HAT's detection and execution by the KGB). Mangold argues that the main suspect for the leaks is not Angleton himself (even though he must have supplied his "tacit approval") but "the FBI's William Sullivan, a friend of Angleton's" (Tom Mangold, *Cold Warrior: James Jesus Angleton, the CIA's Master Spy Hunter* (New York: Simon and Schuster, 1992), 233–36, 410–11). As the former chief of FBI espionage operations in Mexico and Latin America (Gentry, *Hoover,* 392), Sullivan had had a longtime relationship with Win Scott, chief of the Mexico City station which sent the provocative Oswald-Kostikov cable. We shall return to the significance of the Angleton–Sullivan–Win Scott relationship in Chapter 7.

5. Mangold, *Cold Warrior,* 329 ("alternative CIA"); Epstein, *Legend,* 249 (memo).

6. CIA Outgoing Cable 74673 of 10 Oct. 1963.

7. Memo of 16 Oct. 1963 from [deleted] CIA officer to Ambassador Thomas Mann, U.S. Embassy, Mexico City.

8. FBI Letterhead Memorandum to the Secret Service, 23 Nov. 1963. Cf. Anthony Summers, *Conspiracy* (New York: McGraw-Hill, 1981), 386–87.

9. 3 AH 136; Summers, *Conspiracy,* 374.

10. Summers, *Conspiracy,* 373–86.

11. I have spoken to Win Scott's son and stepson, who confirm the Angleton visit. Scott's son Mike adds that Angleton also took his father's diary back to CIA headquarters at Langley. When Mike Scott asked the CIA for permission to read it, he was told that he could not, for reasons of national security. "There are very sensitive matters in there," he was told. "Like what?" "Like Lee Harvey Oswald, for example." See also Dick Russell, *The Man Who Knew Too Much* (New York: Carroll and Graf, 1992), 460.

12. Win Scott's diary, if still extant, might be even more revealing.

13. Schweiker-Hart Report, 7.

14. Gentry, *Hoover,* 544–45; FBI Oversight Hearing, 36–59, 124–75; Schweiker-Hart Report, 93.

15. "Johnson never quite accepted the conclusion of the Warren Commission that Lee Harvey Oswald killed Kennedy entirely on his own. Not long after Johnson became president, Richard Helms was one of a small group that heard him claim that Kennedy's murder was an act of retribution—not by Castro, however, a suspicion Johnson was to voice later, but by unnamed persons seeking vengeance for the murder on November 1, 1963, of the president of South Vietnam, Ngo Dinh Diem" (Thomas Powers, *The Man Who Kept the Secrets* [New York: Knopf, 1979], 121).

16. Gentry, *Hoover,* 548.

17. Schweiker-Hart Report, 34–35; 3 AH 476; *New York Times,* December 3, 1986.

18. FBI files; cf. FBI Chicago File 92-3189-54, March 18, 1964; 9 AH 946.

19. That such a cover-up was relatively nonconspiratorial does not mean that it was irrelevant. On the contrary, as the House Committee noted, Warren Commission members have stated that awareness of the CIA-Mafia plots would have led their investigation into new areas (AR 258).

20. For the Milteer tape and relevant FBI memos, see Harold Weisberg, "The Milteer Documents," reprinted in Scott, Hoch, and Stetler, *The Assassinations,* 117–34; WCD 20.24; 1347.119–24.

21. WCD 20.24 ("attended"); "Third Decade Document Discovery: The Congress of Freedom Papers," *The Third Decade,* II, 2 (January 1986); cited in Russell, *The Man Who Knew Too Much,* 299, 547–48, 755.

22. Gentry, *Hoover,* 567.

23. For this evidence, see Lifton, *Best Evidence,* and the summary in Hurt, *Reasonable Doubt,* 423–28. Lifton's witnesses claim (1) that the ceremonial coffin in which the President's body left Dallas is not the simple shipping casket in which it arrived at Bethesda; (2) the body arrived in a body bag, which no witness in Dallas recalls; (3) X-ray photographs of the body had already been taken at Bethesda before the ceremonial coffin arrived; (4) FBI agents at the autopsy reported prior "surgery of the head area, namely, in the top of the skull," while the Parkland doctors performed no such surgery; (5) the head wound was reported in Dallas to be about 35 square centimeters in size, while the autopsy diagram at Bethesda shows it to be 170 square centimeters; and (6) according to two Bethesda hospital technicians, the brain had been removed prior to the arrival of the body, which had left Dallas with the brain protruding. See also the purported rebuttal of Lifton's arguments in the *Journal of the American Medical Association* (May 27, 1992; October 7, 1992).

24. For a detailed chronology of Hoover's role, see Gentry, *Hoover,* 541–57; Robert Hennelly and Jerry Policoff, "JFK: How the Media Assassinated the Real Story," *Village Voice,* March 31, 1992, reprinted in Stone and Sklar, *JFK,* 485–86; Mark North, *Act of Treason* (New York: Carroll and Graf, 1992), 406 ff, especially 415–16, 426–27, 430, 480, etc.

25. Gentry, *Hoover,* 553.

26. Anthony Summers and Steven Dorril, *Honeytrap* (London: Hodder and Stoughton, 1988), 269.

27. Mark Aarons and John Loftus also talk of Dulles's "agency-within-the-Agency," run with the help of Angleton, in *Unholy Trinity* (New York: St. Martin's Press, 1991), 260.

28. Guy Richards, "Russia's School for Assassins—and the Oswald Case," *New York Journal-American*, January 11, 1964; Richard Helms letter of July 14, 1966, reprinted in U.S. Cong., Senate, Select Committee on Standards and Conduct, *Investigation of Senator Thomas J. Dodd, Hearings*, 577.

29. See Chapter 17.

30. *Washington Post*, November 23, 1963 ("agent"); *Dallas Morning News*, November 24, 1963 ("surveillance"); North, *Treason*, 414, 422.

31. American Security Council, *Washington Report*, March 16, 1964, p. 3; cf. 20 WH 745.

32. Stone and Sklar, *JFK*, 151, 488–90; Scott, *Crime and Cover-Up*, 25, 36.

33. Scott, *Crime and Cover-Up*, 36, 67–68.

34. Carl Bernstein, "The CIA and the Media," *Rolling Stone*, October 20, 1977, 63.

35. Warren Hinckle and William W. Turner, *The Fish Is Red* (New York: Harper and Row, 1981), 164–68 (Luce).

36. See Chapter 7.

37. Susan Trento, *The Power House: Robert Keith Gray and the Selling of Access and Influence in Washington* (New York: St. Martin's Press, 1992), 61–76.

38. Guy Richards, *New York Journal-American*, December 8, 1963; Gerry Patrick Hemming, CBC Fifth Estate, November 1977.

CHAPTER FOUR

1. Scott, Hoch, and Stetler, *The Assassinations*, 366–67.

2. Peter Dale Scott, "Government Documents and the John F. Kennedy Assassination," manuscript, circulated as "The Dallas Conspiracy," ch 3. of Appendix, 17.

3. In the summer of 1973 I began to reconstitute the missing names at the National Archives in Washington, by looking at FBI interviews of Ruby associates in relevant Warren Commission Documents (WCD 4, WCD 5, WCD 84, etc.). I later engaged a student to spend several weeks at the Archives to complete the task. Unfortunately, my files have since been accidentally destroyed, so I can no longer talk precisely of how many names were suppressed, or what percentage they constituted of the whole file, WCD 355. But I am confident that anyone who reconstructs the same research from the same evidence will conclude, as I did, that the residue or negative template of suppressed names is significantly biased toward important criminal and political connections.

4. *Los Angeles Times*, September 12, 1970; Scott, *Crime and Cover-Up*, 46.

5. Chicago Crime Commission, *Report*, 1963, 29; cf. 22 WH 313.

6. *Washington Post*, April 6, 1978.

7. Gentry, *Hoover*, 551.

8. Richard Powers, *Secrecy and Power* (New York: Free Press, 1987), 389; Schweiker-Hart Report, 52–55.

9. Epstein (*Legend*, 164–65) saw something sinister in Marina's notification, since it was routed within the embassy to a second secretary, Vitaliy A. Gerasimov, who was then "under intense scrutiny by FBI counterespionage." Since William Sullivan, in charge of FBI counterespionage, was also a major source for Epstein's Angletonian book, we can assume that Epstein's evaluation of the letter and of Gerasimov reflects Sullivan's, which only makes the FBI handling of Oswald even stranger. Epstein also quotes a CIA evaluation of Gerasimov as someone "known . . . to have made payments for intelligence information of value to the Soviets." If the CIA had anxieties about the Marina Oswald–Gerasimov letter (which Epstein elevates into "the Oswalds' contact with him"), why then did the CIA suppress all reference to the even more sinister Kostikov when notifying the FBI, on October 10, 1963, of the "Oswald" contact with the Soviet Embassy in Mexico City? We shall soon have occasion to ask this question again.

10. Schweiker-Hart Report, 92; Powers, *Secrecy and Power*, 387 (Washington).

11. Memorandum from Gale to Tolson, 12/10/63, as quoted in Schweiker-Hart Report, 92; cf. 3 AH 518.

12. Memorandum from Gale to Tolson, 9/30/64, in Schweiker-Hart Report, 54; 3 AH 535.

13. Gentry, *Hoover*, 549; 3 AH 514–25.

14. Theoharis and Cox, *The Boss*, 372 (Belmont); Church Committee Report, II, III, 145; Gentry, *Hoover*, 282 (Branigan).

15. Church Committee Report, II, 8, 10, 16, 64.

16. Ward Churchill and Jim Vander Wall, *Agents of Repression: The FBI's Secret Wars against the Black Panther Party and the American Indian Movement* (Boston: South End Press, 1988), 61–62, 396.

17. By 1971 Sullivan had been promoted to succeed Belmont, C. D. Brennan was the head of the Domestic Intelligence Division, and G. C. Moore was handling COINTELPROs against black activists. Hoover, Sullivan, Brennan, and George C. Moore were the first four of forty-nine "Unsued Conspirators" in the suit, ultimately successful, brought by the widow of the murdered Chicago Black Panther leader Fred Hampton against the Chicago Police Department and FBI (ibid., 76–77, 404). Then Brennan's handling of the Ellsberg case in 1971 angered Hoover, resulting in a demotion and transfer for Brennan, and final estrangement between Hoover and Sullivan (Gentry, *Hoover*, 685; Summers, *Official and Confidential*, 397).

18. Summers, *Official and Confidential*, 229.

19. Gentry, *Hoover*, 453.

20. Gentry, *Hoover*, 424, emphasis added.

21. Ibid., 420–24; Howard Zinn, *People's History of the United States* (New York: Harper and Row, 1980), 425 (400 hours). As late as 1974, Bran-

igan was visited by Irving Kaufman, the judge who convicted the Rosenbergs; and the two men discussed ways to counter two TV documentaries "advancing the theory the Rosenbergs were victims of a frameup" (Ronald Radosh and Joyce Milton, *The Rosenberg File* [New York: Holt, Rinehart, and Winston, 1983], 431).

22. Stevenson, *Intrepid's Last Case* (New York: Villard Books/Random House, 1983), 19; David Martin, *Wilderness of Mirrors* (New York: Harper and Row, 1980), 42; John Ranelagh, *The Agency: The Rise and Decline of the CIA* (New York: Simon and Schuster, 1986), 149n.

23. Martin, *Wilderness of Mirrors*, 42.

24. Hersh, *The Old Boys*, 447.

25. Schlesinger, *Robert Kennedy*, 516.

26. Apparently, Angleton took over after a message on November 24 from Win Scott's CIA station in Mexico City, which apparently claimed that one of Valeriy Kostikov's contacts had been Rolando "Cubella" (i.e., Cubela). This was embarrassing to Angleton's rival, Desmond FitzGerald. Cubela was a potential double agent whom FitzGerald and his Special Affairs Staff had contacted about assassinating Castro, up to and including the day of the JFK assassination. On receipt of this message, Angleton asked the SAS for a "trace" on "Cubella," which FitzGerald, "after some consideration," declined to give. See Martin, *Wilderness of Mirrors*, 151 (Mexico City station); Epstein, *Legend*, 232–33, 240, 242, 253–54 (FitzGerald). Specifically, FitzGerald decided to give Angleton Cubela's "201" file, which contains general information, but not his "operational" file. In analogous fashion, the CIA gave the Warren Commission (and later the public) Oswald's "201" file, without addressing the possibility that an operational file existed.

27. Russell, *The Man Who Knew Too Much*, 197–98.

28. This is confirmed by an illuminating anecdote narrated by David Wise: "So close were Dulles and Angleton that after Dulles died in 1969, his sister, Eleanor Lansing Dulles, asked Angleton to give away his pipes to Dulles' best friends in the secret world. Don Moore, the Soviet counterintelligence chief for the FBI, who had worked for many years with both the CIA director and Angleton, got two of Dulles's favorite briars" (David Wise, *Molehunt* [New York: Random House, 1992], 39).

29. Cf. Congressman Fithian at 12 AH 624; discussion in Summers, *Conspiracy*, 519–20. For a much more negative, closely reasoned treatment of Blakey and the Committee, see Davis, *Mafia Kingfish*, 431–42. Jim Marrs's even more negative assessment of the Committee's performance under Blakey (*Crossfire*, 524–30) is in my view overstated; it fails to take into account the real political problems and restrictions which Blakey faced on taking his post as counsel.

30. Summers, *Conspiracy*, 519.

31. Scott, "The Kennedy Assassination Cover-Up," *Inquiry* II, May 14, 1979, 11.

32. Dwight C. Smith, Jr., *The Mafia Mystique* (New York: Basic Books, 1975), 324; Alan A. Block, "History and the Study of Organized Crime"

(1978), reprinted in Block, *Perspectives on Organizing Crime* (Dordrecht: Kluwer Academic Publishers, 1991), 21.

33. 9 AH 5–6; Blakey and Billings, *The Plot*, 210–15.

34. Scott and Marshall, *Cocaine Politics*, passim.

35. Schlesinger, *Robert Kennedy*, 678–80, 1129.

CHAPTER FIVE

1. Scott, *Crime and Cover-Up*, 40, 70; Blakey and Billings, *The Plot*, 285.

2. Blakey and Billings, *The Plot*, 343–44.

3. 1 WH 197; Scott, *Dallas Conspiracy*, VII-17, VII-33; Blakey and Billings, *The Plot*, 344.

4. Jack Anderson, *Washington Exposé* (Washington: Public Affairs Press, 1967), 452–55. Congressmen Morrison and Long, both old friends of Marcello's lawyer G. Wray Gill, also intervened on behalf of David Ferrie in a grievance he filed against Eastern Airlines (10 AH 120).

5. To remain credible, deep political narratives need to use a parapolitical corollary to Ockham's Razor: namely, that "conspiracies are not to be multiplied beyond necessity." For this reason I shall follow convention in treating Lee Harvey Oswald as a single individual with (roughly speaking) the biography attributed to him by the Warren Commission and House Committee. I shall ignore the indications that the identity of "Lee Harvey Oswald" was in fact maintained by a set of so-called "pocket litter"—passports, ID, diary, etc.—used at different times by different individuals who may not even have known each other. In particular there are reasons for doubting that the Lee Harvey Oswald in New Orleans was either the opera lover who visited the Soviet Union, or (as we saw in Chapter 3) the alleged thirty-five-year-old who apparently used the name in the Mexico City Cuban consulate.

6. 8 WH 280, 284; 25 WH 864 (STRONGBACK); Hurt, *Reasonable Doubt*, 199–202 (Atsugi); Summers, *Conspiracy*, 176–81 (false defectors); Philip H. Melanson, *Spy Saga: Lee Harvey Oswald and U.S. Intelligence* (New York: Praeger, 1990).

7. Summers, *Conspiracy*, 230–33. See Chapter 15.

8. Scott, *Crime and Cover-Up*, 34–36, 66; AR 217–18; 12 AH 54–55; Summers, *Conspiracy*, 222–30.

9. Hinckle and Turner, *The Fish Is Red*, 210. George de Mohrenschildt's address book contains four separate references to Colonel Howard Burris, Vice-President Johnson's military advisor. One has the simple entry "Howard Burris/Haiti."

10. An article about the Charles and the T-28s noted that I. Irving Davidson, Washington lobbyist and associate of Carlos Marcello, had visited Haiti in May 1963 with two Dallas arms dealers; but Davidson later denied participating in any Haitian arms deals (*Washington Post*, September 9, 1964; 12 AH 57). Cf. Pete Brewton, *The Mafia, CIA, and George Bush* (New York: S.P.I. Books, 1992), 193–95.

11. Jonathan Kwitny, *The Crimes of Patriots* (New York: Norton, 1987), 276–79.

12. Steve Pizzo, Mary Fricker, and Paul Muolo, *Inside Job* (New York: McGraw-Hill, 1989), 84–88, 150–51 (Renda); 231–38 (Beebe-Marcello); Brewton, *Mafia, CIA, and George Bush,* 66–73 (Renda-Beebe), 192 (Renda-Charles).

13. Brewton, *Mafia, CIA, and George Bush,* 195, 298–99. Freeman was a law partner of Paul Helliwell, a CIA operative and major architect of the protected drug traffic (see Chapter 10).

14. *New York Times,* July 3, 1972; November 17, 1972; Pizzo et al., *Inside Job,* 302–58; Brewton, *Mafia, CIA, and George Bush,* 154–58. Years earlier, a Harper from Piedras Nigras had been named in a 1947 drug case of Maurice Melton and Paul Roland Jones, concerning which Jack Ruby was questioned but not indicted (see Chapter 8).

15. Brewton, *Mafia, CIA, and George Bush,* 156 (Seal statement); *New York Times,* May 22, 1973, 12 (visit and resignation). At the time, Ambrose was head of ODALE (the White House Office of Drug Abuse Law Enforcement) and special consultant to the President on narcotics control. Without naming Richmond Harper, Edward Jay Epstein says that he was "suspected of narcotics-smuggling" (*Agency of Fear* [New York: Putnam's, 1977], 239).

16. In 1964 Duvalier awarded a casino franchise in Port-au-Prince to the Bonanno family, who according to Pete Brewton (*Mafia, CIA, and George Bush,* 195) "may have helped Charles get the aircraft from the United States" in that same year.

17. E.g., Robert Sam Anson, *"They've Killed the President!" The Search for the Murderers of John F. Kennedy* (New York: Bantam, 1975), 177.

18. Among de Mohrenschildt's corporate acquaintances and employers in Texas were some prominent LBJ backers with their own criminal associates. At one point, for example, he had worked for Three States Oil and Gas (9 WH 202), and thus for the Murchisons, business allies of Herman Beebe and Carlos Marcello (Brewton, *Mafia, CIA, and George Bush,* 99–101). See also Chapter 12; Dan Moldea, *Interference: How Organized Crime Influences Professional Football* (New York: Morrow, 1989), 104–5.

19. Summers, *Conspiracy,* 315–27. The witnesses are Jack Martin, Delphine Roberts, and William Gaudet. It is true that the credibility of all three witnesses has been challenged; but even proof that they had all concertedly given false testimony would hardly dispel the indications of mystery and conspiracy surrounding Oswald's relationship to the 544 Camp Street address.

20. The five are Carlos Bringuier (10 WH 34), Frank Bartes (10 AH 4, 10 AH 62), Carlos Quiroga (22 WH 831, 26 WH 768), Ernesto Rodriguez, Jr., (22 WH 829, 24 WH 659, cf. 22 WH 188), and Orest Pena (11 WH 352–57). In addition Ronny Caire, the registered foreign agent and a fundraiser for the CRC, "seemed to recall Oswald applying for a job with his [advertising] agency . . . about the time Oswald had a radio debate" (22 WH 829, 831). A sixth CRC member, Manuel Gil, managed the show that aired the Oswald-Bringuier "debate" used to discredit Oswald later as a deceitful Marxist (22

WH 829; see Chapter 6). On the first of these encounters (with Bringuier) Oswald allegedly professed anti-Castro sentiments himself.

21. The staff report is signed "Gaeton Fonzi," but was in fact written by someone else. Blakey subsequently was less unequivocal: "We could not say, however, that the testimony of . . . Bartes, Bringuier, and others in New Orleans, in light of what we *had* learned about Oswald in the summer of 1963, left us with a feeling that we knew all there was to know" (Blakey and Billings, *The Plot,* 177). Unlike the staff report, Blakey and Billings mention the visit to Oswald's home of Carlos Quiroga, but do not mention that he was a CRC member (ibid., 162, 169). Likewise, the Committee Report mentions the Quiroga visit, without identifying him (AR 141); while another staff report, using Quiroga as a witness on an unrelated matter, mentions that Quiroga "had been involved with the CRC," but is predictably silent about his visit to Oswald (10 AH 112).

22. Firmin Peraza Sarausa, *Personalidades Cubanas: Cuba en el Exilio,* vol. 10 (Miami: Ediciones Anuario Bibliografico Cubano, 1968), 13. The Warren Commission Hearings transmit this fact, corroborated by Bringuier elsewhere, in garbled fashion: "BRINGUIER: . . . . After that I joined, at the beginning of 1962, the New Orleans Delegation of the Cuban Revolutionary Council, and I was working here as Secretary of Publicity and Propaganda here in New Orleans for the Cuban Anti-Castro. That was, I believe, June or July—June 1962" (10 WH 34).

23. *New York Times,* September 7, 1962, 5.

24. Interview of William Gaudet by Bernard Fensterwald, May 13, 1975. Gaudet said of Oswald: "I don't even think he knew exactly what he was distributing. . . . [T]he Fair Play for Cuba deal . . . was nothing but a front and was one of the dreams of—I think Guy Banister." Gaudet repeated these opinions to me when I interviewed him for Canadian television in 1977.

25. Blakey and Billings, *The Plot,* 342.

26. Summers, *Conspiracy,* 341; cf. 9 AH 99, 119 (Bruneau); 4 AH 498, 565; 9 AH 194 (Pecora-Ruby).

27. Blakey and Billings, *The Plot,* 364.

28. Ibid., 358–59: "They decided to call Emile Bruneau, an old friend of the Murrets who had political influence, and Bruneau arranged Oswald's bail that afternoon." More accurately, Bruneau contacted "someone else" who arranged Oswald's release: Summers, *Conspiracy,* 341 (citing 25 WH 117; WCD 75.159); cf. Marrs, *Crossfire,* 146; North, *Act of Treason,* 296.

29. 8 WH 145; cf. 8 WH 175; Priscilla McMillan, *Marina and Lee* (New York: Harper and Row, 1977), 346.

30. It is relevant that Oswald's performance was watched by the Trade Mart's p.r. director, Jesse Core, and at least three other publicists, including the aforementioned William Gaudet, suggesting that they too had been alerted.

31. More likely organizers are the DRE Cubans and their allies. One of the CRC Cubans, Orest Pena, testified under oath that Oswald had come to his bar with an unidentified Latin man (11 WH 352–56; cf. 11 WH 345). According to Bringuier, this was a suspected Mexican pro-Communist, about whom Brin-

guier had telephoned the FBI (11 WH 45–46). Bringuier, arguing for a Castro-inspired assassination conspiracy, made much of this Mexican. The Warren Commission, dedicated to the proposition that Oswald was a loner, ignored this suggestion and never identified the third leafleter.

32. Summers, *Conspiracy,* 315–16, 574.

33. As Paul Hoch wrote in 1975, "After the assassination, the FBI hid from the [Warren] Commission the fact that it had known about Oswald's use of 544 Camp Street earlier, and suppressed the link to Banister by giving his address (531 Lafayette Street) without indicating that it was the same corner building as 544 Camp Street. Even the limited amount of documentary evidence which has not been kept from the Warren Commission and the public strongly suggests that the FBI was keeping hands off Oswald's activities, quite plausibly because the Bureau believed that he was not in fact a pro-Castro activist but was working for Banister or for some official intelligence agency" (Paul L. Hoch, "CIA Activities and the Warren Commission Investigation," in Scott, Hoch, and Stetler, *The Assassinations,* 465–66).

34. In the section of WCD 75 on Oswald and the FPCC, there are two interviews about "544 Camp Street" (one of them, strikingly brief, with Banister himself; WCD 75.680,683) without any indication of the reason (i.e., the leaflet) linking the address to Oswald and the FPCC. Extensive but ostensibly unrelated interviews with David Ferrie never link him to Banister or 544 Camp Street; and a volunteered unrelated remark by Ferrie about Banister (WCD 75.293) is omitted from the FBI's generally thorough index to WCD 75. Nor is there any overt reference in WCD 75 to the contact between Oswald and Carlos Quiroga of the CRC, whom the FBI had already interviewed. This allowed the Warren Report to claim that "extensive investigation was not able to link Oswald with [the Camp Street] address" (WR 408).

35. Keep in mind that (a) deBrueys was the agent in charge of the New Orleans FPCC file; (b) Hoover had called for special attention to FPCC activities; (c) Oswald was apparently the only FPCC activist in New Orleans; (d) someone in the FBI Field Office had said to "c[hec]k out" the 544 Camp Street address; and (e) according to the records we have, this was never done.

36. AR 143–45. In 1977 I interviewed deBrueys for the "Fifth Estate" show of the Canadian Broadcasting Corporation. Without informing us, deBrueys taped the interview and sent a transcript to FBI headquarters. Soon afterwards the transcript was released amid the FBI's general release of 100,000 pages on the Kennedy assassination. I suspected that the transcript might have been altered on one or two significant points and asked that the CBC send me a copy of our own recording. Unfortunately, despite my specific urging, they mailed me the original. It was blank on arrival.

37. AR 139–40.

38. CIA memo to the FBI of September 16, 1963, as quoted by Schweiker-Hart Report, 65.

39. Schweiker-Hart Report, 65.

40. Epstein, *Legend,* 224.

41. Ibid., 111–12.

42. Summers, *Conspiracy,* 319–20; Marrs, *Crossfire,* 235–38.

43. Blakey and Billings, *The Plot,* 166; cf. David Scheim, *Contract on America: The Mafia Murder of President John F. Kennedy* (New York: Zebra, 1989), 61.

44. CIA Document 501; cf. 11 WH 348, 357.

45. Theoharis and Cox, *The Boss,* 220–21, quoting from a former agent's letter; also quoted by Hinckle and Turner, *The Fish Is Red,* 203.

46. Summers, *Conspiracy,* 338. To readers and filmgoers surprised by so little reference to Ferrie at this point, let me reveal my belief that Ferrie, as much as Oswald, was a designated "patsy" or fall guy for the assassination. My reasons for thinking so will be developed in Chapter 15. In brief, Ferrie (like Oswald) helped incriminate himself, by departing suddenly from New Orleans for Galveston. One reason that Ferrie gave Garrison in 1966 for the trip was that "he had some business for Gill to take care of." Garrison's failure to mention this Ferrie-Gill-Marcello relationship is only one example of how weak, and how dubious, is his case against Ferrie.

47. Gentry, *Hoover,* 530; 9 AH 70–71.

48. *New Orleans States-Item,* May 5, 1967; quoted in Hinckle and Turner, *The Fish Is Red,* 203.

49. 10 AH 110; Hinckle and Turner, *The Fish Is Red,* 204.

50. 10 AH 112.

51. Hinckle and Turner, *The Fish Is Red,* 204. While still Cuban dictator Batista's secret police chief, Piedra used a Mexican drug trafficker, Cristobal Martinez Zorrilla, to kidnap one of Castro's chief supporters in Mexico (Jules Dubois, *Freedom Is My Beat* [Indianapolis: Bobbs-Merrill, 1959], 265). After Batista's fall, Piedra dealt with the organizers of raids by Frank Sturgis and Gerry Patrick Hemming on behalf of the Havana casino operators.

52. Hinckle and Turner, *The Fish Is Red,* 199.

53. Hinckle and Turner, *The Fish Is Red,* 199–200.

54. California Senate Un-American Activities Report, 1965, p. 163; quoted in J. Harry Jones, Jr., *Private Army* (New York: Collier Books, 1969), 112. Hoover showed the same bias vis-à-vis the John Birch Society, which the FBI had no files on "because it only investigated subversive organizations" (Jones, ibid., 171).

55. Hoover's ambivalence toward the Minuteman right (arresting Lauchli for Kennedy, but without seeing anything dangerous in his Minutemen) will be offered in Chapters 15 and 16 as a clue to explain Oswald's analogously ambivalent behavior with Carlos Bringuier.

56. Scott, *Crime and Cover-Up,* 43; 23 WH 363. Among those involved were Ruby's friend Lou Kopple (22 WH 423; cf. WCD 1193.69–75), Allen Dorfman, Gil Beckley, and Frank Rosenthal.

57. By his own account, Sierra had founded the JGCE with the encouragement of his employer, William Browder of the Union Tank Car Company, after an unidentified Cuban (who Sierra took to be Robert Kennedy's friend Enrique Ruiz-Williams) told Sierra by telephone to contact John Crimmins, the State

Department's Coordinator for Cuban Affairs, and say that Robert Kennedy had suggested the two should meet. Documents in the Kennedy Archives, summarized and cited by Arthur Schlesinger in his RFK biography (587, 1057), confirm that Sierra did meet with Crimmins on August 17, 1963, and that the meeting was "set up at RFK's request." Sierra and Browder agree with the House Committee that the purpose of the JGCE "was to back the activities of the more militant groups, including Alpha 66 and the . . . DRE, both of which had reportedly been in contact with Lee Harvey Oswald" (AR 134). Both Sierra and Browder claim, however, that the JGCE was founded, with official U.S. encouragement and assistance, to regroup the more militant Cuban-exile factions and persuade them to mount their guerrilla and terrorist operations from outside the United States. Sierra's account of his activities is supported both by the public record and by the Kennedy archives. The FBI and CIA files on Sierra and his Junta should be released, so we can see if they are indeed the source of a falsified account of Sierra. For either the files failed to record the Crimmins visit or else the House Committee made this misleading omission. If the JGCE was launched at the behest of Robert Kennedy, then the false assassination leads traced by the Secret Service to Sierra and his organization (AR 133–34, 26 WH 441) may have been used to force Robert Kennedy's acquiescence in the lone-assassin explanation.

58. 10 AH 61, 171, 169; 5 AH 314, 360–61; CIA Inspector General's Report of 1967, 29, 31.

59. 10 AH 171–72; Hinckle and Turner, *The Fish Is Red,* 75; Charles Rappleye and Ed Becker, *All American Mafioso: The Johnny Rosselli Story* (New York: Doubleday, 1991), 192. In particular Varona had remained in contact with members of the Chicago Syndicate who oversaw the mob investments in Havana, such as Richard Cain, an investigator for the Chicago sheriff's office who was simultaneously on the payroll of mafia leader Sam Giancana (10 AH 171–73).

60. Hinckle and Turner, *The Fish Is Red,* 74–75.

61. Church Committee, *Assassination Report,* 84; Hinckle and Turner, *The Fish Is Red,* 123–24. Harvey personally signed for the rental U-Haul trailer in which sophisticated electronics equipment was left, under the watchful eyes of John Rosselli and CIA officer Jim O'Connell, for Tony de Varona or his men to pick up.

62. William Stuckey, *New Orleans States-Item,* July 1962; reprinted, almost illegibly, as CIA Kennedy Assassination Document 351–1059B.

63. *Hispanic-American Report* 16:8 (October 1963), 761; interviews of 1979–80 with Paulino Sierra.

64. Scott, *Crime and Cover-Up,* 16–18, 56.

65. Summers, *Conspiracy,* 440–43. See Chapter 7.

66. Morris J. Blachman et al., *Confronting Revolution: Security Through Diplomacy in Central America* (New York: Pantheon, 1986), 128 (banana companies); *New York Times,* October 10, 1963, 12 (Somoza). On October 2, 1963, the day before the coup, United Fruit denied any involvement in military plans (*Hispanic-American Report* 16:10 [December 1963], 952).

CHAPTER SIX

1. Ralph Lee Woodward, Jr., *Central America: A Nation Divided* (New York: Oxford University Press, 1985), 256.

2. Philip L. Shepherd, "Honduras," in Morris J. Blachman et al., *Confronting Revolution: Security Through Diplomacy in Central America* (New York: Pantheon, 1986), 128 ("banana firms"); *New York Times,* October 10, 1963, 12 (Somoza); *Hispanic-American Report* 16:10 (December 1963), 952 (Army planes).

3. Schlesinger, *Robert Kennedy,* 469, 680, 681, 686, 744 (Mann/Kennedy); Susanne Jonas and David Tobis, *Guatemala* (New York: NACLA, 1974), 68n (Mann/coup); *Christian Science Monitor,* June 29, 1963; Scott, *Crime and Cover-Up,* 55 (resignation).

4. We know now that Ambassador Mann's push in November 1963 for a "phase one" Castro conspiracy hypothesis aroused the concern of the FBI, CIA, and State Department (Schweiker-Hart Report, 41; 3 AH 568–69).

5. 22 WH 829; Harold Weisberg, *Oswald in New Orleans* (New York: Canyon Books, 1967), 362.

6. Scott, *Crime and Cover-Up,* 14–15.

7. Ibid., 16; citing Hank Messick, *Lansky* (New York: Putnam's, 1971), 83, 87 (Syndicate).

8. The FBI had Roland Martin of Martin's Restaurant, 701 Tchoupitoulas, New Orleans, identify himself as having cashed Oswald's paycheck #1684 of June 14, 1963 (22 WH 208). In fact the check is stamped as having been endorsed by Oswald and then deposited by Foltz Tea & Coffee, Inc., at 633 Tchoupitoulas (22 WH 288). See also Chapter 15.

9. Suspiciously, Monaghan's next place of employment was at a newly opened facility of the National Aeronautics and Space Administration. Monaghan migrated there with at least three other Reily Company employees; and, at the time, Oswald told a reliable witness that he too "expected to work next at the New Orleans plant of NASA" (Summers, *Conspiracy,* 313). Monaghan was an expert in industrial security; and it has been suggested that the other employees were employed at Reily as part of a trial period during which industrial security checks could be run on their backgrounds. For more on Oswald's role in this, see Chapter 15.

10. Scott, *Crime and Cover-Up,* 15, 54; and sources there cited.

11. Ibid., 10–11; Summers, *Conspiracy,* 440; Schweiker-Hart Report, 28 ff, 41 ff.

12. FBI File SA 89-67; Report of November 30, 1963; WCD 75.588, 613, 652; Anson, *"They've Killed the President!"* 181n, 381; Summers, *Conspiracy,* 362–63. The gap is disguised in the State Department mistranslation (24 WH 685) of the Gobernación list (24 WH 679): the English describes two names *following* Oswald's number ("posterior" in Spanish, 24 WH 679) as "prior" (24 WH 685).

13. WCD 75.588, FD-302 of November 27, 1963; Scott, *Crime and Cover-Up,* 15, 54. The House Committee reviewed Gaudet's CIA file and found no

CIA use of or contact with Gaudet after 1961 (AR 218–19). But Gaudet told Summers he had had contact with the CIA down through 1969 (Summers, *Conspiracy,* 363). Gaudet told me in a 1977 interview for the Canadian Broadcasting Corporation that he considered the CIA responsible for the omission of his name.

14. An alternative possibility, suggested to me by Gaudet himself, is that Oswald's tourist card was obtained the same day by other persons intending to embarrass Gaudet and the CIA. Cf. Summers, *Conspiracy,* 364.

15. Other examples are Carlos Bringuier and Ed Butler of INCA; Ronny Caire, who had once promoted the New Orleans CRC; and at least two of the FBI's witnesses to Oswald's leafleting in front of the International Trade Mart, including the Trade Mart's PR Director Jesse Core (who later became Jim Garrison's campaign manager; Scott, *Crime and Cover-Up,* 14; WCD 75.690; WCD 6.414).

16. Dr. Joseph d'Antoni, who succeeded his brother Blaise as president of Standard Fruit, was simultaneously Ochsner's colleague as Professor of Clinical Tropical Medicine at Tulane (Thomas Karnes, *Tropical Enterprise* [Baton Rouge: Louisiana State University Press, 1978], 172, 275–77).

17. Scott, *Crime and Cover-Up,* 15; AR 218–19; Summers, *Conspiracy,* 363; Hurt, 229.

18. Thomas P. McCann, *An American Company: The Tragedy of United Fruit* (New York: Crown, 1976), 48.

19. William Ivy Hair, *The Kingfish and His Realm* (Baton Rouge: Louisiana State University Press, 1991), 286; *New York Times,* July 18, 1939; August 19, 1939 (indictments); November 20, 1940 (jailed); Hank Messick, *Hoover* (New York: David McKay, 1972), 166, citing testimony in 1970 before the New York Joint Legislative Committee on Crime.

20. Karnes, *Tropical Enterprise,* 104 (Vaccaros/Roosevelt Hotel); T. Harry Williams, *Huey Long* (New York: Bantam, 1969), 265, 612–13 (Long).

21. After 1926 Standard Fruit's management "was placed in the hands of the so-called Moss-Hecht group, made up of Washington Irving Moss, who served as chairman of the board beginning in 1927; his brother Mike; Harold W. Newman; and Rudolph Hecht, president of Hibernia Bank and Trust Company" (Karnes, *Tropical Enterprise,* 196). Thus at this point Standard Fruit interlocked both with its bank, Hibernia, and with Union Indemnity, a Vaccaro-Moss insurance company of which W. I. Moss was president and his brother Mike Moss and Felix Vaccaro were vice-presidents. The Vaccaros also housed their Standard Fruit Corporation in their Union Indemnity Building. The most celebrated corporate scandal of the Long era was that of Union Indemnity. Rudolph Hecht obtained $1 million from the Reconstruction Finance Commission, to finance repayment of a loan from Union Indemnity (of which he was a director) to his Hibernia Bank. Soon afterwards, Union Indemnity went bankrupt, while Huey Long arranged for a "bank holiday" in order to save the Hibernia Bank (Webster Smith, *The Kingfish: A Biography of Huey P. Long* (New York: Putnam's, 1933), 282; Williams, *Huey Long,* 646–48). At this time one of Harold Newman's sons (Robert) was assistant treasurer of Union Indemnity, while another (Harold, Jr.) was assistant general counsel for

the Reconstruction Finance Commission. Hecht, who received the RFC loan, was (thanks to his influence with Long) chairman of the regional advisory board of the RFC.

22. Messick, *Hoover*, 166. Before Rudolph Hecht died in 1956, he had become chairman of the executive committee of the International Trade Mart and of the Cordell Hull Foundation, which supported INCA, of which Seymour Weiss was a charter member.

23. Hair, *Kingfish*, 318, 321, 325; Williams, *Huey Long*, 883, 914–17.

24. Hair, *Kingfish*, 298–300; Williams, *Huey Long*, 823, 901. In his youth, Parker had helped organize the famous New Orleans anti-Sicilian lynch party of 1890 (see below).

25. Williams, *Huey Long*, 767.

26. Scott and Marshall, *Cocaine Politics*, 52.

27. Messick, *Lansky*, 83.

28. Ibid., 83–87; Blakey and Billings, *The Plot*, 241. Blakey omits all reference to the role of Seymour Weiss in the slot-machine deal, and misspells, as "Montranga," the name of mob leader Charles Matranga whose funeral was attended by representatives of the fruit companies. Yet Weiss was a senior figure in the anti-Communist p.r. world that managed Oswald's televised "debate."

29. David Leon Chandler, *Brothers in Blood* (New York: Dutton, 1975), 182; Davis, *Mafia Kingfish*, 45 (clearinghouse); R. T. Naylor, *Hot Money and the Politics of Debt* (New York: Simon and Schuster, 1987), 21, 386; Nicholas Faith, *Safety in Numbers* (New York: Viking, 1982), 218–19; *New York Times*, September 28, 1985 (Switzerland).

30. Williams, *Huey Long*, 865–67. By the 1960s Huey's son Senator Russell Long had emerged as an owner of Win or Lose. It was Russell Long who launched the Garrison investigation of the JFK murder, which as we shall see was suspected of being part of a plot, involving Jimmy Noe's son-in-law Gordon McLendon, to bring pressure on an important witness against Hoffa, Edward Grady Partin (Walter Sheridan, *Hoffa* (New York: Saturday Review Press, 1972), 406–11, 424–28, 503–05). McLendon's brother-in-law Lester May (see Chapter 14) was also named in this plot.

31. Messick, *Hoover*, 166.

32. Chandler, *Brothers in Blood*, 182. Chandler, who is committed to the "Cosa Nostra" version of organized crime, describes Coppola as "a capo in the Luciano-Costello family" (182). But Coppola appears to have drifted to New York from Detroit, where he was named with Detroit mob leader Santo Perrone in the AFL's anti-CIO strike-breaking activities as late as 1941 (Dan E. Moldea, *The Hoffa Wars* [New York: Paddington Press, 1978], 37–38).

33. Peter Dale Scott, in Henrik Krueger, *The Great Heroin Coup* (Boston: South End Press, 1981), 14 (massacre); Moldea, *Hoffa Wars*, 42 (heroin); see Chapter 10.

34. Messick, *Hoover*, 166. Cf. Gentry, *Hoover*, 329; Davis, *Mafia Kingfish*, 45 (Costello). When Lou Nichols resigned from the FBI in 1957, he went to work for Rosenstiel at Schenley Industries. He was joined there by Joe McCarthy's former assistant Roy Cohn, another friend of Seymour Weiss.

35. Scott and Marshall, *Cocaine Politics,* 52; Chandler, *Brothers in Blood,* 97; Karnes, *Tropical Enterprise,* 10. A fourth firm which merged at the same time as the Machecas', S. Oteri, may also have had gang connections; cf. Chandler, ibid., 91.

36. Karnes, *Tropical Enterprise,* 2, 10, 91–92.

37. Racing Hearings, 886.

38. Lamberto Artioli, *Sport e Mafia* (Milan: V. Bompiani, 1968), 224.

39. *New York Times,* July 24, 1940; Rappleye and Becker, *All American Mafioso,* 151.

40. Stanley Penn, "On the Waterfront," in Nicholas Gage (ed.) *Mafia: U.S.A.* (New York: Dell, 1972), 323.

41. Rodney Campbell, *The Luciano Project* (New York: McGraw-Hill, 1977).

42. Davis, *Mafia Kingfish,* 27–29; cf. Scheim, *Contract on America,* 385, 394, 410; Frederick Sondern, *Brotherhood of Evil: The Mafia* (New York: Farrar, Straus and Cudahy, 1959), 56–65; Ed Reid, *The Grim Reapers* (New York: Bantam, 1970), 146–50; Chandler, *Brothers in Blood,* 80–96. Davis and Scheim fail to consider the devastating analysis of these mafia allegations by Humbert Nelli in *The Business of Crime* (New York: Oxford University Press, 1976), 47–66, and Dwight C. Smith, Jr., in *The Mafia Mystique* (New York: Basic Books, 1975), 27–45. The suppressed evidence vindicating Matranga, and the dubious and self-interested role played in the "mafia" scare of 1890–91 by William Pinkerton and by his detective Frank Dimaio, should be remembered when we turn to Hoover's role in promoting the FBI hype of "La Cosa Nostra" in 1963 (see Chapter 11). Pinkerton and Dimaio later formed a special group of Italian-speaking agents to engage in the business of investigating "Black Hand" murders (Nelli, 91–92; cf. Smith, 38).

43. "Mafia in New Orleans," *Harper's* 34 (November 8, 1890): 874; quoted in Smith, *Mafia Mystique,* 30. The lynching appears to have been organized by New Orleans patricians attempting to seize the Democratic party away from the "Ring," a Tammany-type urban party machine, later the "Old Regulars" of Clem Sehrt, that relied heavily on the Italian and Sicilian vote (Hair, *The Kingfish,* 12–15; cf. Smith, 350n; Williams, *Huey Long,* 135–37). They appear to have not only exploited but believed the fear that the mafia were plotting to take over the city, with the assassination of the mayor and new police chief next on their agenda (Hair, 13). One of the plotters was future Louisiana governor John M. Parker, later a member of the Square Deal plot against Huey Long (Hair, 13, 298, 324).

44. Nelli, *Business of Crime,* 37–38. The extent of "mafia" involvement in the Matranga affair, though hysterically exaggerated at the time and since, should not be wholly discounted, as the New York waterfront should remind us. In the following pages I shall talk about "mafia" as both an occasional reality, perhaps unfortunately named, and a myth fostered by law enforcement (see Chapter 9).

45. Davis, *Mafia Kingfish,* 56 ("boss"); Blakey and Billings, *The Plot,* 241 ("head"); Nelli, *Business of Crime,* 64 ("stevedore").

46. Chandler, *Brothers in Blood*, 98.

47. Blakey and Billings, *The Plot*, 342–44; Scheim, *Contract on America*, 64–65; Davis, *Mafia Kingfish*, 135–36.

48. In 1976 Marcello's lobbyist, I. Irving Davidson, told a future FBI informant, Joseph Hauser, "that he had known Marcello for years and knew he controlled the Teamsters and the Longshoremen in Louisiana" (Davis, *Mafia Kingfish*, 464). At one point the Longshoremen's local in New Orleans owned the building at 544 Camp Street.

49. *San Francisco Chronicle*, November 26, 1975, 44; Nancy Peckenham and Annie Street, eds, *Honduras: Portrait of a Captive Nation* (New York: Praeger, 1985), 131 (Bananagate).

50. Oliver North's notebooks refer to a key Contra-support meeting at Lindner's Ocean Reef Club in Florida in March 1984, one month after Carl Lindner's American Financial Corp. increased its holdings in United Brands from 29.3 percent to 45.4 percent. North also refers to a "United Brands grant to [Andy] Messing," a key organizer of Contra support both in the field and in Congress (Brewton, *The Mafia, CIA, and George Bush*, 289–91). Messing was an ally of Contra fundraiser John Singlaub, whose headquarters for the U.S. Council for World Freedom and the World Anti-Communist League was in Scottsdale, Arizona, next door to Charles Keating's company, American Continental, a former Lindner subsidiary. For United Brands and Noriega, see Frederick Kempe, *Divorcing the Dictator* (New York: Putnam, 1990), 57; Scott and Marshall, *Cocaine Politics*, 208, also 91. The hangars at Lindner's Ocean Reef Club were used for drug smuggling by the convicted trafficker Jack DeVoe (see Chapter 5), who had listed as his sponsor for membership there Richard Nixon's friend Bebe Rebozo (Brewton, *The Mafia, CIA, and George Bush*, 291–94). For Lindner, Keating, and Milken, see James B. Stewart, *Den of Thieves* (New York: Simon & Schuster/Touchstone, 1992), 54, 66–67, 130, 137–38, 237, 453.

51. Peckenham and Street, *Honduras*, 73.

52. Ibid., 21, 71–73; *Fortune*, March 1933, 26–27; Karnes, *Tropical Enterprise*, 42–45.

53. Karnes, *Tropical Enterprise*, 44.

54. Woodward, *Central America*, 196–98; Peckenham and Street, *Honduras*, 56.

55. William O. Walker III, *Drug Control in the Americas* (Albuquerque: University of New Mexico Press, 1989), 142; Scott and Marshall, *Cocaine Politics*, 53.

56. Scott, *Crime and Cover-Up*, 46, 73; Maurice Helbrant, *Narcotics Agent* (New York: Vanguard, 1941), 265, 279.

57. Helbrant, *Narcotics Agent*, 265–81; Walker, *Drug Control*, 141–49.

58. Walker, *Drug Control*, 145.

59. Turner, *Power on the Right*, 97n.

60. Ubico's relatively early fall can be explained by U.S. opposition to his fascist sympathies during World War II. See Susanne Jonas, *The Battle for Guatemala* (Boulder: Westview, 1992), 22.

61. Walker, *Drug Control*, 79–80.

62. James Mills, *Underground Empire* (Garden City, N.Y.: Doubleday, 1986), 548.

63. Ibid., 527 (cards). See Chapter 9.

64. Elaine Shannon, *Desperados*, (New York: Viking, 1988), 179; Cf. *New York Times*, April 21, 1985 (quoted in Scott and Marshall, *Cocaine Politics*, 39): "Every time we grab someone, they're carrying a card from the DFS."

65. *San Diego Union*, March 26, 1982 (quoted in Shannon, *Desperados*, 183); cf. Scott and Marshall, *Cocaine Politics*, 34–36. Others who have been linked to trafficking in stolen cars across the U.S.-Mexican border include Frank Sturgis and Richmond Harper (see Chapter 5), as well as the major Nicaraguan drug trafficker Norwin Meneses Canterero.

66. See Summers, *Conspiracy*, 379–81. For Win Scott's close association with Gobernación, see Philip Agee, *CIA Diary* (Harmondsworth, Middlesex: Penguin, 1975), 275–75, 524–26, 553. Agee was told by a colleague that Gustavo Díaz Ordáz, the head of the Gobernación in 1963, was "really in Scott's pocket," after Scott got an automobile for the Minister's girlfriend (274–75). See Chapter 7.

67. Scott and Marshall, *Cocaine Politics*, 34–35 (de Torres-Nazar).

68. For the drug history of WACL, originally the Asian People's Anti-Communist League, see Scott, *War Conspiracy*, 204–06.

CHAPTER SEVEN

1. Gentry, *J. Edgar Hoover*, 295–96, 391–92. William Gaudet, who identified himself to the FBI as "CIA," was in fact a member of this wartime network.

2. Ibid., 392; William Corson, *The Armies of Ignorance* (New York: Dial Press/James Wade Books, 1977), 286; Hersh, *The Old Boys*, 187.

3. Franz Schurmann, *The Logic of World Power* (New York: Pantheon, 1974); Bruce Cumings, *The Origins of the Korean War* (Princeton: Princeton University Press, 1990) 2:13–19.

4. Hersh, *The Old Boys*, 341 (Jackson).

5. John Prados, *The President's Secret Wars* (New York: Morrow, 1986), 101–06; Hersh, *The Old Boys*, 351. A third position, eventually excluded from the operation, was that of the CIA's Col. J. C. King, chief of the Western Hemisphere Division in the Directorate of Plans. King's more traditional style was to let United Fruit, Somoza, and the Guatemalan army do the job. "If you think you can do this without United Fruit, you're crazy!" King exclaimed, after being removed from the project (Ranelagh, *The Agency*, 265–66).

6. Scott, *Crime and Cover-Up*, 16; citing IV Congreso Continental Anticomunista, *Actas* (Guatemala, 1961), 415 (Antonio Valladares y Aycinena); *Saturday Evening Post*, February 29, 1964, 19 (Marcello's lawyer).

7. Rappleye and Becker, *All-American Mafioso*, 149; Scott, *Crime and Cover-Up*, 16.

8. Rappleye and Becker, *All-American Mafioso*, 149; Sterling Seagrave, *The Marcos Dynasty* (New York: Harper and Row, 1988), 161–64, 329–30, 334.

9. Rappleye and Becker, *All-American Mafioso*, 150.

10. Karnes, *Tropical Enterprise*, 270–71, 277, 280, 281.

11. Rappleye and Becker, *All-American Mafioso*, 154; cf. Blachman et al., *Confronting Revolution*, 31–32.

12. Rappleye and Becker, *All-American Mafioso*, 155; Blachman et al., *Confronting Revolution*, 31.

13. Karnes, *Tropical Enterprise*, 287.

14. A major Guatemalan drug bust of 1963, involving both opium and marijuana from Mexico, led to the arrests of more than twenty persons including six deputies in the Guatemalan Congress. One of these, Manuel Orellana Portillo, was a leading member of the party of Roberto Alejos, longtime CIA ally in Guatemala, and the party's candidate for the presidency of Congress. The arrests were announced by secret-police chief Horacio Neri Porres (*Hispanic-American Report* 16:2 [April 1963], 117–18).

15. Mills, *Underground Empire*, 355, 357.

16. Scott and Marshall, *Cocaine Politics*, 34; Mills, *Underground Empire*, 75.

17. Peter Dale Scott, Foreword, in Krueger, *The Great Heroin Coup*, 7.

18. Scott and Marshall, *Cocaine Politics*, 34; Rappleye and Becker, *All-American Mafioso*, 169; Mills, *Underground Empire*, 360–61.

19. Jonas, *The Battle for Guatemala*, 60–63.

20. Private communication from a longtime friend of Martino.

21. Blachman et al., *Confronting Revolution*, 34; Marshall, Scott, and Hunter, *The Iran-Contra Connection*, 20–25; Christopher Dickey, *With the Contras* (New York: Simon and Schuster, 1985), 86–87, 90.

22. Rappleye and Becker, *All-American Mafioso*, 218–19.

23. Hinckle and Turner, *The Fish Is Red*, 168–75; Rappleye and Becker, *All-American Mafioso*, 218–19. Weyl had played a small but crucial role in the conviction of Alger Hiss, where the collaboration of Richard Nixon, the FBI's Lou Nichols, and former FBI agents Robert King and Lou Russell, is now documented (Theoharis and Cox, *The Boss*, 252, 315).

24. Scott, *War Conspiracy*, 210; Cumings, *The Origins of the Korean War* 2:509–12. Pawley was also an advocate, in the December 1960 *Washington Report* of the American Security Council, of using Chinese Nationalist troops to overthrow the Government of North Vietnam (Turner, *Power on the Right*, 205).

25. Michael R. Beschloss, *The Crisis Years* (New York: Edward Burlingame Books, 1991), 94, 136. According to Richard Nixon's *Six Crises* (New York: Pocketbooks, 1962), Pawley was one of four men, along with J. Edgar Hoover, who had supported Nixon's "minority" but successful campaign for "stronger" CIA operations against Cuba (379). In late 1960 Pawley was still complaining to Eisenhower that the CIA's *frente* was "too far to the left" (Prados, *The President's Secret Wars*, 190).

26. Together with the former FBI agent Raymond Leddy, another principal in the 1954 Guatemala operation, Pawley had attacked the CIA and State Department's initial "softness" toward Castro, testifying publicly to Senator James Eastland's Senate Internal Security Subcommittee against an alleged pro-Communist State Department employee, William Wieland. By Pawley's account, it was Eastland in 1963 who put Pawley in touch with Martino (Hinckle and Turner, *The Fish Is Red*, 170–72).

27. Ibid., 173–74; Peter Wyden, *The Bay of Pigs* (New York: Simon and Schuster, 1979), 84 (Somoza).

28. Hinckle and Turner, *The Fish Is Red*, 171–72. Pawley's request to Carter may have been pro forma, to implicate the CIA. According to Martino's friend John Cummings, Martino and Robertson were already close, from their work for the CIA in 1959–60; and it was Robertson who told Martino to collaborate with Weyl, who was already working on Pawley's biography.

29. 10 AH 77. The concept was promoted from within the State Department by Walt Rostow, perhaps the leading civilian hawk and advocate for the U.S. bombing of North Vietnam.

30. After the assassination, Martino contacted the Commission and told a story that was hauntingly similar to the one John Rosselli told more than twelve years later: the Kennedy assassination had been an act of retaliation for an anti-Castro plot, according to a source "high in the Cuban government" whose identity Martino refused to reveal (Blakey and Billings, *The Plot*, 80, citing memo of April 1, 1964, from David Slawson to J. Lee Rankin); cf. Scott, *Crime and Cover-Up*, 19–30 (Rosselli). In addition, Martino claimed that Oswald had been active for Cuban intelligence in the Miami area (WCD 320.7; cf. WCD 561.1–2; WCD 886), a story apparently traceable to the International Anti-Communist Brigade of Frank "Fiorini," i.e., Frank Sturgis, and his propaganda director Tim Buchanan (WCD 59.2–3, WCD 395.2, 15, WCD 1020.1–6; 26 WH 424; Scott, Hoch, and Stetler, *The Assassinations*, 360–61).

31. Leo Janos, *Atlantic*, July 1973, 39; quoted in Scott, Hoch, and Stetler, *Assassinations*, 362.

32. Summers, *Conspiracy*, 433; quoting William Manchester, *The Death of a President* (New York: Harper and Row, 1967), 730.

33. Hurt, *Reasonable Doubt*, 309, quoting Blakey and Billings, *The Plot*, 140.

34. Hurt, *Reasonable Doubt*, 309, citing Harris Wofford, *Of Kennedy and Kings* (New York: Farrar Straus Giroux, 1980), 418; Schlesinger, *Robert Kennedy*, 616.

35. Scott, *Crime and Cover-Up*, passim.

36. Blakey and Billings, *The Plot*, 80; Hinckle and Turner, *The Fish Is Red*, 169–73, 349–50.

37. Blakey and Billings, *The Plot*, 80; 11 AH 439.

38. Robert K. Brown and Miguel Acoca, "The Bayo-Pawley Affair," *Soldier of Fortune*, February 1976; Dick Russell, *Village Voice*, October 3, 1977.

39. Meagher, *Accessories after the Fact*, 376–87; Summers, *Conspiracy*, 415–17; 26 WH 834 (false Hall testimony); WCD 1553; AR 138–39; 11 AH 600 (retraction of false testimony). The story is that of Silvia Odio (see below).

40. Turner, *Power on the Right*, 102–05; Russell, *The Man Who Knew Too Much*, 547, 771, 778. The FBI learned that Gale had attended a secret meeting in Birmingham, Ala., before the September 1963 bombing of a Birmingham church that left four young black girls dead; it also heard from an informant that at least one of those at the meeting had gone there as part of a plot to kill Martin Luther King (AR 377).

41. Hinckle and Turner, *The Fish Is Red*, 350 (Castillo); 4 AH 146 (CIA Inspector-General's Report of 25 April 1967, 118).

42. Brown and Acoca, "The Bayo-Pawley Affair."

43. Ibid.; Russell, *Village Voice*, October 3, 1977.

44. Prados, *The President's Secret Wars*, 101–06; Hersh, *The Old Boys*, 351.

45. Bernard Diederich, *Somoza* (New York: Dutton, 1981), 45; Wyden, *Bay of Pigs*, 84.

46. Prados, *The President's Secret Wars*, 213.

47. Rappleye and Becker, *All-American Mafioso*, 218–19, 225. Cf. Bradley Ayers, *The War That Never Was* (New York: Bobbs-Merrill, 1976), 38.

48. Rappleye and Becker, *All-American Mafioso*, 245.

49. Blakey and Billings, *The Plot*, 80.

50. Hinckle and Turner, *The Fish Is Red*, 156–57; Hugh Thomas, *Cuba* (New York: Harper and Row, 1971), 198; *Hispanic-American Report*, 1962, 911.

51. Hinckle and Turner, *The Fish Is Red*, 168–70.

52. Ibid., 349–50. Hall's credibility is not good; the assassination story, however, is corroborated by Bob "Tosh" Plumlee, a CIA contract pilot. Further corroboration, not noted by Hinckle and Turner, comes from the Luis Castillo retaliation story; Hall told Hinckle and Turner that it was Luis Castillo who informed them that Bayo and two of his commandos were captured in Cuba.

53. Scott, *Crime and Cover-Up*, 23–27; 4 AH 127–50 (I-G Report); Watergate Hearings, vol. 21, 9751–55; cf. 9723.

54. Charles Crimaldi (as told to John Kidner), *Crimaldi: Contract Killer*, (Washington: Acropolis Books, 1976), 217 ("CIA guy"); William Brashler, *The Don: The Life and Death of Sam Giancana* (New York: Harper and Row, 1977), 324 ("same people"); see below, Chapter 10.

55. Summers, *Conspiracy*, 452. Martino's death has been variously dated between 1975 and 1977.

56. Marrs, *Crossfire*, 66–68 (Jackson/Zapruder); Scott, *Crime and Cover-Up*, 35–36 (Marina, CIA). I should make it clear that in the Bayo-Martino-Pawley mission I see the role of Billings as that of a victim rather than a plotter, someone whose presence was planned by others with a more sinister agenda. Cover-up, for whatever motive, is a different issue. I will offer an extended critique of the Blakey-Billings handling of the Jack Ruby story in Part III of this book.

57. In 1975, Martino allegedly told a second friend, a Texas businessman called Fred Claasen, that "the anti-Castro people put Oswald together. Oswald didn't know who he was working for—he was just ignorant of who was really putting him together. Oswald was to meet his contact at the Texas Theater. . . .

They were to meet Oswald in the theater, and get him out of the country, then eliminate him" (Summers, *Conspiracy,* 451).

58. "One of the federal investigators probing Rosselli's murder thirteen years later came across an FBI report on the meetings and relayed its contents, on a confidential basis, to Washington, D.C., reporter William Scott Malone. An accomplished investigator himself, Malone said in an interview he was confident of the integrity of his source, and said the FBI had determined the actual site of the Miami meetings" (Rappleye and Becker, *All-American Mafioso,* 245; citing William Scott Malone, "The Secret Life of Jack Ruby," *New Times,* January 23, 1978). The generally crowded Ruby Chronology for October 1963 leaves possible gaps for such meetings on October 8 and October 13–14 (9 AH 1093–95).

59. 10 AH 24; Summers, *Conspiracy,* 417–18. The Gonzalez assassination attempt was masterminded by Antonio Veciana, who at that time worked for Julio Lobo, the financier of the Hotel Capri in Havana which was visited by Ruby when his friend McWillie worked there. Later Veciana organized Alpha 66 (10 AH 37–39).

60. According to one of Martino's friends, the purpose of the Dallas visit was to meet Odio's daughter, Silvia.

61. *Human Events,* December 21, 1963 (Martino); Pompano Beach *Sun-Sentinel,* November 26, 1963; discussed in WCD 59.2–3 (Sturgis alias Fiorini). In an FBI interview, Sturgis later denied responsibility for the *Sentinel* story (WCD 1020).

62. Gentry, *Hoover,* 543–47.

63. The FBI reported in 1967 that the 1963 dynamite cache at the McLaneys "was an operation of the Directorio Revolucionario Estudiantil (DRE)" (FBI airtel 62–109060–4758; SAC NO to Director, 3/7/67). It listed two prominent DRE activists, Carlos "Batea" Hernández, the hero of the DRE's Miramar raid in 1962, and José Basulto Leon.

64. Testimony of Laureano Batista Falla, military chief of the Movimiento Democrata Cristiano (MDC) which organized the camp. Batista Falla's men, led by his nephew Victor Paneque, had left Miami for the camp on July 24, 1963, one week after Batista had visited Gen. Somoza in Nicaragua.

65. Schweiker-Hart Report, 28.

66. WR 308; cf. CIA-396, WCD 1000, WCE 3152, 26 WH 857–60 (all roughly the same). The role of the FBI in the "phase two" November 30 retraction suggests that this was the unresolved "additional lead being pursued in Mexico" which Hoover referred to in his memo of November 29 (AR 244). Clark Anderson was, as it happened, an acquaintance of William Gaudet, the intelligence operative whose Mexican entry card preceded Oswald's.

67. According to a contemporary CIA cable, there were two interviewers, but the other was an Embassy Security Officer (CIA-52).

68. David Phillips, *The Night Watch* (New York: Atheneum, 1977), 141–42.

69. WCD 1000A ("Communist"); CIA-52 = WCD 1000B.4 ("serious"); CIA-69 = WCD 1000C.2 ("cooperative").

70. FBI Memo of December 12, 1963; 3 AH 595. DeLoach's references to "D" as "a source of CIA's," "CIA's source," and "CIA source" belie even further the CIA's description of "D" as a "well-known Nicaraguan Communist underground member." Cf. the CIA's letter of June 4, 1964: " 'D' was known to this agency as a former informant of a Latin American security service" (26 WH 858).

71. 3 AH 304, cf. 301 ("friend"); Agee, 274–75 ("pocket," cf. Chapter 6). Díaz Ordáz, the head of Gobernación in 1963, was President of Mexico by the time Garro de Paz spoke to the U.S. embassy official in 1965.

72. 3 AH 83, 112, 301. Silvia Durán told the House Committee staff that her husband Horacio was a Communist sympathizer and was also involved in a campaign "against the drugs" (3 AH 112–13).

73. 3 AH 86, 102; cf. 3 AH 292–93, 297, WR 302, 735, 16 WH 54, 24 WH 568.

74. By February 1964 Hoover and Angleton would have a falling out when Hoover told the Warren Commission about Yuri Nosenko, a KGB defector who arrived in time to deny KGB interest in Oswald, and whom Angleton was keeping secret (Ranelagh, *The Agency*, 405; Mangold, *Cold Warrior*, 175). Angleton and William Sullivan on the FBI remained close; but Hoover had disciplined Sullivan by November 28 for his handling of the Oswald case. The resulting gaps separating Hoover from Angleton and Sullivan were never to close (cf. Ranelagh, ibid., 403; Gentry, *Hoover*, 418, 646).

75. Schweiker-Hart Report, 41; 3 AH 568–69.

CHAPTER EIGHT

1. WR 801; Blakey and Billings, *The Plot*, 83.

2. One of the Warren Commission Counsels and authors of the Warren Report was Albert Jenner. At the time Jenner also was representing Henry Crown, a Chicago businessman close to Democratic political kingmaker Jake Arvey, in whose political machine Ruby and his brother had reportedly worked; later, Jenner was attorney for one of the organized-crime figures, Irwin Weiner, whom Ruby telephoned shortly before the Kennedy assassination.

3. Scheim, *Contract on America*, 128; FBI Interview with Bobby Gene Moore, WCE 1536, 23 WH 27 (edited version); WCD 84.91 (unedited version). Scheim reproduces both versions photographically; the two texts are compared by John H. Davis, who suggests that the censor may have been Commission counsel Howard Willens, a former soldier with Blakey in the Kennedy Justice Department war on organized crime (*Mafia Kingfish*, 311–13). The FBI had itself contributed to the cover-up in its FD-302 report of the interview, misspelling Civello's name as "CIRELLO." Cf. 22 WH 303, where Civello's name is rendered by the FBI as "JOE SAVELLA."

4. McClellan Hearings, 12526.

5. Blakey and Billings, *The Plot*, 339.

6. Ibid., 180; cf. AR 160.

7. Blakey and Billings, *The Plot*, 314. As mentioned earlier, I shall talk about "Mafia" both as a reality, perhaps unfortunately named, and as a myth fostered by law enforcement (see Chapter 9). While men like Joseph Civello in Dallas and Carlos Marcello in New Orleans undoubtedly dealt with mafiosi in other cities and can thus perhaps be called mafiosi themselves, talk such as Blakey's of "the Mafia family in Dallas" (ibid.) is unsubstantiated, and should perhaps be treated as part of the myth. What Moore's testimony shows is that Civello's criminal operations were not restricted to Sicilians or Italians but involved non-Italians like Ruby.

8. Blakey and Billings, *The Plot*, 314, inserts in original.

9. WCD 302.16 (FBI interview of Civello); cf. WCD 302.30 (FBI interview of Frank Lamonte, co-owner of the store, who also knew Ruby).

10. McClellan Hearings, 12269–70. The FBN also knew that, after Apalachin, Ormento telephoned both "Joe Civillo" in Dallas and Mike Polizzi in Detroit (see below; Narcotics Hearings, 282).

11. Narcotics Hearings, 1098, citing Civello's FBI Criminal History File 1222605.

12. Personal telephone conversation, October 1979.

13. Blakey and Billings, *The Plot*, 322.

14. 23 WH 369. Eileen Curry later surfaced as an "unindicted co-conspirator" (i.e., probably an informant) in an important Chicago mob case involving Frank Tornabene, a veteran wire-service employee who earlier had been involved in local vote fraud. (Chicago Crime Commission, 1965, 80–81).

15. Scott, "From Dallas to Watergate," in Scott, Hoch, and Stetler, *The Assassinations*, 368; cf. Scheim, *Contract on America*, 115–17, 146–47. One of these sources was among the many witnesses (including former Dallas County Sheriff Steve Guthrie) who also reported that "Ruby hustled the strippers and other girls who worked in his club" (23 WH 373). Joe Bonds, a former business partner of Ruby's, told the FBI that Ruby "made women available" to Dallas police officers" (22 WH 335). Narcotics and prostitution frequently go together: the drugs help procure the women; the women often move, sell, and consume the drugs.

16. Committee staff counsel Donald Purdy deposed Ruby's friend Lewis McWillie; and, while pursuing the question of "narcotics activity in the Dallas area," asked if Ruby knew "James or Bunny Breen" (5 AH 81). I have found no effort to contact the Breens directly, or any of the other sources, even though (as noted in an earlier footnote) Eileen Curry Breen continued to serve as a government informant.

17. Hurt, *Reasonable Doubt*, 172.

18. Scheim, *Contract on America*, 368–69. Scheim's book is useful, and in its own way thoroughgoing; but I regret that it uses so much of his own and others' research to reach this reductionist conclusion, which ignores so much other evidence.

19. FBI interview of Angelo Lonardo, as quoted in Block, *Perspectives on Organizing Crime*, 18.

20. Scott, *Crime and Cover-Up*, 43, citing WCD 732, WCD 1052. I was given the opportunity to present this and subsequent information personally to

Blakey and his staff in Washington, at a small conference with assassination researchers which the Committee transcribed. The Committee then bought seven copies of my book *Crime and Cover-Up*, which is cited sparingly in the staff report on organized crime (9 AH 1132, 1140).

21. AR 156–58; Blakey and Billings, *The Plot*, 322; cf. 9 AH 139–44.

22. Steele testified that he had come to the station "to pick up some correspondence, telegrams, and things like that, to take to Officer Tippit's widow," and was told by Captain Talbert's deputy, Lieutenant Pierce, to "stick around for a while" (12 WH 354; cf. Meagher, *Accessories*, 443).

23. Meagher, ibid., 404–20; AR 158; Blakey and Billings, *The Plot*, 321–22; Summers, *Conspiracy*, 486–92.

24. 5 WH 255; Meagher, ibid., 413; Blakey and Billings, ibid., 330–33.

25. Summers, *Official and Confidential*, 329; Moldea, *Interference*, 105.

26. Elsewhere Revill made it clear that his statement "that Ruby was not an informant for the intelligence division" did not apply to other sections of the Department (9 AH 1119).

27. WCD 85.64: FBI Interview of Richard L. Clark, Narcotics and Vice Squad, Special Service Bureau. Cf. 13 WH 183; Scott, *Crime and Cover-Up*, 72.

28. "On November 6, 1959, Flynn wrote that Ruby's information had not been particularly helpful, that further attempts to develop Ruby as a PCI (potential criminal informant) would be fruitless and that the file on Ruby should be closed."

29. FBI teletype 62-109060-852; AIB FBI release #319.

30. Scott, *Crime and Cover-Up*, 41; 22 WH 300, 478; 23 WH 203; 24 WH 516. Cf. the House Committee staff's uncritical summary of the conflicting statements at 9 AH 521–23.

31. 9 AH 1080, citing Warren Commission Document and Exhibit. The latter citation is wrong; it should read "Vol. 23, p. 206" (23 WH 206). The lead author of this and the following staff reports was Committee staff counsel Donald A. Purdy, Jr. (9 AH 127).

32. Blakey and Billings, *The Plot*, 286.

33. Kefauver Hearings, 5, 1178.

34. 9 AH 515.

35. George Butler notes of Jones-Guthrie conversations, 1946.

36. Kefauver Committee, *Third Interim Report*, 82nd Cong., 1st sess.; reprinted in Gus Tyler, *Organized Crime in America: A Book of Readings* (Ann Arbor: University of Michigan Press, 1967), 338.

37. Ibid., 342.

38. Smith, *The Mafia Mystique*, 138–40. The FBN had made the wartime case with "information from an informer" in Kansas City; the case represented one of the FBN's biggest breakthroughs at that time into the Mafia (Stephen Fox, *Blood and Power* [New York: William Morrow, 1989], 144–46).

39. Senate Narcotics Hearings, 989; Peter Noyes, *Legacy of Doubt* (New York: Pinnacle Books, 1973), 56–57.

40. Block, *Perspectives on Organizing Crime*, 230–31, summarizing California State Organized Crime Control Commission, *First Report* (Sacramento, May 1978), 66; cf. McCoy, *The Politics of Heroin*, 41–44. McCoy writes that

because Meltzer was arrested in 1949, his Mexican venture was a failure. But Meltzer himself was no failure: he was described in the Senate Narcotics Hearings as "a major figure in the organized underworld . . . known to all the important narcotics traffickers throughout the United States" (Senate Narcotics Hearings, 781; quoted in Noyes, *Legacy of Doubt,* 57). Stromberg himself was convicted in 1958, but as late as 1970 he was suspected by U.S. Narcotics Bureau officials of supervising, with Lansky, major heroin imports into New York (Dennis Eisenberg et al., *Meyer Lansky: Mogul of the Mob* [New York: Paddington Press, 1979], 312).

    41. Walker, *Drug Control in the Americas,* 178, 162–67.

    42. Scott and Marshall, *Cocaine Politics,* 33–42, 85–86.

    43. Kefauver Committee Hearings, Part 4, 88, 414.

    44. 19 WH 469, 527; Noyes, *Legacy of Doubt,* 19–23, 56–57, 246–47; Blakey and Billings, *The Plot,* 396. Braden told his parole officer that he was in Dallas to visit Lamar Hunt, the son of H. L. Hunt, whose office was also visited by Ruby on November 21 (Noyes, ibid., 72–75, cf. 66; WR 368).

    45. Noyes, *Legacy of Doubt,* 64, 100–101, 197–205, 237; Robert Houghton, *Special Unit Senator* (New York: Random House, 1970), 158.

    46. Noyes, *Legacy of Doubt,* 64, 205, 226; 9 AH 276, cf. 424, 1094.

    47. 9 AH 431–33; Blakey and Billings, *The Plot,* 307–08.

    48. Ibid.; cf. Scheim, *Contract on America,* 285–86.

    49. Scheim, *Contract on America,* 285. Blakey writes that the visits by Jones and Gruber "troubled us" (Blakey and Billings, *The Plot,* 307). But the eleven-page Committee memo on Jones and his relations with Ruby (9 AH 513–24) has only one brief sentence about the 1963 visit (9 AH 523), while its 78-page interrogation of Gruber (9 AH 435–512) did not ask about Jones at all. Both visits are omitted from Donald Purdy's chronology of Ruby's movements in November 1963 (9 AH 1098–1101).

CHAPTER NINE

    1. Gentry, *Hoover,* 286n, 495n, 530.

    2. Messick, *Lansky,* 100–101; Messick, *John Edgar Hoover,* 80–81; Dennis Eisenberg et al., *Meyer Lansky,* 166–67; U.S. Federal Bureau of Narcotics, *Traffic in Opium and Other Dangerous Drugs,* 1939, 30.

    3. Block, *Perspectives on Organizing Crime,* 230.

    4. McCoy, *The Politics of Heroin,* 43. McCoy also notes that, after Meltzer's default, Max "Chink" Rothman was looking for Meltzer on behalf of Lansky and Rosen; we learn from Ed Reid and Ovid Demaris (*The Green Felt Jungle* [New York: Pocket Books, 1964], 173) that Rothman was a stoolie for the FBI.

    5. Messick, *Hoover,* 206–07. Messick points out that when Lansky was finally indicted for the skim, along with two former official owners of the Flamingo, it was because of the IRS. "Clearly the Mafia had nothing to do with the Flamingo deal. Consequently, Hoover and the FBI weren't interested" (199).

6. Anthony Summers, *Official and Confidential: The Secret Life of J. Edgar Hoover* (New York: Putnam, 1993); Public Broadcasting System, "Frontline," February 10, 1993. According to Assistant FBI Director William Sullivan (not to be trusted in this matter), the protector of Lansky was not Hoover, but a senior FBI official close to Hoover who was on Lansky's payroll: "FBI reports had fallen into the hands of organized crime figures long before Kennedy's men arrived at Justice. There was a rumor, often heard in the underworld, that Meyer Lansky had his own man very high up in the FBI. William Sullivan had his own suspect, someone close to both the director and Tolson, who was reputedly living far above his means. This was one case the FBI never solved. When Sullivan left the Bureau, in 1971, the leaks were still going on" (Gentry, *Hoover*, 531–32).

7. Messick, *Lansky*, 253; Jean-Pierre Charbonneau, *The Canadian Connection* (Ottawa: Optimum, 1976), 295–97; Eisenberg, *Meyer Lansky*, 282–83.

8. Ward Churchill and Jim Vander Wall, *Agents of Repression*, 12, 68.

9. For the argument that the FBN was also developed primarily as a counterintelligence agency, see Block, *Perspectives on Organizing Crime*, 212–22; Alan A. Block and John McWilliams, "On the Origins of American Counterintelligence: Building a Clandestine Network," *Journal of Policy History* (1989).

10. Hoover declined to help Senator Kefauver's Committee in its search for a "national crime syndicate" (whose existence the then–attorney general denied). The Kefauver Committee then "turned to Hoover's nemesis Harry Anslinger of the Federal Bureau of Narcotics. . . . Among those the [Kefauver Committee] testimony linked to organized crime were such friends of [Hoover] as Clint Murchison, Joseph Kennedy, Walter Winchell, Sherman Billingsley, Lewis S. Rosenstiel, and Myer Schine" (Gentry, *Hoover*, 397).

11. Summers, *Official and Confidential;* Gentry, *Hoover*, 329–30.

12. Messick, *Hoover*, 198–201; cf. Eisenberg et al., *Meyer Lansky*, 281.

13. "Mafia-as-myth" critiques: Nelli, *The Business of Crime*, 182–83; Smith, *The Mafia Mystique*, 234–35; Alan A. Block, "History and the Study of Organized Crime," *Urban Life*, 1978, reprinted in Block, *Perspectives on Organizing Crime*. Rebuttal: Fox, *Blood and Power*, 376–82.

14. Messick, *Lansky*, 76–77.

15. Blakey and Billings, *The Plot*, 216. Blakey refutes Messick by citing an FBI wiretap of a single Mafia conversation, whose relevance is at best unclear. On other wiretaps strongly corroborating Messick, see Messick, *Hoover*, 198–201, partly cited above.

16. Peter Maas, *The Valachi Papers* (New York: Bantam, 1969), 3–4. As Maas recounts, Katzenbach and the Justice Department went on to fight in court the publication they had initially authorized (ibid., 10–11). The result of the litigation was the release of *The Valachi Papers* as "a third-person book" (ibid., 13)—a book in which Jimmy Hoffa, to name one obvious example, is not mentioned once.

17. Smith, *Mafia Mystique*, 251. In 1967 Blakey also testified to the McClellan Committee, interpreting transcripts of a bug on New England mafia boss

Raymond Patriarca as proving that "1. There is an organization called "Cosa Nostra".... 2. The organization is headed by a 'Commission' " (Donald R. Cressey, *Theft of a Nation* (New York: Harper and Row, 1969), 121. Cressey's own book, an academic expansion of the Valachi LCN model, is an "extensive revision of a report I prepared for the President's Commission on Law Enforcement"; in his preface, Cressey thanks both Blakey and, above all, Salerno [xi-xii]).

18. G. Robert Blakey, "Aspects of the Evidence Gathering Process in Organized Crime Cases: A Preliminary Analysis." President's Commission on Law Enforcement and Administration of Justice, *Task Force Report: Organized Crime*, Appendix C (Washington: Government Printing Office, 1967), 80–113. Cf. Smith, *Mafia Mystique*, 249 (critic).

19. Blakey and Billings, *The Plot*, xiii.

20. Smith, *Mafia Mystique*, 327–28.

21. Nelli, *The Business of Crime*, 182–83; Smith, *Mafia Mystique*, 234–35; Block, *Perspectives on Organizing Crime*, 4–6; Maas, *The Valachi Papers*, 113. Block's analysis is the most damning, because he shows that some of Valachi's alleged memories are in fact derived from earlier published accounts of organized crime.

22. Smith, *Mafia Mystique*, 324.

23. Ibid., 324, 327–28.

24. Blakey and Billings, *The Plot*, 215.

25. Nelli, *The Business of Crime*, 183. As Block suggests, the fact that Valachi's estimate of "some forty" exactly echoes Dewey's is precisely a reason to suspect that the FBI gave Valachi the number, not vice versa.

26. Blakey and Billings, *The Plot*, 211–13.

27. Scott, in Krueger, *The Great Heroin Coup*, 15.

28. Smith, *Mafia Mystique*, 209; Milton Wessel, "How We Bagged the Mafia," *Saturday Evening Post*, July 16, 1960, 20 +; July 23, 1960, 19 +.

29. Block, *Perspectives on Organizing Crime*, 5; Messick, *Lansky*, 49, 57–58. Blakey also claims that "the eyewitness accounts of Gentile and Joseph Valachi were independently substantiated by the reminiscences of other insiders— picked up on FBI bugs" (Blakey and Billings, *The Plot*, 211). But the most extended example of FBI "substantiation" introduced as evidence (5 AH 388–414) is the reverse of reassuring. Its case for "an organized crime conspiracy which is controlled nationally by a membership which is exclusively Italian" (5 AH 389) relies on a "confidential source," Angelo Lonardo, whose testimony has been lengthily dissected by Block as an example of "undoubted coaching" by the FBI (Block, ibid., 17–19). Cf. 5 AH 446, 448; 9 AH 26, 37, 41; Blakey and Billings, ibid., 217. These citations are to intercepts which suggest the existence of a Commission, but one which operates more like a U.N. Security Council of independent components rather than a controlling conspiracy.

30. Messick, *Lansky*, 49.

31. Kutner interview with author for CBC Television show "Fifth Estate," 1978; Scott, in Scott, Hoch, Stetler, *The Assassinations*, 369; cf. Scheim, *Contract on America*, 112; Milton Viorst, *Washingtonian*, November 1975, 116. A House Committee Staff Report, citing a staff interview of Luis Kutner on April

15, 1978, notes that "Ruby also offered, and gave information (albeit worthless) to the Kefauver Committee" (9 AH 1120).

32. Kefauver Hearings, 5, 1187.

33. McClellan Hearings, 12520, 12522, 12525.

34. WR 793; AR 150; 9 AH 152; discussion by Meagher, *Accessories*, 423–25; Scheim, *Contract on America*, 109–14.

35. Kefauver Hearings, 5, 1180; AR 150–51. Cf. Blakey and Billings, *The Plot*, 187: "Four witnesses identified Lenny Patrick, Dave Yaras, and Willie Block as the gunmen, but after one witness was murdered, two recanted, and another fled, the indictment was dropped." Cf. also Scott, *Crime and Cover-Up*, 40–43; Scheim, *Contract on America*, 136–37.

36. The Committee staff report presents this information as reliable (9 AH 516–18). At another point, however, the same staff report notes that "on December 12, 1946, Butler visited Jones and was introduced to two men identified as Murray Humphreys and Jake Guzik, Chicago syndicate leaders. Handwritten notes next to Butler's notes stated that these two individuals were not actually Humphreys and Guzik. Later in his notes, Butler said that Dominic Joseph Blasi was the man introduced to him as Murray Humphreys" (9 AH 151; cf. 9 AH 518). Later Blasi became chauffeur to Chicago mafia leader Sam Giancana, and was with Giancana the night he was murdered in 1975.

37. McClellan Hearings, 12525.

38. Scott, *Crime and Cover-Up*, 43; 25 WH 244, 294–95; 9 AH 277, 313.

39. McClellan Hearings, 12524.

40. Scott, *Crime and Cover-Up*, 39–40; Blakey and Billings, *The Plot*, 284–85.

41. Scheim, *Contract on America*, 101–103, citing Texas Attorney General, *Files of Evidence Connected With the Investigation of the Assassination of President John F. Kennedy* (Washington: Microcard Editions, 1967), Vol. 5, R2–3; 22 WH 297–303 (Jones). According to Scheim, the disposition of Ruby's arrest is unknown, because the original Chicago police files are missing.

42. Robert Kennedy, *The Enemy Within* (New York: Popular Library, 1960), 87.

43. A lengthy House Committee staff report on Paul Roland Jones (9 AH 513–24) is silent about both the wire service and the Teamsters; and it misrepresents Jones's statement to the FBI in 1964 (22 WH 300; cf. 22 WH 478) as corroborating that he met Ruby in 1947, rather than in the fall of 1946 (9 AH 518–19).

44. Blakey and Billings, *The Plot*, 193.

45. Ibid., 284.

46. Ibid., 326.

47. 9 AH 192–96.

48. Scott, *Crime and Cover-Up*, 45–46.

49. Moldea, *The Hoffa Wars*, 163–64; Blakey and Billings, *The Plot*, 204–05.

50. Blakey and Billings, *The Plot*, 204. Predictably, Blakey has nothing to say about the non-Italian Frank Chavez, even though one of Chavez's former

aides, Leopoldo Ramos Ducos, told the FBI that he "heard Frank Chavez . . . mention the name of Jack Ruby as someone connected with [the] Teamsters Union" (WCD 86.558; quoted in Moldea, *The Hoffa Wars*, 163; cf. WCD 301.66).

51. Gentry, *Hoover*, 330–31.

52. Drew Pearson, *Diaries 1949–1959* (New York: Holt, Rinehart, and Winston, 1974), 470; Demaris, *Captive City* (New York: Pocket Books, 1970), 244–45 (real estate).

53. Jack Lait and Lee Mortimer, *Chicago: Confidential!* (New York: Crown, 1950), 231, 191.

54. Parole Board Hearings, 293; *New York Times*, June 27, 1976, 20; Scheim, *Contract on America*, 241–43; William F. Roemer, Jr., *War of the Godfathers* (New York: Donald I. Fine, 1990), 112–14, 176–77.

55. Dan Moldea, *Dark Victory: Ronald Reagan, MCA, and the Mob* (New York: Viking, 1986), 339–42.

56. Rufus King, *Gambling and Organized Crime* (Washington: Public Affairs Press, 1969), 27–29, emphasis in original, quoted in Scott, *Crime and Cover-Up*, 40.

57. Blakey and Billings, *The Plot*, 344.

58. Fox, *Blood and Power*, 105–07.

59. Scott, *Crime and Cover-Up*, 40–41.

60. Rappleye and Becker, *All-American Mafioso*, 74–75.

61. Ibid., 75–76.

62. Ibid., 123 (Havana meeting of February 1947); Messick, *Lansky*, 150 (New York meeting of June 16, 1947).

63. Rappleye and Becker, *All-American Mafioso*, 124–26.

64. William Turner, *The Police Establishment* (New York: Putnam's, 1968), 264.

65. Rappleye and Becker, *All-American Mafioso*, 139 (conduit); Fox, *Blood and Power*, 227–31.

66. Parole Board Hearings, 425.

67. *Chicago Tribune*, August 28, 1947; Parole Board Hearings, 494 (Yaras).

68. 22 WH 349 (Barrish); cf. 22 WH 319, 327, 352, 425.

69. Scott, *Crime and Cover-Up*, 40; WR 787. *San Francisco Chronicle*, September 26, 1974; January 11, 1975.

70. Parole Board Hearings, 444, 465; 9 AH 944 947 ("gambling").

71. Parole Board Hearings, 507, 561–62; Rappleye and Becker, *All-American Mafioso*, 117.

72. 1961 federal report; quoted in Demaris, *Captive City*, 183.

73. John Kobler, *Capone: The Life and World of Al Capone* (New York: Da Capo Press, 1992), 80, 97–99.

74. John Landesco, "Organized Crime in Chicago," in *Illinois Crime Survey for 1929* (Chicago: University of Chicago Press, 1968), 1066–70.

75. Kefauver Hearings, 5, 682, 759, 955. Ruby was engaged in both of these activities.

76. Melvin M. Belli, *Dallas Justice: The Real Story of Jack Ruby and His Trial* (New York: David McKay, 1964), 48.

77. 23 WH 158–60; 9 AH 178–79.

78. See Chapters 5 and 7.

79. Penn Jones, *Forgive My Grief* (Midlothian, Tex.: Midlothian Mirror, n.d. [1966]), 160–61; cf. Turner, 195. Turner adds that John Birch Society backer H. L. Hunt "is usually escorted to his public engagements around town by a Dallas officer, ordinarily Lieutenant George Butler."

80. Hurt, *Reasonable Doubt*, 173–74.

81. Milton Viorst, *Washingtonian*, November 1975, 116; quoted in Scheim, 112. Blakey never once mentions Kutner, clearly an important and informed source; instead he offers an alternative hypothesis: "We found it a distinct possibility that Ruby . . . was told to *leave* Chicago by syndicate figures" (Blakey and Billings, *The Plot*, 288, emphasis added).

82. Rappleye and Becker, *All-American Mafioso*, 115.

83. Blakey and Billings, *The Plot*, 322.

84. 19 WH 507–09; discussion in Meagher, *Accessories*, 96 (Boone). Jones in 1946 blamed his indictment on Decker, acting on Binion's orders.

85. Scheim, *Contract on America*, 145–46; 23 WH 87–92.

86. WR 340–42; 5 WH 188–89.

87. Scott, *Crime and Cover-Up*, 36–37; cf. 22 WH 298, 9 AH 516 (Irwin); 2 WH 321, 336–37; 22 WH 785 (coaching, cf. Chapter 17). The Warren Commission's published chronology of Ruby's movements on November 20, which contained such irrelevancies as his thirty-minute treatment for baldness the same day, suppressed this contact with Pete White (25 WH 321; cf. WCD 273.120, WCD 360.130; 9 AH 1099). When Ruby's roommate George Senator was questioned about more than fifty names in the notebook of a Ruby employee, the name of Pete White (19 WH 73) was passed over (14 WH 295; cr. 14 WH 34). It is likely that the bureaucratic reason for bypassing Pete White was White's status as an FBI confidential informant.

88. Testimony of Thayer Waldo to Warren Commission, 15 WH 595; quoted in Meagher, *Accessories*, 425; cf. Summers, *Conspiracy*, 490.

89. Blakey and Billings, *The Plot*, 287; 9 AH 945 (Ragen); 9 AH 953–77 (interview); 9 AH 945, 964 (Zuckerman). Zuckerman himself had once been an active campaign worker for Jake Arvey (Parole Board Hearings, 412).

90. AR 150–51; cf. Scott, *Crime and Cover-Up*, 45; Scott, Hoch and Stetler, *The Assassinations*, 368–70.

91. 25 WH 294–95. At the time, Baker was employed by a man whose West Coast representative, Victor Pereira, was the closest associate of Jim Braden, alias Eugene Brading, the man picked up and released in Dealey Plaza right after Kennedy was shot. And the son of Baker's employer, Philip Earl Scheib, was a California Minuteman leader, later arrested by the FBI in the course of investigating an assassination plot, and a close associate of the Minuteman Loran Eugene Hall, who took part in the Bayo-Pawley Mission and later went to Dallas (Noyes, *Legacy of Doubt*, 64, 205–07, 226. Baker was in repeated phone contact with the young Scheib's father; WCD 722.95). The

House Committee was not the first congressional committee to have problems investigating Dave Yaras, a killer with proven political clout. In 1950 the Kefauver Committee intended to interview William Drury, the police captain thrown off the Chicago police force after arresting Yaras and Patrick for the shooting of James Ragen. Drury, not a man to quit, told his lawyer Luis Kutner that he had "a hot new witness who will . . . name Leonard Patrick, Willie Block, as the killers." On the same day, September 25, 1950, Drury and a supporting witness, Marvin Bas, were themselves murdered. Kefauver, aware of the danger Drury was exposed to, "appealed to the FBI director, who coldly responded, 'I regret to advise the Federal Bureau of Investigation is not empowered to perform guard duties' " (*Newsweek*, October 9, 1950, 37; *New York Times*, September 26, 1950, 34; September 29, 1950, 24; Demaris, *Captive City*, 141; Gentry, *Hoover*, 397).

CHAPTER TEN

1. See for example Frank Browning and John Gerassi, *The American Way of Crime* (New York: Putnam's, 1980), passim.

2. *Chicago Tribune*, June 29, 1946, 5.

3. Demaris, *Captive City*, 186.

4. Moldea, *The Hoffa Wars*, 124.

5. Block, *Perspectives on Organizing Crime*, 213–16.

6. McCoy, *The Politics of Heroin*, 31–34; Block, *Perspectives on Organizing Crime*, 230; Campbell, *The Luciano Project*, passim.

7. R. Harris Smith, *OSS* (Berkeley and Los Angeles: University of California Press, 1972), 86 ("aloof"); Kefauver Hearings, Part 7, 607–08, 1188–91; Campbell, *The Luciano Project*, 278; Scott, in Krueger, *The Great Heroin Coup*, 25.

8. Block, *Perspectives on Organizing Crime*, 216. Block continues: "So zealous was the Bureau in these matters that its highest officers committed numerous crimes ranging from drug distribution and drug use to planning foreign assassinations. . . . The Bureau had been subordinate to the CIA since the Agency's founding." Cf. Alan A. Block, "Failures at Home and Abroad: Studies in the Implementation of U.S. Drug Policy," in Alfred W. McCoy and Alan A. Block, eds., *War on Drugs: Studies in the Failure of U.S. Narcotics Policy* (Boulder, Colo.: Westview Press, 1992), 40: "It is often impossible to distinguish whether top FBN agents were primarily CIA men using narcotics jobs as cover or were drug enforcers merely hip-deep in helping counterintelligence."

9. For the French "Operation X" in Indochina, and the American takeover of it, see McCoy, *The Politics of Heroin*, 131–46, 195–96. Our "Operation X" can neither be identified with, nor wholly distinguished from, the "Operation X" described in *U.S. News and World Report*, April 9, 1948. This informed general summary of CIA covert operations in early 1948 points in particular to anti-Communist operations in Italy and in Marseille (where alliances with drug traffickers were quickly made).

10. *Wall Street Journal,* April 18, 1980; Block, *Masters of Paradise,* 161–70; McCoy, *The Politics of Heroin,* 167–68, 469–70; Scott, *War Conspiracy,* 210–11 and passim. In 1945–46 Helliwell, an OSS veteran, was chief of the Far East Division of the War Department's Strategic Service Unit, an interim intelligence organization between the years of the OSS and 1947, when the CIA was created. In 1950, when he helped negotiate the sale of General Claire Chennault's airline, Civil Air Transport, to the CIA, Helliwell was an official in the Office of Policy Coordination (OPC), a semi-autonomous unit later merged into the CIA. A decade later he was reportedly a CIA recruiter and paymaster for the Bay of Pigs.

11. Scott and Marshall, *Cocaine Politics,* 93–93 (Castle, Nugan Hand); Brewton, *The Mafia,* 185 (WFC, BCCI); Block, *Masters,* 171, 191; Penny Lernoux, *In Banks We Trust* (New York: Anchor Press / Doubleday, 1984), 87; James Ring Adams and Douglas Frantz, *A Full Service Bank* (New York: Pocket Books, 1992), 55 (Castle, Mercantile Bank and Trust, International Bank, BCCI).

12. See Kirkpatrick Sale, *Power Shift* (New York: Random House, 1975); Pete Brewton, *The Mafia, CIA, and George Bush,* 181–96, 277–302, etc.; also Chapter 12.

13. Block, *Perspectives on Organizing Crime,* 213.

14. Scott, in Krueger, *The Great Heroin Coup,* 15–16, citing *San Francisco Chronicle,* January 15, 1959, 1, 4; *New York Times,* January 15, 1959, 4. White's first Mafia drug case in 1937 had involved the Hip Sing tong, which in 1992 was still involved in drug trafficking (*San Francisco Chronicle,* June 9, 1992).

15. Block, *Perspectives on Organizing Crime,* 213; Dayle, in *Causes and Cures: National Campaign on the Narcotics Epidemic* (1324 North Capitol, NW, Washington, D.C. 20002), *Final Report,* p. 9.

16. For Rosselli's motives, see 10 AH 153–54; Scott, *Crime and Cover-Up,* 23–27.

17. Peter Dale Scott and Jonathan Marshall, *Cocaine Politics,* 51–65, 177–78; Alfred W. McCoy, *The Politics of Heroin,* 436–53, 481–84; McCoy and Block, *War on Drugs,* 125–77; Jonathan Marshall, *Drug Wars* (Forestville, Calif.: Cohan and Cohen, 1991), 44–53.

18. Scott and Marshall, *Cocaine Politics,* 26–27, 29, 36, 72, 115–17, 121, 219n, and passim. A particularly disturbing instance is the case of José Roberto Gasser, arrested in Miami in May 1980, and almost immediately released from custody by the Miami U.S. Attorney's office. This was shortly before the June 1980 Cocaine Coup in Bolivia, financed by the Roberto Suarez cocaine network of which Gasser was a member (Scott and Marshall, *Cocaine Politics,* 219n; Michael Levine, *Deep Cover* [New York: Delacorte, 1990], 17–18, 103–04).

19. Cumings, *The Origins of the Korean War,* vol. II, 512; cf. Block, *Perspectives on Organizing Crime,* 213 (deep cover); Scott, *War Conspiracy,* 210 (officer).

20. Cumings, *The Origins of the Korean War,* 509, 512, 522; David E. Kaplan and Alec Dubro, *Yakuza* (New York: Macmillan, 1986), 55–63.

21. Stolen Securities Hearings, 715–16, cf. 856 (Fassoulis); 9 AH 518 (Jones).

22. Pizzo et al., *Inside Job,* 259–60, 362.

23. George White Diaries, Foothill College, Los Gatos, California.

24. Rappleye and Becker, *All-American Mafioso,* 123; see Chapter 9.

25. 10 AH 147–95; Scott, *Crime and Cover-Up,* passim. See Chapter 7.

26. Blakey and Billings, *The Plot,* 389, 391; cf. Brashler, *The Don,* 324 (Giancana's daughter).

27. Moldea, *The Hoffa Wars,* 386–87, quoting from Crimaldi, *Crimaldi,* 217.

28. Moldea, ibid., 433, quoting from Crimaldi, ibid., 218.

29. Moldea, ibid., 12; see Chapter 11.

30. Ibid., 401; cf. 402.

31. Ibid., 387.

32. Siragusa, as quoted in Moldea, ibid., 124.

33. Block, *Perspectives on Organizing Crime,* 213.

34. Moldea, *The Hoffa Wars,* 127–28, citing personal information from Siragusa and Jack Anderson column of June 4, 1978.

35. Block, *Perspectives on Organizing Crime,* 216. Block tells us that this official believed Siragusa to have been QJ/WIN, the principal agent in charge of ZR/RIFLE field operations. Initially I rejected this identification out of hand. QJ/WIN was first identified in a Church Committee interim report as a "foreign citizen with a criminal background recruited by the CIA" (Church Committee Assassination Report, 189); he was recruited either in Frankfurt or Luxembourg. On the surface, this might seem to exclude Siragusa. Block has since informed me that Siragusa did in fact serve the FBN in Europe under deep cover, posing as a European criminal. The basic CIA document on Project ZR/RIFLE specifies that the CIA station chief in Luxembourg (probably Arnold Silver) contacted QJ/WIN sporadically "in behalf of the [Federal] Bureau of Narcotics"; and adds that "Files of this Bureau [the FBN] reflect an excellent performance by QJWIN" (4 AH 198). It would be typical of CIA deniability to recruit Siragusa in this oblique way. Another page in the same hand recommends keeping the operation "within [CIA] only," followed by the words "(e.g., how much does Siragusa now know?)" (4 AH 201). Given QJ/WIN's "primary task of spotting agent candidates" (4 AH 198), and considering that most of these were from the U.S. mafia and its allies, Siragusa seems a more likely candidate than true European criminals such as Jo Attia or Robert Blémant, who have also been proposed.

36. Block, *Perspectives on Organizing Crime,* 216.

37. David Martin, *Wilderness of Mirrors* (New York: Harper and Row, 1980), 123; 4 AH 202.

38. Moldea, *The Hoffa Wars,* 28–33.

39. Ibid., 49–50.

40. Ibid., 131; cf. 387.

41. McClellan Hearings, 19166–67 (Plumeri, Granello, Teamster locals 130, 805); Sheridan, *Hoffa,* 114–15.

42. Anson, *"They've Killed the President!"* 296. The witness, Mario Brod, was a New York lawyer and salaried CIA contract officer; first in Italy and later in New York, Brod worked for CIA counterintelligence chief James Angleton; in this capacity he "had contacts with the Mafia" (Mangold, *Cold Warrior,* 104–05).

43. Moldea, *The Hoffa Wars,* 25 (Coppola-Hoffa); Scott, in Krueger, *The Great Heroin Coup,* 14–15, citing Gaia Servadio, *Mafioso* (New York: Dell, 1976), 72, 108 (Italy); Narcotics Hearings, 801.

44. Scott, in Krueger, *The Great Heroin Coup,* 14; citing Servadio, *Mafioso,* 125–28.

45. Miles Copeland, *Beyond Cloak and Dagger: Inside the CIA* (New York: Pinnacle Books, 1975), 240.

46. Ralph Blumenthal, *Last Days of the Sicilians* (New York: Pocketbooks, 1989), 95.

47. Moldea, *The Hoffa Wars,* 42–43, 48.

48. At first, heroin from Coppola in Italy went to John Priziola, who had succeeded Coppola in Detroit as head of the American segment of the Partinico Mafia clan. It was stashed in a fish shop owned by Priziola's son-in-law Peter Tocco. From there it was received in New York by Frank Livorsi, son-in-law of Tocco's uncle Angelo Meli. Hoffa himself was involved with Livorsi, and also with Livorsi's other in-laws, who included John and Frank Dioguardi and their uncle James Plumeri. John Dioguardi (alias Johnny Dio) controlled a number of Teamster locals in New York for Jimmy Hoffa, having been originally launched into union racketeering by Paul Dorfman. Another Livorsi in-law was John Ormento, the Civello associate, whose trucking company moved heroin from Detroit to the East Coast. A niece of Angelo Meli married William Bufalino, cousin of Russell Bufalino, who with James Plumeri owned a Havana racetrack, which resulted in the two men's involvement with Hoffa in the anti-Castro plots. Peter Tocco's brother-in-law was Detroit Mafia leader Joseph Zerilli, and both were related to New York Mafia leader Joe Profaci. In turn, the son of Joe Bonanno, another major drug trafficker, was married to Profaci's daughter. This Mafia cousinage reached to the West Coast as well. Priziola's other sons-in-law included not only Mike Polizzi of Detroit (another Hoffa associate) but also Joe Matranga of California, whose sister Katherine had married Salvatore Vitale. Salvatore Vitale was a former Detroit Mafioso who had been deported with Frank Coppola to Italy, and had become allied with Luciano and Coppola in exporting the heroin to John Priziola and Raffaele Quasarano. Quasarano meanwhile was the son-in-law of Vito Vitale (Moldea, *The Hoffa Wars,* 42–43, 48, and passim; Sheridan, *Hoffa,* 19, 24–26, 529, 532, and passim).

49. Moldea, *The Hoffa Wars,* 64.

50. Sheridan, 114–15; *New York Times,* July 2, 1959; McClellan Hearings, 19166–67; 5 AH 403 (Licavoli), etc.

51. Charbonneau, *The Canadian Connection,* 38.

52. Ibid., 82, 129.

53. Ibid., 247, 262, 269; Newsday, *Heroin Trail* (New York: New American Library, 1974), 112–14. The case involved the French intelligence and Gaullist double agent Michel-Victor Mertz, whom some have suspected of being a gunman in Dealey Plaza. Cf. Krueger, *The Great Heroin Coup*, 95–96.

54. Moldea, *The Hoffa Wars*, 63.

55. McCoy, *The Politics of Heroin*, 44–45.

56. Ibid., 53–63; Scott, in Krueger, *The Great Heroin Coup*, 15.

57. McCoy, *The Politics of Heroin*, 131–35.

58. Alain Jaubert, *Dossier D comme Drogue* (Paris: Alain Moreau, 1974), 51, 618. Jaubert quotes Roger Colombani as writing (*Historia*, "Le Milieu," 1973) that "at Bordeaux, in 1952, Antoine [Guérini] took part in a mysterious meeting with Irving Brown [of the AFL, a transmitter of CIA funds], Jacques Stachino, [Pierre] Ferri-Pisani [the CIA's go-between with the gangsters], [Jean] Colonna, [Jo] Césari. The same year, one finds him [Guérini] in Italy, where he made contact with men from the Mafia."

59. Moldea, *The Hoffa Wars*, 63.

60. Scott and Marshall, *Cocaine Politics*, 219 and passim. In the 1980s the Detroit Teamster–Steven Kalish connection used the illicit banking services of the Bank of Credit and Commerce International, or BCCI (Adams and Frantz, *Full Service Bank*, 84).

61. In 1967, for example, Marcel Francisci met with Tony Corallo; two years later Jean-Claude Kella met with Louis Cirillo (Jaubert, *Dossier*, 571–72; Pierre Galante, *The Marseilles Mafia* [London: W. H. Allen, 1979], 203).

62. Charbonneau, *The Canadian Connection*, 73; Scott, in Krueger, *The Great Heroin Coup*, 15.

63. Davis, *Mafia Kingfish*, 59.

64. Andrew Cockburn and Leslie Cockburn, *Dangerous Liaison* (New York: Harper Collins, 1991), 42.

65. Roberto Faenza and Marco Fini, *Gli Americani in Italia* (Milan: Feltrinelli, 1976), 138, quoted in Krueger, *The Great Heroin Coup*, 25n.

66. Block, *Perspectives on Organizing Crime*, 213; Cumings, *The Origins of the Korean War*, II, 511–12; Hersh, *The Old Boys*, 229–30; Scott, *War Conspiracy*, 210.

67. Kaplan and Dubro, *Yakuza*, 55–63.

68. Ibid., 60.

69. McClellan Hearings, 19085–89; cf. Sheridan, *Hoffa*, 109–12 (on Dominic Bartone, who financed Morgan).

70. Scheim, *Contract on America*, 211–12 (Rothman, Sturgis); Moldea, *The Hoffa Wars*, 107 (Hoffa).

71. Rappleye and Becker, *All-American Mafioso*, 224; citing Ayers, *The War That Never Was*, 38 ("Colonel").

72. Rappleye and Becker, *All-American Mafioso*, 148–58.

73. Block, *Perspectives on Organizing Crime*, 168–71.

74. Blakey and Billings, *The Plot*, 230.

75. Rappleye and Becker, *All-American Mafioso,* 136, 139, 145–47, etc. In 1978, investigating the circumstances of Ruby's trip to Cuba, House Committee investigators interviewed Ruby's friend Tony Zoppi, with whom Ruby spent the morning of November 22 before the assassination. (As we shall see, there are serious problems with Ruby's and Zoppi's conflicting accounts of both the 1959 trip and the November 22 visit; 5 WH 183; 5 AH 176 [Ruby]; 5 AH 170 [Zoppi].) They found Zoppi in 1978 at the Riviera Hotel in Las Vegas, where Baron now worked. Zoppi knew Baron, whom he identified as "a general in the Army Reserves and a close friend of General Curtis LeMay." The investigators "subsequently learned that Baron was visiting LeMay the following week" (5 AH 170).

76. Demaris, *Captive City,* 250

77. 14 WH 345–53 (colonel); Meagher, *Accessories,* 385–86; Scheim, *Contract on America,* 225–27; cf. Summers, *Conspiracy,* 461–65.

78. Blakey and Billings, *The Plot,* 302.

79. 10 AH 183; 5 AH 105. One informant told the FBI that Ruby had been active in arranging illegal-arms flights to Castro piloted by Eddie Browder, a Rothman associate (26 WH 634–43; WCD 914.89–94; Summers, *Conspiracy,* 460–61). This important lead was ignored by the Committee, even when they investigated Rothman (10 AH 183–86).

80. 20 WH 58; cf. 20 WH 37; Scott, *Crime and Cover-Up,* 41.

81. Rappleye and Becker, *All-American Mafioso,* 245; citing Scott Malone, *New Times,* January 23, 1978.

82. Scheim, *Contract on America,* 225, citing Malone, ibid.

83. Narcotics Hearings, at 916.

84. *Miami Herald,* March 13, 1960; *New York Times,* July 4, 1959; March 14, 1962. The stolen securities had allegedly been pledged as collateral for the Browder-Rothman arms deals, some of them by the couriers at a Swiss bank.

CHAPTER ELEVEN

1. The three Italians were Paul Labriola, Nick de John, and Paul Mann (alias Pat Manno). Others who could be added to the list are Danny Lardino, Jack Nappi, James Barcella, William Joseph Messina, and Dominic Blasi, all minor figures (9 AH 515–16). I have been unable to identify a single source that has said that in 1946 the "Mafia" was moving into Dallas. The FBI file on the subject was entitled "James Weinberg et al." (9 AH 1151). The staff report's own references are to "the Weinberg gang," the "Guzik mob," and the "Chicago syndicate" (9 AH 514–17). The senior person who allegedly moved down was Jake Guzik, the suspected dope trafficker who controlled, among others, Dave Yaras and Lenny Patrick, and who was Chicago Police Captain William Drury's prime suspect in the shooting of James Ragen.

2. The one Italian called by Ruby, Nofio Pecora, is of interest because of his connection to Lee Harvey Oswald's uncle and father-figure "Dutz" Murret. Nevertheless, the Committee conceded that Ruby's one-minute call, to Pecora's

trailer park, may have been to have Pecora transmit a message to his neighbor, Harold Tannenbaum, a night-club operator who did business with Ruby (9 AH 194).

3. Blakey and Billings, *The Plot*, 202; cf. AR 176–77; Sheridan, *Hoffa*, 216–17; Gentry, *Hoover*, 495. As we shall see, Partin was soon used as a key witness against Hoffa by Bobby Kennedy and his assistant Walter Sheridan, as part of a deep-political get-Hoffa strategy that is still disputed. To fully assess the complex but extremely relevant Partin story, one should also evaluate the anti-Partin version of Ralph de Toledano (*RFK: The Man Who Would Be President* [New York: Putnam, 1967], 241); and the independent versions of Clark Mollenhoff (*Tentacles of Power: The Story of Jimmy Hoffa* [Cleveland: World Publishing, 1965], 374–75), Fred J. Cook (*Nation*, April 27, 1964), and Victor Navasky (*Kennedy Justice* [New York: Atheneum, 1971]).

4. Blakey and Billings, *The Plot*, 233–36; AR 160.

5. 4 AH 563; Blakey and Billings, *The Plot*, 302–05; cf. Scott, *Crime and Cover-Up*, 42–46.

6. Sheridan, *Hoffa*, 20–21.

7. Scott, *Crime and Cover-Up*, 45; McClellan Hearings, 14072 (Harriman).

8. Blakey and Billings, *The Plot*, xi.

9. Fox, *Blood and Power*, 337. Hoover belatedly adopted the same rhetoric: "Let us unite in a devastating assault to annihilate this mortal enemy" (Gentry, *Hoover*, 529). Neither Kennedy nor Hoover, of course, was uninvolved with this enemy, but for different reasons: Bobby was in some complex fashion dealing with, and perhaps atoning for, the bootlegging origins of his family's wealth (John H. Davis, *The Kennedys* (New York: McGraw-Hill, 1985), 56–57, 75–77, 485–86). For more on Joe Kennedy and the Chicago mob, see the references to an unidentified "Mr. Kennedy" in Kefauver Hearings, Part 5, 595, 607; cf. 599.

10. Blakey and Billings, *The Plot*, 201–04; Sheridan, *Hoffa*, 292, 347 (Miller), 266–68, 364 (Weiner).

11. Blakey and Billings, *The Plot*, 304–05.

12. It also ignored Ruby's telephone call to Joseph Glaser, Sidney Korshak's top man in the American Guild of Variety Artists (23 WH 374, 5 WH 200, 14 WH 446; *New York Times*, June 29, 1976, 16; Moldea, *Dark Victory*, 116–18. See Chapter 14.

13. Sheridan, *Hoffa*, 292.

14. Ibid., 64.

15. Blakey and Billings, *The Plot*, 189–91, 228, 231, 233.

16. "The Castellamarese War was based, in part, on Sicilian feuds, which had begun long before in the old country. There is even an American version of the myth of the Sicilian Vespers. The 'Old Moustaches,' the name for Old World Italian criminal leaders then heading organizations in the United States, were said to have been murdered almost simultaneously in many parts of the country over a 48-hour period. The dates are usually given as September 10–12, 1931, the number murdered between 40 and 60" (9 AH 6). Cf. Nelli, *The*

Business of Crime, 179–84; Smith, *The Mafia Mystique,* 242, 324–27; discussion in Block, *Perspectives on Organizing Crime,* 2–7, 19–21.

17. It is true that Robert Kennedy promoted Valachi, and once called his data "the biggest intelligence breakthrough we have ever had" (Gentry, *Hoover,* 533n). But Schlesinger quotes Kennedy as saying that Valachi's importance lay in his impact on Hoover: "For the first time the FBI changed their whole concept of crime in the United States" (*Robert Kennedy,* 289). A third possibility is that Kennedy and Blakey both valued Valachi's testimony for the same reason: its account of a national organized-crime commission, whether true or false, provided a basis for federal wiretapping and other legislation.

18. For example, a William H. Cooper of Baton Rouge alleged that Partin and four other individuals were in on the conspiracy to kill the President (FBI File 105-82555-5510, -5498).

19. Sheridan, *Hoffa,* 417 and passim.

20. FBI File document, 3/15/67, Rosen to DeLoach, 62-109060-4834.

21. Sheridan, *Hoffa,* 434. So did a private investigating agency, Southern Research, Inc. (ibid., 428, cf. 440–42), which had earlier investigated Ferrie on another matter (10 AH 115); and which in 1964 hired Milton Kaack, the former New Orleans FBI agent disciplined for his handling of the file of Lee Harvey Oswald.

22. Moldea, *The Hoffa Wars,* 122; cf. 106, 123.

23. Ibid., 107.

24. Ibid., 179; cf. Sheridan, *Hoffa,* 416–17; Scott, *Crime and Cover-Up,* 27–28, 46. For example, Sheridan alleges that in 1967 an ally of Jim Garrison's chief investigator Pershing Gervais "discussed the possibility of planting narcotics on Partin and Gervais said, 'Do anything but kill him. He has to be alive to testify that he committed perjury' " (Sheridan, ibid., 435). Gervais had earlier reported Jack Martin's allegations which made David Ferrie a suspect in the Kennedy assassination (see below, 369–70).

25. Moldea, *The Hoffa Wars,* 180; cf. Sheridan, *Hoffa,* 423–27. In 1992 Ragano, an old man both sick and convicted, published his reasons for his belief that his clients Santos Trafficante and Hoffa had plotted with Marcello to kill the President (*Penthouse,* May 1992; Russell, *The Man Who Knew Too Much,* 579–80).

26. Here it becomes more significant that, as we saw in Chapter 5, Ferrie told one of Garrison's investigators that one of the reasons for his trip to Galveston (used by Garrison to implicate Ferrie in the Kennedy assassination) was that "I had some business . . . to take care of" for G. Wray Gill, Marcello's attorney and one of those involved in Hoffa's defense. Garrison never mentioned this reason or, for that matter, any of Ferrie's links to Gill and Marcello.

27. *Chicago Tribune,* February 27, 1964; compare Sheridan, 349.

28. *Congressional Record,* 1964, 4034.

29. Fred J. Cook, "The Hoffa Trial," *Nation,* April 27, 1964; *Congressional Record,* 1964, May 4, 1964, 9978–91; Sheridan, 359–61.

30. Michael Dorman, *Payoff: The Role of Organized Crime in American Politics* (New York: David McKay, 1972), 109–10.

31. Moldea, *The Hoffa Wars,* 108, 260.

32. Sheridan, *Hoffa,* 408, 424–25, 492, and passim; Moldea, *The Hoffa Wars,* 260–61. Others named by Sheridan in this effort to pressure Partin include Clint Murchison, Jr., Gordon McLendon, McLendon's brother-in-law Lester May, Trafficante's attorney Frank Ragano, and Murray Chotiner in the Nixon White House.

33. Clark Mollenhoff, *Strike Force* (Englewood Cliffs, N.J.: Prentice-Hall, 1972), 222; Scott, *Crime and Cover-Up,* 21, 58.

34. Robert Kennedy, *The Enemy Within,* 229; quote in Schlesinger, *Robert Kennedy,* 181.

35. The one exception was Frank Livorsi (Kefauver Hearings, Part 3, 1–20). But the exception proves the rule. Livorsi was quizzed not about the "Mafia" or about narcotics, but about black-market operations during World War II, when he was allied with a number of non-Mafia figures.

36. Smith, *Mafia Mystique,* 136, 138–40.

37. Messick, *Hoover,* 192–95.

38. Blakey and Billings justify their focus on "La Cosa Nostra" by recounting a number of conversations in which mafiosi are overheard saying things such as that the President "should drop dead. . . . They should kill the whole family—the mother and father too." The problem is that such sentiments were widespread in the organized-crime community. In the most widely cited overhear—"With Kennedy, a guy should take a knife, like one of them other guys, and stab and kill the fucker"—the speaker is in fact a non-Mafia Jew, who is then restrained by his associate Angelo Bruno (AR 165, Blakey and Billings, *The Plot,* 237–38; cf. Davis, *The Kennedys,* 488–89: "G. Robert Blakey told me that . . . the tapes convinced him that if there had been a conspiracy to kill the President, the Mafia was probably behind it." Blakey has never disowned this non sequitur.

39. Blakey and Billings, *The Plot,* xi.

40. Moldea, *The Hoffa Wars,* 12.

41. See Scott and Marshall, *Cocaine Politics,* 250–51.

42. Block, *Perspectives on Organizing Crime,* 215.

43. Hersh, *The Old Boys,* 238–39; cf. 269.

44. McCoy, *Politics of Heroin,* 59, 62; *Saturday Evening Post,* May 20, 1967, 10, 14.

45. Fox, *Blood and Power,* 217.

46. Conversation with Dick Russell, June 23, 1992.

47. Seymour Hersh, *New York Times Magazine,* June 25, 1978; Hersh, *The Old Boys,* 317 (mail interception); Epstein, *Legend,* 168–69; Summers, *Conspiracy,* 193 (mail interception and Oswald).

48. Epstein, *Legend,* 253.

49. Summers, *Conspiracy,* 163 ("responsible"); Hersh, *The Old Boys,* 316, 357 (Dulles).

50. Mangold, *Cold Warrior,* 173–75, 193; Marrs, *Crossfire,* 131 (defectors); Epstein, *Legend,* 253–54; Martin, *Wilderness of Mirrors,* 151; Summers, *Conspiracy,* 349–52 (Cubela).

51. Russell, *The Man Who Knew Too Much,* 460. See Chapter 3.

CHAPTER TWELVE

1. Noyes, *Legacy of Doubt*, 66–79; Scheim, *Contract on America*, 288–89. I have to observe that, if the plot to kill the President was a serious one and Ruby and the Hunts were central to it, it seems unlikely that Ruby would have visited a co-conspirator, as he allegedly did Lamar Hunt, in the presence of an independent eyewitness (Connie Trammel). A more likely possibility might be that Ruby was deliberately laying a false trail to the Hunts.

2. Blakey says that "Ruby told the Warren Commission that he was in the second-floor advertising offices of the *Dallas Morning News* from 11 or 11:30 A.M. to 1:30 P.M." (Blakey and Billings, *The Plot*, 315). But Ruby testified that he went first "to Tony Zoppi's office," and only later to "the main room where we compose our ads" (5 WH 183). The point is not a small one, since Ruby used his visit to the newspaper as an alibi to conceal his visit to Parkland Hospital after the shooting (9 AH 1103).

3. "Ruby told him he was moving into a new apartment starting Monday that cost $190 a month (up from the $100 that Ruby had been paying). The new address was 21 Turtle Creek. When Zoppi questioned about it, Ruby said, 'I've scrimped all my life and now I want to live a little.' These were Ruby's last words to Zoppi" (5 AH 170).

4. Blakey and Billings, *The Plot*, 300; 9 AH 164–69.

5. Jack Entratter was allegedly a "front" at the Sands in Las Vegas for New York mobsters Frank Costello and Joe Adonis, the same pair he had allegedly fronted for when working as bouncer at the Copacabana in New York City (Reid and Demaris, *Green Felt Jungle*, 77).

6. For the hostility between President Kennedy and his Air Force chief of staff Curtis LeMay, cf. (e.g.) Schlesinger, *Robert Kennedy*, 457, 484, 551, etc.

7. Blakey and Billings, *The Plot*, 308 ("We concluded . . . that a Ruby trip to Las Vegas on the weekend before the assassination was a distinct possibility").

8. Rappleye and Becker, *All-American Mafioso*, 247.

9. Scott, *Crime and Cover-Up*, 42, 71; WCD 686d.

10. 9 AH 948.

11. 10 AH 183.

12. Rappleye and Becker, *All-American Mafioso*, 176 (Ruby and Rothman); AR 151–52, 173; 9 AH 802.

13. Charbonneau, *Canadian Connection*, 143; *New York Times*, July 4, 1959, 5; *Miami Herald*, March 13, 1960; *New York Times*, March 3, 1962, 5; March 14, 1962.

14. Charbonneau, *Canadian Connection*, 199–227, 450–55, etc.

15. Anson, *"They've Killed the President!"* 296 (witness); personal communication (Brod); Mangold, *Cold Warrior*, 105 (Angleton-Brod-mafia).

16. *New York Times*, September 26, 1950, 34; September 29, 1950, 24; *Newsweek*, October 9, 1950, 36.

17. 5 WH 195–96; Summers, *Conspiracy*, 455–56.

18. Seth Kantor, *The Ruby Cover-Up* (New York: Zebra, 1992), 37; Peter Dale Scott, *The Dallas Conspiracy* (manuscript, 1971), VI-21; 9 AH 185;

Blakey and Billings, *The Plot*, 297–98. The date of McLane's death is recorded by Seth Kantor (correctly) as March 16, 1960, and by the House Committee and Blakey (incorrectly) as 1963.

19. Jack Anderson, *Washington Exposé*, 214–16 (Eisenhower); Fred J. Cook, *The FBI Nobody Knows* (New York: Macmillan, 1964), 230 (Hoover).

20. Jack Anderson, *San Francisco Chronicle*, December 30, 1970, 25; Scott, *The Dallas Conspiracy*, VI-6; Scheim, *Contract on America*, 244–45.

21. Narcotics Hearings, 997. Martin Pera of Customs was the probable author of this biography.

22. Michele Pantaleone, *Mafia e droga*, 36–39. As noted in Chapter 10, others at this meeting included Frank Coppola, Vito Vitale, and Carmine Galente of "Operation X."

23. *World Petroleum*, February 1964.

24. Discussion in Scott and Marshall, *Cocaine Politics*, 85–86; McCoy, *The Politics of Heroin*, 38–41.

25. *Le Monde*, June 17–18, 1973; Krueger, *The Great Heroin Coup*, 1–3 (French charges); Scott and Marshall, *Cocaine Politics*, 85–86 (alleged breakdown); Messick, *Lansky*, 212; McClellan Hearings 12369–70 (Anastasia).

26. Messick, *Lansky*, 89; Scott, *War Conspiracy*, 209.

27. Ovid Demaris, *The Director*, 15; Summers, *Official and Confidential*, 184–86.

28. Chicago Crime Commission, *Report*, 1963, 67; McClellan Hearings, 20467; Robert Kennedy, *Enemy Within*, 87; Sheridan, *Hoffa*, 71; Fox, *Blood and Power*, 354–58.

29. Anderson, *Washington Exposé*, 214–16.

30. Cook, *The FBI Nobody Knows*, 230 (Hoover); Messick, *Hoover*, 144, citing *New York Times*, August 24, 1954.

31. Summers, *Official and Confidential*, 329, 488. The other witnesses were Byars's son, Billy Byars, Jr., and Arthur and Mara Forbes, managers of the Del Charro.

32. 5 AH 70–71 (Byars); Marrs, *Crossfire*, 394 (McWillie).

33. Butler Notes of Jones-Guthrie conversation; Senate Commerce Committee Files.

34. Jones-Guthrie conversations, FBI Transcript, Record 9.

35. We have already seen how the FBI referred to Joe Civello in one place as "CIRELLO" (WCD 84.91), and in another as "SAVELLA" (22 WH 303).

36. Messick, *Hoover*, 146.

37. Ibid., 145; Robert Sherrill, *Gothic Politics in the Deep South* (New York: Grossman, 1968), 11.

38. Moldea, *Interference*, 104–5.

39. Brewton, *The Mafia, CIA, and George Bush*, 24, 100–101, 156–57.

40. Moldea, *Interference*, 105.

41. Blakey and Billings, *The Plot*, 314; 9 AH 335.

42. 9 AH 1146; Blakey and Billings, *The Plot*, 313. Campisi was definitely a part of the Civello organization, Dallas Police Captain W. P. Gannaway assured the Committee.

43. Messick, *Hoover*, 146; Powers, *Secrecy and Power*, 315. One of the Las Vegas gangsters was John Drew, a point-holder at the Las Vegas Stardust with Moe Dalitz and Milton Jaffe, whose name was found in Ruby's personal notebook (22 WH 504). Allan Witwer, manager of the Del Charro, later wrote in an unpublished manuscript that "the FBI was looking for Drew" at the same time Drew hid out in a Del Charro suite and Hoover occupied his Del Charro bungalow. According to *Life* (September 1, 1967, 43), Giancana was a hidden owner of the Stardust in 1961, when Bobby Kennedy began to investigate it.

44. Powers, *Secrecy and Power*, 315. Messick, *Hoover*, 138–39; Jeff Gerth, "Nixon and the Miami Connection," in Steve Weissman, ed., *Big Brother and the Holding Company* (Palo Alto, Calif.: Ramparts Press, 1974), 263. After Myer Schine's embarrassing testimony to the Kefauver Committee about bookmaking at the Gulfstream, Hoover (and Nixon and McCarthy) moved their winter holidays from the Gulfstream to the Key Biscayne Inn and Villas, owned by partners of Lou Chesler, a business associate of Meyer Lansky.

CHAPTER THIRTEEN

1. Messick, *Hoover*, 44–45, 69–70 (Torrio), 81 (Hoover), 152–54 (casino); Messick, *Lansky*, 100–101 (Lepke).

2. Gentry, *Hoover*, 365n; Messick, *Hoover*, 104; *Life*, May 2, 1969, 31.

3. Messick, *Hoover*, 112–17.

4. Ibid., 117.

5. Hersh, *The Old Boys*, 177, 185–86.

6. According to Burton Hersh (ibid., 327, 512), forgers in Angleton's Counterintelligence Division added diversionary material to the flow of CIA documents being leaked to McCarthy.

7. Cumings, *The Origins of the Korean War*, II, 109–13.

8. Ibid., 82–100.

9. Harry Hurt III, *Texas Rich* (New York: Norton, 1981), 164.

10. Cumings, *The Origins of the Korean War*, II, 105.

11. E. H. Cookridge, *Gehlen: Spy of the Century* (New York: Random House, 1971), 363.

12. Sale, *Power Shift*, 226.

13. Russell, *The Man Who Knew Too Much*, 529 (Corso); 26 WH 410–15, 26 WH 599, 24 WH 648.

14. Hersh, *The Old Boys*, 347, 411.

15. Russell, *The Man Who Knew Too Much*, 528–29 (Knights); Martin, *Wilderness of Mirrors*, 105 and passim (Goleniewski); Guy Richards, *Imperial Agent: The Goleniewski-Romanov Case* (New York: Devin-Adair, 1966) (Knights and Goleniewski). Colonel Charles Pichel, Grand Chancellor of the Knights and a steady correspondent of Willoughby's in 1963, had sought in the 1930s to be appointed Hitler's official representative in America (Russell, ibid.,

528, citing Sander A. Diamond, *The Nazi Movement in the United States: 1924–41* [Ithaca, N.Y.: Cornell University Press, 1974], 116–17). In the early 1950s, General Fellers, calling for rollback, "thought the CIA harbored 'a group of Marxist-Socialist pro-Communists'" (Cumings, *The Origins of the Korean War,* II, 101).

16. AIB FBI release #736, FBI memo of February 10, 1964; Russell, *The Man Who Knew Too Much,* 529.

17. Hugh C. McDonald, as told to Geoffrey Bocca, *Appointment in Dallas* (New York: Zebra Books, 1975).

18. Richards, "Russia's School for Assassins" (cf. *Ukrainian Bulletin,* January 1–15, 1964, 1); Frank Capell, *Herald of Freedom,* January 17, 1964 (20 WH 745); American Security Council, *Washington Report,* March 16, 1964, 3. Richards's chief favor for the Shickshinny Knights was to write *Imperial Agent,* a book supporting the Pole Goleniewski's claim on the Romanoff fortunes lying dormant in U.S. bank accounts, as the surviving son of the murdered Tsar! For more on Richards, see Chapters 14 and 16.

19. U.S. Cong., Senate, Committee on the Judiciary, *Murder International Incorporated,* Staff Report, 1964; cf. Investigation of Senator Dodd Hearing, 577–78 (Richard Helms letter of July 14, 1966).

20. Russell, *The Man Who Knew Too Much,* 687; cf. 299, 548; see Chapter 3. Oliver later served on a board of the anti-Semitic Liberty Lobby with Shickshinny Knight Pedro del Valle, and Austin J. App of Hunt's Foreign Intelligence Digest (Turner, *Power on the Right,* 163).

21. *American Opinion,* February 1964, 19; reproduced at 20 WH 726; cf. WCD 770.4. A very similar story, naming Huber Matos as the replacement candidate, was told by John Martino in a "phase one" story ("Cuba and the Kennedy Assassination") in the right-wing journal *Human Events,* December 21, 1963. A secret letter circulated by the Minutemen at the same time also wrote that the assassination "could have been a by-product of a known plot (or should we say a very well known plot) to set up a coalition government in Cuba timed to re-assure Kennedy's re-election in 1964" (Noyes, *Legacy of Doubt,* 195). Because of the links of both Martino and the Minutemen to the mob's former casino owners in Havana, one can understand their mistrust of any plans for Cuba that would not return to the status quo ante 1959.

22. Turner, *Power on the Right,* 189; cf. Noyes, *Legacy of Doubt,* 202–06; Anthony Summers, *Goddess: The Secret Lives of Marilyn Monroe* (New York: Macmillan, 1985), 312, cf. 343 (Clemmons/Monroe). The four men indicted pleaded no contest. Dennis Mower, a Minuteman associate of Martino's friend Loran Eugene Hall, was also implicated but not prosecuted, in return for his testimony.

23. Turner, *Power on the Right,* 110–11; Russell, *The Man Who Knew Too Much,* 604.

24. Investigation of Senator Dodd Hearing, 314, etc.

25. Turner, *Power on the Right,* 203–05, etc.

26. Ibid., 130–31, 184–85, 203–04, etc. Turner shows that a number of those involved with Oswald's p.r. activities in New Orleans, such as Ed Butler of INCA and his patron Dr. Alton Ochsner, were taken on by Schick-Eversharp

in the later 1960s, to escalate their pro-war propaganda activity (172, 185–87). At one of their conferences a major speaker was Ruby's old lawyer-friend Luis Kutner (188).

27. As previously noted, McLendon's father-in-law was Jimmy Noe, associate of Seymour Weiss and Russell Long as a co-owner of Huey Long's Win or Lose Corporation. Walter Sheridan accused both Russell Long and Gordon McLendon of being part of a plot to bring pressure on Bobby Kennedy's witness against Hoffa, Edward Grady Partin (Sheridan, *Hoffa*, 406–11, 424–28, 503–05). McLendon's brother-in-law Lester May (see Chapter 14) was also named in this plot.

28. Davis, *Mafia Kingfish*, 474–75; cf. *Washington Post*, July 3, 1980 (Davidson-Oman).

29. Moldea, *Hoffa Wars*, 107–08; Sheridan, *Hoffa*, 140, 155–56.

30. Moldea, *Hoffa Wars*, 264. Davidson's partner and co-defendant in the Teamster-financed Beverly Hills Estates case, Leonard Bursten, was a former lawyer under McCarthy who knew Murchison's employee Thomas Webb. See Baker Hearings (Financial Interests), 275–76.

31. Davis, *Mafia Kingfish*, 474–75.

32. Messick, *Hoover*, 145. Thompson testified to the Senate Rules Committee that he thought he had met Baker "in the office of Lyndon Johnson."

33. Reid and Demaris, *The Green Felt Jungle*, 217–20. Ed Levinson had fronted for Lansky at the Las Vegas Sands, the casino contacted by Ruby's friend Tony Zoppi (Messick, *Lansky*, 196).

34. Davis, *The Kennedys*, 379; Davis, *Mafia Kingfish*, 101–05.

35. Navasky, *Kennedy Justice*, 55; Davis, *The Kennedys*, 376–77.

36. Sheridan, *Hoffa*, 279, 281 (Hoffa: May 9 and June 4, 1963); *New York Times*, October 20, 1963 (Bruno); *Wall Street Journal*, October 29, 1963 (Plumeri).

37. Sheridan, *Hoffa*, 236, 242.

38. The investigation was eventually blocked by the Las Vegas casino operators' attorney, Edward Bennett Williams, who by this point no longer represented Jimmy Hoffa but remained one of Bobby Kennedy's most powerful opponents inside the Democratic party. See Navasky, *Kennedy Justice*, 79–81. After the Kennedy assassination Williams represented Bobby Baker as well, replacing Johnson's friend Abe Fortas (Bobby Baker, *Wheeling and Dealing* [New York: Norton, 1978], 186).

39. Baker, *Wheeling and Dealing*, 176; *New York Times*, September 28, 1963; *New York Times*, November 13, 1963; Scott, *Crime and Cover-Up*, 11.

40. The stories preceded the imminent publication of *The Green Felt Jungle*.

41. A 1962 congressional investigation into the the Texas scandal involving Billie Sol Estes, who had made telephone calls to Johnson's assistant Clifton Carter, was also blamed on the Kennedys. See North, *Act of Treason*, 155–58 and passim. North charges that Johnson, to protect himself, maintained a close liaison with J. Edgar Hoover in the Billie Sol Estes case (155; cf. Gentry, *Hoover*, 559).

42. Davis, *The Kennedys*, 513–14. Sheridan says only that the Baker case "first surfaced in the fall of 1963" (Sheridan, *Hoffa*, 392).

43. Alfred Steinberg, *Sam Johnson's Boy* (New York: Macmillan, 1968), 592–93; *New York Times,* November 28, 1963, 17.

44. Steinberg, *Sam Johnson's Boy,* 602, 611. Demaris, *Captive City,* 246.

45. Steinberg, *Sam Johnson's Boy,* 611.

46. Ibid., 668–71. Drew Pearson, Jack Anderson, and the *Washington Post* helped the new President by releasing dirt and unchecked gossip about Reynolds and Committee Chairman Senator John Williams.

47. TFX Contract Hearings (November 20, 1963), 2740; *Business Week,* November 23, 1963, 33 (Korth).

48. Navasky, *Kennedy Justice,* 30.

49. *New York Times,* November 13, 1963, 1; Reid, *Grim Reapers,* 138–39; Baker Hearings, 891.

50. Davis, *Mafia Kingfish,* 475.

51. Gentry, *Hoover,* 559n; William W. Turner, *Hoover's FBI* (Los Angeles: Sherbourne Press, 1970), 185.

52. A list of the new frequent visitors to the Johnson White House is supplied by Steinberg (*Sam Johnson's Boy,* 630): it includes Fortas, Acheson, Corcoran, Rowe, Clark Clifford, and the conservative commentator William S. White.

53. Richard Danner saw Murchison lobbyist Thomas Webb at the time he was channeling compromising funds from Las Vegas to Nixon before Watergate (20 Watergate Hearings, 9614–16). For the mediating but powerful and mysterious role of Edward Bennett Williams in Watergate, see Jim Hougan, *Secret Agenda* (New York: Random House, 1984), 240–42, 262–64. For Jack Anderson's role in 1964 (to defend Johnson and Bobby Baker against Bobby Kennedy) and in 1971–72 (against Nixon), see Steinberg, *Sam Johnson's Boy,* 670 (Johnson-Baker); Stanley I. Kutler, *The Wars of Watergate* (New York: Norton, 1990), 108, 116–18 (Nixon); Scott, *Crime and Cover-Up,* 32–34 (Nixon); Hougan, ibid., 65–95 (Nixon). (Anderson was an ally and for nine years an officemate of I. Irving Davidson; Hougan, ibid., 89n.)

54. Davis, *Mafia Kingfish,* 600–601; Church Committee Assassination Report, 173–74; Schlesinger, *Robert Kennedy,* 594–98 (Attwood).

55. One would, however, like to know the 1963 Vietnam recommendations of the President's Foreign Intelligence Advisory Board, and of its chairman, Clark Clifford. Clifford is one of the mystery men in the events of this period.

56. Hougan, *Secret Agenda,* 131–33.

57. *New York Times,* November 19, 1963, 11; *Business Week,* November 23, 1963, 41; extended discussion in Scott, "Vietnamization and the Drama of the Pentagon Papers," *Pentagon Papers* (Beacon), V, 226–27, 238; Peter Dale Scott, "The Vietnam War and the CIA-Financial Establishment," in Mark Selden, ed., *Remaking Asia* (New York: Pantheon, 1974).

CHAPTER FOURTEEN

1. Baker Hearings, 257–86; Sheridan, *Hoffa,* 424–25.

2. Labor Insurance Hearings, 994–1027. The principal in the case, Joseph Hauser, had paid a $250,000 finder's fee to former attorney general Richard

Kleindienst, law partner of John Rosselli's lawyer, Edward P. Morgan. Hauser escaped punishment after his conviction by becoming an informant for the FBI in its BRILAB investigation of Davidson and Carlos Marcello (Davis, *Mafia Kingfish,* 464–71).

3. Davis, *Mafia Kingfish,* 261–64, citing Summers, *Goddess.* Athan Theoharis and John Cox, having closely studied the available Hoover files, conclude that, "as far as J. Edgar Hoover was concerned . . . there was no Kennedy-Monroe affair, and therefore no blackmailing the Kennedys on that score" (*The Boss,* 336–38). Curt Gentry, while echoing their conclusion from the *available* evidence, notes that this is incomplete (*Hoover,* 493–94).

4. Rappleye and Becker, *All-American Mafioso,* 207–10. This was the show which Tony Zoppi attended, and mistakenly used as an explanation for why Ruby went to Cuba some months earlier (Blakey and Billings, *The Plot,* 306).

5. Church Committee Assassination Report, 75–76; Scott, *Crime and Cover-Up,* 22, 58.

6. Rappleye and Becker, *All-American Mafioso,* 208.

7. Davis, *Mafia Kingfish,* 308. The Christine Keeler sex-ring story had first surfaced in March 1963, leading to Profumo's resignation in June.

8. Summers, *Official and Confidential,* 241–45, 269–70, 288–309.

9. Beschloss, *The Crisis Years,* 598–99, 602.

10. Summers and Dorril, *Honeytrap,* 256–57.

11. Ibid., 257; Summers, *Official and Confidential,* 306–09.

12. Summers and Dorril, *Honeytrap,* 116, etc.

13. Ibid., 177–87.

14. Ibid., 249.

15. Ibid., 269.

16. Ibid., 259.

17. Beschloss, *The Crisis Years,* 616; Summers, *Official and Confidential,* 309–13.

18. Clark Mollenhoff, "U.S. Expels Girl Linked to Officials—Is Sent to Germany After FBI Probe," *Des Moines Register,* October 26, 1963, reprinted in *Congressional Record,* October 28, 1963, 20372; cf. Beschloss, *The Crisis Years,* 616; James Reston, *New York Times,* October 31, 1963: "This city has been full of ugly rumors about illicit relations between Baker's girl friends and prominent Senators and officials in the administration."

19. Baker, *Wheeling and Dealing,* 80. Back in 1962, Johnson's visit to Bobby Baker's Carousel Motel, where Rometsch was present, generated an FBI report to Hoover, linking the Vice-President to "immoral activities" and "hoodlum interests" (North, *Act of Treason,* 215–16; Gentry, *Hoover,* 559).

20. When the introduction occurred is not clear. It might seem unlikely that the President would have so exposed himself after Hoover had already apprised Bobby Kennedy of his knowledge about Judith Campbell and Marilyn Monroe. But Jack Kennedy seems almost to have preferred sexual involvements which carried the excitement of political danger as well.

21. Beschloss, *The Crisis Years,* 616–17; Summers, *Official and Confidential,* 309–13.

22. Beschloss, ibid., citing Benjamin Bradlee, *Conversations With Kennedy* (New York: Norton, 1975), 231–35.

23. Sheridan, *Hoffa,* 210; McClellan Committee, *American Guild of Variety Artists,* Hearings, 142 (testimony of William J. Scott, Special Assistant to U.S. Attorney, Northern District of Illinois).

24. Blakey and Billings, *The Plot,* 290.

25. AGVA Hearings, 378 ff. The man, John Zanetti, was also a relative of John Angersola, who owned the building, and of Dave Triscaro. Women were recruited for the nationwide strip business from Havana (289, 300–310).

26. Scheim, *Contract on America,* 118–19 (Ruby's hustling); Blakey and Billings, *The Plot,* 291.

27. Gary Mills and Ovid Demaris, *Jack Ruby* (New American Library, 1968), 64–68.

28. Davis, *Mafia Kingfish,* 262, where it is asserted that Marilyn Monroe knew both Mickey Cohen and John Rosselli.

29. Mills and Demaris, *Jack Ruby,* 66.

30. Donald Barlett and James B. Steele, *Empire: The Life, Legend, and Madness of Howard Hughes* (New York: Norton, 1979), 125–27, 147–50.

31. Baker, *Wheeling and Dealing,* 170.

32. Rappleye and Becker, *All-American Mafioso,* 168, 310, 319–20.

33. Summers and Dorril, *Honeytrap,* 268.

34. The lodge burned the night before a visit from House Intelligence Committee staffers on another mission; Hougan, *Secret Agenda,* 131–33; Gentry, *Hoover,* 734. Hougan speculates that Hunt brought the Watergate burglars to Washington on May 3, 1972, to acquire these files.

35. Gentry, *Hoover,* 50–56, 728–35; Theoharis and Cox, *The Boss,* 329–36.

36. Baker, 182; *Life,* November 22, 1963, 92A.

37. Hougan, *Secret Agenda,* 115–20; Len Colodny and Robert Gettlin, *Silent Coup: The Removal of a President* (New York: St. Martin's Press, 1991), 126–31.

38. Hougan, *Secret Agenda,* 80, 82, 118–19, 309.

39. Theoharis and Cox, *The Boss,* 315.

40. Hougan, *Secret Agenda,* 307.

41. James McCord, *A Piece of Tape* (Rockville, Md.: Washington Media Services, 1974).

42. Hougan, *Secret Agenda,* 81–82, 182–83.

43. Ibid., 306–11.

44. Ibid., 115.

45. Ibid., 120–21.

46. Trento, *The Power House,* 97–103, 107–08.

47. Ibid., 112.

48. Scott and Marshall, *Cocaine Politics,* 101–02, 137, 173, 252n.

49. Trento, *The Power House,* 176–77; personal information (Nesline). The other investigator was Ethics Committee Counsel Donald Purdy, formerly

with the Assassinations Committee, but during the conversation between Shoffler and Moriarity, Purdy left for another appointment.

50. Trento, *The Power House,* 178–79; personal information.

51. Trento, *The Power House,* 176–82.

52. Ibid., 183.

53. Colodny and Gettlin, *Silent Coup,* 130 (Rikan-Nesline); Block, *Perspectives on Organizing Crime,* 233–36.

54. Block, *Perspectives on Organizing Crime,* 234.

55. Moldea, *Interference,* 168; 5 AH 20, 108–09.

56. Moldea, *Interference,* 242.

57. Colodny and Gettlin, *Silent Coup,* 127.

58. Ibid., 142–47; cf. Hougan, *Secret Agenda,* 172–74; *Washington Star,* June 9, 1972.

59. Colodny and Gettlin, *Silent Coup,* 128, 133, 145–46.

60. Moldea, *Hoffa Wars,* 279, 293, 343.

61. Colodny and Gettlin, *Silent Coup,* 130.

62. Some miscellaneous speculations: Owen, it will be recalled, was with Ruby's stripper friend Candy Barr in 1957, just before she was arrested. Both Lester May, her attorney in that case, and his brother-in-law Gordon McLendon (whom Ruby listed as one of his six closest friends, 20 WH 39) were busy in 1971 in the mob effort to secure the release of Jimmy Hoffa (Sheridan, *Hoffa,* 503–04; Moldea, *Hoffa Wars,* 280). So was Carlos Marcello's associate D'Alton Smith, brother-in-law of Nofio Pecora, the head of Marcello's call-girl operation whom Ruby phoned in October 1963. In 1970 Smith would be indicted as part of a securities fraud network, along with Charles Tourine, Ruby's friend Maurice "Frenchy" Medlevine, Mike McLaney, and Sam Benton of the McLaney arms cache on Lake Pontchartrain (Scott, *Crime and Cover-Up,* 46). Bobby Baker was approached about the million-dollar bail-out of Hoffa as well (Baker, *Wheeling and Dealing,* 17).

Bedford Wynne entertained his girls, and his friend George Owen, at his home in the Maple Terrace Apartments. This was also the address of Oswald's womanizing friend George de Mohrenschildt (WCD 7.135), and at one time of Ruby's friend Lewis McWillie (WCD 84.86).

Could Ruby and McWillie have moved in such "higher" circles by their ability to supply women, drugs, and gambling? McWillie told the House Committee that he ran "stag parties" at the Cipango Club for Dallas gamblers Ivy Miller and Earl Dalton, although he explained that the stag parties featured dice games, at which "they let their wives come too" (5 AH 66). Jim Marrs writes that the Four Deuces in Fort Worth, which McWillie managed for the "gentleman gambler" W. C. Kirkwood, was "in an area noted for its taverns and its prostitution. It was here, under the protective eye of off-duty policemen, that men like H. L. Hunt, Clint Murchinson [*sic*], and others joined [Speaker] Sam Rayburn and his protégé [Lyndon] Johnson for hours of Kirkwood-provided hospitality" (Marrs, 292).

One last detail to support the retired Washington policeman's theory that the mob, and more specifically Nesline, has been behind sexual corruption in high places for a long time. Mandy Rice-Davies, the number-two woman in the

Ward-Keeler sex ring that compromised both Profumo and Kennedy, established mob contacts when she moved to Israel. There she met Herbert Itkin, the mob-FBI-CIA double agent who had testified in the Teamster kickback trial, where Angleton's agent Mario Brod had testified successfully for the defense.

Had she known the mob before the Profumo story broke? At least one of Ward's women, Mariella Novotny (who slept with Kennedy), had worked in London strip joints like the Club Pigalle and the Black Sheep (Summers and Dorril, *Honeytrap,* 96). Lansky and Cellini also had interests in London clubs, which may explain why Lansky and Nesline were spotted there in 1962.

It is safe to say that the mob was involved in the post-assassination cover-up, beginning with Ruby's murder of Oswald in the Dallas Police basement. But it is clear that many of those involved in the pre-assassination sexual intrigues, including Rosselli, Hoover, Guy Richards, Michael Eddowes, and above all, Bedford Wynne, were involved in the post-assassination story as well.

CHAPTER FIFTEEN

1. 5 WH 112. See Chapter 3. On Oswald's tax records, cf. Hurt, *Reasonable Doubt,* 406–07; North, *Act of Treason,* 257–59, 562–72; Summers, *Conspiracy,* 394, 587.

2. The story was first floated by two journalists with intelligence connections, Joe Goulden (*Philadelphia Inquirer,* December 8, 1963) and Alonso Hudkins (*Houston Post,* January 1, 1964). Hudkins's motives may have been the same as those for the Martino-Rosselli story: to blackmail the FBI. For a while, Hudkins was part of the Harvey-Rosselli-Martino milieu in Miami; according to another member of that milieu, Ed Arthur, Hudkins "headed up one of the groups that had gone to Miami to recruit assassination teams" against Castro (Mike Wales, *Ed Arthur's Glory No More* [Westerville, Ohio: Dakar, 1975], 84).

3. CIA Document 501; see Chapter 5.

4. Cold War Against Communism Hearings, 1467–1514; Ronstadt Report, 80.

5. Hoover took over the American Legion vigilante effort "by setting up a system where Legion post commanders reported their suspicion to local special agents in charge and let the FBI do the investigating" (Gentry, *Hoover,* 413).

6. Hougan, *Secret Agenda,* 9; Nedzi Hearing, 1023–31.

7. Epstein, *Legend,* 193. Oswald may have also enjoyed a special role at his first job after returning in 1962 from the Soviet Union to Fort Worth. Although he worked at a small local metal-awning factory, his paychecks were personally and individually signed by officers of the parent company in Illinois (usually the president) and drawn on their Illinois bank (24 WH 886–90; cf. 22 WH 232).

8. Summers, *Conspiracy,* 230.

9. 10 WH 200; Epstein, *Legend,* 194; Summers, *Conspiracy,* 231.

10. Summers, *Conspiracy,* 313. As noted in Chapter 6, William Monaghan, the INCA member and William B. Reily industrial-security officer who later reported on Oswald, was one of the four employees who actually made the move.

11. One sign that Oswald's employment at the TSBD was not a normal one is the anomaly that the name entered for him in the TSBD payroll time records for November 16–30, 1963, is "Leslie Oswald," even though the TSBD had received a correct application and tax-withholding certificate from "Lee Harvey Oswald," and had previously entered his name as "Lee Oswald" (23 WH 747–51). By itself, the anomaly is a small one, but there are anomalies in Oswald's payroll records at all his places of employment. Keep in mind that, as already noted in Chapter 6, the paychecks submitted as Oswald's to the Warren Commission are apparently not genuine, and that the FBI misrepresented the problems with them of which they were obviously aware. As noted in Chapter 6, the FBI had Roland Martin of Martin's Restaurant, 701 Tchoupitoulas, New Orleans, confirm he had cashed Oswald's paycheck #1684 of June 14, 1963 (22 WH 208). In fact the check is stamped as having been endorsed by Oswald and then deposited by Foltz Tea & Coffee, Inc., at 633 Tchoupitoulas (22 WH 288). If this sounds like quibbling, consider the analogous problem of two of Oswald's earlier paychecks, from Jaggars-Chiles-Stovall in Dallas. There a Mr. Pactor of Mart Liquor Store identified check #5663 of April 3, 1963, as having been cashed by him (on the basis of his store stamp on the check's back); and he denied having cashed #5511 of March 27, 1963 (22 WH 224). This was consistent with the fronts of the checks in question, which showed that the first had not been cashed at the Mercantile National Bank, while the second had been (22 WH 248). However, it was entirely *inconsistent* with the backs of the same checks, which (at least in the Warren Commission Exhibits) showed a Mart Liquor stamp for #5511 (where it should not have been), and yet none for #5663 (where it should have been). The FBI thus had Mr. Pactor claim to have cashed a check (as the FBI needed to for consistency's sake) on the basis of a store stamp that was apparently not there. As reproduced, check #5511 of March 27 remains an apparent falsification or artifact, since the stamps on it suggest that it was cashed both at the bank counter and also at the Mart Liquor store.

12. According to Summers (337), Banister and Ferrie were both helping Gill to fight Robert Kennedy's efforts to deport Marcello.

13. The movie did not mention a simultaneous trip to Galveston by one of Ruby's employees in Dallas.

14. Memo of December 15, 1966, to Jim Garrison from John Volz, in Assassination Archive, Washington, D.C.

15. *Ramparts,* January 1968, reprinted in Scott, Hoch, and Stetler, *The Assassinations,* 279. Cf. WCD 75.293.

16. Blakey and Billings, *The Plot,* 46–47, 166–67, and passim.

17. At a deeper political level, it seems possible that Martin's charges against Ferrie had to do with the contemporary efforts of Carlos Marcello and others (including Clint Murchison, Jr., Ruby's friend Gordon McLendon, and McLendon's brother-in-law Lester May [Sheridan, *Hoffa,* 503–06]) to save Jimmy Hoffa from going to prison. Ferrie was fingered as an assassination suspect in a memo of December 13, 1966, to Jim Garrison from his chief investigator Pershing Gervais. Gervais transmitted additional allegations from Martin, linking both David Ferrie and his friend Morris Brownlee to narcotics.

Pershing Gervais, and in a more ambiguous way Morris Brownlee, alias Bromlee, both figure prominently in Sheridan's deep-political account of how Carlos
Marcello's people used the Garrison investigation (and "the possibility of
planting narcotics on Partin") to threaten Edward Grady Partin, Sheridan's witness against Hoffa (Sheridan, *Hoffa*, 417–35). See above, pp. 187–90, 357–58.

18. See Chapter 17. As Sylvia Meagher pointed out long ago, no one has
ever linked Oswald to any equipment to take care of his weapons, or any ammunition other than the bullet shells found at the murder scenes of the President and Tippit, the latter very dubious (*Accessories After the Fact*, 113–16,
131–33). We have also been misinformed about Oswald's rifle practice. For example, Priscilla Johnson McMillan vividly describes what no eyewitness has
ever reported, how Oswald practiced shooting in March 1963 in the "Trinity
River bottom" (Priscilla McMillan, *Marina and Lee* [New York: Harper and
Row, 1977], 279, quoted in Peter Dale Scott, *Coming to Jakarta* [New York:
New Directions, 1989], 133). Her citation is to an FBI memo which speculated
that " 'Trinity River bottom' is clear and uninhabited and . . . *could be used* for
rifle firing" (26 WH 61; emphasis added).

19. Hurt, *Reasonable Doubt*, 298.

20. Ibid., 297; cf. 10 WH 220–22; 23 WH 727–29.

21. Senator Thomas Dodd, a former FBI agent, sat on Senator Eastland's
Senate Internal Security Subcommittee, and was still at this time a key member
of what Gentry (*Hoover*, 407) calls the "FBI stable" in Congress, loyal to
Hoover.

22. Dodd Hearings, 3642; cf. 3596, 3433; 17 WH 675, 678; Hurt, 300–
302. The investigation was conducted over a two-year period in 1962–63
(*Congressional Record*, December 10, 1963, 2044, reprinting *Christian Science
Monitor*, October 29, 1963).

23. Hurt, *Reasonable Doubt*, 296; AR 193.

24. Dodd Hearings, 3595.

25. Ibid., 3204.

26. *Washington Post*, November 23, 1963, 4; cf. 10 WH 35.

27. Schweiker-Hart Report, 12, 79; FBI Airtel 62–109060–4758, pp. 5, 10,
13.

28. 11 WH 375. Rogelio Cisneros, alias "Eugenio," the leader whom Odio
phoned with the news, confirmed independently that he had met Martin with
Odio, in a short-lived discussion about buying arms (26 WH 349). If "Johnny
Martin" were in fact John Martino, who did visit Cubans in Dallas at this
time, then Oswald might have been continuing to target the conspiratorial faction of Gerry Patrick Hemming (the Marine Reservist at the camp) and John
Martino.

29. Account of Odio story by Mrs. Connell; cf. WCD 1546.179.

CHAPTER SIXTEEN

1. Sheriff's deputy Walthers later also told the Warren Commission that he
had found "Freedom for Cuba" literature among Oswald's effects in Ruth
Paine's garage (7 WH 548; cf. 19 WH 503, 520).

2. Hinckle and Turner, *The Fish Is Red,* 166–67.

3. Ibid., 166; Hurt, *Reasonable Doubt,* 327.

4. *National Review,* June 18, 1963, 483–84.

5. Schweiker-Hart Committee, 63–64. The four groups were JURE, the DRE, Alpha 66, and the 30th of November Movement.

6. The Schweiker-Hart Report added that "one Cuban in the Dallas area ... investigated ... because he was alleged to be an agent of the Cuban government ... was an approved, although unused, source of Army intelligence in 1963" (65). This was apparently the vice-secretary of Alpha 66 in Dallas (WCD 1085 K, WCD 1085 N.5), whose brother (WCD 1085 N.5) was training on a Florida Key with Gerry Patrick Hemming (*Saturday Evening Post,* June 8, 1963). Alpha 66 at the same time was the chief group funded by Paulino Sierra's Cuban junta, possibly as a means to move Alpha 66 abroad and lessen their threat to Kennedy's policies (10 AH 99–100).

7. *New York Times,* September 16, 1963, 39. At one point, Sturgis and Hemming also discussed the overthrow of Duvalier in Haiti, as a stepping stone to the eventual overthrow of Castro, with one of the backers of the Bayo-Pawley raid. It may or may not be a coincidence that the U.S. official Veciana first contacted in 1960 for support in his anti-Castro operations was Col. Samuel Kail in the U.S. embassy in Havana (10 AH 42), who later helped set up the de Mohrenschildt-Charles-Army-CIA meeting about Haiti in Washington, because of Haiti's "strategic position relative to ... Cuba" (12 AH 56–57).

8. Warren Commission staff memo, Griffin to Slawson, April 16, 1964.

9. In addition, someone involved with the group was an Oswald look-alike. The FBI was told that an apparent sighting of "Oswald" in Oklahoma was in fact Manuel Rodriguez Orcarberro (WCD 23.4). Agent Ellsworth, queried about this by author Dick Russell, gave Russell the impression that it was Masen (Russell, *The Man Who Knew Too Much,* 542–45). This issue of the Oswald look-alike in Alpha 66, whether Oswald, Rodriguez, or Masen, has been subjected to multiple conflicting narrations far too complex to untangle here. Suffice it to say that it is an area for further inquiry. All relevant files, particularly those of the ATF, should be among those released to the public.

10. ATF (Dallas) memo of January 14, 1964, to Secret Service (Dallas); Secret Service assassination file, Control #902 (not in WCD 87 or WCD 320). This memo says that the seven ATF agents arrived at about 12:40 P.M. (about ten minutes after the assassination) and assisted in the second search of the building about 1:30 P.M. It does not mention the rifle.

11. Dodd Hearings, 3595 (see Chapter 15).

12. The meeting would be even more interesting if one or more of these three people had met before the assassination with Dallas Police Lieutenant Jack Revill, whose responsibilities for liaison on subversive investigations with these agencies (and with LEIU, an intelligence network linking the police departments of different cities) will be described in the next chapter. Revill did

meet with Hosty and an unidentified army-intelligence agent right after the as-sassination (see Chapter 17).

13. Some uses of "legend" as "cover" or "false biography," as opposed to "real life," are quoted by Epstein, *Legend*, v.

14. AR 222 (112th MIG); Epstein, *Legend*, 225 (ONI). The record of Os-wald's testimony is apparently not only false but manipulative. For example, he is said to have claimed to Quigley that he had told Martello he was born in Cuba; but in fact he had told Martello, correctly, that he was born in New Orleans.

15. Lt. Col. Jones told the House Committee he "believed that Oswald first came to his attention" because of information received from the New Orleans Police Department, i.e., in August 1963. This may not be the whole story.

16. Epstein, *Legend*, 225.

17. Hurt, *Reasonable Doubt*, 236–37, citing WR 180–81, 17 WH 681; Meagher, *Accessories*, 182 (circuits); AR 221–23; *Dallas Morning News*, March 19, 1978 (Jones-FBI).

18. Meagher, *Accessories*, 182–91.

19. Hurt, *Reasonable Doubt*, 239.

20. Ray La Fontaine and Mary La Fontaine, *Houston Post*, November 22, 1992, A-1.

21. There are many anomalies about the card. Oswald's passport applica-tion of September 4, 1959, just before his alleged defection to the Soviet Union, carries the notation that "MCR/Inactive I.D. Card #N4,271,617 SUB-MITTED" (22 WH 78), but the card itself, according to Oswald's military file, was not issued until one week later, on September 11 (19 WH 665). The photo on the ID card is the same as that on the fraudulent Hidell Selective Service card, but it is different from that on the passport application; some consider it to be of a different person. The Warren Commission did not release the card as an exhibit (unlike the other cards allegedly found in Oswald's wallet) and may never have received it from the FBI. However, the FBI did transmit the photo on the card (with the same whited-out space in a corner), and this was released by the Commission as WCE 2892, a "Photo taken in Minsk"—i.e., *after* the card had been issued. When the FBI finally released the original ID Card to the Na-tional Archives in December 1966 (as opposed to the copy released through the Dallas police), it arrived "nearly obliterated by FBI testing," according to an ar-chivist. But researcher David Lifton, who has gone through his FBI testing re-ports with care, has found no mention of the DD 1173 (Ray La Fontaine and Mary La Fontaine, *Houston Post*, November 22, 1992, A-1).

22. Eastland's Senate Judiciary Committee "had legislative jurisdiction over the Justice Department, including the FBI, but, in the Bureau's case, never ex-ercised its oversight functions. Moreover, Eastland used his formidable powers to make sure no one else did" (Gentry, *Hoover*, 407).

23. Theoharis and Cox, *The Boss*, 15, 440n.

24. *New York Times*, December 8, 1963.

25. Guy Richards, "Mystery N.Y. Contact of Oswald Revealed," New *York Journal-American*, December 8, 1963, 1; FBI Serial 105-81556-552.

26. Ibid.

27. Scott, *Crime and Cover-Up*, 8–9, 12.

28. 10 AH 83, 85, 138 (Dulles, DRE); Hinckle and Turner, *The Fish Is Red*, 168–73 (Pawley-Eastland).

29. Weisberg, *Frame-Up*, 247 (Lamont-King); Powers, *Secrecy and Power*, 369 (Davis-King).

30. WR 410; 20 WH 258 (letter dated "June 10, 1962," i.e., 1963).

31. WH 767; cf. WCD 6.435.

32. Oswald also told Martello that his FPCC chapter had at least one supporter at Tulane University (10 WH 55). A Tulane student, Hugh Murray, reported to the FBI that a pile of Oswald's FPCC "Hands Off Cuba" handbills had been left in the foyer of the Tulane University library (WCD 75.699). Bringuier's CRC ally Carlos Quiroga, an FBI informant, also told the FBI after the assassination that Oswald had claimed to attend Tulane University (FBI Serial 105-82555-50 OO).

33. FBI Serial 62-109060-4514. Bringuier had had some kind of altercation with an NOCPA member who was a Quaker.

34. E.g., *New York Times*, July 16, 1963, 16; cf. Senator Strom Thurmond in *Congressional Record*, August 23, 1963, 15798; August 25, 1963, 15801. King, of course, had been a target of Hoover's since the late 1950s, when the FBI began to order agents to burglarize the offices of King's Southern Christian Leadership Conference and also to tap their phones (Gentry, *Hoover*, 501).

35. *New York Times*, October 5, 1963, 10.

36. *New York Times*, October 26, 1963, 11; November 2, 1963, 12.

37. FBI Serial 105-82555-50 QQ; WCD 6.435.

38. E.g., U.S. Senate, Committee on the Judiciary, *Communist Threat Through the Caribbean*, Hearings, 89th Cong., 1st Sess., March 31, 1965, 960.

39. Turner, *Power on the Right*, 95.

40. Interview of January 1979; cf. Summers, *Conspiracy*, 322.

41. 10 AH 130.

42. Russell, *The Man Who Knew Too Much*, 397.

43. Hall used the money to redeem a rifle belonging to Gerry Patrick Hemming from a California pawnshop (WCD 1179.295–98). Hall had been active with this "Committee to Free Cuba" since mid-1963 and was arrested in Dallas on drug charges on October 17, 1963 (WCD 1546.211).

44. FBI Director Memo of October 12, 1961, to SAC New York; obtained and released by Political Rights Defense Fund. The FBI ultimately spent an estimated $1.7 million on some 1,300 informants in the SWP, three of whom ran for public office on the party ticket. During the 1960s one out of every ten SWP members was a paid FBI informant (Gentry, *Hoover*, 442n). Significantly, when the FBI became aware of Oswald's correspondence with the SWP, it did not move to put Oswald on the Security Index.

45. Gentry, *Hoover*, 504.

CHAPTER SEVENTEEN

1. Chapters 17 and 18 were originally drafted in 1972–74 and circulated in "Government Documents and the Kennedy Assassination," an appendix to

an unpublished manuscript, "The Dallas Conspiracy." Part of chapter 17 was later published as "Assassinations and Domestic Surveillance," in Scott, Hoch, and Stetler, *The Assassinations*, 443–46.

2. WCD 344.22–23, reprinted in David Lifton, ed., *Document Addendum to the Warren Report: Three Documents from the Files of the Warren Commission* (El Segundo, Calif.: Sightext Publications, 1968), 312–13, emphasis added.

3. Manchester, *The Death of a President*, 326.

4. In Chapter 18 we shall look at one of the more improbable of these stories, that in April 1963 she prevented Oswald from assassinating Nixon by forcibly detaining him in the family bathroom: "she forcibly held the bathroom door shut" for an entire day "by holding on to the knob and bracing her feet against the wall" (23 WH 511; 22 WH 786). More to the point, we shall also see unsolicited, credible evidence that her gun testimony was coached.

5. Manchester, *The Death of a President*, 326.

6. WCD 354, SS 1009, reprinted in Josiah Thompson, *Six Seconds in Dallas* (New York: B. Geis/Random House, 1967), 312; cf. WCD 329.58.

7. For Revill and military intelligence, see below.

8. L. Fletcher Prouty, *The Secret Team* (Englewood Cliffs, N.J.: Prentice-Hall, 1973), 412. There is a flavor of *Seven Days in May* to this cable of November 22, which USSTRICOM Intelligence requested, since the distribution list (although confusing) suggests that it may not have reached headquarters in Washington until four days later.

9. 3 AH 171–73; North, *Act of Treason*, 412, 415, 427; Blakey and Billings, *The Plot*, 20–21.

10. Jerry Richmond in *Dallas Times-Herald;* unrecorded item in FBI file 62-103117, with date stamp August 5, 1963.

11. WR 738; 2 WH 407–08; 9 WH 462–68. Michael Paine revealed his right-wing politics in his Warren Commission testimony, by a passing reference to "the Stalinist, Dubinsky, David Dubinsky" (2 WH 390). Dubinsky, one of the CIA's and Angleton's top agents of influence in the world anti-Communist labor movement, was a recurring target of those in the Willoughby and John Birch circles who felt that the CIA was tainted by Communist connections (e.g., Robert Welch, *The Politician* [Belmont, Mass.: Belmont Publishing, 1963], 227).

12. Scott, *Crime and Cover-Up*, 12; cf. 3 WH 8; 4 WH 32, 38, 261, 432. Oswald's name was falsified in CIA files differently, as "Lee Henry Oswald," yet even in a CIA memo there is an unexplained reference to Oswald as "the Harvey story" (3 AH 572).

13. No less than three books have alleged that not only the same inverted name, but also the same falsified address, "605 Elsbeth," were contained in army-intelligence files on Oswald (Anson, *"They've Killed the President!"* 175; Marrs, *Crossfire*, 309; Russell, *The Man Who Knew Too Much*, 570). In the earliest book (Anson's), this claim is attributed to me; but all I had told him was that the name variant "Harvey Lee Oswald" could be found in the files of army intelligence, as well as in the files of many other agencies. What I have

said and written is that Oswald's name was recurringly altered in intelligence files: as "Lee Henry Oswald" in CIA files, and as "Harvey Lee Oswald" in the files of several agencies (including but not restricted to army intelligence). FBI headquarters even sent out a cable directing its agents to use the name "Lee Harvey Oswald" rather than "Harvey Lee Oswald" in its files.

14. George O'Toole, *The Private Sector* (New York: Norton, 1978), 127–48.

15. *Washington Star,* December 2, 1970, A-8.

16. O'Toole, *The Private Sector,* 145. The FBI were part of this sordid collaboration as well (Churchill and Vander Wall, *Agents of Repression,* 51, etc.).

17. *Nation,* October 1, 1973, 297; *Saturday Review–World,* September 11, 1973, 28.

18. Kelley himself had attended four interviews with Oswald, but the Warren Commission did not question him about them (7 WH 403); he was asked only about his later role in the controversial official "re-enactment" of the assassination, concerning which conflicting testimony had been received (5 WH 130).

19. *New York Times,* June 28, 1970, reprinted in Federal Data Banks Hearings, 1668–69.

20. *Washington Star,* December 6, 1970, reprinted in Federal Data Bank Hearings, 1728.

21. *Washington Star,* December 2, 1970, reprinted in Federal Data Banks Hearings, 1752.

22. *Watergate Hearings,* 3401.

23. Federal Data Bank Hearings, 1668.

24. Scott, Hoch, and Stetler, *The Assassinations,* 446.

25. Theoharis and Cox, *The Boss,* 431–33. The key documents were Executive Order 12333 of 4 December 1981, and Attorney General Smith's new FBI "domestic security/terrorism" guidelines of 7 March 1983.

26. For some of the details, see Robert Parry and Peter Kornbluh, "Iran-Contra's Untold Story," *Foreign Policy* 72 (Fall 1988): 3–18; Peter Dale Scott, "Northwards Without North," *Social Justice* 17:2 (Summer 1989), 1–30; Scott and Marshall, *Cocaine Politics,* 125–64, 183–84; Martin Lee and Norman Solomon, *Unreliable Sources* (New York: Carol Group, 1990), 131–39. An instructively bowdlerized summary of the Parry-Kornbluh story will be found in Theodore Draper, *A Very Thin Line* (New York: Hill and Wang, 1991), 52–54.

27. Parry and Kornbluh, "Iran-Contra's Untold Story," 3–4.

CHAPTER EIGHTEEN

1. Chapters 17 and 18 were originally drafted in 1972–74 and circulated in "Government Documents and the Kennedy Assassination," an appendix to an unpublished manuscript, "The Dallas Conspiracy."

2. House Committee on Banking, Penn Central Failure Report, December 21, 1970, III, 30.

3. Chapter 13; see also Sale, Power Shift, 80–84, etc.

4. Mollenhoff, Tentacles of Power (Cleveland: World Publishing, 1965), 345–46. John Roosevelt and his brother James both addressed the controversial Teamsters convention of 1961 (Sheridan, Hoffa, 180).

5. Ralph James and Estelle James, Hoffa and the Teamsters (Princeton, N.J.: Van Nostrand, 1965), 250. Webb & Knapp had originally been incorporated in 1923 as American Superpower. From 1929 to 1935–36 it had held half of Italian Superpower, whose Italian power investments were rescued in 1945 by Allen Dulles of OSS. At the time, one director of Italian Superpower was James Russell Forgan, of Glore Forgan, who was OSS commander in Europe (Scott, Coming to Jakarta, 47–48; R. Harris Smith, OSS, 116; Hersh, The Old Boys, 127).

6. Esquire, May 1963, 121.

7. House Committee on Banking and Currency, Penn Central Failure Report, III, 30. In 1954 John J. McCloy, chairman of the Rockefeller-dominated Chase Manhattan Bank, became "an important financial ally" of Clint Murchison, Sr., and Sid Richardson when the two Texans became (through Alleghany Corp.) major stockholders in the New York Central Railroad, later merged into the Penn Central (Ernestine Orrick Van Buren, Clint: Clinton Williams Murchison—A Biography [Austin, Texas: Eakin Press, 1986], 286). McCloy was of course a member of the Warren Commission. Warren Commission assistant counsel Francis W. H. Adams had represented the Murchisons in 1959 in a conflict over control of Alleghany Corp.

8. Joseph R. Daughen and Peter Binzen, The Wreck of the Penn Central (New York: Signet, 1971), 135 and passim; Scott, Crime and Cover-Up, 35–37, 67.

9. Donald L. Barlett and James B. Steele, America: What Went Wrong? (Kansas City: Andrews and McMeel, 1992), 58 ff.

10. Van Buren, Clint, 102–08.

11. Congressional Record, January 26, 1965, 1313.

12. Anderson, Washington Exposé, 212–13.

13. Senate Committee on Rules, Stadium Hearings, 862.

14. Ibid., 989.

15. Robert Oswald, Lee (New York: Coward-McCann, 1967), 154.

16. John J. McCloy, in Lifton, Document Addendum to the Warren Report, 26.

17. Meagher, Accessories, 361.

18. WR 368; Noyes, Legacy of Doubt, 72–79.

19. Look, January 26, 1965, 28–29; Russell, The Man Who Knew Too Much, 323.

20. Hurt, Reasonable Doubt, 223.

21. Russell, The Man Who Knew Too Much, 321–22.

22. Marrs, Crossfire, 37; Stone and Sklar, JFK, 119–20.

23. Marrs, Crossfire, 36.

CHAPTER NINETEEN

1. Warren Commission, Executive Session Transcript, December 5, 1963; Anson *"They've Killed the President!"* 41, 368; Scheim, *Contract on America,* 183.

2. Warren Commission, Executive Session Transcript, December 5, 1963; Blakey and Billings, *The Plot,* 25.

3. Warren Commission, Executive Session Transcript, December 5, 1963; Epstein, *Inquest,* 46–47.

4. The Warren Report's Appendix VII, cited in support of this finding, concedes that Booth "plotted with others for months to kidnap the President"; yet it too speaks of Lincoln's assassination as a lone killing by a lone gunman (WR 506).

5. Summers's source is a good one: Kennedy's personal secretary, Evelyn Lincoln, who was present when Kennedy made the decision with his brother Robert. Lincoln "heard enough, she says, to understand that Edgar's smear information was at the heart of their dilemma. 'It was the information J. Edgar Hoover passed to Johnson. . . . Kennedy was angry. . . . He was absolutely boxed in" (Summers, *Official and Confidential,* 273). Lincoln's understanding, less than certain knowledge, is hard to reconcile with more conventional accounts which talk of Kennedy's need to balance the ticket and secure electoral votes from the South. Lincoln's diary remains locked in a deposit box. Whether or not her account of Hoover's role in Johnson's nomination is ever confirmed, one should look more closely at other reports about the Murchison-Hoover-Johnson axis, such as Hoover's phone call on the afternoon of November 22 to Ruby's alleged acquaintance Billy Byars of the "Del Charro set" (see Chapter 13), and Gordon McLendon's revelation to me on camera in 1978 that he spent November 24, 1963, in the the company of his friends Clint Murchison, Jr., and Bedford Wynne. We need to know more, above all, about who and what was behind the rapid moves by Katzenbach and Hoover to establish Oswald as the lone assassin: Was it Johnson, Bobby Kennedy, or for some reason both men acting together?

6. Stone and Sklar, *JFK,* 181–82. In saying this, it is the Pentagon phone I wish to exculpate, not General Edward Lansdale ("Y"). "Y" was indeed the superior of William Harvey, John Rosselli, and Tony Varona in the 1962 MONGOOSE assassination plots against Castro. I can agree with Stone and Sklar's speculation that "Lansdale was furious with J.F.K. for two reasons: (1) he did not get the hoped-for ambassadorship to Vietnam . . . and (2) his good friend, South Vietnamese President Ngo Dinh Diem, had been killed in a CIA-sanctioned coup" (183). It is also true that in November 1963 he came to Texas and stayed at the Hotel Texas in Fort Worth, occupied by the presidential entourage the night before the assassination. But I cannot agree with Fletcher Prouty ("Colonel X"), who worked for Lansdale and who sincerely believes he can identify the back of Lansdale's neck in the so-called "tramp" photos taken in or near Dealey Plaza on November 22. The movie goes with this identifica-

tion. I cannot do so; even the frontal face shots (Howard Hunt? Frank Sturgis?) have proven inconclusive.

7. Krueger, *The Great Heroin Coup,* 16–17 and passim.

8. Cumings, *Origins of the Korean War,* II, 105. I recommend Cumings's history to anyone who retains doubts as to the intense proliferation of intelligence superstructures in the postwar years.

9. Philip H. Melanson, *The Murkin Conspiracy* (New York: Praeger, 1989), 32–38, etc.; Philip H. Melanson, *The Robert F. Kennedy Assassination* (New York: Shapolsky, 1991), 273–85.

10. The transnational connections in the Watergate crisis have been overlooked in many book-length treatments of it, but, although obscure, they are unmistakable. Renata Adler, a member of the House impeachment-investigation staff, wrote later that the congressional investigation of Watergate faded away when traces were uncovered of large funds pumped into the Nixon re-election campaign from the Far East. She also referred to theories "that Nixon was driven from office by a conspiracy within government itself—more specifically, within the CIA"; and she drew attention at this point to the CIA's own involvement in the Southeast Asian drug traffic (Renata Adler, "Searching for the Real Nixon Scandal," *Atlantic Monthly,* December 1976, 76–77, 90–94). Another version is that General Haig in June 1974 ordered an Army CIC investigator, Russell Bintliff, to investigate Nixon's suspected connections to Mafia leaders involved in narcotics traffic and gold-bullion smuggling in Southeast Asia (Jeremiah O'Leary, "Haig Probe: Did Nixon Get Cash from Asia?" *Washington Star,* December 5, 1976; Hougan, *Secret Agenda,* 312; Scheim, *Contract on America,* 307.) A third allegation is that the Greek KYP, an intelligence agency founded and subsidized by the CIA, had transferred $549,000 into Nixon's 1968 campaign fund, in exchange for vice-presidential candidate Spiro Agnew's endorsement, supplied in a response to a question at the National Press Club in September 1968, of the KYP-backed Greek Colonels' coup of 1967. (Asked whether the CIA had knowledge of this, Helms replied with an ambiguity that failed to deny it.) The Nixon White House knew that a whistle-blower, who had already testified about the money to a congressional committee, had given particulars on the transaction to Larry O'Brien of the Democrats, after which he was the subject of FBI surveillance, and probably CIA surveillance as well (Kutler, *The Wars of Watergate,* 205–07; Kutler adds that the money allegation was confirmed by "an authoritative KYP official" in 1987).

11. Theoharis and Cox, *The Boss,* 239–46, 272 (Service/Hoover), 284–86 (Lattimore/Hoover). Hoover (along with Lou Russell and Nathaniel Weyl) played a similar behind-the-scenes role in HUAC's and Richard Nixon's persecutions of Harry Dexter White and Alger Hiss (Theoharis and Cox, *The Boss,* 250–53; Gentry, *Hoover,* 347–52).

12. For the major role played by BCCI in Iran-Contra see U.S. Cong., Senate, Committee on Foreign Relations, *The BCCI Affair,* Report to the Committee by Senator John Kerry and Senator Hank Brown, December 1992; 102nd Cong., 2nd Sess., Senate Print 102-140 (Washington: GPO, 1993), 308–13;

Beaty, Jonathan, and S. C. Gwynne, *The Outlaw Bank: A Wild Ride into the Secret Heart of BCCI* (New York: Random House, 1993), 116, 301, 328–29, 348, etc. See also Scott, *War Conspiracy,* 203–04, 209 (China Lobby/drugs); Marshall, Scott, and Hunter, *The Iran-Contra Connection,* 42–49; Scott and Marshall, *Cocaine Politics,* 27–33, 119–21, 234n (Watergate/Contragate/drugs).

13. Raymond L. Garthoff, *Détente and Confrontation: American-Soviet Relations from Nixon to Reagan* (Washington: Brookings Institution, 1985), 435–36. In 1974, the climactic year of Nixon's resignation, the weakened President was unable to counter the growing revolt of Defense Secretary James Schlesinger and others against his ambitious proposals for SALT II ("Nixon called Schlesinger on the carpet in the Oval Office on June 6 but was afraid to fire him" [411]).

14. This was revealed shortly afterwards by Arthur Liman, chief counsel for the Senate Iran-Contra committee. His words to a Brown University audience are worth quoting at some length: "Even if you concluded that the President was involved in the diversion, an impeachment process has a huge price. In a nuclear age it's something that has to be used sparingly. We were all very mindful of the fact that there was an opportunity for the negotiations with the Soviet Union. We were mindful that if an impeachment process was started, that opportunity would be lost. We were mindful that this country would have been paralyzed" (Arthur Liman, speech of March 1, 1988, reprinted in *New York Times Magazine,* April 29, 1990, 64). His remarks of course prove nothing about the origins of the Iran-Contra crisis. But they show that détente was very much a factor in determining that crisis's relatively benign and anti-climactic outcome.

15. See Chapter 4.

16. Wise, *Molehunt,* 177 (Harriman); Kutler, *The Wars of Watergate,* 457 (Kissinger).

17. Kutler, *The Wars of Watergate,* 457.

18. Gentry, *Hoover,* 748n.

19. FBI airtel 62-109060-4758 (dynamite). Cf. *Covert Action Information Bulletin,* Summer 1992, 55; Wyden, *The Bay of Pigs,* 111.

20. Roger Morris, Foreword, in Colodny and Gettlin, *Silent Coup,* xiii (coup); cf. Colodny and Gettlin, ibid., 11, 30, 56–59 (Vietnam, espionage), 367–69, 414–25 (resignation).

21. Roger Morris, *Haig: The General's Progress* (New York: Playboy Press, 1982), 61–63; Colodny and Gettlin, *Silent Coup,* 88.

22. Colodny and Gettlin, *Silent Coup,* 323; Hinckle and Turner, *The Fish Is Red,* 342.

23. H. R. Haldeman (with Joseph DiMona), *The Ends of Power* (New York: Times Books, 1978), 109 ss; Hougan, *Secret Agenda,* 58–59. Elsewhere, Hougan lists a number of CIA lawyers who served as counsel for witnesses denouncing Nixon, such as Magruder and Dean (240n). Magruder's counsel, James Bierbower, had earlier served as vice-president of Southern Air Transport, the CIA proprietary airline that in the 1980s would play a key Contra-

support role with the Cuban exiles Felix Rodriguez and Luis Posada at Ilo-
pango Air Force Base in El Salvador. Drug allegations involving this airline
were never pursued.

24. Joe Trento, Wilmington, Del. *News-Journal,* January 10, 1981, as
quoted in Hinckle and Turner, *The Fish Is Red,* 342. According to Hinckle and
Turner, Haig's role "was confirmed by Ricardo Canette [i.e., Canete], a founder
of the violent Cuban Nationalist Movement who turned government witness.
'Haig kept promising us things. We kept pressing the government,' Canette
said. 'One of the ways they satisfied us was by giving us a role in the support
teams to hit Castro. We were allowed to participate in the shipment of weapons
in March 1964 into Cuba for a hit.' "

25. Hougan, *Secret Agenda,* 17–22.

26. Ibid., 306–11; see Chapter 14.

27. Kutler, *The Wars of Watergate,* 250–51.

28. Colodny and Gettlin, *Silent Coup,* 236.

29. Churchill and Vander Wall, *Agents of Repression,* 396; Maria Laurino,
Village Voice, February 26, 1985, reprinted in David Gallen, ed., *Malcolm X As
They Knew Him* (New York: Carroll and Graf, 1992), 251–56. Roberts was
revealed after he testified for the government in 1970 as an agent who had in-
filtrated the Black Panthers and helped to found their New York chapter.

30. Gentry, *Hoover,* 606; quoting House Committee on Assassinations,
Martin Luther King, 6 AH 107; *San Francisco Examiner,* October 10, 1976.
For the FBI and the King murder, see Melanson, *The Murkin Conspiracy.*

31. Schlesinger, *Robert Kennedy,* 867. Schlesinger, who heard this from Sullivan, cites similar remarks from military and CIA personnel.

32. Melanson, *The Robert F. Kennedy Assassination,* 154–60 ("did not remember"), 290–99 ("federal intelligence files"). Melanson's conclusion is that
"Sirhan Sirhan seems clearly to have been in federal intelligence files *before* the
assassination" (291, emphasis in original). His presence in army-intelligence
files is recorded in the LAPD Chronology of the case. Federal intelligence on
Sirhan was almost certainly received from Sirhan's classmate at Pasadena City
College, William T. Divale, an FBI informant and left-wing penetration agent
since 1965.

33. Melanson, *The Robert F. Kennedy Assassination,* 287–89 (Pena/CIA);
Congressional Record, December 10, 1963, 24044, reprinting *Christian Science
Monitor,* October 29, 1963 (Pena/Dodd/firearms).

34. Daniel Yergin, *Shattered Peace* (Boston: Houghton Mifflin, 1977),
401–02.

35. Gentry, *Hoover,* 500–509; Schlesinger, *Robert Kennedy,* 384–85.

36. Gentry, *Hoover,* 621. O'Neal had given the Chicago police a floor plan
of the apartment, including a sketch of where Fred Hampton slept (Zinn, *People's History,* 455; Churchill and Vander Wall, *Agents of Repression,* 64–77.
Four days later, a similar raid, with a similar floor plan from a similar FBI informant, was conducted in Los Angeles. Bullets were fired into the bed of the
main target, Geronimo Pratt, but no one was killed. Pratt, a Vietnam veteran

with back injuries, was sleeping on the floor (Churchill and Vander Wall, ibid., 82–84).

37. Churchill and Vander Wall, *Agents of Repression*, 66, 398. Groth's training program may have been the same as that of Manuel Pena from the LAPD: Victor Marchetti has said that while he was in the CIA he became aware of CIA training at Langley for policemen from two cities—Chicago and Los Angeles (Melanson, *The Robert F. Kennedy Assassination*, 290). For Bolden's allegations, see Russell, *The Man Who Knew Too Much*, 635.

38. Gentry, *Hoover,* 622; Churchill and Vander Wall, *Agents of Repression,* 42–44, 80, etc.

39. Frank Donner, *The Age of Surveillance: The Aims and Methods of America's Political Intelligence System* (New York: Alfred A. Knopf, 1960), 223.

40. Churchill and Vander Wall, *Agents of Repression,* 366–70 (Puerto Rico); 181–349 (AIM).

41. Ibid., 76–77, 149, 164–68, 465.

42. Ibid., 81–82, 370, 465.

43. Gentry, *Hoover,* 756–57.

44. Churchill and Vander Wall, *Agents of Repression,* 77.

45. By statute, of course, Hoover would normally have been retired in 1964, on his seventieth birthday.

46. Gentry, *Hoover,* 435–37.

47. The interested reader can check the names in the index to this book against the names indexed in, for example, *Inside Job,* or any other detailed book on the savings-and-loan debacle.

Bibliography

GOVERNMENT DOCUMENTS

AGVA Hearings: U.S. Cong., Senate, Committee on Government Operations, *American Guild of Variety Artists, Hearings,* 87th Cong., 1st Sess. (Washington: GPO, 1963).

Assassination Hearings: U.S. Cong., House, Select Committee on Assassinations, *Investigation of the Assassination of President John F. Kennedy, Hearings,* 95th Cong., 2nd Sess. (Washington: GPO, 1979).

Assassination Report: U.S. Cong., House, Select Committee on Assassinations, *Investigation of the Assassination of President John F. Kennedy, Report,* 95th Cong., 2nd Sess., House Report No. 95–1828, Part 2 (Washington: GPO, 1979).

Baker Hearings: U.S. Cong., Senate, Committee on Rules, *Financial or Business Interests of Officers or Employees of the Senate, Hearings,* 88th Cong., 2nd Sess. (Washington: GPO, 1964).

Church Committee Assassination Report: U.S. Cong., Senate, Select Committee to Study Governmental Operations with Respect to Intelligence Activities, *Alleged Assassination Plots Involving Foreign Leaders; Interim Report,* 94th Cong., 1st Sess., Senate Report No. 94–465 (Washington: G.P.O., 1975).

Church Committee Report: U.S. Cong., Senate, Select Committee to Study Governmental Operations with Respect to Intelligence Activities, *Final Report,* 94th Cong., 2nd Sess., Senate Report No. 94–755 (Washington: G.P.O., 1976).

Cold War Against Communism Hearings: U.S. Cong., House, Committee on Un-American Activities, *Cold War Against Communism, Hearings,* 87th Cong., 2nd Sess. (Washington: GPO, 1962).

Dodd Hearings: U.S. Cong., Senate, Committee on the Judiciary, *Juvenile Delinquency, Part 15: Interstate Traffic in Mail-Order Firearms, Hearings,* 88th Cong., 2nd Sess. (Washington: GPO, 1964).

Federal Data Banks Hearings: U.S. Cong., Senate, Committee on the Judiciary, *Federal Data Banks, Computers, and the Bill of Rights, Hearings,* 92nd Cong., 1st Sess. (Washington: GPO, 1971).

Investigation of Senator Dodd Hearing: U.S. Cong., Senate, Select Committee on Standards and Conduct, *Investigation of Senator Thomas J. Dodd, Hearing,* 89th Cong., 2nd Sess., and 90th Cong., 1st Sess. (Washington: GPO, 1966–67).

Kefauver Hearings: U.S. Cong., Senate, Special Committee to Investigate Organized Crime in Interstate Commerce, *Investigation of Organized Crime in Interstate Commerce, Hearings,* 81st Cong., 2nd Sess., and 82nd Cong., 1st Sess. (Washington: GPO, 1950–51).

Labor Insurance Hearings: U.S. Cong., Senate, Committee on Governmental Affairs, *Labor Union Insurance, Hearings,* 95th Cong., 2nd Sess., 96th Cong., 1st Sess. (Washington: GPO, 1978–80).

McClellan Committee Hearings: U.S. Congress, Senate, Select Committee on Improper Activities in the Labor or Management Field, *Hearings,* 85th Cong., 2nd Sess. (Washington: GPO, 1959).

Murder International Hearing: U.S. Cong., Senate, Committee on the Judiciary, *Murder International Incorporated, Hearing,* 89th Cong., 1st Sess. (Washington: GPO, 1965).

Narcotics Hearings: U.S. Congress, Senate, Committee on Government Operations, *Organized Crime and Illicit Traffic in Narcotics, Hearings,* 88th Cong., 2nd Sess. (Washington: GPO, 1964).

Nedzi Hearing: U.S. Cong., House, Committee on Armed Services, *Inquiry into the Alleged Involvement of the Central Intelligence Agency in the Watergate and Ellsberg Matters, Hearings,* 94th Cong., 1st Sess. (Washington: GPO, 1975).

Parole Board Hearings: U.S. Cong., House, Committee on Government Operations, *Investigation as to Manner in which Board of Parole Is Operating and as to Whether There Is Necessity for Change in Either Procedure or Basic Law, Hearings,* 80th Cong., 2nd Sess.

Penn Central Failure Report: U.S. Cong., House, Committee on Banking and Currency, *The Penn Central Failure and the Role of Financial Institutions,* Staff Report, 91st Cong., 2nd Sess., December 21, 1970.

The Pentagon Papers: As Published by the New York Times, *Based on the Investigative Reporting of Neil Sheehan.* New York: Bantam, 1971.

The Pentagon Papers: The Senator Gravel Edition. Boston: Beacon Press, 1971.

Racing Hearings: U.S. Cong., House, Select Committee on Crime, *Organized Crime in Sports (Racing), Hearings,* 92nd Cong., 2nd Sess. (Washington: GPO, 1973).

Ronstadt Report: U.S. Cong., House, Committee on Un-American Activities, *Annual Report for the Year 1962,* House Report No. 176, 88th Cong., 1st Sess. (Washington: GPO, 1963). 79–81.

Schweiker-Hart Report: U.S. Cong., Senate, Select Committee to Study Governmental Operations with Respect to Intelligence Activities, *Final Report, Book Five, The Investigation of the Assassination of President John F. Kennedy: Performance of the Intelligence Agencies*, 94th Cong., 2nd Sess., Senate Report No. 94-755 (Washington: G.P.O., 1976).

Stadium Hearings: U.S. Cong., Senate, Committee on Rules, *Construction of the District of Columbia Stadium, Hearings*, 88th Cong., 2nd Sess. (Washington: GPO, 1964).

Stolen Securities Hearings: U.S. Cong., Senate, Committee on Government Operations, *Organized Crime: Stolen Securities, Hearings*, 92nd Cong., 1st Sess. (Washington: GPO, 1971).

TFX Contract Hearings: U.S. Cong., Senate, Committee on Government Operations, *TFX Contract Investigation, Hearings*, 88th Cong., 1st Sess. (Washington: GPO, 1963).

Warren Commission Hearings: President's Commission on the Assassination of President John F. Kennedy, *Hearings* (Washington: GPO, 1964).

Warren Report: President's Commission on the Assassination of President John F. Kennedy, *Report* (Washington: GPO, 1964).

Watergate Hearings: U.S. Cong., Senate, Select Committee on Presidential Campaign Activities, *Hearings*, 93rd Cong., 2nd Sess. (Washington: GPO, 1974).

BOOKS AND ARTICLES

Aarons, Mark, and John Loftus. *Unholy Trinity*. New York: St. Martin's, 1991.

Adams, James Ring, and Douglas Frantz. *A Full Service Bank*. New York: Pocket Books, 1992.

Adler, Renata. "Searching for the Real Nixon Scandal." *Atlantic Monthly*, December 1976.

Anderson, Jack. *Washington Exposé*. Washington: Public Affairs Press, 1967.

Anson, Robert Sam. *"They've Killed the President!" The Search for the Murderers of John F. Kennedy*. New York: Bantam, 1975.

Artioli, Lamberto. *Sport e Mafia*. Milan: V. Bompiani, 1968.

Ayers, Bradley. *The War That Never Was*. New York: Bobbs-Merrill, 1976.

Baker, Bobby, with Larry L. King. *Wheeling and Dealing*. New York: Norton, 1978.

Barlett, Donald L., and James B. Steele. *America: What Went Wrong?* Kansas City: Andrews and McMeel, 1992.

Beaty, Jonathan, and S. C. Gwynne. *The Outlaw Bank: A Wild Ride into the Secret Heart of BCCI*. New York: Random House, 1993.

Belli, Melvin M. *Dallas Justice: The Real Story of Jack Ruby and His Trial*. New York: David McKay, 1964.

Bernstein, Carl. "The CIA and the Media." *Rolling Stone*, October 20, 1977.

Beschloss, Michael R. *The Crisis Years*. New York: Edward Burlingame Books, 1991.

Blachman, Morris J., William M. LeoGrande, and Kenneth E. Sharpe, eds. *Confronting Revolution: Security Through Diplomacy in Central America.* New York: Pantheon, 1986.

Blakey, G. Robert, and Richard N. Billings. *The Plot to Kill the President.* New York: NYT Books, 1981.

Block, Alan A. *East Side–West Side: Organizing Crime in New York, 1930–1950.* New Brunswick, N.J.: Transaction Books, 1983.

————*Perspectives on Organizing Crime.* Dordrecht: Kluwer Academic Publishers, 1991.

Block, Alan A., and John McWilliams. "On the Origins of American Counterintelligence: Building a Clandestine Network." *Journal of Policy History,* 1989.

Blumenthal, Ralph. *Last Days of the Sicilians.* New York: Pocketbooks, 1989.

Bradlee, Benjamin. *Conversations With Kennedy.* New York: Norton, 1975.

Brashler, William. *The Don: The Life and Death of Sam Giancana.* New York: Harper and Row, 1977.

Brewton, Pete. *The Mafia, CIA, and George Bush.* New York: S.P.I. Books, 1992.

Brown, Robert K., and Miguel Acoca. "The Bayo-Pawley Affair." *Soldier of Fortune,* February 1976.

Browning, Frank, and John Gerassi. *The American Way of Crime.* New York: Putnam's, 1980.

Campbell, Rodney. *The Luciano Project.* New York: McGraw-Hill, 1977.

Chandler, David Leon. *Brothers in Blood.* New York: Dutton, 1975.

Charbonneau, Jean-Pierre. *The Canadian Connection.* Ottawa: Optimum, 1976.

Churchill, Ward, and Jim Vander Wall. *Agents of Repression: The FBI's Secret Wars against the Black Panther Party and the American Indian Movement.* Boston: South End Press, 1988.

Cockburn, Andrew, and Leslie Cockburn. *Dangerous Liaison.* New York: Harper Collins, 1991.

Colodny, Len, and Robert Gettlin. *Silent Coup: The Removal of a President.* New York: St. Martin's, 1991.

Cook, Fred J. *The FBI Nobody Knows.* New York: Macmillan, 1964.

————"The Hoffa Trial." *Nation,* April 27, 1964.

Cookridge, E. H. *Gehlen: Spy of the Century.* New York: Random House, 1971.

Copeland, Miles. *Beyond Cloak and Dagger: Inside the CIA.* New York: Pinnacle Books, 1975.

Corson, William. *The Armies of Ignorance.* New York: Dial Press/James Wade Books, 1977.

Cressey, Donald R. *Theft of a Nation.* New York: Harper and Row, 1969.

Crimaldi, Charles, as told to John Kidner. *Crimaldi: Contract Killer.* Washington: Acropolis Books, 1976.

Cumings, Bruce. *The Origins of the Korean War.* Princeton: Princeton University Press, 1990.

Daughen, Joseph R., and Peter Binzen. *The Wreck of the Penn Central.* New York: Signet, 1971.

Davis, John H. *The Kennedys.* New York: McGraw-Hill, 1985.

——*Mafia Kingfish.* New York: New American Library, 1989.

Demaris, Ovid. *Captive City.* New York: Pocket Books, 1970.

Diamond, Sander A. *The Nazi Movement in the United States: 1924–41.* Ithaca, N.Y.: Cornell University Press, 1974.

Dickey, Christopher. *With the Contras.* New York: Simon and Schuster, 1985.

Diederich, Bernard. *Somoza.* New York: Dutton, 1981.

Domhoff, G. William. "Who Made American Foreign Policy, 1945–1963?" In David Horowitz, ed., *Corporations and the Cold War.* New York: Monthly review Press, 1969.

Dorman, Michael. *Payoff: The Role of Organized Crime in American Politics.* New York: David McKay, 1972.

Draper, Theodore. *A Very Thin Line.* New York: Hill and Wang, 1991.

Dubois, Jules. *Freedom Is My Beat.* Indianapolis: Bobbs-Merrill, 1959.

Eisenberg, Dennis, et al. *Meyer Lansky: Mogul of the Mob.* New York: Paddington Press, 1979.

Epstein, Edward Jay. *Agency of Fear.* New York: Putnam's, 1977.

——*Legend: The Secret World of Lee Harvey Oswald.* New York: Reader's Digest Press/McGraw-Hill, 1978.

Faenza, Roberto, and Marco Fini. *Gli Americani in Italia.* Milan: Feltrinelli, 1976.

Faith, Nicholas. *Safety in Numbers.* New York: Viking, 1982.

Fox, Stephen. *Blood and Power.* New York: William Morrow, 1989.

Galante, Pierre. *The Marseilles Mafia.* London: W. H. Allen, 1979.

Gallen, David, ed. *Malcolm X As They Knew Him.* New York: Carroll and Graf, 1992.

Garthoff, Raymond L. *Détente and Confrontation: American-Soviet Relations from Nixon to Reagan.* Washington: Brookings Institution, 1985.

Gentry, Curt. *J. Edgar Hoover: The Man and the Secrets.* New York: Penguin, 1991.

Hair, William Ivy. *The Kingfish and His Realm.* Baton Rouge: Louisiana State University Press, 1991.

Haldeman, H. R., with Joseph DiMona. *The Ends of Power.* New York: Times Books, 1978.

Helbrant, Maurice. *Narcotics Agent.* New York: Vanguard, 1941.

Hennelly, Robert, and Jerry Policoff. "JFK: How the Media Assassinated the Real Story." *Village Voice,* March 31, 1992.

Hersh, Burton. *The Old Boys: The American Elite and the Origins of the CIA.* New York: Scribner's, 1992.

Hinckle, Warren, and William W. Turner. *The Fish Is Red.* New York: Harper and Row, 1981.

Hoch, Paul L. "CIA Activities and the Warren Commission Investigation." In Scott, Hoch, and Stetler, *The Assassinations.*

Hougan, Jim. *Secret Agenda.* New York: Random House, 1984.

Houghton, Robert. *Special Unit Senator.* New York: Random House, 1970.

Hurt, Harry, III. *Texas Rich.* New York: Norton, 1981.

Hurt, Henry. *Reasonable Doubt.* New York: Holt, Rinehart and Winston, 1985.

James, Ralph, and Estelle James. *Hoffa and the Teamsters.* Princeton, N.J.: Van Nostrand, 1965.

Jaubert, Alain. *Dossier D comme Drogue.* Paris: Alain Moreau, 1974.

Jonas, Susanne. *The Battle for Guatemala.* Boulder: Westview, 1992.

Jonas, Susanne, and David Tobis. *Guatemala.* New York: NACLA, 1974.

Jones, J. Harry, Jr. *Private Army.* New York: Collier Books, 1969.

Jones, Penn. *Forgive My Grief.* Midlothian, Tex.: Midlothian Mirror, n.d. [1966].

Kahin, George M. *Intervention: How America Became Involved in Vietnam.* New York: Alfred A. Knopf, 1986.

Kantor, Seth. *The Ruby Cover-Up.* New York: Zebra, 1992.

Kaplan, David E., and Alec Dubro. *Yakuza.* New York: Macmillan, 1986.

Karnes, Thomas. *Tropical Enterprise.* Baton Rouge: Louisiana State University Press, 1978.

Karnow, Stanley. *Vietnam: A History.* New York: Viking, 1983.

Kempe, Frederick. *Divorcing the Dictator.* New York: Putnam, 1990.

Kennedy, Robert. *The Enemy Within.* New York: Popular Library, 1960.

King, Rufus. *Gambling and Organized Crime.* Washington: Public Affairs Press, 1969.

Kolko, Gabriel. *The Roots of American Foreign Policy.* Boston: Beacon, 1969.

Kuhn, Thomas S. *The Structure of Scientific Revolutions.* Chicago: University of Chicago Press, 1970.

Kutler, Stanley I. *The Wars of Watergate.* New York: Norton, 1990.

Kwitny, Jonathan. *The Crimes of Patriots.* New York: Norton, 1987.

Lait, Jack, and Lee Mortimer. *Chicago: Confidential!* New York: Crown, 1950.

Laurent, Frédéric. *L'Orchestre noir.* Paris: Stock, 1978.

Lee, Martin, and Norman Solomon. *Unreliable Sources.* New York: Carol Group, 1990.

Lifton, David. *Best Evidence.* New York: Macmillan, 1980.

——, ed. *Document Addendum to the Warren Report: Three Documents from the Files of the Warren Commission.* El Segundo, Calif.: Sightext Publications, 1968.

Linklater, Magnus, et al. *The Nazi Legacy.* New York: Holt, Rinehart, and Winston, 1984.

Livingstone, Harrison. *High Treason 2.* New York: Carroll and Graf, 1992.

Maas, Peter. *The Valachi Papers.* New York: Bantam, 1969.

McCann, Thomas P. *An American Company: The Tragedy of United Fruit.* New York: Crown, 1976.

McCord, James. *A Piece of Tape.* Rockville, Md.: Washington Media Services, 1974.

McCoy, Alfred W. *The Politics of Heroin.* New York, Lawrence Hill Books, 1991.

McDonald, Hugh C., as told to Geoffrey Bocca. *Appointment in Dallas.* New York: Zebra, 1975.

McMillan, Priscilla. *Marina and Lee.* New York: Harper and Row, 1977.

Malone, William Scott. "The Secret Life of Jack Ruby." *New Times,* January 23, 1978.

Manchester, William. *The Death of a President.* New York: Harper and Row, 1967.

Mangold, Tom. *Cold Warrior: James Jesus Angleton: The CIA's Master Spy Hunter.* New York: Simon and Schuster, 1992.

Marrs, Jim. *Crossfire: The Plot That Killed Kennedy.* New York: Carroll and Graf, 1989.

Marshall, Jonathan, Peter Dale Scott, and Jane Hunter. *The Iran-Contra Connection: Secret Teams and Covert Operations in the Reagan Era.* Boston: South End Press, 1987.

Martin, David. *Wilderness of Mirrors.* New York: Harper and Row, 1980.

Meagher, Sylvia. *Accessories After the Fact.* New York: Random House, 1975.

Melanson, Philip H. *The Murkin Conspiracy.* New York: Praeger, 1989.

——*The Robert F. Kennedy Assassination.* New York: Shapolsky, 1991.

——*Spy Saga: Lee Harvey Oswald and U.S. Intelligence.* New York: Praeger, 1990.

Messick, Hank. *John Edgar Hoover.* New York: David Mackay, 1972.

——*Lansky.* New York: Putnam's, 1971.

Mills, Gary, and Ovid Demaris. *Jack Ruby.* New American Library, 1968.

Mills, James. *Underground Empire.* Garden City, N.Y.: Doubleday, 1986.

Moldea, Dan E. *Dark Victory: Ronald Reagan, MCA, and the Mob.* New York: Viking, 1986.

——*The Hoffa Wars.* New York: Paddington Press, 1978.

——*Interference: How Organized Crime Influences Professional Football.* New York: Morrow, 1989.

Mollenhoff, Clark. *Strike Force.* Englewood Cliffs, N.J.: Prentice-Hall, 1972.

——*Tentacles of Power: The Story of Jimmy Hoffa.* Cleveland: World Publishing, 1965.

Morris, Roger. *Haig: The General's Progress.* New York: Playboy Press, 1982.

Moses, Tai. "The Cult of Conspiracy." Santa Cruz *Sun,* January 26, 1989.

Navasky, Victor. *Kennedy Justice.* New York: Atheneum, 1971.

Naylor, R. T. *Hot Money and the Politics of Debt.* New York: Simon and Schuster, 1987.

Nelli, Humbert. *The Business of Crime.* New York: Oxford University Press, 1976.

Newman, John M. *JFK and Vietnam.* New York: Warner Books, 1992.

Newsday. *Heroin Trail.* New York: New American Library, 1974.

Nixon, Richard. *Six Crises.* New York: Pocketbooks, 1962.

North, Mark. *Act of Treason.* New York: Carroll and Graf, 1992.

Noyes, Peter. *Legacy of Doubt.* New York: Pinnacle Books, 1973.

O'Donnell, Kenneth. *Johnny, We Hardly Knew Ye.* Boston: Little Brown, 1970.

O'Hehir, Andrew. "JFK: Tragedy Into Farce." *San Francisco Weekly*, December 18, 1991.

Oswald, Robert. *Lee*. New York: Coward-McCann, 1967.

O'Toole, George. *The Private Sector*. New York: Norton, 1978.

Parry, Robert, and Peter Kornbluh. "Iran-Contra's Untold Story." *Foreign Policy*, Fall 1988.

Pearson, Drew. *Diaries 1949–1959*. New York: Holt, Rinehart, and Winston, 1974.

Peckenham, Nancy, and Annie Street, eds. *Honduras: Portrait of a Captive Nation*. New York: Praeger, 1985.

Penn, Stanley. "On the Waterfront." In Nicholas Gage, ed., *Mafia: U.S.A*. New York: Dell, 1972.

Phillips, David. *The Night Watch*. New York: Atheneum, 1977.

Pizzo, Steve, Mary Fricker, and Paul Muolo. *Inside Job*. New York: McGraw-Hill, 1989.

Powers, Richard. *Secrecy and Power*. New York: Free Press, 1987.

Powers, Thomas. *The Man Who Kept the Secrets*. New York: Knopf, 1979.

Prados, John. *The President's Secret Wars*. New York: Morrow, 1986.

Prouty, L. Fletcher. *The Secret Team*. Englewood Cliffs, N.J.: Prentice-Hall, 1973.

Radosh, Ronald, and Joyce Milton. *The Rosenberg File*. New York: Holt, Rinehart, and Winston, 1983.

Ranelagh, John. *The Agency: The Rise and Decline of the CIA*. New York: Simon and Schuster, 1986.

Rappleye, Charles, and Ed Becker. *All-American Mafioso: The Johnny Rosselli Story*. New York: Doubleday, 1991.

Reid, Ed. *The Grim Reapers*. New York: Bantam, 1970.

Reid, Ed, and Ovid Demaris. *The Green Felt Jungle*. New York: Pocket Books, 1964.

Richards, Guy. "Russia's School for Assassins—and the Oswald Case," *New York Journal-American*, January 11, 1964.

Russell, Dick. *The Man Who Knew Too Much*. New York: Carroll and Graf, 1992.

Rust, William J. *Kennedy in Vietnam*. New York: Scribner's, 1985.

Sale, Kirkpatrick. *Power Shift*. New York: Random House, 1975.

Scheim, David. *Contract on America: The Mafia Murder of President John F. Kennedy*. New York: Zebra, 1989.

Schlesinger, Arthur M., Jr. *Robert Kennedy and His Times*. New York: Ballantine Books, 1978.

Schurmann, Franz. *The Logic of World Power*. New York: Pantheon, 1974.

Scott, Peter Dale. "The Kennedy Assassination Cover-Up." *Inquiry* II, May 14, 1979.

———"Transnationalised Repression." *Lobster*. Hull, England, 1986.

———"Vietnamization and the Drama of the Pentagon Papers." In *The Pentagon Papers*. Gravel edition. Boston: Beacon, 1972.

————"The Vietnam War and the CIA–Financial Establishment." In Mark Selden, ed. *Remaking Asia*. New York: Pantheon, 1974.

————*The War Conspiracy: The Secret Road to the Second Indochina War*. New York: Bobbs Merrill, 1972.

————Foreword. In Henrik Krueger, *The Great Heroin Coup*. Boston: South End Press, 1981.

Scott, Peter Dale, and Jonathan Marshall. *Cocaine Politics: Drugs, Armies, and the CIA in Central America*. Berkeley and Los Angeles: University of California Press, 1991.

Scott, Peter Dale, Paul L. Hoch, and Russell Stetler. *The Assassinations: Dallas and Beyond—A Guide to Cover-Ups and Assassinations*. New York: Random House, 1976.

Seagrave, Sterling. *The Marcos Dynasty*. New York: Harper and Row, 1988.

Selden, Mark, ed. *Remaking Asia*. New York: Pantheon, 1974.

Servadio, Gaia. *Mafioso*. New York: Dell, 1976.

Shannon, Elaine. *Desperados*. New York: Viking, 1988.

Shepherd, Philip L. "Honduras." In Morris J. Blachman et al., *Confronting Revolution: Security through Diplomacy in Central America*. New York: Pantheon, 1986.

Sheridan, Walter. *The Fall and Rise of Jimmy Hoffa*. New York: Saturday Review Press, 1972.

Smith, Dwight C., Jr. *The Mafia Mystique*. New York: Basic Books, 1975.

Smith, R. Harris. *OSS*. Berkeley and Los Angeles: University of California Press, 1972.

Steinberg, Alfred. *Sam Johnson's Boy*. New York: Macmillan, 1968.

Stevenson, William. *Intrepid's Last Case*. New York: Villard Books/Random House, 1983.

Stone, Oliver, and Zachary Sklar. *JFK: The Book of the Film*. New York: Applause Books, 1992.

Summers, Anthony. *Conspiracy*. New York: McGraw-Hill, 1981.

————*Goddess: The Secret Lives of Marilyn Monroe*. New York: Macmillan, 1985.

————*Official and Confidential: The Secret Life of J. Edgar Hoover*. New York: Putnam, 1993.

Summers, Anthony, and Steven Dorril. *Honeytrap*. London: Hodder and Stoughton, 1988.

Theoharis, Athan G., and John Stuart Cox. *The Boss: J. Edgar Hoover and the Great American Inquisition*. Philadelphia: Temple University Press, 1988.

Thomas, Hugh. *Cuba*. New York: Harper and Row, 1971.

Thompson, Josiah. *Six Seconds in Dallas*. New York: B. Geis/Random House, 1967.

Toledano, Ralph de. *RFK: The Man Who Would Be President*. New York: Putnam, 1967.

Trento, Susan. *The Power House: Robert Keith Gray and the Selling of Access and Influence in Washington*. New York: St. Martin's, 1992.

Turner, William W. *Hoover's FBI*. Los Angeles: Sherbourne Press, 1970.

————*The Police Establishment*. New York: Putnam's, 1968.

————*Power on the Right*. Berkeley: Ramparts Press, 1971.

Tyler, Gus. *Organized Crime in America: A Book of Readings*. Ann Arbor: University of Michigan, 1967.

Vankin, Jonathan. *Conspiracies, Cover-Ups, and Crimes: Political Manipulation and Mind Control in America*. New York: Paragon House, 1991.

Walker, William O., III. *Drug Control in the Americas*. Albuquerque: University of New Mexico Press, 1989.

Weisberg, Harold. *Oswald in New Orleans*. New York: Canyon Books, 1967.

Wessel, Milton. "How We Bagged the Mafia." *Saturday Evening Post,* July 16, July 23, 1960.

Williams, T. Harry. *Huey Long*. New York: Bantam, 1969.

Wise, David. *Molehunt*. New York: Random House, 1992.

Wofford, Harris. *Of Kennedy and Kings*. New York: Farrar Straus Giroux, 1980.

Woodward, Ralph Lee, Jr. *Central America: A Nation Divided*. New York: Oxford University Press, 1985.

Wyden, Peter. *The Bay of Pigs*. New York: Simon and Schuster, 1979.

Yergin, Daniel. *Shattered Peace*. Boston: Houghton Mifflin, 1977.

Zinn, Howard. *People's History of the United States*. New York: Harper and Row, 1980.

Index

Abwehr (German espionage service), 213
Accardo, Tony, 208
Acheson, Dean, 223, 364
Adamcik, Detective John, 276
Aerospace industry, 20, 34, 155, 179, 220, 245
Afghanistan, 9, 168
AFL (American Federation of Labor), 173, 176, 186, 195; Free Trade Union Committee, 195
AGVA (American Guild of Variety Artists), 232–33, 356, 366
Air Force, U.S., 30–31, 37, 96–97, 216, 275
Alba, Adrian, 248–50
Alch, Gerald, 236
Alcohol, Tobacco, and Firearms Unit of U.S. Treasury (ATF), 224, 246, 249, 250, 254–57, 272, 292, 371
Alexander, William F., 60, 70, 134, 233, 270, 273
Alliance for Progress, 93
Alpha 66, 114, 115, 119, 251, 254–57, 305, 371; and army intelligence, 115, 255, 257, 371; and JGCE, 371; and Oswald, 254–57, 371; and Time-Life, 115
Alvarado, Gilberto ("D"), 91, 95, 121–24, 222, 300, 301, 341
Ambrose, Myles, 81
American Civil Liberties Union (ACLU), 277

American Committee to Free Cuba, 265, 373
American G.I. Forum, 246
American Indian Movement (AIM), 309
American Jewish League Against Communism, 146, 211
American Legion, 244, 245
American National Insurance Co., 204
American Protective League, 244
American Security Council (ASC), 34, 55, 215, 216, 245, 292, 357
American Society for Industrial Security, 277
AMGOT (Allied Military Government), 8
AMLASH. See Cubela, Rolando Secades
Anastasia, Albert, 203, 204
Anderson, Clark, 121
Anderson, Jack, 77, 116, 172, 228, 231, 236, 237, 364
Anderson, Lambert, 64
Andrade, C. Dick, 206
Angleton, James Jesus, 39, 40, 44, 47, 54, 66, 67, 87, 124, 173, 174, 177, 194, 195, 196, 201, 229, 235, 236, 304, 324; and Allen Dulles, 54, 67; and FBI, 44, 47, 54, 66, 67, 124, 320; and seizure of evidence, 44, 196, 309, 320
Annenberg, Max, 158
Annenberg, Moe, 60, 154–56, 158, 159, 179, 192
Annenberg, Walter, 155

Anslinger, Harry J., 144, 150, 165, 167, 193, 345
Anti-Castro activities, 79, 88–90, 111–13, 115–18, 124, 215–16, 244, 251, 254, 255, 265, 266, 306, 380; "track two" (irregular ops), 112. *See also* CIA-Mafia plots against Castro; Cuban exiles; ZR/RIFLE plots to kill Castro
Anti-Communist Legion (or League) of the Caribbean, 88
Anti-desegregation movement, 49–50, 195, 207, 214, 263–66, 268, 289, 292, 304; Ole Miss riots, 50, 293
Antinori family, 141
Apalachin meeting, 65, 130, 150, 186, 200
App, Austin, 213
Araña Osorio, Carlos, 110, 111
Arbenz, Jacobo, 110, 111
Arcacha Smith, Sergio, 87, 88
Arkansas, 152
Armed Forces, U.S., 50
Army, U.S., 166, 255, 311
Army Intelligence, U.S., 9, 13, 31, 32, 78, 145, 166, 168, 169, 177, 218, 224, 237, 241, 245, 255, 257, 260, 268, 274, 276–81, 292, 307, 374, 375; and Alpha 66, 115, 255, 257, 371; and ATF, 257; and Chicago police, 278; and Dallas police, 274, 276–77, 371–72; and "A. J. Hidell" (Oswald), 258–60; in Honolulu, 31; and James Hosty, 257, 260, 274, 372; and mob, 168, 169, 178, 196; and Jack Revill, 136, 274, 276–77; and Secret Service, 279–81; and Sirhan Sirhan, 307; surveillance by, 278–81; and Time-Life, 115; and Vietnam, 31. *See also* Military Intelligence Groups (Army Intelligence)
Army Intelligence Reserve, U.S., 276
Army Reserve, U.S., 246; and Dallas police, 276
Arthur, Ed, 368
Artime, Manuel, 112
Arvey, Jacob, 77, 155, 158–60, 179, 200, 341, 349
ASA (American Security Agency), 178, 245
Association of Former (or Retired) Intelligence Officers, 217
ATF. *See* Alcohol, Tobacco, and Firearms Unit of U.S. Treasury
Atlantic City, 111
Attwood, William, 224

Austin, Richard, 158
Australia, 166
Auto theft rings, 105, 336
Ayers, Capt. Bradley, 178
Azcue, Eusebio, 43, 123

Babushka Lady, 294
Baer, Henry, 289–91
Bahamas, 98, 166, 220
Bailley, Phillip, 240
Baker, Barney (Robert B.), 143, 152, 154, 163, 165, 184, 185–87, 192–94, 349
Baker, Bobby (Robert G.), 208, 217–22, 226, 227, 230–32, 234–36, 239–41, 286
Balistrieri, Frank, 186
Banister, Guy, 80, 81, 85–90, 96, 103, 109, 188, 197, 243, 246, 247, 251, 264, 265, 327–28
Baron, Charles, 179, 199, 355
Barr, Candy (Juanita Slusher), 233, 234
Barrish, Benny, 60, 158
Bartes, Frank, 81, 91, 326–27
Bartone, Dominic, 178
Basulto Leon, José, 305
Batista, Fulgencio, 172, 178
Batista Falla, Laureano, 91, 340
Baumgardner, Fred J., 64, 65
Bay of Pigs, 110–14, 179, 225, 227, 232, 256
Bayo, Eddie (alias Perez), 114, 115
Bayo-Pawley mission, 55–56, 112, 114–17, 119, 121, 262; and John Martino, 114; and Senate Internal Security Subcommittee, 116; and Time-Life, 55–56, 115–16
BCCI (Bank of Credit and Commerce International), 166, 238, 303, 351, 354, 378
Beebe, Herman, 79, 207
Belli, Melvin, 233
Belmont, Alan, 13, 47, 64–66, 243, 304, 323
Benton, Sam, 88–89, 367
Bernstein, Carl, 55
Beschloss, Michael, 231
Billings, Richard, 55, 56, 115, 117, 128, 149, 162, 208, 339. *See also* Bayo-Pawley mission; Blakey, G. Robert
Biner (or Biener), Maureen "Mo" (Maureen Dean), 234, 239, 240
Binion, Benny, 160, 161, 206
Black, Fred, 218, 223, 235
"Black holes" (zones of missing information), 13, 14, 33, 36, 59–61, 115

Black Panther Party, 308, 309, 311
Blakey, G. Robert, 19, 68, 69, 71, 72, 77, 82, 83, 87, 91, 94, 101, 115, 128, 129, 131–35, 139, 140, 153, 154, 162, 167, 168, 170, 171, 173, 177, 179, 184–88, 194, 199, 208, 232, 233, 247, 294, 297, 324, 327, 345–48; and externalized conspiracy theory, 71, 72, 128–39 passim, 167, 170, 345, 347; and LCN crime model, 147–51, 184–87, 193
Blaustein, Bernard, 175
Block, Alan A., 149, 150, 165–67, 172, 173
Block, William, 158
BND (West German Intelligence), 213, 302
Boggs, Hale, 19, 242
Bolden, Abraham, 308
Bolivia, 9, 351
Bonanno, Joe, 175
Bonanno family, 326
Bonds, Joe (alias Joe LoCurto), 233
Boone, Eugene, 161
Booth, John Wilkes, 295
Boxing, 82, 100, 197, 205
Braden, Jim (alias Eugene Hale Brading), 143
Branigan, William, 13, 64–66, 243, 304, 323–24
Breen, James, 131
Brennan, C. D., 64, 65, 323
Bringuier, Carlos, 81, 91, 94, 119, 120, 214, 251–54, 262, 263, 326–27; and CRC, 81; and DRE, 81, 91, 119, 120, 254; and Oswald, 81, 91, 94, 119–21, 251–54, 263, 326; Oswald-Bringuier debate and tape, 81, 82, 91, 94, 120, 266, 326
Brock, Alvis (or Alvin) R., 134, 135
Brod, Mario, 174, 194, 195, 201, 353, 368
Browder, Eddie, 355
Brown, Irving, 195, 354
Brown, Judge Joe B., 233
Browne-Bioff extortion case, 158
Brownlee (or Bromlee), Morris, 370
Bruneau, Emile, 82, 83, 86, 257, 263, 327
Bruno, Angelo, 219
Buchalter, Louis "Lepke," 144, 211
Budenz, Louis, 262
Bufalino, Russell, 171, 173, 174, 353
Bufalino, William, 175, 353
Bullion, J. W., 204
Burchwell, Ashland F., 293

Burris, Col. Howard, 31, 325
Business Council, 10
Bussie, Victor, 189
Butler, Edward, 82, 94, 266, 332
Butler, Lt. George, 128, 137, 151–53, 160–62
Butterfield, Alexander, 306
Byars, Billy, 206

Caccia, Sir Harold, 229
Caesar's Palace, Las Vegas, 110
Cage, Ben Jack, 208
Cain, Richard, 330
Cain, Wofford, 202, 205, 206
Caire, Ronnie, 326
Califano, Joe, 306
California, 141
Cal-Neva Lodge, Lake Tahoe, 199
Calvillo, Manuel, 123
Campbell (or Exner), Judith, 227, 238, 235
Campisi, Joe, 129, 135, 160, 207, 208, 361
Campisi, Sam, 208
Canada, narcotics networks in, 175–77, 181
Canadian Broadcasting Corporation (CBC), 21
Canadian Husky Oil Company, 203, 204
Canavese, Pierre. See DeGeorgio, Giuseppe
Cannon, Sen. Howard, 219
Cannon (alias Canon), Jack, 178, 213
Capell, Frank, 213–16
Capri, Havana, 180, 240
Carbo, Paul "Frankie," 100, 205, 219
Cárdenas, Lázaro, 104
Carías Andino, Tiburcino, 103
Carlson, Maurice, 289, 290
Carolla (alias Carollo), Silvestro "Sam," 77, 99, 117
Carr, Waggoner, 242, 243
Carroll, Warren, 292
Carter, Jimmy, 281
Carter, Marshall "Pat," 112
Caruso, Vincent, 101
Casinos, 80, 199, 201. See also Havana casinos; Las Vegas casinos
"Castellammarese War," 149, 150
Castillo, Luís, 114, 116, 117
Castillo Armas, Carlos, 110
Castorr (alias Caster), Col. L. Robert, 118
Castro, Fidel, 34, 95, 113, 116, 178, 190, 200, 216, 218, 222, 243, 251,

Castro, Fidel (*continued*)
  264, 306. *See also* Anti-Castro activi-
  ties; CIA-Mafia plots against Castro;
  Cuba; Oswald, "phase one" ("Com-
  munist assassin") myth
Catena, Gerardo, 207, 208
CAUSA, 238
Celler, Rep. Emmanuel, 286
Cellini, Dino, 90, 179, 180, 239
Cellini, Eddie, 90, 240
Central Intelligence Agency. *See* CIA
Cesari, Jo, 176
Charles, Clemard Joseph, 78–80,
  189, 325
Chavarri, Capt. Rafael, 142
Chavez, Frank, 154
Chennault, Anna, 237
Chicago, 77, 101, 128, 141, 152–61 pas-
  sim, 164, 169, 173, 179, 183, 185,
  187, 190, 200, 201, 278; Arvey polit-
  ical machine in, 158–60; Chicago
  Crime Commission, 161; Chicago
  police, 278, 279; 24th Ward of, 77,
  158, 159
Chicago Herald-American, 158
Chicago Tribune, 158, 164, 190
China, 112, 167, 303
China Lobby (Taiwan Lobby), 34, 106,
  121, 212, 237, 288, 303, 305
Chomsky, Noam, 34–37
Christian Crusade, 34, 213, 216
Christian Defense League, 114
Church Committee, 21, 117, 168, 170,
  194, 195, 235, 251, 281
CIA (Central Intelligence Agency), 8, 11,
  18–20, 39, 41, 103, 107–27, 121,
  122, 124, 165–68, 170–78, 194–96,
  203, 204, 212, 214, 215, 217–19,
  221, 222, 224, 225, 227, 229, 275,
  280, 289, 292, 304–07, 309, 310;
  Counterintelligence, 39–40, 44, 54,
  66, 67, 87, 124, 174, 304, 309; Cuban Task Force W, 90, 91; and drug
  traffickers, 167, 168, 174, 176, 195,
  203, 204, 324; Executive Action,
  172; Inspector-General's Report on
  retaliation story, 114, 116; in Japan,
  78; in Mexico City, 39–41, 62, 67,
  105–07, 109, 121, 122, 124, 224,
  300, 301; MK-ULTRA, 165, 173;
  and police, 309, 381; and Time-Life,
  55–56, 113, 115–17; Western Hemisphere Division, 66; ZR/RIFLE plots
  to kill Castro, 90, 91, 173, 352
CIA-Mafia plots against Castro, 19–20,
  49, 90, 91, 109–17 passim, 165–68,

  170–75, 177–78, 180–81, 194–95,
  227; Inspector-General's Report on
  retaliation story, 114, 116; Martino-
  Rosselli retaliation story, 111–13,
  116–17, 170
CINCPAC (Commander-in-Chief, Pa-
  cific), 37
Civello, Joseph Francis, 65, 128–31,
  133–35, 141, 147, 161, 208, 341–42,
  361; as narcotics informant, 131, 133
Clark, Mark, 308–10
Clark, Max, 245
Clark, Richard L., 137
Clark, Atty-Gen. Tom, 155
Clemmons, J. D., 216
Clifford, Clark, 223, 364
Coca-Cola, 218
Cocaine, 73, 168, 351. *See also* Narcot-
  ics traffic
Cockburn, Alexander, 10, 11, 25, 26
Cocke, J. Bernard, 264
Cohen, Mickey, 141, 143, 157, 219, 233
COINTELPROs (FBI Counterintelli-
  gence Programs), 12, 64–65, 261,
  266, 307, 309–11, 323; against
  FPCC, 261; against Martin Luther
  King, 323, 373
Cold War, 34, 222, 226, 228, 229, 235,
  303, 307, 308
Colodny, Len, 239
Colosimo, "Big Jim," 159
Comandos L, 115
Commerce International China (CIC),
  168, 169, 177, 178
Congo (Zaire), 173, 201
Congress, U.S., 7, 194, 237, 281. *See also*
  Church Committee; House Select
  Committee on Assassinations
  (HSCA); House Un-American Activi-
  ties Committee (HUAC); Iran-Contra
  Committees; Kefauver Committee;
  McClellan Committee; Pike Commit-
  tee; Senate Internal Security Subcom-
  mittee (SISS); Watergate Committee
  (Ervin Committee)
Congressional Record, 190, 231
Congress of Freedom, Inc., 49, 50, 215
Connally, John, 3, 208
Connell, Lucille, 118, 119
Connelly, Capt. Thomas, 158, 159
Conservative Society of America, 265
Conspiracy theories, 9–11, 54, 87, 296–
  99; alien (or externalized) conspiracy
  theories, 9, 128–39 passim, 150,
  153–55, 160–62, 177, 183, 289
Constitution Party, 49, 114

Continental National Bank of Fort Worth, 220
Contragate. *See* Iran-Contra affair
Contras, 8, 111, 282; Contra support networks, 305, 335, 379–80
Cook, Fred J., 190
Cooke, Leon, 153, 164
Copacabana, Havana, 140
Copeland, Miles, 174
Coppola, Frank, 99, 174, 176, 177, 195, 353
Coppola, "Trigger Mike," 219
Corallo, Tony "Ducks," 219
Corcoran, Thomas, 223, 364
Cordell Hull Foundation, 95, 333
Corsicans, 8, 176, 177, 195
Corso, Col. Philip J., 214–16
Corson, William, 107
"Cosa Nostra, La" (LCN), 19, 68, 70, 71, 130, 132, 145–49, 151, 154, 182–84, 186, 187, 192–94, 225, 251, 346. *See also* Mafia
Costello, Frank, 97–100
Cotroni, Giuseppe, 175–77, 181, 200, 201
Cotroni, Vincent, 175–77
Council on Foreign Relations (CFR), 16
Coup d'état, 296–97
Courtney, Kent, 265
Crafard, Curtis LaVerne (Larry), 291
Crichton, Jack Alston, 276, 290
Crimaldi, Charles, 171–73, 194
Crossland, Taylor, 139, 140
Crown, Henry, 155, 179
Crusade to Free Cuba Committee, 161
Cuba, 107, 112, 113, 115–17, 178, 179, 188, 189, 200, 216, 222, 224, 275. *See also* Cuban Consulate, Mexico City; Cuban exiles; DGI (Cuban intelligence); Havana casinos
Cuba Lobby, 106, 262
Cuban Consulate, Mexico City, 43, 91, 121–23
Cuban exiles, 111, 115, 118, 213, 225, 254–57, 262, 300; Anti-Castro Cubans, 85, 118, 254; ex-CIA Cuban exiles, 7–8, 110, 302, 305, 306; CRC Cubans, 85, 95, 119. *See also* Alpha 66; Comandos L; Cuban Revolutionary Council (CRC); DRE; JGCE; JURE; MDC; SNFE; 30th of November Movement
Cuban missile crisis, 115, 229, 255
Cuban Revolutionary Council (CRC), 81, 87, 88; in Miami, 8, 90, 91; in New Orleans, 81, 87, 88, 229, 326–27

Cubela Secades, Rolando ("AMLASH"), 67, 196, 324
Curry, Eileen, 131, 342
Curry, Jesse, 136, 292
CUSA (Conservatism-USA), 292, 293
Customs, U.S., 202
Cuyamel Fruit Co., 102, 103
Czolgosz, Leon F., 292

"D." *See* Alvarado, Gilberto
Dallas Morning News, 199, 214, 292; November 22 anti-Kennedy advertisement in, 214, 292
Dallas Police Department, 131–38, 160, 162, 233, 246, 248, 270, 277; intelligence unit of (in SSB), 136, 275–77; and right wing, 160; and Jack Ruby, 131–38, 162, 276; SSB (Special Services Bureau), 160, 276, 277, 279, 288, 290, 301
d'Antoni, Blaise, 100, 332
Davidson, I. Irving, 106, 188, 189, 191, 217–22, 227, 231, 285, 300, 325
Davis, Ben, 262
Davis, John H., 91, 100, 218, 221, 222, 228
Dayle, Dennis, 167
DEA (Drug Enforcement Administration), 8, 105, 110, 167, 173, 194, 203. *See also* FBN (Federal Bureau of Narcotics)
Dealey Plaza, 45, 196, 274, 277, 292
Dean, John, 51, 234, 240
Dean, Maureen. *See* Biner, Maureen "Mo"
Dean, Patrick, 131, 133–35
Deauville, Havana, 111, 118
DeBrueys, Warren, 85, 328
Decker, Sheriff J. E. "Bill," 131, 161
Deep politics, 7, 9–12, 17–19, 97, 158, 159, 166, 298–300, 325
"Deep Throat," 304
Defense Department (DOD), 13, 25, 28, 34, 35
DeGeorgio (alias DeGeorge, DiGiorgio), Giuseppe, 180, 181, 199
De Jaegher, Raymond, 213
De John, Nick, 141, 192
Del Charro, Hotel, 202, 205–08, 211
Del Charro set, 205, 206, 233, 361
Del Mar race track, 202, 205, 207
Delhi-Taylor Oil Co, 202
DeLoach, Cartha, 45, 53, 122
DeLucia, Paul (alias Paul Ricca), 173
Demaris, Ovid, 220
Democratic National Committee (DNC), 236

Democratic party, 19, 60, 159, 185, 190, 191, 226, 278, 279; Chicago 24th Ward machine, 60, 158–60; 1968 Convention of, 278, 279; "Old Regulars" in New Orleans, 77, 334

De Mohrenschildt, George, 78–80, 189, 245, 288, 326

Denial and resistance, psychological, 13, 68, 296, 299, 304, 306, 313

De Torres, Bernardo, 105

Deutsch, Eberhard, 94

DeVoe, Jack, 79, 335

Dewey, Thomas E., 150

DFS (Dirección Federal de Seguridad, Mexican intelligence), 104, 105, 123, 124, 142, 301; and CIA, 142; and Kennedy assassination investigations, 105, 123–24; and narcotics trafficking, 142. See also Nazar Haro, Miguel

DGI (Cuban intelligence), 67, 79

Díaz Ordáz, Gustavo, 123

Díaz Verson, Salvador, 214

Dioguardi, Frank, 175, 176, 353

Dioguardi, John (alias Johnny Dio), 175, 176, 192, 353

Dirección Federal de Seguridad (Mexican intelligence). See DFS

Directorio Revolucionario Estudiantil. See DRE

Dirksen, Sen. Everett, 231

Dobriansky, Lev, 216

Dodd, Sen. Thomas, 215, 216, 249, 250, 307, 370

Dombrowski, Dr. James, 262–64

Domestic Intelligence Division (FBI Division Five), 64, 65

Domhoff, G. William, 10, 11

Dominican Republic, 88, 179

Donner, Frank, 309

Donovan, William, 166, 174, 177, 178

Dorfman, Allen, 20, 110, 191, 192, 227

Dorfman, Paul, 153, 154, 162, 164, 173, 187, 191, 192, 205, 353

Dorman, Michael, 190

Dragna, Jack, 157

Dragna, Louis Tom, 141

DRE (Directorio Revolucionario Estudiantil), 81, 86, 91, 119, 120, 214, 251, 254, 256, 262, 266, 293, 305

Drug Enforcement Administration. See DEA

Drug traffic. See Narcotics traffic

Drury, Capt. William, 158, 164, 201

Dubinsky, David, 195, 374

Duffy, LaVerne, 232

Dulles, Allen Welsh, 47, 53–55, 67, 117, 196, 242, 262, 295, 296; and James Angleton, 54, 67; and Warren Commission, 19, 55, 295

Dunn, Joseph, 244

Durán, Horacio, 123

Durán, Ruben, 123

Durán, Silvia, 123, 124

Duvalier, François "Papa Doc," 78, 79, 218

Eastland, Sen. James, 114, 116, 260, 262, 264–66

Eddowes, Michael, 229, 230

Edwards, Sheffield, 194

Egozi, José, 110

Eisenhower, Pres. Dwight D., 55, 202, 206, 214, 311

Ellsberg, Daniel, 37

Ellsworth, Frank, 255–57, 274

Enlightenment, 10, 22

Entratter, Jack, 199

Epstein, Edward Jay, 63, 86, 87

Ervin, Senator Sam J., 237, 267, 280. See also Watergate Committee

ESSO, 98, 195

Estes, Billy Sol, 363

Evans, Courtney, 46, 61, 62, 65

Eversharp, Inc., 216

Exner, Judith. See Campbell, Judith

Fair Play for Cuba Committee (FPCC), 12, 64, 81–86, 245, 258–66, 275, 309, 328

Fassoulis, Satiris "Sonny," 168, 169, 178

FBI (Federal Bureau of Investigation), 3–5, 12, 13, 18, 20, 39, 41–55, 59, 61–73, 84–89, 99, 105, 107, 108, 112–14, 117–23, 130–34, 137, 142, 144–48, 150–55, 173, 177, 181, 185, 187, 192, 193, 199–201, 205, 207, 208, 211, 215, 216, 221, 222, 224, 227–30, 232, 235, 236, 242–52, 254–62, 269, 271, 272, 276, 277, 279, 280, 284, 288–92, 295, 304, 307–11; in Dallas, 42–43, 119, 120, 130, 131, 257; Domestic Intelligence Division (Division 5) of, 64–65; and industrial security, 243–44; Inspection Division of, 63, 65; and Meyer Lansky, 144–46, 345; and leaks to media, 44, 86, 228, 261; in New Orleans, 84, 85, 87, 88, 131, 248, 249, 258–60, 262; and official murders, 307–10; and prior warning of Kennedy's murder, 49–51; and right wing, 89, 329; Security Index of, 63,

64, 373; Special Intelligence Service
(SIS), 107, 320; Special Investigative
(Organized Crime) Division of, 65,
107. *See also* COINTELPROs;
Hoover, J. Edgar
Federal Bureau of Narcotics (FBN), 71,
129, 131, 138–40, 146, 147, 150,
165–75, 177, 190, 192–95, 200, 345,
350, 352; and counterintelligence,
165–67, 350; and OSS, 165
Federation of American Citizens of
German Descent, 213
Fellers, Gen. Bonner, 214
Felt, Mark, 304
Fensterwald, Bernard, 236
Fergus, John F., 216
Fernandez, Pablo, 279
Ferrie, David W., 86–88, 188, 189, 246,
247, 257, 325, 328–29, 357, 369
Fiedler, Leslie, 295
Fiorini, Frank. *See* Sturgis, Frank
FitzGerald, Desmond, 194
FitzGerald, George S., 191
544 Camp Street, 59, 84, 85–87, 90,
109, 197, 247, 265
Flamingo Hotel, Las Vegas, 207, 344
Fogelson, E. E., 205, 206
Fong, Chung Wing, 167
Ford, Gerald, 56, 122
Foreign Intelligence Digest (FID), 213,
216, 301, 362
Fort Gulick (Panama), 122
Fort Jackson, 110
Fortas, Abraham, 221
Fox, Stephen, 147
FPCC. *See* Fair Play for Cuba Com-
mittee
Franzwald, Art, 293
Freeman, Al, 199
Freeman, Larry, 79
Free Trade Union Committee, 195
Frente Revolucionario Democratico
(FRD), 90
Freud, Sigmund, 22
Friends of Democratic Cuba, 88

Galbraith, John Kenneth, 35
Gale, Col. William P., 114, 339
Gale, James, 63, 65
Galente, Carmine, 175, 176
Gambino family, 79
Gambling, 89, 108–10, 117, 128, 131,
132, 156–60, 164, 165, 172, 200,
204–06, 208; bookmaking, 89,
128; slot machines, 98, 140, 152.
See also Casinos

Gannaway, W. P., 276
Garrison, Jim, 94, 188, 189, 264, 357
Garrison investigation, 21, 80, 87, 105,
142, 188, 191, 236, 247
Garro de Paz, Elena, 123
Garson, Greer, 205
Gates, Robert, 40
Gatlin, Maurice B., 59, 109
Gaudet, William, 82, 96, 97, 105, 340
Gehlen Organization, 213, 302
Gelb, Leslie, 25, 26, 28, 29, 35, 36
Gemberling, Robert P., 51
Gener, "Macho," 90
General Dynamics Corporation, 20, 34,
155, 179, 220, 245
General Electric Corp., 34, 195
Genovese, Vito, 8, 65, 176, 177, 207
Gentile, Nicola, 150, 151, 177, 193, 195
Gentry, Curt, 13, 88, 120, 242
George Town Club, 237, 238
German-American Bund, 159
Gervais, Pershing, 357, 369
Gettlin, Robert, 239
Gheesling, W. M., 64
Giancana, Sam, 21, 49, 114, 116, 117,
127, 160, 170–72, 185, 186, 189,
192–95, 199, 219, 222, 227, 228,
347, 361; anti-Castro activities and,
49, 114, 116, 172; and Bayo-Pawley
mission, 114; and CIA, 49, 172; and
Robert Kennedy, 192–94, 219, 227;
murder of, 21, 117, 170, 171, 194,
195, 347
Gibbons, Harold, 184
Gibson, Truman, 205
Gil, Manuel, 94
Gilbert, Keith, 143
Gill, G. Wray, 87, 88, 191, 246, 247,
357
Gobernación (Ministry of Interior):
Honduras, 104; Mexico, 105, 123,
336, 341
Goldwater, Sen. Barry, 290
Goleniewski, Michal, 215
Golitsyn, Anatoly, 196
Gopadze, Leon, 270
Gorbachev, Mikhail, 303
Gordon, Abe, 175
Gottlieb, Dr. Sidney, 172, 173
Gracchi, the, 313
Graham, Bill, 157
Granello, Salvatore, 173
Grant, Eva, 139
Gray, L. Patrick, 304
Gray, Robert Keith, 238
Gray alliances, 80, 87, 102–05, 203

Great Southwest Corporation, 206, 226, 239, 241, 283–91, 293, 294
Greenglass, David, 66
Gregory, Peter, 268–70, 272, 279, 280, 284, 286–88
Griffin, Burt, 184
Grombach, John V. "Frenchy," 212
Gross, Rep. H. R., 231
Groth, Daniel, 308, 309, 381
Gruber, Alexander, 143
Guatemala, 104, 108–11, 114, 219, 337; death squads in, 111
Guérini gang, 176, 178
Guillen Velez, José Maria, 104
Guitart, Agustin, 91, 119, 252
Guiteau, Charles J., 296
Gulfstream Hotel, 208
Gun-trafficking, 79, 179, 188–90, 293
Guthrie, Sheriff Steve, 152, 153, 161, 206
Guzik, Jacob, 152, 164, 170, 347, 355

Haig, Gen. Alexander, 205, 306, 380
Haiti, 78–80, 189, 218, 221, 325, 371; political plots in, 78–80, 325, 371
Haldeman, H. R., 306
Hall, Harry (alias Harry Haler, Haller, or Helfgott), 205, 206
Hall, Loran Eugene, 114, 116, 119, 143, 266, 339, 349, 373
Halper, Dave "Dingy," 199
Hampton, Fred, 308–10
Hanna, Rep. Richard, 237
Hannegan, Robert, 161
Hargis, Billy James, 34, 213, 215–17, 265
Harper, Richmond, 79–80, 207, 326
Harper, "Tito," 79–80, 207
Harper's, 101
Harriman, Averell, 184, 304
Hart, Sen. Gary, 44, 45
Harvard University, 8
Harvey, William King, 66, 90, 91, 107, 113, 173, 178, 194, 195
Hatfield, Robert, 292
Havana, 111, 113, 116, 117, 140, 142, 157, 179, 180, 200, 204, 218
Havana casinos, 111, 114, 140, 173, 178, 179, 198–200, 202, 204, 240. See also Capri; Copacabana; Deauville; Hotel Nacional; Sans Souci; Tropicana
Health and Welfare, Dept. of (HEW), 247
Hearst newspaper network, 53, 156, 158, 159, 230

Hecht, Rudolph, 97, 332
Hegel, Georg Wilhelm Friedrich, 22
Held, Richard G., 309, 310
Held, Richard Wallace, 309, 310
Helliwell, Paul L. E., 165, 204, 326, 351
Helms, Richard, 42, 66
Hemming, Gerry Patrick, 89, 91, 112, 114, 120, 178, 243, 255, 329, 373
Hennessey, David, 100, 101
Hernández, Carlos "Batea," 340
Heroin, 8, 73, 103, 174–77, 353. See also Narcotics traffic
"Hidell, A. J.," 247, 249, 250, 258–60, 284, 307. See also Oswald, Lee Harvey
Hilsman, Roger, 316
Hilton, Barron, 155
Hilton, Conrad, 155
Hilton Hotels, 155, 179
Hinckle, Warren, 88
Hip Sing Tong, 167
Hoch, Paul L., 248
Hoffa, James R., 74, 153, 154, 171–75, 178, 184–86, 188–93, 195, 204, 205, 218–20, 222, 223, 225, 227, 240; and CIA, 173; and Robert Kennedy, 154, 185–93 passim, 218, 222
Holt, Milton, 175
Honduras, 92, 102–04, 108, 124, 168; Gobernación (Interior Ministry) of, 104; 1963 coup in, 92–94, 124, 330
Honeywell Corp., 34
Honolulu conference (Nov. 20, 1963), 26, 29, 32, 33, 37
Hoover, J. Edgar, 12, 38, 47, 56, 61–66 passim, 72, 73, 88, 107, 120, 124, 144–47, 155, 221–32, 235, 243, 253, 258–62, 266, 304, 307–11; and Billy Byars, 206; and Davidson, 106, 217, 218, 221, 222; and Del Charro set, 205, 206; and FPCC, 84, 85; and Lyndon Johnson, 12–13, 297, 363, 377; and Kennedys, 61, 73, 187, 193, 206, 222, 224–32, 253, 307; and Martin Luther King, 266, 308, 373; and LCN crime model, 146, 151, 187, 193; and McCarthyism, 211, 212, 303, 304, 310, 311; and Clint Murchison, Sr., 73, 202, 205–07, 214, 217, 221; "O & C" files of, 224, 225, 235; and organized crime figures, 61, 99, 112, 130, 144–46, 207, 208, 361; "Personal & Confidential" files of, 235; and "phase two" Oswald myth, 45–47, 53–55, 61–63, 65, 275; and right wing, 89,

329; and Lewis Rosenstiel, 65, 146, 211, 212; and sexual blackmail, 56, 227–32, 235, 242, 243; and William Sullivan, 47, 62, 64, 65, 120, 124, 309, 341. *See also* COINTELPROs; FBI
Horwitz, Erwin, 60
Hosty, James P., Jr., 47, 48, 51, 62–64, 119, 120, 243, 255–57, 260, 274; and army intelligence, 257, 260, 274; and ATF, 255–57, 274; and Cuban exiles, 256; and Oswald, 47, 119–20, 260; in Oswald's notebook, 47, 243; and Jack Revill, 371–72
Hotel des Palmes (Palermo) mafia meeting, 176, 203, 360
Hotel Nacional, Havana, 211
Hougan, Jim, 235–37, 306
House Ethics Committee, 238, 239
House Intelligence Committee, 235
House Select Committee on Assassinations (HSCA), 20, 21, 58, 68–71, 82, 83, 85–90, 115–17, 123, 143, 148–55, 162, 163, 179, 180, 183, 194, 198–200, 250, 294, 296; and externalized conspiracy theory, 71, 128–39 passim, 153–55, 160–62, 167, 183; files of, 33; and intelligence matters, 40, 42, 43, 48, 170–72; and LCN crime model, 148, 183–87 passim, 193, 194; and mob hit hypothesis, 68, 70, 71, 82, 87, 89, 90, 223; Report of, 49, 61, 69, 85, 117, 133, 194; staff of, 115, 139, 140, 238, 366. *See also* Blakey, G. Robert
House Un-American Activities Committee (HUAC), 236, 244, 378; and FBI, 236; and Robert Ronstadt, 244
Howard, Mike, 287–89
Hoy, Patrick, 155, 179
HUAC. *See* House Un-American Activities Committee
Hudkins, Lonnie, 368
Hughes, Howard, 235
Hughes, Maury, 159
Humphreys, Murray, 186, 347
Hunt, Dorothy, 306
Hunt, E. Howard, 109, 116, 236, 279, 281, 306
Hunt, H. L., 169, 205, 206, 212–14, 216, 217, 255, 292, 293, 302
Hunt, Lamar, 198, 207, 213, 292, 293
Hunt, Nelson Bunker, 213, 214, 216, 292
Hunt Oil Company, 302
Hurt, Henry, 202, 259, 293, 294
Huston Plan, 281

ICA (International Cooperation Administration), 109
INCA (Information Council of the Americas), 94, 95, 97
India, 142
Indochina, 9, 176
Indonesia, 9
Industrial security, 243–46, 276, 277; and Oswald, 245, 246, 277
Inn of the Six Flags, 283, 288, 289, 294
International Comité for the Defense of Christian Culture (ICDCC), 213
International Ladies' Garment Workers' Union (ILGWU), 195
International Railway of Central America, 110
International Trade Mart (New Orleans), 83–84, 327, 332
Iran, 142
Iran-Contra affair, 238, 281, 303, 304
Iran-Contra Committees, 282
I.R.S. (Internal Revenue Service), 98, 99, 145, 190
Irving Sport Shop, 271
Irwin, Ivan, Jr., 292
Irwin, Ivan, Sr., 162, 292, 293
Irwin, T. K., 162, 292
Israel, 106, 146, 189, 217; Israel Aircraft Industries, 106; Israel Lobby, 106
Italy, 7–9, 176. *See also* Sicily
Itkin, Herbert, 78, 368
ITT (International Telephone and Telegraph Corp.), 108
Ivanov, Yevgeniy, 229

J. Edgar Hoover Foundation, 211
Jackson, C. D., 55, 56, 108, 113, 117, 214
Jaffe, Morris, 288
Jaggars-Chiles-Stovall (JCS), Dallas, 78, 245
Japan, 142, 169, 178; yakuza (organized crime) in, 169, 178
Jenkins, Walter, 45
Jenner, Albert E., Jr., 20, 215, 227, 341
JFK (Stone movie), 24, 25, 33, 56, 247, 294, 297–99
JGCE (Junta del Gobierno de Cuba en el Exilio), 89, 329–30, 371; and Alpha 66, 371. *See also* Sierra Martinez, Paulino
John Birch Society, 157, 215, 292, 300, 329
Johnson, Guy, 103
Johnson, Lyndon Baines, 24–32, 124, 190, 204, 214, 218–23, 227, 288,

Johnson, Lyndon Baines (*continued*)
    296, 297, 367; and Billie Sol Estes,
    363; and J. Edgar Hoover, 12, 13,
    297, 363, 377; on JFK assassination,
    321; Vice-Presidential Office of, 31;
    on Vietnam, 24–28, 30–32
Joint Chiefs of Staff, U.S. (JCS), 14
Jones, Clifford, 218
Jones, Col. Robert E., 258, 260
Jones, Paul Roland, 138–45, 152, 153,
    155, 159–62, 167, 169, 170, 179,
    192, 200, 201, 206, 207, 292, 326,
    344; and Ruby, 152, 153, 155, 160–
    62, 344
JURE (Junta Revolucionaria Cubana),
    251, 252
Justice Department, U.S., 7, 49, 59, 60,
    64, 68, 69, 72, 132, 148, 154, 171,
    182, 188, 193, 219, 222; "Get
    Hoffa" squad, 184, 219; Organized
    Crime Section, 219

Kaack, Milton, 357
Kahin, George, 14
Kalb, Marvin, 36
Kansas City, 141, 192
Karnow, Stanley, 14
Kastel, "Dandy Phil," 98
Katz, Bob, 22
Katzenbach, Nicholas, 46, 148, 345
KCIA (South Korean Intelligence),
    237, 238
Keating, Charles, 10, 335
Keeler, Christine, 228–30
Kefauver, Sen. Estes, 152, 350
Kefauver Committee, 70, 141, 143, 146,
    151, 152, 159, 162, 165, 177, 182,
    192, 201
"Kehler," 169
Kelley, Thomas J., 280, 281
Kennedy, John F., 143, 160, 186, 190,
    191, 199, 208, 213–15, 222–35 pas-
    sim, 241, 253–56, 286, 304, 306;
    and Cuba, 115, 224, 292; and Lyn-
    don Johnson, 24–32, 297; opposi-
    tion to, 54, 116, 221–32; and Soviet
    Union, 35, 55, 115, 292; and Viet-
    nam, 24–32, 35, 224, 292, 318–19;
    and women, 227, 228, 365
Kennedy, John F., assassination investi-
    gations, 13, 19, 61, 66, 73, 236,
    237, 295; autopsy, 3, 52; cover-up,
    19, 52, 54, 68, 72, 73, 78; medical
    evidence, 52, 55. *See also* Garrison
    investigation
Kennedy, Joseph, 211, 356

Kennedy, Regis, 88
Kennedy, Robert F., 66, 73, 90, 113, 184–
    93, 206, 222, 228, 230–32, 307, 357;
    assassination of, 307; and CIA, 66,
    173; and Cubans, 90, 113, 115; ene-
    mies of, 66, 73, 143, 173, 184, 188,
    191–93, 222, 225, 280, 281, 302, 307;
    and Hoover, 61, 73, 187, 193, 206, 222,
    224–32 passim, 253, 307; and Justice
    Department, 184, 185, 193, 205, 219,
    220, 222; and organized crime, 144,
    145, 185–93 passim, 222, 228, 240;
    and Paulino Sierra, 90, 329–30, 371;
    and Teamsters, 154, 185–93 passim,
    218, 222; and Vietnam, 35, 307
Key Biscayne, 115
Key Records, 266
KGB (Soviet Intelligence), 39–41, 43,
    54, 55, 67, 196, 215, 216, 223, 229,
    260; alleged assassination depart-
    ment of, 39, 40, 67, 260; alleged
    assassination school in Minsk, 39,
    55, 215, 216
Khrushchev, Nikolai, 113, 115, 215
Kidner, John, 171
Kimsey, Herman, 215, 216
King, Martin Luther, Jr., 50, 64, 253,
    262, 264, 266, 308, 373; plots
    against, 50, 143, 280, 302, 307, 339
King, Robert, 112
King, Rufus, 156, 164
Kissinger, Henry, 236, 304
KKK (Ku Klux Klan), 49, 160; and
    police forces, 160
Klein's Sporting Goods, 248, 249
KMT (Kuomintang), 167. *See also* Tai-
    wan (Nationalist China); World
    Anti-Communist League (WACL)
Kohlberg, Alfred, 211, 212
Kolko, Gabriel, 10
Kopkind, Andrew, 25
Koreagate, 234, 237, 238, 302
Kornbluh, Peter, 282
Korshak, Sidney, 155, 179, 356
Korth, Fred, 208, 220, 221
Kostikov, Valeriy, 39–44, 54, 62–64, 67,
    195, 223, 224, 260
Krieger, Albert, 79
Krulak, Gen. Victor, 32
Kubek, Anthony, 292
Kuchel, Sen. Thomas, 216
Kuhn, Thomas, 15
Kuomintang. *See* KMT
Kutner, Luis, 48, 151, 161, 181, 201,
    346–47, 349, 350
Kynette, Earle, 156, 157

Labay, André, 79
"La Cosa Nostra" ("LCN"), 147–51,
    154, 184–87, 193, 194; as external-
    ized projection, 151, 193, 194
La Ducas (Kansas City), 192
Lait, Jack, 155
Lake Pontchartrain arms cache and
    training camp, 89, 91, 112, 120, 213,
    244, 253–55, 293, 305
Lamont, Corliss, 262
Landesco, John, 159
Lane, Mark, 45, 202
Lansdale, Gen. Edward G., 31, 275,
    377–78
Lansky, Jake, 98, 179, 180, 211
Lansky, Meyer, 90, 98–100, 109, 111,
    141–48, 152, 155, 165, 166, 169,
    172, 176, 179, 180, 187, 192, 193,
    195, 199, 204, 208, 211, 218–20,
    228, 239, 240; and Cuba (or Cu-
    bans), 90, 141, 166, 172, 179, 204,
    211, 218; and FBI, 144–46, 345;
    Lansky-Luciano drug connection, 99,
    166, 176, 177, 192, 193, 195; and
    Las Vegas, 148, 199, 207, 208, 220;
    and McWillie, 179, 180; and Mexi-
    can drug connection, 141–45; and
    money-laundering, 98; and New
    Orleans, 98; and Operation Under-
    world, 100, 145, 165, 169; and sex
    clubs, 239; and George White, 145,
    165, 169
Lardner, George, 29
LaRocca, John, 173, 174
Las Vegas, 145, 180, 199, 207, 208,
    219, 285
Las Vegas casinos, 144, 145, 148, 199,
    200, 220, 361. See also Caesar's Pal-
    ace; Flamingo Hotel; Sands;
    Thunderbird
Latin America, 106, 107, 189
Lattimore, Owen, 303
Lauchli, Richard, 88, 89, 293
Lawson, Winston, 276–79
"LCN." See "La Cosa Nostra"
"Lebanon crisis" (1958), 275
Leche, Richard W., 99
Leddy, Raymond, 107, 338
Lee, V. T. (Ted), 86, 258, 260–62,
    264, 271
Legion of Justice (Chicago), 279
LEIU (Law Enforcement Intelligence
    Units), 276–78, 371, 372
LeMay, Gen. Curtis, 30, 199, 355
Lemnitzer, Gen. Lyman, 31
Le Monde, 203

Lens, Sidney, 182
Leon, John, 237, 306
Levi, Edward, 281
Levine, Isaac Don, 55, 288, 289; and
    Allen Dulles, 55
Levinson, Ed, 218, 220, 363
Lewin, Ted, 109, 110
Lewis, Benjamin, 60
Libonati, Rep. Roland, 185, 186,
    189, 190
Licavoli, James, 175
Liebman, Marvin, 106
Life, 55, 56, 113, 115–17, 149, 227, 286,
    288. See also Jackson, C. D.; Luce,
    Henry; Time-Life
Lincoln, Abraham, 295
Lincoln, Evelyn, 220, 377
Lindner, Carl, 102, 335
Linton, Leonard M., 64
Lippmann, Walter, 9
Lipsky, Marcus, 140
Little Rock, 141
Livingston, Neil, 238
Lloyd's of London, 108
Lockheed Aircraft Corporation, 34
LoCurto, Joe. See Bonds, Joe
Long, Earl, 100
Long, Huey, 95, 97–99, 332
Long, Sen. Russell, 191, 363
Longshoremen's Union, 100, 101,
    203, 335
Lopez, Edwin, 41, 43
López Arellano, Oswaldo, 94, 102
Los Angeles, 142, 143, 155–57, 160
Los Angeles Police Department (LAPD),
    157, 205, 307, 310
Louisiana, 152, 190
Louisiana Joint Legislative Committee
    on Un-American Activities, 87
Lovestone, Jay, 195
Lowman, Myers G., 265
LSD, 173
Lubin, Eli, 143
Lucchese family, 100, 205
Luce, Clare Booth, 120
Luce, Henry, 55, 254, 155
Luciano, Charles ("Lucky"), 8, 99, 142,
    147, 150, 165, 174–77, 180, 192,
    195, 203
Lumpkin, Deputy Chief George, 273–
    75, 278, 279
Lumumba, Patrice, 173
Lykes Steamships, 101

McAfee, Guy, 157
MacArthur, Gen. Douglas, 178, 212–14

McCann, Thomas, 97
McCarthy, Joseph P., 244
McCarthy, Sen. Joseph, 208, 211, 212, 217, 218, 303, 310, 311
McCarthyism (or Hooverism), 303, 304, 310, 311
McClellan, Sen. John L., 182, 221
McClellan Committee, 152, 178, 186, 205, 218, 221, 232
McCloy, John J., 296, 376; and Clint Murchison, 376
McCone, John, 39, 122
McCord, James, 236, 244, 306
McDill Air Force Base, 275
McGarr, Lt. Gen. Lionel, 30, 31
McGrath, Atty-Gen. J. Howard, 66
Macheca, Joseph, 100, 101
McKenzie, William, 162, 234, 283, 284, 288, 289–91, 293
McKeown, Robert, 160
McLane, Alfred E., 202, 204, 205
McLaney, Mike, 88, 120
McLaney, William, 88, 120
McLendon, Gordon, 124, 217, 227, 233, 234, 358, 363
McNamara, Robert S., 13, 26–31, 35–37, 215, 225
McNamara-Taylor Report, 31
McNaughton, John, 37
McWillie, Lewis, 166, 179–81, 184, 198–200, 206, 240; and Lanskys, 179–80
MACV (Military Assistance Command Vietnam), 31, 32
Mafia, 100, 101, 121, 128, 156, 176, 182, 186, 202, 204; Commission of, 147, 149–51; "Mafia" panic of 1888–1890, 100, 101; in Sicily, 8, 99, 101, 111, 150, 174, 176, 203, 360. See also Apalachin meeting; "La Cosa Nostra"; Organized crime
Maheu, Robert, 112, 179, 194
Malcolm X, 307
Malone, John, 230, 261
Malone, Scott, 117, 180
Maloney (or Molony), Guy, 98, 103
Mamantov, Ilya, 268, 270, 272, 273, 275, 276, 279, 288–90
Mann, Paul (alias Pat Manno), 140, 159, 355
Mann, Thomas, 67, 94, 124
Mannarino, Gabriel, 173, 174, 200
Mannarino, Sam, 181, 200, 201
Mannlicher-Carcano rifle, 136, 161, 248–50, 256–60, 271, 272, 276, 284, 290, 307; as "dark and scope-

less," 267–71, 276; with different stock, 272, 284
Manno, Pat (alias Paul Mann), 140, 159, 355
Mansfield, Sen. Mike, 26, 37, 231, 232
Maranzano, Salvatore, 149, 150
Marcello, Carlos, 19, 60, 77, 79, 82, 87, 88, 95, 98, 99, 108, 109, 129–31, 144, 147, 156, 173, 182, 189–91, 194, 207, 217–19, 222, 223, 225, 246, 247, 301, 335, 357; and Banister, 88; and Davidson, 217–19; and Ferrie, 246, 247; and Kennedys, 182, 191, 219; and Lansky, 98; and Louisiana politics, 19, 190; and Murchisons, 207; and narcotics, 99, 173
Marcos, Ferdinand, 109
Marijuana, 233. See also Narcotics traffic
Marines, U.S., 77, 102, 260
Marseille, 165, 176, 178, 195
Martello, Lt. Francis, 258, 259, 262, 263
Martin, Jack, 188, 246, 247
Martin, James Herbert, 283, 284, 286, 288, 289, 294
Martin, Juan B. ("Johnny"), 118–20, 252
Martinez, Rolando, 114
Martino, John, 56, 107, 109, 111–20, 146, 197, 215, 216, 237, 298, 305, 306, 338, 362; and Bayo-Pawley mission, 113–17, 160, 338; in Central America, 107, 109; and CIA, 111; and Silvia Odio, 117–19; on Oswald, 112, 338–40; retaliation story of, 111–14, 116, 237, 338, 368; and John Rosselli, 111, 117, 197, 338; and Jack Ruby, 117, 118; and Frank Sturgis, 112, 119, 120, 338
Marx, Karl, 22
Marxism, 17
Masen, Thomas, 256, 371
Matranga, Tony (of New Orleans), 100, 101
Matthews, R. D., 118
Mauzy, Oscar, 185
May, Lester, 233, 358, 363, 367, 369
MDC (Christian Democratic Movement), 213
Meagher, Sylvia, 134, 135, 258
Medlevine, Maurice "Frenchy," 60
Meiggs, Henry, 102
Melton brothers, John and Maurice, 139, 140

Meltzer, Harold "Happy," 141–45, 343–44
Mertz, Michel-Victor, 354
Messick, Hank, 98, 145, 147, 148, 193, 208, 212
Mexico, 104, 105, 107, 109, 137, 141, 142, 201, 234
Mexico, government of, 38, 39, 105, 110, 142, 143; Gobernación (Interior Ministry), 105, 123, 124, 336, 341; and Kennedy assassination investigations, 105, 123. See also DFS
Mexico City, 105–07, 109, 121, 122, 124, 142, 224, 300
Miami, 49, 105, 117, 120, 142, 165, 171, 175, 180, 305
MI5 (British security), 229
Military-industrial complex, 34, 55, 70, 216, 225, 297. See also Aerospace industry; Vietnam War, Vietnam War Lobby
Military Intelligence Groups (Army Intelligence), 211, 212, 257, 258, 259, 278, 279; and Dallas police, 274–77; 112th M.I.G. (Fort Hood, Texas, and Dallas), 258, 277–79, 372
Milken, Michael, 102
Miller, Dave "Yiddles," 60, 159, 169
Miller, Herbert Jack, 46
Miller, Murray "Dusty," 154, 169, 184–87
Milteer, Joseph, 49–52, 215
Minutemen, 74, 88, 89, 114, 143, 215, 216, 254–56, 266, 292, 349, 362
Minsk, 215; alleged assassination school in, 39, 215, 216
MK/ULTRA LSD experiments, 173
Moceri, Leo, 172
Mohr, John, 255, 304
Mohrenschildt, George de. See De Mohrenschildt, George
Moldea, Dan, 154, 171–73, 175–77, 189, 194
Molina, Joe R., 246
Mollenhoff, Clark, 230
Molony (or Maloney), Guy, 98, 103
Monaghan, William, 94, 95, 368
Mondoloni, Paul, 176
Money-laundering, 98, 303
Monroe, Marilyn, 216, 227–29, 231
Moore, Bobby Gene, 128, 129
Moore, Donald E., 64, 65, 67
Moore, G. C., 64
Moore, J. Walton, 78
Moreno Chauvet, Jorge, 142
Morgan, William, 178

Morgenthau, Hans, 9
Moriarity, Jack, 238
Morris, Dr. Robert, 34, 292, 293
Morris, Roger, 305
Morrison, Jimmy, 77
Morse, Sen. Wayne, 26, 37
Moss Associates, Edward K., 90
Moss, Mike, 97
Motorola Corp., 34
Mower, Dennis, 143, 362
Moyers, Bill, 46
Mozambique, 302
Murchison, Clint, Jr., 135, 207, 217, 218, 234, 358
Murchison, Clint, Sr., 73, 202, 205–08, 211–14, 217–22, 227, 285, 286, 345, 367; and Del Charro set, 206–08; and Hoover, 206–08, 218, 221, 362; and Lyndon Johnson, 218, 219; and McCarthy, 208, 218; and John J. McCloy, 376
Murchison, John, 286
Murchison family, 108, 202, 221, 222, 285, 286, 293, 300, 326, 376
Murphy, Atty-Gen. Frank, 99
Murret, Charles "Dutz" (uncle of Oswald), 77, 82
Murret, Joyce (cousin of Oswald), 83
Murret, Lillian (aunt of Oswald), 83, 264

Narcotics traffic, 7–9, 11, 16, 17, 71–73, 103–05, 108, 114, 128–30, 132, 133, 136–38, 140–45, 150, 159, 164–68, 174–77, 181, 197, 195, 199, 202, 203, 299–301, 303, 305, 353, 378; Lansky-Luciano drug connection, 99, 166, 176, 177, 192, 193, 195, 203; Mexican drug connection, 131, 141–45. See also Operation X
NASA Space Center, Michoud, 245
Nation, 10, 25, 29, 190
National Archives, 59, 60
National Cash Register (NCR), 195
National City Bank of New York (Citibank), 204
National Guard, 179, 199
National Security Action Memorandum. See NSAM
National Security Council (NSC), 10, 218, 313
National States Rights party (NSRP), 49, 265
Navasky, Victor, 221
Naval Intelligence, U.S. (ONI), 87, 103, 145, 158, 277
Navy, U.S., 102, 255

Nazar Haro, Miguel, 105, 168; and
    Winfield Scott, 105. *See also* DFS
Nazi movement in America, 250,
    361–62
"Negative templates," 60–61, 69
Nelli, Humbert, 101, 149, 150
Nelson, Frank, 329, 368
Nesline, Joe, 56, 111, 145, 238–40,
    367–68
Newman, John, 14, 26, 30–32, 34, 36,
    37, 297
New Orleans, 77, 87, 91–93, 97, 99,
    101–03, 118, 129, 131, 141, 156,
    179, 190, 204, 248, 271
New Orleans Council for Peaceful Alter-
    natives (NOCPA), 263
New Orleans Police Department, 257–59
New York, 7, 45, 99, 101, 141, 142,
    145, 150, 157, 158, 169, 173, 174,
    177, 204
New York Police Department
    (NYPD), 307
New York Review of Books, 10
New York Times, 13, 26, 28–30, 69,
    189, 220, 221, 252, 261, 264, 296
Ngo Dinh Diem, 25, 30, 214, 292
Ngo Dinh Nhu, 214
Ngo Dinh Nhu, Mme., 24, 213, 214; in
    Dallas, 214
Nicaragua, 9, 92, 102, 104–06, 218, 222
Nicaraguan Secret Service, 67, 95, 121,
    300
Nicaragua Lobby (Somoza Lobby),
    106, 122
Nichols, Louis B., 99
Nixon, Richard M., 80, 112, 191, 208,
    218, 222, 236, 275, 281, 282, 289,
    290, 303, 305, 306, 312, 379; and
    Dallas, 289, 290, 374
Nixon Administration, 116, 226, 240,
    304
Noble, Herb, 160
Noe, Jimmy, 99, 363
Noriega, Manuel, 102, 335
Norris, James, 100
North Vietnam, 27, 28, 33, 36, 37,
    224, 303
Nosenko, Yuri, 196
Novotny, Mariella, 229, 230
Noyes, Peter, 143
NSAM (National Security Action Mem-
    orandum) 263 and 273, 14, 24–30,
    32–37
NSC-68 (National Security Council doc-
    ument of 1950), 308
Nugan Hand Bank, 79, 166

O'Banion, Dion, 159
O'Brien, Chuck, 174
Obyedkov, Ivan, 39
Ochsner, Dr. Alton, 96, 97
O'Connell, Jim, 194, 330
Odio, Amador, 118, 120
Odio, Silvia, 118, 119, 251, 252, 256
Odio story, 64, 118, 119, 252
O'Donnell, Kenneth, 32, 37
Odum, Bardwell D., 119
Ofstein, Dennis, 245
Oglala Sioux Indians, 309
Oil exploration, 9, 80, 203
O'Leary, Jeremiah, 44
Olf, Murray, 77
Oliva, Lt-Col. Enrique Trinidad,
    110, 111
Oliver, Beverly, 294
Oliver, Revilo, 215, 225, 300
Oman, 218
O'Neal, William, 308, 380
ONI (Office of Naval Intelligence), 87,
    103, 145, 158, 277
Operation Mongoose, 91
Operation Second Naval Guerrilla, 112
Operation Strongback, 78
Operation Underworld, 100, 145, 165,
    166, 169, 175, 177, 178
Operation X (American), 71, 99, 165–
    68, 171, 176, 178, 180, 181, 192,
    193, 195, 199, 200, 350
Operation X (French), 165, 176
OPLAN 34-63 planning, 37
Organized crime, 6, 18, 61, 65, 132, 311;
    in Chicago, 158–60; "Commission"
    model of, 132, 147–51, 184, 346; in
    Dallas, 71, 132, 160–62, 361; FBI
    and, 144–46, 181; history of, 100,
    101, 149, 150, 187; intelligence oper-
    ations and, 113, 166–70, 193, 194,
    197–99; "La Cosa Nostra" (LCN)
    model of, 19, 70, 129, 132, 147–51,
    154, 183, 184, 192, 193; Meyer Lan-
    sky and, 144–48; "Mafia" model of,
    129, 132, 141, 143, 146–50, 154,
    192, 193, 252; in Montreal, 175–77;
    in New Orleans, 97–101; and Jack
    Ruby, 5, 20, 48, 49, 61, 67–69, 71,
    127–29, 131–33, 140, 151, 159, 161,
    181, 200–02, 204, 232; in Southeast
    Asia, 11, 168; "syndicate" model of,
    98, 140–43, 148, 153, 161, 164, 187,
    191, 192. *See also* "La Cosa Nos-
    tra"; Mafia; Narcotics traffic; Symbi-
    osis of crime and politics; Syndicate,
    National Crime

Ormento, John, 129, 130, 141, 142, 174–76, 353
OSS (Office of Strategic Services), 100, 107, 145, 165, 167, 174, 376
Oswald, Lee Harvey, 3, 58, 65, 119, 160, 161, 178, 188, 257, 300, 301, 305, 307; address book of, 47, 48, 124, 243, 250, 258, 307; alleged Nixon assassination attempt, 289, 290, 374; and Alpha 66, 254–56; ambiguous politics of, 63, 80–86, 119, 245, 250–55, 258, 262–66, 275; and anti-Castro Cubans in Dallas, 118, 251, 254–56; and anti-Castro Cubans in New Orleans, 81, 326–27; and anti-desegregation movement, 262, 265; arrests of, 257, 258; and ATF, 250, 254; and Banister, 96; and Bringuier, 81, 91, 94, 119, 120, 251–53, 263; Bringuier-Oswald debate and tape, 81, 82, 91, 94, 120, 326; and CIA, 78, 324; and Cuban Consulate in Mexico City, 39, 91, 223; in Dallas, 42, 43, 78, 114, 118, 119, 131, 134, 137, 196, 269, 277; in Far East, 78; and FBI, 18, 242–46, 249–53, 257–61; and firearms, 248–52; and 544 Camp St., 80, 81, 84, 87, 265, 326–28; and FPCC, 80–86, 245, 258–61, 263–66, 275; "A. J. Hidell," 258–60, 372; and Hosty, 47, 119–20, 243, 260; and industrial security, 245, 246, 277; "Harvey Lee Oswald," 277, 374; "Lee Henry Oswald," 40; and Mannlicher-Carcano, 289, 290; Marine Corps Reserve card of, 78, 243; in Mexico City, 39–42, 62, 91, 95, 121, 122, 195; Mexico tourist card of, 96; Mexico trip of, 96, 105, 142; and military intelligence, 21, 33, 258, 259; murder of, 61, 128, 131, 134, 162, 179, 183, 205, 288; in New Orleans, 20, 59, 77, 80–86, 92, 93, 96, 118, 178, 197; Oswald doubles, impostors, and look-alikes, 40–43, 96, 284, 291; "phase one" ("Communist assassin") myth, 42, 52, 54, 59, 63, 105, 120, 121, 124, 214, 222, 229, 268, 271; "phase two" ("lone nut") myth, 38, 42, 44, 45, 47, 62, 63, 107, 116, 124, 268, 271, 275, 280, 296; p.r. performances by, 82–84, 86, 91; Ruby-Oswald link, 290, 291; and Security Index, 63, 64, 373; selective service card,

259, 260; and Soviet Embassy in Mexico City, 39, 41–43, 67; and Soviet Embassy in Washington, 39, 62; in Soviet Union, 21, 59, 78, 195
Oswald, Marguerite, 41, 261, 287, 288, 291
Oswald, Marina, 55, 78, 117, 162, 206, 248, 267–73, 276, 280, 283, 284, 286–91, 294
Oswald, Robert Lee, 287
Otash, Fred, 227
Otepka, Otto, 292
Owen, George, 234, 240

Page, Farmer, 157
Paine, Michael, 277
Paine, Ruth, 263, 264, 268, 269
Palermo, Frank "Blinky," 205
Palomares, Noe, 105, 123
Parapolitics, 6–8, 11, 12, 21, 325
Park, Tong Sun, 237
Parker, Gov. John M., 98, 334
Parker, William, 157
Parkland Hospital, 278
Parry, Robert, 282
Partin, Edward Grady, 184, 187–91, 356, 363, 370
Patrick, Lenny, 48, 60, 127, 152, 153, 158–60, 162–64, 179, 187, 200, 355
Pawley, William, 34, 112, 115, 116, 129, 169, 212, 214, 262, 298, 300, 337–38. See also Bayo-Pawley mission
Pearson, Drew, 45, 155, 228
Pecora, Nofio (alias Nofio Pecorara), 82, 103, 184, 191, 355–56, 367
Peltier, Leonard, 309
Pena, Manuel, 307, 380, 381
Pena, Orest, 85, 326, 327
Pendergast machine, 192
Penn Central Railroad, 284, 285
Pennington, Lee, 244
Pentagon. See Defense Department (DOD)
Pentagon Papers, 13, 14, 26–29, 33, 35–37
Pepsico, 290
Perez, Eddie. See Bayo, Eddie
Petrula, Frank, 175
Pfister, Rep. James, 264–66
"Phase one" and "phase two" Oswald myths. See Oswald, Lee Harvey
Philadelphia, 142, 214
Philippines, 109, 114
Phillips, David, 41, 44, 121, 122, 124, 127
Piedra, Orlando, 88, 327
Pike Committee, 194, 281

Pinkston, Nat, 274
Planck, Max, 15
"Plumbers" (Nixon covert assets), 281
Plumeri, James, 173–75, 192, 193, 219,
    325, 353
Pluralism, 18, 325
Poletti, Charles, 8
"Pond, The," (intelligence organiza-
    tion), 212
Powell, James W., 136, 257, 274, 275
President's Committee on Law Enforce-
    ment, 148–49
President's Crime Commission, 150
President's Foreign Intelligence Advisory
    Board, 364
Presser, William, 188
Preyer, Rep. Richardson, 137
PRI (Revolutionary Institutional Party
    of Mexico), 104, 123
Price, M. H., 284, 291
Prío Socarras, Carlos, 91, 112, 160, 200
Priziola, John, 175, 176, 353
Profumo, John, 228–31
Progressive Labor Movement (PL), 261
Progressive Labor Movement (jour-
    nal), 261
Prostitution, 164, 232–40, 367; Jack
    Ruby and, 232–33
Prouty, Fletcher, 275
Provenzano, Tony, 154, 171
Psychological warfare (and public rela-
    tions), 5, 6, 11, 12, 17, 55
Puerto Rico nationalist movement,
    309, 310
Purdy, Donald, 136, 140
Puterbaugh, Jack, 273
Putnam, James, 134
"Putty's Place," 158

Quasarano, Raffaele, 175, 176, 353
Quigley, John Lester, 258, 262
Quinn, Lt.-Col. William, 177, 195
Quiroga, Carlos, 326–27, 373
Quorum Club ("Q Club"), 219, 227,
    230, 231, 234, 237, 239, 241, 286

Racing wire service, 156–58, 162–64,
    169, 183, 187, 201
Ragano, Frank, 189
Ragen, James M., 141, 152, 154–59,
    162, 164, 179, 201; murder of, 141,
    154, 158, 169, 170, 347, 350
Raikin, Spas T., 58, 59
Rankin, J. Lee, 47, 242
Rappleye, Charles, 109
Rasco, José Ignacio, 213

RCMP (Royal Canadian Mounted
    Police), 175
Reagan, Ronald, 281, 303, 310
Rebozo, Charles "Bebe," 213
Reconstruction Finance Corporation,
    332–33
Redlich, Norman, 271
Reid, Ed, 220
Reily, Eustis, 95
Reily, William B., 94, 95
Reily Coffee Company, 94, 95, 245,
    248, 250, 266
Reissman, Dr. and Mrs. Leonard,
    262–64
Reliance Life and Accident Insurance
    Co., 288, 290, 291
Renda, Mario, 79
Republican party, 218, 276, 289–90
Resistance and denial, psychological, 13,
    68, 296, 299, 304, 306, 313
Revill, Jack, 135, 136, 274–77, 371; and
    army intelligence, 136, 274, 276–77;
    and James Hosty, 274; and LEIU,
    276; and Oswald, 277; and Ruby,
    136
Reykjavik Conference, 303
Reynolds, Don, 220, 221
Ricca, Paul "the Waiter" (alias Paul De-
    Lucia), 173
Richards, Guy, 53, 54, 215, 229, 230,
    261, 262
Richardson, Sid, 206, 207
Rikan, Heidi (alias Cathy Dieter), 236,
    237, 239, 240, 306
Rimrock International Oil Co., 202, 203
Rimrock Tidelands Oil Co., 202, 204
Riva Palacio, Carlos, 104
Riviera (Hotel), Las Vegas, 355
Roberts, Eugene, 307
Robertson, William "Rip," 66, 108, 112,
    114, 115, 121, 300; and Martino,
    112, 115; Martino-Robertson-
    Rosselli trio, 115; and Somozas, 108,
    112, 114, 115
Rocca, Ray, 54, 67, 124
Rockefeller family, 177, 285, 293
Rodriguez, Ernesto, Jr., 326
Rodriguez Orcarberro, Manuel, 256, 371
Rometsch, Ellen, 230–32, 235
Ronstadt, Robert C., 244–46
Roosevelt, Elliott, 235
Roosevelt, Franklin D., 98
Roosevelt, John, 285
Roselli, John. See Rosselli, John
Rosen, Harry "Nig" (alias Harry Strom-
    berg), 142

Rosenberg, Ethel, 13, 65, 66, 295, 311
Rosenstiel, Lewis, 65, 97, 99, 146, 157, 208, 211, 212, 345
Rosenthal, Frank "Lefty," 240, 329
Rosselli (or Roselli), John, 117, 161, 170, 171, 222; and Central America, 109, 110, 117; and CIA, 170, 172, 173, 178, 179, 194, 227, 305; and Cuban exiles, 110, 111, 330; and FBI, 228; and Hearst circulation teams, 156; and Las Vegas, 110, 199; and Los Angeles, 156; and John Martino, 111–13, 117, 118; Martino-Robertson-Rosselli trio, 115; and organized crime, 156–58, 161, 172, 194; and prostitution, 235; retaliation story of, 112–14, 116, 117, 120, 170, 237; and Jack Ruby, 117–18, 156, 180, 340
Rosson, Gen. William D., 275
Rostow, Walt W., 338
Rothman, Norman "Roughhouse," 178, 179, 181, 200, 201, 355
Rousselot, Rep. John, 157
Rowe, James, 223
Rowley, James, 295
Rubenstein, Hyman (brother of Jack Ruby), 138, 154, 159
Ruby, Jack (alias Jack Rubenstein), 3–5, 20, 52, 60, 74, 77, 103, 127–29, 131, 135, 143, 151–64 passim, 167, 187–89, 192–202, 203–07, 217, 219, 232, 233, 237, 240, 243, 291–94, 298; and Chicago, 60, 77, 138–40, 151, 152, 164, 200, 205; and Cuba, 48, 62, 133, 137, 153, 199, 214; in Dallas, 124, 128, 138, 151, 196, 201; and Dallas Police, 70, 71, 131–38, 206, 276; and Paul Dorfman, 153, 154; and establishment figures, 18, 19, 70, 131–33, 138, 160, 197, 198, 201, 205; and FBI, 18, 133, 136, 137; and guns, 179; and Paul Roland Jones, 152, 153, 155, 160–62; and Lewis McWillie, 166, 179, 199, 200, 240; and narcotics, 18, 131–33, 136–38, 141, 200, 301; as narcotics informant, 70, 137, 138, 142, 144, 170; and organized crime, 5, 20, 48, 49, 61, 67–69, 71, 127–29, 131–33, 140, 151, 159, 161, 181, 200–02, 204, 232; Oswald-Ruby link, 290, 291; as PCI (potential criminal informant), 133, 136, 137, 342; and John Rosselli, 117–18, 180, 340; and sex traffic, 219, 233, 342; and Team-

sters, 184–86, 188, 348; telephone calls of, 103, 143, 163
Rule of law, 296
Russell, Dick, 114, 293
Russell, Lou, 236, 237, 244, 306
Rust, William J., 14
Ryan, Ray, 65, 206
Ryder, Dial D., 272, 272

Saigon, 30, 33, 176
St. George, Andrew, 115
St. Louis, 101, 141
Sakwa, Paul, 176
Salerno, Ralph, 130, 148, 150, 151, 183, 184, 186, 187
Samish, Arthur "Artie," 157, 158, 208
San Diego, 105
Sandoval Alarcón, Mario, 111
Sands Casino, Las Vegas, 363
San Francisco, 60, 101, 141, 158, 173
San Francisco Call-Bulletin, 158
Sans Souci (casino), Havana, 179, 200, 201
Saturday Evening Post, 150
Savings and loan scandals, 80, 102, 169, 208, 312
SCEF (Southern Conference Educational Fund), 264, 265
Scheib, Philip Earl, 143, 349
Scheim, David, 91, 128
Schenley Products Corp., 146, 157, 211, 212
Schick-Eversharp Corp., 216, 362–63
Schine, G. David, 208
Schlesinger, Arthur M., Jr., 73
Schmidt, Larrie, 292, 293
Schrank, John, 296
Schulman, Solly, 205
Schurmann, Franz, 9, 108
Schweiker, Sen. Richard, 44, 45, 255
Scotland Yard, 228
Scott, Winston MacKinlay, 39, 41, 44, 67, 105, 107, 109, 122, 124, 324; and automobiles, 105, 336; and "D" story, 122; and FBI, 320; and Oswald-Kostikov story, 39, 41, 44, 105; and William Sullivan, 67, 320
Seal, Barry, 79
Seaport Traders, 249
"Secret Government" or "Secret Team" theories, 16, 17, 298, 299
Secret Service, U.S., 45, 49, 51, 205, 206, 224, 241, 248–50, 256, 262, 263, 268–73, 279–81, 286, 292, 295; and army intelligence, 279–81; and Dallas parade route, 273, 277;

Secret Service, U.S. (*continued*)
  and Dealey Plaza, 256, 274, 277,
  292; and Peter Gregory, 268–70,
  279, 287, 288; and Marina Oswald,
  268–71, 287, 288
Security Index, 63, 64, 373
Sehrt, Clem, 77
Senate Internal Security Subcommittee
  (SISS), 54, 56, 215, 216, 260, 262,
  338; and anti-desegregation move-
  ment, 114, 164, 266; and Bayo-
  Pawley mission, 116. *See also* East-
  land, Sen. James; Sourwine, Julien
Senate Judiciary Committee, 249, 372
Senate Juvenile Delinquency Subcom-
  mittee (Dodd Subcommittee), 249,
  250, 307, 370
Senate Rules Committee, 220
Senator, George, 291
Senkel, B. L., 272–74
Service, John Stewart, 303
Sexual politics and blackmail, 224,
  227–40
Shackley, Theodore, 194
Shadow-government theories, 16, 17,
  298, 299
Shanklin, Gordon, 120
Shannon, Elaine, 105
Shapiro, Howard, 136
Shaw, Clay, 247
Shaw, Joe, 157
Shenker, Morris, 223
Sheridan, Walter, 184–89, 219
Shickshinny Knights of Malta, 214, 215,
  361–62
Shimon, Joe, 237
Shoffler, Carl, 238, 239
Sicilia Falcón, Alberto, 104, 105, 110
"Sicilian Vespers" of 1931 (alleged mas-
  sacre), 149, 150, 187
Sicily, 7, 8, 99, 147, 150, 165, 174, 177,
  178, 204; Communists in Sicily, 195;
  Mafia in Sicily, 99, 101, 111, 203
Siegel, Ben "Bugsy," 157, 169
Siegelbaum (or Sigelbaum), Benja-
  min, 220
Sierra Martinez, Paulino, 89–91, 329–
  30, 371; and Alpha 66, 371; and
  Robert Kennedy, 90, 329–30, 371
Silver Spur, 161
Sinatra, Frank, 227
Siragusa, Charles, 146, 165–68, 171–
  73, 175–77, 192, 352; and CIA,
  166–67, 352
Sirhan, Sirhan, 307, 380
Sizoo, Joseph, 64

Slot machines, 98, 140, 152
Smathers, Sen. George, 208
Smith, Benjamin, 264, 265
Smith, D'Alton, 191, 317, 367
Smith, Dwight C., Jr., 149, 150
Smith, Joseph M., 256, 273
Smith, Sergio Arcacha, 87, 88
Smith, William French, 375
SNFE (Second National Front of the
  Escambray), 254
Socialist Workers' party (SWP), 64,
  266, 373
Socony-Vacuum (Mobil Oil), 195
Somersett, Bill, 49–51
Somoza, Anastasio I, 88, 108, 115
Somoza, Anastasio II, 91, 93, 300
Somoza, Luis, 91, 120
Somoza family, 92, 94, 95, 104–08, 112,
  121, 122, 124, 217, 218, 222, 262,
  300, 301
Sorge, Santo, 203, 204
Sorrels, Forrest, 274
Sourwine, Julien, 116, 215, 216, 260,
  262, 264–66
Southeast Asia, 165, 199
Southern Conference Educational Fund
  (SCEF), 264, 265
Southern Research, Inc., 357
Southern Union Gas Co., 202
South Korea, 238, 303
South Vietnam. *See* Vietnam
Soviet Union (USSR), 34, 66, 78, 108,
  115, 116, 226, 228, 267, 270, 271
Special Intelligence Service (SIS; FBI spy
  network in Latin America), 107, 320
Specter, Michael, 30
Spindel, Bernard, 227, 228
Sprague, Richard, 294
Square Deal Association, 98
SSB (Special Services Bureau of Dallas
  Police), 160, 276, 277, 279, 288,
  290, 301; and Jack Ruby, 276
SSU (Strategic Services Unit, U.S. War
  Dept.), 174, 194, 351
Stalin, Joseph, 55
Stalinism and post–Stalinism, 310
Standard Fruit and Steamship Co., 92–
  95, 97, 99–102, 106, 107, 109, 110,
  197, 204; and INCA, 94–95, 97,
  332; and organized crime, 99–102,
  106, 107, 109, 110; and John
  Rosselli, 107, 109, 110; and Seymour
  Weiss, 94–95, 97, 100
Standard Oil of New Jersey (ESSO,
  EXXON), 98, 195
Stashynsky, Bogdan, 215, 216

Steele, Charles Hall, Jr., 84
Steele, Don F., 134
Steig, Edwin, 119
Stevenson, Adlai, 159, 190, 279; demon-
    strations against, 292
Stewart, Robert H., III, 286
Stone, I. F., 36
Stone, Oliver, 14, 24–26, 29, 33
Strategic Arms Limitation Agree-
    ment, 303
Stringfellow, Don, 275
Structuralism, 10–12, 17
Stuckey, William, 91, 94
Sturgis, Frank (alias Frank Fiorini), 7,
    79, 88, 89, 91, 112, 119, 120, 178,
    236, 237, 255, 305, 338; and Mar-
    tino, 112, 119, 120, 338
Suez Crisis, 302
Sukarno, 78
Sullivan, William C., 44, 47, 62–65, 67,
    120, 124, 307, 309, 310, 317, 320,
    323; and Hoover, 47, 62, 64, 65,
    120, 124, 309; as accuser of Hoover,
    47, 120, 309; and Win Scott, 67, 320
Summers, Anthony, 21, 87, 206, 227–
    30, 294, 297
Surveillance policy, U.S., 278–81
Sweetwater Development Co., 286
Symbiosis of crime and politics, 71,
    145–46, 160, 165, 177, 187, 222,
    298, 299, 312
Syndicate, National Crime, 98, 140–43,
    148, 153, 161, 164, 187, 191, 192,
    345. See also Organized crime

TACA (airline), 103
Taiwan (Nationalist China), 105, 106,
    167, 169, 178, 237. See also China
    Lobby (Taiwan Lobby); KMT
Talbert, Cecil, 134
Tammany Hall, 7, 8
Tarrants, Albert, 143
Taylor, Gen. Maxwell, 25–29, 31, 32,
    36, 37, 319
Teamsters, International Brotherhood of,
    73, 106, 153, 154, 162–65, 171,
    173–75, 177, 182, 185–88, 193, 218,
    221, 227, 285; Central States Pension
    Fund (CSPF) of, 201, 218, 219, 363;
    Local 320 in Miami, 161, 171, 175,
    233; and narcotics traffic, 165, 174–
    77, 353; and organized crime, 153,
    164, 165, 173–75; and Jack Ruby,
    153, 154, 162, 163, 173, 185
Tecon Corp, 286
Tet Offensive, 35, 37

Texas Employment Commission, 245
Texas School Book Depository (TSBD),
    136, 143, 246, 256, 257, 270, 272–
    74, 276, 277, 279
TFX (experimental fighter plane),
    220, 221, 245. See also General
    Dynamics Corporation
Theoharis, Athan, 12, 13
30th of November Movement, 371
Thompson, Robert, 208, 218, 220, 223,
    286, 363
Thunderbird Casino, Las Vegas, 180
Thurmond, Sen. Strom, 214
Time-Life, Inc., 55, 56, 116, 254–55
Time-Warner, 56
Tippit, J. D., 258, 277, 279
Tisci, Anthony, 185
Tolson, Clyde, 307
Tolstoy Foundation, 268, 289
Tonahill, Joe, 233
Tonkin Gulf incidents, 27, 37
Torrio, Johnny, 211
Tourine, Charles, 145, 239, 240, 367
Trafficante, Santos (or Santo), Jr., 8, 48,
    49, 65, 90, 111, 113, 114, 129, 130,
    141, 144, 165, 166, 168, 171–73,
    175, 176, 179–81, 189, 199, 219,
    223, 227, 233; and Hoffa, 171, 175;
    and Robert Kennedy, 227; and Mar-
    cello, 189; and Pawley, 114; and
    Rosselli, 179; and Ruby, 48, 129,
    144, 180, 181, 199, 233; in Trescor-
    nia Prison (Cuba), 181; and Vietnam,
    8; and Dave Yaras, 171, 172,
    175, 233
Trans-American Wire Service, 157
Transnational connections, 140–42,
    213, 300–03, 378
Travelers' Aid Society, 58
Treasury Dept., U.S., 98
Trento, Susan, 238
Trescornia Prison (Cuba), 180, 181, 240
Tripodi, Thomas, 8, 174
Tropicana, Havana, 166, 179, 201, 240
Trujillo, Rafael, 88, 179, 218, 221, 262
Truman, Harry, 161, 192, 212
Tshombe, Moise, 201
Tulane University, 263, 265, 373
Tunisia, 203
Turkey, 142
Turner, Elbert, 64
Turner, F. P., 272–74
Turner, William, 87, 88, 216

Ubico, Jorge, 104, 335
Unification Church, 238

United Fruit Co. (later United Brands,
    Chiquita Brands International), 91–
    93, 95, 97, 99–103, 108–10, 124,
    197, 204, 300, 335, 336
Universal Service Corp., 212
USSTRICOM (U.S. Strike Com-
    mand), 275
U-2 reconnaissance, 78

Vaccaro, Lucca, 100
Vaccaro family, 97, 99, 100, 332
Valachi, Joseph, 68, 69, 71, 148–51,
    183, 184, 187, 192, 193, 252, 346,
    357; Valachi version of history, 148–
    50, 346
Vance, Cyrus, 305, 306
Vann, Col. John Paul, 32
Vanuatu, 98
Varona, Manuel Antonio ("Tony") de,
    90, 91, 112, 160, 172, 330; and CIA,
    90, 330; and New Orleans CRC, 90,
    91, 160; and organized crime, 90,
    172, 330; and Somozas, 91; and
    ZR/RIFLE assassination plots,
    90, 91
Veciana, Antonio, 255, 340
Vegas Club, Dallas, 233
Vietnam, 8, 9, 11, 31, 33, 34, 213, 222,
    237, 275, 294, 300, 307; U.S. policy
    toward, 13, 16, 25, 26, 30; U.S.
    troop withdrawal from, 225, 226,
    303. See also Indochina; Saigon
Vietnam War, 6, 10, 22, 23, 56, 72,
    216, 223, 225, 311; anti-Vietnam
    war movement, 149, 297, 305; Viet-
    nam War Lobby, 34, 222, 297
Villeda Morales, Ramón, 93
Vinson, J. D., 263, 265
Vitale, Salvatore, 176, 353
Vitale, Vito, 176, 353

Wade, Henry, 134, 161, 162, 243
Walker, Gen. Edwin, 34, 50, 83, 118,
    119, 213, 214, 217, 255, 292, 293
Wall Street, 102
Walmsley, Mayor T. Semmes, 98
Walthers, E. R. "Buddy," 254
Waltzer, Bruce, 264, 265
Wannall, W. R., 64, 65
Ward, Stephen, 229
Warren Commission, 4, 7, 18–21, 58–
    60, 137, 153, 162, 187, 215, 227, 242,
    250, 252, 256, 280, 281, 284, 290,
    291, 296, 301; and Alpha 66, 255;
    army intelligence and, 33, 136, 279;
    Blakey on, 128, 129, 131; CIA and,
    40–42, 67, 124, 168, 196; CIA-Mafia
    plots not reported by, 19, 168; Allen
    Dulles and, 19, 55, 295; FBI and, 41,
    46–54 passim, 59, 62, 63, 85, 89,
    118, 122, 128, 205, 248, 255, 256,
    272; Hoover and, 53, 54, 65; Lyn-
    don Johnson and, 113; Justice De-
    partment and, 59–61, 70; Life mag-
    azine and, 55, 56; lone assassin
    theory of, 46, 47, 59, 295; and
    Mannlicher-Carcano, 267, 268, 271,
    272, 284; and Martino-Rosselli re-
    taliation story, 113; and Lee Harvey
    Oswald, 33, 40, 41, 43, 47, 59, 68,
    84, 85, 95, 96, 118, 127, 143, 245,
    248, 249, 256, 267, 280; and Marina
    Oswald, 267, 268, 271, 189; and
    Ruby, 4, 5, 48, 61, 68, 70, 127, 128,
    132, 135, 138–40, 151–55, 158–60,
    162, 198, 202, 205
Warren, Earl, 113, 202, 242, 259,
    295, 296
Warren Report, 3, 40, 58, 59, 69, 119,
    121, 123, 127, 131, 139, 140, 260,
    268, 272, 280, 284
Washington Post, 28, 29, 47, 51,
    69, 189
Washington Star, 278
Washington Times, 44, 238
Watergate, 7, 8, 23, 51, 80, 114, 223,
    234–37, 239, 267, 275, 279, 281,
    303–06
Watergate Committee (Ervin Com-
    mittee), 237, 267, 306
Watson, Marvin, 45
WDSU, Station, 84
Webb, Del, 145
Webb & Knapp, 284–85
Webb, Thomas, 220, 223, 227, 286
Weber, Max, 22
Weberman, A. J., 297
Weiner, Irwin, 20, 60, 154, 184, 185,
    192–94, 341
Weisl, Edwin, 223
Weiss, Dr. Carl, 97
Weiss, Seymour, 95, 97–100; and FBI,
    99; and INCA, 94–95; and orga-
    nized crime, 95, 97–100
Wells, Nat, 186
WerBell, Mitchell, 79
Weyl, Nathaniel, 112, 116, 337
White, George, 141, 143, 145, 146,
    164–73, 175, 177, 192, 194, 195;
    and CIA, 166, 167, 172; and Kefau-
    ver Committee, 141, 143, 146, 177,
    192; and Operation Underworld,

145, 165, 166, 168, 169, 175, 177; and Ragen killing, 169; and "Ruby," 169
White, Pete, 162, 289, 291–93, 349
Whitmeyer, George, 273, 274
Wicker, Tom, 36
Willens, Howard, 132, 154, 341
Williams, Col. Garland, 165, 166, 168, 278
Williams, Edward Bennett, 179, 223
Williams, Gen. Abraham, 103, 104
Williams, Sen. John J., 231
Willoughby, Maj. Gen. Charles, 34, 169, 178, 212–14, 216, 293, 302, 360
Wilson, Edwin, 237
Wilson, Will, 161
Wilson-Hudson, John, 48, 181
Winchell, Walter, 230
Win or Lose Corporation, 98, 363
Wire service. See Racing wire service
"Woodin," 169
World Anti-Communist League (WACL), 59, 106, 167, 301, 335
World Commerce Corporation, 177, 178
World Finance Corporation (WFC), 166, 335
Worley, Gano E., 134, 135
WWL, Station, 84
Wynne, Angus Jr., 288, 289
Wynne, Bedford, 226, 227, 234, 239–41, 283, 286, 288–90, 293, 367

Wynne, Jaffe, and Tinsley, 285, 286, 288–90
Wynne, Toddie Lee, Jr., 206
Wynne, Toddie Lee, Sr., 206, 285
Wynne family, 285, 293, 294

Yakuza, 169, 178, 213
Yaras, Dave, 5, 48, 49, 89, 152, 153, 158, 162–65, 171, 172, 175, 179, 187, 193, 194, 200, 233; and Cuba, 172, 200; in late 1963, 152–53, 163; and politics, 158, 179; and Ragen murder, 152, 158, 162–64, 179; and Ruby, 5, 48, 49, 152–53; and Ruby's 1963 phone calls, 162–63; and Teamsters, 165, 171, 175; and Trafficante, 48–49, 165, 172, 175, 179, 233
Yaras, Ron, 172
Yaras, Sam, 152, 183

Zangara, Giuseppe, 296
Zapruder film, 55, 117
Zemurray, Samuel, 102, 103
Zicarelli, "Bayonne Joe," 179
Zoppi, Tony, 198, 199, 359
ZR/RIFLE plots to kill Castro, 90, 91, 173, 352
Zuckerman, Ben, 162
Zumwalt, Adm. Elmo, 304

Compositor:	BookMasters
Text:	10/13.5 Caledonia
Display:	Caledonia
Printer and Binder:	Berryville Graphics